STUDIES IN RABBINIC NARRATIVES
VOLUME ONE

Program in Judaic Studies
Brown University
Box 1826
Providence, RI 02912

BROWN JUDAIC STUDIES

Number 367
STUDIES IN RABBINIC NARRATIVES
VOLUME ONE

edited by
Jeffrey L. Rubenstein

STUDIES IN RABBINIC NARRATIVES

VOLUME ONE

Edited by

Jeffrey L. Rubenstein

Brown Judaic Studies
Providence, Rhode Island

Library of Congress Control Number: 2021933274

Contents

Abbreviations vii

Introduction
Jeffrey L. Rubenstein ix

"Hornets Came and Consumed Her": Gender, Animality, and Hunger in Bavli Sanhedrin's Stories of Sodom and Noah
Julia Watts Belser 1

Bio-Power, Sabbath Burdens, and the Badly Behaved Donkey in Bavli Tractate Shabbat
Beth Berkowitz 31

Problematizing Charity: Rabbinic Charity Narrative Cycle in Bavli Ketubbot 67b-68a
Dov Kahane 47

The Righteous Women of Bavli Sotah: On Reading Talmudic Narrative in the Context of a Tractate
Jane L. Kanarek 79

Mishnah as Story: Aspects of the Reception of the Mishnah in Midrash and *Piyyut*
Tzvi Novick 93

The Iridescence of Scripture: Inner-Talmudic Interpretation and Palestinian Midrash
James Adam Redfield 115

The All-Night Seder in Bene Beraq: A Literary and Cultural History
Jay Rovner 177

The Story-Cycles of the Bavli: Part 1
Jeffrey L. Rubenstein 227

The Deposition of Rabban Gamaliel: Talmud and the Political Unconscious
Zvi Septimus 281

Jews, Gentiles, and Gehinnom in Rabbinic Literature
Dov Weiss 337

Conflict over the Essential Nature of Law: Bava ben Buta's Activism in Tosefta Hagigah.
Barry Scott Wimpfheimer 377

Notes on Contributors 405

Source Index 409

Abbreviations

AB	Anchor Bible
AGJU	Arbeiten zur Geschichte des antiken Judentums und des Urchristentums
AJEC	Ancient Judaism and Early Christianity
AJSR	*Association for Jewish Studies Review*
ALGHJ	Arbeiten zur Literatur und Geschichte des hellenistischen Judentums
BBR	*Bulletin for Biblical Research*
BibInt	*Biblical Interpretation: A Journal of Contemporary Approaches*
BibInt	Biblical Interpretation
BJS	Brown Judaic Studies
CRINT	Compendia rerum Iudaicarum ad Novum Testamentum
DSD	*Dead Sea Discoveries*
FAT	Forschungen zum Alten Testament
HeBAI	*Hebrew Bible and Ancient Israel*
HOS	Handbook of Oriental Studies
HTR	*Harvard Theological Review*
HUCA	*Hebrew Union College Annual*
ISBL	Indiana Studies in Biblical Literature
Jastrow	Marcus Jastrow, *A Dictionary of the Targumim, the Talmud Babli and Yerushalmi, and the Midrashic Literature* (1903; repr., New York: Pardes, 1950)
JJS	*Journal of Jewish Studies*
JQR	*Jewish Quarterly Review*
JESHO	*Journal of the Economic and Social History of the Orient*
JFSR	*Journal of Feminist Studies in Religion*
JR	*Journal of Religion*
JRAS	*Journal of the Royal Asiatic Society*
JSIJ	*Jewish Studies Internet Journal*
JSJ	*Journal for the Study of Judaism in the Persian, Hellenistic, and Roman Period*
JSJSup	Supplements to the Journal for the Study of Judaism in the Persian, Hellenistic, and Roman period
JSOT	*Journal for the Study of the Old Testament*
JSOTSup	Journal for the Study of the Old Testament: Supplement Series

JSP	*Journal for the Study of the Pseudepigrapha*
JSQ	*Jewish Studies Quarterly*
JTS	*Journal of Theological Studies*
KJV	King James Version
MGWJ	*Monatschrift für Geschichte und Wissenschaft des Judentums*
NJPS	New Jewish Publication Society Version
NovT	*Novum Testamentum*
OSHT	Oxford Studies in Historical Theology
PAAJR	*Proceedings of the American Academy of Jewish Research*
PMLA	*Proceedings of the Modern Language Association*
RHR	*Revue de l'histoire des religions*
SBAW	Sitzungsberichte der Bayerischen Akademie der Wissenschaften
SFSHJ	South Florida Studies in the History of Judaism
SJC	*Studies in Jewish Civilization*
SJLA	Studies in Judaism in Late Antiquity
StPB	Studia Post-biblica
SWBA	Social World of Biblical Antiquity
TSAJ	Texte und Studien zum antiken Judentum
VT	*Vetus Testamentum*
YJS	Yale Judaica Series

Introduction

The studies in this volume are the proceedings of the conference entitled "Rabbinic Narratives" held at New York University on June 4–5, 2018. The goals of the conference were straightforward: to stimulate scholarship on rabbinic narratives and to provide a venue for its publication. While the study of rabbinic narratives has been an extremely fertile area of scholarship, there remains a great deal more to be done. Hundreds of narratives still lack even a single scholarly treatment. New methods of analysis developed by cultural and literary theorists have the potential to shed light on many rabbinic narratives. Aspects of the poetics of rabbinic stories are not fully understood and require further attention. Themes and motifs that cut across different stories within a rabbinic composition should be fully explored and the implications reckoned with. It was toward these ends that the conference was directed.

Drafts of the papers were precirculated, and a generous amount of time was allotted for questions, comments, and discussion of each paper. The wonderful collaborative atmosphere and the seriousness with which the participants and other attendees engaged each presentation contributed a great deal to the quality of the papers.

Fifty Years of Scholarship on the Rabbinic Narrative[1]

About fifty years ago scholarship on rabbinic narratives went through a Kuhnian paradigm shift for which three scholars deserve credit: Jacob Neusner, Yonah Fraenkel, and Ofra Meir. In the early 1970s Neusner and Fraenkel argued that previous scholars had mistakenly understood rabbinic narratives as fundamentally reliable historical-biographical sources, or at least as containing historical kernels that could be isolated and iden-

1. I prefer the term *narrative* because it is typically defined more broadly than *story*. A narrative refers to any sequence of events, whereas a story involves events, causality, and change. Many rabbinic narratives consist primarily of dialogue rather than actions and so would not qualify as stories by some definitions, as they lack events and change. Thus, all stories are narratives, but not all narratives are necessarily stories.

tified, on the basis of which biographies of the sages and the history of the rabbinic period could be written.[2] Rabbinic narratives were closer to what we would call didactic fictions that storytellers formulated, transmitted, and reworked for their own didactic purposes. These sources were first and foremost texts, not transparent reflections of a biographical or historical reality, and had to be understood as such. Literary analysis was therefore required to understand their literary qualities and narrative art. In a series of studies Fraenkel offered masterful analyses of dozens of rabbinic stories, exploring their literary structures, figurative language, uses of irony and wordplay, and other dimensions.[3] In the 1980s Meir contributed further studies of the literary features of rabbinic stories, including the role and function of the narrator, characterization, and the importance of the literary context.[4] These scholars laid the groundwork for decades of new studies, approaches, and methods.

A decade later, in 1990, Daniel Boyarin demonstrated the potential of this new understanding of the genre of the rabbinic narrative by drawing on contemporary literary and cultural theory. His *Intertextuality and the Study of Midrash*, as per the title, employed intertextuality to provide a theoretical understanding of rabbinic midrash, also invoking Wolfgang Iser's theory of literary gaps, Michael Riffaterre's notion of "ungrammaticalities," and other theories.[5] While Boyarin focused on midrash, that is, rabbinic biblical exegesis, he also treated exegetical narratives as well as a few sage stories.[6] In his *Carnal Israel: Reading Sex in Talmudic Culture*, published five years later, Boyarin used new historicism and other literary theories to analyze rabbinic stories in conjunction with halakhic rulings and other aggadic sources—the book was published in a series entitled "The New Historicism: Studies in Cultural Poetics."[7] These path-breaking

2. Jacob Neusner, *Development of a Legend: Studies on the Traditions Concerning Yoḥanan ben Zakkai*, StPB 16 (Leiden: Brill, 1970); Neusner, *Judaism: The Evidence of the Mishnah* (Chicago: University of Chicago Press, 1981), 307–28; Yonah Fraenkel, "Hermeneutic Problems in the Study of the Aggadic Narrative" [Hebrew], *Tarbiṣ* 47 (1978): 139–72.

3. See the articles collected in Yonah Fraenkel, *The Aggadic Narrative: Harmony of Form and Content* [Hebrew] (Tel Aviv: Hakibbutz Hameuchad, 2001).

4. See Ofra Meir, "Hasipur talui-haheqsher batalmud," *Biqoret ufarshanut* 20 (1984): 3–20; Meir, "Hashpa'at ma'ase ha'arikha 'al hashqafat ha'olam shel sipurei ha'aggada," *Tura* 3 (1994): 67–84. See too the discussion of her contribution and references to other works in Jeffrey L. Rubenstein, *Talmudic Stories: Narrative Art, Composition, and Culture* (Baltimore: Johns Hopkins University Press, 1999), 11–14.

5. Daniel Boyarin, *Intertextuality and the Reading of Midrash*, ISBL (Bloomington: Indiana University Press, 1993).

6. On midrash and modern literary theory, see too David Stern, *Midrash and Theory: Ancient Jewish Exegesis and Contemporary Literary Studies*, Rethinking Theory (Evanston, IL: Northwestern University Press, 1996).

7. Daniel Boyarin, *Carnal Israel: Reading Sex in Talmudic Culture*, New Historicism 25 (Berkeley: University of California Press, 1995).

studies provided models for other scholars to emulate in the fruitful application of literary and cultural theory to rabbinic narratives.

The work of Neusner, Fraenkel, Meir, and Boyarin paved the way for a dramatic proliferation of scholarship on rabbinic narratives in the decades that followed. This scholarship can be grouped into five main categories.

1. Source-criticism, redaction-criticism, and comparative studies, including attention to literary processes
2. Intellectual and cultural history
3. Literary and cultural theories
4. Literary and legal contexts
5. Cultural contexts of late antiquity

I will briefly review some examples of the contributions in each area and note how the essays in this volume continue these scholarly endeavors. Certainly these categories are for heuristic purposes and could be organized differently. This brief survey is not meant to be comprehensive but only to review the main trends in order to set the studies in this volume in a scholarly context.

1. Source Criticism, Redaction Criticism, and Comparative Studies, Including Attention to Literary Processes

The awareness that different versions of a sage story were explained by literary processes was a crucial factor in reassessing the genre of the rabbinic narrative. The versions found in different rabbinic compilations—sometimes within the same compilation—were not different reports offered by two or three eyewitnesses to a historical event but rather resulted from the transmitters and storytellers reworking their sources in different ways. Similarly, redactors of rabbinic compilations reworked their sources for their own literary purposes and so as to further their editorial aims. Emancipation from the effort to get behind the sources to a putative historical reality gave way to comparative studies that sought to understand parallel versions on their own terms. Source-critical and redactional-critical studies likewise sought to understand how and why later storytellers and redactors altered the sources they received.

Neusner had observed some of these literary processes in his early studies, noting that later versions consistently embellished and expanded earlier, presumably more original, ones.[8] Shamma Friedman's founda-

8. Neusner, *Development of a Legend*; Neusner, *The Rabbinic Traditions about the Pharisees before 70* (Leiden: Brill, 1971).

tional article, "Towards the Historical Aggada of the Babylonian Talmud," demonstrated that Bavli compilers of the long aggadic series of biographical traditions of R. Eleazar b. R. Shimeon and other rabbis in b. B. Meṣ. 83b–86a based the series on two earlier Palestinian story-cycles that had been glossed, reworked, expanded, and embellished by later Babylonian transmitters or by the redactors.[9] I attempted to document some of these literary processes in *Talmudic Stories: Narrative Art, Composition, and Culture*, attributing much of this work to the Bavli redactors, the Stammaim.[10] Amram Tropper, in his *Like Clay in the Hands of the Potter: Sage Stories in Rabbinic Literature*, meticulously traced the reworking of earlier traditions in the construction of rabbinic stories, suggesting that the storytellers reused and shaped their source material "like clay in the hands of the potter/creator (*yotser*)."[11] Similarly, Geoffrey Herman demonstrated that the Talmud's story of King David and Ishbi Benob in b. Sanh. 95a "culled its material from elsewhere. It has created, with great artistry, a mosaic of quotations through the combination of many rabbinic sources."[12]

Comparative studies of different versions of a story both helped confirm and later built upon these studies of literary processes to provide more accurate understandings of the didactic interests of storytellers. Three relatively early comparative studies of the Bavli and Yerushalmi versions of two well-known stories identified aspects of the literary reworking and elucidated the disparate interests of the later storytellers: Lee Levine's "R. Simeon b. Yohai and the Purification of Tiberias: History and Tradition" (1978), Ofra Meir's "The Story of R. Shimon bar Yohai and His Son in the Cave—History or Literature?" (1989), and Haim Shapira's "The Deposition of Rabban Gamaliel—Between History and Legend" (1999).[13] As the oppositions within the titles suggest—history and tradition, history or literature, history and legend—the precise degree to which history could be recovered

9. Shamma Friedman, "Towards the Historical Aggada of the Babylonian Talmud" [Hebrew], in *The Saul Lieberman Memorial Volume*, ed. Shamma Friedman (Jerusalem: The Jewish Theological Seminary, 1989), 11–63. An abbreviated English version of this article appeared as "Literary Development and Historicity of the Aggadic Narrative of the Babylonian Talmud: A Study Based upon B.M. 83b–86a," in *Community and Culture: Essays in Jewish Studies in Honor of the Ninetieth Anniversary of Gratz College, 1895–1985*, ed. Nahum W. Waldman (Philadelphia: Gratz College, 1985), 67–80.

10. See n. 4.

11. Amram Tropper, *Like Clay in the Hands of the Potter: Sage Stories in Rabbinic Literature* [Hebrew] (Jerusalem: Shazar Institute, 2011).

12. Geoffrey Herman, "'One Day David Went Out for the Hunt of the Falconers': Persian Themes in the Babylonian Talmud," in *Shoshanat Yaakov: Jewish and Iranian Studies in Honor of Yaakov Elman*, ed. S. Secunda and S. Fine (Leiden: Brill, 2012), 111–36, here 117.

13. Lee Levine, "R. Simeon b. Yohai and the Purification of Tiberias: History and Tradition," *HUCA* 49 (1978), 143–85; Ofra Meir, "The Story of R. Shimon bar Yohai and His Son in the Cave—History or Literature?" [Hebrew], *Alei Siah* 26 (1989), 145–60; Haim Shapira, "The Deposition of Rabban Gamaliel—Between History and Legend" [Hebrew], *Zion* 64 (1999), 5-38.

from a rabbinic story was still an issue, but scholars were using the comparative method to understand a story's genre and literary development. Meir, in her magnum opus, *Rabbi Judah the Patriarch: Palestinian and Babylonian Portrait of a Leader*, systematically compared parallel stories about the sage and delineated the different ways he is portrayed in these respective sources.[14] In the next decades, comparative studies continued to provide new insights into the diversity of rabbinic ideas, values, and theologies, as well as to call into question previous notions. Pinhas Mandel, in "Was Rabbi Aqiva a Martyr? Palestinian and Babylonian Influences in the Development of a Legend," showed that it was only the Bavli that construed R. Akiva as a martyr, whereas the Yerushalmi parallel is a political drama that involved no death (in the uncorrupted text).[15] Mandel also documented that the Bavli storyteller used a "literary pastiche" of phrases and sources from elsewhere in the Bavli in the reworking process. Leib Moskovitz, in "'The Holy One Blessed be He ... Does Not Permit the Righteous to Stumble': Reflections on the Development of a Remarkable BT Theologoumenon," argued that this doctrine, which appears in the Bavli version of a story of R. Pinhas b. Yair and in other Bavli sources, does not appear in the original story in the Yerushalmi, nor is the idea attested anywhere in Palestinian compositions.[16] Moscovitz accordingly concluded that the post-Amoraic "recontextualization of earlier Amoraic teachings significantly influenced, and sometimes altered, the scope and meaning of these teachings.... In addition, our analysis suggests that the anonymous material in BT sometimes differs theologically or ideologically from Amoraic material."[17]

Besides comparative analysis of the Babylonian and Palestinian versions of a narrative, this method can be applied profitably within each Talmud too. Thus Shamma Friedman's "A Good Story Deserves Retelling: The Unfolding of the Akiva Legend" compared the different versions of the story of R. Akiva and his devoted wife in b. Ketub. 62b and b. Ned. 50a.[18] Friedman argued that the Nedarim version is a reworking of the

---

14. Ofra Meir, *Rabbi Judah the Patriarch: Palestinian and Babylonian Portrait of a Leader* [Hebrew] (Tel-Aviv: Hakibbutz Hameuchad, 1999).

15. Pinhas Mandel, "Was Rabbi Aqiva a Martyr? Palestinian and Babylonian Influences in the Development of a Legend," in *Rabbinic Traditions between Palestine and Babylonia*, ed. Ronit Nikolsky and Tal Ilan, AJEC 89 (Leiden: Brill, 2014), 306-54. See too the other essays collected in this volume.

16. Leib Moskovitz, "'The Holy One Blessed be He ... Does Not Permit the Righteous to Stumble': Reflections on the Development of a Remarkable BT Theologoumenon," in *Creation and Composition: The Contribution of the Bavli Redactors (Stammaim) to the Aggada*, ed. Jeffrey L. Rubenstein, TSAJ 114 (Tübingen: Mohr Siebeck, 2005), 125–80.

17. Ibid., 174.

18. Shamma Friedman, "A Good Story Deserves Retelling: The Unfolding of the Akiva Legend," *JSIJ* 3 (2004): 1–39.

Ketubbot story and attempted to account for the differences, partly on the basis of the contexts of the two stories.

Several essays in this volume continue this line of inquiry, including Dov Kahane's "Problematizing Charity: Rabbinic Charity Narrative Cycle in Bavli Ketubbot 67b–68a," which analyzes stories about charity in the Bavli and their parallels in the Yerushalmi, and Jay Rovner's, "The All-Night Seder in Bene Beraq: A Literary and Cultural History," which compares the anecdote of the five rabbis who stay up all night at the seder in the Passover Haggadah and in t. Pes. 10:12. James Redfield's "The Iridescence of Scripture: Inner-Talmudic Interpretation and Palestinian Midrash" explores not only how Bavli storytellers reworked traditions from Pesikta de Rab Kahana, but also, as the title implies, how Bavli editors continued to gloss and augment traditions after their inclusion in the Bavli to forge connections between two passages. Redfield thus advances our understanding of the processes of reworking stories within the Bavli by triangulating the evidence from both internal and external sources. Barry Scott Wimpfheimer's "Conflict over the Essential Nature of Law: Bava ben Buta's Activism in Tosefta Hagigah" compares the Toseftan and Bavli versions of the famous story of Bava B. Buta's efforts to have the halakha follow the House of Hillel to reveal different attitudes of the storytellers toward rabbinic pluralism.

2. Intellectual and Cultural History

The strategy of comparing Babylonian and Palestinian sources has been particularly productive, especially where consistent differences appear across multiple stories and traditions. These patterns point to differences in the cultures and worldviews of the two rabbinic communities and can contribute to the production of intellectual and cultural history. Boyarin's *Carnal Israel* and Michael Satlow's *Tasting the Dish: Rabbinic Rhetorics of Sexuality* both adopted this approach to explore the different construction of sex and marriage in Babylonian and Palestinian rabbinic tradition.[19] David Goodblatt also employed this method in his groundbreaking *Rabbinic Instruction in Sasanian Babylonia* (1975).[20] Goodblatt's examination of stories and rabbinic anecdotes suggested that the Babylonian Amoraim met in disciple circles, with a small group of students attending an individual rabbinic master, and not in large and permanent institutionalized

---

19. See n. 7; Michael Satlow, *Tasting the Dish: Rabbinic Rhetorics of Sexuality*, BJS 303 (Atlanta: Scholars Press, 1995). See too Jeffrey L. Rubenstein, *The Culture of the Babylonian Talmud* (Baltimore: Johns Hopkins University Press, 2003).

20. David Goodblatt, *Rabbinic Instruction in Sasanian Babylonia*, SJLA 9 (Leiden: Brill, 1975). See too Jeffrey L. Rubenstein, "The Rise of the Babylonian Rabbinic Academy: A Reexamination of the Talmudic Evidence," *JSIJ* 1 (2002): 55–68.

academies. This and other related studies have resulted in a new understanding of the history of rabbinic institutional settings.

A related axis of analysis compares sources in earlier and later rabbinic documents for these consistent patterns, tracing diachronic development of rabbinic ideas and values. Tannaitic narratives compared with those of the Amoraic or Stammaitic sources reveal developments in rabbinic thought over the course of time. Thus, Daniel Boyarin, in *Border Lines: The Partition of Judaeo-Christianity*, made a major contribution to this effort of reevaluating our view of the development of ideas sometimes considered characteristic of rabbinic Judaism.[21] In a provocatively titled chapter, "The Yavneh Legend of the Stammaim: On the Invention of the Rabbis in the Sixth Century," Boyarin claimed that the various stories about Yavneh in the Bavli, which are typically understood as traditions of the early rabbis who first constructed rabbinic Judaism after the destruction of the temple, are in fact late traditions of the Stammaim.[22] They tell us about post-Amoraic theology and ideology, not about the period of Yavneh, and hence we must consider "Rabbinic Judaism as Stammaitic Invention."[23] Alyssa M. Gray, in "The Formerly Wealthy Poor: From Empathy to Ambivalence in Rabbinic Literature of Late Antiquity," observed that Tannaitic stories express "sympathy" for aristocrats who suffered a reversal of fortune and became impoverished whereas talmudic sources in both the Yerushalmi and Bavli are ambivalent. Moshe Lavee, in *The Rabbinic Conversion of Judaism: The Unique Perspective of the Bavli on Conversion and the Construction of Jewish Identity*, as the title suggests, claimed that some Bavli sources, including many stories, are far less welcoming of converts than those found in Palestinian sources.[24]

Dov Weiss's essay in this volume, "Jews, Gentiles, and Gehinnom in Rabbinic Literature," similarly argues for a development in rabbinic views of gentile salvation. While Tannaitic sources debate this question, Amoraic and post-Amoraic traditions almost without exception believe that gentiles are consigned to Gehinnom. Jay Rovner also employs this strategy by examining anecdotes of gatherings of multiple sages in Tannaitic sources, as opposed to the all-night seder described in the Haggadah, to identify the distinct concerns of the Haggadah's compilers.

---

21. Daniel Boyarin, *Border Lines: The Partition of Judaeo-Christianity*, Divinations (Philadelphia: University of Pennsylvania Press, 2004).

22. Ibid., 151–201.

23. Ibid., 155.

24. Alyssa Gray, "The Formerly Wealthy Poor: From Empathy to Ambivalence in Rabbinic Literature of Late Antiquity," *AJSR* 33 (2009): 101–33; Moshe Lavee, *The Rabbinic Conversion of Judaism: The Unique Perspective of the Bavli on Conversion and the Construction of Jewish Identity*, AJEC 99 (Leiden: Brill, 2018). However, Lavee claims that the Bavli's view is not monolithic, and some sources are more favorable.

3. Literary and Cultural Theories

The appropriation of methods drawn from literary and cultural studies has provided a great deal of insight into rabbinic Judaism and promoted an appreciation of the "cultural work" done by rabbinic narratives. Boyarin's *Carnal Israel* employed new historicism to explicate the rabbinic construction of sexuality and also Mikhail Bakhtin's "dialogical" understanding of texts and theory of the grotesque body.[25] The very strange elements in the series of stories in b. B. Meṣ. 83b–86a, including Rabbi Eleazar b. R. Shimeon's self-inflicted "liposuction" through removing buckets of fat from his abdomen, and the discussion of the enormous size of rabbinic phalli—motifs that had baffled previous interpreters—became understandable in light of Bakhtinian theories of the symbolism of the body, borders and permeability, fertility and reproduction, and birth and death.[26] Barry Wimpfheimer continued this productive use of Bakhtin in his *Narrating the Law: A Poetics of Talmudic Legal Stories*, employing Bakhtin's insights into novelistic discourses and his concept of heteroglossia to problematize the dichotomy between stories and law, between aggada and halakha.[27] In another chapter of this book, Wimpfheimer applied Pierre Bourdieu's method of "internal literary sociology" to several talmudic stories and his theory of "cultural capital" to knowledge of Torah.[28] Michel Foucault, a mainstay of cultural theory, has been employed by many rabbinics scholars, including Joshua Levinson in his study of the exegetical narrative, *The Twice-Told Tale: A Poetics of the Exegetical Narrative in Rabbinic Midrash*.[29] For Levinson, Foucault's understanding of commentary as "the opportunity to say something other than the text itself, but on condition that it is this text itself which is uttered" helps illuminate how rabbinic interpreters could add so much to the biblical text while claiming to be interpreting, not creating anew.[30] Levinson also employed "symptomatic reading," a derivative of psychoanalytic method, and various theories of interpretation such as the filling of literary gaps to clarify aspects of the exegetical narrative.[31] Mira Balberg adopted Foucault's concept of "heterotopia" in her analysis of two well-known talmudic stories of men who travel to the "cities by

25. Boyarin, *Carnal Israel*, 12–13.

26. Ibid., 197–226.

27. Barry Wimpfheimer, *Narrating the Law: A Poetics of Talmudic Legal Stories*, Divinations (Philadelphia: University of Pennsylvania Press, 2011), 13–16.

28. Ibid., 122–46.

29. Joshua Levinson, *The Twice-Told Tale: A Poetics of the Exegetical Narrative in Rabbinic Midrash* [Hebrew] (Jerusalem: Magnes, 2005).

30. Ibid., 41; see also 59, 119.

31. See my review essay, "The Exegetical Narrative: New Directions" *JQR* 99 (2009): 88–106.

the sea" to consort with prostitutes.[32] Galit Hasan Rokem and Dina Stein adopted methods from folklore, identifying features and motifs found in other folk traditions, while at the same time analyzing the function of the stories within rabbinic texts.[33] Among the salutary results of these studies was an appreciation of marginal voices within the stories, including those of women, children, strangers, and the uneducated, and an awareness of the different generic characteristics of rabbinic stories, including riddles, parables, and historical legends. Others have used methods drawn from narratology,[34] anthropology,[35] environmental studies,[36] postcolonial theory (especially James Scott's theory of "hidden transcripts"),[37] animal studies,[38] disability studies,[39] and other fields.

Feminist approaches and gender theory have been widely adopted by scholars of rabbinic narratives, as they have by biblical scholars. The journal *Nashim* already in 2001 devoted an entire issue to "Feminist Interpretations of Rabbinic Literature," with introductions by Charlotte Fonrobert and Tal Ilan. Ilan also coordinates the "Feminist Commentary on the Babylonian Talmud," a project involving many scholars, which has produced nine volumes to date, with more on the way.[40] Naturally, stories about Beruriah have been a site for feminist readings, many of which are sur-

32. Mira Balberg, "Between Heterotopia and Utopia: Two Rabbinic Narratives of Journeys to Prostitutes" [Hebrew], *Meḥkare Yerushalyim be-sifrut 'ivrit* 22 (2008): 191–214.

33. Dina Stein, *Maxims, Magic, and Myth: A Folkloristic Perspective of Pirkei deRabbi Eliezer* [Hebrew] (Jerusalem: Magnes, 2005); Stein, *Textual Mirrors: Reflexivity, Midrash, and the Rabbinic Self*, Divinations (Philadelphia: University of Pennsylvania Press, 2012). In these books Stein draws on an array of literary and cultural theories including semiotics, reflexivity, Bakhtin, and Foucault. See too Galit Hasan-Rokem, *Web of Life: Folklore and Midrash in Rabbinic Literature*, trans. Batya Stein, Contraversions (Stanford, CA: Stanford University Press, 2000). Earlier scholars of folklore had identified many folk motifs in talmudic stories but had not analyzed the stories in their entireties, nor discussed their function within the Talmud or midrash. That is, they were more interested in the folk-motifs within the stories than in the stories themselves. See, e.g., Haim Schwarzbaum, *Studies in Jewish and World Folklore*, Fabula: Supplement Series B.3 (Berlin: de Gruyter, 1968).

34. Moshe Simon-Shoshan, *Stories of the Law: Narrative Discourse and the Construction of Authority in the Mishnah* (New York: Oxford University Press, 2012).

35. See, e.g., James Redfield, "Redacting Culture: Ethnographic Authority in the Talmudic Arrival Scene," *Jewish Social Studies* 22 (2016): 29–80.

36. Julia Watts Belser, *Power, Ethics, and Ecology in Jewish Late Antiquity: Rabbinic Responses to Drought and Disaster* (New York: Cambridge University Press, 2015).

37. Julia Watts Belser, *Rabbinic Tales of Destruction: Gender, Sex, and Disability in the Ruins of Jerusalem* (Oxford: Oxford University Press, 2011). See pp. xix–xxi for survey of rabbinics scholars who have employed postcolonial theory.

38. Beth A. Berkowitz, *Animals and Animality in the Babylonian Talmud* (New York: Cambridge University Press, 2018).

39. Belser, *Rabbinic Tales of Destruction*, 86-90.

40. See the description on the Mohr-Siebeck website, https://www.mohrsiebeck.com/en/multi-volume-work/a-feminist-commentary-on-the-babylonian-talmud-799900000?no_cache=1 and the summary on the website "Ancient Jew Review," https://www.ancient

veyed in "'Beruriah Said Well': The Many Lives (and Deaths) of a Talmudic Social Critic," by Tova Hartman and Charlie Buckholtz.[41] Among the stories discussed in Inbar Raveh's *Feminist Rereadings of Rabbinic Literature* is that of Judith, wife of R. Hiyya, who tricks her husband into permitting her to take a sterilization medicine (b. Yebam. 65a). Her "gender-based" reading attempts "to reconstruct and draw out what is concealed behind the recorded dialogue."[42] The same story, together with many others, is analyzed by Judith Hauptman in *Rereading the Rabbis: A Woman's Voice*, who describes her approach as "contextualized feminism."[43]

This volume includes several essays that adopt contemporary literary and cultural theory to shed light on rabbinic stories. Zvi Septimus, in "The Deposition of Rabban Gamliel: Talmud and the Political Unconscious," offers a Marxist analysis, drawing on Fredric Jameson's concept of the "absent cause" of a narrative, as well as the theories of Walter Benjamin, Louis Althusser, and Raymond Williams. Beth Berkowitz's "Bio-Power, Sabbath Burdens, and the Badly Behaved Donkey in Bavli tractate Shabbat" invokes methods from animal studies, as does Julia Watts Belser's "'Hornets Came and Consumed Her': Gender, Animality, and Hunger in Bavli Sanhedrin's Stories of Sodom and Noah," which also draws on gender and ritual theory. Jane L. Kanarek's "The Righteous Women of Bavli Sotah: On Reading Talmudic Narrative in the Context of a Tractate" analyzes the extended aggadic section of the tractate with feminist and gender theories.

4. Literary and Legal Contexts

Fraenkel, committed to his new-critical method and principle of "closure," analyzed stories outside of their literary context and even tended to reject assessing the literary context in any significant way. It was the great contribution of Ofra Meir to demonstrate that the literary and halakhic contexts not only impacted the meaning of a story but in some cases impacted the text itself.[44] Different versions of a story seem to have been tailored to fit their contexts, and therefore context always has to be considered when analyzing a story. Scholars have accordingly devoted attention to the immediate and extended literary contexts of a story, and especially to the legal context within the talmudic *sugya* and the specific mishnaic context,

---

jewreview.com/articles/2016/4/6/the-feminist-commentary-on-the-babylonian-talmud-at-sbl-2015.

41. Tova Hartman and Charlie Buckholtz, "'Beruriah Said Well': The Many Lives (and Deaths) of a Talmudic Social Critic," *Prooftexts* 31 (2011): 181–209.

42. Inbar Raveh, *Feminist Rereadings of Rabbinic Literature*, trans. Kaeren Fish (Waltham, MA: Brandeis University Press, 2014), 74–75.

43. Judith Hauptman in *Rereading the Rabbis: A Woman's Voice* (Boulder, CO: Westview, 1998).

44. See n. 4 above.

that is, the proximate Mishnah, with which the story is juxtaposed. That the parallel versions of stories in the Bavli and Yerushalmi may appear in different mishnaic contexts is potentially relevant to the meanings and messages the storytellers or editors intended to communicate. Eli Yassif has emphasized that many stories appear within "story-cycles" containing from three to forty stories in succession, and that this context is crucial to understanding the individual story, which takes on specific meanings in relation to the other stories in the cycle.[45]

Yonatan Feintuch, in his PhD dissertation, "Tales of the Sages and the Surrounding Sugyot in Bavli Neziqin," systematically examined the stories in those three tractates and argued that reading the stories in their contexts sheds new light on both the stories and their legal contexts, and also reveals new themes and messages.[46] In addition, the texts of the stories have been influenced by their contexts, as they contain phrases and key words that appear in the proximate talmudic discussion but not in the parallel versions of the stories.[47] Feintuch developed these ideas in *Face to Face: The Interweaving of Aggada and Halakha in the Babylonian Talmud,* discussing the different functions of stories in their legal contexts, in story-cycles, and sometimes in multiple contexts in one and the same talmudic passage.[48] Itay Marienberg-Milikowsky, in *We Know Not What Has Become of Him: Literature and Meaning in Talmudic Aggada,* discusses the multiple literary contexts of the story of Moses visiting R. Akiva's academy with great insight.[49]

Other scholars have broadened the scope of the relevant context beyond the immediate literary context to the entire chapter of Talmud or even the entire tractate. Devora Steinmetz explored the interrelationship of aggadot and stories in the third chapter of Bavli tractate Taʿanit, identifying a set of motifs and themes that render the entire chapter a literary unit.[50] Charlotte Elisheva Fonrobert analyzes the stories of tractate Niddah in her discussion of the aims and purpose of the tractate taken as a whole (employing a method of "feminist literary criticism"),[51] and Mira Wasserman treats the

---

45. Eli Yassif, "The Cycle of Tales in Rabbinic Literature" [Hebrew], *Jerusalem Studies in Hebrew Literature* 12 (1990): 103–45.

46. Yonatan Feintuch, "Tales of the Sages and the Surrounding Sugyot in Bavli Neziqin" [Hebrew] (PhD diss., Bar-Ilan University, 2008).

47. See too Rubenstein, *Talmudic Stories,* 265–67. Wimpfheimer, in his *Narrating the Law,* also paid great attention to the broader talmudic contexts of the Bavli's stories, delineating their interaction with proximate discussions and halakhic debates.

48. Yonatan Feintuch, *Face to Face: The Interweaving of Aggada and Halakha in the Babylonian Talmud* [Hebrew] (Jerusalem: Maggid Books, 2018).

49. Itay Marienberg-Milikowsky, *We Know Not What Has Become of Him: Literature and Meaning in Talmudic Aggada* [Hebrew] (Ramat-Gan: Bar-Ilan University Press, 2016).

50. Devora Steinmetz, "Perception, Compassion, and Surprise: Literary Coherence in the Third Chapter of Bavli Ta'anit," *HUCA* 82–83 (2011–2012): 61–117.

51. Charlotte Elisheva Fonrobert, *Menstrual Purity: Rabbinic and Christian Reconstructions of Biblical Gender,* Contraversions (Stanford, CA: Stanford University Press, 2000), 7.

stories of tractate Avodah Zarah in the same way, focusing on the entire tractate as the dominant frame for analysis.[52] So too Julia Watts Belser discusses the stories of responses to drought and disaster of tractate Taʿanit through a literary and cultural analysis of the tractate as a whole.[53]

In this volume Jane L. Kanarek continues in this line of inquiry by assessing an extended midrashic passage of the "righteous women" of the rabbinic retelling of the exodus narrative in the context of tractate Sotah. Dov Kahane's discussion of the story-cycle on charity in b. Ketub. 67b–68a and my article analyzing several story-cycles follow Yassif in paying attention to the context of individual stories within the collection in which they appear. Barry Wimpfheimer draws on the larger Toseftan context of the narrative of Bava b. Buta to shed light on the storyteller's perspective.

5. Cultural Contexts of Late Antiquity

Scholars of the nineteenth-century *Wissenschaft des Judentums* movement endeavored to find parallels to the themes, motifs, and plots of rabbinic narratives in Greco-Roman literature. This was often done in a crude way, the scholar simply pointing out the parallel or concluding that there was classical influence on the rabbinic sources, though it did sometimes explain puzzling narrative elements. More recently, scholars have made great advances in setting rabbinic stories in disparate cultural contexts in more sophisticated ways, discerning parallels in form and genre, and also understanding the relationship to be more complex than influence or borrowing. In his "The Tragedy of Romance: A Case of Literary Exile," Joshua Levinson observes "the adoption and adaptation of Greco-Roman literary models in midrashic literature" by documenting how a rabbinic story borrows but inverts the standard plot pattern of Hellenistic romance novels to create the opposite effect, namely, a sense of disintegration, isolation, and exile.[54] Catherine Hezser has provided a comprehensive study of the literary form of the Hellenistic "chreia" in rabbinic literature, analyzing its function, formal characteristics, and themes.[55] Haim Weiss's meticulous study of the "Talmudic Dreambook" in b. Ber. 55a–57b and other narratives about consulting dream interpreters elucidates the function and

52. Mira Beth Wasserman, *Jews, Gentiles, and Other Animals: The Talmud after the Humanities*, Divinations (Philadelphia: University of Pennsylvania Press, 2017).

53. Belser, *Power, Ethics, and Ecology*.

54. Joshua Levinson, "The Tragedy of Romance: A Case of Literary Exile," *HTR* 89 (1996): 227–44.

55. Catherine Hezser, "Die Verwendung der hellenistischen Gattung Chrie im frühen Christentum und Judentum," *JSJ* 27 (1996): 371–439.

dynamics of these sources by placing them in the context of Hellenistic and Mesopotamian dream manuals.[56]

The Sasanian-Persian context, which had received minimal attention from *Wissenschaft* scholars (apart from in matters of philology), has seen a great deal of fruitful research in recent years.[57] Daniel Sperber's influential article "On the Unfortunate Adventures of Rav Kahana" (1982) identified Persian motifs in the depiction of R. Yohanan's "Palestinian" academy and noted other literary features. This article contributed to the awareness of the fictional nature of Bavli narratives by documenting that some of the coloring added by later Bavli storytellers derived from their Persian cultural context.[58] Geoffrey Herman built on Sperber's study and identified further Armeno-Persian parallels, also noting Persian parallels to other Bavli stories.[59] Yaakov Elman, who stimulated much of this renewed interest in the Persian context, treated various narratives among his copious studies of rabbinic and Persian law.[60] Shai Secunda's *The Iranian Talmud: Reading the Bavli in Its Sasanian Context*, Jason Mokhtarian's *Rabbis, Sorcerers, Kings and Priests: The Culture of the Talmud in Ancient Iran*, and Yishai Kiel's *Sexuality in the Babylonian Talmud* all discuss Persian themes and motifs found in many Bavli narratives.[61]

More recently, the Syriac context has received a great deal of atten-

---

56. Haim Weiss, *"All Dreams Follow the Mouth?" A Literary and Cultural Reading in the Talmudic "Dream Tractate"* [Hebrew] (Beer-Sheva: Ben Gurion University Press, 2011). The parallels to Artemidorus's *Oneirocritica* had been noted by previous scholars, but Weiss's analysis is much more sophisticated and draws on a great deal of theory, as the title suggests.

57. See Geoffrey Herman, "Ahasuerus, The Former Stable-Master of Belshazzar, and The Wicked Alexander of Macedon: Two Parallels between the Babylonian Talmud and Persian Sources," *AJSR* 29 (2005): 283–85, for a review of early research on these questions. For a survey of studies of aggada and Persian-Sasanian sources, see Geoffrey Herman and Jeffrey L. Rubenstein, "Introduction," in *The Aggada of the Bavli and Its Cultural World*, ed. Geoffrey Herman and Jeffrey L. Rubenstein, BJS 362 (Providence, RI: Brown Judaic Studies, 2018), xii–xvii.

58. Daniel Sperber, "On the Unfortunate Adventures of Rav Kahana: A Passage of Saboraic Polemic from Sasanian Persia," in *Irano Judaica*, ed. Shaul Shaked (Jerusalem: Ben-Zvi, 1982), 83–100.

59. Geoffrey Herman, "The Story of Rav Kahana (BT Baba Qamma 117a–b) in Light of Armeno-Persian Sources," *Irano-Judaica VI: Studies Relating to Jewish Contacts with Persian Culture throughout the Ages*, ed. Shaul Shaked and Amnon Netzer (Jerusalem: Ben-Zvi Institute, 2008), 53–86.

60. See, e.g., Yaakov Elman, "Dualistic Elements in Babylonian Aggada," in Herman and Rubenstein, *Aggadah of the Bavli*, 273–311; Elman, "'He in His Cloak and She in Her Cloak': Conflicting Images of Sexuality in Sasanian Mesopotamia," in *Discussing Cultural Influences: Text, Context, and Non-Text in Rabbinic Judaism*, ed. Rivka Ulmer, Studies in Judaism (Lanham, MD: University Press of America, 2007), 129–64.

61. Shai Secunda, *The Iranian Talmud: Reading the Bavli in Its Sasanian Context*, Divinations (Philadelphia: University of Pennsylvania Press, 2014); Jason Sion Mokhtarian, *Rabbis, Sorcerers, Kings, and Priests: The Culture of the Talmud in Ancient Iran*, S. Mark Taper Foundation Imprint in Jewish Studies (Oakland: University of California Press, 2015); Yishai Kiel,

tion.[62] Michal Bar-Asher Siegal's *Early Christian Monastic Literature and the Babylonian Talmud,* has called attention to connections between rabbinic biographical traditions and Syriac hagiographical literature.[63] She argues, for example, that the differences between the Bavli's version of the story of "R. Shimon b. Yohai and the cave" and that of the Yerushalmi is a function of the Bavli adopting motifs found in Syriac lives of "holy men" and monks.[64] Other studies have also suggested that rabbis in both Talmuds are sometimes portrayed as "holy men" in the manner of the Syriac biographical tradition.[65] Simcha Gross has suggested that the Bavli story of the martyrdom of Rabbah bar Naḥmani is modeled on Syriac martyrological traditions such as those found in the Persian Martyr Acts, though it communicates different ideas about persecution and identity.[66] A number of studies of talmudic stories in their Persian and Syriac contexts are collected in the volume *The Aggada of the Bavli and Its Cultural World,* also published by Brown Judaic Studies.[67]

Tzvi Novick's contribution, "Mishnah as Story: Aspects of the Reception of the Mishnah in Midrash and *Piyyut,*" discusses the reception of mishnaic traditions and several mishnaic narratives in piyyutim, which flourished in the Byzantine cultural context, blazing a new trail in these efforts to set rabbinic stories in late antique contexts. Julia Watts Belser draws on the Sasanian context and the Zoroastrian disgust toward insects to explicate the Sodomites cruelty of killing a woman by exposing her to hornets.

The essays in this volume continue these trends that have produced such fruitful research over the past half century and, in turn, contribute to their advancement. They exemplify the wide variety and diversity of methods and approaches developed in the past and also add new theoretical tools and lines of analysis to scholarship of the rabbinic narrative. It is hoped that future studies will build upon these essays in creative and innovative ways.

Sexuality in the Babylonian Talmud: Christian and Sasanian Contexts in Late Antiquity (Cambridge: Cambridge University Press, 2016).

62. For a review of studies of aggada and Syriac sources, see Herman and Rubenstein, "Introduction," in *Aggada of the Bavli,* xvii–xxx.

63. Michal Bar-Asher Siegal, *Early Christian Monastic Literature and the Babylonian Talmud* (Cambridge: Cambridge University Press, 2013).

64. Ibid., 133–69.

65. See, e.g., David Levine, "Holy Men and Rabbis in Talmudic Antiquity," and Chana Safrai and Zeev Safrai, "Rabbinic Holy Men," both in *Saints and Role Models in Judaism and Christianity,* ed. Marcel Poorthuis and Joshua Schwartz, Jewish and Christian Perspectives 7 (Leiden: Brill, 2004), 45–58 and 59–78. See too Herman and Rubenstein, "Introduction," xxvi–xvii, for further references.

66. Simcha Gross, "A Persian Anti-Martyr Act: The Death of Rabbah bar Naḥmani," in Herman and Rubenstein, *Aggada of the Bavli,* 211–42.

67. See n. 57 above.

Summary of Contents

Julia Watts Belser, in "'Hornets Came and Consumed Her': Gender, Animality, and Hunger in Bavli Sanhedrin's Stories of Sodom and Noah," probes narratives from the Babylonian Talmud's account of Noah and Sodom (b. Sanh. 108a–109b). She devotes particular attention to the final scene of the Sodom tale in which a woman who sneaks food to a starving man to subvert the men of Sodom's cruel decree is punished by being daubed in honey and stood upon the city wall, where she is eaten alive by bees. Reading these tales through the prism of hunger, Belser argues that the act of eating brings critical dimensions of gender, sexuality, social class, and species into sharp relief. Where the Sodom tale uses animal hunger to prop up an unjust regime and enact public violence on a woman's flesh, the Noah stories reveal animals disciplining their hungers, fashioning consumption into an expression of ethical agency and a mark of moral sensitivity. In the Sodom stories, hunger serves as an index of the bestial, a powerful force intertwined with violence, greed, and sexual perversion. The threat of the bestial haunts the Bavli's account of the flood, which it imagines as the consequence of illicit sex between humans and other animals. But in the Bavli's telling, the ark opens to an alternate form of interspecies intimacy, one in which the act of eating and feeding holds out the promise of mutuality and kinship between human and animal flesh.

In "Bio-Power, Sabbath Burdens, and the Badly Behaved Donkey in Bavli Tractate Shabbat," **Beth Berkowitz** examines Bavli Shabbat chapter 5 to explore how human techniques of animal control come to seem necessary and beneficial. The essay first looks at a legal passage dealing with disciplinary devices for animals and then turns to a story about a badly behaved donkey to argue that the story exposes the "disguises and pretenses" (a notion borrowed from Bertrand Russell) that the legal discourse puts into place. Putting critical animal studies in dialogue with the Talmud, this essay argues that the talmudic treatment of Sabbath burdens is an illuminating case study in the exercise of bio-power.

Dov Kahane, in "Problematizing Charity: Rabbinic Charity Narrative Cycle in Bavli Ketubbot 67b–68a," examines the cycle of charity narratives that appear on these two folios of the Babylonian Talmud. These narratives all share certain thematic and stylistic features and, taken as a whole, represent a highly redacted corpus. Each story speaks of a donor and his (and in one story, her) particular—often supererogatory—practice of charity. All of these stories present some type of twist on the expected outcome. Kahane argues that this cycle of narratives works to problematize aspects of the act of charity in the social context that is depicted. This problematizing reflects a cultural awareness on the part of the Bavli editors that—notwithstanding the notion that charity is the ultimate act of corporate solidarity—other concerns about its implementation are significant. This awareness may well reflect the shift to greater rabbinic institutionalization of charity activities in late Amoraic and Geonic periods or the waning influence of euergetism. It may also reflect the academic culture of the editors of the Bavli and their desire to create a multivocal, nuanced text that eschews binary categorizations of normative behavior.

In "The Righteous Women of Bavli Sotah: On Reading Talmudic Narrative in the Context of a Tractate," **Jane L. Kanarek** argues that the talmudic narrative of the righteous women through whose merit Israel was redeemed from Egypt (b. Soṭah 11b) should be read not only within its local midrashic context but also within the wider context of the Bavli's presentation of the sotah ritual. With its description of women birthing a nation, the righteous-women homily portrays an act of political rebellion that mirrors the sotah ritual and acts as a subversive countertradition to the ritual. In addition, the homily may be part of a Babylonian trend toward shifting the focus of the sotah ritual from women's guilt to include men and male sin.

The Mishnah is a legal work, but because it includes many narrative elements, and because of its foundational importance in the rabbinic canon, later texts that are not designed principally for explication of the law often allude to it. **Tzvi Novick**, in "Mishnah as Story: Aspects of the Reception of the Mishnah in Midrash and *Piyyut*," collects five passages from the homiletical literature of Amoraic Palestine and from classical *piyyuṭ* that in different ways receive the Mishnah as story. Careful analysis of these passages yields new insight into a range of narrative motifs and, more generally, into the production of a legal culture in which law and narrative are inextricably intertwined.

Via source-critical analysis of two adjacent literary units in the Babylonian Talmud (b. B. Bat. 73a–75b), and a comparison to their parallels in the Palestinian work Pesiqta de Rab Kahana, **James Redfield**'s "The Iridescence of Scripture: Inner-Talmudic Interpretation and Palestinian Midrash" interrogates the relation between Babylonian and Palestinian midrash more generally and develops a model for accessing distinctive features of midrash in the Babylonian Talmud. Redfield argues the following: (1) the Palestinian and Babylonian parallels do reflect more popular as opposed to more scholastic ideologies, respectively; (2) the Babylonian material is composed of basically discrete units that were, however, gradually integrated through a process of "inner-talmudic interpretation"; (3) the dynamics of inner-talmudic interpretation involve the use of key words and catchphrases to open pathways for rereading among accumulated sources. This final, theoretical argument builds upon recent work in the field but stresses the need to combine precision about *active* links between sources with an appreciation for their *longue durée* and the relatively nonintentional formation of pathways in the "live" context of talmudic study.

Jay Rovner, in "The All-Night Seder in Bene Beraq: A Literary and Cultural History," observes that the *maʿaśeh* (story anecdote) about a Passover seder celebrated by sages with Rabbi Akiva in Bene Beraq appears to be a typical tale crafted sometime during the Tannaitic era, the period during which they lived. However, it is found only in the Passover Haggadah, and there was no Haggadah then. Comparison of different versions of this *maʿaśeh* shows that it was taking form and evolving much later, in the Geonic period. Indeed, it is one of several texts that were being developed or deployed in the formation of the *ʿavadim hayinu* section of the Babylonian version of the Passover Haggadah during that period.

Jeffrey L. Rubenstein, in "The Story-Cycles of the Bavli: Part I" begins a comprehensive study of the clusters of stories found throughout the Bavli. Eli Yassif first called attention to this phenomenon in several studies beginning in 1990 and ultimately identified twenty-four story-cycles in the Bavli of between three and thirty-eight stories. Rubenstein argues that Yassif's pioneering study, based largely on folkloristic methods and interests, requires revision in light of recent scholarship on the nature and editing of the Bavli. He begins this project with analyses of five story-cycles: (1) Ber. 18a–b (five stories of the dead); (2) Ketub. 67b (nine stories of charity); (3) Šabb. 30b–31a (nine stories of annoying questions); (4) Šabb. 156b (three stories of astrology); (5) ʿAbod. Zar. 10a–11a (three stories of righteous gentiles). Rubenstein discusses the boundaries and definition of the story-cycle, parallels, composition and dating, halakhic context, and interruptions between the stories.

Zvi Septimus, in "The Deposition of Rabban Gamliel: Talmud and the Political Unconscious," argues that a Marxist reading of the Babylonian Talmud can be used to understand the impact of the process of urbanization on rabbinic ideology. At the same time, he proposes a method for the historical analysis of the development of rabbinic literature that contrasts with the standard diachronic model practiced in the field. The story of the deposition of Rabban Gamliel as *Nasi* (b. Ber. 27b–28a; y. Ber. 4:1), and its place within the Yavneh story-cycle, has received considerable scholarly attention. What these studies have in common is their desire to locate the authorship of the story in a concrete historical context and thereby use the story to discover something about both the historical period of the text's composition and the people who produced it, though a wide range of dates are proposed by various scholars. The diachronic method used in these studies relies on a comparison of two extant textual relics (in this case the Bavli and Yerushalmi versions of a story). Septimus assumes that many now-lost versions of the story existed over time and proposes a method for historical analysis that takes into account the important role these missing versions might have played in the development of the story that we now read. While a distant reading approach that resists narratological analysis is the starting point for such an investigation, Fredric Jameson's method for finding the absent cause of a narrative provides the structure for the analysis. In *The Political Unconscious*, Jameson demonstrated that, though Marx's epochal scheme of history was inherently flawed, his central idea of historical materialism could nonetheless be salvaged. Septimus follows Jameson through his three stages of reading, representing three distinct semantic horizons, and displays how an increasingly urbanized rabbinic world dealt with traces of competing power structures located in different periods of Jewish history. Other Marxist thinkers, such as Walter Benjamin, Louis Althusser, and Raymond Williams, play central roles in the argument.

In "Jews, Gentiles and Gehinnom in Rabbinic Literature," **Dov Weiss** argues that, while the rabbis debated the question of gentile salvation in the Tannaitic period, the exclusivist position—which regarded the gentiles as destined for Gehinnom—reached near-unanimous consensus in the Amoraic and post-Amoraic periods. This fact—that the rabbinic belief in gentile damnation intensified and radicalized over time—has gone unnoticed in both Jewish and Christian scholarship. This essay further argues that a rabbinic anti-gentile soteriology worked in tandem with a new rabbinic doctrine that advocated a radical vision of Jewish privilege: all Jews–even the sinners–would escape the fiery torments of hell.

Barry Wimpfheimer, in "Conflict over the Essential Nature of Law: Bava ben Buta's Activism in Tosefta Hagigah," analyzes the story of Baba ben Buta, a disciple of Beit Shammai, who intervenes in the logistical execution of sacrificial rituals to achieve a practical legal outcome according to the position of Beit Hillel. This article lends texture to this narrative by reading into both the doubling of the story in the text and a series of editorial interruptions in the narration. These features combine with similar editorial interruptions in the famous adjacent passage about the temple-era legal system to tell a story of editorial resistance to the original story and its assumptions about law and jurisprudence. This example demonstrates that Jewish law as a unified consistent entity was already being contested in the Tannaitic period.

I would like to thank The Skirball Department of Hebrew and Judaic Studies and its chair, Dr. Alex Jassen, and The Center for Ancient Studies of New York University and its director, Dr. Matthew Santirocco, for the funding that made the conference and this publication possible. I am grateful to Ryan Grubbs and Kirsten Howe, the administrative staff, for making the conference run smoothly. My thanks also to Joshua Blachorsky, Maurya Horgan, and Paul Kobelski for their meticulous editing, and to Michael Satlow for facilitating publication in the Brown Judaic Studies Series.

Jeffrey L. Rubenstein
August 2020

"Hornets Came and Consumed Her"

Gender, Animality, and Hunger in Bavli Sanhedrin's Stories of Sodom and Noah

JULIA WATTS BELSER

In the final chapter of Bavli Sanhedrin, the talmudic tractate devoted to the practice of human justice, the rabbis leave aside the procedures and punishments that preoccupy the earthly court and turn their attention to matters eschatological. Mishnah Sanh. 10:1 enumerates a cast of biblical schemers and scoundrels who are denied a place in the hereafter. Chief among them are the generation of the flood and the men of Sodom, two communities whose spectacular destructions represent preeminent biblical sites of divine judgment. In rabbinic literature, the stories of Noah and Sodom become a means for the rabbis to probe the boundaries of the human, to assay the faults and failings of two communities whose transgressions pressed the moral limits of humanness. These stories allow us to glimpse how the rabbis construct and confront a dystopian past marked by deviant sexuality and queer desires; by social violence, brutality, and greed. In the Bavli's telling, the flood is a response to bestial sex—the destruction of a world given over to sexual relations between humans and animals, and between different animal kinds. Rabbinic tales of the destruction of Sodom showcase a different form of inhumanity: a world in which judges extract fines from the victims of crimes, in which the rich entertain at banquets while the poor starve in the streets.

In approaching rabbinic notions of the human, it is easy for modern readers to be seduced by our own science, to retroject into the late ancient world a conception of human and animal difference rooted in genus and genes.[1] But rabbinic sources think quite differently about the distinction

1. My thinking about the relationship between humans and other animals has been shaped by work in critical animal studies and the ecological humanities, which underscores the political and cultural import ascribed to notions of species difference and which contests notions of ontological difference between humans and the rest of the creaturely world. For an overview of animal studies in the humanities, see Cary Wolfe, "Human, All Too Human:

between humans and animals. In many rabbinic texts, human distinctiveness is not primarily a matter of physiology but a difference in ethical capacity.[2] This notion of humans as the sole species with a robust capacity for moral action is a well-worn trope, not only in rabbinic culture but in many contemporary accounts of human exceptionalism.[3] The claim that humans alone are capable of moral concern is increasingly contested by animal behaviorists and ethicists alike, and new works in animal ethics aim to document the moral lives of diverse animal species.[4] Rabbinic sources are no strangers to such speculation, and indeed, as Jonathan Crane and others have documented, certain rabbinic narratives ascribe ethical agency and moral intention to animals.[5] Yet even as rabbinic literature offers tantalizing speculations about the inner lives of animals, an overriding assumption regarding human–animal difference remains intact. Humans differentiate ourselves from animals (if we differentiate ourselves from animals) not because of our biology but because of our capacity for moral rectitude. In such a world, the line between species is never certain, never assured. Humans are always at risk of sliding back

---

'Animal Studies' and the Humanities," *PMLA* 124 (2009): 564–75. On animal studies in the context of religion, see Aaron Gross, *The Question of the Animal and Religion: Theoretical Stakes and Practical Implications* (New York: Columbia University Press, 2015).

2. Recent scholarly work offers new insights into rabbinic thinking about animals and the nature of the human. See Beth A. Berkowitz, *Animals and Animality in the Babylonian Talmud* (New York: Cambridge University Press, 2018); Mira Beth Wasserman, *Jews, Gentiles, and Other Animals: The Talmud after the Humanities*, Divinations (Philadelphia: University of Pennsylvania Press, 2017); Rachel Neis, "The Reproduction of Species: Humans, Animals, and Species Nonconformity in Early Rabbinic Science," *JSQ* 24 (2017): 289–317.

3. Critical animal studies scholarship interrogates the way that epistemic violence and material violence against humans and other animals are bound together. It also illuminates the way claims to human exceptionalism are used to buttress other social hierarchies, as well as the way the discourse of animality is commonly used to stigmatize certain groups and imagine them as beyond the boundaries of the human. See Carol J. Adams, *The Sexual Politics of Meat: A Feminist-Vegetarian Critical Theory* (New York: Continuum, 1990); Maneesha Deckha, "Toward a Postcolonial, Posthumanist Feminist Theory: Centralizing Race and Culture in Feminist Work on Nonhuman Animals," *Hypatia* 27 (2012): 527–45; Claire Jean Kim, *Dangerous Crossings: Race, Species, and Nature in a Multicultural Age* (New York: Cambridge University Press, 2015); David Alan Nibert, *Animal Rights/Human Rights: Entanglements of Oppression and Liberation* (Lanham, MD: Rowman & Littlefield, 2002); Sunaura Taylor, *Beasts of Burden: Animal and Disability Liberation* (New York: New Press, 2017); and Delores S. Williams, "Sin, Nature, and Black Women's Bodies," in *Ecofeminism and the Sacred*, ed. Carol J. Adams (New York: Continuum, 1993), 24–29.

4. See Marc Bekoff and Jessica Pierce, *Wild Justice: The Moral Lives of Animals* (Chicago: University of Chicago Press, 2009); Dale Peterson, *The Moral Lives of Animals* (London: Bloomsbury, 2011); Frans de Waal, *Our Inner Ape: A Leading Primatologist Explains Why We Are Who We Are* (Harmondsworth: Penguin, 2006).

5. Jonathan K. Crane, ed., *Beastly Morality: Animals as Ethical Agents* (New York: Columbia University Press, 2016).

into animality, of failing to enact the ethical qualities that make us different from the beasts.[6]

Yet this very notion of *human* difference is insufficiently precise. Analyzing rabbinic legal traditions in Bavli Avodah Zarah that guard against sexual relations between humans and animals, Mira Beth Wasserman argues that rabbinic discussions of bestiality become a prism not only for navigating the difference between humans and other animals but also for navigating gender difference and for contouring Jewish and non-Jewish relations.[7] While some rabbinic traditions reify a binary divide between humans and other animals, others stress the kinship between animals, women, and non-Jewish men—distinguishing instead a particular ethical capacity that belongs solely to Jewish males. Here too, Wasserman argues, the elevated moral status of the rabbinic Jewish man is far from assured. In the Bavli's telling, "it is not just women and Gentiles who harbor animal impulses, but Jewish men as well."[8] In the cultural world of the Bavli, the basic human condition is largely indistinguishable from animal life. Torah alone elevates certain humans from the bestial—and, at that, only imperfectly.

In rabbinic accounts of Sodom and Noah, the rabbis grapple with communities whose unchecked greed, lust, and violence have plunged them into the realm of the bestial and condemned them to destruction.[9] These stories thus serve as a striking site through which to analyze how the rabbis grapple with distinctions between humans and other animals, between creatures of diverse kinds. In this article, I read Bavli Sanhedrin's tales of Noah and Sodom through the prism of hunger, arguing that these rabbinic accounts of human and animal eating bring critical dimensions

---

6. Jeremy Cohen analyzes the rabbinic and medieval Jewish reception of Gen 1:27–28, an important locus for Jewish thinking about the difference between humans and animals. These verses, he argues, were commonly understood to affirm human distinction from other animals, as well as to authorize human dominance over the creatures. They also ground a rabbinic assumption that human nature is poised between the divine image and the animals, that human merit and moral effort can allow us to rule over the animals (and our own animal nature), while an absence of merit will leave us to be ruled by animal impulse. Jeremy Cohen, *Be Fertile and Increase, Fill the Earth and Master It: The Ancient and Medieval Career of a Biblical Text* (Ithaca, NY: Cornell University Press, 1989). On the distinction between humans and other animals through the motif of human creation in the divine image in rabbinic and later Jewish sources, see David Mevorach Seidenberg, *Kabbalah and Ecology: God's Image in the More-than-Human World* (New York: Cambridge University Press, 2015).

7. Wasserman, *Jews, Gentiles, and Other Animals*, 73–119.

8. Ibid., 100.

9. Here, I deliberately use the term *bestial* in its moral sense. As Wasserman observes, while the word can be used as a value-neutral term describing the condition of being an animal, rabbinic literature commonly uses it as "a synonym for brutality, depravity, or debasement." When used in this way, the "bestial" implies that "humans should avoid acting like animals" (Wasserman, *Jews, Gentiles, and Other Animals*, 76).

of gender, sexuality, social class, and species into sharp relief. Hunger appears as a significant motif in early exegesis of the Sodom story. In Ezek 16:49, the prophet condemns the sin of Sodom as one of arrogance—an arrogance manifested through refusal to share bread. "Only this was the sin of your sister Sodom," Ezekiel proclaims, "Arrogance! She and her daughters had plenty of bread and untroubled tranquillity; yet she did not support the poor and the needy" (16:49).[10] The Bavli's Sodom stories accentuate Ezekiel's critique. The rich men of Sodom use hunger as a deliberate tool of social violence, defrauding the vulnerable and denying them bread in a calculated effort to ensure that they starve. While some fall prey to their schemes, the Bavli's Sodom stories celebrate the cleverness of Eliezer, Abraham's servant, whose trickster wiles allow him to navigate Sodom's courtrooms and banquets, escaping the city's brutal justice and turning the tables on its murderous elites.

The Eliezer tales stand in sharp contrast to the final story in Bavli Sanhedrin's Sodom cycle, in which a young woman defies the cruel law to sneak food to a starving man. In a narrative move that subverts the gender polemic of Ezek 16, the Bavli imagines a "daughter" of Sodom as the one person who subverts the city's harsh decree, who shares her bread with the poor. Her compassion is met with cruelty. When the men of Sodom discover her act, they smear her body with honey and stand her on the city wall, until hornets come and eat her alive.[11] The Sodom cycle thus closes with a haunting moment of violence, in which animal hunger is conscripted to enforce a brutal human regime. In rabbinic sources, hunger often serves as a symbolic articulation of sexual desire.[12] In the Sodom story, the rabbinic image of bees feasting on a woman's exposed flesh gives hunger a bestial cast, intertwining perversion and punishment with the instinctive drive of an animal to feed. Even as the rabbinic storytellers use this tale to dramatize the horrors of Sodom, the woman's death underscores the way gender contours the rabbis' capacity to imagine subversion and resistance. Eliezer surmounts personal peril to fill his own belly; the woman risks herself to feed another and instead becomes food.

When the Sodom stories are set alongside Sanhedrin's stories of the

---

10. The translation follows the NJPS. The emphasis on Sodom's refusal to offer hospitality to the poor stands in sharp contrast to Abraham's embrace of hospitality, particularly his choice to offer food to the three strangers who appear at the terebinths of Mamre in Gen 18:1–8, an encounter that eventually culminates in the revelation of God's judgment against Sodom. I thank Jeffrey Rubenstein for his insightful suggestions with regard to these biblical intertexts.

11. Throughout this article, I use the terms *hornet* and *bee* interchangeably.

12. On the metaphorical use of food and hunger to discuss sexuality in rabbinic literature, see Gail Labovitz, "Is Rav's Wife 'a Dish'? Food and Eating Metaphors in Rabbinic Discourse of Sexuality and Gender Relations," *SJC* 18 (2008): 147–70; Michael Satlow, *Tasting the Dish: Rabbinic Rhetorics of Sexuality*, BJS 303 (Providence, RI: Brown Judaic Studies, 1995).

flood, however, they shed light on different lines of social hierarchy: the delineation between species that seeks to divide the human from the beast. In describing the sins that provoked the flood, the Bavli describes a world of sexual and species perversion, in which humans have sexual relations with the animals and breed their beasts in ways that create new animal kinds. The ark aims to foreclose such species crossings, as it shepherds a small band of chaste survivors into a postdiluvian world unmarred by such transgressions. But the specter of forbidden sexuality continues to haunt Noah and his fellow creatures, even as other hungers drive the Bavli's narrative attention. When the Bavli speaks of the days on the ark, it focuses particularly on the problem of animal eating, lingering over accounts of how Noah and his son Shem painstakingly tend the animals and nourish them. In these stories, food becomes a striking site of interspecies intimacy, a way of conceptualizing care that crosses the species line. While studies of food and fasting in late antiquity have long highlighted the ways in which eating and asceticism allow *human* subjects to craft the self as a moral subject by disciplining its desires, the Bavli's Noah tales suggest that these arts of eating do not belong to humans alone.[13] Bavli Sanhedrin imagines hunger as an opportunity to exercise moral agency—recognizing both the perils and possibilities of hunger as a capacity that joins all creatures in the community of flesh.

Becoming Food for Bees: Hunger and Resistance in the Story of the Woman of Sodom

Echoing a common motif in rabbinic interpretations of Gen 18, the closing narrative of Bavli Sanhedrin's Sodom cycle asserts that God destroys the city of Sodom in response to a woman's cry.[14] My translation follows the Jerusalem Yad HaRav Herzog manuscript, which preserves a more expansive Yemenite tradition than the laconic Ashkenazi text that appears in the printed edition.[15] B. Sanh. 109b reads:

---

13. Michel Foucault, "Technologies of the Self," in *Technologies of the Self: A Seminar with Michel Foucault*, ed. Luther H. Martin, Huck Gutman, and Patrick H. Hutton (Amherst: University of Massachusetts Press, 1988); Eliezer Diamond, *Holy Men and Hunger Artists: Fasting and Asceticism in Rabbinic Culture* (New York: Oxford University Press, 2004).

14. Versions of this story appear in Gen. Rab. 49:6 and Pirqe R. El. 25. On the Sodom cycle in Bavli Sanhedrin, see Eliezer Segal, "A Funny Thing Happened on the Way to Sodom," *JSJ* 46 (2015): 103–29; Margaret Jacobi, "Literary Construction in the Babylonian Talmud: A Case-Study from Perek Helek" (PhD diss., Birmingham University, 2014); Eli Yassif, *The Hebrew Folktale: History, Genre, Meaning*, Folklore Studies in Translation (Bloomington: Indiana University Press, 2009).

15. There are four surviving manuscripts for Bavli Sanhedrin, three of which (MSS Munich 95, Karlsruhe-Reuchlin, and Florence) preserve an Ashkenazi tradition. The fourth,

A young girl worried about a certain poor man.
She would bring him bread in a pitcher.
They said, "What is going on—
that this poor man remains alive, more than the usual measure?"
They searched for her and found her
and they smeared her with honey
and they stood her on the rampart of the city wall.
Hornets came and consumed her.

And this is what is written: *And God said,*
"Because the cry of Sodom and Gomorrah is great [rabba]" (Gen 18:20).
And Rav Yehudah said that Rav said:
On account of the matter of the girl [*riva*].
And this is what is written:
"I will go down and I will see,
on account of the outcry that has reached me" (Gen 18:21).
The outcry of that girl.

The Bavli's tale recounts the execution of a young woman who hides bread in her pitcher to feed a starving man. When the men of Sodom discover her generosity, they condemn her to a gruesome death, daubing her body in honey and standing her upon the city wall, so that hornets come and eat her alive. It is her cry—the cry of the eaten, of the woman become food—that summons divine attention and prompts God's decision to destroy the city. The tradition of associating the destruction of Sodom with the cry of a woman rests on two distinctive particularities of the biblical text. When Gen 18:21 describes God's decision to "go down and see, on account of the outcry that has reached me, it uses a feminine ending for the cry (*tsaʿaqatah*). The midrash Genesis Rabbah, recounting a parallel version of this tale, makes the gendered reasoning specific: "It does not say, 'according to *their* cry, but rather according to *her* cry—the cry of the girl" (Gen. Rab. 49:6). The Bavli also finds a second intimation of this story in Gen 18:20. Glossing a verse that describes the cry of the city, the rabbis note the aural similarities between the Hebrew word for "great" (*rabba*) and the Aramaic word for "young girl" (*riva*), explicitly linking the death of this

---

Jerusalem Yad HaRav Herzog, is a Yemenite manuscript. Though the manuscript is significantly later than the Ashkenazi manuscripts, Mordechai Sabato argues that it preserves the most authentic version of the Sanhedrin traditions. It is more closely related to texts found in the Geniza, as well as to citations by the medieval authorities Alfasi and Nachmanides (Sabato, *A Yemenite Manuscript of Tractate Sanhedrin and Its Place in the Text Tradition* [Jerusalem: Yad Ben-Zvi, 1998], 80–99). The text of the Vilna reads as follows: "There was a young girl who would bring bread to a poor man in her pitcher. The matter was revealed. They smeared her with honey and they stood her on the rampart of the city wall. Hornets came and consumed her. And this is what is written: *And God said, 'Because the cry of Sodom and Gomorrah is great* [rabba]' (Gen 18:20). And Rav Yehudah said that Rav said: On account of the matter of the girl [*riva*]."

young woman with the destruction that follows. Her cry becomes the cry of the city, and to her pain God responds.

How shall we understand the power of hunger in this story? In this tale, the Bavli fashions hunger into an imperative that drives the woman's compassionate act and also becomes the means of her punishment. The affective power of hunger is particularly acute in the Yemenite version of the tale. While the Vilna text simply states that "there was a young girl who would bring bread to a poor man in her pitcher," the Yemenite version emphasizes her feeling. His hunger "grieves her" (*karei lah*); the use of the personal pronoun makes plain the way his hunger acts upon her, affects her own self. Hunger is a powerful force, one that goads her to action. Though rabbinic texts often conceptualize hunger as a potent drive, as a need that demands fulfillment, this story is striking for the way it positions the hunger of another as a force that compels action and response.[16] The woman is driven not by her own biological imperative, but by an ethical one. In feeling with the poor man, she acts against the interest of her own flesh. She faces risk not because she herself hungers but because she attends to another's need. In the Bavli's tale, her compassion is repaid by a death that suborns hunger's moral force, a death that makes her body into a banquet for the bees.

The rabbinic storytellers align themselves with the girl whose felt response to a poor man's hunger drives her to subvert the power of a brutal regime. In the face of such brutality, the rabbis figure the young woman's willingness to go against Sodom's harsh decree as a righteous act, an act championed by God. The Yemenite version of this story dramatizes the dissonance between her generous response and Sodom's hardheartedness in the face of hunger. The men of Sodom ask why the poor man remains alive, "beyond his measure" (*tapei mi-sheiʿura*). It is a haunting phrase, suggestive of the calculated death of the poor. It depicts a world in which men of Sodom know the precise amount of time an impoverished man can survive on their streets, where no one offers him bread. The men of Sodom know the very measure of a poor man's life; they can calculate how long it will take for him to die of his own accord. Since this particular man has outlived his allotted portion, they are determined to root out the source of his continued survival. While the Vilna's version transitions to the final scene by declaring that "the matter was revealed," the Yemenite tradition highlights the embodied action of the men of Sodom through a rapid series of active verbs. They search, they find, they smear, and they stand her on the wall for punishment. By stressing the way in which the

16. Susan R. Holman documents the rhetorical use of hunger in late antique Christian preaching as a reality that demands generosity, giving, and ethical concern (*The Hungry Are Dying: Beggars and Bishops in Roman Cappadocia*, OSHT [New York: Oxford University Press, 2001], 64–98).

men investigate the crime, the Yemenite version prefigures the final biblical prooftext, which is absent in the Vilna's version. In Gen 18:21, God decides to "go down and see" (*ʾaradah-na vĕʾarĕʾah*) what has prompted the cry, an act that mirrors the investigative tendencies of the men of Sodom and likewise results in a similarly decisive judgment.

Versions of this tale appear elsewhere in rabbinic literature, but only the Bavli's story positions hunger as both the cause of her crime *and* the means of her punishment. Gen. Rab. 49:6 begins with two young women drawing water from the well. One observes that the other is looking quite pale, and she confesses, "We have no food left and are ready to die." The young woman saves the other by filling her own pitcher with flour; the two covertly exchange pitchers when they meet again. When the generous act is discovered, the men of Sodom burn her alive—and God is moved to requite justice, in response to her cry. In Pirqe R. El. 25, the young woman is identified as the daughter of Lot, who offers food and provisions to a poor man; when she is discovered, the men of Sodom burn her by fire.[17] While all three rabbinic tales link the girl's persecution with her transgressive choice to offer food in the face of death, only the Bavli's version imagines her eaten in turn. Both midrashic stories use the burning of the girl to anticipate God's own fiery response to Sodom's cruelty, a neat measure-for-measure motif that communicates the precise economy of divine justice. The Bavli tells the story differently. In the Talmud's tale, it is the men of Sodom who enact a measure-for-measure punishment, tailoring her death to the particulars of her transgression. Because the woman offered food, she becomes food. Her body is slathered with honey, and she is eaten up (*ʾokhlehu*) by hornets. The Bavli's language is precise. She is not stung to death; she is devoured.

The Bavli's account of the woman of Sodom's death seems to play upon motifs of Persian execution in which human flesh is devoured by insects, after being smeared with honey to summon a ravenous swarm. An early attestation of honey as a Persian death sentence appears in the infamous "death of the troughs," through which the Achaemenian emperor Artaxerxes II (404 BCE–358 BCE) executed the rebellious soldier Mithridates.[18] Plutarch describes how the Persians lay the condemned man in a trough and then fit a second trough overtop his body, tightly enough that only his head, hands, and feet stuck out. Then they fed him milk and honey and poured it over his face, and left him exposed so that "a multi-

17. On the historical context of the midrash and its manuscript traditions, see Rachel Adelman, *The Return of the Repressed: Pirqe de-Rabbi Eliezer and the Pseudepigrapha*, JSJSup 140 (Leiden: Brill, 2009), 35–48.

18. Bruce Lincoln, *Religion, Empire, and Torture: The Case of Achaemenian Persia, with a Postscript on Abu Ghraib* (Chicago: University of Chicago Press, 2007), 85.

tude of flies settled down, covering his face" (Plutarch, *Art.* 16.4–5).[19] The Persian death likewise fashions animals into executioners, eating away at living human flesh. Plutarch reports that during the seventeen days it took for Mithridates to die, "worms and maggots boiled up from the decay and putrefaction of his excrement, and these ate away his body, boring into his interior."[20] Analyzing the significance of this death, Bruce Lincoln argues that the act of being eaten by vermin activates a powerful Zoroastrian revulsion toward insects—a form of animal life thought to be "aggressive, venomous, death dealing, and destructive." [21] Infamous for their "ravenous appetites" and often associated with the demonic, they "travel in swarms and attack in great numbers, gnawing, biting, and poisoning their prey."[22] Perhaps the Bavli's distinctive death scene aims to activate such cultural tropes, imagining the insect as a ravenous, even demonic, dealer of death. Or the Bavli's storytellers aim to disaffiliate themselves from the men of Sodom's cruelty, choosing a form of execution that marks such brutality as distinctively Persian.

That death by honey and hornets might evoke the specific viciousness of the Persian is suggested by a similar scene in the Persian Martyr Acts, when the Christian woman Anahid is being tortured for her faith.[23] After refusing to renounce Christianity, Anahid is tortured by the Persian authorities and subjected to whipping, dismemberment, and exposure. At the height of her ordeal, her torturers stretch out and stake her body to the hillside, smear her with honey and leave her exposed.[24] Yet this tale unfolds in a manner decidedly different from the Bavli's story. Rather than fulfill the designs of Anahid's persecutors, the wasps serve as her protectors. At a moment of profound bodily vulnerability, Anahid is engulfed by a great swarm of wasps. But instead of destroying her flesh, they form "a canopy above her body" and shelter her from her persecutors.[25] Echoing a common

---

19. Plutarch attributes his account to the testimony of the Greek physician Ctesias, who claims to have been an eyewitness to the death. My quotations follow Lincoln, *Religion, Empire, and Torture,* 87. See also Lloyd Llewellyn-Jones and James Robson, *Ctesias' History of Persia: Tales of the Orient* (London: Routledge, 2010), 205.

20. Lincoln, *Religion, Empire, and Torture,* 87.

21. Ibid., 91.

22. Ibid. Lincoln notes that, in Zoroastrian religious thought, insects are understood to have been created shortly before the beginning of history, to assist in "the Evil Spirit's attack on the Wise Lord's creation, when he himself took the form of a fly."

23. Sebastian P. Brock and Susan Ashbrook Harvey, trans., *Holy Women of the Syrian Orient,* Transformation of the Classical Heritage 13 (Berkeley: University of California Press, 1998), 82–99.

24. Ibid., 96. See also discussion in Jeffrey L. Rubenstein, "Martyrdom in the Persian Martyr Acts and in the Babylonian Talmud," in *The Aggada of the Bavli and Its Cultural World,* ed. Geoffrey Herman and Jeffrey L. Rubenstein, BJS 362 (Providence, RI: Brown Judaic Studies, 2018), 175–210, here 189.

25. Brock and Harvey, *Holy Women,* 97.

narrative trope in early Christian narrative, the wild animal recognizes and affirms the sanctity of the holy figure—in ways that serve to demonstrate the depravity of the ostensibly cultured human community.[26] In the Anahid tale, the wasps' recognition of a Christian woman's piety stands in sharp contrast to the human aggressors. While humans brutalize and mutilate Anahid's body, animals recognize her sanctity, shelter her flesh, and offer her succor. By contrast, the Bavli's hornets serve as the willing executioners of the cruel city, the manifestation of its brutality and its terrible hunger.

That the Bavli's woman of Sodom is *eaten* by the hornets not only makes her death an exemplar of cruelty but also imbues it with the connotations of sexual perversion. In rabbinic culture, hunger has a dual valence: the consumption of food is often used as a metaphorical frame for sexual satisfaction.[27] In the Bavli's tale, the men of Sodom stand a young woman upon the city wall and slather her body in honey. Honey is a vivid signifier in early Jewish literature, one that not only evokes the sweet abundance of Torah and the lush fertility of the promised land but also conveys the allure of the forbidden.[28] Contrast the honey that drips from the lover's lips in Song 4:11 with the honey that flows from the mouth of the forbidden woman in Prov 5:3. As Deborah Green argues, the combination of women and honey serves as a vivid, multivalent marker of the sensual, an intimation of sexual appetite and seductive power.[29] In the Bavli's story, honey

26. On animals in Christian martyr tales, see Patricia Cox Miller, *In the Eye of the Animal: Zoological Imagination in Ancient Christianity*, Divinations (Philadelphia: University of Pennsylvania Press, 2018). On animal assistance to martyrs, including aid from insects, see Maureen Tilley, "Martyrs, Monks, Insects, and Animals," in *The Medieval World of Nature: A Book of Essays*, ed. Joyce E. Salisbury (New York: Garland, 1993), 93–107. On animal motifs in Jewish narratives of holy figures, see Eliezer Diamond, "Lions, Snakes, and Asses: Palestinian Jewish Holy Men as Masters of the Animal Kingdom," in *Jewish Culture and Society under the Christian Roman Empire*, ed. Richard Kalmin and Seth Schwartz, Interdisciplinary Studies in Ancient Culture and Religion 3 (Leuven: Peeters, 2003), 254–83.

27. As Sacha Stern observes, the metaphor of sex as food commonly serves to mark revulsion in rabbinic sources; the Bavli frequently uses the language of forbidden food to evoke disgust for the act of forbidden sexual relations (*Jewish Identity in Early Rabbinic Writings*, AGJU 23 [Leiden: Brill, 1994], 164–66).

28. On honey symbolism in biblical and rabbinic literature, see Tova Forti, "Bee's Honey—From Realia to Metaphor in Biblical Wisdom Literature," *VT* 56 (2006): 327–41; Greg Schmidt Goering, "Honey and Wormwood Taste and the Embodiment of Wisdom in the Book of Proverbs," *HeBAI* 5 (2016): 23–41; and André Villeneuve, *Nuptial Symbolism in Second Temple Writings, the New Testament and Rabbinic Literature*, AJEC 92 (Leiden: Brill, 2016), 73–74.

29. Deborah A. Green, *The Aroma of Righteousness: Scent and Seduction in Rabbinic Life and Literature* (University Park: Pennsylvania State University Press, 2011), 97–98. The rabbinic association between honey and sex is vividly crystallized in Bavli B. Batra 3b, in which Herod overthrows the Hasmonean dynasty and spares one of the women "upon whom he cast his eyes." When she learns that he wishes to marry her, she throws herself from the roof and Herod preserves her body in honey for seven years. The rabbis debate whether he engaged in sexual relations with her preserved corpse. On this tale, see Yonatan Feintuch, "External Appearance versus Internal Truth: The Aggadah of Herod in Bavli Baba Batra,"

holds the power to attract; it draws the bees inexorably to their victim. The taste of the sweet becomes the kiss of death, the lure that makes her body irresistible. The hornets come, consuming her body through a thousand little bites.[30] In imagining the female body as food, our storyteller taps into a common rabbinic discourse that, as Gail Labovitz has shown, describes sex through metaphors of taste and table—figuring women as a dish that men delight to eat.[31] But in the Bavli's tale, the men do not violate her themselves. Instead, they position the woman's honeyed body so that it rouses an animal hunger, fashioning her into a feast for bees.

Subverting the Cruel Law: Gender, Class, and the Tricksters of Sodom

As the final tale in Bavli Sanhedrin's Sodom cycle, the death of the young woman of Sodom crystallizes motifs that recur throughout the larger narrative, underscoring the cruelty and corruption of justice that reigns in the city. In contemporary discourse, Sodom has become eponymous for sexual sin. As Mark Jordan shows, Christian interpretation has long associated Sodom with perverse sexuality—not only with the infamous charge of male homosexuality, but also with a wide range of sexual pleasures and practices that were not directed toward procreation.[32] Rabbinic interpreters understood the Sodom story quite differently—as a condemnation of cruelty, greed, and inhospitality. Though a few rabbinic sources include sexual sin in their critique of Sodom, most rabbinic texts rebuke the men of Sodom for their refusal to share their wealth, particularly castigating them for turning away from the need of wayfarers and from the poor.[33] Bavli Sanhedrin's discussion of Sodom begins with an exegesis of Gen 13:13, the biblical verse that describes the men of Sodom as "wicked and sinners before the Lord exceedingly" (b. Sanh. 109a). As it outlines a variety of transgressions for which the city was condemned, the Bavli

---

AJSR 35 (2011): 85–104 and Jeffrey L. Rubenstein, "King Herod in Ardashir's Court: The Rabbinic Story of Herod (B. Bava Batra 3b–4a) in Light of Persian Sources," *AJSR* 38 (2014): 249–74.

30. The hornet is an animal the Bavli elsewhere associates with a haughty woman, describing the prophet Devorah's unseemly haughtiness; the name Devorah is also the Hebrew word for bee. See b. Meg. 14b.

31. Labovitz, "Is Rav's Wife a 'Dish'?"

32. Mark D. Jordan, *Invention of Sodomy in Christian Theology*, Chicago Series on Sexuality, History, and Society (Chicago: University of Chicago Press, 1997).

33. Margaret Jacobi documents the widespread rabbinic framing of Sodom's sinfulness in terms of their refusal to care for wayfarers, often coupled with descriptions of their great wealth or abundance ("Literary Construction in the Babylonian Talmud," 110–17). Josephus also offers a brief condemnation of Sodom, claiming that "their pride in their wealth led them to forget God and hate foreigners" (*A.J.* 1.190–94).

reiterates a common rabbinic claim that Sodom's "wickedness" is a sin of the purse.[34] Sodom, it avers, has forgotten "the Torah of the wayfarer." Echoing a motif found already in the Tosefta, the Bavli stresses that the people of Sodom have been blessed with great abundance. They live in a land that gives forth breath, whose very dust is gold. But rather than prompt generosity, this lush bounty provokes them to distrust strangers and to turn away from travelers. In the Bavli's telling, the men of Sodom ask each other, "Why do we need wayfarers? They come only to divest us of our wealth!" (b. Sanh. 109a).[35]

While the broad strokes of Sodom's greed are widespread in rabbinic literature, Bavli Sanhedrin intensifies this portrayal with a cycle of stories about the city of Sodom—unparalleled in the rabbinic corpus—that highlight the malice and perversion of justice that reigns within the city (b. Sanh. 109b).[36] The Bavli paints a portrait of a city where the law is both cruel and absurd: a city whose judges rule that a person must pay money to his own assailant, because the attacker has done him the "benefit" of bloodletting, a city where those who cross on the ferry must pay a substantial fee, but those who cross in the water pay double. When a woman miscarries after being struck by a man, the judges of Sodom instruct her husband to give his wife to the aggressor until he impregnates her and thus recreates the lost child. Amid such brutality, the Bavli's Sodom cycle recounts the exploits of two clever low-class men—an unnamed orphan and Abraham's servant Eliezer—who use clever wiles to outsmart the wicked men of Sodom and turn their cruel logic against them.[37] The biblical text itself offers little hint of why the Bavli might choose, in Eliezer Segal's words, "to cast Abraham's drab and dutiful slave as a crafty trickster who thwarts the malicious citizens of Sodom."[38] Segal argues that the motivation for Eliezer's starring role comes instead from the Roman satirical figure of the clever slave (*servus callidus*), a stock character in Latin comedy whose trickster qualities allow him to outwit his master and thereby skewer the conventional power hierarchies of the ancient world.[39] In Roman literature, the clever slave might also deploy his smarts in service to his master, or to aid star-crossed lovers who ultimately benefit from his mischief. By casting Abraham's servant Eliezer in the mold of

34. On rabbinic exegesis of Gen 13:13, see Jacobi, "Literary Construction in the Babylonian Talmud," 112.

35. The motif of the gold dust and the bread is drawn from Job 28:4–9.

36. On the Bavli's Sodom cycle as social protest, see Yassif, *Hebrew Folktale*, 235.

37. On Eliezer as a trickster figure, see ibid., 212.

38. Segal, "Funny Thing," 110.

39. Ibid., 110–13. On the Bavli's Sodom passages as satire, see Yassif, *Hebrew Folktale*, 235. On the motif of Jewish cleverness used to outwit non-Jews, see Galit Hasan-Rokem, *Web of Life: Folklore and Midrash in Rabbinic Literature*, Contraversions (Stanford, CA: Stanford University Press, 2000), 39–65.

the clever slave, Segal argues that the Bavli's storytellers create a character who can triumph over the "morally topsy-turvy world of Sodom, a society to which mischievous subversion is the appropriate religious response."[40]

While such subversion is indeed a significant element of the Bavli's Sodom stories, it is strikingly gendered. Let us consider two representative stories that showcase successful tricksters, both of them low-status men. In the first story, which appears in b. Sanh. 109a–b, a clever orphan turns the cruel justice of Sodom against the inhabitants of the city:

> One who has an ox shall herd [the city's oxen] for one day.
> One who has no oxen shall herd for two days.
> An orphan, the son of a widow, went and killed the oxen.[41]
> He went and announced in the town,
> "I have killed the oxen.
> One who had an ox shall take one hide,
> One who had no oxen shall take two."
> They said to him, "What is the reason?!"
> He said to them, "The final law is like the first."

In the Bavli's telling, the law of Sodom holds that a person who has one ox must tend the city's herd for a day, while a person who has none must tend the herd for two. Forced to herd, presumably without compensation, the orphan slays the oxen and then announces that a person who had one ox may take one hide, but those who had none may take two. When the men of Sodom protest, the orphan argues that "the last law is like the first"—a retort that forces the city's residents to confront the injustice of their own law. The orphan's trick shifts the law in favor of the vulnerable, allowing him to derive both profit and pleasure from turning the unjust law against its makers. That his trick rests on the slaughter of animals evokes no comment from the text; the oxen are collateral damage, casualties of the trickster's scheme. Their death is the means by which the orphan springs the trap and accomplishes his own rescue.

In the second trickster tale, Abraham's servant Eliezer happens upon the city of Sodom and outsmarts the men at their banquet. B. Sanh. 109b reads:

> There was a feast.
> Whenever a stranger used to come[42]

40. Segal, "Funny Thing," 128.

41. The Ashkenazi manuscripts and the Vilna printed edition specify that they gave the oxen to the orphan to herd. They also use the verb *ve-qatlinhu* to indicate that he killed them, while the Jerusalem Yad HaRav Herzog uses *shakhavinhu,* a verb that can also have sexual connotations, as in "he lay with them." The verb can be used to indicate male–male sex, as well as sex between a human and an animal.

42. The Jerusalem Yad HaRav Herzog manuscript uses *ʾakhsenaya,* "stranger" or "transient lodger."

and one of them would invite him [to the feast]—
they had a punishment that they would crucify him.
Eliezer, servant of Abraham, happened upon that feast.
He went and sat at the lowest place among them.
They said to him, "Who invited you here?"
He said, "You."
He took up his cloak and ran.
[Eliezer] went and sat by the next.
He took up his cloak and ran.
He did so until he came to the judge.
When he came to the judge, he said to him, "Who invited you here?"
He said, "You."
The judge took up his cloak and ran.
Once they had all taken their cloaks and run,
he sat at the head of the banquet and ate.[43]

This story also dramatizes the merciless law that reigns in the city of Sodom, where inviting a wayfarer to a feast becomes a capital crime. To share food with a stranger is, in Sodom, an act worthy of a traitor's death; the man who does so will be crucified.[44] The stakes of the crime are intensified by the Bavli's assertion, elsewhere in the story cycle, that the men of Sodom used to each give a wayfarer a dinar on which they had written their own names. Though they gave him money, they would refuse to give him bread—and when the traveler starved on the streets of the city, each man would reclaim his original coin.[45] The invitation to feast thus stands in sharp counter to the city's collusion, the collective effort to ensure that wayfarers cannot survive.

This is the narrative context in which Eliezer "happens upon" the feast. Might we imagine him as famished? The Bavli's tale gives us no indication of his affect, offers us no sense of whether he has begun to feel the gnaw of hunger in his own gut. But if Eliezer may himself be at risk in the city of Sodom, he also possesses the insight to recognize how the regime in Sodom leaves even the well-fed vulnerable to the brutality of the law. When the first man approaches him to ask who tendered his invitation, Eliezer claims that his interlocutor has invited him to dine. On its face, it is an absurd assertion, a brazen lie. The man to whom he speaks knows he has not invited the stranger. Yet, as the story makes plain, the truth of the

43. My translation follows the Jerusalem Yad HaRav Herzog manuscript.

44. The Bavli's critique of Sodom highlights the brutality of their justice, not only in the courtroom but also through their execution procedures. On rabbinic execution, as articulated elsewhere in Bavli Sanhedrin, see Beth Berkowitz, *Execution and Invention: Death Penalty Discourse in Early Rabbinic and Christian Cultures* (New York: Oxford University Press, 2006).

45. The sequence of the four (or sometimes five) penultimate narratives in the Sodom cycle varies widely in the manuscripts. For a table that compares the differences, see Jacobi, "Literary Construction in the Babylonian Talmud," 131.

matter hardly makes a difference. In Sodom, the mere intimation of charity might become a death sentence. The man runs, rather than risk facing the charges. As Eliezer moves up the ranks of Sodom's table, he forces each of the men to abandon his place at the feast. Even the judge, who should presumably be sure of his own ability to navigate the systems of justice in the city, flees when Eliezer confronts him. Once he clears the men of Sodom from the banquet, Eliezer sits alone at the table and consumes the feast. His clever trick has turned the trap back on the men who would have starved him, forcing them instead to abandon their food and flee.

While both Eliezer and the orphan use trickster strategies to successfully subvert an unjust law, the woman of Sodom likewise tries a trick—hiding bread in her pitcher to smuggle it to the poor man. But where the men's tricks successfully turn the tables on unjust authority, the woman's ruse is discovered and she pays with her life. The Sodom story-cycle suggests that gender makes a powerful difference in rabbinic trickster tales. As I have argued elsewhere, the Bavli narrates with relish the exploits of male tricksters who use clever stratagems to subvert authority, while casting women's challenges in a very different light.[46] The woman of Sodom's subversion of the law is arguably more significant than Eliezer's, and her challenge to the culture of Sodom seems even more in keeping with rabbinic ethical principles. While Eliezer acts in order to save his own skin and secure his own place at the table, the woman of Sodom risks herself to save another—offering bread to a man in need. And while Eliezer is able outwit the men of Sodom and turn them into buffoonish figures who take up their cloaks and run from the room, the Bavli affords the woman of Sodom no such cultural power. She is no trickster to subvert authority and live to tell the tale. Her resistance brings the full wrath of the city's men to bear upon her own body. Though her cry summons divine attention and brings a final punishment upon the city, God's intervention comes too late to save her flesh.

Gender, Affect, and Subversion: Extrajuridical Violence in the Story of the Woman of Sodom

The Bavli's story of the woman of Sodom centers on a decidedly public death, a scene that makes both visible and visceral the power of the men of Sodom, the way they use violence to exercise authority over the bodies

46. Julia Watts Belser, "Rabbinic Trickster Tales: The Sex and Gender Politics of the Bavli's Sinful Sages," in *Talmudic Transgressions: Engaging the Work of Daniel Boyarin*, ed. Charlotte Elisheva Fonrobert et al., JSJSup 181 (Leiden: Brill, 2017), 274–92.

of those who violate their decrees. Unlike Eliezer, the young woman in our tale is a resident of Sodom, a daughter who lives in a city (perhaps even in a household) that expects impoverished people to starve in the streets. But she refuses the dictates of the city, refuses to comport herself with the rules of the regime. In sustaining the poor man, the young woman of Sodom sets herself at odds with the elites of her city, the men who have fashioned the rules so that the hungry will not survive. When her resistance is revealed, the men of Sodom punish her with a virulence that stands out as shocking, even after the recitation of their other crimes. How shall we understand this response? In analyzing the spectacular violence the woman of Sodom provokes, I think of the particular force with which white supremacists hurl the epithet "race traitor," the rage directed against one who goes against the interests of "her own kind."[47] Let me be plain: the notion of the race traitor is indelibly steeped in the particularity of distinctive racial histories and white supremacist logics; it does not belong within the Bavli's cultural lexicon. The kinships I am drawing here are affective, not historical; they are meant to help us parse the power of feeling, not the specifics of culture and class.[48] But I wonder: might imagining the woman of Sodom as a traitor to her class allow us to better understand the affective charge that her crime carries, the way her betrayal *feels* to the men who brutalize her body?

In this matter of feeling, gender makes a difference. The woman of Sodom rejects the compact made by the wealthy to starve those who lack sufficient resources. She acts for the poor man, against the interest of her kin. It is her gender, I contend, that crystallizes and catalyzes the particular vehemence of the men of Sodom's response. Because she is expected to be their own subordinate, her subversion of their law threatens not only their control of the city, but also their authority over the household. Her feeding of the hungry man threatens their sway not just over the streets of the city but over their own hearth. Consider her use of the pitcher to sneak food to the poor man. The pitcher frequently appears in biblical and rabbinic narrative as a gendered vessel, a vessel through which women and girls draw water for their household.[49] When the woman of Sodom hides bread in her pitcher, she uses the pitcher to claim and craft woman's space.

47. On the affective power of the epithet "race traitor," see Mab Segrest, *Memoir of a Race Traitor* (Boston: South End, 1994); for a critical interrogation of the term "race traitor" and its relationship to law, see Naomi Zack, "White Ideas," in *Whiteness: Feminist Philosophical Reflections*, ed. Chris J. Cuomo and Kim Q. Hall (Lanham, MD: Rowman & Littlefield, 1999), 77–84.

48. On the relationship between affect and racism, see Sharon Patricia Holland, *The Erotic Life of Racism* (Durham, NC: Duke University Press, 2012); Donovan O. Schaefer, *Religious Affects: Animality, Evolution, and Power* (Durham, NC: Duke University Press, 2015), 120–46,

49. On the significance of the pitcher in the biblical account of Eliezer's recognition of

The pitcher becomes a tool of concealment, a means of keeping the bread and the subversion it entails from the gaze of (elite) men. But what began as hidden in the end becomes exposed. When the men of Sodom discover her ruse, they "stand her upon the rampart of the city wall," enacting an execution that centers her body in the public eye. While the punishment reveals the stark consequences of her transgression, we misread her death if we focus solely on the woman of Sodom. This is a public killing, a death that is meant to make plain the cost of going against the regime, a death that broadcasts threat far beyond the particularity of the singular resisting body. Those who live within the city are meant to see and know the price of stepping out of line.

Strikingly, at the conclusion of a *sugya* that has dramatized the profound injustice of the city's courts, this tale proceeds without the consultation of a judge. There is no legal process to give sanction to the violence. The men of Sodom have appointed themselves as executioners. Yet, as the Bavli's *sugya* has made plain, their actions align with the will of Sodom's corrupt court; the men might act without formal judicial authority, but their violence serves as an extension of the court's own principles. The woman of Sodom's death is orchestrated on the city ramparts, at the hands of men who believe themselves able to kill with impunity, men who know they need fear no reprisal from the city's corrupt judges.

To grasp the cultural power of this death, to probe its effects within the imagined city of Sodom, I ask the reader to consider this rabbinic story alongside another form of public execution: the lynching of African American men (and some women) in the post–Civil War American South.[50] This is a risk. The discontinuities between these two forms of violence are vast enough to need no detailed recounting. Even if we leave aside the chasms of cultural and historical difference between these communities, even if we recognize that the dynamics of white supremacy that buttress lynching as a historical practice have no neat analog in rabbinic culture, even then, we must also acknowledge the epistemic risk in laying the lived reality of racial terror against a thin scrap of rabbinic story, a story that has no mate-

---

Rebecca as the woman he should seek as Isaac's wife, see Tikva Frymer-Kensky, *Reading the Women of the Bible: A New Interpretation of Their Stories* (New York: Schocken, 2008), 7–10.

50. The literature on lynching is vast; the works that have most shaped my own thinking on the subject are James Cone, *The Cross and the Lynching Tree* (Maryknoll, NY: Orbis, 2011); Margaret Vandiver, *Lethal Punishment: Lynchings and Legal Executions in the South* (New Brunswick, NJ: Rutgers University Press, 2006); Ashraf H. A. Rushdy, *American Lynching* (New Haven: Yale University Press, 2012); Angela Sims, *Lynched: The Power of Memory in a Culture of Terror* (Waco, TX: Baylor University Press, 2017); Amy Louise Wood, *Lynching and Spectacle: Witnessing Racial Violence in America, 1890–1940*, New Directions in Southern Studies (Chapel Hill: University of North Carolina Press, 2009). On women and lynching, see Evelyn M. Simien, ed. *Gender and Lynching: The Politics of Memory* (New York: Palgrave Macmillan, 2011).

rial anchor beyond the power it holds in the minds of its tellers. Lynching is a physical and psychic threat, a visceral act of violence enacted against past and present Black bodies. The Sodom story is different. The woman of Sodom is a textual figure, not a woman of bone and flesh.

I do not aim to trade in false equivalencies. Nonetheless, I suggest that the dynamics of power, spectacle, and violence that drive the Bavli's tale can be illuminated by the scholarly work that probes the political and religious significations of lynching. I do not mean that the woman of Sodom's death matches the contours of American racial terror; it does not. I mean instead that lynching offers, in certain respects, a powerful analog to the kind of violence with which the rabbis mean to grapple—a violence whose public character is meant to terrorize, to reinscribe a social hierarchy that the victim dared to breach; a violence that deploys spectatorship to expose the body to humiliation, in which the witnesses feast on the spectacle of pain; a violence that lays claim to a certain kind of quasi-judicial power.

Consider how the practice of lynching reveals the complex relationship between legal authority and social violence. Lynching is conventionally understood as mob violence, a practice that operates outside the law—"extralegal punishment," in the words of James Cone, "sanctioned by the community."[51] But such a characterization fails to recognize the complicity of local authorities in giving sanction to the mob, in providing cover for violence. In historical terms, the lynching of African American men gained traction during the Reconstruction era; it served as a way to viscerally contest the civil rights and public protections granted to African Americans by the federal government. Lynching serves to contest the imposed law of a distant federal authority, but it is a mistake to understand it as *countering* the rule of law *tout court*. Lynching is made possible by strategic disinclination of local authorities to prosecute those who perform such violence, by powerful institutions and cultural practices that shield the perpetrators. The mob frequently acted with the tacit (if not overt) approval of judges and officials, protected by local refusal to prosecute such killings as a crime.[52] Lynching in America was no secret act. Newspapers publicized the details of an anticipated lynching, and white spectators gathered in droves to savor the spectacle of death.[53] Journalists documented the killings in salacious detail, even as they maintained a studied innocence when it came to the identities of the perpetrators. The

51. Cone, *Cross and the Lynching Tree*, 3.

52. "Far from being a *defiance* of the law," Rushdy contends, "lynching ... is an *assertion* of it, the fundamental assertion of self-governing men" (*American Lynching*, 1; emphasis original). On the relationship between lynching and legal execution, see Vandiver, *Lethal Punishment*, 10.

53. On "spectacle lynchings" in American culture, see Grace Elizabeth Hale, *Making Whiteness: The Culture of Segregation in the South, 1890–1940* (1998; repr., New York: Knopf Doubleday, 2010), 199–240.

state strategically divested from knowledge of the crime; the killing was always done "at the hands of persons unknown."[54] Lynching rests upon collusion between court and community.

In the Bavli's telling, the city of Sodom is similarly situated. The people of Sodom are subject to the cruelty of the city's courts, in which corrupt judges shield the perpetrators of violence and subject victims who dare seek redress to further punishment. In such a city, the men who kill the woman of Sodom on the city wall need have no fear of censure. While they never bring the woman before a judge, and while they seek no legal sanction for their killing, their actions are well in line with the principles of (in)justice that govern their city. It is the very presence of the corrupt court that allows the men of Sodom to act with impunity, to know that their actions will escape judgment. In the Bavli's telling, the men of Sodom come face to face with divine justice—with the Judge who refuses to sanction such brutality. The Bavli thus deploys this story to challenge the cruel law of Sodom, to align its own ethics with the woman rather than the mob, to lift up her voice as the cry that summons God and calls the wicked to account. For the Bavli, the woman's death becomes the catalyst for divine judgment, the impetus that ends the cruel reign of injustice in the city. The woman dies, and Sodom burns.

But let us pause and consider the consequences of this telling, to ask what else the Bavli gains through the drama of this death. Think with me about the details over which the Bavli lingers: honey, the hornets, the eating of the woman's flesh. This is, I believe, a tale meant to titillate, this story of a woman smeared with sweetness, becoming food for bees. Horror functions as a fuel for fascination, a driver of desire. Consider also how little shelter this tale of divine intervention affords the woman wronged, how little rescue it offers her. For all that our tale is crafted for rabbinic audiences, for all that it would have been told and retold in the all-male preserve of the rabbinic study house, I cannot help but wonder: Did this story travel, as stories often do? Did its telling echo in the ears of the rabbis' own subordinates? Did it also send a message to the women, wives, and daughters who might have been tempted to sneak bread in their own pitchers, who might marshal their own protest against the dictates of *rabbinic* authority? Even as this story serves primarily to affirm rabbinic justice contra Sodom, even as it allows the rabbis to imagine themselves as distant from and different from the men of that cruel city, I also ask: Does the woman of Sodom also stand as a testament to the consequences of subversion, a reminder of the way men punish women who protest? I cannot read this rabbinic story without thinking of the men who tell it, the men who might profit in part from its violence, even as they mean to

54. Cone, *Cross and the Lynching Tree*, 11.

disavow its cruelty. But if this is so, then I must interrogate my own narrative choices, ask how my own whiteness contours the stories *I* have told. I think about the deaths I have evoked, the details I have chosen, those I have pared away. Does telling the story of a killing make us complicit in the terror it provokes?

Animality and Hunger: Lynching, Barbarism, and the Bavli's Death by Bees

In *The Cross and the Lynching Tree,* James Cone emphasizes that the murder of black men in Reconstruction-era America was a white media spectacle, one that could attract a crowd of up to twenty thousand white spectators. Narrating the lynching as a white American festival, Cone writes:

> It was a family affair, a ritual celebration of white supremacy, where women and children were often given the first opportunity to torture black victims—burning black flesh and cutting off genitals, fingers, toes, and ears as souvenirs. Postcards were made from the photographs taken of black victims with white lynchers and onlookers smiling as they struck a pose for the camera. They were sold for ten to twenty-give cents to members of the crowd, who then mailed them to relatives and friends, often with a note saying something like this: "This is the barbeque we had last night."[55]

That handwritten note, scrawled on the back of a photograph of the burnt body of William Stanley, murdered in August 1915 in Temple, Texas, throws into vulgar relief the sharp conjunction between violence and hunger.[56] The writer's language portrays the lynching as a quintessential white American picnic; the lynched man's body becomes the feast.[57] Can I write these words without my own gut twisting, without turning away in revulsion? The designation *barbeque* performs potent rhetorical work, layered over the brutal reality of corporeal violence. It denies the humanity of the victim, fashions him into a subject who can be eaten with impunity. This is no cannibalism, this white crowd gathered round in its hunger for black flesh. Through the designation *barbeque,* our writer invests the violence with the legitimacy of sanctioned eating. To dismember the body, to burn the flesh, to char the limbs—this is the making of man into meat; the transformation of human into animal, fit to be consumed.

---

55. Cone, *Cross and the Lynching Tree,* 9.

56. James Allen, *Without Sanctuary: Lynching Photography in America* (Santa Fe, NM: Twin Palms, 2003), front and back postcard photos 25 and 26, the burnt corpse of William Stanley, August 1915, Temple, Texas.

57. On lynching as ritual performance that "created a spectacle of virtuous and sanctified white supremacy," see Wood, *Lynching and Spectacle,* 61.

The Sodom story also centers on a death that turns a woman into food. The Bavli configures the dynamics of eating and animality somewhat differently, fashioning the woman's body not as a feast for white racists but as a banquet for the beasts. Nonetheless, I suggest that the rabbinic story invests the consumption of the human with a similar charge. To become food is to lose a certain privileged status as human: the privilege to be the eater, rather than the eaten.[58] While animal predation of humans is hardly without precedent, we humans commonly imagine ourselves inedible. Assessing the rarity with which humans acknowledge that we might ourselves be food, Erika Murphy argues that, in contemporary culture, the category of the human is often imbued with "the privilege of an untouchable corporeality," the notion that we occupy "the top of the food chain."[59] Against this imagined surety of flesh, Murphy contends that ecological correctness requires us to acknowledge that "humans are a consumable product." All of us return to the earth "through the mouths and stomachs of insects, bacteria, and sometimes larger predators who find us a rather easy meal."[60] In the cultural world of late antiquity, the human is not cordoned off so neatly from the prospect of being eaten. The Bavli fears that other animals might prey on humans; it tells of a community across the Jordan that decreed a fast because wolves had devoured two children (b. Ta'an. 19a).[61] Yet, in most rabbinic traditions, the recognition that humans might become food for beasts is freighted with moral meaning. Consider the tradition attributed to Rami b. Abba that "an animal does not overpower a man unless the man looks like an animal in its eyes."[62] So too, the medieval commentator Rashi maintains, "Since the generation of the flood went wrong, they were allowed to become food for wild animals—

---

58. Genesis 9:3–5 lays out the relations of humans and animals after the flood, framing human–animal hierarchy in terms of permissible consumption of flesh. Though humans must abstain from eating animal blood, they are granted permission to eat "every creature that lives." If their own life-blood is shed, however, God will require a reckoning—from animals and from humans who kill.

59. Erika Murphy, "Devouring the Human: Digestion of a Corporeal Soteriology," in *Divinanimality: Animal Theory, Creaturely Theology*, ed. Stephen D. Moore, Transdisciplinary Theological Colloquia (New York: Fordham University Press, 2014), 51–62, here 51. Beth Berkowitz discusses a recent turn in critical animal studies, in which theorists call attention to the ways in which humans are like animals, rather than solely thinking about the ways in which animals are like us. Her first example of this position highlights the salience of eating, as she asks readers to consider, "with Gilles Deleuze, that we too are slabs of meat, and that the packaged meat in the butcher section of the supermarket looks remarkably like our own body parts" (Berkowitz, *Animals and Animality in the Babylonian Talmud*, 11).

60. Murphy, "Devouring the Human," 51.

61. In b. Ḥul. 126a, a dog eats the flesh of a human corpse and dies on the threshold, bringing corpse impurity with him.

62. B. Šabb. 151b, glossing Ps 49:13, "But if man does not abide in honor, he is like the beasts that perish."

to be ruled by them."[63] When humans become food for the animals, it is a sign of human ethical failing—a moral collapse that results in the faltering of the species line.

In the Bavli's Sodom story, the image of a woman devoured by bees serves as a visceral indictment of the extraordinary barbarism of the city of Sodom, a city whose embrace of injustice and deliberate cruelty toward the poor was so profound that they punished a young woman's charity by smearing her in honey, to be eaten alive by hornets. Exposed to the elements and the animals alike, her body stands as a striking warning to those who would defy the law of the land, a visible marker of the cost of defiance. The men of Sodom craft a perverse measure-for-measure punishment: She who gives food to a man in need will herself become food for the ravenous bees. In the Bavli's telling, animal hunger becomes a potent tool of human discipline. By inverting the conventional hierarchy of eater and eaten, the Sodom story blurs the usual lines between the species, making the animal the ravager of the human body. For the Bavli, such species transgression becomes another sign of the depravity of the men of Sodom; they are the men who wantonly feed women to the beasts. Species transgression is also infused, in the Bavli's telling, with the taste of sexual perversion. The condemned woman stands exposed on the city wall, her body dripping with sensuous sweetness. The erotic connotations of honey, coupled with the vivid rabbinic association between sex and food, turn the woman's body into a love feast for the bees. She is eaten up, consumed. Her flesh feeds a creaturely hunger.

Transgressing Sex and Species: Human–Animal Crossings and the Generation of the Flood

In Bavli Sanhedrin's accounts of the generation of the flood, the notion of species transgression as sexual perversion emerges as one of the defining sins that provokes God's destruction of the earth. In the rabbinic telling, the flood was a reaction to forbidden sexual relations, a response to an antediluvian refusal to keep distinct the divisions between species and kinds. B. Sanh. 108a reads:

> "*God saw the earth and how all flesh* [kol basar]
> *had corrupted its way* [darkho] *upon the earth.*" (Gen 6:12)
> R. Yoḥanan said:
> It teaches that they mated the domesticated animals [*behemah*]
> upon [*ʿal*] the wild animals [*ḥayah*]

63. Rashi on Gen 9:5. See Gross, *Question of the Animal and Religion*, 162.

and the wild upon the domesticated,
and all of them upon the man [*'adam*]
and the man upon all of them.

The Bavli imagines the antediluvian world as a place where human sexual permissiveness has collapsed the boundaries between kinds. The passage begins with an interpretation of Gen 6:12, in which God sees how "all flesh" (*kol basar*) has corrupted "its way" (*darkho*), a phrase that rabbinic interpreters commonly invest with a sexual connotation. While rabbinic texts elsewhere use the language of *darkho* to stigmatize sex between men or to rebuke nonprocreative forms of male–female sex, our passage associates it with sexual relations that blur the categorical distinctions between human and animal kinds.[64] Bavli Sanhedrin inveighs against two kinds of sex: that which crosses the line between animality and humanity and that which transgress the boundary between the domesticated and the wild. Consider the three named categories this passage uses, which represent only a small subset of the taxonomical divisions that rabbinic tradition uses to organize the creaturely world. *Behemah* represents a grouping of large domesticated animals, typified by cattle. In biblical Hebrew, it is often distinguished from *tzon*, the category of small domesticates, like sheep and goats.[65] Our passage fashions the distinction between kinds differently. It juxtaposes domesticated livestock (*behemah*) against wild animals (*ḥayah*), both of which are imagined as distinct from the human, *'adam*.[66]

While it is tempting to describe the configurations noted in this passage as cross-species sex, this is not entirely accurate. Though the Bavli clearly inveighs against liaisons among diverse kinds, the primary thrust

64. As Satlow has demonstrated, rabbinic literature also uses the phrase *lo kedarkha* to describe nonprocreative sexual relations, including male–male sex, as well as anal intercourse between a man and a woman. He argues that, while this phrase "is often translated as unnatural sex/intercourse, neither the phrase itself nor any other rabbinic rhetoric implies the attachment of an argument from nature to anal intercourse" (*Tasting the Dish*, 239). The same phrase also appears in rabbinic literature in a variety of (nonsexual) legal contexts to signal behavior that differs from prevailing custom.

65. On different animal kinds in the Bavli, see Wasserman, *Jews, Gentiles, and Other Animals*, 93.

66. In first approaching this passage, I instinctively translated *'adam* in gender-inclusive terms, not as a marker for the human male, but as a marker for humanity that is imagined as distinct from the creature. But as I have worked more closely with these texts, I am no longer certain that the gender-inclusive term accurately reflects a rabbinic sensibility. Is this rabbinic passage really about humans in general, or about human men in particular? While the passage does not give us a clear indication of its intentions, I suspect the latter. In contrast to the Genesis Rabbah flood traditions, which include explicit discussion of female sexuality through the exegesis of the biblical passage that recounts how the "sons of God" saw the "daughters of men" and took them as wives, Bavli Sanhedrin shows little interest in women's sexuality.

of R. Yohanan's critique is not primarily focused on illicit sexual desire. The generation of the flood is condemned not simply for participating in forbidden sex but for orchestrating it—for a deliberate breeding program that violates the "way" God established for diverse "kinds." Nor is the prohibition simply a violation of species integrity in the biological sense. Consider the pairings this text castigates, in contrast to the ones that remain unmarked. The problem lies in sexual relations that mingle the human with the creature, the wild with the domesticated. Sexual relations between two predators—a lion and a wolf, for example, both wild animals according to the Bavli's schema—would occasion no protest. Nor does our passage take exception to relations between a wolf and a deer, two wild animals that might ordinarily be predator and prey. By contrast, a liaison between a wolf and a cow would provoke the Bavli's ire. In singling out the categories of *behemah* and *ḥayah,* the Bavli castigates sexual unions that cross the domestication line, a line fashioned, at least in part, by the habits of hunger. What is one way domesticated animals differ from wild ones? Domesticates often depend on humans as providers of food.[67]

In contrast to the improper sexual relations that plunge the world into flood, the Bavli imagines the ark as a domestic sanctuary, a space in which feeding and eating across species lines becomes a sanctioned form of intimacy and care between creatures. The Bavli's ark becomes an idealized utopian world, a world whose construction inscribes clear distinctions between human and other animal kinds. B. Sanh. 108b reads:

> *With bottom, second, and third stories, you shall make it.* (Gen 6:16)
> It was taught:
> The bottom story is for excrement;
> the middle is for animals [*behemah*];
> the top is for the human.

Our text describes an ark of three levels, with architectural divisions designed to keep human and animal bodies apart, while also separating living creatures from their waste. While the ark presumably allows the *behemot* and the *ḥayot* to mingle in close physical proximity amid quarters that are presumably quite cramped indeed, the architecture of the vessel serves as an antidote (or at least an architectural impediment) to the human antediluvian desires. The ark is constructed to constrain the

67. David Nibert offers a critical account of human domestication of animals, arguing domestication practices remain inextricably linked to human violence, and that human exploitation of animals continues to drive conquest, subjugation, and capitalism today (*Animal Oppression and Human Violence: Domesecration, Capitalism, and Global Conflict,* Critical Perspectives on Animals: Theory, Culture, Science, and Law (New York: Columbia University Press, 2013).

forbidden body contacts that brought about catastrophe.[68] Elsewhere in this passage, Bavli Sanhedrin emphasizes that the ark itself is to be a space of complete sexual renunciation. Not only is there no sex between human and animal kinds; sex between human partners is also forbidden. Aboard the ark, even ordinarily permissible sexual connections are suspended.

At the Nexus of Nurture and Nourishment: Eating on the Ark

While sexual relations are foreclosed within the ark, Bavli Sanhedrin's narrative traditions imagine eating as an alternative route to intimacy between humans and animals, an expression of care and nurture that brings creaturely bodies together in sanctioned relationships. But eating on the ark is not without peril. The Bavli dramatizes the difficulty that Noah and his family faced in feeding the animals, through a conversation between Noah's son Shem and Abraham's servant Eliezer. B. Sanh. 108b reads:

> Shem said to him:
> We had great suffering [*tsaʿar gadol*] on the ark.
> A creature whose way was to eat by day—
> we fed it by day.
> One whose way was to eat by night—
> we fed it by night.
>
> The chameleon—father did not know what she ate.
> One day, he was sitting and peeling a pomegranate
> and a worm fell from it and she ate it.
> From then onwards, he made a mash of bran and water,
> and when it wormed [*metaleʿa*],
> she would eat.

Shem emphasizes the great pains that Noah and his family took to sustain the animals on the ark, particularly through their commitment to feed the animals at the proper times. In Shem's estimation, the act of giving care is a source of significant suffering: it is *tsa'ar gadol,* great pain. The text imagines all the creatures on the ark as Noah's domesticates; he is responsible for their care and their food, even though it means that he and his family are feeding around the clock. It is a decidedly maternal image. This mother-Noah is the primary provider to creatures who depend for their very survival on his provision and care. The Bavli's tradition offers no insight into whether the women on the ark have a hand in feeding the creatures. Noah and Shem tend the animals; their wives are never mentioned.

68. Space does not permit a full discussion of sexuality in relation to the Bavli Sanhedrin flood narratives; I plan to take up these questions elsewhere.

In this passage, Noah shoulders the responsibility to feed and sustain creation. But the task of feeding strains the limits of his knowledge, exposing the gaps in his capacity to nurture and nourish creation. Noah does not know what the chameleon eats. How can he sustain her on the ark?[69] A chance encounter provides the clue, when the chameleon eats a worm that falls from a pomegranate. From that day onward, the Bavli recounts, Noah makes her a bran mash, and when it becomes full of worms, the chameleon eats. Let us consider those worms, the source of the chameleon's provision. The Hebrew verb *talʿa* means to decay or to rot; *metaleʿa* means "to become wormy." In the Bavli's telling, the worms appear by means of spontaneous generation, as though produced by the bran itself.[70] Noah's worms are not treated as animal bodies; they are not regarded as a species to save. They matter to the Bavli only as nourishment for another, as the source of the chameleon's succor. But I cannot take my eyes off their little invertebrate bodies, their small heads probing at the boundaries of Noah's bran bowl. Was there no place on the ark for these tiny creatures, no effort made to ensure they too will endure? These are the questions with which I tarry, the hauntings that press beyond the borders of the Bavli's own concern. What are the limits we place on refuge, the boundaries we set around sanctuary? Does the ark shelter only the creatures that capture our imaginations, the ones we wish to consume or caress? What of the undesirable bodies, the ones we regard as insignificant, the flesh from which we turn away? Does every ark bear the sin of its own sealing, the curse of those on whom the doors swung closed?

While the Bavli professes no interest in the survival of the worms, the continuation of this passage grapples more forthrightly with the problem of predation. How shall the lion eat aboard the ark, since its sustenance demands the killing of another kind? B. Sanh. 108b continues:

> The lion—fever sustained him,
> as Rav said,
> no less than six and no more than twelve,
> a fever sustains.

Predation threatens God's careful program of species survival. To sidestep the problem, the Bavli imagines that a fever keeps the lion alive. Claiming that a fever can sustain a body for a week or more, Rav attempts to leverage talmudic knowledge of human medicine to account for the lion's survival on the ark. The lion's customary hunger cannot be accommodated on the ark. He must forgo the hunt. Sickness becomes a salve, altering the

---

69. I have gendered the animals according to the grammatical gender of the Hebrew noun.

70. On the late antique notion of worms as emerging via spontaneous generation, see Miller, *In the Eye of the Animal*, 163.

usual biophysical demands of the lion's body. On the ark, the lion needs no food; he is sustained by the fire within.

To conclude Shem's conversation with Eliezer, Bavli Sanhedrin recounts the tale of one more animal, the mythical phoenix. While the lion feeds through fever, the phoenix is famished—but not because he *cannot* eat. He refrains from seeking food because he desires to cause no trouble for his human provider. B. Sanh. 108b continues:

> The phoenix [*avarshinah*]—
> Father found him lying down in the storeroom of the ark.
> He said to him, "Do you not want food?"
> He said to him, "I saw that you were agitated, and I thought:
> I will not trouble you."
> He said to him, "May it be God's will that you do not die."
> As it said, *I thought I would end my days in my nest,*
> *and be as long-lived as the phoenix.* (Job 29:18)

The phoenix stands as a striking example of renunciation, a witness to the animal's capacity to discipline his own desires. In spatial terms, the phoenix locates himself on the very margins of the ark. He holds back, refraining from asserting himself before Noah. He sees Noah's agitation; perhaps he even feels Noah's pain. The phoenix's concern with Noah's suffering—the word is the same that Shem uses at the very start of this passage—leads him to sublimate his hunger in favor of another's need. The phoenix, I contend, offers Noah a quintessential gesture of care, a care that mirrors his own. For this supererogatory act, he is bountifully repaid. Rather than offer the quotidian sustenance of ordinary food, Noah prays that he be granted a more enduring form of survival. The Bavli thus frames the phoenix's capacity for rebirth as a reward for the creature's willingness to discipline his own hunger. He gains eternal life because of his capacity to express affective concern for the human steward who suffers as he struggles to provide.

Bavli Sanhedrin valorizes the phoenix's sensitivity, imagining his suffering as richly repaid through Noah's blessing. Might we imagine the phoenix as a kind of fasting body, an animal participant in a quintessential rabbinic religious project? Rabbinic ritual practice elsewhere calls for elite individuals to engage in a *taᶜanit yaḥid*, an individual fast, in times of communal crisis.[71] While our passage never uses the language of fasting,

---

71. On fasting as a ritual response to communal crisis in rabbinic literature, see Julia Watts Belser, *Power, Ethics, and Ecology in Rabbinic Late Antiquity: Rabbinic Responses to Drought and Disaster* (New York: Cambridge University Press, 2015), 116–26; on the distinction between the *taᶜanit yaḥid* and the *taᶜanit tsibur*, see David Levine, *Communal Fasts and Rabbinic Sermons: Theory and Practice in the Talmudic Period* [Hebrew] (Jerusalem: Hakibbutz Hameuchad, 2001), 44–46; on fasting in relation to rabbinic asceticism, see Diamond, *Hunger Artists*.

the sexual renunciations of the ark and the flood that rages beyond its walls are similarly suggestive. If we allow ourselves to read the phoenix as an individual who fasts, we see his hunger as a deliberately cultivated state, deployed to help the world weather spiritual crisis.[72] Regardless of whether we attribute religious significance to the animal's act, our text clearly uses the phoenix's hunger as an index of his emotional sensitivity. In this passage, Bavli Sanhedrin imagines the animal as an ethical subject who is attuned to human suffering. The Bavli's phoenix disciplines his hunger and sets aside his own need for the sake of another; he responds with care to Noah's distress. Through this tale, the Bavli recognizes the phoenix as an animal who distinguishes himself from the beasts. He is not driven by instinct. He holds back his hunger, curbs his craving. He governs his desire.

Thus far, I have read the Bavli's phoenix tale as a laudatory text, drawing out the rich palate of possibilities it offers for acknowledging animals as ethical agents, for recognizing that moral concern is not the sole province of humankind.[73] Following the grammar of the Aramaic noun, I have gendered the phoenix as masculine, a frame that invites us to imagine the phoenix as a pious renunciant, one able to deploy self-denial for a valorized end. But I am not sure whether the Bavli's moral imagination extends sufficiently to endow the phoenix—the animal creature—with the same capacity for ascetic virtue it might afford a rabbinic man. Instead, I wonder: Do the dynamics of animality, vulnerability, and care in this tale render the phoenix a "feminized" subject, a subordinate who is praised for renouncing his (animal) need in favor of the superior (human) male's desires? If so, the tale evokes a very different set of resonances: of women who go hungry so their children can eat, who lay food first on their husband's plate, who make do with the burnt ends of stale toast. In fashioning the phoenix into a subject fit for praise, I wonder: Has the Bavli simply crafted one more docile, sacrificial body—willing to sublimate his need and offer himself for the sake of another? The words the phoenix speaks to Noah take on a sinister cast, a reminder of the way that subordinates learn to manage a master's anger, to assuage his agitation. I think of the woman who ghosts through her own home, the enslaved people who swallow their resistance to keep themselves alive. They too have learned to discipline their bodies, still their hunger, deny desire. Is the Bavli's phoenix

72. On the elite individual fast as a means of averting communal crisis, see my discussion of R. Tsadok's fast before the destruction of Jerusalem: Julia Watts Belser, *Rabbinic Tales of Destruction: Gender, Sex, and Disability in the Ruins of Jerusalem* (New York: Oxford University Press, 2018), 86–90.

73. On the concept of animals as ethical agents, see Jonathan K. Crane, "Beastly Morality: A Twisting Tale," in Crane, *Beastly Morality*, 10–12.

stitched from the cloth of that same tapestry, a reminder that the power of renunciation also cuts against the bone?

Better the Bitter than the Sweet: Animal Eating and Sanctified Sustenance

In the Bavli Sanhedrin's Sodom stories, hunger serves as an index of the bestial, a powerful force intertwined with violence, greed, and sexual perversion. While such carnal impulses also haunt the generation of the flood, the Noah tales imagine animal hunger as a force that might be channeled for moral good. Imagining the dove sent forth from the ark to scout the land and seek out shelter for all creatures, the Bavli recounts a conversation between the bird and her God. B. Sanh. 108b reads:

> *And behold—a plucked off* [taraf] *branch of olive in her mouth!* (Gen 8:11)
> Rabbi Elazar said:
> The dove said before the Holy Blessed One,
> "Lord of the World,
> may it be that my sustenance be bitter as the olive
> and dependent on your hands.
> And let it not be sweet as honey
> and dependent on the hand of flesh and blood."
> And where do we see that "plucked off" [*taraf*] is sustenance?
> *Feed me* [hatrifeni] *my daily bread.* (Prov 30:8)

Playing off an aural association between the Hebrew word for "plucked off" branch and food, the Bavli claims that the dove deliberately rejects the sweetness of honey and takes instead the bitter olive to be her chosen food. All she asks, all she prays, is that her sustenance come directly from God's own hands. It is a startling request, given the history of the dove as a domesticated animal; the messenger bird has long been associated with humankind.[74] But in the Bavli's telling, the dove rejects the human, choosing to rely instead on God alone. She turns away from the seductive sweet that ensnared Sodom's bees and draws her sustenance instead from God's own fruit.

---

74. Sophia Germanidou, "Dovecotes from the Roman and Byzantine Periods: An Overview," *Herom* 4 (2015): 33–51; Jennifer Ramsay, "Not Just for the Birds: Pigeons in the Roman and Byzantine Near East," *The Ancient Near East Today*, 5:11, November 2017, http://asorblog.org/2017/11/28/not-just-birds-pigeons-roman-byzantine-near-east/.

Bio-Power, Sabbath Burdens, and the Badly Behaved Donkey in Babylonian Talmud Tractate Shabbat

BETH BERKOWITZ

In the summer of 2017, my family welcomed a large and boisterous puppy into our home. Since then I have been dragged down the street, immobilized on the sidewalk, caught in dog fights, slobbered on, and mauled while at my desk. The problem of animal control has, in short, been on my mind. The questions that I want to explore in this essay are these: How does it happen that human techniques of animal control come to seem necessary for animals? Whom does animal discipline appear to benefit, and whom does it actually benefit? To take the case of my dog: What are the conditions that led me to perceive the collar and leash as necessary or beneficial for my dog? In particular, I am interested in the role of law in promoting this perception. How do laws about animal control make it seem normal or even natural?

In this essay I will argue that the talmudic treatment of Sabbath burdens is an excellent case study in the exercise of bio-power.[1] Though the idea of bio-power originates with Michel Foucault, he was not much interested in animals. Like many other theorists of power, Foucault considered animals to exist outside the scope of power. He did not see the relevance of animals to his most famous ideas about power: bio-power, that is, the exercise of power over bodies; the microphysics of power, that is, the study of power in particular and dynamic relationships; and the role of discourse in normalizing power. By contrast, Bertrand Russell viewed relationships between human beings and animals as emblematic

1. For Foucault's notion of bio-power applied to animal discipline, see Joel Novek, "Discipline and Distancing: Confined Pigs in the Factory Farm Gulag," in *Animals and the Human Imagination: A Companion to Animal Studies*, ed. Aaron S. Gross and Anne Vallely (New York: Columbia University Press, 2012), 121–50, esp. 132–33.

of the exercise of power: "Forms of power are most naked and simply displayed in our dealings with animals where disguises and pretences are not thought necessary."[2] Russell's illustration is a pig with a rope around his middle being hoisted squealing into a ship. The pig is "subject to direct physical power over its body," says Russell, who equates such exercise of power in the human realm with military and police power. For Russell, dealings with animals are singularly instructive because there are no "disguises and pretences." The exercise of power with animals is power in its barest form.

My approach here seeks a middle ground between Foucault and Russell as I read selections from the fifth chapter of Bavli Shabbat, whose topic is animal restraint. Like Foucault, I am interested in the microphysics of power, the role of discourse in naturalizing power, and in bio-power. Unlike Foucault, and like Russell, I see animals as participants in those processes if not paradigmatic of them. But, parting ways with Russell, I will suggest that the Talmud does consider disguises and pretenses to be necessary to the exercise of power over animals. I will first look at a legal discussion in the Talmud that deals with disciplinary devices—the leashes, bridles, chains, ropes, harnesses, and other accessories designed to make animals comply with human commands. The animals who wear these accessories are already domesticated, but the need for this array of devices suggests that domestication is a relative term. My interest will be the "disguises and pretences" in which the Talmud dresses the exercise of bio-power over animals. I will then turn to a talmudic story about a badly behaved donkey to argue that the story exposes the disguises and pretenses that the legal discourse puts into place. The broader project in which this essay partakes is to put critical animal studies in dialogue with rabbinic literature.[3] The rise of critical animal studies has raised new questions for the Talmud, and the Talmud can in turn contribute its rich resources to critical animal studies.

Animals Bearing Burdens on the Sabbath

The fourth of the Ten Commandments prohibits labor on the Sabbath: "Six days you shall labor and do all your work, but the seventh day is a Sabbath of the Lord your God: you shall not do any work" (Exod 20:9–10).[4]

2. Bertrand Russell, *Power: A New Social Analysis* (1938; repr., London: Routledge, 2004).

3. This discussion is an extension of the work in Beth A. Berkowitz, *Animals and Animality in the Babylonian Talmud* (Cambridge: Cambridge University Press, 2018).

4. Translations are from the NJPS. Exodus envisions Sabbath rest as reflecting God's completion of creation, while Deuteronomy presents it as a remembrance of the exodus from Egypt and redemption from slavery (Exod 20:11; Deut 5:15). Other biblical passages that prohibit labor on the Sabbath are Exod 31:12–17; 34:21; 35:2–3; and Lev 23:3.

The prohibition includes animals among other members of the household within its scope: "you, your son or daughter, your male or female slave, *or your cattle,* or the stranger who is within your settlements" (Exod 20:10).[5] In its recapitulation, Deut 5:14 mentions particular work-animal breeds: "your ox or your ass, or any of your cattle."[6] The Sabbath rest of the household depends on the cessation from labor of all those who contribute actively to its working economy.[7] An alternative formulation from Exodus understands Sabbath rest as not only including animals but as designed specifically for them, along with human laborers: "Six days you shall do your work, but on the seventh day you shall cease from labor, *in order that your ox and your ass may rest,* and that your bondman and the stranger may be refreshed" (Exod 23:10–12).

Prophetic texts speak of a restriction on carrying burdens on the Sabbath. That restriction seems less to be adding components to Sabbath rest than refining it:

> כא כֹּה אָמַר יְהוָה הִשָּׁמְרוּ בְּנַפְשׁוֹתֵיכֶם וְאַל־תִּשְׂאוּ מַשָּׂא בְּיוֹם הַשַּׁבָּת וַהֲבֵאתֶם בְּשַׁעֲרֵי יְרוּשָׁלִָם כב וְלֹא־תוֹצִיאוּ מַשָּׂא מִבָּתֵּיכֶם בְּיוֹם הַשַּׁבָּת וְכָל־מְלָאכָה לֹא תַעֲשׂוּ וְקִדַּשְׁתֶּם אֶת־יוֹם הַשַּׁבָּת כַּאֲשֶׁר צִוִּיתִי אֶת־אֲבוֹתֵיכֶם
>
> Guard yourselves for your own sake against carrying burdens [*masa*] on the sabbath day, and bringing them through the gates of Jerusalem. Nor shall you carry out burdens from your houses on the sabbath day, or do any work, but you shall hallow the sabbath day, as I commanded your fathers. (Jer 17:21–22)

Jeremiah's picture of the Sabbath is not the stilled plow as it is in the Decalogue but the quiet main street. Jeremiah refers verbatim to the Decalogue's prohibition on labor—"or do any work"—but reframes the prohibition so that it refers to the transportation of goods rather than the agricultural labor that the Decalogue has in mind. "Burden" (*masa*) replaces "labor" (*melakhah*) as the key word for Sabbath work. Later Jewish interpreters like the rabbis will interpret Jeremiah broadly as prohibiting virtually all kinds of carrying.[8] Nehemiah 13's adaptation of Jer 17, which in turn is adapting

5. The wife is notably absent. She is likely folded into the second-person masculine singular address.

6. On Deuteronomy's enumeration of the ox and ass, see Moshe Weinfeld, *Deuteronomy 1–11: A New Translation with Introduction and Commentary,* AB 5 (New York: Doubleday, 1991), 309. Weinfeld understands Exodus's version to be influenced by priestly terminology.

7. I say "contribute actively" because simply being part of the economy, as inanimate objects are, does not qualify for inclusion in the prohibition. See A. Rahel Schafer, "Rest for the Animals? Nonhuman Sabbath Repose in Pentateuchal Law," *BBR* 23 (2013): 167–86, esp. 174 n. 21.

8. For discussion of these biblical passages and their reformulation and interpretation by subsequent authors, see Alex Jassen, "Tracing the Threads of Jewish Law: The Sabbath

Deut 5, speaks to the role of the animal in this new vision of the Sabbath: "At that time I saw men in Judah treading winepresses on the sabbath, and others bringing heaps of grain and loading them onto asses, also wine, grapes, figs, and all sorts of goods and bringing them into Jerusalem on the Sabbath" (Neh 13:15).[9] Sabbath rest, according to this imagining of it, means refraining from loading up one's animal.[10]

The Mishnah dedicates the fifth chapter of tractate Shabbat to the prohibition on animals bearing burdens on the Sabbath. Is a saddle a "burden" and therefore prohibited? Is a collar or a bell? Can animals be tied one to the other on the Sabbath or does this constitute a "burden"? As is typical of the Mishnah, the chapter legislates for a series of highly specific cases and never articulates the underlying axioms, leaving unclear why one device is deemed a burden and another is not.[11] A camel may bear something called an *'afsar* on the Sabbath but not a *metutelet*. The Mishnah does not explain why the *'afsar* does not constitute a burden and the *metutelet* does, or what these devices are, and so on for the other accessories mentioned.[12] Neither does the Mishnah say that venturing out with a burden on the Sabbath is the only legal concern at stake in this chapter. Indeed, the chapter does not ever use the word "burden." Other Sabbath prohibitions may be operating.

Guessing at the Mishnah's logic is further complicated by the fairly tight parallels that govern the materials. First comes a list of accessories that particular animal species are permitted to wear on the Sabbath, followed by a list of accessories that more or less the same species are pro-

Carrying Prohibition from Jeremiah to the Rabbis," *Annali di Storia dell'Esegesi* 28 (2011): 253–78.

9. For discussion of the dependence of Neh 13 on Jer 17 and their relationship to Deut 5, see Michael A. Fishbane, *Biblical Interpretation in Ancient Israel* (New York: Oxford University Press, 1985), 129–34.

10. The prohibition on bearing burdens is melded together in later sources with the prohibition found in Exod 16:29–30 on moving from one's place of habitation. See Charlotte Elisheva Fonrobert, "From Separatism to Urbanism: The Dead Sea Scrolls and the Origins of the Rabbinic Eruv," *DSD* 11 (2004): 43–71.

11. See the characterization of early rabbinic literature in Leib Moscovitz, *Talmudic Reasoning: From Casuistics to Conceptualization*, TSAJ 89 (Tübingen: Mohr Siebeck, 2002).

12. The parallel passage in t. Šabb. 4:3 is more illuminating since it describes a *metutelet* being used to protect a camel from the wind. The *'afsar* seems to come from Persian and refers to a bit or halter, while the *metutelet*, according to Saul Lieberman, comes from the root *tiltel*, "rolling or moving," and refers to a piece of cloth that would have hung from the camel's hump and moved up and down as the camel walked (see Lieberman, *Tosefta ki-Feshuṭah: A Comprehensive Commentary on the Tosefta*, part 3, *Order Mo'ed* [New York: Jewish Theological Seminary of America, 2002], 57). Biblical literature features disciplinary devices for animals, such as in Ps 31:9 ("Be not like a senseless horse or mule whose movement must be curbed by bit and bridle") and Prov 26:3 ("A whip for a horse and a bridle for a donkey"), but I know of no study of these accessories.

hibited from wearing, followed by parallel legislations for women, men, and children. The literary repetitions are clearly intended to play the various accessories off each other, as well as the categories of animal, woman, man, and child, but the principles of comparison are left implicit.

The underlying idea, or one of them, seems to be that an item worn on the body on a daily basis does not constitute a "burden." Key concepts developed in the Talmuds are "clothing" (*malbush*) and "jewelry" (*takhshit*).[13] A person's habitual clothing or jewelry is taken to be different from a package or bag. The person is not thought to be carrying a burden when they wear a sweater, necklace, or belt. The categories of jewelry and clothing are understood almost as extensions of the body and not extra or additional to it.[14] An accessory that falls into these categories may be worn about on the Sabbath presumably because the person wearing it, and those around them, will see it as an integral part of their physical presence.

The Naturalization of Discipline

The talmudic commentary articulates this axiom as it applies to animals. The opening discussion of the Talmud tackles the Mishnah's first legislation (m. Šabb. 1:1):

> במה בהמה יוצא ובמה אינה יוצא לא יצא הגמל באפסר והנקה בחטם[15]
>
> With what may an animal go out, and with what may she not go out? The male camel may go out with a bit, and a female camel may go out with a nose ring.

The Mishnah's legislation permits a male camel to wear a bit on the Sabbath and a female camel to wear an iron nose ring on the presumption that neither constitutes a burden to the animal. The talmudic commentary features the Amora Shmuel posing a question about that legislation:

> אמ׳ רב יהוד׳ אמ׳ שמואל מחליפין לפני ר׳ של זו בזו ושל זו בזו מהו[16]
>
> Rav Yehudah said that Shmuel said: They switch [the devices] before Rabbi, one [device] for the other, what is [the law]? (b. Šabb. 51b)

Shmuel here asks: What if, instead of putting the bit on the male camel and the nose ring on the female, one were to put the nose ring on the male

13. For *malbush*, see y. ʿErub. 10:1, 26a; b. Šabb. 61a; b. ʿErub. 95b; for *takhshit*, see t. Šabb. 4:11; y. Šabb. 6:2, 8b; b. Šabb. 59b–60a.

14. For a similar notion as it appears in the purity laws, see Mira Balberg, *Purity, Body, and Self in Early Rabbinic Literature* (Berkeley: University of California Press, 2014).

15. MS Kaufmann.

16. MS Munich 95.

and the bit on the female? Would those devices still not be considered burdens? With this question, Shmuel seems to want to grasp the deeper principles by which the Mishnah classifies a device as burdensome.

The Stam elaborates on Shmuel's question:

> נאקה באפסר לא תיבעי ליה דכיון דלא מינטרא משוה הוא כי תיבעי לך גמל בחטם מאי כיון דסגי ליה באפסר משוי הוא הוי או דילמ׳ כל נטירותא יתירא לא אמרינן משוי הוא
>
> A female camel with a bit is not a question for him. Since it does not secure, it is a "burden." When it is a question for you is the male camel with a nose ring; what is [the law]? Since it is sufficient for him with a bit, it is a "burden," or perhaps [regarding] any excessive security we do not say it is a "burden."

In their typical *oqimta* style, the talmudic editors contract the scope of Shmuel's question. According to the Stam, the question relates only to cases of so-called excessive security (*netiruta yetera*), when a device exerts stronger force than is considered necessary to control the animal. The editors take Shmuel's case of the male camel fitted with a nose ring to be such an instance. In the Stam's view, when Shmuel asked his question about reversing the devices, Shmuel was in fact asking about whether devices that exert excessive force should be considered burdens.

The editors here create a spectrum of disciplinary force: devices that provide insufficient security, devices that provide too much, and devices that are just strong enough to secure the animal but no more than that, like the porridge in Goldilocks and the Three Bears. A device that is too light is deemed to be a burden, counterintuitively, since it does not serve its disciplinary purpose and is therefore thought to be extraneous. The female camel wearing the bit serves to illustrate this case in the Stam's view. Also legally unambiguous is a device that provides just the right amount of security, which the Stam presumes not to fall into the category of burden. The question that the Talmud isolates as legally interesting regards the device that provides more security than is necessary. Is such a device not a "burden" because it serves the purpose for which it is being used, or is it a "burden" because it serves that purpose too well?

The most significant development in the passage in my view is the one that goes unstated: the presumption that a just-right disciplinary device is not a burden. It is only the heaviest chains, or ineffectual ones, that become viable candidates for the category. But everyday disciplinary devices used to control animals are presented by the anonymous voice of the Talmud as a necessary accoutrement, a form of "jewelry" or "clothing" for the animal considered integral to the animal's physical being. By framing certain disciplinary devices as normal, necessary, or beneficial and not a burden, and relegating other ones to the category of burden, the chapter succeeds in the strange task of declaring various straps, leashes, bridles, and bits to be not a "burden" to the animal. By identifying burdensomeness only in some devices, the editors neutralize other ones. "Burden" becomes a technical term that serves to define bodily conventions for people as well as for animals. Whether an item worn on the body is in fact burdensome to the wearer becomes irrelevant so long as that item is deemed habitual or normal.

Foucault on Discourse and Discipline

Foucault may not be interested in animals, but I am, and his notion of discipline and the role of discourse in shaping it is helpful for understanding the rabbinic vocabulary of burdens. For Foucault, "relations of power cannot themselves be established, consolidated nor implemented without the production, accumulation, circulation and functioning of a discourse."[17] Clare Palmer explains that, for Foucault, "relations of power ... produce 'discourses of truth': the truth delineating what can be thought and said and what remains unthought and therefore unsaid within the social body."[18] Such discourses create and support the "techniques and tactics of subjugation" within what Foucault calls "disciplinary societies."[19] I am suggesting that the Talmud here produces such a discourse of truth in relation to animals. In the Talmud's legal discourse, an animal's normal state is understood to be one in which they are physically controlled by human beings. Disciplinary devices emerge from the discourse as a form of accessory that is integral to the daily functioning of the animal, forms of animal "clothing" or "jewelry" akin to hairbands or sandals.[20] Thus does this seemingly limited halakhic discussion quietly fan out into the rest of rabbinic law, from Sabbath rulings to sacrifice to torts, anchoring the presumption of animal control that runs through it all, and rooting that presumption in the demands of scripture. Rest may be enjoined on only one day of the week but the claim that certain disciplinary devices are not burdens would seem to pervade the other six too.

---

17. Michel Foucault, *Power/Knowledge: Selected Interviews and Other Writings, 1972–1977*, ed. and trans. Colin Gordon (Brighton, Sussex: Harvester, 1980), 93.

18. Clare Palmer, "'Taming the Wild Profusion of Existing Things?': Foucault, Power and Human/Animal Relationships," in *Foucault and Animals*, ed. Matthew Chrulew and Dinesh Joseph Wadiwel, Human–Animal Studies 18 (Leiden: Brill, 2016), 105–31, here 112.

19. Ibid.

20. As Meiri puts it (s.v. *bameh*, b. Šabb 51b): "Any device that is intended for security and possesses that which is required for security is permitted since it is like a piece of jewelry or article of clothing.... This is the core of the chapter [stated] generally." See also Rashi on 51b, s.v. *bameh*.

Animal Accessories in the Mishnah and Tosefta

One catches a glimpse of discourse in the making, as it is being produced, by sifting through the Talmud's literary layers. Earlier rabbinic traditions when read without the Talmud's editorial framing do not make the same assumption about everyday disciplinary devices that the editors do. It is difficult to say just what assumption is behind the grid of permitted and prohibited devices in the Mishnah and Tosefta. Even talmudic rabbis living only a century or two later are unsure what many of the devices are, much less why they are permitted or prohibited. The Tosefta offers more information than the Mishnah about the purpose of the devices. According to the Tosefta, one of the devices described as being worn by sheep seems intended to keep their wool clean (t. Šabb. 4:1). The Tosefta describes another device as controlling an animal's sexual activity, either forcing female animals into being inseminated, or preventing males from mounting females (ibid.). Another device is described as keeping the animal warm or cooling the animal off (t. Šabb. 4:2–3).[21] Medical and protective devices are described, as are devices involved in milk production, animal identification, and animal beautification.[22]

The Tosefta reveals little, however, about why a device is permitted or prohibited. A muzzle is prohibited by the Tosefta presumably because it is associated with fieldwork (t. Šabb. 4:5). Certain ropes are prohibited out of a concern that the human owner will violate the Sabbath through tying the ropes (t. Šabb. 4:3–4). Otherwise the legal principles are murky. The notion that appears in the Talmud, that a device that controls the animal's movement is permitted because it is necessary to secure the animal, is absent.

Conceptualizing Discipline

The closest that early rabbinic law comes to a concept of discipline is a *baraita* that appears in the Babylonian Talmud:

אין חייה יוצא׳ בסוגר׳ חנינא אומר יוצאה [בסוגר] ובכל דבר הנשתמרת [בו]

> A *ḥayah* may not go out with a collar. Ḥanina says: She may go out with a collar or anything that secures [the animal].

The two sides featured in this *baraita*, the first anonymous and the second attributed to Ḥanina (Ḥananyah later in the passage), debate whether a

21. I treat the concern with animal pleasure in a paper I delivered at the Jewish Law Association Conference at Yeshiva University in March 2017.

22. For medical and protective devices, see t. Šabb. 4:5; for milk production, t. Šabb. 4:5; for identification, t. Šabb. 5:8; and for beautification, t. Šabb. 4:5.

ḥayah, which I will leave untranslated for the moment, may wear a collar on the Sabbath.[23]

Two features of this tradition are worth noting. One is that it extends the discussion beyond sheep, goats, cows, and other breeds that would fall clearly into the category of *behemah* to include the *ḥayah*. The very mention of security devices for a *ḥayah*, usually the binary opposite of *behemah*, is surprising and potentially self-contradictory if one takes *ḥayah* to be a "wild" animal, which by definition is not secured. Parallel texts suggest that, when this teaching uses the word *ḥayah*, it has in mind not truly "wild" or undomesticated animals but rather dogs or cats, animals commonly considered to be domesticated, if not to be the paradigms of domestication.[24] The Mishnah and Tosefta in fact feature a debate about whether a dog is a *behemah* or a *ḥayah*, suggesting that the distinction the Tannaim make between *behemah* and *ḥayah* is different from the one we make between domesticated and undomesticated (m. Kil. 8:6; t. Kil. 5:7).

The second noteworthy feature of the *baraita* is that it explicitly conceptualizes animal control and develops a vocabulary of discipline. The later literary layers of the Talmud run with this. This early rabbinic dispute taken on its own does not say whether the same principle would apply to the *behemah*. The notion of control is never in fact mentioned by the early rabbis apart from in this one teaching, which may be a relatively late fabrication given its absence in early corpora. Yet the editorial voice of the Talmud will understand this dispute to be about all animals, *behemah* and *ḥayah*, and not about security per se, but *excessive* security:

> ... וחנניה סבר כל נטירותא יתירתא לא אמרינן משוי הוא א״ר יהודה אמ׳ שמואל הלכה כחנניה
>
> And Ḥananyah reasons: Any security that is excessive we do not call a "burden." R. Yehudah said Shmuel said: The law is like Ḥananyah. (b. Šabb. 51b)

For the later editors, this *baraita* becomes the basis for the claim that any device found to be in the sweet spot between insufficient and excessive security is no burden.

The earlier rabbis barely conceptualize animal control at all, however, and when they do, it is only with respect to the *ḥayah*. The missing link is likely to be found in a debate between early Babylonian Amoraim Rav and Shmuel about whether accessories designed for beauty (*lenoy*) or for discipline (*leshamer*) are permitted to be worn on the Sabbath (b. Šabb. 52a,

---

23. Ḥanina appears in the printed edition and later in this manuscript as Ḥananyah. Perhaps it is a reference to the third-generation Tanna R. Ḥanina.

24. See y. Šabb. 5:4, 7c, which has a similar teaching about a dog. B. Šabb. understands the *baraita* to be referring to a cat.

54b).[25] The Talmud presents different versions of this debate, which seems, in any of the versions, to be the main source of inspiration for the Stam's more elaborate theorizing of animal discipline.

Necessary Discipline

The Stam's claim that normal disciplinary devices are no burden is, however, betrayed or disrupted at various points throughout the talmudic discussion. One such moment is when Rav Yosef poses a question about whether a goat may go out on the Sabbath with a bit inserted into her beard. The Stam explains the question this way:

כיון ד[כי] מיתנחא לה כאיב לה ולא אתיא לנתוחי

> Since if she tries to tear herself free [from the bit], she will be in pain, and [therefore] she will not come to tear herself free [and so therefore there is no concern about Sabbath violation since the owner will not need to pick up the bit from the ground to carry it.] (b. Šabb. 52a)

The Talmud imagines a goat struggling to liberate herself from a device that has been pierced into her body, anticipating pain if she does, and submitting from the outset due to fear. The aim of the bit is "a docile body that may be subjected, used, transformed, and improved."[26] Only anticipation of pain impels the goat's acceptance of the bit. The Stam's exclusion of this device from the scope of "burden" means that "burden" is now functioning as a technical term whose meaning no longer reflects the physical realities originally associated with it.

The devices of sexual control described throughout the chapter present a similar paradox as alleged nonburdens that would seem to be extremely burdensome to the animal. The Talmud describes practices that are designed to inhibit sexual activity such as tying up the ram's genitals so that he is not able to mount the females or fastening the tail of the ewe over her genitals so that, were the ram to mount her, he could not enter her. The chapter also describes practices designed to coerce sexual activity such as fastening the tail of the ewe above her genitals so that she cannot prevent the male from entering her. There are practices also to control nursing such as tying up a goat's udder either to dry up or stimulate her milk supply (b. Šabb. 54a).[27]

25. Second- and third-generation Amoraim debate Rav and Shmuel's stance on whether security is a sufficient justification to permit a device on the Sabbath (b. Šabb. 52a, statements attributed to R. Yirmiyah b. Abba and Rav Yosef).

26. Foucault, quoted in Novek, "Discipline and Distancing," 132 (Michel Foucault, *Discipline and Punish: The Birth of the Prison*, trans. Alan Sheridan [New York: Vintage Books, 1979], 136).

27. Some of the Bavli's explanations of the devices in the early rabbinic materials are based on those materials themselves, but most seem to be later guesses.

The dark side of discipline is even more apparent in the various bindings of animal's limbs described in the chapter that are designed to immobilize the animal and prevent them from escaping: a camel's foreleg is tied to his back leg; the upper part of his foreleg is tied to its lower part; both forelegs and both back legs are tied together (m. Šabb. 5:3; t. Šabb. 4:3; b. Šabb. 54a). These bindings are on the list of prohibited accessories, so their burdensomeness is recognized by law, but it is also recognized in the rhetoric when Rav Yehudah compares one of the binding practices to Abraham's binding of Isaac (b. Šabb. 54a). In invoking the binding of Isaac, one of the most theologically problematic stories in the biblical tradition, the Talmud is far from the rhetoric of routine discipline that governs much of the rest of the chapter. The vocabularies of discipline throughout the chapter—the repeating roots *r-d-h* ("to subjugate, rule, govern") and *k-f-h* ("to press, force, compel, bend"), along with *sh-m-r* ("guard, observe, secure") and its Aramaic equivalent *n-t-r*, and all the other bindings, tyings, and pullings, and the outright suffering (*tsa'ar*)—likewise undermine or at least complicate the notion that these devices redound to the animal's benefit or are strictly necessary and no "burden" to them.[28]

The Story of Levi and the Badly Behaved Donkey

The disruptive moment I want to dwell on is a story about a donkey:

> לוי בר בריה דרב הונא בר חייא ורבה בר רב הונא הוו אזלי באורחא קדמיה חמרא דלוי לחמריה (דרב הונא) דרבה בר רב הונא חלשא דעתיה אמ׳ אימ׳ מילת׳ כי היכי דתייב דעתיה אמ׳ לו חמור שעסקיו רעים כגון זה מהו לצאת בפרומביא בשבת א״ל הכי אמ׳ אבוך משמיה דשמואל הלכה כחנניה
>
> Levi son of Rav Huna b. Ḥiyya and Rabbah b. Rav Huna were traveling on the road. The donkey of Levi went ahead of the donkey of Rabbah b. Rav Huna. Rabbah b. Rav Huna became distraught.
>
> (Levi) said [to himself], "Let me say to him something so as to restore his composure."
>
> Levi said to Rabbah, "A donkey whose behavior is bad [literally, whose affairs are wicked] such as this one, what is the law regarding [his] going out with a halter on the Sabbath?"
>
> Rabbah said to Levi, "Thus said your father in the name of Shmuel: the law is like Hananyah." (b. Šabb. 51b–52a)[29]

28. For *r-d-h: rodeh* (52b); *marda'at* (m. Šabb. 5:2, 4, though that may be a loanword); *moredet* (52a). For *k-f-h* or *k-f-f: yakhof* (54a); *ukaf* (53a); *mikaf* (54b). For *sh-m-r: mishtamer* (51b); *leshamer* (52a). For *n-t-r: netiruta* (51b); *minatra* (51b); *tsa'ar*: 53a.

29. A parallel to the legislation is found in y. Šabb. 5:4, 7c: "An ox whose behavior is bad

Sensitivity to slight is well known among Babylonian rabbis and forms the basis for the story.[30] Levi son of Rav Huna b. Ḥiyya, mentioned only here and in one other story in tractate Shabbat, offends his more well-known colleague, Rabbah son of Rav Huna, when his donkey pulls ahead of the other's.[31] Levi tries to correct the offense by posing a legal question to Rabbah. The mere fact of posing a question is a display of subordination since with the question Levi is recognizing Rabbah's superior knowledge and authority. But the substance of Levi's question is also significant since it telegraphs to Rabbah that the donkey, not Levi, is responsible for cutting in front.[32] In describing his donkey as ill-behaved, Levi makes clear that his own behavior is respectful.

The story presents parallels and intersections between the discipline of the rabbinic study house and that of human–animal relationships. The story is about reversals of power and the reimposition of order. The hierarchy among species mimics the hierarchy among rabbis, both of which are disrupted within the mini-drama of the story. In the story's unstable resolution, the restoration of the hierarchy between the two rabbis depends on the restoration of the hierarchy between the rabbi and his animal. We never do find out, however, whether Rabbah was mollified.

---

may go out with his bridle. And our rabbis in the exile practiced thus." Perhaps the allusion to diaspora practice inspired the story in the Babylonian Talmud.

30. On the delicate social dynamics of the rabbinic academy, see chapters 1 and 4 in Jeffrey L. Rubenstein, *The Culture of the Babylonian Talmud* (Baltimore: Johns Hopkins University Press, 2005). On the talmudic expression for the feeling of offense, *ḥalash da'ateh*, see Nachum (Norman) Meir Bronznick, "The Semantics of the Root H-L-SH in Scripture," *Leshonenu* 41 (1977): 173–75. Bronznick explains that the talmudic phrase has a variety of meanings but that they all have in common the idea that "he did not feel comfortable for some reason." Bronznick proposes that the root reflects the idea of shrinkage.

31. The other story is found in b. Šabb. 156a:

> לוי בריה דרב הונא בר חייא אשכחיה לגבלא דבי נשיה דקא גביל וספי ליה לתוריה בטש ביה אתא אבוה אשכחיה אמר ליה הכי אמר אבוה דאמך משמיה דרב ומנו רבי ירמיה בר אבא גובלין ולא מספין ודלא לקיט בלישניה מהלקיטין ליה והני מילי הוא דמשני

> Levi, son of Rav Huna b. Ḥiyya, found the one who kneads in his parents' home kneading bran on Shabbat and feeding it to his ox. He kicked him so that he would stop. When his father came and found him, he said to him: This is what your mother's father said in the name of Rav. And who is his mother's father? It is R. Yirmiyah b. Abba, who said: One may knead but not feed animals, and a calf that does not take the food with his tongue may be fed on Shabbat. And this applies only when one alters the manner in which he does so.

The stories share some core features: discussion of laws having to do with animals on the Sabbath; Levi behaving improperly; Levi being rebuked by reference to a legislation issued by a parent figure.

32. As Rashi comments, "'so as to restore his composure': to inform him that I did not intend [it]."

Critical to Levi's question is the notion of the unruly animal who requires discipline. The story leaves ambiguous whether the donkey even was unruly to begin with. Perhaps Levi was remiss in his hold on the reins, or perhaps he even purposely put his donkey ahead of his superior's. This last reading of the story is implied by Rashi, who comments that Rabbah took offense because he thought that Levi intentionally cut in front of him.[33] We are drawn to see that whether the unruliness of the animal is true or false, it is useful. When Levi poses his question, he says, "A donkey whose behavior is bad *such as this one.*" Levi makes it clear to Rabbah, and the story makes it clear to the audience, that this apparently abstract legal question is being asked for a particular reason in a particular situation. In the world of the story, the law is a tool that rabbis use to mediate power relations, among species and rabbis. Returning to Bertrand Russell's "disguises and pretences," I suggest that this story exposes the disguises and pretenses produced by the law.

The final observation I would make about the story relates to an irony that emerges from it. The problem with which the story plays is that the exercise of power relies on the possibility of resistance. For Levi to repair the political damage wrought by his seemingly uppity act, he must be able to blame it on his donkey's "wicked affairs" (*asaqav ra'im*), the curiously hyperbolic and moralistic expression used by the narrative. An entirely subordinate donkey would not have misbehaved and gone ahead of the other. The ideal is a trained animal free to resist but controlled enough by his disciplinary devices so that most of the time he chooses not to. One might say the same of the rabbinic hierarchy, that it relies upon rabbis choosing—most of the time—to honor those who are greater. Foucault puts it this way:

> A power relationship can only be articulated on the basis of two elements which are each indispensable if it is really to be a power relationship: that the other, the one over whom power is exercised, be thoroughly recognized and maintained to the very end as a person who reacts; and that faced with a relationship of power, a whole field of responses, reactions, results, and possible inventions may open up ... Power is exercised only over free subjects, and only insofar as they are free.[34]

The work of Chris Philo, Tim Ingold, Jason Hribal, and others make plain that animals "act back."[35] Belgian philosopher Vinciane Despret points out that the instances in which animals act back obscure the fact

---

33. "*Ḥalsha da'ateh de-Rabbah bar Rav Huna*": who was greater, and he (Rabbah b. Rav Huna) figured that he (Levi) had done [so] intentionally [*mi-da'at*].

34. Michel Foucault, "The Subject and Power (Afterword)," in *Michel Foucault: Beyond Structuralism and Hermeneutics*, ed. Hubert L. Dreyfus and Paul Rabinow (New York: Routledge, 2014), 208–26, here 220.

35. On "acting back," see Tim Ingold, "Introduction," in *What Is an Animal?*, ed. Tim Ingold (New York: Routledge, 2016), 1–16, here 2.

that at all other times they act with or, in other words, choose to cooperate.[36] Rather than passive victims of human exploitation, animals work and play alongside people in conditions of cohabiting "companion species," as Donna Haraway describes it in her manifesto of that name.[37] For ancient Jewish discourse, a lively and robust animal agency begins with Balaam's donkey in the book of Numbers and can be traced to the famously pious donkey of R. Pinḥas ben Yair, cousin to Levi's "wicked" donkey in our story.[38] The animals' agency, their ability either to act back or act with, is essential to the Talmud's discourse of discipline.

Conclusion

The story of Levi's donkey reveals that the discourse of animal discipline is just that, a discourse, created to address human needs and purposes. The presumption that everyday disciplinary devices like the bit, nose ring, or halter are no burden, and that they are as necessary and as normal as shoes and socks or one's body itself, is belied by the story. The story denaturalizes animal discipline and operates as a meta-discourse, a discourse about discourse. Even animal agency itself becomes a fiction, a fiction within a fiction, manipulated by the characters within their microphysics of power. Other stories in this talmudic chapter play a similarly meta-discursive role. One story critiques the fetishization of an exotic donkey breed; another lampoons people's pampering of sheep with oil rubs.[39]

In "Whipping to Win," Dinesh Wadiwel describes legal regulation of horse-whipping as

> an attempt to fix in place an economy that guarantees a continuing plunder, through apparently benign civil apparatuses. A facet of this sovereign domination is its apparent imperceptibility: arrangements of violent

36. Vinciane Despret, *What Would Animals Say If We Asked the Right Questions?*, Posthumanities 38 (Minneapolis: University of Minnesota Press, 2016), 182.

37. Donna Jeanne Haraway, *The Companion Species Manifesto: Dogs, People, and Significant Otherness* (Chicago: Prickly Paradigm, 2003).

38. On Balaam's donkey, see the beginning of Berkowitz, *Animals and Animality in the Babylonian Talmud*, 1–8. On the donkey of R. Pinḥas ben Yair, see Ofra Meir, "The She-Ass of R. Pinhas ben Yair" [Hebrew], *Folklore Research Center Studies* 7 (1983): 117–37; Louis Jacobs, "The Story of R. Phinehas Ben Yair and His Donkey in B. Hullin 7a-B," in *A Tribute to Géza Vermès: Essays on Jewish and Christian Literature and History*, JSOTSup 100 (Sheffield: JSOT Press, 1990), 193–205; Leib Moscovitz, "'The Holy One Blessed Be He … Does Not Permit the Righteous to Stumble': Reflections on the Development of a Remarkable BT Theologoumenon," in *Creation and Composition: The Contribution of the Bavli Redactors (Stammaim) to the Aggada*, ed. Jeffrey L. Rubenstein, TSAJ 114 (Tübingen: Mohr Siebeck, 2005), 125–80.

39. The story that lampoons exotic donkey breeds (that is my reading of it) is in b. Šabb. 51b; the one about sheep massage is in b. Šabb. 54b.

domination are so ingrained and intricate that they appear as natural, given, ever present.[40]

Inspired by the Talmud's own meta-discourse, I have tried to make rabbinic techniques of animal control slightly less imperceptible and natural, and a little more visible.

40. Dinesh Joseph Wadiwel, "Whipping to Win: Measured Violence, Delegated Sovereignty and the Privatised Domination of Non-Human Life," in *Law and the Question of the Animal: A Critical Jurisprudence*, ed. Yoriko Otomo and Ed Mussawir, Law, Justice and Ecology (New York: Routledge, 2013), 116–32, here 121.

Problematizing Charity

Rabbinic Charity Narrative Cycle in Bavli Ketubbot 67b–68a

DOV KAHANE

For the poor shall never cease out of the land: Therefore I command thee, saying, Thou shalt open thine hand wide unto thy brother, to thy poor, and to thy needy, in thy land.

—Deut 15:11 (KJV)

Introduction and the Challenge of Rabbinic History

The history of poverty in the ancient world is vast and varied. In certain periods and places the expectation of even basic subsistence was the privilege of only a tiny part of the population. At other times "deep" poverty—the lack of some basic level of food, clothing, and shelter—was confined to a smaller percentage of the society.[1] Nevertheless, it is an obvious truism that poverty has always been part and parcel of the human condition. How a community cares for its poor is an important and interesting subject. Much has been written on the shift from the euergetic impulse of the Greek and Roman societies to the almsgiving imperative of the Christian ones, a transition that has been characterized as reorienting attitudes to the poor from benign neglect to institutionalized piety.[2] Greco-Roman euergetism was characterized by the expectation of some reciprocity that would accrue—often in the form of a public honor, statue, or title—for

1. Peter Brown, *Poverty and Leadership in the Later Roman Empire*, Menahem Stern Jerusalem Lectures (Hanover, NH: University Press of New England, 2002), 7; and see below for more on this issue.

2. See Paul Veyne, *Bread and Circuses: Historical Sociology and Political Pluralism*, trans. Brian Pearce (London: Penguin, 1990), 30–34; Anneliese Parkin, "An Exploration of Pagan Almsgiving," in *Poverty in the Roman World*, ed. Margaret Atkins and Robin Osborne (New York: Cambridge University Press, 2006), 60–82; Brown, *Poverty and Leadership*, 1–73.

the patron on behalf of his or her benevolence to the city. But this was typically benevolence directed toward the general good of the city and not focused specifically on its poor. The pre-Christian Roman world of the ancient Near East simply did not institutionalize charity giving, and the poor could rely only on their own success at begging to address some of their needs.[3] While many credit the Hebrew Scriptures for introducing the concept of charity, if not the very vocabulary of poverty itself, attention to the poor qua poor became a societal norm in the Mediterranean and later the European world only after the spread of Christianity throughout the empire.[4] In his seminal work on gift giving in ancient and traditional societies, Marcel Mauss somewhat imprecisely pinpoints the inception of this shift and its subsequent cultural transmission:

> We can even date from the Mischnaic [*sic*] era, from the victory of the "Poor" in Jerusalem, the time when the doctrine of charity and alms was born, which with Christianity and Islam, spread around the world.[5]

With respect to the Jews of the late antique periods we can ask the question, How did Jewish communities of the late ancient world relate to poverty, the poor, and the giving of charity? But already a number of problems begin with the inquiry itself. We must first define which of the many communities in the Land of Israel or Babylonia we are asking about, which decade—let alone century—of the rabbinic period we want to examine and what we mean by a Jewish community in the first place. But the ultimate concerns stem from the sources of our information on these Jewish communities. While nonrabbinic sources provide some information about Jewish demographics, practices, and attitudes in the Roman world, when it comes to the Babylonian Jewish communities of late antiquity we rely much more heavily on the rabbinic literature itself for clues about Jewish society.[6] Reading these texts as simple history becomes somewhat problematic. Rabbinic texts were not composed as histories (in the modern sense), and their own history of compilation undermines such claims. With respect to the Jews of Babylonia during late antiquity, we rely on data that come from oral texts that were edited and written down centuries after the times they purport to describe. Furthermore, we cannot assume that these texts tell us much about

3. Gregg E. Gardner, *The Origins of Organized Charity in Rabbinic Judaism* (Cambridge: Cambridge University Press, 2015), 11.

4. Veyne, *Bread and Circuses*, 31.

5. Marcel Mauss, *The Gift: The Form and Reason for Exchange in Archaic Societies*, trans. W. D. Halls (New York: Norton, 1990; French original 1925), 18.

6. See Seth Schwartz, "The Political Geography of Rabbinic Texts," in *The Cambridge Companion to the Talmud and Rabbinic Literature*, ed. Charlotte Elisheva Fonrobert and Martin S. Jaffee (New York: Cambridge University Press, 2007), 75–98.

nonrabbinic Jewish attitudes or approaches.[7] We can, however, attempt to do some intellectual history about the culture that produced these texts by examining how they are composed, their different versions, their redaction history, how they express their ideas, and about whom they speak.[8] In this article, I examine a text from the Babylonian Talmud—a *sugya* consisting of a series of narratives and some laws that engage this topic of charity. I focus primarily on the narratives as they form what we might call a narrative cycle in that, as I will show, they have been edited together both thematically and stylistically toward achieving some coherent goal with regard to rabbinic attitudes around poverty and charity. I will suggest that this cycle of narratives serves to nuance and problematize the act of charity giving. This problematizing reflects a cultural awareness on the part of the Bavli editors that, notwithstanding the religious imperative of giving charity, other concerns about its implementation are significant. This awareness may well reflect the shift to greater rabbinic institutionalization of the charity activities in the late Amoraic and Geonic periods—a phenomenon pointed out by Alyssa Gray and Gregg Gardner in their respective works on the topic[9]—or the waning influence of euergetism. It may also reflect the literary culture of the editors of the Bavli and their desire to create a multivocal, nuanced text that eschews binary categorizations of normative behavior.

Background: Review of Literature

The history of the Jewish response to poverty in the late ancient world has been addressed by a number of writers. The majority of these studies focus on third- through fifth-century Palestine and tend to make the relevant comparisons with contemporary imperial, provincial, and Christian attitudes. As early as 1930, George Foot Moore delved into rabbinic attitudes toward charity in his *Judaism in the First Centuries of the Christian Era: The Age of the Tannaim*.[10] Moore uses the whole gamut of early rabbinic teachings to articulate a rabbinic approach to charity. He compares and contrasts these attitudes with charity notions in the New Testament and shows the interdependence of ideas as well as the nuances of their disparity. In a similar sense, Ephraim Urbach shows that a good number of passages in

7. See Jacob Neusner and Alan Avery-Peck, eds., *Judaism in Late Antiquity*, part 3, *Where We Stand: Issues and Debates in Ancient Judaism*, vol. 1, HOS 1.53 (Leiden: Brill, 1999), 123–229.

8. See Richard Lee Kalmin, *Sages, Stories, Authors, and Editors in Rabbinic Babylonia*, BJS 300 (Atlanta: Scholars Press, 1994), 2–3.

9. Alyssa Gray, "The Formerly Wealthy Poor: From Empathy to Ambivalence in Rabbinic Literature of Late Antiquity," *AJSR* 33 (2009): 101–33; Gardner, *Origins of Organized Charity*.

10. George Foot Moore, *Judaism in the First Centuries of the Christian Era: The Age of the Tannaim*, 3 vols. (Cambridge, MA: Harvard University Press, 1946), 2:162–79.

the Amoraic midrash Leviticus Rabbah are responses to Christian charity practices or texts. In this important work, Urbach contrasts the redemptive, donor-centric emphasis of Christian charity with the ameliorative function that the rabbis prioritized.[11] Both of these authors tend to flatten the historical development of rabbinic attitudes assuming that the rabbis, as a movement, were responsible for a unified doctrine of charity that stretched across the centuries. In a similar vein, Ze'ev Safrai's *The Jewish Community in Palestine during the Period of the Mishna and the Talmud* compares Jewish and Roman communal charity institutions.[12] Moshe Beer's *The Babylonian Amoraim: Aspects of Economic Life* also collapses a few centuries of rabbinic attitudes in his section on economic mobility and poverty but does, at least, mostly narrow the scope to the three hundred years of the Babylonian Amoraic period.[13] While his treatment of charity practices is limited and only incidental to other economic areas on which he focuses, among his broad conclusions are that the Babylonian Amoraim, like their Jewish and non-Jewish contemporaries, lived varied economic lives but certainly valorized wealth. Poverty and the fear of becoming poor was a reality that informed the world of these rabbis and their attitudes toward the poor and charity giving.[14] Beer's evidence is drawn primarily from the Babylonian Talmud itself, but it fails to meaningfully differentiate between the historical strata and redaction history of the sources.

More recently, a number of articles and books have been written that look at rabbinic attitudes toward poverty and charity in light of the countervailing Greco-Roman norms of euergetism of late antiquity. These perspectives primarily follow an analysis of Jewish charity and euergetism suggested by Seth Schwartz, first briefly in *Imperialism and Jewish Society*[15] and then more fully articulated in his *Were the Jews a Mediterranean Society?*[16] Schwartz posits that, typologically, societies can be viewed as being based largely on networks of reciprocity and mutual exchange or based on a solidarity of individuals bound by common beliefs and core myths. The former typifies the ideal in the Greek and Roman polis, while the latter is the norm that the Torah commands to the Jews. Although not mutually

11. Ephraim Urbach, "Political and Social Tendencies in Talmudic Concepts of Charity" [Hebrew], *Zion* 16 (1951): 1–27.

12. Ze'ev Safrai, *The Jewish Community in Palestine during the Period of the Mishna and the Talmud* [Hebrew] (Jerusalem: Merkaz Zalman Shazar, 1995).

13. Moshe Beer, *The Babylonian Amoraim: Aspects of Economic Life* [Hebrew] (Ramat-Gan: Bar-Ilan University Press, 1982).

14. Ibid., 341–49.

15. Seth Schwartz, *Imperialism and Jewish Society: 200 B.C.E. to 640 C.E.*, Jews, Christians, and Muslims from the ancient to the Modern World (Princeton, NJ: Princeton University Press, 2001), 275–78.

16. Seth Schwartz, *Were the Jews a Mediterranean Society? Reciprocity and Solidarity in Ancient Judaism* (Princeton, NJ: Princeton University Press, 2010).

exclusive, these archetypes are in many ways in tension with one another.[17] The euergetic ideal—in which a patron makes a gift to the city and is in turn given an honor for his or her patronage—is one that contributes to the reciprocity norm. Charity, on the other hand, in its pure form, is all about corporate solidarity. It is meant to be a gift given with no "strings attached." Works that respond to this typology in one way or another include Susan Sorek's *Remembered for Good: A Jewish Benefaction System in Ancient Palestine*, Michael Satlow's "Fruits and Fruits of Fruits: Charity and Piety among Jews in Late Antique Palestine," Tzvi Novick's "Charity and Reciprocity: Structures of Benevolence in Rabbinic Literature," Gregg Gardner's "Charity Wounds: Gifts to the Poor in Early Rabbinic Judaism," Yael Wilfand Ben-Shalom's *Poverty, Charity and the Image of the Poor in Rabbinic Texts from the Land of Israel*, and, most recently, Gregg Gardner's *The Origins of Organized Charity in Rabbinic Judaism.*[18] These studies tend to focus primarily on the Palestinian sources or fail to distinguish Babylonian from Palestinian texts in any meaningful way. On the other hand, in looking at the subclass of what she terms "the formerly wealthy poor," Alyssa Gray is one of the few recent writers to trace the differences in rabbinic attitudes that emerge diachronically from the two Talmudic corpora.[19] She shows that a demonstrable shift in attitude toward the patrician poor occurred over the rabbinic period, moving from Tannaitic empathy to Amoraic ambivalence. Gray's methodological approach is important. Since rabbis in both the Land of Israel and Babylonia often made use of the same sources—biblical verses, Mishnah, Tosefta, Tannaitic midrash and early Amoraic statements—a comparison of the treatment of these sources is instructive. In tracing a text from its appearance in early rabbinic sources to its later redactional settings, one can often discern important differences in the approach of its authors and editors.

In this article, I will utilize this approach to analyze the cycle of charity narratives that appear on two folios of the Babylonian Talmud—b. Ketub. 67b–68a—which tells the stories of a number of rabbis and their acts of charity. These narratives all share certain thematic and stylistic features. One shared feature is their depiction of unique personalized charity giving by rabbis. Each story describes a scenario of a particular rabbi (or in

---

17. Ibid., 14–15.

18. Susan Sorek, *Remembered for Good: A Jewish Benefaction System in Ancient Palestine* (Sheffield: Sheffield Phoenix, 2010); Michael Satlow, "Fruits and Fruits of Fruits: Charity and Piety among Jews in Late Antique Palestine," *JQR* 100 (2010): 244–77; Tzvi Novick, "Charity and Reciprocity: Structures of Benevolence in Rabbinic Literature," *HTR* 105 (2012): 33–52; Gregg Gardner, "Charity Wounds: Gifts to the Poor in Early Rabbinic Judaism," in *The Gift in Antiquity*, ed. Michael Satlow (Hoboken, NJ: Wiley-Blackwell, 2013), 175–88; Yael Wilfand Ben-Shalom, *Poverty, Charity and the Image of the Poor in Rabbinic Texts from the Land of Israel*, SWBA 2/9 (Sheffield: Sheffield Phoenix, 2014); Gregg Gardner, *Origins of Organized Charity*.

19. Alyssa Gray, "Formerly Wealthy Poor," 101–33.

one case, a local community) engaged in the act of charity. But these acts are not just about a modest contribution to a common charity fund. Rather, each story speaks of an individual donor and his (and in one story, her) seemingly unique—often supererogatory—practice of charity. A number of these stories have clear-cut parallels in earlier rabbinic literature allowing a tentative reconstruction of their redaction history. Most of these stories have less direct parallels but still evidence the influences of a tradition of storytelling on this topic in their tropes, motifs, and themes. These affinities will enable us to speculate about the historical forces that may have impacted the transmission of these narratives within rabbinic culture. All of these stories present some type of twist on the expected outcome. I will argue that these narratives all work, in their current redactional form in the Bavli, to problematize aspects of the act of charity in the social context that is depicted. That being the case, this narrative cycle presents a unique, multivocal expression of the complexities of the prevailing rabbinic attitudes toward charity in the late antique period in which the Bavli was edited.

The Texts

B. Ketub. 67b–68a presents a cycle of nine narratives that each tell a (very) short story about charity giving. Structurally, this cycle of nine narratives is "interrupted" after the fourth story with the interpolation of a halakhic interlude. In addition, the provenance of the first two narratives appear to be Tannaitic. They are—with the exception of an Aramaic-language editorial intervention following the second narrative—recorded in Mishnaic Hebrew and, in the case of the second narrative, introduced by תנו רבנן, "our rabbis taught," a putative signifier of Tannaitic provenance. Both of these stories have direct parallels in both t. Pe'ah 4:10 as well as Sifre Deut. 116 (175) with some variations.[20] The Bavli's reworking of these sources will be evaluated in the following section dealing with their parallels in the Yerushalmi. The next seven stories of the cycle are in Aramaic—with the exception of some of the dialogue, which is in Hebrew—and appear to be of later provenance. The first of these seven Aramaic narratives tells a tale of Rabbi Neḥemiah (of Shiḥin, per the Yerushalmi version), presumably a late Tanna,[21] and the second, of Rava, the prolific fourth generation Babylonian Amora.

20. Except where noted all Tosefta citations are from Saul Lieberman, ed., *The Tosefta: According to Codex Vienna, with Variants from Codex Erfurt, Genizah MSS. and Editio Princeps* (New York: Jewish Theological Seminary of America, 1955), 187. All citations of Sifre Deut. are from Louis Finkelstein, ed., *Sifre on Deuteronomy* (New York: Jewish Theological Seminary of America, 1969).

21. See n. 55.

As mentioned, following this first subset of narratives is a halakhic interlude—largely a reworking of t. Pe'ah 4:12–13 with editorial comments and a passage paralleling Sifre Deut. 116 (175)—which deals with the community's responsibility toward those poor who refuse to accept charity and those nonpoor who request it. Following this, the narrative cycle resumes with a series of three stories about the Babylonian sage Mar 'Uqba, an early Amora of the late third century.[22] Following these is a narrative about Rabbi Abba, who was, presumably, the late third- and early fourth-century Babylonian Amora who moved to the Land of Israel later in his life.[23] The last narrative of the cycle is about Rabbi Ḥanina, who is thought to be Ḥanina b. Ḥama, an early third-century Babylonian Amora who also moved to the Land of Israel.[24]

Below is a presentation of this narrative cycle based on the Vilna printing of the Bavli. I have numbered and translated each one, and have noted where Bavli manuscript versions varied substantially from the printed text.[25] This is followed by the parallel pericopae in the Talmud Yerushalmi based on the Leiden manuscript.[26] Other relevant sources such as Tosefta and midrashic collections are cited later or in footnotes as needed.

The Bavli Narratives: B. Ketub. 67b–68a

B1. Hillel the Elder	They said about Hillel the Elder that he purchased for a particular well-born poor person a horse to ride on and a slave to run before him. Once he did not find a slave to run before him so he [Hillel] ran before him for three miles.	אמרו עליו על הלל הזקן שלקח לעני בן טובים אחד סוס לרכוב עליו ועבד לרוץ לפניו. פעם אחת לא מצא עבד לרוץ לפניו ורץ לפניו שלושה מילין.

22. See Moses Margaliot, "Mar 'Uqba" in *Encyclopedia of Talmudic and Geonic Literature* (Tel Aviv: Yavneh, 1976).

23. Ibid., "Abba".

24. See David Assaf, "Let's Thank the Crooks: On the Shaping of Charity Stories in the World of the Sages," in *Iturim: Studies in Honor of Moshe Krone* [Hebrew] (Jerusalem: Eliner-Torah Education Department of the World Zionist Organization, 1986), 248–62, here 255. But see also Zechariah Frankel, *Introduction to the Yerushalmi* [Hebrew] (Jerusalem: Tzilum Press, 1967), 50, who posits that this is a much later Amora.

25. The manuscripts consulted were as follows: Munich Cod. Heb 95, Firkovich 187 (St. Petersburg – RNL Evr. I 187), Vatican 113, Vatican 130, Cambridge - T-S F1 (2) 110, G196. (*The Friedberg Genizah Project for Talmud Bavli Variants*; https://bavli.genizah.org; *National Library of Israel Online Manuscripts*; http://web.nli.org.il/sites/NLI/Hebrew/collections/jewish-collection/Talmud/Pages/default.aspx; and *The Lieberman Institute: The Sol and Evelyn Henkind Talmud Text Online Databank*; https://www.lieberman-institute.com).

26. Yaacov Sussman, ed., *Talmud Yerushalmi according to Ms. Or. 4720 (Scal. 3) of the Leiden University Library with Restorations and Corrections* (Jerusalem: Academy of the Hebrew Language 2005), 112–13.

B2. People of the Galilee	The rabbis taught: A story [is told] of the people of the Upper Galilee who purchased for a particular well-born poor person from Sepphoris a pound of meat every day. A pound of meat! What is the significance [of that]? Rav Huna said: [it was] a pound of poultry. And if you prefer you can say: it was a pound of money's worth of real meat. Rav Ashi said: [Since they were] a small village every day they would waste a [whole] animal on his account.	תנו רבנן מעשה באנשי גליל העליון שלקחו לעני בן טובים אחד מציפורי ליטרא בשר בכל יום. ליטרא בשר מאי רבותא אמר רב הונא ליטרא בשר משל עופות ואיבעית אימא בליטרא בשר ממש רב אשי אמר התם כפר קטן היה בכל יומא הוה מפסדי חיותא אמטולתיה.
B3. R. Neḥemiah Kills a Man with Lentils	This [poor man] once came before R. Neḥemiah [for charity] who said to him, "What do your meals consist of?" The man said to him, "Of fatty meat and old wine." "Will you consent to dine with me on lentils?" He dined with him on lentils and died. He said, "Alas for this man whom Neḥemiah has killed " On the contrary, he should have said "Alas for Neḥemiah who killed this man!" [The fact], however, is [that the man] himself [was to blame, for] he should not have cultivated his luxurious habits to such an extent.	ההוא דאתא לקמיה דרבי נחמיה אמר ליה במה אתה סועד א"ל בבשר שמן ויין ישן רצונך שתגלגל עמי בעדשים גלגל עמו בעדשים ומת אמר אוי לו לזה שהרגו נחמיה. אדרבה אוי לו לנחמיה שהרגו לזה מיבעי ליה אלא איהו הוא דלא איבעי ליה לפנוקי נפשיה כולי האי.
B4. Rava and his Long-Lost Sister	A [poor] man once came before Rava [for maintenance] who said to him, "What do your meals consist of?" He answered, "Of fatted chicken and old wine." He [Rava] said to him, "Did you not consider the burden of the community?" To which he replied, "Do I eat of theirs? I eat [the food] of the All-Merciful; for we learned: 'The eyes of all wait for Thee, and Thou givest them their food in his 'season' (Ps 145:15). Since it is not said, 'in their season' but 'in his season', this teaches that the Holy One, blessed be He, provides for every individual his food in accordance with his own habits."	ההוא דאתא לקמיה דרבא אמר לו במה אתה סועד אמר לו בתרנגולת פטומה ויין ישן אמר ליה ולא חיישת לדוחקא דציבורא א"ל אטו מדידהו קאכילנא מדרחמנא קאכילנא דתנינא עיני כל אליך ישברו ואתה נותן להם את אכלם בעתו בעתם לא נאמר אלא בעתו מלמד שכל אחד ואחד נותן הקב"ה פרנסתו בעתו.

	Meanwhile Rava's sister arrived, who had not seen him for thirteen years, and brought him a fattened chicken and old wine. [Rava] said, "What is this!" He said [to the poor man], "I apologize to you, come and eat."	אדהכי אתאי אחתיה דרבא דלא חזיא ליה תליסרי שני ואתיא ליה תרנגולת פטומה ויין ישן אמר מאי דקמא א"ל נענתי לך קום אכול.
Halakhic interlude	The rabbis taught: If he does not have [sufficient means of support] and does not want to be supported [from charity funds], they give [it] to him as a loan and then they go back and give [it] to him as a gift; these are the words of R. Meir. But the Rabbis say: They give him [charity funds] as a gift, and then they go back and give [it] to him as a loan.	תנו רבנן אין לו ואינו רוצה להתפרנס נותנין לו לשום הלואה וחוזרין ונותנין לו לשום מתנה דברי רבי מאיר וחכמים אומרים נותנין לו לשום מתנה וחוזרין ונותנין לו לשום הלואה.
	'As a gift'? He will not take it [as a gift]! Rava said: [They] begin [discussions] with him [by offering it] as a gift.	לשום מתנה הא לא שקיל אמר רבא לפתוח לו לשום מתנה.
	If he has [sufficient means of support] but does not want to support [himself], they give him [charity] as a gift, and then they go back and collect the debt from him.	יש לו ואינו רוצה להתפרנס נותנין לו לשום מתנה וחוזרין ונפרעין ממנו.
	They go back and collect the debt from him? He would not continue to take [their support]! Rav Pappa said: [They collect the debt from his estate] after his death.	חוזרין ונפרעין הימנו תו לא שקיל אמר רב פפא לאחר מיתה.
	R. Shimeon says, If he has [sufficient means of support] but does not want to support [himself], they do not get involved with him. If he does not have and does not want to be supported [from charity], they say to him: Bring collateral and take [the funds as a loan], [this is so] that his mindset should be elevated [i.e. eased. But it is in fact a charity gift].	ר"ש אומר יש לו ואינו רוצה להתפרנס אין נזקקין לו אין לו ואינו רוצה להתפרנס אומרים לו הבא משכון וטול כדי שתזוח דעתו עליו.

	The rabbis taught: 'lend', this [refers to] one who does not have [funds] and does not want to be supported [by charity] that they give [it] to him as a loan and go back and give [it] to him as a gift. 'Surely lend', this [refers] to one who has [sufficient means of support] but does not want to support [himself], they give him [charity] as a gift, and then they go back and collect the debt from [his estate] after his death. These are the words of R. Yehuda. But the Rabbis say: If he has [sufficient means of support] but does not want to support [himself], they do not get involved with him. How then do I account for [the infinitive absolute] 'you shall surely lend'? The Torah spoke in human language [colloquially].	ת״ר העבט זה שאין לו ואינו רוצה להתפרנס שנותנים לו לשום הלואה וחוזרין ונותנין לו לשום מתנה תעביטנו זה שיש לו ואינו רוצה להתפרנס שנותנין לו לשום מתנה וחוזרין ונפרעין הימנו לאחר מיתה דברי ר׳ יהודה וחכ״א יש לו ואינו רוצה להתפרנס אין נזקקין לו ואלא מה אני מקיים תעביטנו דברה תורה כלשון בני אדם.
B5. Mar 'Uqba in the Oven	Mar 'Uqba had a poor man in his neighborhood into whose door-socket he used to throw four zuz every day. Once [the poor man] thought, "I will go and see who does me this kindness." On that day [it happened] that Mar 'Uqba was late at the house of study and his wife was coming home with him. As soon as [the poor man] saw them moving the door he went out after them, but they fled from him and ran into an oven from which the fire had just been swept. Mar 'Uqba's feet were burning and his wife said to him, "Raise your feet and put them on mine." He [Mar 'Uqba] became upset; She said to him, "I am usually at home and my benefactions are direct."	מר עוקבא הוה עניא בשיבבותיה דהוה רגיל כל יומא דשדי ליה ארבעה זוז בצינורא דדשא. יום אחד אמר איזיל איחזי מאן קעביד בי ההוא טיבותא ההוא יומא נגהא ליה למר עוקבא לבי מדרשא אתיא דביתהו בהדיה כיון דחזיוה דקא מצלי ליה לדשא נפק בתרייהו רהוט מקמיה עיילי לההוא אתונא דהוה גרופה נורא הוה קא מיקליין כרעיה דמר עוקבא אמרה ליה דביתהו שקול כרעיך אותיב אכרעאי חלש דעתיה אמרה ליה אנא שכיחנא בגויה דביתא ומקרבא אהנייתי.

	And what [was the reason for] all that [fleeing and hiding from the poor man]? As Mar Zutra b. Tobiah said in the name of Rav. And others state: R. Huna b. Bizna said in the name of R. Shimeon Ḥasida; and others again state: R. Yoḥanan said in the name of R. Shimeon b. Yoḥai: "Better had a person thrown himself into a fiery furnace than publicly put another person to shame." Whence do we derive this? From [the action of] Tamar; for it is written, "When she was brought forth [she sent to her father-in-law, Judah, discreetly, so as not to embarrass him]" (Gen 38:25).	ומאי כולי האי דאמר מר זוטרא בר טוביה אמר רב ואמרי לה אמר רב הונא בר ביזנא אמר ר"ש חסידא ואמרי לה אמר ר יוחנן משום רבי שמעון בן יוחי נוח לו לאדם שימסור עצמו לתוך כבשן האש ואל ילבין פני חברו ברבים מנא לן מתמר דכתיב היא מוצאת.
B6. Mar 'Uqba and the Luxuriant Pauper	Mar 'Uqba had a poor man in his neighborhood to whom he regularly sent four hundred zuz on the eve of every Day of Atonement. On one occasion he sent them through his son who came back and said to him, "He does not need [your help]." [Mar 'Uqba] said, "What have you seen?" "I saw that they were spraying old wine before him." [Mar 'Uqba] said, "Is he so used to luxury?" He doubled [the amount] and sent it back to him.	מר עוקבא הוה עניא בשיבבותיה דהוה רגיל לשדורי ליה ארבע מאה זוזי כל מעלי יומא דכיפורא יומא חד שדרי־נהו ניהליה ביד בריה אתא אמר ליה לא צריך אמר מאי חזית חזאי דקא מזלפי ליה יין ישן אמר מפנק כולי האי עייפינהו ושדרינהו ניהליה.
B7. Mar 'Uqba's Deathbed	When he [Mar 'Uqba] was [about] to die he requested, "Bring me my charity account-books." He discovered that seven thousand Sijan [gold] denarii were entered therein [undistributed]. He said, "The provisions are scanty and the road is long," and he immediately distributed half of his wealth.	כי קא ניחא נפשיה אמר אייתו לי חושבנאי דצדקה אשכח דהוה כתיב ביה שבעת אלפי דינרי סיאנקי אמר זוודאי קלילי ואורחא רחיקתא קם בזביזה לפלגיה ממוניה.

	But how could he do such a thing? Has not R. Ilai stated: "It was ordained at Usha that if one wishes to spend liberally [on charity] he should not spend more than a fifth [of his wealth]?" This applies only during one's lifetime, lest he become impoverished. But after death we are not [concerned] about it.	היכי עביד הכי והאמר ר אילעאי באושא התקינו המבזבז אל יבזבז יותר מחומש הני מילי מחיים שמא ירד מנכסיו אבל לאחר מיתה לית לן בה.
B8. R. Abba and the Rogues	R. Abba used to bind money in his scarf, sling it on his back, place himself amidst the poor, and cast his eyes sideways [as a precaution against—or, perhaps, a trap for] the rogues.	רבי אבא הוה צייר זוזי בסוד־ריה ושדי ליה לאחוריה וממצי נפשיה לבי עניי ומצלי עיניה מרמאי.
B9. R. Ḥanina and the Fraudulent Pauper	R. Ḥanina had a poor man to whom he regularly sent four zuz on the eve of every Sabbath. One day he sent that sum through his wife who came back and told him [that] he [was in] no need [of it]. [He asked her:] "What did you see?" [She replied:] "I heard that he was asked, 'On what will you dine; On the silver cloths or on the gold ones?'" [Rabbi Ḥanina] replied, "It is [in light of such cases] that R. Eleazar said: Come let us be grateful to the rogues for were it not for them, we would have been sinning every day, for it is said, 'And he cries unto the Lord against thee, and it is sin unto thee'" (Deut 15:9).	רבי חנינא הוה ההוא עניא דהוה רגיל לשדורי ליה ארבעה זוזי כל מעלי שבתא יומא חד שדרינהו ניהליה ביד דביתהו אתאי אמרה ליה לא צריך מאי חזית שמעי דהוה קאמרי ליה במה אתה סועד בטלי כסף או בטלי זהב אמר היינו דאמר רבי אלעזר בואו ונחזיק טובה לרמאין שאלמלא הן היינו חוטאין בכל יום שנאמר וקרא עליך אל ה' והיה בך חטא.

Yerushalmi Parallels: Y. Pe'ah 8:8–8:9, 21a–b

The order of the Yerushalmi parallels has been changed in the following presentation to reflect the order of their analogs in the Bavli. The actual order of these stories in the Yerushalmi varies slightly: the story of R. Neḥemiah (Y3) appears last, following a series of six stories that do not appear in the Bavli at all; the first two stories (Y1, Y2) are consecutive (as in the Bavli) but are followed by a halakhic interlude not found in the Bavli. The overall sequence in the Yerushalmi, then, is as follows: 1. Hillel the Elder, 2. People of the Galilee, 3. Halakhic interlude, 4. Shmuel and the Fraudulent Paupers, 5. R. Yoḥanan and Resh Laqish and the Fraudulent

Pauper, 6. Shmuel and the Luxuriant Pauper, 7. Series of six additional charity stories, 8. R. Neḥemiah Kills a Man with Meat.

Y1. Hillel the Elder	A story [is told] of Hillel the Elder who purchased for a well-born poor person a horse to work with (or work out with?) and a slave to serve him.	מעשה בהלל הזקן שלקח לעני בן טובים סוס אחד להתעמל בו ועבד לשמשו.
Y2. People of the Galilee	Another story [is told] of the people of the Galilee who would donate to a particular elder a pound of bird meat (or 'Sepphoris' meat?) every day. Is this possible? Rather, it is that he did not eat with others (or 'eat other [food]').	שוב מעשה באנשי הגליל שהיו מעלין לזקן אחד ליטרא בשר צפרים בכל יום ואיפשר כן אלא דלא הוה אכל עם חורנין.
Y3. R. Neḥemiah Kills a Man with Meat	Neḥemiah of Shiḥin encountered a Jerusalemite who told him: "Gain merit through [giving] me a hen!" [Neḥemiah] said to him: "Here is its price for you. Go and buy [red] meat." He ate and died. And they (he) said: "Come and mourn for Neḥemiah's victim."	נחמיה איש שיחין פגע ביה ירושלמי אחד אמ' ליה זכי עימי חדא תרנגולתא אמ' ליה הילך טימיתיה וזיל זבון קופד ואכל ומית ואמ' בואו וספדו להרוגו שלנחמיה.
Y4. Shmuel and the Fraudulent Paupers	Shmuel fled from his father. He went and stood between two poor people's huts. He heard their voices saying: "On which table service should we dine today? On the gold table service or on the silver table service?" [Shmuel] went and told his father [who] said: "We have to be grateful to the deceivers among them (the poor)."	שמואל ערק מן אבוי אזל וקם ליה בין תרין צריפין דמיסכינין שמע קלהון אמרין בהדין אגנטין אנן אכלין יומא דין בארגרונטרין דהבא בארגנטורין כספא אעל ואמר קומי אבוי אמר ליה צריכין אנו להחזיק טובה לרמאין שבהם.
Y5. R. Yoḥanan and Resh Laqish and the Fraudulent Pauper	A story: R. Yoḥanan and R. Shimeon b. Laqish were going in to bathe in the public baths of Tiberias and [on their way] were encountered by a poor person. He told them: "Gain merit through [assisting] me." They told him: "On our return [we will give you charity]." On their return, they found him dead. They said: "Since we did not attend to him when he was alive, let us attend to him now that he is dead." While they were attending to him [for burial], they found a money pouch hanging [from his neck]. They	דלמא רבי יוחנן ורבי שמעון בן לקיש עלון מיסחי בהדין דימוסין דטיבריא פגע בון חד מסכן אמר לון זכין בי אמרו ליה מי חזרון מי חזרון אשכחוניה מית אמרו הואיל ולא זכינן ביה בחיוי ניטפל ביה במיתותיה כי מיטפלון ביה אשכחון כיס דינריא תלו ביה אמרו הדא דאמר רבי אבהו אמר רבי לעזר צריכין אנו להחזיק טובה לרמאין שבהן שאילולא הרמאין שבהן היה אחד מהן תובע צדקה מן האדם ולא נותן לו מיד היה נענש.

	said: "Thus did R. Abbahu say in the name of R. [E]liezer: We have to be grateful to the deceivers among them since without the deceivers among them, when one of them requests charity from a person and that person refuses, immediately he [who refused] would be punished."	
Y6. Shmuel and the Luxuriant Pauper	Abba the son of Ba gave coins to his son Shmuel to distribute to paupers. He [Shmuel] went out and found one pauper eating beef and drinking wine. He went in [back home] and told his father who said to him, "Give [him] more for his soul is bitter."	אבא בר בא יהב לשמואל בריה פריטין דפלג למיסכיניא נפק ואשכח חד מסכן אכל קופד ושתי חמר עאל ואמר קומוי אבוי אמר לי׳ הב יתיר דנפשיה מרתיה.

Redactional Analysis and Historical Aspects of the Narratives

In a brief reference to some of these narratives, Peter Brown writes, "[The rabbis] toyed with the surreal cases of de-classe persons being maintained in the state to which they were accustomed, and emphasized the need to spare such persons the shame of appearing to beg for alms."[27] "Surreal cases," as it were, is an apt description for some of these stories. There is something in the realm of the absurd in the Bavli's description of Hillel the Elder running as a herald before the horse that he himself had provided to the pauper whom he is supporting. And if he could not find a horse might Hillel have carried the man on his own shoulders?[28] Surreal or not, these are tales meant to captivate the imagination, and surely they do. Whether these stories are didactic fiction designed to model exemplary behavior or to critique it will be discussed below. How these stories came to be is the subject at hand. We will now look at the context and, where possible, the redactional history of these narratives in order to shed some light on this question.

As Jeffrey Rubenstein has shown, the context of the rabbinic narrative—its literary setting—is significant for understanding its redactional value.[29] The Bavli narratives appear in tractate Ketubbot, which nominally deals with the marriage document and other laws of marriage. Specifically, these narratives follow on the heels of a Mishnah that relates

27. Brown, *Poverty and Leadership*, 60.

28. See n. 38 below.

29. Jeffrey L. Rubenstein, *Talmudic Stories: Narrative Art, Composition, and Culture* (Baltimore: John Hopkins University Press, 1999), 24.

the requirements of the community's responsibility toward dowering an orphaned girl (m. Ket. 6:5). The Talmud begins with a *baraita* that delineates the community's responsibility to provide financially for an orphaned boy who wishes to marry. The *baraita* cites the biblical phrase [*and lend to him*] *sufficient for whatever he needs* (Deut 15:8) to include in this responsibility a house, its furnishings, and then even a wife. The exegesis turns on a redundancy in the original Hebrew of the verse: די מחסורו אשר יחסר לו, literally, "sufficient for his needs that he is needing." This redundancy is read in a cumulative way, each part of the phrase adding another responsibility. The Talmud then segues to a discussion of broader charity responsibilities by citing another *baraita* (paralleling the Toseftan text, t. Pe'ah 4:10) that adduces the same verse to address the requirements of the community vis-à -vis the general poor. In this case the exegesis hinges on reading the redundancy in the verse as being somewhat antagonistic:

> די מחסורו אתה מצווה עליו לפרנסו ואי אתה מצווה עליו לעשרו אשר יחסר לו אפילו סוס לרכוב עליו ועבד לרוץ לפניו
>
> "Sufficient for his need"—you are commanded to support him, but you are not commanded to enrich him. "That he is needing"—even [to provide] a horse to ride on and a slave to run before him. (b. Ketub. 57b)[30]

The first part of the phrase teaches the basic law and its limitation—only what he truly needs—while the second part expands the notion of support to aspects of life that might seem to be luxurious excesses. This exegesis introduces a tension between needs and luxuries that is never fully acknowledged in the text but is addressed by later medieval commentaries.[31] The Bavli, following the Tosefta and the Yerushalmi, segues from this ambivalent normative construct to the first narrative of the cycle—"Hillel the Elder." I suggest that the tension inherent in this ambivalent reading of the verse—which functions structurally as a frame to the narrative cycle—is what animates most, if not all, of the narratives in the cycle.

The Yerushalmi also records a cycle of narratives on charity. As noted, these appear in tractate Pe'ah, and a number of these narratives are parallels to our Bavli stories. The context of tractate Pe'ah is also a "natural" setting for charity texts, as the tractate deals largely with agrarian poverty relief—the farmer's requirement to leave the "corners," "gleanings," and "forgotten things" of the harvest in the field for the poor. The last Mishnah of the tractate delineates a "poverty line" of personal funds. Only an individual who falls below this line may take the agricultural gifts. The

30. This text is a close parallel of Sifre Deut. 116 (175) with the addition of the phrase "you are commanded to support him," which is not found in the original Sifre text.

31. See, e.g., Betzalel Ashkenazi, *Shitah Mekubetzet Tractate Ketubbot, Volume II* (Jerusalem: Ma'aseh Rokeach Press, 1952), 46.

Mishnah then segues to censuring those who take, even though they are not entitled, and other dissembling for personal gain. It is in this context that the charity story-cycle of the Yerushalmi is located.

The first three Bavli narratives of the cycle readily lend themselves to synoptic comparison with the parallel Yerushalmi texts.[32] With regard to the first story, "Hillel the Elder," this comparison is revealing. The Yerushalmi version (Y1)—with almost verbatim parallels in the Tosefta and Sifre (t. Pe'ah 4:10; Sifre Deut. 116 [175])— is significantly different from the Bavli version (B1). The Yerushalmi reports the story as a one-time occurrence. Hillel bought this man a horse and a slave, two essential tools for his livelihood, or perhaps his lifestyle. And that is it. Catherine Hezser has shown the significance, if not the prevalence, of the slave for the Jewish family in late antiquity in the Land of Israel.[33] Domestic slaves served as an integral part of the family economy, though they never became the basis for slave estates of the likes of other provincial settings.[34] It is then fitting with the theme of restoring this formerly wealthy poor man to his status quo ante that Hillel would have purchased the slave for him.[35] The horse may be, לעמל בו, "to work with," or even להתעמל בו, "to work out with," i.e., "to go riding on," as this man had been accustomed to do, as a member of the gentry.[36] This story is about a venerable founding father, Hillel the Elder, a contemporary of Herod. The trappings of slaves and riding horses are perfectly appropriate for a patrician of the age. The Bavli version, however, embellishes the tale. First, the slave is more than a domestic servant (לשמשו in the earlier sources). He is now the herald (לרוץ לפניו), the κῆρυξ, announcing the advent of the nobleman.[37] Or perhaps this is the Bavli's envisioning of an ancient Persian custom known from the Scroll of Esther (Esth 6:9). Furthermore, the editors of the Bavli are not content with Hillel's charity toward the poor man being viewed as a one-time event. Now Hillel has committed himself to procuring an ongoing retinue of slaves, such that on that hapless day, when Hillel is unable to find the requisite slave, he enlists himself to the task of a three-mile herald run. This adden-

32. The reader is encouraged to refer back to the translations presented above.

33. Catherine Hezser, "The Impact of Household Slaves on the Jewish Family in Roman Palestine" *JSJ* 34 (2003): 375–424.

34. Schwartz, "Political Geography of Rabbinic Texts," 43.

35. See Gray, "Formerly Wealthy Poor," 103-5, for an evaluation of the terminological significance of the phrase עני בן טובים, literally "a patrician poor," which, together with שירדו מנכסיהם, "[the poor who] have descended from their property," or the Aramaic equivalents דאיתנחת מן נכסוי (in the Yerushalmi) or נחתי מנכסיהן (in the Bavli), are references to a subset of the general poor that Gardner refers to as the "conjunctural poor"— those who were once well off, that is, the formerly wealthy poor (Gardner, *Origins of Organized Charity*, 38).

36. Both the Vilna and Venice versions of the printed Yerushalmi textual witnesses also read להתעמל. T. Pe'ah 4:10 and the parallel in the Sifre Deut. 116 (175) similarly read: שהיה מתעמל בו, "that he would work out with."

37. Or the convicted prisoners, as in the Mishnah's phrase: וכרוז יוצא לפניו (m. Sanh. 6:1).

dum adds another dimension to the level of supererogatory performance of charity practiced by Hillel.[38] The rabbis of the Bavli have indeed created a "surreal" or absurd case. The narrative now borders on the satirical. In this Bavli reworking, the editors may, in fact, be engaged in an exploration of the contours and limits of the commandment of charity by depicting a non-normative exemplum that offers a skeptical criticism of these kinds of over-the-top practices.[39] What might be read at first blush as hagiography may very well be implicit opprobrium of this excess.[40] This move will become evident in many of the other Bavli narratives in this cycle.

The second narrative, "People of the Galilee," is another *baraita* with parallels in the Tosefta (t. Pe'ah 4:10 and Sifre Deuteronomy (116 [175]) that also has a direct parallel in the Yerushalmi (y. Pe'ah 8:8–9, 21a–b). When the Bavli (B2) text is compared with the Yerushalmi (Y2) text a number of similarities and differences are noticeable. Both versions begin with a Tannaitic statement describing the charity act of the town—feeding a certain poor man—and conclude with a comment by the anonymous voices of each Talmud. The poor man is identified as a sage (זקן) in the Yerushalmi,[41] as a guest (אורח) in the Sifre Deuteronomy parallel, and as a patrician poor (עני בן טובים) in the Bavli.[42] And, while a particular poor person might have been all of these things, it appears that the Bavli's tradition, placing an emphasis on his status as a formerly well-off person, is significant. By highlighting this attribute, the Bavli reads the first two narratives, the Hillel story and this one, as a conceptual unit concerned with the desideratum to restore the conjunctural poor[43] to their status quo ante that was introduced in the exegesis prior to the narrative cycle. While this may be the implicit understanding of the Yerushalmi text as well, given the gist of the anonymous editor's intervention, it is not signaled so explicitly. The poor man is simply identified as a sage.[44] On the other hand, the

---

38. Neusner points out this *reductio ad absurdum*, as it were, in his (own cynical) remark: "I suppose a still later version would have said Hillel could not find a horse, and so would have made Hillel carry the man on his back." See Jacob Neusner, *The Rabbinic Traditions about the Pharisees before 70*, 3 vols. (Leiden: Brill, 1971), 1:286.

39. See Moshe Simon-Shoshan, *Stories of the Law: Narrative Discourse and the Construction of Authority in the Mishnah* (New York: Oxford University Press, 2012), 142.

40. The notion of היה זקן ואינה לפי כבודו ("[Because] he is an elder and [this act] is not appropriate for his stature") is well attested in rabbinic literature (e.g., b. B. Meṣ. 30b and its parallel in Sifre Deut. 222 [256]). Hillel is identified as "the Elder."

41. And similarly in t. Pe'ah 4:10.

42. In all the text witnesses except Firkovich 187, which reads simply עני ("a poor person"); St. Petersburg: Yevr. I-187.

43. For this term, see n. 35 above.

44. The words שוב מעשה, "another story," which introduce Narrative 2 in both the Yerushalmi and the Toseftan texts, seem to imply a connection with Narrative 1, the Hillel story. Narrative 1 is explicitly about restoring a patrician who has fallen from his socioeconomic station. Perhaps this connection implies that the poor man in Narrative 2 is also a

Bavli's depiction of the poor man as a patrician poor may also be the result of an unwitting contamination from the Hillel narrative.

The Yerushalmi describes the charitable act of these Galileans as: שהיו מעלין לזקן אחד ליטרא בשר צפרים בכל יום, "daily, they would donate to this elder a pound of bird meat."[45] The Bavli reads: שלקחו לעני בן טובים אחד מציפורי ליטרא בשר בכל יום, "daily, they would purchase for a particular well-born poor person from Sepphoris a pound of meat."[46] The Tosefta reads more like the Bavli: ליטרא בשר בצפורי, "a pound of meat in Sepphoris," or, as Lieberman understands it, a Sepphoris-measure pound of meat.[47] The corruption of the word *ṣipori* (i.e., the place)—whether it means the type of measure, the location of the event, or the origin of the poor man—to *ṣiporim* (poultry), is quite plausible. It is also noteworthy that this is a case of the Bavli's *baraita* hewing closer to the Toseftan tradition than the Yerushalmi text does, a phenomenon noted by many scholars.[48] And finally, the Bavli's identification of the location as the גליל העליון, the Upper Galilee, may be a transposition of the Yerushalmi's (and Tosefta's) שהיו מעלין, "[the people of the Galilee] would provide," the same root, עלה, appearing in both texts.[49]

---

formerly wealthy poor. In addition, as Shaye J. D. Cohen points out, most of the early rabbis of the Land of Israel were patrician landowners ("The Rabbi in Second Century Jewish Society" in *The Cambridge History of Judaism*, ed. William Horbury, W. D. Davis, and John Sturdy [Cambridge: Cambridge University Press, 1999], 922–90, here 931). Thus, the term *zaqen* may be taken in Tannaitic literature as a reference to someone from the patrician class. But see also Gregg Gardner's "Who Is Rich? The Poor in Early Rabbinic Judaism," *JQR* 104 (2014): 515–36, for a more nuanced perspective on the economic situation of the early rabbis. Alyssa Gray, on the other hand, reads all of these stories as referring to the formerly wealthy poor. In her study of these texts, she seeks to demonstrate a shift in attitude from empathy among the early rabbis to ambivalence among the later Amoraim toward these conjunctural poor. She also sees the Bavli narratives acting to efface the distinction between the formerly wealthy and the congenitally poor. She does not explain, however, the Bavli's unique designation of this poor Sepphorian as a patrician poor (Gray, "Formerly Wealthy Poor").

45. See nn. 52 and 53 with regard to the relative values of livestock versus fowl commodities.

46. The word מציפורי, "from Sepphoris," is absent in two manuscripts: Munich 95 and Vatican 130. Given the congruity with the word צפורים found in the Tosefta and the Yerushalmi this omission seems to be a deletion of the original.

47. Saul Lieberman, *Tosefta ki-feshuṭah: A Comprehensive Commentary on the Tosefta*, part 1, *Order Zera'im*, (Jerusalem: Jewish Theological Seminary of America, 1992), 186. Lieberman actually glosses the Yerushalmi as: ליטרא בי צפרים, that is, "a Sepphoris-measure pound of meat," based on the question and answer of the anonymous voice that interrogates the quantity of the meat ration. Thus, he reads both the Tosefta and the Yerushalmi as referring to the Sepphorian measurement of the meat rather than its place of origin.

48. For a thorough summary of the field on the issue of dependence of these texts, see Yaakov Elman's *Authority and Tradition: Toseftan Baraitot in Talmudic Babylonia* (Hoboken, NJ: Ktav, 1994), 13–46.

49. See Gardner, *Origins of Organized Charity*, 132.

This story is then followed in both Bavli and Yerushalmi by an anonymous editorial question of surprise and a resolution. Perhaps aware of the versions that speak of poultry, Rav Huna glosses the Bavli version to preserve that old tradition. Nevertheless, this difference in where the word צפורי(ם) goes—to describe the beneficiary's origins or his meal—leads to the main distinction between the two texts: the editor's question and resolution. The Yerushalmi seems to be asking why the town benefactors were so generous with their donation and answers that he did not eat with other people—that is, he was used to a luxuriant lifestyle that did not entail sharing surplus food. It was to this generous standard that the town maintained him in his state of penury. Alternatively, the phrase דלא הוה אכל עם חורנין could mean that he could not (or did not) eat other foods. The town needed to provide the pound of poultry in order to satisfy the person's caloric needs.[50] The Bavli asks the opposite: What's the big deal about a pound of meat? Apparently this quantity of meat does not seem significant enough to the anonymous editors of the Bavli to warrant any special mention for Galilean generosity.[51] The Bavli text offers three answers: (1) Rav Huna says it was poultry, implying that poultry was significantly more expensive than meat.[52] This fact may be seen in the story of "Rava and His Long Lost Sister" (B4) in

---

50. See the commentary of Moses Margolies (*P'nei Moshe*) ad loc. Lieberman suggests that the correct reading is דלא הוה אכל עם חורנין לא הוה אכל, "if he did not eat with others he would not eat." That is, he would not dine alone, and thus the people of the Galilee needed to provide a much larger quantity of meat for this banquet with his friends! (*Tosefta ki-feshuṭah*, 186).

51. *Pace* this understanding of the Bavli editor's relative devaluation of this *pound of meat*, the phrase appears in a number of contexts throughout rabbinic literature where it signifies a very large quantity of food, e.g., t. 'Arak. 4:27 (ed. Zukermandel): וכן היה רבי אלעזר בן עזריה אומר מי שיש לו עשרה מנה מתעסק בירק בקדירה בכל יום עשרים מנה מתעסק ירק בקדירה ואלפס חמישים מנה ליטרה בשר מערב שבת לערב שבת מאה מנה ליטרה בשר בכל יום. See also b. Ḥul. 84a and b. Ta'an. 30a for parallels.

52. Lieberman suggests that the question of the Bavli's editor and Rav Huna's answer reflects a difference in the economies of Babylonia and the Land of Israel. In Babylonia red meat was inexpensive while poultry was more expensive. In the Land of Israel it was the reverse (*Tosefta ki-feshuṭah*, 186).

It should be noted that several of the manuscripts (Vatican 113, Vatican 130, and Firkovich 187) read ליטרא מוח (של) עופות, "a pound of bird brains." See the other reference to a meal of bird brains in rabbinic literature in *Lamentations Rabbah*, ed. S. Buber (Tel Aviv: Hildesheim, 1967), 130: ר' אבהו אזל לבצרה ואיתקבל גבי יוסי רישא אייתון קמיה תמנין מיני מוחין דעוף א"ל לא יכעוס רבי דלא הוה צידא ספק ולא קריין ליה יוסי רישא אלא דלא הוה מאכליה אלא מוחין דעוף. From this source it appears that bird brains were considered a delicacy (see Michael Sokoloff, *A Dictionary of Jewish Palestinian Aramaic* [Ramat Gan: Bar-Ilan University Press, 2002], s.v. *moaḥ*), and the host thought that the paucity of this meal of only eighty types of bird brains might offend R. Abbahu! If this is, in fact, the poor man's menu it is indeed a big deal. (The average bird brain weighs one-half ounce; a ליטרא is thought to be about sixteen ounces. Thus one ליטרא of bird brain would require about thirty-two birds, though one might question if this was indeed the same quantity as a Sepphorian litra!)... This becomes a bird-brained argument.

Finally, if, in fact, the original tradition was simply "meat," which is preserved in the

which the desired food delicacy, whose procurement is depicted as onerous for the community, is fattened chickens![53] (2) Or, suggests the anonymous editor, it was a pound of money's worth of real (non-fowl) meat, which is, apparently, a significant quantity to warrant the storyteller's special mention.[54] (3) Alternatively, opines Rav Ashi, it was the economic wastefulness engendered by their daily slaughtering of a whole cow to satisfy this impoverished aristocrat's carnivorous needs in light of their village's small size and inability to use the leftovers efficiently that was at stake (pun intended). Regardless of the reason, the editors of the Bavli are clearly expressing a more critical perspective—at least by implication—of the potential strain that profligate charity may place on community assets. This theme will be voiced again in the later narratives in the cycle.

The third narrative, "R. Neḥemiah Kills a Man with Lentils," is an Amoraic story with a parallel in the Yerushalmi whose details have changed somewhat in the Bavli. While I have called this an Amoraic narrative on account of its language and absence from any Toseftan or other Tannaitic text, its protagonist is the second-century Tanna, R. Neḥemiah (of Shiḥin), presumably the contemporary of R. Akiva.[55] A number of differences are apparent in the transmission of this narrative. In the Yerushalmi version (Y3), as in the last narrative, the poor person is not specifically identified as poor, only as a Jerusalemite. Neḥemiah (noticeably without rabbinic title) is of Shiḥin, a town in the Lower Galilee.[56] Perhaps the Yerushalmi

---

Tosefta and the initial Bavli understanding, then this may be an example of the phenomenon of a Yerushalmi text having been corrected (to "poultry") based on the Bavli's conclusion!

53. And in the Yerushalmi version of the "Neḥemiah Kills a Man" story (Y3), the poor man asks for chicken rather than the meat which he eats to his detriment. Moshe Beer cites these cases as proof that, in fact, during this period fowl was more expensive than ox meat (*Babylonian Amoraim*, 295 n. 20). It is not clear if this was the reality and for which locale.

We do find other (late) rabbinic sources like Num. Rab. 21:25 (ed. A. Mirkin; Tel Aviv: Hotsa'at Yavneh, 1956) referring to this price differential between beef and fowl:

> למדך התורה דרך ארץ מן הקורבנות. שאם ילך לאכסניה וקבלו חבירו יום ראשון מקבלו יפה ומאכילו עופות בשני מאכילו בשר בשלישי מאכילו דגים ברביעי מאכילו ירק כך הולך ופוחת עד שמאכילו קטניות
>
> "The Torah taught you proper behavior from [the order of] the sacrifices. That if a person is a guest at the behest of another, on the first day the host receives him graciously and feeds him poultry, on the second day he feeds him meat, on the third day he feeds him fish, on the fourth day he feeds him vegetable. Thus he diminishes [daily] until he feeds him lentils."

However, in the parallel Midr. Ps. 23:3 (ed. S. Buber; Jerusalem, 1966) the order of בשר and עופות is reversed, implying that beef is more precious than fowl.

54. This reading of the words בליטרא בשר as "with a pound *of money's worth* of real meat" is supported by the Firkovich 187 MS version, בליטרא מעות בשר, which glosses the word *money* in the phrase.

55. See y. Soṭah 2:5,13a: אמר רבי יודה העיד נחמיה איש שיחין את רבי עקיבה האשה שותה ושונה.

56. Shiḥin is identified in the Tosefta for its pottery manufacturing (B. Meṣ. 6:3), and elsewhere in the Bavli ('Erub. 51a), for its poor: עניי כפר שיחין (!).

is describing a refugee from Jerusalem who has come to the Galilee. In addition, in the Yerushalmi version, Neḥemiah is serendipitously met (פגע ביה) by the poor man. In the Bavli parallel (B3), the poor man comes before (אתא לקמיה) R. Neḥemiah. This nuance may be seen as support for a historical difference in charity practices, which has been suggested by Isaiah Gafni.[57] Unlike in Babylonia, where rabbis were largely in charge of Jewish charity distribution, in the Land of Israel charity was a task not limited solely to the rabbis themselves. Thus, the stories of fourth-century Amoraim R. Yosi and R. Ḥagai separately appointing פרנסים, charity managers, are found only in the Yerushalmi (y. Pe'ah 8:6, 21a). Whether he is a rabbi or not, Neḥemiah of Shiḥin of the Yerushalmi is being asked to help as a private donor. The Bavli, on the other hand, envisions R. Neḥemiah as the official address for the supplications of the poor because that is what Babylonian rabbis do. It is part of their job description, as it were.

The interactions depicted in the two versions differ in a number of other critical respects. It is not clear what to make of the diet to which the poor man is accustomed, hen (Yerushalmi) versus meat and wine (Bavli), and the food he ends up fatefully eating, meat (Yerushalmi) versus lentils (Bavli).[58] The response of Neḥemiah is also certainly perplexing. But the most interesting difference is the Bavli's concluding gloss, which is com-

57. Isaiah Gafni, *The Jews of Babylonia in the Talmudic Era: A Social and Cultural History* [Hebrew] (Jerusalem: The Zalman Shazar for Jewish History, 1990), 105–6.

58. In his discussion of the semiotics of poverty, Gregg Gardner points to the diets of meat and wine, on the one hand, and beans, on the other, as classic signifiers of great wealth versus poverty in the ancient world (*Origins of Organized Charity*, 51, 88). It is also noteworthy that the singular expression תגלגל עמי בעדשים, which I have translated as "consent to dine with me on lentils," based on Jastrow's rendering, "will you bear with me when I offer you only lentils?" (Marcus Jastrow, *A Dictionary of the Targumim, the Talmud Babli and Yerushalmi, and the Midrashic Literature*, 2 vols. [New York: Pardes, 1950], s.v. *gilgel*), may be connected with another rabbinic trope based on the round shape of the lentil and its association with death. B. B. Bat. 16b reads:

> ותנא אותו היום נפטר אברהם אבינו ועשה יעקב אבינו תבשיל של עדשים לנחם את יצחק אביו [ומ"ש של עדשים] אמרי במערבא משמיה דרבה בר מרי מה עדשה זו אין לה פה אף אבל אין לו פה דבר אחר מה עדשה זו מגולגלת אף אבילות מגלגלת ומחזרת על באי העולם
>
> "It was taught: On that day Abraham our forefather passed away, and Jacob our forefather prepared a lentil stew to comfort Isaac, his father. And what is different about lentils [that they in particular are the fare customarily offered to mourners]? They say in the West in the name of Rabba b. Mari: Just as this lentil has no mouth so too a mourner has no mouth. Alternatively, just as this lentil is completely round, so too mourning rolls and comes around to the inhabitants of the world."

The association between poverty, death, and lentils in the resonances of the Bavli story are very interesting and need further evaluation. Are the lentils in our story symbolic of the inscrutable inevitability of death and the ambivalent ponderings on the culpability for this poor man's demise? Note the Yerushalmi's formulation: "Come and mourn for Neḥemiah's victim." And is there an editorial wink to the audience in choosing the lentil, the mourner's food, in this Bavli reworking in light of the meaning of the protagonist's name: Neḥemiah, literally, "the consoler of" (or "consoled by") "God!"

pletely absent in the Yerushalmi. Here the glossator has clearly tipped his hand. This is an explicit critique of the poor man's behavior, exonerating R. Neḥemiah and laying the ethical culpability for the death squarely on the poor man himself. The Yerushalmi seems to be focused on the importance of attending to the poor person's needs accurately and immediately.[59] Failure to do so is a matter of life and death. His request for hen rather than red meat indicates the poor man's particular culinary customs; and, while it may be signaling something about his former economic station in life, it is not implying a critique of his charity request. The story in the Yerushalmi serves as a cautionary tale about the potential direness of poverty and the need to address it swiftly. The Bavli, on the other hand, transforms this story into one that, while initially inscribing the value of charity, which restores a status quo ante, then offers a stinging criticism of the excesses of this approach. This twist is encoded in the paronomasia: איבעי מיבעי, "he should have [said] ... he should have not ..." The use of this wordplay—focusing the audience on the shift from what R. Neḥemiah should have said to what the poor man should not have done—serves to heighten the effect of the Bavli's editor's reworking of the original narrative.

Thematic Analysis

What follows in the Bavli cycle is a series of six Amoraic narratives that have no explicit parallel in the Yerushalmi or other Palestinian sources. These "later" narratives, if we may deem them thus, contain clear allusions to some of the underlying motifs and themes in the Yerushalmi and midrashim, indicating that the Bavli narrators were not creating from whole cloth. But the connections are more tenuous than in the case of the first three stories. For example, the last Bavli narrative, "R. Ḥanina and the Fraudulent Pauper" (B9), has clear thematic connections with passages in Palestinian rabbinic literature. Versions of the same story, in which the deceit of fraudulent paupers is viewed as a theological boon, are found in the Yerushalmi, the story of "Shmuel and the Fraudulent Paupers" (Y4), as well as in the story of "R. Yoḥanan and Resh Laqish and the Fraudulent Pauper" (Y5), and, in a parallel to the latter story, in Leviticus Rabbah.[60]

59. This theme appears in two other stories found in the Yerushalmi cycle of charity narratives at y. Pe'ah 8:7–9, 21a–b: viz. the story of "R. Yoḥanan and Resh Laqish and the Fraudulent Pauper" as well as a story of Naḥum of Gamzo and a leprous pauper.

60. Lev. Rab. 34:10 (ed. Margulies, 793–94) ר׳ אבהו בש׳ ר׳ ליעזר צריכין אנו להחזיק טובה לרמאין שבהם, שאילולי הרמיין שבהן כיון שהיה אחד מהן תובע ביד אדם והוא מחזירו מיד היה נענש למיתה, דכת׳ וקרא עליך אל ייי והיה בך חטא וכת׳ הנפש החטאת היא תמות דיל׳ ר׳ יוחנן וריש לקיש נחתין למיסחי בהדין דימוסיא דטבריא ופגע בהון חד מסכן אמ׳ להון זכון בי, אמ׳ ליה מיחזרין אנן זכיין בך. מיחזרין אשכחוניה מיית, אמרי הואיל ולא אטפלנן ביה בחיוי נטפל ביה במותוי. מי מסחין ליה אשכחון חדה כיס דחמש מאה דינרין תלי בצואריה. אמרי ברוך שבחר בחכמים ובדבריהם, לא כן אמ׳ ר׳ אבהו בש׳ ר׳ לעזר צריכין אנו להחזיק טובה לרמיין שבהן, שאילולי

Both of these stories have elements that are reproduced in this last Bavli narrative of R. Ḥanina. The accounts of the uncovering of the imposters by the wife (in the R. Ḥanina story) and the son (in the Shmuel story) both occur through overhearing their conversations about using gold and silver tableware or linens.[61] And, of course, the phrase בואו ונחזיק טובה לרמאין שאלמלא הן היינו חוטאין בכל יום, "Come let us be grateful to the rogues for were it not for them, we would have been sinning every day," is indicative of a common tradition between the Bavli and the Yerushalmi.[62]

Along these lines, it is likely that the story of "Shmuel and the Luxuriant Pauper" (Y6) in the Yerushalmi is the source for the Bavli's tale of "Mar 'Uqba and the Luxuriant Pauper" (B6). In both tales the father dispatches his son to distribute his charity, the son returns with a report implying that the recipient may be a fraud, and the father responds that the son is misinterpreting the evidence—he subsequently dispatches the son with more charity. This connection has been noted by Aryeh Leib Yellin in his commentary to the Bavli, in which he points to some of the inconclusiveness of the cases in both Yerushalmi and Bavli parallels, a point to which we will return in our conclusions.[63]

David Assaf has noted a further structural parallel between the Bavli and the Yerushalmi's narrative cycle.[64] The Bavli includes the stories of "Mar 'Uqba and the Luxuriant Pauper" (B6) and "R. Ḥanina and the Fraudulent Pauper" (B9), both of which tell of rabbis who are presented with evidence that the beneficiaries of their charity may be frauds. In the former case, Mar 'Uqba doubles his gift, deeming the recipient legitimate. In the latter, R. Ḥanina assumes the recipient has been scamming him. The Yerushalmi evokes a similar dialectic with the two stories of Shmuel. In "Shmuel and the Luxuriant Pauper" (Y6), Shmuel's father decides that the poor man is legitimate saying, "Give [him] more for his soul [determines] his [appropriate] measure." On the other hand, in "Shmuel and the Fraudulent Paupers" (Y4), his father comes to the opposite conclusion, evoking the trope, "We have to be grateful to the deceivers among them." The structural similarity—each Talmud tells two stories depicting similar scenarios of suspected fraud with very different outcomes—indicates the

---

הרמאין שבהן כיון שהיה אחד מהן תובע דבר ביד אדם והוא מחזירו מיד היה נענש למיתה, דכת׳ וקרא עליך אל יי״ וכת׳ הנפש החטאת היא תמות.

61. The words אגנטין/ארגנטורין of the Yerushalmi story are from the Greek word for silver-like, Αργυροειδής, according to Jastrow, indicating plates or silverware. The Bavli's word טלי is undetermined according to Sokoloff and means "table linens" according to Jastrow. See Michael Sokoloff, *A Dictionary of Jewish Babylonian Aramaic of the Talmudic and Geonic Periods* (Ramat Gan: Bar-Ilan University Press, 2002), ad loc.

62. See David Assaf's "Let's Thank the Crooks." In this article Assaf proposes a scheme for understanding the redaction of these parallel traditions.

63. Aryeh Leib Yellin, *Yefeh 'Enayim* (ad loc.), 4.

64. Assaf, "Let's Thank the Crooks," 261.

dependence of the Bavli editors on the Yerushalmi precedents for this dialectical juxtaposition. It also indicates that the editors of the cycles wish to bring these competing values into conversation.

Looking at many of these stories in both the Bavli and the Yerushalmi in their redactional context has led Alyssa Gray to conclude that the trend of rabbinic attitudes toward the formerly wealthy poor runs from one of empathy in the earlier sources (third century CE) to growing ambivalence in the later ones (fourth century CE).[65] She demonstrates this shift most clearly across the Palestinian sources. Gray notes that the Bavli, on the other hand, seems to exhibit mostly ambivalent views on charity toward these conjunctural poor.[66] With regard to this conclusion, Gray's analysis is dependent on stories that she could identify as referring to this specific subclass of poor. While it seems that many of these charity narratives tell stories about the formerly wealthy, not all of them do. The Yerushalmi has a good number of cases that speak about recipients of charity with the terminology such as עני בן טובים, "poor person of a good family"; בן טובים שירד מנכסי, "person of a good family who descended (depreciated?) from his properties." But if we examine the narratives that appear in the Bavli, we find that the identification of the poor person as formerly wealthy is stated explicitly only in the two cases we deemed Tannaitic—"Hillel the Elder" (B1) and "People of the Galilee" (B2). In both of these cases, the text is taken almost verbatim from the earlier Palestinian sources. A number of other stories suggest that the subject was accustomed to a more luxuriant lifestyle, perhaps evidencing the fact that this is a formerly wealthy poor person. Yet the explicit designation is missing from the text, making it hard to reach any conclusion about the story's intentions with regard to the poor person's status. Gray does assert that these omissions in the Bavli are, in and of themselves, evidence of a reworking of the Palestinian sources by the Bavli editors. She claims that this reworking is a further indication of an attitudinal difference that had become normative. One might object that the reworking of earlier sources that we have seen—the "Bavlification" of the material, as it were—is quite wide ranging. It does not consist simply of one omitted word or phrase like "formerly wealthy." Rather, in stories like "Mar 'Uqba and the Luxuriant Pauper" (B6), many details of the "original" have changed, including the identity of the protagonists. Whether these linguistic shifts reflect attitudinal changes with regard to the formerly wealthy poor is speculative at best. Perhaps the rabbis of the Bavli are simply not as interested in this subclass as their colleagues in the Yerushalmi seem to be.

In fact, the story of "Mar 'Uqba and the Luxuriant Pauper" (B6) is an exemplum that seems to depict great empathy toward someone who

65. Gray, "Formerly Wealthy Poor," 101–33.
66. Ibid., 123.

might have been experiencing conjunctural poverty. In addition, while the ending of "Rava and His Long-Lost Sister" (B4) is somewhat ambiguous, it can be likewise read as a narrative expressing an empathic view toward providing for the formerly wealthy poor. Furthermore, in the story of the "People of the Galilee" (B2) we see explicit mention of the "formerly wealthy" status of the recipient where none was mentioned in the Yerushalmi parallel.[67] All of these points being so, it is hard to claim that the Bavli redactors take a more jaundiced view of these formerly wealthy recipients of charity than do the earlier editors of the Yerushalmi.

Problematizing Charity

Rather than reflecting a shift in rabbinic attitude toward the specific subclass of the formerly wealthy poor, other attitudinal shifts toward charity may in fact be at stake in the editorial choices and redactional influences of the stories of rabbinic charity that are found in the Bavli. In examining the "migration" of stories of rabbis giving charity as presented in the three loci—the Tannaitic Palestinian sources, the Amoraic Palestinian sources, and the Babylonian sources—a fairly consistent trend emerges: a movement from stories that simply report the ostensibly meritorious acts of charity as performed by a number of rabbis toward a discernible trend at complicating and problematizing that giving.

Even in the Yerushalmi sources we can discern the juxtaposition of similar scenarios with differential, multivocal outcomes. This is true of the cases that describe the luxuriant poor versus the dissembling imposters, where rabbis take different approaches to dealing with the ambiguity of these circumstances. But it is in the Bavli cycle that virtually all of the narratives and their *ad locum* Stammaitic interventions depict scenarios of charity gone astray, or conclusions that work to interrogate underlying assumptions that underpin these stories. For example, in the tale "R. Neḥemiah Kills a Man with Lentils" (B3), it is the comment of the Babylonian editor that turns a Toseftan story about the importance of attending to the particular dietary needs of the recipient of food charity into a critique of the indulgent habits of that recipient.

In the case of "Rava and His Long-Lost Sister" (B4) the story is more ambiguous in its message. When the fourth-century Babylonian rabbi Rava questions the ethics of supporting the expensive culinary habits of a particular poor man from the community's dole, this man retorts with a biblical exegesis bringing to bear a theological argument that underpins charity. "Do I eat of theirs [the community]?" he asks Rava rhetorically; "I eat [the food] of the All-Merciful; for we learned ..." Rava gives no answer.

67. There is no mention in any text witness, as has been noted above.

Instead we are told that Rava's sister, whom he has not seen in years, arrives bearing the very foodstuff this poor man had requested of Rava. This propitious occurrence leads Rava to conclude that the poor man's request was divinely sanctioned, and he apologizes. Are we, the audience, to conclude that this largesse is to become public policy for every luxuriant habit that a poor person may want indulged? And what if the sister had not come with the foodstuff? Would the community have been obligated to provide the gourmet meal? The story is deliberately ambivalent. It seems the best we can say is that the editors wish to articulate the very real tension between the need to give with specific sensitivity to the recipient's "needs" and the realities of finite resources. The acute ambivalence of this story indicates an attempt to articulate some of the problems inherent in actualizing the norm of *that which he is lacking* of Deut 15:8 as read by the rabbis of the Bavli.[68]

The didactic intent of the narrative of "Mar 'Uqba in the Oven" (B5) is also somewhat ambiguous. Without the editorial comments that follow the fabula, the story seems to be a subtle critique of Mar 'Uqba's supererogatory form of secretive charity giving. Instead of being a paean to the sensitivity being shown by preserving the dignity of the poor man through his anonymous giving, the story ends up favoring the open (soup kitchen) charity practiced by the wife of Mar 'Uqba. It is, after all, her feet that do not get singed in the oven. The editorial comments beginning with the question ומאי כולי האי, "What was all that about?," however, appears to be a Stammaitic attempt to realign the narrative with the norms. Preservation of the dignity of another person should be done at all costs, quote the editors. Scorched feet or not, they assert, Mar 'Uqba acted properly. But the overall conclusion is at best ambivalent and may be summed up by James Laidlaw's observation:

> Religious charity and philanthropy in all the great religions have repeatedly rediscovered the supreme value of the anonymous donation, only to find that time and again donors have been more attracted to the benefits of the socially entangling Maussian gift, which does make friends.[69]

The subsequent story, "Mar 'Uqba and the Luxuriant Pauper" (B6), presents the problem of the potential fraud. As pointed out above, this story

68. See p. 61 above.

69. James Laidlaw, "A Free Gift Makes No Friends," *Journal of the Royal Anthropological Institute* 6 (2000): 617–34, here 632. It is the social ties that Mrs. 'Uqba's open, personalized giving creates, which may be what the storyteller is lauding here—but more to be said on the Maussian gift below. This fascinating story has also, of course, been read successfully through the lens of gender studies. See Jennifer Nadler, "Mar Ukba in the Fiery Furnace: A Meditation on the Tragedy of the Norm," *Law and Literature* 19 (2007): 1–13, as well as Dov Kahane,"Mar 'Ukba Had a Poor Man (B. Ketubbot 67b): A Talmudic Patriarchal Narrative with a Metadialogue Commentary," *AJS Perspectives*, Spring 2019, 62–64.

closely follows the contours of the story of "Shmuel and the Luxuriant Pauper" (Y6) found in the Yerushalmi and was likely formulated with that story in mind. Here, the break with the expected norm is obviously Mar 'Uqba's reaction to his son's report. This story, read together with the last narrative of the cycle, "R. Ḥanina and the Fraudulent Pauper" (B9)—a similar story whose outcome is the antithesis of this one—presents the Bavli's multivocal expression of the inherent dilemma of the potential scam.

The story of "Mar 'Uqba's Deathbed" (B7) has structural parallels to "Mar 'Uqba in the Oven" (B5) in that it too tells a tale that diverges from a norm and is followed by an editorial question about the propriety of the action. Here Mar 'Uqba disburses a great sum of pledged money to charity in anticipation of his death. The anonymous editor asks היכי עביד הכי, "How could he have done this?," since it violates the normative standards of charity practices. That norm is articulated: "R. Elai stated: It was ordained at Usha that if a man wishes to spend liberally [on charity] he should not spend more than a fifth [of his wealth]."[70] The response given utilizes a dialectical answer and serves, like the editorial comment following the first story about Mar 'Uqba, to realign a story that diverges from the norm back into the normative realm.[71]

Finally, the description of "R. Abba and the Rogues" (B8) balances the generosity of the rabbi with his cleverness at thwarting frauds and gives further expression to inherent problems involved in acts of charity.

While antecedents for most of these Bavli narratives can be found in the earlier Palestinian literature, the editors of the Bavli have constructed a cycle of stories that goes much further in highlighting the problematic nature of charity giving, giving voice to a number of anxieties that connect with the act of giving to the poor. These narratives, like many others which have been well documented, demonstrate the Bavli's pattern of incorporating the earlier sources and motifs and reengineering them to construct a *sugya* with a deliberate and intentional design. Here the design serves to problematize charity giving. By introducing this cycle with the pericope on the exegesis of Deut 15:8, "sufficient for his needs that he is needing," the Bavli highlights at the outset—in its very framing of the narrative cycle—an essential tension inherent in charity giving. The rabbis read the verse to mandate providing for the poor only that which is truly needed but also to include luxuries to which the recipient had been

70. See Gardner, *Origins of Organized Charity*, 135–37, on dating the 'Usha ordinance.

71. Note the structural affinity between the terse היכי עביד הכי, "How could he have done this?," in this narrative (B7), and ומאי כולי האי, "What was all that about?," of the narrative "Mar 'Uqba in the Oven" (B5), and each question being followed by a longer attributed citation of a normative statement. This similarity implies a deliberate literary design and is idiomatic of the anonymous voices' interventions in the Bavli narrative.

accustomed. This kind of dialectical tension is present in most, if not all, of the ensuing narratives in the Bavli cycle. The Yerushalmi narratives on charity also evince cautionary tales. Yet, while issues of dissembling paupers and the tension between providing the formerly wealthy poor with luxuriant levels of charity may have been on the minds of the rabbis of Palestine, these and other concerns find their full expression in this cycle of narratives in the Bavli.

The question that needs to be asked is whether this conclusion reflects an underlying shift in values on the part of the authors/editors of the Bavli texts. Were the rabbis of fourth-century Palestine less concerned about the problems that charity giving entails than their later Babylonian counterparts? A number of answers can be offered to this question. As mentioned above, Gafni suggests that the institutional role of the rabbi as charity administrator is a relatively late one.[72] He claims that charity collection and distribution in Palestine were done at many levels of society and not just by rabbis. In contrast, by the fifth century in Babylonia, these functions had become institutionalized and consolidated under the rabbis. Once the rabbis, as a group, had become more involved in the process of charity it is understandable that their literature would reflect more of the nuances and the fraught issues that it does. Gray notes the trend in Bavli literature to favor giving through communal charity collectors administered by the rabbis.[73] She attributes this trend to the general rabbinic move toward galvanizing control over ever wider aspects of Jewish culture than the relatively small focus of the disciple circles in which the rabbis initially operated. She also attributes the trend to a theological shift influenced by Sasanian culture toward skepticism of divine protection of the righteous in this world.[74] This might explain the focus, apparent in a number of the narratives, on the need for the more careful pragmatism in charity giving, rather than a reliance on providence.

Another approach to understanding this dynamic may through the lens of the Maussian construct of the reciprocal gift and its relative significance in the dynamic of the late antique societies of Roman Palestine and Sasanian Persia and Babylonia. Marcel Mauss studied the phenomenon of the gift cycle rituals found in many ancient as well as contemporary traditional societies.[75] The prevalence and significance of these rituals and their modern residues—such as holiday gift exchanging—led Mauss to conclude that the gift cycle ritual serves as a form of economic exchange

72. Gafni, *Jews of Babylonia*, 105–6.

73. Alyssa Gray, "Redemptive Almsgiving and the Rabbis of Late Antiquity," *JSQ* 18 (2011): 144–84.

74. See Yaakov Elman, "Righteousness as Its Own Reward: An Inquiry into the Theologies of the Stam," *PAAJR* 57 (1991): 35–67, here 45–47.

75. Mauss, *The Gift: The Form and Reason for Exchange in Archaic Societies.*

that acts to build and reinforce both lateral and hierarchical relationships between individual members of society as well as between families and clans within the societies in which the ritual was practiced. These rituals depend on a reciprocity of sorts, or the potential for it, in order to create this economy of gifts. The giving of the gift engenders a debt from recipient to donor that demands repayment.[76] This idea of reciprocity underpins the culture of the Roman Empire, in which the Mishnah and Yerushalmi were formed.[77] It constitutes a basis for the euergetic norm—the responsibility to give one's time and financial resources for the upkeep of the polis. As Peter Brown puts it:

> It was a fact of life ... [that] the cities were dependent ... for their economic and political success on their ability to draw on a seemingly unlimited willingness to give on the part of their richer and more powerful inhabitants.... As a result *euergesia,* the urge to "do good" by public benefaction; the wish to be a *euergetes,* a "doer of good", to be a public benefactor ... these Greek words became associated with actions that were especially prized by the elites of the classical world and by their inferiors in every city.[78]

This euergetic gifting created dependency relationships which established well-ordered, hierarchical social classes that served as a stabilizing force in imperial society. One of the many well-documented ways in which the rabbis defined themselves was through their opposition to the ambient Roman culture. "The rabbis performed their political and cultural marginality in their teaching and writing."[79] One area of this alterity was certainly their resistance to imperial euergetism.[80] In fact, the euergetic norms can be seen as running orthogonally counter to the egalitarian ideals of the rabbis insofar as the Torah envisioned economic parity among Jews as an ideal.[81] Whether actually practiced by Jews in this period, the customs of tithes, agricultural gifts, and sabbatical year debt release were essential, if not aspirational, elements in the society that served to equalize or mitigate hierarchical disparities among its members. So, too, for the giving of alms to the poor. These were gifts that were to be unreciprocated. They were to produce no relationships of dependency and to create no patronage status for the donor. In direct contrast to the significant show of honor accorded to the *euergetēs* in the Roman culture, the early rabbis encour-

76. Ibid., 18.
77. Schwartz, *Were the Jews a Mediterranean Society*, 7.
78. Brown, *Poverty and Leadership*, 3–4.
79. Schwartz, *Were the Jews a Mediterranean Society*, 43.
80. Ibid., 25.
81. On this idea, see, e.g., Gardner, "Charity Wounds," 177.

aged giving in secret.[82] Yet, as Mauss and many others before and after him have observed: charity wounds.[83] The unreciprocated gift inevitably confers inferiority on the person who has accepted it, particularly when it has been accepted with no thought of returning it.[84] This awareness may explain the rabbis' desire to encourage the conversion of gifts into loans that might be repaid,[85] to encourage anonymous giving,[86] and to support practices that generalize the requirements to equilibrate wealth disparity to a broad base of society.[87]

It was to these kinds of issues that the rabbis of the early talmudic sources were responding when they characterized their charity practices in the Yerushalmi. Not so the later texts. In the Bavli, a different set of ambient cultural norms prevailed. Greco-Roman euergetism, whether it was a significant force in society or not, certainly held less negative import for Babylonian rabbinic culture in its Sasanian context. Furthermore, it has been noted that the ambient Sasanian culture valued wealth in its leaders.[88] A formal caste system impacted the Amoraim of the Bavli and their

---

82. See, e.g., t. Šeqal. 2:16. and the relevant stories at y. Pe'ah 8:9, 21b. Gardner points out the pertinence here of Jesus's injunction in the Sermon on the Mount to "beware of practicing your piety before others in order to be seen by them … so whenever you give alms, do not sound a trumpet before you, as the hypocrites do in the synagogues and in the streets … and do not let your left hand know what your right hand is doing so that your alms may be done in secret" (Matt 6:1–4). He suggests that the object of this harangue is euergetism (Gardner, *Origins of Organized Charity*, 151).

83. See Mary Douglas, "No Free Gifts," foreword to Mauss, *The Gift: The Form and Reason for Exchange in Archaic Societies*, vii–xviii, here vii: "Charity is meant to be a free gift, a voluntary, unrequited surrender of resources. Though we laud charity as a Christian virtue we know that it wounds … the recipient does not like the giver, however cheerful he be. This book explains the lack of gratitude by saying that the [charity giver or] foundations should not confuse their donations with gifts. It is not merely that there are no free gifts in a particular place, Melanasia or Chicago for instance; it is that the whole idea of a free gift is based on a misunderstanding. There should not be any free gifts. What is wrong with the so-called free gift is the donor's intention to be exempt from return gifts coming from the recipient. Refusing requital puts the act of giving outside any mutual ties. Once given, the free gift entails no further claims from the recipient.… According to Marcel Mauss that is what is wrong with the free gift. A gift that does nothing to enhance solidarity is a contradiction."

84. Mauss, *The Gift: The Form and Reason for Exchange in Archaic Societies*, 65.

85. See Gardner, *Origins of Organized Charity*, 168. See also t. Pe'ah 4:12: האומר איני מתפרנס משל אחרים שוקדין עליו ומפרנסין אותו ונותנין לו לשום מלוה וחוזרין ונותנין לו לשום מתנה דר"מ רש"א אומרין לו הבא משכון כדי לגוס את דעתו; "One who says: 'I will not be supported by charity' … they give him [funds] as a [putative] loan … they even say to him: 'bring collateral,' so as to preserve his dignity." Although the intent here is to induce the recipient to accept the gift, this law does speak very clearly to the wounding nature of the act of charity.

86. See, e.g., y. Pe'ah 8:9, 21b; b. B. Bat. 10b.

87. Here I refer to the vast rabbinic literature of the Tannaitic period on the Sabbatical year and tithing.

88. For example, Beer writes somewhat hyperbolically: "In the Eastern lands especially in the ancient period, a well-respected, yet poor, person never existed" (*Babylonian Amoraim*, 270).

way of life.[89] While references are made to poor rabbis in the Bavli, the notion of giving away one's wealth to charity is never valorized.[90] Finally, the shift toward rabbinic institutionalization of charity giving shifted the focus of the rabbinic expression on this topic, as well. Taking all of these cultural factors together, we can suggest that a gradual shift in normative values had indeed occurred and is, in fact, manifested in the narratives cycle on charity. Thus, we find that these Bavli texts are somewhat critical of secret anonymous charity giving (e.g., the story of "Mar 'Uqba in the Oven" [B5]), ambivalent concerning the value of giving beyond the community or individual's ability (e.g., "Rava and His Long-Lost Sister" [B4]), concerned with the notion of "heroic" charity giving, which may lead the benefactor to privation (e.g., "Mar 'Uqba's Deathbed" [B7]), antagonistic to overly entitled formerly wealthy poor (e.g., "R. Neḥemiah Kills a Man with Lentils" [B3]), and perhaps even more concerned about the ability to discern the frauds (e.g., "R. Ḥanina and the Fraudulent Pauper" [B9] and "R. Abba and the Rogues" [B8]). The issues of unreciprocated gifts and the debts these engender become much less of a focal point in favor of these other literary moves at problematizing charity giving.

Conclusion

It has been noted that the Bavli *sugya* is often a reworking of the sources found in the Yerushalmi. Whether editors of both texts worked from a common tradition or the Babylonian editors possessed a version of the Yerushalmi is an ongoing discussion.[91] These might have been oral texts, which engendered a continual fluidity until they finally congealed in the pre-Geonic, Geonic, or even post-Geonic period. Or they might have existed as written compilations with some level of plasticity until their ultimate canonization. Or, perhaps, the Bavli is some combination of these origins. These are issues that continue to be debated.[92] How much autonomy and intentionality to ascribe to the editors of the texts and what the ultimate agenda of these editors was are also desiderata of great importance.[93] Nevertheless, the Bavli and its antecedents all serve as literary arti-

89. See Richard Kalmin, *The Sage in Jewish Society of Late Antiquity* (London: Routledge 1999), 7–8.

90. Gray, "Redemptive Almsgiving," 149.

91. Moulie Vidas, *Tradition and the Formation of the Talmud* (Princeton, NJ: Princeton University Press, 2014), 50.

92. Neil Danzig, "From Oral Talmud to Written Talmud: On the Methods of Transmission of the Babylonian Talmud and Its Study in the Middle Ages," *Bar-Ilan* 30–31 (2006): 49–112.

93. For some of the most recent scholars to weigh in on these issues, see Sergey Dolgopolski, *The Open Past: Subjectivity and Remembering in the Talmud* (New York: Fordham

facts for us to evaluate and make tentative conjectures about the cultures that created them.

My focus has been a cycle of charity narratives that appears in b. Ketub. 67b–68a. These nine stories depict acts of charity by members of the rabbinic class (or a village, in one case) on behalf of individual poor people. Each of these stories ostensibly describes supererogatory acts—ones that go beyond the simple giving of alms—whether in the size of the donation or the manner in which the donation transpired. In a number of these stories the notion of restoring a formerly wealthy person to his status quo ante is reported. In some it is the sensitivity to the individual's emotional needs that is being highlighted. But, as I have argued, in shaping or reshaping these stories from their sources or from their earlier redactional settings, the editors of the Bavli *sugya* have created a cycle of narratives that serve to further nuance and problematize the act of charity giving. The tension inherent in the ambivalent exegetical reading of the verse "sufficient for his needs that he is needing" (Deut 15:8), which immediately precedes the narrative cycle, is a paradigm for the tension in each of the narratives in the cycle.

This problematizing reflects a cultural awareness on the part of the Bavli editors that, notwithstanding the notion that charity is the ultimate act of corporate solidarity, other concerns about its implementation are significant. This may well reflect the shift to greater rabbinic institutionalization of the charity activities in late Amoraic and Geonic periods or the waning influence of euergetism. It may also reflect the literary culture of the editors of the Bavli and their desire to create a multivocal, nuanced text that eschews binary categorizations of normative behavior.

University Press, 2012); Shai Secunda, *The Iranian Talmud: Reading the Bavli in Its Sasanian Context*, Divinations (Philadelphia: University of Pennsylvania Press, 2014); and Vidas, *Tradition and the Formation.*

The Righteous Women of Bavli Sotah

On Reading Talmudic Narrative in the Context of a Tractate

JANE L. KANAREK

The end of the first chapter of Bavli Sotah contains a long aggadic *sugya* (9b–14a) that retells a number of biblical stories—Samson and Delilah, Saul, Absalom, Tamar and Judah, and Joseph. Included in this extended *sugya* is a series of homilies—Tannaitic and Amoraic, Palestinian and Babylonian—that expound upon the biblical narrative of Israelite slavery in Egypt (b. Soṭah 11a–13a).[1] Reworked by a Babylonian editorial hand into a thematic whole of redemptive rebellion and partnership, the latter between God and Israelite women,[2] one of these homilies can be titled, "The righteous women for whose sake Israel was redeemed from Egypt" (b. Soṭah 11b). Although the homily of the righteous women has received a significant amount of scholarly attention, an important lacuna remains: an analysis of the story within its larger redactional context in Bavli Sotah. In this article, I address this scholarly lacuna by arguing that attention to the story's redactional context in tractate Sotah enables a richer understanding both of the narrative of the righteous women and of its literary role in tractate Sotah. I contend that widening our interpretive lens to include the

1. The homilies retell Exod 1:8–2:9. Like the long aggadic *sugya* in b. Meg. 10b–16b, the aggadic *sugya* in b. Soṭah opens with a series of homilies by Rav and Shmuel built around five verses. In contrast to the b. Meg. *sugya*, which is built mainly from Babylonian homilies, the b. Soṭah *sugya* contains homilies primarily from second- and third-generation Palestinian Amoraim; see Joshua Levinson, *The Twice Told Tale: A Poetics of the Exegetical Narrative in Rabbinic Midrash* [Hebrew] (Jerusalem: Magnes, 2005), 292. David Rosenthal contends that this collection of midrashim was redacted into b. Soṭah as an already complete story-cycle; see David Rosenthal, "'Arichot Qedumot Ha-Meshuqqa'ot ba-Talmud ha-Bavli," in *Mehqerei Talmud 1*, ed. David Rosenthal and Yaacov Sussman (Jerusalem: Magnes, 1990), 155–204, here 168–69 n. 25.

2. Levinson, *Twice Told Tale*, 291–99; Ishay Rosen-Zvi, *The Mishnaic Soṭah Ritual: Temple, Gender and Midrash*, JSJSup 160 (Leiden: Brill, 2012), 115.

countervoice or countertradition[3] of the righteous women in our reading of the Sotah ritual has implications not only for interpreting this story in its ancient Bavli context but also for subverting the Sotah ritual itself. Indeed, as we will see, the midrash of the righteous women becomes the mirror of the Sotah ritual.

In its rabbinic representation,[4] the Sotah ritual presents us with a particular type of rabbinic misogyny: a culture of male supervision of female sexuality[5] where a woman accused of adultery by her husband undergoes a voyeuristic ritual that, as Sarra Lev argues, "can even be classified as pornographic."[6] Yet, despite the themes of seduction, hiddenness, possible pregnancy, and rebellion that run throughout the Sotah ritual, scholars writing on the righteous women narrative do not connect the story with these motifs. Indeed, while Yonah Fraenkel observes that the themes of seduction, pregnancy, birth, hiding, and home are found in the homily, he does not link them with similar motifs in the Sotah ritual.[7] Joshua Levinson comments on the ways in which the righteous women story subverts hierarchies—for example, the women objectify their husbands sexually instead of the reverse—but does not link these subversions with the specifics of sexuality and its attendant power in tractate Sotah.[8] Even Ishay

---

3. Here I extend Ilana Pardes's conception of the countertradition—the desire to give voice to antipatriarchal elements in the biblical text—to rabbinic texts; see Ilana Pardes, *Countertraditions in the Bible: A Feminist Approach* (Cambridge, MA: Harvard University Press, 1993), 144.

4. Scholars writing on the Tannaitic Sotah ritual have observed a number of different ways in which Tannaitic texts reframe the biblical Sotah ritual: for example, locating the ritual within rabbinic judicial procedure (warning and witnesses; see m. Soṭah 1:1), making a private ritual public (the woman is displayed before the public; see m. Soṭah 1:6), presuming the woman's guilt (in the biblical version, both guilt and innocence are offered as possibilities; the mishnah explores only the consequences of guilt). See Lisa Grushcow, *Writing the Wayward Wife: Rabbinic Interpretations of Sotah*, AGJU 62 (Leiden: Brill, 2005), 19–30; Moshe Halbertal, *Interpretive Revolutions in the Making: Values as Interpretive Considerations in Midrashei Halakhah* [Hebrew] (Jerusalem: Magnes, 1997), 94–112; Judith Hauptman, *Rereading the Rabbis: A Woman's Voice* (Boulder, CO: Westview, 1997), 15–29; Sarra Lev, "Sotah: Rabbinic Pornography?," in *The Passionate Torah: Sex and Judaism*, ed. Danya Ruttenberg (New York: New York University Press, 2009), 7–22; Rosen-Zvi, *Mishnaic Soṭah Ritual*.

5. Rosen-Zvi, *Mishnaic Soṭah Ritual*, 21. Rosen-Zvi argues for a methodology that examines the different processes through which marginalization occurs, enabling us to interrogate how "… the mechanisms of exclusion operate in different spheres and different texts" (*Mishnaic Sotah Ritual*, 11).

6. Lev, "Sotah: Rabbinic Pornography," 6. The preconditions of warning before witnesses and the woman's secreting herself with the man about whom she has been warned must be met before the next stage of the ritual moves forward. See m. Soṭah 1:1–2 for a debate between R. Eliezer and R. Yehoshua about the number of required witnesses for each stage of this process.

7. Yonah Fraenkel, *Darkhe Ha-'Aggadah Ve-Ha-Midrash* (Giv'atayim: Yad la-Talmud, 1991), 1:306.

8. Levinson, *Twice Told Tale*, 304.

Rosen-Zvi, who cites this story and the larger story-cycle in which it is embedded as an example of a Babylonian trend toward the hyper-sexualization of reality, does not analyze the significance of the story's redaction in a tractate where a central concern is the transgression of sexual boundaries.[9]

This move to widen the contextual lens through which we locate and analyze this particular narrative exemplar joins with the scholarly assumption that Bavli narratives are best understood when their interpretive context reaches beyond the immediate framework in which that narrative is embedded.[10] It also intersects with scholarship that has begun to reconsider the tractate as a unit of analysis, that is, whether single Bavli tractates should be considered as individual units of analysis that have their own narrative arcs. While scholars such as Charlotte Fonrobert, Julia Watts Belser, and Mira Wasserman recognize that tractates are composed of material from disparate chronological and geographical sources, they also argue that an editorial voice has combined these materials in such a way that one can discern an overall theme and voice, even among materials that may initially appear disparate.[11] As Wasserman argues, only "by

9. Ishay Rosen-Zvi, *Demonic Desires: "Yetzer Hara" and the Problem of Evil in Late Antiquity*, Divinations (Philadelphia: University of Pennsylvania Press, 2011), 114–16.

10. Jeffrey L. Rubenstein has described the ways in which the literary features of talmudic narratives extend into the adjacent dialectical material. See Jeffrey L. Rubenstein, *Talmudic Stories: Narrative Art, Composition, and Culture* (Baltimore: Johns Hopkins University Press, 1999); Jeffrey L. Rubenstein, *Stories of the Babylonian Talmud* (Baltimore: Johns Hopkins University Press, 2010). Other scholars who have emphasized the importance of context to the interpretation of rabbinic narrative include Daniel Boyarin, *Carnal Israel: Reading Sex in Talmudic Culture*, New Historicism 25 (Berkeley: University of California Press, 1993); Julia Watts Belser, *Power, Ethics, and Ecology in Jewish Late Antiquity: Rabbinic Responses to Drought and Disaster* (New York: Cambridge University Press, 2015); Julia Watts Belser, *Rabbinic Tales of Destruction: Gender, Sex, and Disability in the Ruins of Jerusalem* (New York: Oxford University Press, 2017); Ofra Meir, "The Literary Context of the Sages' Aggadic Stories as Analogous to Changing Storytelling Situations—The Story of the Hasid and the Spirits in the Cemetery" [Hebrew], *Jerusalem Studies in Jewish Folklore* 13–14 (1992): 81–97; Mira Beth Wasserman, *Jews, Gentiles, and Other Animals: The Talmud after the Humanities*, Divinations (Philadelphia: University of Pennsylvania Press, 2017). The assertion of the importance of context is, in many instances, a continuation of and response to the groundbreaking work of Yonah Fraenkel on rabbinic narratives. Fraenkel's new-critical approach de-emphasized the wider literary context of a particular narrative in favor of a principle of closure, isolating the story from the larger context in which it was embedded. On Fraenkel's methodology, see Rubenstein, *Talmudic Stories*, 11, and the attendant notes; and Barry Scott Wimpfheimer, *Narrating the Law: A Poetics of Talmudic Legal Stories*, Divinations (Philadelphia: University of Pennsylvania Press, 2011), 38.

11. For examples of this approach, see the works of Charlotte Elisheva Fonrobert, *Menstrual Purity: Rabbinic and Christian Reconstructions of Biblical Gender*, Contraversions (Stanford, CA: Stanford University Press, 2000); Belser, *Power, Ethics, and Ecology*; Wasserman, *Jews, Gentiles, and Other Animals*. The Feminist Commentary on the Babylonian Talmud project, edited by Tal Ilan, is also part of this trend to approach a tractate as a unit of analysis.

adopting a reading practice that presumes design and seeks after cohesion [do] aspects of the Talmud's art come into view."[12] While I do not aim here for a reading of Bavli Sotah in its entirety, I contend that the story of the righteous women should be read within the Bavli's presentation of the Sotah ritual.[13] Indeed, while m. Sotah emphasizes female sin, b. Soṭah shifts responsibility for sexual sin to men as much as women. As the Bavli moves from female sin to male sin and from sexual sin to sin in general, it also paints a picture of ideal rabbinic behavior and the idealized rabbinic male. When women other than the accused Sotah do appear, they are most often righteous.[14] Reading tractate Sotah in order to understand the Sotah ritual involves noticing both the ways in which the ideology of this Bavli tractate differs from its respective mishnaic tractate as well as widening our lens beyond descriptions of the Sotah ritual itself.[15]

It differs from the previously mentioned works, though, in that the authors in the series (at least of the works published to date) are not looking for an overall thematic that drives the choice of passages on which to comment but rather mine those tractates for sections that implicate women and/or gender. See also Alyssa M. Gray, *A Talmud in Exile: The Influence of Yerushalmi Avodah Zarah on the Formation of Bavli Avodah Zarah*, BJS 342 (Providence, RI: Brown Judaic Studies, 2005); Christine Elizabeth Hayes, *Between the Babylonian and Palestinian Talmuds: Accounting for Halakhic Difference in Selected Sugyot from Tractate Avodah Zarah* (New York: Oxford University Press, 1997).

12. Wasserman, *Jews, Gentiles, and Other Animals*, 23. It is, of course, possible to overread for thematic unity and to force a tractate into a preconceived notion of unity that it does not possess. Nevertheless, it would be worthwhile to investigate systematically whether and why some tractates possess a greater thematic unity than others. In addition to this redactional point, by arguing for approaching the tractate as a unit of discourse, I also aim to challenge modes of reading, made easier by the internet, that encourage selective and noncontextual readings. The "source sheet," usually a collection of rabbinic citations from a variety of different texts, creates conversations that, while valuable, often differ greatly from those that read a particular citation in its textual home. A source sheet that includes the Sotah ritual along with the Bavli's righteous women midrash would, I hypothesize, result in a learning experience very different from one that includes only the various versions of this midrash.

13. On the Bavli's shift of emphasis from female to male sin, see Ishay Rosen-Zvi, "The Ritual of Suspected Adulteress (Sotah) in Tannaitic Literature: Textual and Theoretical Perspectives" [Hebrew] (Ph.D. diss., Tel Aviv University, 2004), 52–56. Whereas Rosen-Zvi discusses this phenomenon as occurring in the first four pages of b. Soṭah, I identify the phenomenon as extending throughout the tractate.

14. B. Soṭah 9b–14a provides extensive exegetical reimaginings of Tamar (Gen 38) and the many females central to the exodus narrative (Exod 2): Miriam, Yocheved, the daughter of Pharaoh (Bityah), and the midwives Shifra and Puah. For analyses of these aggadot, see Fraenkel, *Darkhe Ha-'Aggadah*, 1:302–8; Levinson, *Twice Told Tale*, 291–306; Rosenthal, "'Arichot Kedumot be-Bavli," 168–69 n. 25; Avigdor Shinan, "Aggadic Motifs between Midrash and Story" [Hebrew], *Jerusalem Studies in Hebrew Literature* 5 (1984): 203–20.

15. As evidenced by the paucity of a medieval commentary tradition on Bavli Sotah, tractate Sotah was not among the volumes more commonly studied as part of the rabbinic curriculum. In contrast, contemporary scholarship has turned to the Sotah ritual as a locus of inquiry, interrogating the biblical, Tannaitic, and later rabbinic textual representations of the ritual. See, for example, Adriana Destro, *The Law of Jealousy: Anthropology of Sotah* (Atlanta:

Adrienne Rich writes, "How have women given birth, who has helped them, and how, and why? These are not simply questions of the history of midwifery and obstetrics: they are political questions."[16] B. Soṭah 11b portrays women birthing a nation, an act of political rebellion that, with divine help, subverts accepted hierarchies. How and why, I add, might reading this story within its Bavli Sotah context subvert the Sotah ritual itself?

The Righteous Women of B. Soṭah 11b[17]

[א] דרש רב עוירא בשכר נשים צדקניות שהיו באותו הדור נגאלו ישראל ממצרים

[ב] בשעה שהולכות לשאוב מים הקב"ה מזמן להם דגים קטנים בכדיהן ושואבות מחצה מים ומחצה דגים ובאות ושופתות שתי קדירות אחת של חמין ואחת של דגים

[ג] ומוליכות אצל בעליהן לשדה ומרחיצות אותן וסכות אותן ומאכילות אותן ומשקות אותן ונזקקות להן בין שפתים שנאמר אם תשכבון בין שפתים וגו׳ (תהילים סח:יד)

[ד] בשכר תשכבון בין שפתים זכו ישראל לביזת מצרים, שנאמר כנפי יונה נחפה בכסף ואברותיה בירקרק חרוץ (תהילים סח:יד)

[ה] וכיון שמתעברות באות לבתיהם

[ו] וכיון שמגיע זמן מולדיהן הולכות ויולדות בשדה תחת התפוח שנאמר תחת התפוח עוררתיך וגו׳ (שה"ש ח:ה)

[ז] והקב"ה שולח משמי מרום מי שמנקיר ומשפיר אותן, כחיה זו שמשפרת את הולד, שנאמר ומולדותיך ביום הולדת אותך לא כרת שרך ובמים לא רחצת למשעי וגו׳ (יחזקאל טז:ד)

[ח] ומלקט להן שני עגולין אחד של שמן ואחד של דבש שנאמר ויניקהו דבש מסלע ושמן וגו׳ (דברים לב:יג)

[ט] וכיון שמכירין בהן מצרים באין להורגן ונעשה להם נס ונבלעין בקרקע ומביאין שוורים וחורשין על גבן שנאמר על גבי חרשו חורשים וגו׳ (תהילים קכט:ג)

[י] לאחר שהולכין היו מבצבצין ויוצאין כעשב השדה שנאמר רבבה כצמח השדה נתתיך (יחזקאל טז:ז)

Scholars Press, 1989); Grushcow, *Writing the Wayward Wife*; Bonna Devora Haberman, "The Suspected Adulteress: A Study of Textual Embodiment," *Prooftexts* 20, 1-2 (2000): 12-42; Halbertal, *Interpretive Revolutions*, 94-112; Hauptman, *Rereading the Rabbis*, 15-29; Lev, "Sotah: Rabbinic Pornography"; Rosen-Zvi, *Mishnaic Sotah Ritual*. I hypothesize that much of this recent interest coincides with Jewish feminism and increased attention to gender in Jewish studies generally and Talmud scholarship more specifically. For a list of commentaries on b. Soṭah, see Menahem Kasher and Jacob B. Mandelbaum, eds. *Sarei Ha-Elef* (New York: American Biblical Encyclopedia Society, 1959), 190.

16. Adrienne Rich, *Of Woman Born: Motherhood as Experience and Institution* (New York: W. W. Norton & Company, 1995 [1976]), 184.

17. Hebrew text is taken from the Vilna edition.

[כ] וכיון שמתגדלין באין עדרים עדרים לבתיהן שנאמר ותרבי ותגדלי ותבואי בעדי עדים (יחזקאל טז:ז) אל תקרי בעדי עדים אלא בעדרי עדרים

[ל] וכשנגלה הקב"ה על הים הם הכירוהו תחלה שנאמר זה אלי ואנוהו (שמות טו:ב).

[A] Expounded Rav 'Avira:[18] For the reward of the righteous women who were in that generation was Israel redeemed from Egypt.

[B] At the time when they went to draw water, the Holy Blessed One prepared for them small fish in their jars and they drew out half water and half fish. And they came and placed two pots, one for hot water and one for fish.

[C] And they brought them to their husbands in the field and washed them and anointed them with oil and fed them and gave them to drink and had sexual intercourse with them between the mounds in the field [שפתים]. As it is said, "Even for those of you who lie among the sheepfolds [שפתים] [there are wings of a dove sheathed in silver, its pinions in fine gold]" (Ps 68:14).[19]

[D] For the reward of "you who lie among the sheepfolds" Israel merited the spoil of Egypt, as it is said, "there are wings of a dove sheathed in silver, its pinions in fine gold" (Ps 68:14).

[E] And when they became pregnant they went to their houses.

[F] When the time of their giving birth arrived, they went and gave birth in the field under the apple-tree. As it is said, "Under the apple tree I roused you; [it was there your mother conceived you. There she who bore you conceived you]" (Song 8:5).

[G] And the Holy Blessed One sent from heaven one who cleansed and smoothed them like a midwife who smooths a newborn.[20] As it is said,

---

18. The majority of manuscripts (MSS Cambridge 2675.2; Munich 95; Vatican 110–111) read R. Akiva instead of Rav Avira. The printed Venice edition reads Rav Ezra. R. Akiva likely refers to a third- and fourth-generation Palestinian Amora and not the Tannaitic sage, evidence of the story's origination in Palestinian circles before being transformed into a Babylonian exegetical narrative. On the Palestinian Amora R. Akiva, see Hanoch Albeck, *Introduction to the Talmud Babli and Yerushalmi* [Hebrew] (Tel Aviv: Dvir, 1987), 346; Levinson, *Twice Told Tale*, 298. Versions of this story are found also in the later midrashic collections Deut. Rab. 15 (ed. S. Lieberman, *Midrash Debarim Rabbah: Edited for the First Time from the Oxford Ms. No. 147 with an Introduction and Notes*, 2nd ed. [Jerusalem: Shalem Books, 1992], 14-15), Tanḥuma, *Pekudei* 9, and Exod. Rab. 1:12 (ed. A. Shinan, *Midrash Shemot Rabbah Chapters I–XIV: A Critical Edition Based on a Jerusalem Manuscript with Variants, Commentary and Introduction* [Jerusalem: Dvir, 1984], 54–56). For a complete list of manuscript variants, see Abraham Liss, ed., *The Babylonian Talmud with Variant Readings Collected from Manuscripts, Fragments of the "Genizah" and Early Printed Editions, Tractate Soṭah* (Jerusalem: Institute for the Complete Israeli Talmud, 1977), 4.1:151–57.

19. All biblical translations are taken from NJPS. Other translations are my own.

20. MS Oxford 2675.2 reads יורד משמי מרום ("descended from heaven"), eliminating the intermediary, with God acting directly as midwife. See also Deut. Rab. 15: "Said R. Hiyya ha-Gadol: The angels did not do this but rather the Holy Blessed One in his glory, as it says,

"As for your birth, when you were born and your navel cord was not cut, and you were not bathed in water to smooth you; [you were not rubbed with salt, nor were you swaddled]" (Ezek 16:4).

[H] And He would gather for them two cakes, one of oil and one of honey. As it is said, "[He set him atop the highlands, To feast on the yield of the earth;] He fed him honey from the crag. And oil from the flinty rock" (Deut 32:13).

[I] And when Egypt recognized them, they came to kill them and a miracle was done for them and they were swallowed by the earth. And they brought oxen and plowed over their backs. As it is said, "Plowmen plowed across my back; [they made long furrows]" (Ps 129:3).

[J] After they left, they broke through[21] and came forth like the grass of the field, as it is said, "I let you grow like the plants of the field; [and you continued to grow up until you attained to womanhood, until your breasts became firm and your hair sprouted, You were still naked and bare]" (Ezek 16:7).

[K] And when they had grown, they came in flocks to their houses, as it is written, "And you continued to grow up until you attained to womanhood [ותרבי ותגדלי ותבאי בעדי עדיים]" (Ezek 16:7). Do not read, *"ba'adi 'adayim"* but rather, *"be'edrei 'adarim."*

[L] And when the Holy Blessed One was revealed at the Sea, they recognized Him first, as it is written, "This is my God and I will glorify Him" (Exod 15:2).

Although the midrash is structured around disparate verses from, respectively, Psalms, Song of Songs, Ezekiel, Deuteronomy, and Exodus, the exegetical key to this narrative, as Avigdor Shinan argues, lies in an expanded exegetical reading of Ezek 16:3–13.[22] Drawing on Ezekiel's tale of the birth and growth of Jerusalem—representative of the collective Israel—the midrash turns Jerusalem's "birth-day" (Ezek 16:4) into Israel's beginnings as a people in Egypt. The midrash cites Song 8:5 not only because of its mention of an apple tree or because of its description of birth, but also because of the word *dodah* ("beloved") in the verse's beginning, which connects it

---

'And I bathed you (Ezek 16:10).' If it had said, 'I caused you to be bathed,' I might have said perhaps it was done by an angel. But since it is written, 'And I bathed you' and not by an angel, May the name of the Blessed One be praised, He in His glory did this for them" (ed. Lieberman, 14). On the different variants found in Exod. Rab., later ones of which include the word *malakh* ("angel"), see Shinan's notes, *Midrash Shemot Rabbah*, p. 55; and Shinan, "Aggadic Motifs between Midrash and Story," 207 n. 14. On the relationship between God and angels, see Efraim Elimelech Urbach, *The Sages: Their Concepts and Beliefs*, 2 vols., trans. Israel Abrahams (Jerusalem: Magnes, 1975), 135–83, esp. 135–40. On the theological significance of the physical manifestation of God at the sea, see Arthur Green, "The Children in Egypt and the Theophany at the Sea," *Judaism* 24 (1975): 446-56.

21. Jastrow, s.v. בצבץ: "to break through, bubble forth, burst forth."

22. Shinan, "Aggadic Motifs," 208.

to Ezek 16:8 and its mention of *'eit dodim* ("time for love") [F].[23] When the midrash describes God providing food for the infants (Deut 32:13) [H] it likely references Ezek 16:13, "Your food was choice flour, honey, and oil." Much as Ezek 16:3–13 casts the infant Jerusalem as an abandoned and exposed female, without care until she enters puberty,[24] the Bavli homilist transforms this troubling imagery into a picture of divine care from the moment of birth, reshaping the allegorical passage from Ezekiel into a historical tale of miraculous individual deliverance.[25]

This exegetical dependence of the righteous women midrash on Ezek 16:3–13 is particularly interesting in light of Rosen-Zvi's argument for an intricate and profound connection between the book of Ezekiel and the mishnaic Sotah ritual, where Mishnah Sotah becomes, "a latent midrash on the adulteresses' punishment in Ezekiel."[26] Like the Sotah ritual, Ezek 16 and 23 "depict a public and theatrical punishment, centered on a ritual of humiliation and degradation that takes place before an audience and ends with a torturous death combined with bodily mutilation."[27] The details of the Mishnah's depiction of the Sotah ritual closely echo those of

---

23. Song 8:5: "Who is she that comes up from the desert, / Leaning upon her beloved [*dodah*]? / Under the apple tree I roused you; / It was there your mother conceived you, / There she who bore you conceived you." Ezek 16:8: "When I passed by you [again] and saw that your time for love [*'eit dodim*] had arrived. So I spread My robe over you and covered your nakedness, and I entered into a covenant with you by oath—declares the Lord God; thus you became Mine." Note that *'eit dodim* in Ezek 16:8 refers to sexual lovemaking. See Moshe Greenberg, *Ezekiel 1–20: A New Translation with Introduction and Commentary*, AB 22 (Garden City, NY: Doubleday, 1983), 277.

24. Ilana Pardes, *The Biography of Ancient Israel: National Narratives in the Bible*, Contraversions 14 (Berkeley: University of California Press, 2000), 23–24; Mary E. Shields, "Multiple Exposures: Body Rhetoric and Gender Characterization in Ezekiel 16," *JFSR* 14 (1998): 5–18, here 7–9.

25. Moshe Greenberg observes that, in exposure stories, between the foundling's rescue and revelation, the foundling usually lives under the care of a guardian (*Ezekiel 1–20*, 301). In the Ezekiel passage, the foundling is abandoned until marriage, an adjustment of the narrative tradition to fit the exodus traditions of Israel's beginnings as a people. "[T]he child's abandonment in the 'field' and its development 'like the plants of the field' recall the Israelites' labor 'in the field' and God's wonders worked against Egypt, the 'field of Zoan' [Exod 1:14; Ps 78:43]." In the rabbinic reading of the Ezekiel passage, however, the foundlings are under care from the moment of birth, a shift back to the more "usual" version of exposure stories and a rewriting of Israel's beginnings to include divine maternal care. On the shift from the father–son relationship depicted in the exodus narratives to the marital bond of Ezekiel, see Pardes, *Countertraditions in the Bible*, 23–25. For a contemporary theology of maternal care, see Mara H. Benjamin, *The Obligated Self: Maternal Subjectivity and Jewish Thought*, New Jewish Philosophy and Thought (Bloomington: Indiana University Press, 2018).

26. Rosen-Zvi, *Mishnaic Sotah Ritual*, 219. Rosen-Zvi extends this connection also to additional prophetic descriptions of adultery in Isa 47:2–23; 2 Sam 12:11–12; and Nah 3:5–6 (206–7, 215 n. 126).

27. Ibid., 184. See also his accompanying chart comparing Ezek 16 and 20 (184–87).

Ezekiel's account of punishment for adulteresses: "humiliating gestures (m. Soṭah 1:5–6); bodily mutilation and death following a forced drinking (m. Soṭah 3:4); construing the various measures as part of a single punitive continuum of retribution 'measure for measure' (m. Soṭah 1:7); and eliminating the presumption of innocence."[28] However, this link between the Sotah ritual and the prophet Ezekiel does not have to be adduced solely through implicit parallelism. Through its citation of Ezek 23:48, m. Soṭah 1:6 makes explicit this connection:

> And anyone [*ve-khol*] who wants to see comes to see except for her male and female slaves, since with them she feels no shame [*libah gas bahen*].[29] And all[30] women are permitted to see her, as it is said, "And all the women shall take warning not to imitate your wantonness" (Ezek 23:48).[31]

The Bavli notices a gendered contradiction between the first sentence and the second one (b. Soṭah 8b). The first sentence implies that, except for her male and female slaves, all males and females may come to see the Sotah. The second sentence, however, specifies that only women are permitted to see her, implicitly differentiating them from the "anyone" of the opening sentence. Abaye resolves the problem by proposing to interpret the first sentence as referring only to women. Rava, on the other hand, proposes that, while men may watch the Sotah, women are obligated to see her. As a prooftext, he restates Ezek 23:48, instantiating it not as advice but rather as a text that proves women's *obligation* to see the Sotah in her humiliated state and, accordingly, as participants in this public ritual of degradation. The Bavli thus reads Ezek 23:48 as a central halakhic text of the ritual, obligating all women in its ritual performance.

Indeed, the book of Ezekiel may be said to undergird both the rabbinic Sotah ritual and the righteous women narrative. With this in mind, it is striking that the midrash cites verses only from the beginning of Ezekiel. While Ezek 16:1–14 in its biblical context begins with images of infant exposure and abandonment, rabbinic rereading, as I have observed, transforms this passage into one of divine care. In noting this rereading, I do not mean to erase the problematics of the biblical passage but rather to state that, much as the Bavli sees fit to reread Ezek 16:1–14 as a passage of divine care, it does not do the same with the graphic imagery of

28. Ibid., 205. See also his list of additional similarities (205–7).

29. On "since with them she feels no shame," and the various readings of m. Soṭah 1:6, see Rosen-Zvi, *Mishnaic Sotah Ritual*, 70.

30. MS Kaufmann and MS Parma both include the word *other* here. This word makes clear that the previous clause refers only to female slaves, who are not permitted to see the accused woman. All other women, in contrast, are permitted to see her. The Bavli, as I will make clear, does not have the version of either Kaufmann or Parma.

31. I have translated according to the printed mishnah in order to facilitate the Bavli's reading.

sexual betrayal and subsequent punishment found in the remainder of Ezek 16 (vv. 15–63). Nor does it reread Ezek 23, with its metaphor of Israel as God's wife and portrayal of the prophet's declaration that Oholibah will be made to drink the poisonous cup of her sister as judgment for her unfaithfulness (Ezek 23:30–34).[32] The righteous women narrative interprets only the beginning of Ezekiel, leaving the rest to the Sotah ritual.

Much as the Mishnah—and the Bavli in its footsteps—build the Sotah ritual upon Ezekiel's brutal punishments, the Bavli weaves the diametric opposite of that punishment into the midrash of the righteous women—the (rabbinically read) prophet Ezekiel's image of divine care and beneficence. To be clear, I am not making a claim about chronology. But I am making a claim about a thematic relationship between the two poles of the prophet Ezekiel—covenantal love and care on the one side and public degradation on the other—and the ways in which the midrash of the righteous women is, in many ways, the "mirror" of the Sotah ritual.[33] Ezekiel undergirds them both.

Mirroring the Sotah Ritual

This mirroring of the Sotah ritual extends beyond the book of Ezekiel. As I noted in the beginning of this essay, Yonah Fraenkel remarks on the story's motifs of seduction, pregnancy, birth, hiding, and house:

> [E]verything that occurs in the field—seduction, pregnancy, birth, cleansing of the newborn, hiding—should have been in the house, and, if so, the contrast between the house and the field is the subject of the story as a whole. The women offered themselves and made the field a house with the husbands, and the Holy Blessed One made the field into a house for their children.[34]

32. Michael A. Fishbane, "Accusations of Adultery: A Study of Law and Scribal Practice in Numbers 5:11-31," *HUCA* 45 (1974): 25–45. Tikva Frymer-Kensky argues that the biblical Sotah ritual is a religio-legal procedure closely similar to the classic purgatory oath rather than a trial by ordeal. In a trial by ordeal, "the god's decision is manifested immediately, and the result of the trial is not in itself the penalty for the offense." In other words, God as jury gives a verdict of guilt or innocence through the ordeal and then the judges sentence in accordance with the verdict. In the purgatory oath, "… the individual swearing the oath puts himself under divine jurisdiction, expecting to be punished by God if the oath-taker is guilty." In the case of the Sotah, society gives control of the woman to God, who judges her and punishes her if she is in fact guilty. See Tikva Frymer-Kensky, "The Strange Case of the Suspected Soṭah (Numbers V 11–31)," *VT* 34 (1984): 11–26. These two articles can also be found in Alice Bach, ed., *Women in the Hebrew Bible: A Reader* (New York: Routledge, 1998), 1:463–74 and 487–502.

33. Rosen-Zvi observes that the Mishnah presents the Sotah ritual as a mirror image of the sin (*Mishnaic Sotah Ritual*, 139).

34. Fraenkel, *Darkhe Ha-'Aggadah*, 306.

The principle of measure-for-measure, seen in the turning of field into house, first by the women for their husbands and then by God for their babies, can be traced throughout the righteous women narrative. Thus, the women cook two pots, one for hot water and one for fish; God, in return, gathers two cakes, one of oil and one of honey [B]. The women wash and anoint their husbands; God cleans and smooths the newborn babies [C; G].[35] Fraenkel frames these details in the context of the rabbinic principle of measure-for-measure,[36] yet without remarking on the story's redactional context within Bavli Soṭah as explication of m. Soṭah 1:7 ("By the measure with which a person measures, so too will he be measured ..."). Indeed, while the thematics of this story certainly touch on m. Soṭah 1:7's dictum of measure-for-measure, they also reach beyond this principle. In doing in the field what is supposed to be "done" in the house, the righteous women mirror the Sotah.

The wife is legally enjoined, through the process of a warning (*kinui*), against secreting herself with another man (*setirah*) for an amount of time long enough for them to potentially engage in sexual intercourse (m. Soṭah 1:2). In contrast, the righteous women defy Pharaoh's decree and go down to the field—an open space—in order to have sexual intercourse [C].[37] The righteous women seek out their husbands [B; C]; the Sotah is accused of evading her husband. The righteous women bring water to the field in order to wash and feed their husbands [B; C]; the Sotah is forced to drink a water potion to test her fidelity. As penalty for transgressing her husband's warning, the Sotah will suffer some kind of injury to her reproductive abilities;[38] the righteous women, in transgressing Pharaoh and seducing their husbands, become pregnant [E].[39] In the one case God redeems the women and saves their children from death [I; J]; in the other God judges and punishes the woman, possibly by miscarriage or infertility. The righteous women figure women's sexuality as redemptive; the Sotah ritual figures women's sexuality as something that must be constrained and policed. The field becomes a mirror of the home where what would be expected in

35. Ibid., 306–7. Based on the later Deuteronomy Rabbah, Fraenkel argues for the composition of the Bavli midrash from two originally disparate and independent blocs of material: the first an exegetical homily based on Ezek 16 and the second a story without explicit exegetical content. The Bavli then connects these two traditions through the thematic of the house. Fraenkel reads this story as similar to other rabbinic miracle stories where human actions are matched by divine intervention, marking the narrative of the righteous women as similarly religious in nature. See also Levinson, *Twice Told Tale*, 299.

36. Fraenkel, *Darkhe Ha-'Aggadah*, 306.

37. The field here also contrasts with its portrayal in Deut 22:25, the case of the betrothed maiden (*na'arah*) raped in a field.

38. For a survey of interpretations of the biblical punishment, see Grushcow, *Writing the Wayward Wife*, 161 n. 6.

39. See also the versions in Deuteronomy Rabbah and the Tanḥuma, where each woman gives birth to multiple children.

the home (but is now forbidden by Egyptian decree) becomes a surprising and unexpected act of redemption where the righteous women, through their acts of seduction, are figured as saviors of a nation [A].[40] When the suspected Sotah leaves the home, trouble ensues. Indeed, this thematic of mirroring is crystallized in later versions of this midrash: both the Tanḥuma and Deuteronomy Rabbah describe the women bringing mirrors to the field and using them to arouse their husband's desire.[41] In the Tanḥuma version, the mirrors are eventually donated by these women as freewill offerings to the tabernacle and then utilized to build the basin in which the priests wash their hands and feet to prepare for divine service.

Reading Forward

A reader of Bavli Sotah will encounter two seeming poles—the spectacle and brutality of the Sotah ritual and the grace of the midrash. One reading would locate both as policing women and women's sexuality, first, through the coercion of the Sotah ritual and, second, through the exemplar of what it means to be a "good" woman. If a woman leaves the home, she must do so in service of saving the people Israel. Yet, reading Bavli Sotah need not necessitate reading with these two poles. We may choose another way.

When read outside of Bavli Sotah or even within the more local context of the tractate's midrash on Exod 1:8–2:9, the homily of the righteous women can rightfully be conceptualized as a text of rebellion against Pharaoh and Egyptian domination and, as represented by the women's initiative, against male hierarchy more generally. Even God is reimagined; no longer a "man of war" (Exod 15:3), God becomes—at least in some versions of the text—a midwife who smooths the limbs of the newborn babies.[42] Yet when read in the context of the Sotah ritual, the midrash becomes not only rebellious but also subversive. The midrash admittedly does not portray the righteous women as rebelling against—trying to overturn—the Sotah ritual. Nevertheless, its very placement in the tractate enables the midrash to act as a subversive countertradition, that is, as a voice antithetical to that of the Sotah ritual. Indeed, as Lisa Grushcow points out,

40. On the exodus narrative as the story of the birthing of a nation, see Pardes, *Biography of Ancient Israel*, 16–39.

41. The imagery of the mirrors has inspired contemporary Passover ritual, the placing of mirrors on the seder plate. This practice originated with Judith Kates after a gift from Gail Twersky Reimer of two mirrors facing one another on a small stand (oral conversation with Judith Kates, June 2018). The gift was inspired by Avivah Zornberg's reading of the redemptive work of the "mirror drama" in the Tanḥuma. See Avivah Gottlieb Zornberg, *The Particulars of Rapture: Reflections on Exodus* (2001; repr., New York: Schocken, 2011), 220.

42. Levinson, *Twice Told Tale*, 304-5.

rabbinic materials on the Sotah ritual exhibit two different themes: a legal approach that locates the ritual within the rabbinic judicial framework and a moralistic approach that uses the ritual to condemn adultery in general.[43] The latter theme may be part of a Babylonian trend toward shifting the focus of the Sotah ritual from women's guilt to include men and male sin. The righteous women homily may be understood as part of this trend toward shifting responsibility for sin away from the sole provenance of females.[44] Within the Bavli's literary structure, the illicit sexuality of the Sotah flows into the licit sexuality of the righteous women, breaking down the dichotomy between the two and enabling the second to subvert the first. By locating and telling the story of these women as exemplars of rebellion and redemption in the midst of the Sotah ritual, the Bavli opens for its readers an imaginative gap toward alternative possibilities that run counter to those depicted through the ritual itself. The righteous women become political figures, subverting ideas both of who sins and of who saves.

---

43. Grushcow, *Writing the Wayward Wife*, 264-71.

44. On this point, see Rosen-Zvi, *Mishnaic Sotah Ritual*, 35–36 n. 50; Rosen-Zvi, "Ritual of Suspected Adulteress," 52–56. One may also consider the opening *sugyot* of Bavli Soṭah as an introductory lecture to the tractate that lays out these legalistic and moralistic themes. Thus, the first *sugya* (listed by Avraham Weiss as Saboraic) instructs a man "who sees the Sotah in her disgrace" to stay away from wine, implicitly cautioning men against behavior that could lead them to similar sin. Reading m. Soṭah 1:1 juridically, the Bavli's anonymous voice then declares the ritual permitted ex post facto but a priori forbidden. The Amora Resh Laqish next contends that a man gets the match that he deserves—a wicked man a wicked woman—that, at the very least, places responsibility for adultery on both parties. For Weiss's list of Saboraic *sugyot*, see Avraham Weiss, *Ha-Yetzirah Shel Ha-Sabora'im (Helkam be-Yetzirat Ha-Talmud)* (Jerusalem: Magnes, 1953), 1–18. On reading these introductory *sugyot* as forewords to the tractate, that is, as introductions to a tractate's conceptual and intellectual underpinnings, see Charlotte Elisheva Fonrobert, "The Place of Shabbat: On the Architecture of the Opening Sugya of Tractate Eruvin (2a-3a)," in *Strength to Strength: Essays in Appreciation of Shaye J. D. Cohen*, ed. Michael L. Satlow, BJS 363 (Providence, RI: Brown Judaic Studies, 2018), 437–54.

Mishnah as Story

Aspects of the Reception of the Mishnah in Midrash and Piyyuṭ

TZVI NOVICK

The Mishnah is dense with narrative elements. Stories punctuate legal analysis. Whole tractates, and large swaths of others, are devoted to ritual narratives. Casuistic formulations tell stories in the protasis before ruling on the relevant legal question in the apodosis. The articulation of a rabbi's position about a legal question is a story of a sort, especially when two rabbis diverge on the question, and especially when these rabbis thrust and parry.[1] But the Mishnah on the whole is a legal text, and so the question arises: How is it received by later rabbinic texts that do not take explication of the law as their aim?

The current essay considers to what extent and how exegetical and liturgical texts from late antiquity receive the Mishnah, and in particular the ritual narratives therein, as narrative. Perhaps the most "narratival" reception of the Mishnah in this period occurs in the *Yelammedenu* homily. The homily begins with a legal question, which it answers by adducing a rabbinic text, usually from the Mishnah, and this text serves as a pivot into "aggadic" reflections on biblical narrative.[2] My focus in this essay is on

---

My thanks to Prof. Avi Shmidman for his comments on an earlier draft of this paper, and to the workshop participants for their feedback, especially Prof. Jeffrey L. Rubenstein, who convened the workshop and shared additional feedback.

1. On narrative elements in the Mishnah, see Moshe Simon-Shoshan, *Stories of the Law: Narrative Discourse and the Construction of Authority in the Mishnah* (Oxford: Oxford University Press, 2012). On temple-centered ritual narratives in the Mishnah, see Naftali S. Cohn, *The Memory of the Temple and the Making of the Rabbis*, Divinations (Philadelphia: University of Pennsylvania Press, 2013).

2. On the *Yelammedenu* genre, see Marc Bregman, "The Tanhuma-Yelammedenu Literature: Studies in the Evolution of the Verses" (PhD diss., The Hebrew University in Jerusalem, 1991); Jacob Elbaum, "'How Many Benedictions Does One Say Every Day?' Methods of Forming a *Tanhuma* Homily," in *Knesset Ezra: Literature and Life in the Synagogue; Studies Presented to Ezra Fleischer*, ed. Shulamit Elizur et al. (Jerusalem: Yad Ben-Zvi, 1994), 149-67;

other corpora, and on a variety of other frameworks for narrative appropriation of the Mishnah: I work through five case studies from the homiletical midrashim of the Amoraic period (Leviticus Rabbah and Pesiqta de Rab Kahana; redacted in ca. the fifth century) and classical *piyyuṭ* (ca. sixth–eighth centuries).

1. Pesiqta de Rab Kahana 8:1 (137)[3]

In a homily designated for the reading about the barley sheaf (*'omer*) offering (Lev 23:9–14), R. Abin comments, בוא וראה כמה היו ישראל מצטערין על מצות העומר, "Come, see how Israel would take pains concerning the commandments of the *'omer*." To ground this declaration he quotes m. Menaḥ. 10:4, which describes the production process, from the harvesting of the barley to the thirteen siftings, that ultimately yields the *'omer* flour. The fact that the Mishnah speaks in the past tense rather than in the present is probably important for R. Abin's purposes. The past tense is what encourages R. Abin to read the pericope as a story about Israel's past and not simply as a ritual prescription.

It is not immediately clear what R. Abin means to convey by drawing attention to Israel's efforts to prepare the *'omer*, but the context offers a clue, if not to R. Abin's original intent, then at least to the editor's understanding of its force. His statement immediately follows two others, by R. Yannai and by R. Pinḥas, that also concern taking pains (צע"ר *hitpa'el*) to produce food. R. Yannai's reads thus.

> בנוהג שבעולם אדם לוקח לו ליטרה אחת בשר מן השוק כמה הוא יגיע בה כמה צער הוא מצטער עליה עד שלא יבשלה והבריות ישינים על מיטותיהם והקב"ה משיב רוחות ומעלה עננים ומוריד גשמים ומפריח טללים ומגדל צמחי' ומדשן פירות ואין את נותן לו את העומר
>
> In the ordinary course of things, a person purchases a *litra* of meat from the market, and how he toils over it, what pains he takes over it, until he cooks it. Yet mortals sleep on their beds, and the Holiness, blessed be He, blows winds, raises clouds, brings down rain, drives dews, grows grasses, and fattens fruits, and do you not give him the *'omer*?

R. Pinḥas's parable is verbatim the same, except that it concerns the laundering of a garment rather than the preparation of meat. Immediately after

Tzvi Novick, "Liturgy and Law: Approaches to Halakhic Material in Yannai's *Kedushta'ot*," *JQR* 103 (2013): 476–89; Richard Hidary, *Rabbis and Classical Rhetoric: Sophistic Education and Oratory in the Talmud and Midrash* (New York: Cambridge University Press, 2017), 57–67.

3. See the parallel passages in Lev. Rab. 28:1 (651); Qoh. Rab. 3:1. Parenthetical page references are to Mandelbaum's edition of Pesiqta de Rab Kahana; Margulies's edition of Leviticus Rabbah; Weiss's edition of the Sifra; and Kahana's edition of Sifre Numbers. Translations of all texts are my own.

R. Abin's comment comes a statement by R. Levi that also highlights labor, though it does not employ the root צע"ר. R. Levi notes that human beings devote much effort to bringing a grain heap to the winnowing floor (הרי שעמלתה וחרשתה וזרעתה וניכשתה ... ועשיתה אותו ערימה, "Behold, you labored, plowed, sowed, hoed, ... and made it a pile"), but the winnowing depends on wind from God, ואין את נותן לו שכר הרוח, "And do you not give him the wages of his wind?" Ending as it does with the very question, mutatis mutandis, at which the teachings of R. Yannai and R. Pinḥas arrive, R. Levi's statement belongs to the same redactional framework as theirs.

Into the midst of this framework, R. Abin's assertion sounds a very different note. Rather than construing the *'omer* as a small compensation for God's essential and/or extensive effort on the farmer's behalf, R. Abin seizes upon the Mishnah as evidence for Israel's own effort in furnishing the *'omer*. He finds in the Mishnah's ritual narrative in m. Menaḥ. 10:4 the verbal density characteristic of the descriptions of agricultural and natural processes in the teachings of R. Yannai, R. Pinḥas, and R. Levi.

2. Leviticus Rabbah 15:8 (335–37)

The homiletical macro-unit accompanying Lev 13, on skin lesions, includes a passage on m. Neg. 2:4–5. The passage begins by quoting m. Neg. 2:4, together with explanatory elaborations preserved in Sifra *nega'im* 4:1 (63b).

> תנא כיצד ראיית הנגע האיש נראה כעודד וכמסיק זיתים כעודר בית הסתרים וכמסיק זיתים בית השחי והאשה כאורגת וכמניקה את בנה כאורגת בית הסתרים וכמניקה את בנה תחת הדד
>
> It was taught: "How are lesions seen (i.e., inspected)? The man is seen [in the position of] one who hoes, and one who gathers olives." As one who hoes, [for] the genitals, and as one who gathers olives, [for] the armpit. "And the woman [is seen in the position of] who one weaves, and one who nurses her child." As one who weaves, [for] the genitals, and as one who nurses her child, [for] under the breast.[4]

Immediately afterward, the passage cites the beginning of the next pericope, m. Neg. 2:5.

> תנא כל הנגעין אדם רואה חוץ מניגעי עצמו ר' מאיר או' אף לא ניגעי קרוביו

4. The material in quotation marks is from the Mishnah; the additional material is paralleled in the Sifra. The quoted passage continues, but the subsequent text is not important for our purposes. Likewise unimportant are the variations between the versions around the standards of כאורגת ("as one who weaves") and כעורכת ("as one who arranges [bread]").

It was taught: Every lesion a person may see, except his own lesions. R. Meir says: also not the lesions of his relatives.

What comes next is something like an aggadic *sugya*, consisting of two related parts. The first is an anonymous exchange that follows immediately from m. Neg. 2:5.

מי ראה נגע מרים אם תאמר משה ראה אין זר רואה את הנגעים ואם תאמר אהרן ראה אין קרוב רואה את הנגעים אמ' הקדוש ברוך הוא אני כהנא אני מסגירה אני מטהרה הה"ד והעם לא נסע עד האסף מרים

Who saw Miriam's lesion? If you will say, Moses saw, but a non-priest may not see lesions. And if you will say: Aaron saw, but a relative may not see lesions. Said the Holiness, blessed be He: I am a priest. I will seclude her. I will cleanse her. This is what is says, "And the people did not journey until Miriam had been gathered" (Num 12:15).

Material related to this passage is preserved in Sifre Num. 105–6 (261, 265), and a close parallel occurs in b. Zebaḥ. 101b–102a. From these sources, and from the passage itself, it is clear that the question מי ראה נגע מרים, "Who saw Miriam's lesion?," originated as an inquiry concerning Num 12:14, תסגר, "Let [Miriam] be quarantined," or Num 12:15 ותסגר מרים, "And Miriam was quarantined," in the form of something like: מי הסגירה, "Who quarantined her?"[5] Leviticus Rabbah shifts the lemma from Num 12:15 to m. Neg. 2:5, and with this shift the question changes to מי ראה נגע מרים, "Who saw Miriam's lesion?"

The second major part of the *sugya* introduces another *memra* that also makes reference to Aaron.

ר' לוי בש' ר' חמא בר' חנינה צער גדול היה לו למשה בדבר הזה כך הוא כבודו שלאהרן אחי להיות רואה את הנגעים אמ' לו הקדוש ברוך הוא ולא נהנה ממנו עשרים וארבע מתנות

R. Levi in the name of R. Ḥama b. R. Ḥanina: Moses was greatly pained in this matter. Does this befit the honor of my brother Aaron to see lesions? Said to him the Holiness, blessed be He: And does he not have the benefit from it of twenty-four gifts?

5. The *niphal* form of the verb, which occludes the quarantining agent, is what occasions the question. The passage in b. Zebaḥ. 101b begins with more or less the original question: מרים מי הסגירה, "Miriam, who quarantined her?" Sifre Num. 106 (265), at the lemma תיסגר, "Let [Miriam] be quarantined," comments, הקדש הסגירה והקדש טימאה והקדש טיהרה, "The Holiness quarantined her and the Holiness defiled her and the Holiness cleansed her." (This formulation is echoed in Sifre Num. 105 [261], which links it in turn to a version of R. Meir's statement in m. Neg. 2:5.) The continuation of the Leviticus Rabbah passage itself, which has God resolve not to see Miriam's lesion but to quarantine her, likewise establishes that the question מי ראה גנע מרים, "Who saw Miriam's lesion?," is secondary.

The same formulation—"Moses was greatly pained in this matter"—occurs elsewhere in Leviticus Rabbah, also in relation to Aaron, at Lev. Rab. 21:7 (482), where Moses, hearing in Lev 16:2 that Aaron may not approach the holy בכל עת, "at every time," fears that God may be demoting Aaron categorically. What is striking about the current passage, by contrast, is that, at least in context, there is no explicit lemma to which Moses's concern attaches. It appears rather that m. Neg. 2:4–5, as interpreted in the local context, is what generates Moses's concern. The explanatory elaborations introduced into m. Neg. 2:4 highlight the fact that seeing lesions involves intrusion upon concealed, shame-tinged body parts, male and even female. Via the addition of the anonymous comment quoted above (מי ראה נגע מרים, "Who saw Miriam's lesion?" etc.), m. Neg. 2:5 introduces another female patient and the character of Aaron. Together, the two Mishnah pericopes, with their attendant explications, lay the groundwork for the notion that the role of the priest—first and foremost Aaron—in treating lesions implicates him in less than altogether dignified tasks. In the *sugya*, then, the Mishnah text becomes inextricably bound up with narratives of Moses, Miriam, and Aaron.

3. Pesiqta de Rab Kahana 4:7 (73)

The unit devoted to the Sabbath of the red heifer includes a story that features the beginning of Mishnah Parah.

> ר׳ אחא בשם ר׳ יוסי בר׳ חנינה בשעה שעלה לשמי מרום שמע קולו של הקדוש ברוך הוא יושב ועוסק בפרשת פרה ואומ׳ הלכה משם אומרה ר׳ אליעזר או׳ עגלה בת שנתה ופרה בת שתים אמ׳ משה לפני הקדוש ברוך הוא רבון העולמים העליונים והתחתונים ברשותך ואת יושב ואו׳ הלכה משמו של בשר ודם אמ׳ לו הקדוש ברוך הוא משה צדיק אחד עתיד לעמוד בעולמי ועתיד לפתוח בפרשת פרה תחילה ר׳ אליעזר אומ׳ עגלה בת שנתה ופרה בת שתים אמ׳ לפניו רבון העולמים יהי רצון שיהי מחלציי א׳ לו חייך שהוא מחלציך הד׳ היא דכ׳ ושם האחד אליעזר ושם אותו המיוחד אליעזר

> R. Aḥa in the name of R. Yose b. R. Ḥanina: When Moses ascended to the high heavens, he heard the voice of the Holiness, blessed be He, sitting and studying the section of the red heifer, and saying a law in the name of its speaker: "R. Eliezer says: the calf, a year old; the heifer, two years old" (m. Parah 1:1). Said Moses before the Holiness, blessed be He: Master of the World, the upper and lower regions are your domain, and you say a law in the name of flesh and blood? Said to him the Holy One, blessed be He: Moses, a righteous man will arise in my world, and begin to explicate the section of the red heifer: "R. Eliezer says: the calf, a year old; the heifer, two years old." He said to him: Master of the world, may it be [your] will that he be of my loins. He said to him: By your life, he is of your loins. This is what is written, "And the name of the one was Eliezer" (Ex 18:4), i.e., the name of that singular one was Eliezer.

This story has an important afterlife in rabbinic literature, which we will take up briefly below. My interest here is in the generation and meaning of the story. Why does Moses see God studying the beginning of tractate Parah in particular, and why does the story attribute special significance to the teaching of R. Eliezer that opens the tractate?

One possibility is that the story assumes the special inscrutability of the laws of the red heifer. This motif does occur throughout Pesiq. Rab Kah. 4, and later versions of the story in the Bavli and by Qillir appear to interpret the story along these lines.[6] But the motif of inscrutability does not appear in the story itself.

The context suggests a second possibility. According to a statement introduced almost immediately prior to the story, and also attributed to R. Aḥa, דברים שלא ניגלו למשה בסיני ניגלו לר׳ עקיב׳ וחביריו "things that were not revealed to Moses at Sinai were revealed to R. Akiva and his colleagues." This assertion, at least in context, probably also assumes that the laws of the red heifer are singularly inscrutable, but in this passage, too, the motif of inscrutability is not mentioned explicitly. In any case, the two passages together, R. Aḥa's statement and the story of Moses in heaven, highlight different rabbis as Moses's true heir (or even superior): R. Akiva and R. Eliezer. These rabbis figure as complex opposites elsewhere in rabbinic literature. Adiel Schremer, for example, has recently suggested that Mishnah tractate 'Abot, in figuring R. Eliezer as the chief student of R. Yoḥanan b. Zakkai (m. 'Abot 2:8), and in other ways, celebrates R. Eliezer and his traditionalist, holistic perspective on the law, in contrast to R. Akiva and his perspective, which distinguishes the original divine law from subsequent human, rabbinic teaching.[7] Perhaps, then, the "pro-Eliezer" story of Moses in heaven functions in Pesiq. Rab Kah. 4:7 as something of a counterpoint to the "pro-Akiva" statement in the same passage. We may note in this light that, while the story featuring R. Eliezer construes Torah study in a traditionalist mode, as the repetition of another's teaching in his name, and genealogically binds Moses to R. Eliezer, the statement about R. Akiva instead introduces a contrast between the revelation to Moses and the revelation to R. Akiva, and makes no attempt to unite the two figures. The story, in other words, champions not only R. Eliezer but the traditionalist mode of study of which he is a symbol, while the statement championing R. Akiva, reflecting an Akivan predilection, distinguishes later Torah from earlier Torah.

Mandelbaum, in his commentary on the Pesiqta de Rab Kahana passage, intimates a different but not incompatible account of the story's genesis and meaning, one that is rooted in a narratological anomaly in

---

6. On the Bavli's version, see b. Menaḥ. 29b, which I take up in the continuation. For Qillir's, see n. 15 below.

7. See Adiel Schremer, "Avot Reconsidered: Rethinking Rabbinic Judaism," *JQR* 105 (2015): 287-311.

m. Parah 1:1. Tractate Parah, almost uniquely among Mishnah tractates—we will turn to the other two exceptions momentarily—opens with an attributed statement, in the form, "X says, etc." The typical tractate opens instead with an anonymous halakhic statement or question (e.g., m. Beṣ. 1:1 ביצה שנולדה ביום טוב, "An egg born on the festival," i.e., what is the status of an egg laid on the festival?). Named figures enter only afterward, to give their views on the question (e.g., from the immediate continuation in m. Beṣ 1:1: בית שמי אומ' תיאכל, "The house of Shammai says: It may be eaten.").[8] The anomalous opening of Mishnah tractate Parah calls for context, for framing: R. Eliezer's statement seems to come out of nowhere. The narrative of Moses's ascent to heaven may have arisen at least in part as a solution to this problem. The beginning of the tractate represents, as it were, a quotation of a view introduced by God in the course of heavenly deliberations about the red heifer.

The other two tractates that open with "X says" are related. Mishnah 'Eduyyot begins with the words of Shammai (or the house of Shammai) on a topic in the laws of menstruation, and the same passage occurs at the beginning of Mishnah Niddah. It is perhaps not a coincidence that this passage, too, receives a narrative framework early in its reception history: The beginning of Tosefta tractate 'Eduyyot puts the words of Shammai (more precisely, the words of Shammai in m. 'Ed. 1:2, which have the same form) into the mouth of the sages at Yavneh.

> כשנכנסו חכמים לכרם ביבנה אמרו עתידה שעה שיהא אדם מבקש דבר מדברי תורה ואינו מוצא מדברי סופרים ואינו מוצא ... אמרו נתחיל מה לבית שמיי ומה לבית הלל בית שמיי או'
>
> When the sages entered into the vineyard at Yavneh they said: At a future time, a person will see a word from the words of Torah but not find it; from the words of the scribes and not find it.... They said: Let us begin from what is of the house of Shammai and what is of the house of Hillel: "The house of Shammai says, etc."[9]

In the aforementioned article, Schremer suggests that this passage in fact encodes an Akivan alternative to the Eliezer-affiliated genealogy of Torah in m. 'Abot 1:1.[10] If this is true, then the narratological relationship between t. 'Ed. 1:1 and the story in Pesiq. Rab Kah. 4:7, which features an implicit contrast between R. Akiva and R. Eliezer, is especially telling. In any case, it may be possible to view the stories in t. 'Ed. 1:1 and Pesiq. Rab Kah. 4:7 as responses, in part, to the same narratological anomaly.[11]

---

8. The quotation is from MS Kaufmann.
9. The quotation is from MS Vienna.
10. Schremer, "Avot Reconsidered," 300–310.
11. Yair Furstenberg has recently suggested that the story in t. 'Ed. 1:1 was not originally written to introduce the tractate ("From Tradition to Controversy: New Modes of Trans-

4. Qillir, אצילי עם עולי גולה, "Princes of the people ascending from exile"

The Five of Qillir's *qedushta* אחת שאלתי, "One thing I asked," for the Sabbath of the red heifer, depends on m. Parah 3, and to a lesser extent the "commentary" thereon in t. Parah 3.[12] These chapters describe the ritual for the preparation of the red heifer, from the isolation of the priest who will burn the heifer to the storage of the ashes. The Mishnah begins (m. Parah 3:1) with a description of the purification from death uncleanness of the priest who will burn the ashes. This purification process itself requires the use of red heifer ashes, and so the Mishnah backtracks (m. Parah 3:2–4) to describe the process of irrigating and sprinkling those ashes, before proceeding with the cleansing of the burning priest (m. Parah 3:5) and his subsequent work (m. Parah 3:6–11).

Our interest lies, in particular, with the backtracking in m. Parah 3:2-4, which we shall call, for the sake of brevity, the preliminary ritual. The preliminary ritual is most unusual: In a courtyard suspended above the ground, to prevent penetration of death uncleanness from below, women would bear and raise children. These children, once grown, would ride upon oxen, again to avoid contact with sources of uncleanness, down to the Siloam. There they would draw water. From there they would proceed to the Women's Court, at the entrance to which was affixed a container with ashes of previously burned red heifers. By means of a Rube Goldberg-like device—or perhaps not; whether such a mechanism was employed is a matter of debate in the Mishnah—the children would extract ashes from the container, mingle them with the water, and sprinkle the water on the priest designated for burning the next red heifer. In the Tosefta, t. Parah 3:2–5 tracks the Mishnah's description of the preliminary ritual, and afterward comes the following passage.

> מעשים אילו עשו כשעשו (!) מן הגולה דברי ר׳ יהודה ר׳ שמעון או׳ איפרן ירד עמהן לבבל ועלה אמרו לו והלא נטמא בארץ העמים אמ׳ להן לא גזרו טומאה בארץ העמים אלא לאחר שעלו מן הגולה

---

mission in the Teachings of the Early Rabbis," *Tarbiṣ* 85 [2018]: 587–641, here 597–98). In this case, the stylistic anomaly noted above would have served as a factor not in the production of the story but in the attachment of the story to the beginning of the tractate. Furstenberg's interest lies in the emergence of formulae for the transmission of debate, especially "this one forbids (declares unclean), this one permits (declares clean)." Notably, this formula presumes the prior introduction of the topic at hand. On the story in Pesiq. Rab Kah. 4:7 see also Itay Marienberg-Milikowsky, *"We Know Not What Has Become of Him": Literature and Meaning in Talmudic Aggada* [Hebrew] (Ramat Gan: Bar Ilan University Press, 2016), 15–36. Unfortunately this work came to my attention too late to be incorporated into my discussion.

12. For the Hebrew text, see Shulamit Elizur, "אחת שאלתי", קדושתא לשבת פרה לר׳ אלעזר בירבי קיליר, *Qoveṣ al Yad* n.s. 10 (1982): 36–39.

> These things they did when they went up from the exile; the words of R. Yehudah. R. Shimon says: Their ashes went down with them to Babylon, and went up. They said to him: And were they not made unclean in the land of the peoples? He said to them: They did not decree uncleanness on the land of the peoples until after they had returned from the exile.

From the location of this debate in the Tosefta, it is relatively clear that R. Yehudah, in speaking of "these things," refers to the preliminary ritual. According to R. Yehudah, this preliminary ritual is not part of the standard preparation of the red heifer ashes, but rather represented a one-time, postexilic measure, presumably necessitated by the fact that all Israel became unclean in the exile.[13] R. Shimon claims that "the ashes went down with them to Babylon, and went up," and he clarifies that the ashes had not contracted ritual uncleanness, despite their sojourn in "the land of the peoples," because the presumptive uncleanness of lands outside Israel came into effect only after the return from the exile.

The debate between R. Yehudah and R. Shimon is somewhat discordant: R. Yehudah speaks about the people's exile, and R. Shimon speaks of the ashes. What is R. Yehudah's position about the ashes? If he believes that the presumptive uncleanness of the lands of the nations was in force even prior to Israel's restoration, and that the preliminary ritual, involving the children, was a solution to the uncleanness of the exile, then how does he account for the availability of ritually clean ashes? The birthing of children on uncleanness-proof platforms yields clean people, but are not the ashes themselves unclean?

Let us turn, by way of responding to this question, to Qillir's *piyyuṭ*, which I have translated in full in the appendix. In rewriting m. Parah 3 and t. Parah 3, the *payṭan* adopts R. Yehudah's position, that the preliminary ritual—the cleansing of the burning priest by means of the isolation of children from birth—does not constitute a regular feature of the red heifer ritual, but was an ad hoc response to the returning community's uncleanness.[14] Before entering into Qillir's poem in detail, we must note one other feature of these chapters that would have inclined Qillir to receive the Mishnah's ritual narrative more as story than as law. The Mishnah (m. Parah 3:5) preserves a tradition about seven red heifers having been reduced to ashes. It records what is presumably a later debate about this

13. For this explanation, see Saul Lieberman, *Tosefeth Rishonim: A Commentary,* part III-IV: *Seder Tohoroth* (1939; repr., New York: Jewish Theological Seminary of America, 1999), 216–17.

14. See Menachem Schmelzer, "Some Examples of Poetic Reformulations of Biblical and Midrashic Passages in Liturgy and Piyyut," in *Porat Yosef: Studies Presented to Rabbi Dr. Joseph Safran,* ed. Bezalel Safran and Eliyahu Safran (New York: Ktav, 1992), 217–24, here 220-21. Perhaps, indeed, Qillir discerns, in the very fact that the Mishnah introduces the preliminary process as a flashback, a gesture toward R. Yehudah's position.

received tradition: Were these seven heifers prepared after the red heifer of Ezra (per the sages), or are Moses's and Ezra's heifers the first two of the seven, so that only five were prepared after Ezra (per R. Meir)? The fact that both positions name Ezra reinforces the association of the red heifer ritual with the return from the exile.

Below are excerpts from Qillir's Five, אצילי עם עולי גולה: strophes 1–3, followed by the refrain, then the final strophe, strophe 15. These strophes set the chronological framework for the remainder of the poem.

אצילי עם עולי גולה / כחש בוא קץ גאולה / עלו בנות בית בגילה
לחגי זכריה ומלאכי ניגלה / ולהם אל במחז גילה / קץ זמן פרה ועגלה
ערוך מול גורן עגולה / זאת עשות כחוק מגלה / לטהר טומאת סורה וגולה

1. Princes of the people ascending from exile, / when he sped the arrival of redemption time, / went up to build the house with joy.
2. To Haggai, Zechariah, and Malachi he was revealed, / and to them in a vision revealed / the period and time of the heifer and the calf,
3. To arrange before the threshing round, / to do this like the scroll's law, / to cleanse the impurity of the turned and exiled.

זאת הקשת מאד בעיניהם / איך לטהר בית מעוניהם / וטהור וקדוש האיר עיניהם

(Refrain) This was very difficult in their eyes, / how to cleanse their house of dwelling, / and the Clean and Holy enlightened their eyes.

ריגל מהיר עוד לאיילי / ופרה שנייה עש וחיילי / ונקדש א[לה]ים יי חילי

15. The skilled one hurried to strengthen me, / and made a second heifer, and empowered me, / and God was sanctified—the Lord, my power.

Together, the first set of strophes and the last strophe situate the poem at the return from the Babylonian exile, under the last prophets and Ezra ("the skilled one," after Ezra 7:6), who prepares the ashes of the "second heifer," after Moses's first. The body of the poem rewrites, in the main, the preliminary ritual detailed in m. Parah 3:2–4, with additions from the Tosefta, and the refrain positions this ritual as a solution, divinely revealed, to the problem of purification occasioned—so the poem implies—by the exile. It is probably no coincidence that the final line rhymes the root חי"ל twice; the Mishnah and Tosefta chapters also end with the same root, with the notice that one third of the heifer's ashes were deposited in the חיל, "rampart." By the same token, the reference to פרה ועגלה, "the heifer and the calf," in the first set of strophes appears to allude to the very beginning of the tractate, which opens, as noted above, with R. Eliezer's reference to the ages of the calf and the heifer.[15]

---

15. Qillir reverses the order of the calf and the heifer for the purposes of the rhyme. He does the same in his other *qedushta* for the Sabbath of the red heifer, אצולת אומן, "The division

A glance at another extant *qedushta* for the Sabbath of the red heifer by Qillir, אצולת אומן, "The division of the constant one," sheds light on Qillir's decision to focus the Five on m. Parah 3:2–4. Substantively, the closest analogue to the above Five poem in this other *qedushta* is the Six poem, אמרה סנונה צרופה, "Refined, distilled speech." This Six poem also addresses the ritual in m. Parah 3 and t. Parah 3, but its interest lies in what the burning priest does, rather than in the preliminary ritual that prepares him for his task. Qillir therefore picks up, in this poem, with m. Parah 3:6 and the construction of the ramp whereon the priest walks to the Mount of Olives.[16] A comparison of the two poems thus demonstrates that Qillir recognizes and takes advantage of the twofold division of the ritual narrative in the Mishnah and the Tosefta.

One detail from Qillir's narrative in the Five of our *qedushta* is deserving of special attention.

יעלו משם לבית עזרה / זכים משגיית הרהור זרה / להוציא דשן השמור לעזרה
קנקן החבוי שם בחפירה / מלא מאז אפר פרה / לתשע מאות וששים לתפארה

10. Thence they went up to the courtyard, / innocent of the error of foreign thoughts, / to take out ashes vouchsafed to the courtyard.
11. A jar hidden there by digging / was full from then with the heifer's ashes / for nine hundred and sixty for glory.

In the main, Qillir's account derives from and corresponds to m. Parah 3:3 and t. Parah 3:4, and "nine hundred and sixty" refers, as Shulamit Elizur

---

of the constant one," in the Five, in rewriting the story of Moses and R. Eliezer. It is possible, but I think less likely, that the words פרה ועגלה, "the heifer and the calf," refer to the notion, widespread but also specifically the subject of the Four poem, that the red heifer cleanses from the sin of the golden calf.

16. He also adds, at the beginning of the account, a detail not included in the Mishnah or the Tosefta: the inspection of the red heifer for blemishes. He assigns this role to the sages (זקני גזית תמימי ממום, "the elders of the [chamber of the] hewn [stone], free of blemish"; I cite from the transcription in the online Database of the Academy of the Hebrew Language, Maagarim), who thereby find a place near the beginning of the Six poem of אצולת אומן in the same way that they (under a different spatial moniker, גורן עגולה, "the threshing round") appear at the outset of the Five poem of אחת שאלתי. It is striking that, as the Six in the *qedushta* אצולת אומן focuses on the priest's actions rather than on those of the children, so elsewhere in the same *qedushta* Qillir devotes attention to priests to a degree that he does not in the *qedushta* אחת שאלתי. Thus, the verses immediately following the Two and the Three in both *qedushta'ot*—Num 19:3 and 19:4, respectively—make reference at the outset to Eleazar the priest, but, whereas in אצולת אומן Qillir follows the lead of the verses and makes explicit reference to Eleazar in the final lines of each poem, in the case of אחת שאלתי Qillir manages to make no reference at all, explicit or implicit, to Eleazar. There is additional evidence of the complementarity of the two *qedushta'ot*. The two Seven (*rahiṭ*) poems of אחת שאלתי are structured by the phrase זאת חקת ... לאמר, "This is the statute ... saying," at the beginning of Num 19:2, and ויקחו אליך, "and they shall take to you," in the continuation of the verse, whereas the Seven of אצולת אומן is structured by the header פרה אדומה, "a red heifer," which follows immediately after the words ויקחו אליך, "and they shall take to you." Could it be that אצולת אומן was intended for a priestly congregation, and אחת שאלתי for a non-priestly congregation?

notes in her annotations, to the number of years between, on the one hand, the exodus from Egypt, when Moses ("from then") prepared the ashes contained by the jar, and, on the other hand, the return from the Babylonian exile. But neither the Mishnah nor the Tosefta describes the jar as hidden, or exposed by digging. The Mishnah simply situates it at the פתח, "entrance," to the courtyard, and the Tosefta has it affixed to the wall. Qillir evidently means to claim that the jar containing the ashes of Moses's red heifer was concealed in the ground when the temple was destroyed, and afterward retrieved by the returning exiles.

To my knowledge, this motif is otherwise unattested, and while the offhand way in which Qillir refers to it suggests that he is making use of a source unknown to us, it is possible that he (or his source) derives the motif directly from the Tosefta passage. If R. Shimon believes that the ashes of the red heifer went to Babylon and returned from there, and if R. Yehudah, or the sages speaking for R. Yehudah, believe that this reconstruction is not feasible because the ashes would have been defiled in a foreign land, then R. Yehudah must believe that the ashes remained in the land of Israel. And if they remained there, then someone must have concealed them. This notion aligns the red heifer ashes with other temple objects that, according to Second Temple and rabbinic traditions, angels or prophets or kings or priests concealed in caves or pits at the time of the temple's destruction.[17]

The narrative of the altar fire in 2 Macc 1:18–36 offers an especially close parallel. The altar fire, like the red heifer's ashes, is of less durable stuff than the temple vessels associated with the other legends of concealment.[18] Like the red heifer's ashes, the altar fire (condensed into liquid form) is rediscovered upon the return from Babylon, in this case not by Ezra but by his contemporary Nehemiah. The story in 2 Macc 1 also prom-

17. See 2 Macc 12; Syriac Baruch 6:7–9; y. Ta'an. 2:1, 65a; b. Yoma 52b. On the Second Temple passages, see Steven Weitzman, *Surviving Sacrilege: Cultural Persistence in Jewish Antiquity* (Cambridge, MA: Harvard University Press, 2005), 25–28, 96–117. On the texts above and other relevant rabbinic passages, see Gilad Sasson, "The Presence of the Shekinah in the Second Temple: Between the Scholars of Babylon and Those of Palestine," *Jewish Studies* 48 (2012): 49–71; Ra'anan S. Boustan, "The Dislocation of the Temple Vessels: Mobile Sanctity and the Rabbinic Rhetorics of Space," in *Jewish Studies at the Crossroads of Anthropology and History: Authority, Diaspora, Tradition*, ed. Ra'anan S. Boustan, Oren Kosansky, and Manina Rustow, Jewish Culture and Contexts (Pennsylvania: University of Pennsylvania Press, 2011), 135–46; Menahem Kister, "Aggadic and Midrashic Methods in the Literature of the Second Temple Period and in Rabbinic Literature" [Hebrew], in *Higayon L'Yona: New Aspects in the Study of Midrash, Aggadah and Piyut in Honor of Professor Yona Fraenkel*, ed. Joshua Levinson, Jacob Elbaum, and Galit Hasan-Rokem (Jerusalem: Magnes Press, 2007), 231–60, here 240-41 n. 38.

18. See also, in the rabbinic lists (y. Ta'an. 2:1, 65a; b. Yoma 52b), the manna and the anointing oil, both preserved, like the ashes of the red heifer, in jars.

inently attributes to the fire the capacity to cleanse, which is the chief task of the red heifer's ashes.[19]

In Qillir's *qedushta*, this almost incidental narrative about the concealment and exposure of the ashes interacts with the rhetoric of concealment and exposure of the complex laws concerning the red heifer, a rhetoric that pervades the *qedushta* and its classical rabbinic sources. The claim noted above by R. Aḥa in Pesiq. Rab Kah. 4:7, on the red heifer lection, that things were revealed to R. Akiva and his colleagues that were unknown to Moses, is an example of such rhetoric. Perhaps the most spectacular instance of the same in Qillir's *qedushta* occurs in the first of the Seven poems. The following lines, from the beginning of this poem, are representative.

> זאת חקת אמרת צרופה אשר אסם אל באוצרותיו מלהתבזות / לאמר לבאר לברה ביאור ביקורי תורה זאת
>
> ז[את] ח[קת] גזירת עלי באר אש[ר] גנז גדול בגנזנכיו חקוקה / לא[מר] לדבר דקדוקי דת דרושה על ספר חוקה
>
> "This is the statute" of the distilled speech that God gathered in his storehouses not to be plundered, / "saying": to clarify to the clear one the clarification of the inquiries of this instruction.
>
> "This is the statute" of the decree of the rising well, which the Great one deposited in his deposit as something inscribed, / "saying": to speak the fine points of the law sought, a statute on a book.

Each stich is structured by two headers from Num 19:2: זאת חקת, "This is the statute," and לאמר, "saying." After the fixed header in each hemistich comes the word conditioned by the alphabetical acrostic (אמרת and לבאר in the first and second hemistichs, and גזירת and לדבר in the third and fourth). The poem turns on the contrast between the first header, which characterizes the red heifer law as a חק, and thus (for Qillir) as something obscure or withheld, and the second header, which, as a verb of speech, signifies communication. The two headers, in Qillir's hands, define a dynamic of concealment and exposure of the laws of the red heifer: They were hidden and obscure, but God explained them, at least in part, to Israel ("the clear one," after Song 6:9).

These two passages—R. Aḥa's statement about R. Akiva, and Qillir's Seven—also illustrate the way in which the red heifer's obscurities

---

19. We read also in b. Zebaḥ. 62a about other ashes recovered by the returning exiles. According to R. Isaac Nappaḥa, the exiles were able to discern the location on which to rebuild the altar because the patriarch Isaac's ashes lay there. But there is no indication that Isaac's ashes were concealed. On this passage, see Shalom Spiegel, *The Last Trial: On the Legends and Lore of the Command to Abraham to Offer Isaac as a Sacrifice; The Akedah*, trans. Judah Goldin (1979; repr., Woodstock, VT: Jewish Lights, 1993), 43–44. See also n. 20 below.

become a cipher from the mystery and obscurity of the Torah as such.[20] R. Aḥa's statement does not, in itself, refer to the red heifer. In its context in Pesiq. Rab Kah. 4:7 it does appear to carry such a restricted reference, and this context may be the original one for R. Aḥa's statement. But in the reception of R. Aḥa's statement and the adjoining one about Moses and R. Eliezer analyzed above, the statements lose whatever specificity they possessed and come to concern the entire Torah. As Jeffrey Rubenstein has noted, the famous story in b. Menaḥ. 29b of Moses in heaven and in R. Akiva's academy represents a creative amalgam of the two statements, and the Bavli's story thematizes the oracular ability of R. Akiva to make sense of apparent nonsense not in the red heifer passage specifically but in the Torah in general.[21] In Qillir's Seven, the first word after the first header substitutes for the word התורה, "the instruction (Torah)," in Num 19:2 זאת חקת התורה, "This is the statute of the instruction (Torah)," and most of the terminology that Qillir uses in these lines—אמרת צרופה, "the distilled speech"; גזירת עלי באר, "the decree of the rising well"—and subsequent lines occurs in classical rabbinic literature in relation to the Torah.[22] The poem thus implicitly casts over the Torah as a whole the patina of esotericism that is, for Amoraic and post-Amoraic literature, the defining feature of the red heifer law.[23]

20. See also Novick, "Liturgy and Law," 476–77 n. 4; Yehoshua Granat, "Preexistence in Early Piyyut against the Background of Its Sources" (PhD diss., The Hebrew University in Jerusalem, 2009), 171–80, esp. 173–75. Granat adverts to the relationship between the red heifer laws and the Torah as a whole in order to explain the view, amply attested in classical *piyyuṭ*, according to which the red heifer laws preceded creation. Note in particular the occurrence of the terminology of concealment (גנ"ז, צנ"ע, etc.) in relation to the items that existed before creation, including the red heifer laws, on which see Granat, 172. There thus emerges a certain relationship between the theme of preexistence and the theme of post-destruction concealment: In both cases, special objects are stored away, to be exposed again in their proper time.

21. See Jeffrey L. Rubenstein, *Stories of the Babylonian Talmud* (Baltimore: Johns Hopkins University Press, 2010), 194–95.

22. See Elizur's commentary on these lines, and see also, e.g., lines 35, 41.

23. It is possible that the proposition that the Torah cannot be understood by human beings (save by special divine dispensation) emerged in dialogue with the Christian position that no one is without sin, and thus that no one can be justified (save by divine grace). We note, in particular, that the key prooftext for the inscrutability of the red heifer law in Pesiq. Rab Kah. 4, Job 14:4 מי יתן טהור מטמא לא אחד (understood as: "Who can make a clean thing from an unclean thing? No one other than the One."), is also a key prooftext among many contemporaneous Christian authors for the intrinsic sinfulness of fallen humanity. On the latter, see Joseph Ziegler, *Iob 14,4–5a als wichtigster Schriftbeweis für die These "Neminem sine sorde et sine peccato esse" (Cyprian, test 3, 54) bei den lateinischen christlichen Schriftstellern*, SBAW (Munich: Verlag der bayerischen Akademie der Wissenschaften, 1985). In this light it is notable that Yannai and Qillir both link the red heifer ritual to Eve's transgression. See Shulamit Elizur, "A New Poem by Yannai ha-Hazzan," *Kiryat Sefer* 62 (1989–1990): 867–72; Elizur, "אחת שאלתי," 45–50 (lines 215–76, esp. lines 217–20, paraphrasing Job 14:4, and lines 243–46, on the five types of blood that are also the subject of Yannai's poem).

5. Pinḥas, אור ארבעה עשר, "'At light, on the fourteenth'"

In the case of the above *piyyuṭ* by Qillir, the poet enhances the narrative aspect of a ritual narrative that he finds in the Mishnah by transforming it, following the lead of one thread in the Mishnah itself, into a story from the past. In this final case study, the *payṭan* preserves the rule-like character of the ritual narrative but enhances its narrativity by means of selection and condensation, and by situating the ritual in a broad historical horizon. The poem of interest is a *guf ha-yotser* poem, probably for the Sabbath prior to Passover, אור ארבעה עשר, "'At light, on the fourteenth,'" by Pinḥas, who flourished in the eighth century, thus at the end of the classical period.[24] The poem rewrites and reorganizes parts of Mishnah tractate Pesaḥim.[25] In the appendix I provide a full translation of the *piyyuṭ*, together with notes addressing some aspects of Pinḥas's compositional choices not taken up in the analysis below. The strophe numbers to which I refer below derive from this translation.

The Mishnah tractate itself has a loose but unmistakable chronological organization. The opening pericope describes the search for leaven on the evening of the fourteenth of Nisan, and the first three chapters take up, in this light, the prohibition of leaven. The fourth chapter shifts us to the morning after, by addressing the topic of labor on Passover eve. Chapters 5 through 8 concern the preparation of the Passover sacrifice, which occurs on the afternoon of the eve of Passover. Chapter 9 concerns the Second Passover, an offshoot of the topic of the Passover sacrifice. Finally, chapter 10 details the procedure for the nighttime ritual, the seder.

Pinḥas frames this narrative within world history, from the very beginning of time to the very end. The first two strophes link m. Pesaḥ. 1:1 to the creation of light, which is the subject of the *yotser* liturgy.

אור ארבעה עשר / ביארתה ללוקחי מוסר / לידע בהם הניתר והנאסר

באור חיים לאור / יצאו מחשך לאור / וידעו כי אתה יוצר אור

---

24. For the text, see Shulamit Elizur, *The Liturgical Poems of Rabbi Pinḥas Ha-Kohen: Critical Edition, Introduction and Commentaries* (Jerusalem: World Union of Jewish Studies, 2004), 261–66. Elizur identifies the poem as intended for the first day of Passover, but in the introduction (ibid., 23–24) she puts forward the Sabbath before Passover as an alternative possibility. The content seems to me to favor the latter. This possibility gains further support from the fact that a relatively early medieval poem written for the Sabbath before Passover, אדיר דר מתוחים, "Mighty one, sky-dweller," closely depends on Pinḥas's poem. On this dependence, see n. 42 below.

25. Pinḥas's poem אומנם פסח מצה ומרורים, "Indeed, the Passover, matzah, and bitter herbs" (Elizur, *Liturgical Poems of Rabbi Pinḥas Ha-Kohen*, 286–88), intended for a "*qerova* eighteen" for the intermediate days of Passover, extensively overlaps with the poem of interest, and represents, I suspect, an abridgment thereof.

1. "At light, on the fourteenth" / you clarified for the discipline-receivers, / to make known among them the permitted and the forbidden.
2. Lit by the light of life, / they left from darkness to light / and knew that you are the fashioner of light.

The first stich of strophe 1 is a quotation from m. Pesaḥ. 1:1, which specifies the evening (אור "light") of the fourteenth as the time of inspection for leaven.[26] Pinḥas finds in this "light" elements of the light of redemption from Egypt, and more elementally, the light of the first day of creation. The body of the poem, on which more below, is devoted to the laws and rites of Passover eve and of Passover, but at the end, in strophe 21, Pinḥas returns to the arc of history.

שומרי פסח כזאת / פסח אחרון יזכו לחזות / לשמוח במועדי מי זאת

21. They who observe a Passover like this / will merit to see the last Passover / to rejoice in the festivals of "who is this."

This messianic peroration closes the historical trajectory introduced by the opening lines. This trajectory, from creation to the exodus to the messianic age, partly overlaps with that in the refrain strophe.

פסח יעשו ננצרים / חדרי סוף הטבעו כל הצרים / נער כן שונאים וצוררים

The well-guarded ones make the Passover. / In Suf's chambers all the enemies were drowned. / Thus to disturb enemies and foes.

The refrain links the past redemption from Egypt with the future downfall of Israel's current oppressors and projects this trajectory through the performance, in the liturgical present, of the Passover ritual to which the body of the poem is devoted.

In the body of the poem, Pinḥas rearranges selections from the Mishnah tractate to yield a more cohesive and dense ritual narrative. He begins, as the Mishnah does (m. Pesaḥ. 1:4, 2:1), with the limitations on consumption of leaven on the morning of Passover eve, and the disposition of remaining leaven; to this topic he devotes strophes 4–6. At this point comes a significant deviation from the Mishnah's organization, as Pinḥas shifts, in strophes 7–11, to the scene of the women making unleavened bread, described in m. Pesaḥ. 3:4–5. In the Mishnah, the preparation of the matzot by the women does not belong to a ritual series; it appears as a self-standing set of actions, one among many that the rabbis comment

26. I have translated it *as* a quotation, so that Pinḥas means to say that God conveyed "At light, on the fourteenth," that is, Mishnah Pesaḥim, to Israel, to teach the nation the laws of Passover.

on because it implicates the concern about avoidance of leaven that is the topic of the first three chapters. Pinḥas transforms the scene into the next stage in the process of preparation for Passover, זמן מצות שלשים, "the time for kneading the matzot," and devotes to it five strophes, almost a quarter of the entire composition. He appears to assume what was presumably the case, that women would prepare matzot in the afternoon of the eve of Passover, after the disposition of all the leaven.

Afterward, in strophes 12 and 13, Pinḥas takes up m. Pesaḥ. 2:7, on other cases wherein manipulation of wheat products can lead to leavening. These cases, too, feature women. Following a brief reflection, in strophes 14–15, on the scope of the prohibition of work on Passover eve, the subject of m. Pesaḥ. 4, Pinḥas shifts, in strophes 16–18, to the nighttime meal, the subject of the tenth chapter of the tractate. In so shifting he omits reference to the preparation of the Passover sacrifice, the subject of chapters 5–9 of the tractate, evidently because these laws are inapplicable to his audience. Indeed, we may reasonably suppose that Pinḥas has introduced the baking of matzot in place of the preparation of the Passover sacrifice as the event in the ritual sequence that occupies the afternoon of Passover.

Strophe 19 concerns the seven days of Passover as a whole, and the prohibition against possessing leaven during this period. This strophe, which appears to depend on m. Pesaḥ. 9:5, enables Pinḥas to move the narrative forward, from the nighttime meal to the following seven days.[27] In strophe 20, Pinḥas takes up the Second Passover, the subject of m. Pesaḥ. 9:1–4; this strophe gives Pinḥas occasion to progress to the second month of the year. Finally, with strophe 21, quoted above, the narrative hastens to its messianic conclusion.[28]

Conclusion

These soundings in the reception history of the Mishnah have identified different ways in which the homiletical literature and liturgical poetry of late antique Palestine appreciate this canonical text, and especially the rit-

27. For Pinḥas's dependence on m. Pesah. 9:5, see the Appendix on strophes 17, 19, and 20.

28. The two case studies above from classical *piyyuṭ* concern Mishnah Parah and Mishnah Pesaḥim, but there are other important renderings of the Mishnah in *piyyuṭ*, first and foremost the *Avodah* genre, for the Day of Atonement, which describes the day's sacrificial ritual in heavy dependence on Mishnah Yoma. On this genre, see Michael D. Swartz and Joseph Yahalom, *Avodah: Ancient Poems for Yom Kippur*, Penn State Library of Jewish Literature (University Park: Pennsylvania State University Press, 2005). Notable, too, is the use of the chain of tradition in m. 'Abot 1 in a *silluq* by Qillir for Shavuot, אלה החוקים, "These are the statutes." See Shulamit Elizur, *Rabbi El'azar Birabbi Kiliri: Hymni Pentecostales* (Jerusalem: Mekize Nirdamim, 2000), 240–47.

ual narratives therein, as narratives. In Pesiq. Rab Kah. 8:1 (137), R. Abin, reflecting on the *'omer* ritual narrative as history, links it to verbally dense accounts of agricultural and natural processes. Leviticus Rabbah 15:8 (335–37) finds in two pericopes of Mishnah Nega'im a nexus of motifs—inspection of women, inspection of relatives—that calls to mind the story of Miriam in Num 12. The very phenomenon of quoted rabbinic speech, which is pervasive in the Mishnah but takes a distinctive form in m. Parah 1:1, appears to serve as the foundation of a story in Pesiq. Rab Kah. 4:7. Qillir rewrites part of the ritual narrative in Mishnah Parah by locating it at a particular moment in the past. Finally, in a *yotser* for the Sabbath before Passover, Pinḥas, through the application of a historical frame and careful selection and elaboration, intensifies the narrativity of the loose ritual narrative that is Mishnah Pesaḥim.

Appendix

1. Qillir, אצילי עם עולי גולה, *"Princes of the people ascending from exile"*

For the Hebrew text, see Shulamit Elizur, "אחת שאלתי", קדושתא לשבת פרה לר' אלעזר בירבי קיליר, *Qoveṣ al Yad* n.s. 10 (1982): 36–39. From a formal perspective, the poem is a *qiqlar*. Each strophe contains three lines. Each set of three strophes is internally unified by a common rhyme and is followed by the refrain.[29] The poem is structured by a name acrostic composed of the first letter of each strophe. The numbered lines below each represent a strophe.

1. Princes of the people ascending from exile, / when he sped the arrival of redemption time, / went up to build the house with joy.
2. To Haggai, Zechariah, and Malachi he was revealed, / and to them in a vision revealed / the period and time of the heifer and the calf,
3. To arrange before the threshing round,[30] / to do this like the scroll's law, / to cleanse the impurity of the turned and exiled.

This was very difficult in their eyes, / how to cleanse their house of dwelling, / and the Clean and Holy enlightened their eyes, H[oly One].

4. They plotted to build courtyards / constructed on flinty rock, / fortified against defilement from the abyss.

---

29. See Shulamit Elizur, "Position and Structure of the Qiqlar in the Qillirian Qedushta," *Jerusalem Studies in Hebrew Literature* 3 (1983): 140–55. As Elizur notes (149), using the fourth three-strophe block (lines 10–12) of this very *qedushta,* in some cases the unifying rhyme is the final syllable alone, and the additional trailing consonant that characterizes the "Qillirian rhyme" varies from strophe to strophe.

30. The "threshing round" is the Sanhedrin; see m. Sanh. 4:3.

5. They conducted thither women with child. / Therein they were born and therein nurtured / until they grew in strength like heroes.
6. Once they bloomed into people of words / they brought to them mighty oxen, / to contain within them heroic children.
7. They made platforms upon their backs, / like a man at his banner for signs, / to go along the way to the Shiloaḥ,
8. So that they not stretch a leg outside the platforms, / so as not to be tented with death defilement,/ so as to guard by law the details of cleanness.
9. In their hands, stone cups to fill, / to use them to draw holy water, / to raise purifying waters for those in their time.
10. Thence they went up to the courtyard, / innocent of the error of foreign thoughts, / to take out ashes vouchsafed to the courtyard.
11. A jar hidden there by digging / was full from then with the heifer's ashes / for nine hundred and sixty for glory.[31]
12. They brought a ram horned for the purpose, / on its head a rope and a clean stick, / for cleansing this, the keeper of vineyards.[32]
13. They took from the dust in the vessel, / and cleansed and sanctified my glorious sanctum, / by the counsel of the red wine.[33]
14. They knew the force of my conducted song,[34] / and washed and scoured all my assembly, / and bound with a bandage my sad sickness.
15. The skilled one[35] hurried to strengthen me, / and made a second heifer, and empowered me, / and God, the Lord, my power, was sanctified.

2. Pinḥas, אור ארבעה עשר*, "'At light, on the fourteenth'"*

For the Hebrew text, see Shulamit Elizur, *The Liturgical Poems of Rabbi Pinḥas Ha-Kohen: Critical Edition, Introduction and Commentaries* (Jerusalem: World Union of Jewish Studies, 2004), 261–66. On the structure of the *guf ha-yotser* genre in Pinḥas's work, see ibid., 120–26, esp. 123–25. In brief, this *piyyuṭ*, too, like Qillir's above, is a *qiqlar*. Each strophe contains three lines. Each set of three strophes tends to be thematically unified, but the three strophes do not share a common rhyme. After each three-strophe

31. As Elizur clarifies, the nine hundred and sixty years are from the exodus from Egypt, when Moses prepared the first red heifer ashes, to the return from the Babylonian exile.

32. The "keeper of vineyards" is Israel, after Song 1:6.

33. Elizur identifies "red wine" as the Torah, but the rabbinic source she cites, Gen. Rab. 98:10 (1261), seems rather to interpret it as the Sanhedrin. Cf. strophe 3.

34. The "conducted song" is an allusion to Ps 5:1. Elizur ventures that the reference is to the Torah, a suggestion supported by Midrash Tehillim *ad loc*. The subject is presumably the Sanhedrin.

35. Ezra, after Ezra 7:6, the head of the Sanhedrin.

block comes the refrain. A name acrostic, composed of the first letter of each strophe, extends across the entire *piyyuṭ*. The numbered lines below each represent a strophe.

1. "At light, on the fourteenth" / you clarified for the discipline-receivers, / to make known among them the permitted and the forbidden.
2. Lit by the light of life, / they left from darkness to light / and knew that you are the fashioner of light.
3. The redeemed from the rebel land / must mention on the guarded night / the Passover, the matzah, and the bitter herbs.

The well-guarded ones make the Passover. / In Suf's chambers all the enemies were drowned. / Thus to disturb enemies and foes [Holy One].

4. The beloved who eat leaven, / on the fourteenth should not eat, / and if they are accustomed to eat, they eat.
5. All four hours they eat, / and in the fifth, suspend, and in the sixth, burn in fire, / and are liable to death if in the afternoon they eat.
6. And the rest they burn as commanded, / or cast it to the wind as they desire, / or throw it into the sea.

7. At the time for kneading the matzot, / the holy flock was warned / that three women should work.
8. To avert leaven in the dough, / each should bend toward the other, / one kneading, one setting, and one baking.
9. If it swells she should beat it with cold water, / being careful and cautious not to neglect it, / and baker's water she should pour out and neglect.[36]
10. They should see: If the kneading fermented, / and leavened like grasshopper horns, / they should discard it, to be healed from pain,
11. Unless there is fissure in it / that stops short of the other fissure's head, / whereon one may be justified.
12. One shouldn't chew wheat to put aside / and place on a wound with counsel, / because it becomes leaven.[37]
13. Bran for chickens / a woman should not soak in the usual way / on the joyous festivals.

---

36. The reference to baker's water occurs in m. Pesaḥ. 2:8, without any connection to the baking women of m. Pesaḥ. 3:4, or to the process of matzah preparation. Pinḥas links m. Pesaḥ. 2:8 to m. Pesaḥ. 3:4 on the strength of the reference in both pericopes to water.

37. This law occurs at the end of m. Pesaḥ. 2:7. As noted in passing in the body of the essay, it is likely that Pinḥas selected it because of the preceding law in the same pericope, which is the subject of strophe 13, and which is concerned, like the scene in strophes 7–11, with women.

14. One is liable to be rebuked / who does work on the fourteenth / according to the transmitted law,
15. To designate barbers, tailors, and launderers, / and shoemakers to cut and design, / because they are for the festival's purpose.[38]
16. Those ascending from Egypt baked the dough trays, / for thirty days ate what they bound, / to direct in them a commandment for the generations.
17. The Passover of Egypt was distinguished / to note its taking on the tenth. / We note it with cedar wood and hyssop.[39]
18. The careful ones are wise about the Passover, / and where they are accustomed to eat roasted they should eat roasted, / and if they are not accustomed they should not.
19. Fix seven days for your generations, / to inspect on Passover in your tents, / lest sourdough be found in your homes.[40]
20. To do the desired Second Passover is pleasant: / The single nation was permitted / to mingle matzah with leavened bread.[41]

---

38. I.e., these professions are exceptions to the rule against work on the fourteenth. Why Pinḥas should single out this law, from m. Pesaḥ. 4:6, is not altogether clear. My hunch is that Pinḥas was drawn to the fact that the sages explicitly number "three professions"—tailors, barbers, and launderers—that may practice their craft on the eve of Passover. (R. Yose b. R. Judah adds shoemakers.) Two other numbered lists of three from the Mishnah—the "three things" of m. Pesaḥ. 10:5 that must be explained at the seder and the "three women" of m. Pesaḥ. 3:4 who prepare the matzah—also occupy prominent places in the poem, in strophe 3 and in strophes 7ff. Cf. too the triplets in strophe 5 (based on m. Pesaḥ. 1:4) and strophe 6 (based on m. Pesaḥ. 2:1). Likely, the *qiqlar* structure, which is defined by triplets, encouraged Pinḥas to seek out triplets in the Mishnah. It is noteworthy too, that in another narrow but strikingly well-attested genre in the corpus of Qillir, the *shiv'ata* for Passover eve that falls out on the third day of the week, the Mishnah occasionally (but in fact, in the attested corpus, relatively rarely) becomes a source for topically desirable references to the number three. See Shulamit Elizur, "Shivatot by Kalir for Passover Eve according to the Day of the Week," in *Professor Meir Benayahu Memorial Volume, vol. 2: Studies in Kabbalah, Jewish Thought, Liturgy, Piyut, and Poetry* (2 vols.; ed. Moshe Bar-Asher et al.; Jerusalem: Yad ha-Rav Nissim, 2019), 979–1003, esp. 986 n. 24. Note, too, a general affinity for numbers in Pinḥas's poem, as in the occurrence of the number thirty in strophe 16, the number ten in strophe 17, and the number seven in strophe 19. Compare Pinḥas's *qiqlar* (possibly the *guf ha-yoṣer*, possibly for a *qedushta*) for the Sabbath (Elizur, *Liturgical Poems*, 537–41), which begins with a triplet (אכן שלוש אותות "indeed three signs") and incorporates other threes, and other numbers.

39. This strophe derives from m. Pesaḥ. 9:5. Pinḥas likely adduces it both to reinforce the historical horizon of the poem and because the end of the pericope observes that the "Passover of generations" occurs for seven days, the subject of strophe 19.

40. See m. Pesaḥ. 9:5 (per MS Kaufmann): ופסח דורות נוהג כל שבעה, "The Passover of the generations holds all seven days." Pinḥas borrows the number and the word דורות, "generations."

41. By noting in strophe 19, following m. Pesaḥ. 9:5, that the Passover of the generations entails a seven-day leaven prohibition, Pinḥas can transition to the Second Passover, which, according to m. Pesaḥ. 9:3, is distinguished from the standard Passover (of the generations) by the fact that it does not entail any sort of prohibition on leaven ownership.

21. They who observe a Passover like this / will merit to see the last Passover / to rejoice in the festivals of "who is this."[42]

42. "Who is this" is Israel, after Song 3:6. In light of the extent and systematicity of Pinḥas's rewriting of Mishnah Pesaḥim, it becomes clear that another, perhaps not much later poem for the Sabbath before Passover, אדיר דר מתוחים, "Mighty one, sky-dweller," depends on Pinḥas's poem, for this later poem mirrors at various points the structure of Pinḥas's poem, but without the same direct interaction with the Mishnah, and without the same intrinsic logic. Thus, in אדיר דר מתוחים, after the poem reviews the laws on disposing of leaven (line 136; I depend for the text and line numbering on Maagarim), it introduces, like Pinḥas in strophe 7 of his poem, the scene of the women baking (lines 141ff.). The end of the baking scene (lines 151–52) tracks Pinḥas's strophe 9, lines 1–2. The next lines (153–56) turn to the baker's water, as in strophe 9, line 3 of Pinḥas's' poem, and then (lines 157–60) to the topic of medicinal use of leaven, following Pinḥas's strophe 12. Afterward, the poem moves on, again in the footsteps of Pinḥas, to the seder scene. Note finally that lines 65–68 of the later poem closely track Pinḥas's strophe 1. On אדיר דר מתוחים, see generally Katrin Kogman-Appel, *A Mahzor from Worms: Art and Religion in a Medieval Jewish Community* (Cambridge, MA: Harvard University Press, 2012), 57–58.

The Iridescence of Scripture

*Inner-Talmudic Interpretation and Palestinian Midrash**

JAMES ADAM REDFIELD

> There is always, in a text, something unnoticed which haunts us, a key-word which obsesses us.
>
> —Edmond Jabès, "The Key"

Methodological Introduction

Nonlegal engagement with Scripture (midrash aggada) in the Babylonian Talmud (Bavli) is often acknowledged to differ from that of contemporary Palestinian rabbinic works, but there is no consensus on how or why.[1] Two older positions at least enjoyed the aura of simplicity: the Bavli is either better or worse in this department. Zecharias Frankel praised the lyricism of Bavli aggada and liturgy as well as the critical spirit in which Babylonian sages received Palestinian traditions;[2] yet only by contrast to the Palestinian Talmud, not to Palestinian works of midrash. A decade later, Isaac Hirsch Weiss added various dichotomies between the two regions, suggesting that Palestinians simply had to engage in aggada, because Scripture loomed so large in local inter-/intra-religious polemics.[3] By contrast, since Wilhelm

*For Drs. Anna, Jessica, and Mark Siegler, who counted a golem in their minyan.

1. This lacuna is signaled in a standard reference: Marc Hirshman, "Aggadic Midrash," in *The Literature of the Sages*, ed. Shmuel Safrai et al., 2 vols., CRINT 2.3 (Minneapolis: Fortress, 2006), 107–32, here 130. My epigraph is from Edmond Jabès, "The Key," trans. Rosmarie Waldrop, in *Midrash and Literature*, ed. Geoffrey H. Hartman and Sanford Budick (New Haven: Yale University Press, 1986), 349–61, here 360.

2. Zecharias Frankel, *Einleitung in den Jerusalemischen Talmud* [Hebrew] (Breslau: Schletter, 1870), 49a–51a. All translations are mine unless otherwise noted. If a Hebrew work has a title-page in another language, I cite it, followed by [Hebrew].

3. Isaac Hirsch Weiss, *Dor dor vedorshav*, 3 vols. (Berlin, 1883), 3:28–31. Hirsch cites an aphorism (m. 'Abot 2:14: "Be diligent in studying Torah; and know what to answer an Epicurean"), but only late witnesses support the translation "*in order to* know …"; see Shimon

Bacher,[4] others have stressed that relatively few original contributions to aggada are attributed to named Babylonian sages of the talmudic era (Amoraim), attributions declining sharply after the third century. This statistic, coupled with the heavy use of Palestinian sources in the aggada of the Bavli, was attributed to a loss of interest in aggada in Babylonia. A few biting quotations became *loci classici* for the view,[5] partly due to Leopold Zunz,[6] that

---

Sharvit, *Language and Style of Tractate Avoth through the Ages* [Hebrew] (Beer-Sheva: Ben-Gurion University of the Negev Press, 2006), 82. See also b. 'Abod. Zar. 4a: "[The heretics] said to [R. Abbahu]: 'How are you different [from the Babylonian rabbis], that you know [about Scripture]?' He replied, 'We, who are found among all of you, take it upon ourselves to investigate; they do not investigate.'" For this general approach to Palestinian midrash, see Marc Hirshman, *A Rivalry of Genius: Jewish and Christian Biblical Interpretation in Late Antiquity*, trans. Batya Stein, SUNY Series in Judaica [Albany: State University of New York Press, 1996], with literature at 123). For a study of the Bavli's polemics around Scripture in light of *intra*-Christian debates, see Michal Bar-Asher Siegal, *Jewish-Christian Dialogues on Scripture in Late Antiquity: Heretic Narratives of the Babylonian Talmud* (Cambridge: Cambridge University Press, 2019).

4. Wilhelm Bacher, *Die agada der babylonischen Amoräer* (Budapest: Landes-Rabbinerschule, 1878), 147: "Since the time of Ashi [mid-fifth century—JR], we cannot identify a single Babylonian Amora under whose name a memorable exegesis or even an explanation of an earlier aggada has been preserved. Engagement with the aggada was restricted to the preservation and arrangement of the dicta that had been transmitted in the study-houses up to that point." Perhaps "one or another aggadic statement" was added to the Bavli at the end of the Amoraic period, before it was "established as a literary work," and "perhaps some element of the still-developing and expanding aggadah of Palestine" reached the Babylonian study-houses. "But the desire and ability to produce aggadah had come to an end long before the transition from the time of the Amoraim to that of the Savoraim was fully complete." David Weiss Halivni conceded this point to Bacher (*The Formation of the Babylonian Talmud*, ed. and trans. Jeffrey L. Rubenstein [Oxford: Oxford University Press, 2013], 216 n. 66: "*aggadah* finds no place in [the] literary endeavors" of the Bavli's post-Amoraic anonymous redactors [i.e., the "Stammaim"]). Within this general perspective, a more complex picture was already emerging in E. E. Halevi, *Sha'arei ha-aggadah*, 2nd ed. (Tel-Aviv: Dvir, 1982), 3–4. On Halivni's position, see Shamma Friedman, "A Good Story Deserves Retelling," in *Creation and Composition: The Contribution of the Bavli Redactors (Stammaim) to the Aggadah*, ed. Jeffrey L. Rubenstein, TSAJ 114 (Tübingen: Mohr Siebeck, 2006), 71–100, here 72 n. 9.

5. For example, the Babylonians are "coarse in spirit and meagre in Torah" (y. Pesaḥ. 5:3, 32a): editor's note to Leopold Zunz, *Ha-derashot be-yisrael*, ed. and trans. Ḥanokh Albeck (Jerusalem: Mosad Bialik, 1947), 449 n. 5; Abraham Heschel, *Heavenly Torah as Refracted through the Generations*, ed. and trans. Gordon Tucker (New York: Continuum, 2006), 16; Joseph Heinemann, *Aggadah and Its Development* [Hebrew] (Jerusalem: Keter, 1974), 163; Avigdor Shinan, *The World of the Aggadah* (Tel-Aviv: MOD, 1990), 22 (his position [11–22] is reprised in Shinan, "The Late Midrashic, Paytanic, and Targumic Literature," in *The Cambridge History of Judaism*, 4th ed., ed. Steven T. Katz [Cambridge: Cambridge University Press, 2006], 678–98, here 679: "aggadic, poetic, and targumic creativity is the heritage almost solely of the Land of Israel"). For other *loci classici* to this effect, see Marc Hirshman and Tamar Kadari, "*Midrash Aggadah*," in *The Classic Rabbinic Literature of Eretz Israel: Introductions and Studies*, 2 vols. [Hebrew], ed. Menaḥem Kahana et al. (Jerusalem: Yad Ben-Zvi, 2018), 2:511–52, here 511 (epigraph), 549.

6. Leopold Zunz, *Die gottesdienstlichen Vorträge der Juden, historisch entwickelt* (Berlin: Asher, 1832), 308. Yet Zunz (336–42) also noted two aspects of Babylonian aggada, includ-

the Bavli's creators willfully subordinated aggada to their privileged legal discourse (halakha), distorting their aggadic sources by subjecting them to methods of dialectic and analysis properly reserved for law.[7]

Thirty years ago, Yaakov Sussmann issued a valuable corrective to both positions by rejecting their shared assumption of a linear chronological (d)evolution from Palestinian to Babylonian corpora and, indeed, any linear or quantitative model for comparing midrash aggada in the two regions:

> Recently, various scholars have dealt with certain fundamental questions regarding Bavli aggada–its sources, circulation, and comparison to Palestinian parallels–from both historical ... and literary perspectives.... Yet it seems to me that in this area, too, the long time spans have not been sufficiently taken into account; nor do there seem to be any definite grounds to draw a total, basic, and essential distinction between halakha and aggada in this respect. The Amoraic source material (both Palestinian and Babylonian—within one literary framework or another) continues to flourish, circulate, and develop in Babylonia over a very long period.[8]

Beginning with the studies to which Sussmann referred,[9] three methods have yielded more apt characterizations of midrash aggada in the

---

ing later (sixth- to eighth-century) sources, that fostered its appreciation in later research: (1) the intimate coevolution of aggada and targum (see bibliography of Avigdor Shinan in Dalia Marx and Gila Vachman eds., *Alfei Shinan* [Tel-Aviv: Yediot Sefarim, 2014], 382–91); (2) the continued popularity of aggada and its combinations with halakha in public settings, e.g., itinerant preaching (Bacher, *Die agada,* 65) or public sermons (Isaiah Gafni, *The Jews of Babylonia in the Talmudic Era: A Social and Cultural History* [Hebrew] [Jerusalem: Shazar Center, 1990], 204–13); Yaakov Elman, "The World of the 'Sabboraim': Cultural Aspects of Post-Redactional Additions to the Bavli," in Rubenstein, *Creation and Composition,* 383–415, here 394–95.

7. A classic statement is Heinemann, *Aggadah and Its Development,* 163–79, citing the Bavli's elimination of whole narrative forms like the parable (163); limited "'conception of facticity' of *aggadic* matters" (165, 170); lack of lyricism, play, and creativity (174); errors due to ignorance or apologetics (179); and, above all, its reduction of the aggada to methods of interpretation of halakha (168, 170, 174). But, it was noted early on, we can at least compare attitudes toward Scripture in the Mishnah that bear on the attitude of the Bavli: see David Kraemer, "Scripture Commentary in the Babylonian Talmud: Primary or Secondary Phenomenon?," *AJSR* 14 (1989): 1–15.

8. Yaakov Sussmann, "Ve-shuv li-yerushalmi neziqin," in *Talmudic Studies I* [Hebrew], ed. Yaakov Sussmann and David Rosenthal (Jerusalem: Magnes, 1990), 1:55–133, here 100–101 n. 186.

9. Especially Shamma Friedman, "Regarding Historical *aggadah* in the Babylonian Talmud," repr. in his *Talmudic Studies: Investigating the Sugya, Variant Readings, and Aggada* [Hebrew] (New York: Jewish Theological Seminary of America, 2010), 389–432; and the English version, "Literary Development and Historicity in the Aggadic Narrative of the Babylonian Talmud: A Study Based upon B.M. 83b-86a," in *Community and Culture: Essays in Jewish Studies in Honor of the Ninetieth Anniversary of the Founding of Gratz College, 1895–1985,*

Bavli: source, redaction, and literary criticism (what I will call simply "poetics").[10] Signs of progress on our question abound. It is less burdened by tendentious hierarchies between Palestine and Babylonia. The distinctive history and forms of Babylonia's literary production are better appreciated, including the importance of its anonymous Talmud (making a mere tally of dicta attributed to Babylonians a dubious criterion for creativity).[11] Great strides have been made in comparing the aggada of the Bavli to that of Palestinian corpora.[12] However, beyond the larger space allotted to Babylonian tales of the sages than to midrash aggada,[13] our view of the latter's distinctiveness is further blocked by inattention to the core of Sussmann's corrective: the "long time spans" surrounding the Bavli's composition. Poeticians no longer trumpet J. Fränkel's Gadamerian hermeneutic of "closure/*Geschlossenheit*," isolating the message of each talmudic story

ed. Nahum M. Waldman (Philadelphia: Gratz College, 1987), 67–80. See also Friedman, "On the Historical Character of Dama ben Netinah: A Study in Talmudic Aggadah" [Hebrew], repr. in his *Talmudic Studies*, 433–74 [originally published 2006].

10. On defining the scope of talmudic "literary" criticism, see Jeffrey L. Rubenstein, *Talmudic Stories: Narrative Art, Composition, and Culture* (Baltimore: Johns Hopkins University Press, 1999), 26–27. I do not deal with form criticism here, because so far its exemplary applications relate less directly to our question than do studies employing the other three methods.

11. Rubenstein, *Creation and Composition*; Joshua Levinson, *The Twice Told Tale: A Poetics of the Exegetical Narrative in Rabbinic Midrash* [Hebrew] (Jerusalem: Magnes, 2005), 278–307; Moulie Vidas, *Tradition and the Formation of the Talmud* (Princeton, NJ: Princeton University Press, 2014), esp. 81–114.

12. Sarit Kattan Gribetz, "Between Narrative and Polemic: The Sabbath in Genesis Rabbah and the Babylonian Talmud," in *Genesis Rabbah in Text and Context*, ed. Sarit Kattan Gribetz et al., TSAJ 166 (Tübingen: Mohr Siebeck, 2016), 33–61; see further literature in James Adam Redfield, "Redacting Culture: Ethnographic Authority in the Talmudic Arrival Scene," *Jewish Social Studies* 22 (2016): 29–80, here 78 n. 124; and a classic study by Daniel Sperber, "On the Unfortunate Adventures of Rav Kahana: A Passage of Saboraic Polemic from Sasanian Persia," in *Irano-Judaica I*, ed. Shaul Shaked and Amnon Netzer (Jerusalem: Yad Ben-Zvi, 1982), 83–100.

13. In major new edited volumes (Rubenstein, *Creation and Composition*; Ronit Nikolsky and Tal Ilan, eds., *Rabbinic Traditions between Palestine and Babylonia*, AJEC 89 [Leiden: Brill, 2014]; Geoffrey Herman and Jeffrey L. Rubenstein, eds., *The Aggada of the Bavli and Its Cultural World*, BJS 362 [Providence, RI: Brown Judaic Studies, 2018]), only three essays focus on Babylonian midrash aggada, and there is little about it in the other contributions, compared to tales of the sages. Granted, prooftexts and exegesis often play a role in tales of the sages, but Bavli midrash aggada goes far beyond this. Eliezer Segal (*From Sermon to Commentary: Expounding the Bible in Talmudic Babylonia*, Studies in Christianity and Judaism 17 [Waterloo, ON: Wilfrid Laurier University Press, 2005]) offers a thoroughly negative view of the Bavli in contrast to Palestinian midrash aggada: pointless (12), obscure (18), non-homiletical (34, 59), "laconic" (46), "awkward and incomplete" (59), "arbitrary-looking" (76), etc.. Levinson paints a more creative portrait: by decoupling verses from their scriptural context and fusing independent narratives with received exegetical traditions, the Bavli achieves "thickening of the plot via its internal narative logic" (*Twice Told Tale*, 262) unlike Palestinian midrash, which regrounds sources in a wider construal of the context of Scripture.

not only from historical contexts but even from intertexts (see conclusion below). Yet poetics does tend toward synchronic argumentation, as evidenced by ubiquitous disclaimers that a literary reading of the text is not based on a particular historical context, and neither precludes, nor is constrained by, earlier or contemporaneous forms of the same text.[14] Even source criticism is typically a means to an end: the text's "final" redaction. Source criticism and redaction criticism often align in a pyramid: by identifying and comparing the uses of sources, a scholar sheds light on the intention of redactors of one or more "final" products. That intention, in turn, is often assumed to be mirrored in how the text was received by the audience, sometimes figured by early (albeit still much later!) medieval commentators. Not often do such studies circle back to the alternative kind of source criticism that will be developed here: a method that asks how a redacted text can become, in turn, a source for new interpretations of the same material within the Bavli canon.[15] Redaction critics, for their part, often mark "layers" in a particular unit of Bavli aggada, acknowledging the possibility of "influence" among adjacent or disparate Bavli passages. Sometimes they suggest the mechanisms of the influence,[16] but

14. See, e.g., Mira Beth Wasserman, *Jews, Gentiles, and Other Animals: The Talmud after the Humanities*, Divinations (Philadelphia: University of Pennsylvania Press, 2017), 22–23. Contrast the integration of source criticism with literary criticism in Barry Scott Wimpfheimer, *Narrating the Law: A Poetics of Talmudic Legal Stories*, Divinations (Philadelphia: University of Pennsylvania Press, 2011), 24, 167.

15. Friedman, for example, frames the Bavli's changes with respect to Palestinian sources in terms of the agency of the "composer(s) of the Gemara" ("Regarding Historical *aggadah*," 390, 392), whom he sometimes presents as composing directly from earlier sources like those still attested in Palestinian works or in other parts of the Bavli (408, 412). Many of the changes that he analyzes come to an end in the Bavli before us; later commentators serve him to point up contradictions in the Bavli that are due to lack of harmonization of sources (404). At the same time, Friedman identifies phenomena that I will use to track *longue-durée* interaction *between* units within the Bavli: distinctive ways of reworking Amoraic sources, shared with Palestinian midrash (397); shifts in language/style such as repetitions of rare words/phrases, which he agrees point to ongoing integration of Bavli *sugyot* (412-13). To take another example, Friedman cautions against speaking of variant "traditions" ("Dama ben Netinah," 455 n. 102; see also Friedman, "Regarding Historical *aggadah*," 429–30). Instead he reconstructs three chronological stages (history, halakha, and pure fiction) redacted into a single Bavli text ("Dama ben Netinah," 468-69). At the same time, he identifies Bavli mechanisms for reworking Palestinian sources (e.g., the use of transition words, 440 n. 121; changes of names or the doubling/collapsing of characters, 446) that I will also use in order to track the coevolution and reception of sources *within* the Bavli canon, even after its editors have reworked earlier layers of material.

16. E.g. Friedman, "Regarding Historical *aggadah*," 413 n. 152: Amoraim themselves transmitted stories about certain Tannaim, which were later bundled together with stories about those same Amoraim, until eventually they came to rest in the Gemara. Alternatively, a Gemara's composer himself compiled material about named rabbis into collections (413, 401–2); or a Bavli text is based on a specific text elsewhere in the Bavli, rather than both deriving from a common source (422).

we still do not have a formal method for showing how units were recomposed and revised during their inner-canonical reception.[17] In many cases, we are left to imagine how the "final" text, even after it was shaped from earlier sources, continued to circulate under the tectonic pressure of other texts in the canon: both earlier and later, of both Palestinian and Babylonian origin, both in the Bavli and in other midrashic corpora. Attention to the literary unit or *sugya*—the usual frame of inquiry in all three methods,[18] but one with under-specified literary and conceptual borders—thus tends to yield a new hermeneutic closure. The text is no longer isolated from contexts or intertexts, but it remains *the* text: the vehicle of one intentional message, at least at the privileged stage that it comes together as a redacted whole. Undoing this holism requires a new methodology.

To that end, recent studies,[19] including this one, lean more heavily on Sussmann's point that the centuries-long reception of Bavli texts is part and parcel of how we read its "final" products.[20] Rather than bracket out

17. Analysis of inner-talmudic interpretation is more advanced in work on halakha; see, e.g., Vered Noam, "'The Later Rabbis Add and Innovate': On the Development of a Talmudic *Sugya*" [Hebrew], *Tarbiṣ* 72 (2002–2003): 151–75. For excellent examples of how the process unfolds in Bavli aggada due to a textual crux or ideological split, respectively, see David Rosenthal, "'Al ha-qitsur ve-hashlamato: Pereq be-'arikhat ha-talmud ha-bavli," in *Talmudic Studies*, ed. Yaakov Sussmann and David Rosenthal (Jerusalem: Magnes, 2005), 3.2:791–863, here 856–61; Yoav Rosenthal, "Transpositions: Text and Reality," *AJSR* 41 (2017): 333–73, here 358–60.

18. Louis Jacobs's classic study (*The Talmudic Argument: A Study in Talmudic Reasoning and Methodology* [Cambridge: Cambridge University Press, 1984], 2–4), claims origins for the *sugya*-form in question-and-answer sequences throughout the Tanakh, yet argues for its unique, integral, and logically coherent status. Jacobs concedes earlier stages of the *sugya* (20, 211), but not interaction among *sugyot* or how they circulated after their "final" forms. David Brodsky offers a more convincing comparison to Greco-Roman rhetoric ("From Disagreement to Talmudic Discourse: Progymnasmata and the Evolution of a Rabbinic Genre," in Nikolsky and Ilan, *Rabbinic Traditions*, 173–231).

19. Devora Steinmetz, "Agada Unbound: Inter-Agadic Characterization of Sages in the Bavli and Implications for Reading Agada," in Rubenstein, *Creation and Composition*, 293–337; on Zvi Septimus and others, see my conclusion. Friedman ("Unfolding," 97) also rejects analysis of "the end product in splendid isolation" to display "the overall kinetic unfolding of *all* its stages," but still assigns the end stage to "*a* skilled literary artist" who turned "*isolated* components into a polished and *seamless* creation" (emphasis added), rather than portraying a constant interaction between text and audience.

20. Compare a swing of the pendulum in debates on pentateuchal source criticism, from not infrequently balkanizing documentary hypotheses; to holistic literary and final-form canonical criticisms (Sternberg; Childs); to narrower source criticism through the lens of performance, stressing how sources were fluidly and partially set into new contexts (Carr); to a "Neo-Documentarian" approach that maintains the construct of individual sources/documents but analyzes their composition as a more gradual and piecemeal inner-canonical process (Jeffrey Stackert, "Distinguishing Innerbiblical Exegesis from Pentateuchal Redaction: Leviticus 26 as a Test Case," in *The Pentateuch: International Perspectives on Current Research*, ed. Thomas B. Dozeman, Konrad Schmid, and Baruch J. Schwartz, FAT 78 [Tübingen: Mohr Siebeck, 2011], 369–86, here 369-74). While much is gained by critiquing pentateuchal source

sources and variants (poetics), or examine how these materials contributed to the Bavli before us (i.e., a holistic, *sugya*-centric use of source/redaction criticism), we can coordinate all three of these established methods to excavate links *among* traditions of Bavli aggada (as well as bridges to halakha).[21] The basic premise of this approach is that the traditions reflected in sources and variants did not disappear with the "final" text of any given passage but continued to circulate throughout its transmission, in new–more or less integral, discrete, interconnected–forms. This approach sets out to explore how those constellations of texts were engaged by their own creators and audiences. Its emergent method might be called "inner-talmudic interpretation."[22] It is characterized not by a new set of concepts or tools but by a different use of the same tools–and a shift in focus. Rather than privilege the role of the composers (editors, author/redactors, etc.) and their intentions, this approach turns to parallel roles in the world where inner-talmudic traditions were received (student, performer, audience, etc.; each is a construct to be refined via application to local cases). By disentangling such roles from any given redacted text and reconstructing how they both shaped and were reshaped by this "final" form, we can sound out underexcavated layers of commentary, de- and recomposition in the Bavli, with the uses of shared sources in Palestinian midrash as a foil.

---

criticism in terms of how it reflects epochal "paradigms" (Joshua Berman, *Inconsistency in the Torah: Ancient Literary Convention and the Limits of Source Criticism* [Oxford: Oxford University Press, 2017], esp. 218–24), as Stackert shows, this debate is not due to a clash between paradigms (top-down, systemic knowledge formations in their classical form *à la* Kuhn). Rather, it depends on a more tacit epistemological norm: how tightly a scholar construes each text's chronological and literary boundaries. Like documents of the Pentateuch, Bavli *sugyot* can be seen as more or less rigidly periodized, more or less integral units. Analysis of their relationship to others in the canon varies accordingly. Current methods tend to privilege a final *sugya* at the expense of ongoing interplay between it and other Bavli units and, in that sense, can learn from the oscillation of debates in biblical source criticism.

21. The *Yelammedenu* genre, which begins with a halakhic question that is integrated with largely nonlegal *derashot*, would be a strong example of this development within Palestinian tradition (so would that of the *Sheiltot*, as Jeffrey L. Rubenstein added in his comments on this essay). One line of fairly recent scholarship examines how halakha and aggada are integrated within the literary framework of the Bavli: Friedman, "Dama ben Netinah," 453–55, 465–66; Rubenstein, *Talmudic Stories*, e.g., 248, 255; Wimpfheimer, *Narrating the Law*; Amram Tropper, *Like Clay in the Hands of the Potter: Sage Stories in Rabbinic Literature* [Hebrew] (Jerusalem: Shazar Center, 2011), 116–17, 134–37, 146–47; Jane L. Kanarek, *Biblical Narrative and the Formation of Rabbinic Law* (Cambridge: Cambridge University Press, 2014); Yonatan Feintuch, "Uncovering Covert Links between Halakha and Aggada in the Babylonian Talmud: The Talmudic Discussion of the Yom Kippur Afflictions in B. Yoma," *AJSR* 40 (2016): 17–32.

22. By analogy to "inner-biblical interpretation" with respect to aggadic creativity in the Tanakh (Michael Fishbane, *Biblical Interpretation in Ancient Israel* [Oxford: Clarendon, 1985]). Specifically, I also ask how the Bavli became a "synoptic" canon (407), and how editors fostered relations of "correlation" or "polarity" between co-texts (421–23).

Arguments

As a case study in inner-talmudic interpretation, this essay examines an elaborate passage of midrash aggada in b. B. Bat. 74b–75b, focusing on two units that are paralleled in the contemporaneous Palestinian midrashic corpus, Pesiqta de Rab Kahana (PRK). By contrasting uses of shared material in each work, I hope to shed light on issues that have bedeviled students of each passage separately, while exemplifying key processes of inner-talmudic interpretation in the Bavli. As for PRK, I argue, this comparison sets arguments for the work's "popular" character on firmer footing. Since PRK was reconstructed by Zunz and, later, discovered in manuscripts,[23] scholars have tried to correlate its literary forms with its social orientation, contrasting a strain of popular piety in its presumed synagogue setting against the values of the study-house.[24] The longest elaboration of this thesis, Rachel A. Anisfeld's monograph, repeatedly invokes the contrast between "school/not-school" and locates it in the distinctive rhetoric of PRK, the work's tone of "indulgence."[25] Anisfeld proposes that this more "emotional,"[26] nonintellectual turn toward the audience can be explained by factors both internal and external to Jewish society. Internally, because the rabbis aimed to attract new audiences to the synagogue ("a predominantly non-rabbinic institution"),[27] they had to "accommodate" to their less halakhic interests and paint a less domineering picture of God.[28] Externally, they competed with and were influenced

---

23. For the history of research on Pesiqta de Rab Kahana, see Arnon Atzmon, "The Original Order of Pesikta de-Rav Kahana," *JJS* 70 (2019): 1–23, here 2 n. 2. See further Burton L. Visotzky, "The Misnomers '*Petihah*' and 'Homiletic Midrash' as Descriptions for Leviticus Rabbah and Pesikta De-Rav Kahana," *JSQ* 18 (2011): 19–31; Chaim Milikowsky, "Vayyiqra Rabbah, Chapter 28, First Petiḥta (Sections 1–3): Studies in Text, Editing, and Affinity with the Parallel in *Pesikta deRav Kahana*" [Hebrew], *Tarbiṣ* 71 (2001): 19–47.

24. William G. Braude and Israel J. Kapstein, trans., *Pesikta de-Rab Kahana* (Philadelphia: Jewish Publication Society, 1975), xvii–xviii. By contrast, Lewis M. Barth holds that the audience of PRK chap. 15 "could only be the rabbis and their disciples" as it betrays "the school-oriented values and anachronistic interpretation of the religious-scholar class" (!?) ("Literary Imagination and the Rabbinic Sermon: Some Observations," *Proceedings of the Seventh World Congress of Jewish Studies* [Jerusalem: Magnes, 1981], 29–35, here 30). Without a strong foil for comparison, any argument for the work's social orientation is fated to remain impressionistic. For the various approaches, see Elsie R. Stern, *From Rebuke to Consolation: Exegesis and Theology in the Liturgical Anthology of the Ninth of Av Season*, BJS 338 (Providence, RI: Brown University Press, 2004), 81–83.

25. Rachel A. Anisfeld, *Sustain Me with Raisin-Cakes: Pesikta deRav Kahana and the Popularization of Rabbinic Judaism*, JSJSup 133 (Leiden: Brill, 2009), 35–36, 45, 68–93.

26. Ibid., 104–19; see also 173.

27. Ibid., 149.

28. Ibid., 78: "… they cede the power they never really had among the people in the hopes of gaining authority."

by a Christian rhetoric of humility, populism, and incarnate sensuality.[29] Backgrounding comparison with Christianity, contrast with Bavli parallels (not attempted by Anisfeld) will help us to hear more clearly this popular rhetoric of PRK. Rather than infer its social orientation directly from its tone and content, as does Anisfeld, we will track how its composers actively turned the exposition of Scripture away from a scholastic utopia like the Bavli's.

The second argument, to which I devote considerably more attention, concerns how this passage of midrash aggada ("Part 2" in my translation; see Appendix) was shaped and reshaped *within* the Bavli. Here, the problem left open by previous work is how the passage relates to the long unit of aggada preceding it: the fantastical adventures and visions of Rabbah b. bar Ḥanah and similar tales of other rabbis ("Part 1" in my translation). Are the two parts a unified literary composition,[30] or unrelated blocks of material wedged into the Bavli at this location simply because—unlike the surrounding content—they are nonlegal in character? I suggest that a theory of inner-talmudic interpretation circumvents such an either/or way of thinking about the literary integrity of this unit. Rather, by relocating the work of the composition to the mind of the student or "implied reader," as constructed by its editors, we can indeed speak of this passage as a midrashic composition and not merely a collection of aggada. At the same time, we can reckon with the fact that there is meager textual evidence for editorial reworking of part 1 in light of part 2–but more for vice versa.[31] In other words, the two parts of the composition began life as discrete passages but were gradually harmonized in a point–counterpoint between

29. Ibid., 163–74.

30. Argued by Günter Stemberger, "Münchhausen und die Apokalyptik: Baba Batra 73a–75b als literarische Einheit," *JSJ* 20 (1989): 61–83; and presupposed by Dina Stein, "Believing Is Seeing: A Reading of Baba Batra 73a–75b" [Hebrew], *Jerusalem Studies in Hebrew Literature* 17 (1999): 1–24; see also Stein, *Textual Mirrors: Reflexivity, Midrash, and the Rabbinic Self*, Divinations (Philadelphia: University of Pennsylvania Press, 2012), 58–63; Daniel Frim, "'Those Who Descend upon the Sea Told Me …': Myth and Tall Tale in *Baba Batra* 73a–74b," *JQR* 107 (2017): 1–37

31. First and foremost, part 1 is mostly Aramaic with a strongly Babylonian profile in characters, content, and style, whereas part 2 is mostly Hebrew with three parallel sections to the Palestinian PRK. Stemberger proposes Daniel as the model for this bilingual composition, calling it a rabbinic "domestication" of apocalyptic ("Münchhausen und die Apokalyptik," 71–83). But nearly all of the textual evidence that he adduces for the integration of the parts could have been added to part 2 by tradents who already knew part 1 (*a fortiori* for a link between the two parts in Rashi. The latter point also applies to Frim's idea ["'Those Who Descend,'" 12–13] that one manuscript reflects an "allusive link" between both parts. Actually, this link is also in Rashbam—probably a secondary tradition that crept into the text. Frim's other analysis of such phenomena [34] is more akin to my own). In sum, evidence for integration of the parts is heavily tilted toward part 2 and later evidence. Conversely, there are scant traces of changes to part 1 in relation to part 2. For exceptions, see nn. 33 and 36 below.

editors and students of part 2. By picking up the traces of that process in part 2, we will see inner-talmudic interpretation at work.

The Texts[32]

Part 2 is a complex passage interweaving anonymous and attributed material on topics that appear, at first glance, to wander ever farther from those of part 1. Its first section (2.A), on the Leviathan and other cosmic powers of the sea, echoes Rabbah b. bar Ḥana's fantastical sea-creatures in part 1, raising his paranormal curiosities to an eschatological power.[33] This leads to a discussion of how the Leviathan's flesh and skin will be apportioned in the eschaton (2.B), which forms a bridge to the composition's redemptive conclusion (2.C): on the Heavenly Jerusalem. It has a structural affinity with many homiletical midrashim, which also conclude with a messianic "peroration" or "seal" [*ḥatimah*] that consoles the audience by looking toward the end of days.[34] One subtype of peroration, what Edmund Stein calls the "theophoric," has a similar refrain: "The Holy One, Blessed be He, said: 'In this world ... [but] in time to come ....'"[35] Yet the consolation that part 2 offers its audience is not purely eschatological. Rather, like claims animating the tales in part 1, the interwoven exegeses and commentary of part 2 thematize the scholastic status hierarchy, and authority of the oral Torah, as a source of truth—over and against claims to visionary authority.

I propose that this theme of the tension between scholastic and visionary authority not only ties together the Heavenly Jerusalem section but

32. See Appendix below for translations, variants, and notes.

33. The only eschatological moments in part 1 are an Amoraic gloss (Xb: "In time to come, Israel shall be judged on their account") and the conclusion to a story attributed to an Amora (XVIII: "A heavenly voice appeared and said: What have you done with the little basket that belongs to the wife of R. Ḥanina ben Dosa ..."; compare b. Ta'an. 24b: "Rav Yehudah said in the name of Rav: Every single day a heavenly voice appears and says, 'The whole world is nourished by R. Ḥanina ben Dosa ...'" followed by stories about his wife). Both eschatological elements point to an intermediate stage of Amoraic responses *to* part 1, before its full-blown, probably Stammaitic reception in part 2. Thus, even these sources support my analysis better than Stemberger's: integration was a gradual process, not a "planned literary unit," with later generations modeling changes to part 1 on how part 1 had *already* been received by Amoraim (who glossed a textual datum in part 1 in an eschatological light and "hyperlinked" a relevant character).

34. Edmund Stein, "Die homiletische Peroratio im Midrasch," *HUCA* 8–9 (1931–1932): 353–71.

35. Compare the end of 2.C: "The Holy One, Blessed be He, will/wanted to ..."; "In time to come ..."; or a combination. See Stein, "Die homiletische Peroratio," 359–61. I am not suggesting that the Bavli is actually using this form; its verses are not tied back to one another in a circle, as in homiletical midrash, but rather are paired with rabbinic stories and interpretations of them.

also supplied the editors with a recipe for reworking their sources so as to link part 2 back to part 1. As the editors did so, they subtly guided a student of part 2 to revise and reinterpret part 1 in light of the main theme. They did not direct students *how* to apply it to part 1–multiple options remain open, and ambiguities abound–but they sharpened a sense of the options. With one exception,[36] this interpretive process seems entirely retrospective; we cannot prove that it was foreseen by the editors of part 1 (nor did it cause many changes to part 1). Yet such inner-talmudic interpretation is not invisible. It left a trail of traces in part 2—*keywords* and *catchphrases*—which cement the matrix of possible retrospective connections to part 1. This cement is reinforced by thematic associations between both parts 1 and 2, as well as by additional traditions preserved in the Bavli, yielding a more synoptic canon.

We will see how the editors structured this interpretive process for the student of parts 1 and 2 by contrasting how they, and the editors of Palestinian midrash, use a shared set of sources. By stripping part 2 down to its prooftexts and retracing them through the rabbinic canon, we find that many sources of the Heavenly Jerusalem section also parallel the sources of PRK, as well as a sermon that is formally related to PRK (though it may have a different provenance).[37] Rather than verbatim parallels,[38] or linear developments leading into or out of the Bavli,[39] most of these overlapping sources are edited into discrete literary units, accenting different shared traditions, in order to stress markedly different themes. The PRK

36. The only place where I see a heavy and possibly late editorial hand in part 1, in order to connect it with part 2, is the penultimate unit (XX): a pseudo-*baraita* featuring an exegesis on the Leviathan, that is, the theme of the first section of part 2 (2.A). This *baraita* is not in Tannaitic works; resembles other pseudo-*baraitot* (Rubenstein, *Talmudic Stories*, 55, 261); and has a Babylonian Hebrew feature: מהלכין (reflecting Aramaic א.ז.ל throughout part 2. See Shraga Abramson's introduction to his *Talmud Bavli Massekhet Baba Batra* [Tel-Aviv: Dvir, 1958], 2–5).

37. This is inferred from the fact that the sermon is a homily for the second day of Sukkot (ed. Mandelbaum, PRK, Appendix 2, 452 n. 1), which was not a festival day in Palestine. As my interest is in using this unit to assess the character of Bavli midrash aggada, whether it originated in Palestine or in non-(post-?)Talmudic Babylonia does not affect my analysis. Its form and its populism mirror the other parallel that I analyze from PRK. It is cited as *Pesiqta* by the Yalqut Shim'oni and is found in a manuscript of PRK. Either it is from an early macroform of the work, or it reflects its genre and–I argue–ideology.

38. As opposed to the Bavli unit's relation to b. Sanh. 100a, which does have a substantial parallel. See Appendix, 2.C.i.

39. We find a small-scale linear relation between the anonymous list of seven seas surrounding the Land of Israel (y. Kil. 9:4, 32c) and the dictum attributed to R. Yoḥanan (2.A), containing a similar but different and longer list. In the Bavli, this dictum is prefaced by "When Dimi arrived, he said": one example where the famed talmudic "travelers" (*naḥotei*; see Redfield, "Redacting Culture"; see also the appendix to that article cited in n. 165 below; see n. 190 below) do transmit a Palestinian text to Babylonia–a direct line from a Palestinian to a Babylonian source.

parallels draw upon voices that are marginal or anonymous in the Bavli and distance themselves from its case for a status-hierarchy grounded in oral Torah. The Bavli parallels underscore the status-hierarchy, against the authority of vision, and wed it to the Heavenly Jerusalem theme. This contrast between the corpora supports both of my arguments: first, that a more "popular" orientation is reflected in PRK and, second, that the Bavli's readers could have integrated both parts of their composition while leaving the text of part 1 largely intact. It reveals editors' work in reshaping inherited complexes of midrash aggadah into a thematically coherent discussion, leaving it to students to debate the exact nature of that coherence. Here, their creativity was applied less to the textual content than to the models for its interpretation.

I develop both arguments, and show how Bavli editors develop the theme of scholastic versus visionary authority, by working through two cases of dense parallels between the Bavli passage, on the one hand, and PRK (or a closely related work), on the other. In the first case, shared sources were edited so as to reflect sharp, almost precisely inverse orientations to the scholastic status-hierarchy. Further, Bavli editors added a keyword (*Woe!*) on the theme of visionary versus scholastic authority. This keyword ties part 2 back to part 1, as well as potentially to other material in the Bavli, in terms of that larger theme. The keyword thus opens up new, potentially ironic reinterpretations of the Bavli's apparently pro-scholastic, anti-visionary attitude among later generations of students. This first case thus illustrates both of my essay's key claims in a compact form. Here, however, the specific avenues of inner-talmudic interpretation that were opened (is this Bavli passage slanted toward irony or scholastic elitism? toward vision or tradition?) remain fairly obscure. The second, more elaborate case reveals a larger and more tangible set of interpretive pathways between the Bavli's parts 1 and 2, and the rest of the Bavli canon, as well as another inverse orientation to the scholastic status-hierarchy in the Bavli and the contemporary Palestinian PRK. Here, too, options for inner-talmudic interpretation are signaled by keywords and catchphrases. Here, too, they cohere in light of the theme of visionary versus scholastic and exegetically based claims to authority. Yet here, the echo chamber of verbally and thematically linked passages offers a more concrete set of interpretive options—albeit not the singular and foreclosed meaning of a holistic text.

§1. *The Heavenly Banquet and the Eschatological Tabernacle (Job 41:6–7/Isa 4:5–6/Isa 23:8)*

In the Bavli (2.B), R. Yoḥanan (according to Rabbah) interprets Job 41:6a (MT 40:30a) under the old topos of the eschatological banquet of Leviathan, and the "companions" in this verse as "disciples of the sages."[40] These disciples, R. Yoḥanan claims, will be the only ones to feast on the Leviathan. He stresses this point by going on to interpret Job 41:6b (MT 40:30b): leftovers from the banquet will be sold by "merchants" in Jerusalem (with an anonymous Aramaic gloss of "merchants" in light of Isa 23:8).[41] R. Yoḥanan (still according to Rabbah) goes on to interpret the next verse, Job 41:7a (MT 40:31a): at the end of days, God will make a booth (*sukkah*) for the righteous from the Leviathan's skin. Again, he then interprets the second half of the verse (Job 41:7b) as pointing to a status-hierarchy in the eschaton. The righteous will get a booth, whereas the less deserving will get lesser items from the Leviathan's skin. And again, R. Yoḥanan concludes with the Heavenly Jerusalem theme: the Leviathan's skin will be spread out along the city walls, shining across the world, in view of all the nations.

Two devices stand out in R. Yoḥanan's seamless exposition of both parts of both verses: (1) Status-hierarchy at the end of days (scholars/non-scholars; more/less righteous); (2) subordination of the Leviathan to the Heavenly Jerusalem, with which R. Yoḥanan wraps up both parts of both symmetrical expositions. These rhetorical devices are held in tension along an axis of hierarchy/egalitarianism. Does God reward all people equally, or some more than others? Perhaps both: scholars and righteous people will be rewarded more, but ultimately the Heavenly Jerusalem will transcend this distinction. Even people in the marketplace or "the nations" will be able to get a piece of the action, so to speak.

This set of midrashim attributed by Rabbah to R. Yoḥanan (2.B) is now interrupted by an independent unit (the first three paragraphs of 2.C, which are also paralleled in PRK; see §2 below). When that unit ends, Rabbah resumes reciting R. Yoḥanan's midrash and repeats both key points. Just as the righteous will get a booth, so will each get seven "canopies" (as it says in Isa 4:5: "for upon all the glory shall be a canopy").[42] In R. Yoḥanan's reading,[43] this verse means not only that the glory of *God* will cover Mount Zion at the end of days[44] but also that—just as the booth of the Leviathan's skin will be apportioned on the basis of merit, as he stated above—God will

---

40. I cite KJV verse divisions, modifying the translation as needed and noted.

41. In all manuscripts, this anonymous gloss is introduced by a phrase typical of Babylonian give-and-take ("and if you prefer, I will say it from here ..."), introducing an alternative source for a prooftext. This, as well as the language shift, indicates a secondary addition by the anonymous Bavli—which happens to make the *merchants/disciples of the sages* look better. See the parallel at b. Pes. 50a.

42. KJV modified.

43. Here, the addition is in Hebrew and seems to be part of a coherent exegesis; contrast n. 41 above.

44. He is building on the midrash of R. Akiva (Mekhilta de-Rabbi Ishmael §Pisḥa 14, ed. Jacob Z. Lauterbach [Philadelphia: Jewish Publication Society, 2004], 74 = Mekhilta

bestow a canopy on each of the righteous according to his glory/honor/*dignitas* (*kavod*).[45] Here, again, he pairs the Heavenly Jerusalem with a gradation in status at the end of days. But now, hierarchy outweighs egalitarianism: the verse itself extends God's glory to all Heavenly Jerusalem,[46] whereas R. Yoḥanan restricts it to the "righteous." In fact, he continues, (in two more midrashim also recited by Rabbah) *only* the righteous will be invited ("called") up to the Heavenly Jerusalem, just as *only* the righteous will be "called" by the glory of God in the eschaton—in contrast to the verse (which is addressed to all Israel), and to the earthly Jerusalem, where "anyone" at all can go.[47] Commenting on his midrash, Babylonian Amoraim restrict the scope of "the righteous" still further to "disciples of the sages." In sum, this five-part exegetical complex—attributed to R. Yoḥanan, supplemented by Babylonian Amoraim, and arranged by the editors—not only conjoins the Heavenly Jerusalem/status-hierarchy themes but also consistently privileges the sages' position at that conjunction. The specific phraseology by which it does so, in turn, generates a network of connections back to the Bavli's part 1, as we shall see shortly.

A Palestinian midrash (3.A), cited as Pesiqta and at least formally related to PRK,[48] turns the Bavli's innovations on their head. It uses the same verses and interpretations to reverse effect. R. Levi interprets Isa 4:6 ("and there shall be a covering [*sukkāh*] for shadow") in light of Job 41:7a

§Beshallaḥ 1, ed. Lauterbach 124), who reads Isa 4:5 together with 4:6 so as to equate not only the "canopy" (4:5) but also the "booth" (4:6) with a "cloud" for the "glory."

45. Women also have *kavod* (look no further than the fifth commandment; and see Friedman, "Dama ben Netinah," 435–39). The original dictum may not have referred only to men, but the commentary in this passage limits it to rabbis.

46. Underscored by the parallelism (Isa 4:5): וּבָרָא יְהוָה עַל כָּל־מְכוֹן הַר־צִיּוֹן וְעַל־מִקְרָאֶהָ עָנָן יוֹמָם וְעָשָׁן / וְנֹגַהּ אֵשׁ לֶהָבָה לָיְלָה כִּי עַל־כָּל־כָּבוֹד חֻפָּה. Of course, in the postapocalyptic context of the verse, the promise of universality applies only to the righteous "remnant in Jerusalem" (הַנּוֹתָר בִּירוּשָׁלִָם). So the Bavli's reading also has an exegetical basis.

47. Already in R. Yoḥanan's context, when Jewish residence in Jerusalem was banned, this contrasts temporary conditions with eternal salvation. In the post-Constantine context of this text's redaction, Jewish pilgrimage had been affected by an imperial Christianization of space (Oded Irshai, "The Christian Appropriation of Jerusalem in the Fourth Century: The Case of the Bordeaux Pilgrim," *JQR* 99 [2009]: 465–84). That shift may partly account for a renewed emphasis on the Heavenly Jerusalem in our texts. According to Catherine Hezser, in "the only explicit Yerushalmi reference to Jewish pilgrimage to Jerusalem … Jerusalem is described as a disgusting place, full of violence and blood, where one will almost certainly become unclean—the exact opposite of a holy place where pilgrims might want to visit" ("The (In)significance of Jerusalem in the Talmud Yerushalmi," in *The Talmud Yerushalmi and Graeco-Roman Culture*, ed. Catherine Hezser and Peter Schäfer, 3 vols., TSAJ 71, 79, 93 [Tübingen: Mohr Siebeck, 1998–2002], 2:11–49, here 27). Ephraim E. Urbach argues the reverse: for Amoraim, Heavenly Jerusalem was modeled on earthly Jerusalem, and rather secondary ("Yerushalayim shel matah ve-yerushalayim shel ma'alah," in Urbach, *The World of the Sages: Collected Studies* [Hebrew] [Jerusalem: Magnes, 1988], 376–91). See further the literature cited in nn. 54, 62, and 77 below.

48. See n. 37 above.

("canst thou fill his skin with barbed irons [*śukkôt*]?" [MT 40:31]): anyone at all who sits in a *sukkah* in this world will be seated by God in a *sukkah* of the Leviathan's skin in the world to come.[49] A long excursus on the Leviathan's skin, other features, and war with Behemoth ensues. It ends by repeating Job 41:7a: God will make a *sukkah* for the righteous with the Leviathan's skin. In sum, its themes and prooftexts are identical to the Bavli's. But this is a repetition with a difference: R. Yoḥanan defines "righteous" as disciples of the sages; R. Levi, as *anyone* who sits in a *sukkah*.[50]

Like the Bavli, this midrash subjoins an exposition of Job 41:7b.[51] Various opinions are cited, but all agree that the most righteous, who will receive the choicest part of the Leviathan, are those who fulfill the commandment of pilgrimage to Jerusalem. They all gloss "companions" (Job 41:6a) in this way as well—those who fulfill commandments. Again, quite unlike R. Yoḥanan in the Bavli, they do not limit the term's meaning to disciples of the sages. "Companions" are not only "adepts in Scripture ... Mishnah ... Talmud ... Aggada" but also "adepts in commandments" and in "good deeds." There are many different groups of companions, they reiterate, and at the end of days, "*every* single company comes and serves itself a portion" (emphasis added). They prove that there will be no competition among "companions" by glossing the term as "merchants," again in light of Isa 23:8: "whose merchants are princes, whose traffickers are the honorable of the earth." Recall that in the Bavli, the same gloss was cited anonymously, as an alternative to R. Yoḥanan's, lending *merchants* a negative connotation, portraying them as anything but "honorable,"[52] and reaffirming the hierarchy of rabbinic disciples *over* merchants. In the sermon, the Bavli's anonymous gloss is recovered—and highlighted. The midrash

49. Note the change in the Masoretic consonantal text, as well as the ending of the word (הַתְמַלֵּא בְשֻׂכּוֹת עוֹרוֹ ← התמלא בסוכו עורו). For other midrashim featuring these alternations, see Yosef Sheq ed., *Siaḥ ha-talmud: 'Otsar ha-miqra, ha-derashah, veha-lashon be-Talmud Bavli* (Bene Beraq: Morashah Qehillat Ya'aqov, 1999–2000), 344–46.

50. Sitting in a *sukkah* is the paradigm for a "minimal commandment" (*mitsvah qalah*) in the opening *sugya* of Bavli Avodah Zarah, which has several parallels to the first part of this section (see notes in ed. Mandelbaum, 452–53). In that *sugya,* the nations fail to observe even this commandment because God does *not* give them shade (as God does in these midrashim), but "makes the sun blaze upon them" (trans. Jeffrey L. Rubenstein in his "An Eschatological Drama: Bavli Avodah Zarah 2a-3b," *AJSR* 21 [1996]: 1–37, here 6; see also 24–26). This supports my proposal that, by using a *sukkah* to define the "righteous," R. Levi is appealing to a markedly popular Judaism—between the elite and the nations.

51. The following exposition of Job 41:7b is not part of the sermon itself but is joined to it by the formula "another matter." On this formula in PRK, which he unconvincingly claims always conveys the true position of the composer, see Eli Ungar, "When 'Another Matter' Is the Same Matter: The Case of Davar-Aher in Pesiqta DeRab Kahana," in *Approaches to Ancient Judaism*, vol. 2, ed. Jacob Neusner, BJS 9 (Gainesville: University of South Florida Press, 1978), 2:1–43.

52. Hosea 12:7: "the balances of deceit are in his hand; he loveth to oppress" (KJV).

makes everyone "merchants" (disciples included!), painting them in an irenically egalitarian light at the end of days.[53]

This midrashic unit draws from the same set of prooftexts and interpretations as the Bavli to present an inverse vision of the status-hierarchy in the Heavenly Jerusalem.[54] Anyone who fulfills commandments or good deeds will take their share—not only more "righteous" people like disciples. We could read this as a bald rejection of the Bavli's scholastic snobbery. Or we could see it as actually building upon R. Yoḥanan's idea that, in the Heavenly Jerusalem, anyone will be able to buy the Leviathan's flesh or see its skin. That is, whereas he initially defused the tension between hierarchy and egalitarianism by painting Heavenly Jerusalem as an egalitarian island in a sea of hierarchy, this midrash rejects the hierarchy altogether, whether in this world or in the next. Pious deeds are no less righteous than study; pilgrimage to the earthly Jerusalem is no less meritorious. The unit's murky provenance makes it hard to assess whether it is reacting directly to the Bavli, or drawing from the same well of Amoraic-era exegeses but refining them in the opposite direction due to contemporary concerns. Regardless, it avoids the Bavli's scholastic narrowing of the status-hierarchy so pointedly as to offer support for the "popularization" thesis in PRK and related sources.

More importantly for my second argument, this contrast calls attention to an element in the Bavli's Heavenly Jerusalem section (2.C) that does *not* reflect its argument for a scholastic status hierarchy. It is also, perhaps not coincidentally, one of the few elements that might be an editorial voice: the chorus ("Woe for such shame! Woe for such disgrace!"), appended to two earlier traditions.[55] In its local contexts, this chorus puts a wrinkle on the premise that scholars truly dominate the status-hierarchy: they envy one another even in the eschaton, and the decline of the generations has afflicted them since the days of their exemplar Moses (as a previous generation, ironically, reminds them). The chorus strikes another ironic note when we recall that it echoes a scene in part 1 (XII-

53. Contrast R. Ḥanina's interpretation (2.C) of Isa 4:5 ("the shining of a flaming fire by night"): "This teaches that if anyone [of the scholars] envies the canopy of his *companion* …" (emphasis added).

54. As Marc Hirshman points out, PRK strongly emphasizes the earthly Jerusalem and its temple, identifying loanwords and motifs that reinforce Anisfeld's thesis about the affective profile of the midrash ("Yearning for Intimacy: *Pesikta d'Rav Kahana and the Temple*," in *Scriptual Exegesis: The Shapes of Culture and the Religious Imagination; Essays in Honour of Michael Fishbane*, ed. Deborah A. Green and Laura S. Lieber [Oxford: Oxford University Press, 2009], 135–45). As I have indicated above, the same cannot be said of Bavli parallels.

55. Those refrains are not paralleled in earlier rabbinic sources, whereas the statements that they gloss are. The first is attributed to an Amora, the second under the citation formula "And thus have we learned [נמצינו למידין]" in Sifre Numbers. See *Sifre on Numbers: An Annotated Edition*, ed. Menahem I. Kahana (Jerusalem: Magnes, 2011), סו.

Ia–b) wherein Rabbah b. bar Ḥanah hears a heavenly voice proclaiming "Woe is me for having sworn" and members of the study-house deride him as an "ass" and "jackass" for failing to utter a formula that, in their opinion, would have released God from his vow to exile the Jews from Mount Sinai.[56] While their debate about the substance of the vow in question, hinging on the proper usage of the word *woe*, seemed speculative—even playful—in its initial context, now that it has been coded negatively as "disgrace/shame" and scholastic competition, the student might gain some sympathy for Rabbah b. bar Ḥanah as the butt of the sages' derision in part 1. Or, the student might choose to reinterpret both passages as a symptom of the decline of the generations: associating "the face of Moses" (in part 2) with the image of an inaccessible Mount Sinai (in part 1). Neither correlation is foregone, and others are certainly possible, but the key point is that the student's very ability to form any such correlation depends on the work of the Bavli's editors. Just as their shaping of this unit brings out and intertwines its two themes of the Heavenly Jerusalem and the rabbinic status-hierarchy, their use of a keyword (*Woe …*) redirects the student's attention back to part 1 in light of the same theme, enriching both passages and complicating the Bavli's apparent scholastic triumphalism. By comparing its redacted form to the alternative reworking of shared sources in PRK, we have glimpsed how—via such retrospective links—the composition of the Bavli's part 2 could have gradually expanded to envelop part 1.

In other units of PRK, we also find parallels to the Bavli's Heavenly Jerusalem section (2.C). These parallels accent a similar antischolastic *Tendenz* in PRK.[57] Reciprocally, they shed further light on compositional

---

56. According to a traditional interpretation of the "vow"; the earliest that I know is a late twelfth-century *piyyuṭ*, למי אוי למי אבוי ומידינים by R. Ephraim b. R. Yaaqov of Bonn, where this line is paralleled with "woe is the father who exiled his son" (b. Ber. 3a; see *Hymnen und Gebete*, trans. and commentary by Hans-Georg von Mutius, Judaistische Texte und Studien 11 [Hildesheim: Olms, 1989], 80). See also b. Sot. 47b.

57. Consider a third example along these lines: a sermon in PRK on Qoh 8:1 ("A man's wisdom maketh his face to shine"; at 4:4) cites Moses as the scholastic paradigm to whom this verse applies, due to his expertise in purity law. However, PRK also glosses the same verse as *all* Israel, who have the same expertise. Again, this treatment of the motif contrasts sharply with the Bavli's scholastic status-hierarchy and supports the popularization thesis, as the same unit of PRK has another extensive parallel to our Bavli passage (a series of Amoraic midrashim on Ezek 28:13 in section 2.C). PRK 4:4 (ed. Mandelbaum, 66) draws out the logic behind expositions that the Bavli merely attributes to late Babylonians (e.g., Mar Zutra), which could indicate later development on the side of PRK. Yet the Bavli, for its part, adds an exposition of the next words of Ezek 28:13 that is *not* in PRK 4:4. In its place, the PRK parallel develops an interpretation of the same words that the Bavli cites anonymously *en passant* (under the formula ואיכא דאמרי הכי קאמר). Here again, the relation between the two works seems to be not a linear evolution but different elaborations of shared sources. Compare the parallel in Pesiqta Rabbati 14:33–36, ed. Rivka Ulmer, *A Bilingual Edition of Pesiqta Rabbati*, vol. 1, *Chapters 1–22*, Studia Judaica 86 (Berlin: de Gruyter, 2017), 396–401.

devices—more keywords and catchphrases—which knit together the Bavli composition by bringing retrospective readings of part 1 in line with the themes of part 2.

§2. Doubting Thomas in the House of Study (Isa 54:12)

The Bavli's Heavenly Jerusalem section (2.C) begins on an odd note: a philological dispute about the meaning of *kadkod* in Isa 54:12 ("And I will make thy windows of *kadkod* and thy gates of carbuncles") in the name of the Palestinian R. Shmuel b. Naḥmani. The parties to this dispute are also odd: either two unnamed Palestinian Amoraim ("in the West"—from the perspective of the Bavli), or two angels, Gabriel and Michael.[58] Regardless, God intervenes to settle their dispute with a brilliant stroke of equivocation: *The Holy One, Blessed be He, said to them: Let it be both as this and as that* (kedein u-khedein). Now that the meaning of the word is determined by the dispute about its meaning, rather than the other way around, it can have both meanings.[59] In PRK, God's position is attributed to Abba b. Kahana;[60] aside from this variation, the parallels are identical. Then, after an independent story, based on a fourth etymology of *kadkod*, PRK returns to an exposition of the next part of the verse: "and thy gates of carbuncles." Here, as in the parallels that I discussed above, PRK shares the Bavli's interpretation of a word in Scripture (*carbuncles → I shall bore/sprout*) but attributes it to a different authority (R. Shmuel b. Yitsḥaq). Only after citing his independent yet identical gloss does PRK trace the gloss to a source that it shares with the Bavli: R. Yoḥanan's exposition of the subject of this verb as referring to God, and its topic to the Heavenly Jerusalem. In the Heavenly Jerusalem—R. Yoḥanan said—God shall make a single pearl so large that it forms the temple's east gate and both its wickets (in the Bavli, 2.C, he says something similar).[61] A story follows to illustrate

58. Urbach identifies this as an allusion to the *angelus interpres* in apocalyptic sources, e.g., Rev 21:19, KJV, noting that this angel specifically reveals the precious stones in the Heavenly Jerusalem ("Yerushalayim shel matah," 389).

59. Rashbam to b. B. Bat. 75a, s.v. כדין וכדין: "And even though this verse was long before the sons of R. Ḥiyya [the disputing Amoraim "in the West"—J.R.], one may say that this is what Isaiah was prophesying about: that it shall be built according to *all* the words of the commentators" (emphasis added).

60. PRK 18:5. It is tempting to imagine that the work's "author" takes the place of God (Buber supported the attribution based on a theory about the order of PRK, but this has been revised by Atzmon, "Original Order"). Further, manuscript titles of PRK are late and inconsistent, and it is unclear which "Kahana" is meant (see Günter Stemberger, *Einleitung in Talmud und Midrasch*, 9th ed. [Munich: Beck, 2011], 325; Arnold Goldberg, review of ed. Mandelbaum [Hebrew], *Kiryat Sefer* 43 [1967]: 68–79, here 72 n. 6).

61. 2.C: "In time to come, the Holy One, Blessed be He, will bring precious stones and pearls that are *thirty by thirty* [cubits], and carve out [a space from] them *ten* [cubits wide]

the truth of R. Yoḥanan's dictum.[62] A certain "pelagic heretic" (מינוי פרוש),[63] who is called a "disciple" (תלמיד) in the Bavli, disputes (or in the Bavli, "jeers at") R. Yoḥanan's dictum: nobody finds pearls that big![64] When the

---

by *twenty* [high], and set them up in the gates of Jerusalem" (emphasis added. Compare Rev 21:21 (KJV): "And the twelve gates were twelve pearls ..."). In the Bavli, these numbers reflect a structural device: most of the following units have numbers as a signal motif ("seven canopies," "ten canopies," "three *parasangs*"; see the final unit of 2.C, which revives the topic of the length/breadth of the Heavenly Jerusalem). The Bavli's version of the dictum is tailored to this overall schema. The specific verb that R. Yoḥanan uses to gloss אקדח (*I shall bore/sprout*) also differs between the Bavli 2.C (*carve out*, ח.ק.ק) and PRK 3.B (*make*, ע.ש.ה). Both of these verbs are repeated elsewhere in their respective subunits to create a foreshadowing effect (2.C: "he saw the ministering angels ... *carving out* [a space ...]; 3.B: "he was *transformed* [נעשה] into a pile of bones"). So again, they reflect tailoring of the dictum to the context in both cases; one is not more original. It displays the artistry of the editors/storytellers that both of these word choices reflect different aspects of a pearl's formation: a single grain of sand "makes" the lustrous creation by "boring" into the shell and "carving out" a pearl that "sprouts."

62. As Marc Hirshman notes ("Pesiqta deRav Kahana and Paideia" [Hebrew], in *Higayon leYonah*, ed. Joshua Levinson et al. [Jerusalem: Magnes, 2011], 165–78, here 174), what I identify as a related theme of the Bavli (2A.–2C.), viz., the power of belief over vision (cf. D. Stein, "Believing Is Seeing"; Stein, *Textual Mirrors*), is thematized in this larger unit of PRK (18:5, ed. Mandelbaum, 296–99) by inserting similar stories both before and after this one. Hirshman (see also"Yearning for Intimacy") argues that PRK develops a temple-centered *paideia*, and that these three stories are a key to this program insofar as they teach, by example, the imperative of belief in the temple's restoration.

63. Per Saul Lieberman (*Tosefta ki-feshuṭah: A Comprehensive Commentary on the Tosefta, Zeraim* (New York: Jewish Theological Seminary, 1955), 1:54 n. 84, *parush* here means one who "departs" (פ.ר.ש) for the sea. (See also דהוה אזיל פריש בימא, "who regularly went off to sea," at Qoh. Rab. 3:6, ed. Hirshman, https://schechter.ac.il/wp-content/uploads/2018/03/parasha3.pdf). More commonly, of course, it connotes "sectarian"; "separatist" (as in "Pharisee"; see sources and literature in Shaye J. D. Cohen, "The Significance of Yavneh: Pharisees, Rabbis, and the End of Jewish Sectarianism," *HUCA* 55 [1984]: 27–53, here 39 n. 32). Since, in this passage, both connotations are active, we can speculatively compare the term to "Pelagian" (a heresy named after its founder Pelagius, from Greek *pelagos*, "sea"). Those unusual overlapping connotations could index a historical relationship behind the terms, such as a calque. Further, contemporary sources use the etymology of *pelagos* to attack the heresy. For example, Ambrose, cited by Augustine (*On the Grace of Christ*, ch. 50, trans. Peter Holmes, in *Nicene and Post-Nicene Fathers*, First Series, vol. 5, *Augustine, Anti-Pelagian Writings*, Series 1, vol. 5, ed. Philip Schaff [1886–1889; repr., New York: Cosimo, 2007], 234: "Why does Pelagius choose to be sunk in that sea whence Peter was rescued by the Rock?" Notably, PRK's heretic also sinks in the sea). On PRK in light of Christian polemic, see Anisfeld, *Raisin Cakes*, 175–85; literature in Hirshman, "Pesiqta deRav Kahana and Paideia," 176 n. 37; Louis H. Silberman, "Challenge and Response: Pesiqta Derab Kahana Chapter 26 as an Oblique Reply to Christian Claims," *HTR* 79 (1986): 247–53; Holger Zellentin, "Typology and the Transfiguration of Rabbi Aqiva (*Pesiqta de Rav Kahana* 4:7 and BT Menaḥot 29b)," *JSQ* 25 (2018): 239–68.

64. "Nowadays, we don't find them as big as a turtle-dove's egg...." In its wider literary context, the disciple's retort could trigger another wordplay for the audience. "Egg" (ביעתא) generally means "oval"; hence also "testicle" or "skull." Compare the rendering of "skull" (*qadqod*) in Peshitta Pss 7:17 and 68:22 (William Emery Barnes, *The Peshitta Psalter according to the West-Syrian Text* [Cambridge: Cambridge University Press, 1904]). This Aramaic "skull,"

heretic/disciple goes on a sea voyage,[65] however, and what R. Yoḥanan foretold is revealed to him in a miraculous encounter with the angels,[66] he returns and begs R. Yoḥanan to repeat his exposition. Unfortunately, the heretic/disciple now believes for the same wrong reason that he didn't at first: because he has seen it with his own eyes. R. Yoḥanan is quick to point out his error, and is unforgiving.

Given that the two versions relate a more or less identical story, it becomes easier to identify the differences in their plots,[67] all of which imply markedly different attitudes toward the scholastic status-hierarchy. In the Bavli, the rabbi's foil is a "disciple," an insider; in PRK, he is a "heretic" and a seafarer, an outsider to the world of the study-house. In fact, PRK sets the whole story, not in R. Yoḥanan's study center in Tiberias, but at "the great synagogue in Sepphoris," leaving even a contemporary scholar unsure about whether to categorize his exposition as "study" or "preaching."[68] In the Bavli, the disciple calls Yoḥanan "Rabbi" and asks him to "expound" (דרוש) the verse, addressing him in highfalutin or archaic Hebrew that lends a scriptural overtone to his midrash.[69] In PRK, the heretic calls him by an ambiguous term ("Elder"),[70] and his teaching by

---

qadqod (compare JBA קרקפא), is spelled and pronounced differently than "onyx" (*kadkod*, the topic of the previous exposition), but, through its association with "egg," opens up another soundplay (compare *śukkôt/sukkôt; ṣilṣal/ṣilṣāl* in Appendix, 2.B). The Aramaic-speaking audience may hear about a jewel the size of an "egg" and think of a "skull" (*qadqod*), reminding them of the jewel that was just discussed (*kadkod*). Alternatively, "skull" (*qadqod*, with a direct soundplay on *kadkod*) could stand behind "egg" in an earlier version of the story. For other clever word choices by the bad disciple, see below.

65. This motif of the sea voyage is itself a midrash on the previous verse (Isa 54:11: "O thou afflicted, tossed with tempest, and not comforted, behold, I will lay thy stones …" [KJV]). The story was not simply appended to the exposition of Isa 54:12.

66. The motif of an underwater pearl, connected to eschatological symbolism, is also prominent in part 1 (1.XVIII).

67. Defining "story" as the bare succession of events and "plot" as the causal nexus that connects them; see E. M. Forster, *Aspects of the Novel*, Clark Lectures 1927 (London: Harcourt, Brace, 1927), 130–31.

68. Lee I. Levine, *The Ancient Synagogue: The First Thousand Years*, 2nd ed. (New Haven: Yale University Press, 2005), 486 versus 488.

69. His כאשר אמרת applies to R. Yoḥanan's midrash a word rarely found in rabbinic sources (outside biblical quotations) and a standard formula for citing Scripture in the Dead Sea Scrolls (כאשר אמר הכתוב; see Moshe Bernstein, "Scriptures: Quotation and Use," in *Encyclopedia of the Dead Sea Scrolls*, ed. Lawrence H. Schiffman and James C. VanderKam, 2 vols. [Oxford: Oxford University Press, 2000], 2:839–42, here 840).

70. The term *saba* in PRK is not itself derogatory. It can be used to disambiguate rabbis' names, much like our "Senior" (*R. Dostai Saba* as opposed to R. Dostai; y. Ḥag. 1:8, 76d; *Naḥman Saba* as opposed to Naḥman bar Adda, y. Meg. 2:1, 73a). It can even be a scholastic title (b. Sanh. 17b). Yet in every context where a character *repeats* the term (סבא סבא), which occurs only in Palestinian corpora, it is clearly disrespectful: a son disrespecting his father (y. Qid. 1:7, 61b = y. Peah 1:1, 15c); a *matrona* disrespecting a rabbi (y. Šabb. 8:1, 11a = y. Pes. 10:1, 37c); or, in a very similar turn of phrase, Turnus Rufus disrespecting R. Akiva (y. Soṭah

a more general verb ("to praise," שבח), as well as another ambiguous Aramaic term ("to proclaim," לגלג), with no mention of midrash at all. Finally, in the Bavli, his transgression is labeled by the term "jeering at the words of the sages," both by the narrator of the story and by R. Yoḥanan *within* the story. By contrast, in PRK he transgresses not "words of the sages" but "words that I said about Torah" (מילייא דמרתי באורייתא)—also ambiguous, meaning either oral or written Torah,[71] but certainly not respect for the sages per se. The Bavli narrator's "words of the sages" sets up R. Yoḥanan for the punchline. PRK pulls the very same punches, softening any sense that the status-hierarchy is particularly at stake. All of these differences support the "popularization" thesis.

The two versions share other peculiar features that shed light on their editors' aims and compositional techniques. As for the PRK version, alternation between Aramaic and Hebrew is particularly noteworthy. A pattern is not obvious.[72] The narrator begins in Aramaic to introduce the setting and continues in Aramaic after R. Yoḥanan's dictum (Hebrew, as in the Bavli). The "heretic" also speaks Aramaic to R. Yoḥanan, who does not reply, but their dialogue at the end of the story is in Aramaic. So far, language use in the story seems fairly consistent: an Aramaic tale, set in Palestine, with an old quotation in Hebrew, but most of the narration/dialogue in the vernacular. However, the part about the heretic's sea voyage and encounter with the ministering angels is entirely in Hebrew; in the Bavli, entirely in Aramaic. This supports Stemberger's proposal that PRK shares the Bavli's source of that story, but not its version;[73] otherwise, why not keep it in Aramaic?[74]

5:5, 20c; and see y. Ber. 9:5, 14b, with Tropper, *Like Clay*, 134 n. 71); Hadrian disrespecting an old man (Lev. Rab. 25:5); R. Eleazar bar. R. Shimon disrespecting Elijah (PRK 11:22, ed. Mandelbaum, 197). Ours seems to be a lone exception, where a character does not intend to be disrespectful—but it turns out that he actually is. For an audience even vaguely familiar with other uses of the doubled סבא, then, there is a grating tone to the heretic's petition. (Compare "Hey Mister!": a term of respect that bespeaks impudence by mixing high and low registers.) The citation of Leviticus Rabbah is from Mordecai Margulies, ed., *Midrash Wayyikra Rabbah* (Jerusalem: Ministry of Education, 1953), 577. The citations of Talmud Yerushalmi (y.) are from *Talmud Yerushalmi according to Ms. Or. 4720 (Scal. 3) of the Leiden University Library*, ed. Academy of the Hebrew Language (Jerusalem: Academy of the Hebrew Language, 2001).

71. See n. 89 below.

72. Visotzky, "Misnomers '*Petihah*' and 'Homiletic Midrash,'" 29: "For the most part, PRK uses Aramaic loan-words either to spice the dialogue or for a particular lexical nuance." Gerhard Svedlund's *The Aramaic Portions of the Pesiqta de Rab Kahana: According to MS Marshall Or. 24, the Oldest Known Manuscript of the Pesiqta de Rab Kahana, with English Translation, Commentary and Introduction*, Studia Semitica Upsaliensis 2 (Uppsala: Almqvist & Wiksell, 1974) is a translation and study of isolated Aramaic words and features without a thesis about patterns of language use.

73. Stemberger, "Münchhausen und die Apokalyptik," 81.

74. On "code switching" as one answer to this question, see Willem F. Smelik, *Rabbis, Language and Translation in Late Antiquity* (Cambridge: Cambridge University Press, 2013),

Use of Hebrew also tips the hand of the editors of the PRK story, showing where and how they integrated the source into the unit. At the conclusion of the part about the sea voyage, PRK has a sentence that is not in the Bavli: "Immediately [מיד] a miracle was performed [נעשה] for him and he departed unharmed." Since, in the PRK version, the heretic is underwater at the time, this line is crucial to the plot (in the Bavli, his ship never sinks, so it is not). But the Hebrew line has more than a plot function. It also echoes the conclusion of the last part: "Immediately [מיד] he was transformed [נעשה] into a pile of bones."[75] Unlike the preceding dialogue and narration, "transformed into a pile of bones" is in Hebrew, as also in the Bavli, where it appears a few times in similar contexts.[76] On this basis, we can suggest that the editors of the PRK version worked from two sources like those of the Bavli (R. Yoḥanan's interpretation of the verse; a three-part story of the heretic/student's doubt, vision, and destruction) but adjusted the conclusion of the sea-voyage part, for the sake of symmetry with the conclusion of the whole. Now, the salvation of the heretic foreshadows his destruction, just as the beginning foreshadows the end. Our proverbial Doubting Thomas is struck down by precisely that in which he placed his trust—the eyes.[77] By leaving the conclusion's Hebrew

---

116–21; Richard Kalmin, *Migrating Tales: The Talmud's Narratives and Their Historical Context* (Berkeley: University of California Press, 2014), 37–38.

75. Similarly, according to Jeffrey L. Rubenstein, "medieval *midrashim* routinely use this term [מיד] to connect independent traditions and place them in chronological sequence" ("From Mythic Motifs to Sustained Myth: The Revision of Rabbinic Traditions in Medieval Midrashim," *HTR* 89 [1996]: 131–59, here 153). Further, as in our text, מיד can create cause–effect relations within the same passage (ibid., 157). Compare Friedman's analysis of the Bavli's use of "once" (פעם אחת) ("Dama ben Netinah," 439–40), and see Tropper, *Like Clay*, 117 n. 19.

76. On this motif, see Sinai (Tamas) Turan, "'Wherever the Sages Set Their Eyes, There is Either Death or Poverty': On the History, Terminology, and Imagery of the Talmudic Traditions about the Devastating Gaze of the Sages" [Hebrew], *Sidra* 23 (2008): 137–205, esp. 157–79 on our story. For prior discussion, see Shamma Friedman, "The Further Adventures of Rav Kahana: Between Babylonia and Palestine," in *The Talmud Yerushalmi and Graeco-Roman Culture*, ed. Peter Schäfer et al., 3 vols. (Tübingen: Mohr Siebeck, 2002), 3:247–71, here 263–64; Sperber, "On the Unfortunate Adventures," 90 (with Bavli references at 90 n. 40); Rubenstein, *Talmudic Stories*, 340 n. 62.

Compare *Vision of Theophilus*, trans. Alphonse Mingana, Woodbrooke Studies 3 (Cambridge: W. Heffer & Sons, 1931), 3.22, where Jesus turns camels to stone with his gaze, or the saint Thekla, who "knocked the wind out" of certain men with her gaze and "almost would have taken their lives … if she had not spared them" (Linda Ann Honey, "Thekla: Text and Context" [PhD diss., University of Calgary, 2011], 414).

77. To paraphrase R. Yoḥanan: "Have you believed because you have seen me? Blessed are those who have not seen and yet have come to believe" (John 20:29 NRSV). Note the parallel context (master/disciple) and problem (vision/belief). (The same parallel and theme were treated independently by Hirshman, "Paideia," 175; Joshua Levinson, "There Is No Place Like Home: Rabbinic Responses to the Christianization of Palestine," in *Jews, Christians, and the Roman Empire: The Poetics of Power in Late Antiquity*, Jewish Culture and Contexts

intact, the creators cost themselves some realism (the sentence begins in Aramaic and ends in Hebrew, creating a hiccup in the narration). Yet, by retaining the Hebrew formula, they lend their conclusion an elevated, "literary" tone; especially for members of their audience who would recognize allusions to similar talmudic stories.[78] After taking a safe distance from the scholastic status-hierarchy, they still mine it for special effects.

As we just saw, reconstructing the source of this heretic/disciple story—shared by the Bavli and PRK—can shed light on how the editors of the PRK version lightly tailored its frame to link the beginning and the end. This holds for the Bavli as well, except that its composition is on a much larger scale (all of parts 1 and 2), and the tailoring not only confers a meaning upon each literary unit in isolation, but also directs the interpretation of a student who encounters and reencounters both of those parts in the course of study. If we reconsider verbal similarities between the versions in PRK and the Bavli from a student's standpoint, we gain insight into the composition of the Bavli's version of this story. We also learn how Bavli editors used its source to tie part 2 back to part 1.[79]

Keywords, Catchphrases, and the Birth of a Theme

Two keywords stand out: echoes with opposite connotations in the two versions (ל.ג.ג/ג.ל.ג, "to jeer/to proclaim") and a noun (סבא, "Elder") that is not in the Bavli's version of the story, but resurfaces later in the Heavenly Jerusalem section, where, like the verb ל.ג.ג, it is linked to a catchphrase that appears also in part 1. These catchphrases, in turn, link the Bavli's theme in part 2 (status-hierarchy) with a running theme of parts 1 and 2 (belief in *vision* versus *words of the sages*). That link guides a student of the Heavenly Jerusalem section to revisit the instances of the catchphrases in part 1, and to reassess the passages where they appear, in light of part 2—channeling interpretive possibilities latent in the composition as a whole but not determining them.

(Philadelphia: University of Pennsylvania Press, 2013), 99–120, here 115–16; and already by Hermann L. Strack and Paul Billerbeck, *Kommentar zum Neuen Testament aus Talmud und Midrasch*, 3 vols. (Munich: Beck, 1922–1928), 2:586.

78. Friedman similarly acknowledges the possibility of transference of this particular motif between other Bavli sources ("Regarding Historical *aggadah*," 413). Turan shows that it was developed in the Bavli in tandem with conferring greater prestige and dangerousness upon the sages ("'Wherever the Sages Set Their Eyes,'" 190–91).

79. My approach in this section is inspired by a distinctive reading method that Zvi Septimus has developed in his talks and writing (see, e.g., "Trigger Words and Simultexts: The Experience of Reading the Bavli," in *Wisdom of Bat Sheva: The Dr. Beth Samuels Memorial Volume*, ed. Barry S. Wimpfheimer [Jersey City: Ktav, 2009], 163–86; and Septimus, "The Poetic Superstructure of the Babylonian Talmud and the Reader It Fashions" [PhD diss., University of California, Berkeley, 2011]). For differences from Septimus's approach, see my conclusion.

The first keyword echoes only once in the PRK version, with a positive connotation. The heretic goes to R. Yoḥanan and admits that his interpretation of the verse was true, saying:

> "Elder!, Elder!, proclaim all you can proclaim [כל מה דאת יכיל **למגלגא גליג**],
> praise all there is to praise [למשבחה שבח].
> For had my eyes not seen, I would not have believed—"

This keyword has echoes with positive connotations derived from roots in Palestinian Aramaic ("proclaim; make plain"),[80] and in Syriac ("speak in simple terms").[81] However, in both dialects of Jewish Aramaic, it bears a negative connotation: "to deride," specifically, to deride the sages.[82] It is to this negative effect that R. Yoḥanan uses the keyword in the Bavli:

> "Expound, Rabbi, it is fit for you to expound; yea, just as you have said, thus have I seen." He replied:
> "Good-for-nothing![83] If you *hadn't* seen, you *wouldn't* have believed! You jeer [**מלגלג**] at the words of the sages."

In PRK, ג.ל.ג is synonymous with R. Yoḥanan's oral teaching. In the Bavli, the reverse: ל.ג.ל.ג opposes "words of the sages," which the editors turn into a correspondingly marked term by using it to bookend the story. Thus, the Bavli's editors set up a conceptual conflict between sources of truth–*vision* versus "*words* of the sages." That conflict is highlighted by a catchphrase associated with the keyword ("If I hadn't seen, I wouldn't

---

80. Gen. Rab. §64 (ed. Julius Theodor and Ḥanokh Albeck, *Bereschit Rabba mit kritischem Apparat und Kommentar* [Berlin: Itskovski, 1903–1929], 712): "Go and proclaim that you put your head in the lion's mouth unharmed and brought it out unharmed." Etymologically, Michael Sokoloff derives this from a different root (ג.ל.ג) than "stammer/mock" below, in the Babylonian dialect (*A Dictionary of Jewish Palestinian Aramaic of the Byzantine Period* [Ramat-Gan: Bar-Ilan University Press, 1990], 128). Yet they overlap (ג.ל.ג.ל is also "to disdain") and sound so similar as to be readily associated.

81. This root [ל.ג.ג; ל.ע.ג] also refers to reciting Scripture in the Bavli (b. Ḥag. 15b: to recite in a stammering way). See also *Das Buch der Erkenntnis der Wahrheit oder der Ursache aller Ursachen*, ed. C. Kayser (Leipzig: Hinrichs, 1889), 162 line 8 [Syriac]: "even if Scripture speaks simply with us according to that which we are able to comprehend" (trans. Michael Sokoloff, *Comprehensive Aramaic Lexicon*, http://www.cal.huc.edu). Sokoloff (*Comprehensive Aramaic Lexicon*, s.v. לגלג) notes a passage in Rabban Hormizd that combines this verb with "praise," as does the disciple in our story: "In my stammering manner I stammered out his glories in a praising way."

82. Compare b. Ber. 39a: "I am not angry at the one who says the blessing, I am angry at the one who derides [ל.ע.ג] him! If your companion is equivalent to one who has never once tasted an iota of meat, then what did you have to deride?" (The idioms "to deride" and "to taste meat," also appear at b. ʿErub. 21b; a rhetorical formula of some sort).

83. ריקא (*reqa*). See Michal Bar-Asher Siegal, "Matthew 5:22: The Insult 'Fool' and the Interpretation of the Law in Christian and Rabbinic Sources," *RHR* 234 (2017): 5–23, who observes that in general, however, "the insult *reqa* does not seem to be used specifically in reference to Scriptural arguments."

have believed") which, in turn, generates a link back to part 1, where we find the sole other instance in the Bavli of the disciple's fatal error. Rav Pappa reacts to one of Rabbah b. bar Ḥanah's visions (one that began "I myself have seen …"):

> Rav Pappa son of Shmuel said: "If I hadn't *been there* [MSS Vatican, Oxford: *seen it*], I wouldn't have believed it."

This verbatim or nearly verbatim echo between part 1 and the source of part 2, reflected in PRK, is no coincidence. Rather than a schism between apocalyptic authority (vision) and rabbinic authority ("words of the sages"), systematically elaborated by a composer of both parts as a literary unity, however,[84] I prefer to approach it as a means for the editors (or later performers/transmitters) of part 2 to provoke retrospective reflections on epistemological ambiguities that belong firmly within the scholastic horizon of the Bavli passage itself. Clearly, this disciple was wrong to privilege the authority of vision over belief in the words of the sages. But how can a student of this passage square him with his counterpart in part 1, Rav Pappa son of Shmuel? When Rav Pappa son of Shmuel said the same catchphrase, did he mean that he, too, "would not have believed" Rabbah b. bar Ḥanah's vision (a tree bedecked by mythical monsters), but that others—like the members of the "study-house" who repeatedly deride Rabbah as an "ass" and a "jackass"–*should* believe it, because he saw it, too? And yet, if so, is vision legitimate after all? Or perhaps Rav Pappa was making the same mistake as the heretic/disciple: only believing Rabbah b. bar Ḥanah's words after he saw them with his own eyes? Yet if vision is not at all to be believed, then why would Rabbah b. bar Ḥanah have bothered to insist that "I myself have seen" these things? For that matter, why would we, the audience, have been told to "come and see" (תא חזי) for ourselves the lesson of his vision—another ambiguous statement on the blurred authority of vision and oral Torah?

The editors do not answer these questions about part 1. However, by repeating a keyword in part 2; using it to restructure its version of the story; and then "tagging" it with a catchphrase from part 1, they do intensify the questions, thus fostering interpretive integration of the passage. Their technique does not remove inherited ambiguities, it creates new ones;[85] nor does it foreclose alternative resolutions.[86] Regardless, for a student of part 2, part

84. Stemberger, "Münchhausen und die Apokalyptik," 78–82.

85. Along the same lines: if Rabbah b. bar Ḥanah *said* that he saw something, and Rav Pappa *said* that he believed it, then why don't these dicta also qualify as "words of the sages" in the rabbinic oral tradition, even if they refer to seeing?

86. For example, one may read the sages as mocking Rabbah b. bar Ḥanah, not because he claims to have seen things, but simply because he looked for the *wrong* things (1.XIIb: "Now then, those threads of the joints [in the fringes]: Is it according to the House of Sham-

1 will never be the same; the keyword/catchphrase fuses both halves of the composition by restructuring their interpretive process.

The same argument can be made for the second keyword in the Bavli's source ("Elder," סבא), though in this case, the word survives only in PRK's version of the story. In the Bavli, it was displaced to later in the passage,[87] where it is again tied to a catchphrase and a leading theme that forge connections from the Heavenly Jerusalem conclusion of part 2 all the way back to part 1.

In the PRK story, this keyword is, as noted, superficially ambiguous but rhetorically precise. Not in itself derogatory, it creates distance from the scholastic status-hierarchy by naming the rabbi in a more generic register, just as the rest of the dialogue represents rabbinic teaching in a register that is elevated,[88] yet more generic than alternatives.[89] Similarly, the heretic's florid repetition of the honorific ("Elder! Elder!") has, ironically, derogatory connotations, as noted above. In all of these subtle ways, PRK's version uses more formal language to convey less respect for scholastic status, supporting my minor argument about its social *Tendenz*.

---

mai or according to the House of Hillel? If only you'd counted them! And come and told us!"). Here, vision can just as easily *support* the authority of oral Torah (a legal dispute at b. Men. 41b on the issue, "How many threads does one put in [the fringes of the prayer-shawl]?," see Rashbam to b. B. Bat. 74a, s.v. למאי הלכתא).

87. Rubenstein (*Talmudic Stories*, 340 n. 61) shows great fluidity around another Bavli instance of this term (b. Šabb. 34a): in the Yerushalmi parallel it is a "Samaritan" or "scribe"; in Bereshit Rabbah it is an *ʿam ha-ʾarets*; supporting the notion that the Bavli's editors could replace it with "disciple" and use it later in the passage (and see n. 112 below).

88. Note that every verbal element is repeated—unnecessarily, in strictly semantic terms: סבא, the intensive forms ג.ל.ג and ש.ב.ח. Even the verb ח.מ.י and the noun עיני are semantically redundant (the Bavli parallel has simply ר.א.ה.). These repetitions heighten the heretic's register and, correspondingly, the force of R. Yoḥanan's interruption. A similar effect is created differently in the Bavli's Hebrew version, where the student's florid archaism (כאשר אמרת) and poised parallel clauses (דרוש ... לדרוש ... כאשר ... כן) make the rabbi's guttural vernacular retort (ריקא!) all the more blunt. On כאשר ... כן as a well-worn typological formula in the Hebrew Bible, see Fishbane, *Biblical Interpretation* (352, 362, 366).

89. There is a subtle difference between "words of Torah" (מילי דאורייתא) in the Bavli and "words about Torah" (מילייא באורייתא) in our passage of PRK, one that is consistent with the PRK version's aversion to the scholastic status-hierarchy. In the Bavli, "words of Torah" are laws based on the Bible rather than on rabbinic tradition (see esp. b. Pesaḥ. 115a). Similarly, in both Tannaitic and Amoraic works (e.g., PRK 4:3, ed. Mandelbaum, 63–64 = Gen. Rab. 7:1, ed. Theodor-Albeck, 51–52), a "word of Torah" (מילה דאוריתא) is a rabbinic law based on *the* Torah, rather than on the Prophets or Writings ("tradition," קבלה; Wilhelm Bacher, *Die exegetische Terminologie der jüdischen Traditionsliteratur*, 2 vols. [Leipzig: Hinrichs, 1899], 1:166 n. 1). These distinctions set into relief a studied vagueness, a corresponding *lack* of distinction, in the term used by PRK here: "words that I said *about* Torah." In the Bavli version of the story, what is at stake is R. Yoḥanan's ability to interpret the Bible in his role *qua* rabbi ("words of the sages"). In PRK's version, this status of rabbinic interpretation is minimized: as if his authority depends on the Bible itself or, at least, is not grounded in a clearly defined body of rabbinic oral tradition.

The keyword's function in the Bavli is more complex. In the story itself, it is missing or suppressed, with "Rabbi" in its place. This is rhetorically consistent with the Bavli's version; its dialogue is between a master and his "disciple," who "comes before" him to hear his words, presumably in a study-house.[90] It would be unprecedented to call him "Elder"; in the Bavli, the term is never used for direct address in this setting, but only as a title conjoined with "Rabbi,"[91] or as a respectful way to distinguish a senior from junior rabbi by referring to him in the third person (even, possibly, in his presence).[92] Its absence here is not surprising.

Its presence later in part 2, however, is. After a discrete unit on the Garden of Eden—tied into the Heavenly Jerusalem section by the image of a divine *canopy* bestowed upon the righteous—the editors add R. Yoḥanan's final exposition on Isa 4:5 (2.C), circling back to the Heavenly Jerusalem and the status-hierarchy within it. His exposition, based on a gloss of *her assemblies* (מִקְרָאֶהָ) as the elect who are "called" or invited to the Heavenly Jerusalem,[93] is hooked onto a chain of Amoraic exegeses on the same root (ק.ר.א), which also praise the special intimacy of God and the righteous in the eschaton and the Heavenly Jerusalem. This unit concludes with another exposition of Isaiah 4 (v. 3) by R. Elazar, one that yet again exalts the status of the righteous in the Heavenly Jerusalem.

The following unit turns to the Heavenly Jerusalem's physical dimensions:

> And Rabbah said in the name of R. Yoḥanan: "In time to come, the Holy One, Blessed be He, will raise up Jerusalem three *parasangs*, as it is said: *and He shall lift it* [וְרָאֲמָה] *and it shall settle* [וְיָשְׁבָה] *in its place* [תַחְתֶּיהָ]."[94]

90. The ubiquitous formula "X came before R. Y" (אתא לקמיה ר׳ פלוני) in the Bavli implies a scholastic setting where R. Y has special authority (see Avinoam Cohen, "Towards the Historical Meaning Hidden in the Phrase 'Rabbi So-and-so Happened to Come to ...,'" [Hebrew], *Sidra* 15 [1999]: 51–64, here 63).

91. For examples, see Michael Sokoloff, *A Dictionary of Jewish Babylonian Aramaic of the Talmudic and Geonic Periods* (Ramat-Gan: Bar-Ilan University Press, 2002), 783, meaning 3.b.

92. See b. Ḥul. 18a: "But oughtn't a master be worried about [overruling] an Elder?" (referring to a senior rabbi); and b. 'Erub. 63a: "But oughtn't one be worried about [overruling] an Elder?" (as opposed to a member of a subordinate class of scholars, צורבא מרבנן). See also b. Git. 79a and b. Nid. 61b: "From where does the Elder [i.e., Rav Ḥisda] get this [idea]?"

93. This is clarified by the emendation of the Ba''ḥ (ed. Vilna ad loc.), which cites the verse in full.

94. Zech 14:10 (my translation). The verse is difficult. The first verb (ר.ו.ם) was taken in Old Greek Zechariah for the name of the place near Jerusalem: "And Rama shall remain in its place" (Ραμα δὲ ἐπὶ τόπου μενεῖ)—as opposed to other dramatic transformations in the Land of Israel that the prophet depicts in the verse. This is weak, as the *vav* (וְרָאֲמָה וְיָשְׁבָה) indicates that both are verbs, and י.ש.ב is repeated at the start of the following verse: *And they shall settle there* (וְיָשְׁבוּ בָהּ), where the OG translators render י.ש.ב by a synonym (κατοικέω), flaunting the parallel construction. And yet their error highlights the same interpretive problem that gives R. Yoḥanan an opening for his exegesis. What does it mean to say, paradoxically, that God

> What is [meant by] *in its place* [תַּחְתֶּיהָ]? [That *it shall rise* as high] as its base [is wide]. And how [do we know] that this [= three *parasangs*] is its base?
> Rabbah said: A certain Elder told me: I myself have seen the previous Jerusalem, and it is three *parasangs* [wide].
> But perhaps you'll say: It hurts to go up? [It doesn't. That is what] the statement teaches: *Who are these that fly as a cloud, and as the doves to their windows?*[95]

In this local context, Rabbah's invocation of "a certain Elder" functions no differently than many other Amoraic sources: to solve a problem just raised by the anonymous Babylonian scholars, namely, as proof of their claim that the base of the Heavenly Jerusalem will be three *parasangs*. If one studies the Heavenly Jerusalem section in isolation, it is possible, even natural, to accept it at face value as a tradition that aligns the height of the heavenly city (as imagined by R. Yoḥanan) with the base of the ancient city (as recalled by "a certain Elder"),[96] a sublime symmetry also reflected in earlier prophecies and apocalypses.[97] Yet three strange features of the Elder's tradition, as well as parallels and other sources in the Bavli, reveal its thematic role beyond the Heavenly Jerusalem unit (2.C). Viewed in this light, the Elder is not just any Amoraic source, but a suture for both parts of the Bavli's composition in the mind of the student, under the firm hands of the editors.

The first peculiarity is that an Elder hardly ever appears in rabbinic literature as a source like this. "Elder" can designate a reciter of the oral

---

will lift *and* settle Jerusalem "in its place"? Does the prophet simply mean that God will lift the city up in the air and set it back down on the spot? This might be the contextual meaning. But he might also mean that the Heavenly Jerusalem's vertical and horizontal dimensions will correspond: it will rise *in* (= as much as) its place (= its area). For expositions of this verse that respond to similar problems, see t. Sotah 11:16 (ed. Lieberman, 223); PRK 20:7 (ed. Mandelbaum, 317–18).

95. Isa 60:8 KJV.

96. As J. Fränkel says (*'Iyyunim be-'olamo ha-ruḥani shel sippur ha-aggadah* [Tel-Aviv: Ha-qibbuts ha-meuḥad, 1981], 18), "a certain Elder" is often "a figure of special spiritual authority." Tosafot (b. Ḥul. 6a, s.v. אשכחי ההוא סבא) read the unnamed Elder as "Elijah." (In PRK 11:22, he is, and the two appear in succession in b. Šabb. 33b. By the same token, in a story very similar, and adjacent, to the story that parallels this Bavli passage in PRK 18:5 [Appendix 3.B below], "Elijah" plays the role of the "Elder," a.k.a. Rabbi Yoḥanan. For the implications of this doubling, see n. 112 below).

97. See Rev 21:16; Ezek 42:15–20. 4Q554 III, 20–21 and 4Q554a 2 II, 16 portray horizontal symmetry of the city, the temple, or areas thereof in the eschatological Jerusalem (*The Dead Sea Scrolls Study Edition*, ed. Florentino García Martínez and Eibert J. C. Tigchelaar, 2 vols. [Leiden: Brill, 1997–1998], 2:1108, 1110). Rather than extend this symmetry to a vertical dimension in the form of a cube as the Bavli does here, Ezekiel envisions the Heavenly Jerusalem in terms of "altitude markers on a relief map": gradations of holiness tapering toward a peak, on the mythic model of the cosmic mountain. See Jonathan Z. Smith, "Earth and Gods," *JR* 49 (1969): 103–27; repr. in his *Map Is Not Territory: Studies in the History of Religions* (Chicago: University of Chicago Press, 1993), 104–28.

law (Tanna),[98] but, even in that sense, no Amora ever simply cites an Elder in the same way that he would cite a tradition from a rabbinic predecessor.[99] When an Elder does have something to say on a topic of interest to the rabbis, he typically comes from outside the conversation: disrupting, supplementing, querying, or correcting their traditions.[100] No other Elder is associated directly with a particular Amora, as if he were his teacher or colleague.

One of the best analogues to our Elder in rabbinic sources shows, in fact, how unusual he is:

> R. Ḥaninah and R. Yoḥanan and R. Yehoshua ben Levi went up to Jerusalem.
> Produce had been set aside for them and they wanted to redeem it within the [city] walls. An Elder said to them:
> "That is not what your forefathers used to do. Rather, they would renounce [ownership of] it outside the wall and redeem it [out] there."[101]

Here, as in our case, the Elder claims superior knowledge of ancient Jerusalem to that of the Amoraim. However, even he does not claim to have "seen" ancient Jerusalem with his own eyes; he is simply more familiar with the practice of previous generations. Nor is his the last word on the subject: the Talmud goes on to analyze the logic of the practice reflected in his tradition, compare it to the logic of later Amoraim, and reconcile it with positions attributed to earlier rabbis (Tannaim).[102] That Elder stays

98. For examples, see Y. N. Epstein, *Mavo le-nusaḥ ha-mishnah*, 3rd ed. (Jerusalem: Magnes, 2000), 679 n. 2.

99. Yerushalmi Qid. 4:4, 65d (ר' חמא אתא סבא אמ' ליה) is an exception; especially if, as Leib Moscovitz argues, the term אתא ("he arrived") is not a physical description but a rhetorical formula for introducing support for an Amoraic dictum ("'Ata' R' Peloni," in *Talmudic Studies*, ed. Yaakov Sussmann and David Rosenthal [Jerusalem: Magnes, 2005], 3.2:505–18, here 516–17). Yet even the exception would prove the rule: rhetorically, too, this figure of the Elder "arrives" to interject from *outside* the conversation.

100. E.g., b. Ber. 43a: "By and by, a certain Elder came and posed [a contradiction between] a *mishnah* and a *baraita* and taught it [as follows] …"; b. Šabb. 45b: "A certain Elder of Qairouan asked R. Yoḥanan: May a hen's nest be carried on Shabbat?"; b. Šabb. 141b: "A certain Elder said [to R. Abbahu]: Delete your [tradition] due to what R. Ḥiyya taught …"; b. Pesaḥ. 50a (= b. Qid. 71a): "Rava intended to expound it in a public lecture. A certain Elder said to him …"; b. Mak. 11a: "A certain Elder said to him: I heard at the public lecture of Rava …"; b. Ḥag. 25b: "A certain Elder said to Rabbah bar Rav Huna: Do not dispute Ulla's [tradition]. For, like him, we have taught …" (same formulation, different tradition, at b. B. Qam. 114a); b. B. Meṣ. 110a: "A certain Elder said to him: So said R. Yoḥanan …"; b. Ḥul. 28b: "R. Yirmiyah asked … a certain Elder replied: So said R. Yoḥanan …"; b. Nid. 27b: "R. Ammi said: R. Yoḥanan said … a certain Elder replied to R. Ammi: I will explain to you R. Yoḥanan's reasoning …"

101. y. Maʿaś. Š. 3:6, 54b.

102. See Hezser, "(In)significance of Jerusalem," 29–30.

entirely within a realistic chronology and a conventional mode of rabbinic rhetoric.

Our Elder pushes both of those limits. He claims firsthand knowledge of ancient Jerusalem, which he has seen with his own eyes (in fact, he somehow surveyed the entire perimeter of the city). If he means Jerusalem before the temple was destroyed, this is extraordinary, as Rabbah is a third-century rabbi.[103] Yet it is not quite extraordinary enough to make Rabbah a bald-faced liar.[104] Rabbah's claim is no more or less ordinary than the one by R. Yoḥanan that it comes to support: what Zechariah envisioned in the new Jerusalem (according to one rabbi), an Elder already saw in the Jerusalem of old (according to another). Neither rabbi claims to have seen it himself (indeed, R. Yoḥanan disdains the present Jerusalem);[105] they merely claim to know those who have. The Elder's claim serves Rabbah just as the verse serves R. Yoḥanan: as an image of things unseen.

Thus, without radically straining credulity by flagrantly violating chronology or conventions of relying upon sources, the editors successfully insert the Elder to settle a local debate about the Heavenly Jerusalem. Yet, in the same breath, by analogizing our mysterious eyewitness to a major exegete, they raise the composition's larger theme again. It is unsettled. Given the violent conflict between vision and exegesis–marked by the first keyword and first catchphrase in the tale of the doubting disciple—how can this second keyword ("Elder") and catchphrase ("I myself have seen") readily cite a vision to *support* exegesis? And why is Rabbah, uniquely in the tradition, so familiar with this visionary Elder—just as he himself played the role of the visionary throughout part 1?

This association between Rabbah and vision is another strange feature of the Elder's cameo. It goes beyond the attribution to "Rabbah," which recurs throughout the composition.[106] Every other aspect of the Elder's tradition—a catchphrase, a source, even its content—is also associated with Rabbah b. bar Ḥanah elsewhere in the Bavli, especially in part 1. Those repetitions open several portals from the Elder's cameo back to part 1, refocusing a student on this theme in its correlative passages in part 1's visions of Rabbah b. bar Ḥanah. Just as the first keyword was linked to a catchphrase in part 1, animating more pointed interpretive variations on

103. Ḥanokh Albeck, *Introduction to the Talmud, Babli and Yerushalmi* [Hebrew] (Tel-Aviv, Dvir, 1969), 305; Bacher, *Die agada*, 87-93.

104. Again, in his *local* context, the Elder seems to be a perfectly ordinary Amoraic source, cited by Rabbah to support R. Yoḥanan's reading of Zech 14:10. A student who is not attuned to chronology can take him as such and continue learning about the Heavenly Jerusalem. Yet the Elder also does double duty within the composition in these other ways.

105. See n. 47 above.

106. Stemberger, "Münchhausen und die Apokalyptik," 68. On the ambiguity of the spelling of the name (not necessarily of the attribution), see Shamma Friedman, "On the Orthography of the Names 'Rabbah' and 'Rava'" [Hebrew], *Sinai* 110 (1992): 140–64.

the theme in passages where it had appeared, the same process is at work here; if anything, more openly, as it involves a wider range of verbatim verbal repetitions. Like a new actor cast in an old role (with the former star as a supporting actor), the Elder makes it irresistible for a student to compare their performances.[107]

The Elder's catchphrase, "I myself have seen," is virtually Rabbah b. bar Ḥanah's signature, attributed to him in over half its roughly nineteen instances in the Bavli,[108] including three in part 1. By the same token, a catchphrase thematizing vision ("Come, I will show you ...") is attributed to his guide, a nomadic Arab or *Tayeya'* (in fact, MS Hamburg has "*Tayeya'*" for "Elder" here; for this scribe, at least, the episode is strongly reminiscent of part 1!)[109] In other Bavli sources,[110] Rabbah b. bar Ḥanah says "I myself have seen" about a three-*parasang*-sized location in Scripture; just as our Elder says "I myself have seen" the three-*parasang*-wide ancient Jerusalem. Another Elder's tradition is recorded with a variant attribution to Rabbah b. bar Ḥanah;[111] just as, in our context, Rabbah b. bar Ḥanah is the one who records it. In sum, whether we limit ourselves to parts 1 and 2, or also choose to incorporate allusions to other passages in the Bavli, the keyword "Elder" bears a striking kinship to Rabbah b. bar Ḥanah. This kinship is highlighted by their shared catchphrase, which thematizes the relationship of vision to exegesis. Thus, the keyword–catchphrase conjunction guides a student of the text to review what Rabbah b. bar Ḥanah saw in part 1, and to reconsider the relation of vision to oral Torah, as part 2 swells to its conclusion.[112]

---

107. Bacher (*Die agada*, 100–101 n. 12) goes so far as to suggest that, in b. Bat. 75b, "Perhaps this Elder is none other than Rabbah b. bar Ḥanah" (he sees the Rabbah who cites the Elder as, rather, Rabbah bar Naḥmani). Here, a modern scholar performs the interpretive assimilation of the two parts that, I argue, any student is inclined to do by the editors.

108. Exceptions (based on manuscripts in the Maagarim database) include b. Šabb. 22a; b. Ket. 111b; b. Sotah 58a; b. Git. 57a; b. B. Qam. 21a; b. B. Meṣ. 85b; b. B. Sanh. 67b. Some of these (e.g., b. Git. 57a) are attributed to Rabbah b. bar Ḥanah in some manuscripts, although this may be due to harmonization. On this formula, see Reuven Kiperwasser, "The Travels of Rabbah bar bar Ḥanah" [Hebrew], *Jerusalem Studies in Hebrew Folklore* 20 (2008): 215–41, here 224–25.

109. Rabbis also use the catchphrase "I myself have seen" to report visions *of* a *Tayeya'* (b. Šabb. 82a; b. Yebam. 120b).

110. See b. Yoma 75b = b. 'Erub. 55b (in the manuscripts, unlike the prints, the parallel is more or less exact). See also b. Yoma 39b = b. Yoma 20a; b. Ket. 111b = b. Meg. 6a (Bacher disputes the latter's variant attribution [*Die agada* 88 n. 9]).

111. See b. Pes. 53b: "Rav Yehuda said: 'Shmuel said: We only say a blessing on the light at the end of the Sabbath, for that [i.e., evening] is when its creation began.' A certain Elder said to him (or, if you like, it was Rabbah b. bar Ḥanah): 'Just so! And R. Yoḥanan said the same.'" (Three latter attributions are consistent in all manuscripts) This "Elder" tradition, like other traditions where he appears in close proximity to Rabbah b. bar Ḥanah, supports exegesis by R. Yoḥanan.

112. Mira Balberg and Haim Weiss show that, in the Bavli, the elder/old man "cata-

These editorial goads do not direct the student to a single linear argument about the theme. Nor, however, are they fixed at random. Rather, they provoke the student to hypothesize a teleology between verbally correlative passages. For instance, they might look back to this vision in part 1:

> IV. Rabbah b. bar Ḥanah said:
> I myself have seen:
> A day-old gazelle who was as big as Mount Tabor
> (And how big is Mount Tabor? –Forty *parasangs*).
> The length of its neck: three *parasangs*;
> The cradle of its head: a *parasang* and a half;
> and it let loose [ורמא] a turd and stopped up the Jordan.

Striking verbal correlations (the catchphrase "I myself have seen"; the number in this vision, "three *parasangs*"; the echo "let loose" (ורמא); and its location at a holy site in the Land of Israel) invite the student to draw an arc between the "day-old gazelle" in part 1 and the Heavenly Jerusalem in part 2. What relation could this monster, its excrement blocking the sacred river, bear to the Heavenly Jerusalem that will be "lifted" (וְרָאֲמָה) three *parasangs* in the air? Is one to read this grotesque image in part 1 by filtering it through the eschatological prism of part 2[113]—for example, by contrasting it to a sacred river running through the eschatological temple?[114] Or, perhaps, to a river of sacred effluent that fertilized the Land of Israel

lyzes" the plot and exposes the limits of the social order ("'That Old Man Shames Us': Aging, Liminality, and Antinomy in Rabbinic Literature," *JSQ* 25 [2018]: 17–41). It is a "narrative function," not simply a character. This would account for its malleability: it can appear in one parallel (PRK 18:5, 3.B), precede another (b. Sanh. 100a, 2C.i), and follow a third (b. B. Bat. 75b, 2.C). It can be "doubled" with other characters (Rabbah, in b. B. Bat. 75a–b; Elijah, in PRK 11:22; 18:5; and b. Šabb. 33b; see n. 96 above), which is a recognized editorial technique of Bavli aggada (Rubenstein, *Talmudic Stories*, 258; Levinson, *Twice Told Tale*, 259; Friedman, "Dama ben Netinah," 445–46). Some of the Elder's narrative effects identified by Balberg and Weiss within an individual story, and other effects, could also be produced by inner-talmudic interpretation, as students are guided to read "Elder" scenes together precisely because his interruptions are so marked. For the similar function of Elijah ("one of the few … biblical characters that break through the rabbis' narrative and chronological boundaries—both in the Palestinian and in the Babylonian tradition") see Zellentin, "Typology and the Transfiguration," here 262.

113. I am not suggesting an allegorical reading of the "day-old" (or: "aurochs") gazelle, though in this case it has some textual support: (1) Jesus's baptism is often located by the Jordan. (2) Bavli parodies/polemics about Christianity often feature scatological riffs on scenes from the life of Jesus (Yair Furstenberg, "The Midrash of Jesus and the Bavli's Counter-Gospel," *JSQ* 22 [2015]: 303–24, here 317–19; Peter Schäfer, *Jesus in the Talmud* [Princeton, NJ: Princeton University Press, 2007], 93–94). Even if this allegory lay behind the original image, for a later student of parts 1 and 2 together, it is no longer active; the composition must be integrated on its own terms.

114. Ezekiel 47.

and sustained the first temple?[115] In the version of part 2 before us, there are no direct links to either of those traditions—today this is a dead end. Yet it illustrates the kind of *potential* integration of the composition, by inner-talmudic interpretation of keywords/catchphrases, that its editors implanted. And any student *could* follow such cues to draw a Bavli parallel—where the sacred stream *is* evoked—back into the text.[116]

A stronger—that is, still intact—series of correlations between parts 1 and 2 also deploys a multiple of "three *parasangs*" and the verbs ר.ו.ם/ה.מ.י. In both correlative passages, the theme of vision and exegesis is also central. This conjunction of keyword, catchphrase, and theme more clearly invites a student to interpret the end of the series of midrashim by R. Yoḥanan in part 2 as the restatement, elevation, and resolution—the crescendo, as it were—of the beginning of part 1. By retracing those connections, we detect a peroration-like conclusion to the midrashic composition as a whole, playing on its theme of vision versus exegesis and calling vigorously upon its audience.

Part 2 (2.C):

> And Rabbah said in the name of R. Yoḥanan: In time to come, the Holy One, Blessed be He, will raise up Jerusalem three *parasangs*, as it is said: *and He shall lift it and it shall settle in its place*."[117] What is [meant by] *in its place*? [That *it shall rise* as high] as its base [is wide]. And how [do we know] that this [= three *parasangs*] is its base? Rabbah said: A certain Elder told me: I myself have seen the previous Jerusalem, and it is three *parasangs* [wide]. But perhaps you'll say: It hurts to go up? [It doesn't. That is what] the statement teaches: *Who are these that fly as a cloud, and as the doves to their windows?*[118]

Part 1 (1.I):

Rava said:
They that go down to the sea in ships recounted to me:
Between one wave and the next are three hundred *parasangs*,
the height of each wave is three hundred *parasangs*.
Once, a wave lifted us up
and I saw the cradle of a star
and it was as great as the sowing of forty *grivs* of mustard;
had it lifted us any higher, we'd have been burnt by its heat.
The waves raised their voices in chorus:

115. M. Yoma 5:6. *Shisha Sidrei Mishnah*, ed. Ḥanokh Albeck (Tel-Aviv: Dvir, 1954), 2:238; see also m. Mid. 3:2 (ed. Albeck), 5:326.

116. Appendix 2.C.i. (b. Sanh. 100a).

117. Zech 14:10 (my translation; see n. 94 above).

118. Isa 60:8 KJV.

"So, is there anything in the world that you've left alone and not destroyed?"
"Let us go, you and I, and destroy it."
And replied:
"Come see the might of your master!
I cannot pass so much as a grain of sand the width of a thread,"
as it is said:
Fear ye not me? saith the Lord. *Will ye not tremble at my presence? ...*[119]

At first, Rava/Rabbah reports terrifying visions of nature, barely held at bay by God's will. Vision and exegesis are not aligned but opposed: the words of Scripture are the only thing standing between humanity and this image of a violent, alien cosmos.[120] Rabbah's "dream ... upon the Ocean," as the Geonim called it,[121] begins as a nightmare. But he, and the audience, find consolation. Just as Scripture restrains the waves from crashing over the shoreline, the midrash guarantees that Heavenly Jerusalem will be raised three hundred *parasangs* and set back down without a scratch.[122] It is not in

119. *...which have placed the sand for the bound of the sea by a perpetual decree, that it cannot pass it: and though the waves thereof toss themselves, yet can they not prevail; though they roar, yet can they not pass over it?* (Jer 5:22 KJV).

120. No wonder he later interprets the heavenly "oath" (I.XIIIb) as the oath not to destroy humanity with another flood (Gen 9:11; Isa 54:9)! As another way in which the Bavli's composition helps the audience to make sense of a traveling antihero caught between a hostile cosmos and divine power, we might note that, although Jonah is not referenced explicitly ("and it subsides" [1.II] faintly echoes Targum Jonathan to Jonah 1:15), the composition's three-part structure does loosely suggest a "Jonah model." Parts 1.I and 1.V–VII reflect the tempest and (nearly) being swallowed by a whale; 2.B describes a salvific divine canopy; 2.C concludes with hope for the salvation of a city, mapped out in typologically large numbers (on Nineveh-as-Jerusalem in antiquity, see Elias Bickerman, *Studies in Jewish and Christian History: A New Edition Including* The God of the Maccabees, 2 vols., AJEC 68 [Leiden: Brill, 2007], 1:66–67). This Jonah model grows much stronger in the reception of the Bavli's core motifs in Pirqei deRabbi Eliezer, ch. 10. See Rachel Adelman, *The Return of the Repressed: Pirqei de-Rabbi Eliezer and the Pseudepigrapha*, JSJSup (Leiden: Brill, 2009), 243 (underwater pearl); 253 (swallowed sons of Qoraḥ), 255 ("three days and three nights": compare Part 1.VIIIa). A similar compositional model seems to have been used by the 1595 Prague printers who juxtaposed Midrash Jonah with another fantastical travelogue, *Sibbuv Rabbi Petaḥiah mi-Regensburg*. See Ossnat Sharon, "Elephant, Leviathan, and Nineveh the Great City: *Sibbuv Rabbi Petachiah* and *Midrash Yonah*, Printed Side by Side" [Hebrew], in *Jerusalem Studies in Jewish Folklore*, special issue *In Honorem Tamar Alexander*, ed. Galit Hasan-Rokem et al. 30 (2016): 37–73. For rabbinic and contemporaneous Christian stories on a Jonah model, see Reuven Kiperwasser and Serge Ruzer, "Sea Voyage Tales in Conversation with the Jonah Story: Intertextuality and the Art of Narrative Bricolage," *Journeys* 20.2 (2019): 39–57.

121. "And the Geonim wrote that everything of which we here say 'I myself have seen' was in the form of a dream, when he was traveling upon the Ocean" (*Ḥiddushe ha-Ritva `al Massekhet Baba Batra*, b. B. Bat 73a, s.v., אמר רבה אשתעו לי נחותי ימא, ed. Moshe Blau [New York: Gross, 1977], 279).

122. For a similar example of the use of a number as a literary device to confer a "mea-

danger. On the contrary: even as it ascends, it will "settle in its place," not violently transforming but returning to its ancient dimensions, projected on the heavens. And if a skeptical student—recalling part 1?—objects ("Perhaps you will say ...") that no radical change is painless ("... it hurts to go up"), Scripture consoles them too (*as a cloud, and as the doves to their windows*).[123] What began as a war between the cosmos and Scripture is neutralized within Scripture: cosmic forces may threaten human existence, yet they can also be a means of salvation.[124] In this light, one might seek a resolution of the larger theme of visionary authority versus exegesis. The point is not what Rabbah saw or did not see, but where one looks in the text to make sense of it.

Beyond the Sugya and Back to the Sources

This essay has proposed three contributions to the comparison of Palestinian and Babylonian midrash among the Amoraim and their immediate successors, editors of the Bavli roughly as we know it. Its theses can be arranged in concentric circles of narrow philological, mid-range methodological, and broader theoretical argumentation. The narrowest circle brings support for two proposals that others have argued on the basis of different evidence

---

sure-for-measure" structure on an extended Bavli composition, see Sperber, "On the Unfortunate Adventures," 95–96.

123. As J. Fränkel says this unit (1.I) encapsulates, in its two-part structure, the same movement of destruction and consolation that I am suggesting applies to the beginning and end of this extended two-part source (*Darkhe ha-aggadah veha-midrash* [Masadah: Yad la-Talmud, 1991], 1:259). "In the first stage [*a wave lifted us up*], mankind still thinks that it might only be by chance that they were not *burnt* [*by its heat*], whereas in the second part [*Come see the might of your master!*], the conversation reveals the *perpetual decree*," whereby God protects mankind from the elements.

124. An earlier midrash on the "pillar of fire and cloud" (*Mekhilta*, ed. Lauterbach, 158–59; my translation) makes the same point with the same verse of Isaiah: "Come and see: the healing of the Holy One, Blessed be He, is not the same as the healing of a mortal. A mortal does not heal by that with which he wounds; he wounds with a scalpel and heals with a plaster. But the Holy One, Blessed be He, is not that way. Rather, that with which he wounds, He also [uses to] heal [... expounds on the example of the destructive storm from which God ultimately "answered" Job ...] And when He exiled Israel, He exiled them by means of nothing but a cloud, as it is said: *How hath the Lord covered the daughter of Zion with a cloud in his anger* [Lam 2:1 KJV] and when He brings about their ingathering, He does so by means of nothing but a cloud, as it is said, *Who are these that fly as a cloud*. And when He scatters them, He scatters them like nothing but doves, as it is said, *But they that escape of them shall escape, and shall be on the mountains like doves of the valleys, all of them mourning, every one for his iniquity* [Ezek 7:16 KJV]. And when He brings them back, He brings them back as nothing but doves, as it is said, *and as the doves to their windows* ...." In light of this text, "waves" and "clouds" in R. Yoḥanan's midrash are another Amoraic variation on a Tannaitic theme (see n. 44 above): neither the same element (like the storm, clouds, and doves) nor opposed elements (like fire and cloud), but different states of a single element, water.

and methodologies—often by reading works of Babylonian and Palestinian midrash as if they were relatively self-contained productions.

1. Pesiqta de Rab Kahana, one of the great bodies of Palestinian Amoraic midrash, suggests a trend toward "popularization" of rabbinic Judaism, in the sense that it reflects rabbinic practices but resists scholastic status-hierarchy in favor of a more egalitarian social and theological program. Whereas prior versions of this thesis relied on general comparisons to external evidence (e.g., parallel trends in contemporaneous Christianity) or impressionistic reconstructions of this work's social context (without contrasting it to *non*-"popularizing" rabbinic circles), sustained comparison between PRK parallels and the Bavli shows that composers of selected units of the former willfully grounded authority in Scripture rather than in rabbinic status, defining salvation and the scale of merit in terms that would appeal to a wider Jewish audience. Whether this analysis holds for large-scale comparison between PRK and contemporary works of a scholastic *Sitz im Leben*, like the Yerushalmi, remains to be seen; nor do I draw historical conclusions. I try only to exemplify the text analysis on which such conclusions about this Palestinian tradition's social *Tendenz* might rest.

2. A long and intricate passage of Bavli aggada (Appendix, parts 1 and 2) can be called an inner-talmudic composition, held together by a thematized tension between visionary experience and scriptural exegesis as sources of truth, with the tendency to filter the former through the lens of the latter—to tame, so to speak, the would-be authority of vision with the hermeneutics of midrash. By reconstructing the Bavli editors' choices against the background of parallel sources, especially in PRK, I identified a variety of mechanisms whereby they integrated this composition, developed its main theme, and reoriented its audience to the problematic relation between parts 1 and 2 (i.e., between personal visionary experiences and collective eschatological visions grounded in exegesis).

How did Bavli editors employ these mechanisms? At what level did the integration occur? In my second, methodological proposal, I try to access the viewpoint of early students. I argue that the editors joined part 1 to part 2 not so much by textual tinkering as by guiding the student's interpretive process—by implanting mechanisms in part 2 that direct a student's attention selectively to part 1. The composition is not linear but emergent, like a picture coming into focus. In a source-critical adaptation of Septimus's "trigger words and simultexts," I term those mechanisms *keywords* and *catchphrases*. I argue that, conjoined with other features (the theme of vision versus exegesis; attributions; echoes with other sources preserved in whole or in part), such mechanisms create correlations between passages in part 2 and part 1, opening pathways of retrospective interpretation that accent the theme and unite the composition in a student's mind. I examine three keywords appearing in both parts. Two keywords are paired with catchphrases repeated in each part and—I aimed to show—stem from a source also used by editors of a PRK parallel. Those overlaps helped to trace the editing of the Bavli composition and compare it to the editing of PRK parallels.

For editors in both PRK and the Bavli, I argue, the scholastic status-hierarchy is a problem, but for different reasons. Editors of one PRK parallel avoid talk of the hierarchy. Most obviously, they set the same story at a synagogue rather than a study-house; identify authority with Scripture rather than rabbinic tradition; and feature a "heretic" rather than a "disciple." Less obviously, they use Hebrew/Aramaic code switching and a circular plot structure to craft a satire of a figure who—even after God shows him the Heavenly Jerusalem and works a miracle to save his life—merely feigns respect for Scripture, clings to his doubts, and is punished measure for measure.[125] He fails because he fell on the wrong side of the dichotomy between vision and Scripture, trying to ground belief in vision. In that sense, the theme of the PRK and Bavli parallels is the same. Yet PRK neither asserts rabbinic tradition as an independent ground for belief nor dwells on status-hierarchy (neither within the study-house nor between rabbis and other Jews). Our Bavli editors, by contrast, use this tension between vision and exegesis in order to thematize, precisely, vying for status among rabbis—in this world and the next—as well as to ask how personal visions should relate to rabbinic exegesis. Each keyword or catchphrase in part 2 activates a correlative passage in part 1 where those themes are conjoined. The keyword *Woe* prompts a reflection on rabbinic status and hubris, both at the end of days and when rabbis use logic to debate which of God's own vows (!) they can annul. Insofar as *Woe* further characterizes the decline of the generations since the rabbis' founding father, Moses, the keyword *could* initiate a self-critique of part 1. Yet this is only one of many paths that it opens; the editors succeed in sharpening aggadic questions, not in spelling out answers. Another of their catchphrases—*If I hadn't seen it, I wouldn't have believed it*—intensifies the ambivalence of vision versus exegesis as sources of truth. It is uttered by a doubting disciple, who "jeer[s] at the words of the sages," but also recalls rabbis' and the anonymous voice of the Talmud's concessions to the authority of vision. The final catchphrase (*I myself have seen*) plays on the same ambivalence, steering it back to the side of exegesis. Eyewitness accounts of cosmic visions may confirm the words of Scripture, but only Scripture can contain and elevate those visions in the end.

125. For nuances of this rhetoric in the Bavli version, see Turan, "'Wherever the Sages Set Their Eyes,'" 158 nn. 67–68.

I submit my philological and methodological proposals for debate within the horizon of the texts, but I also suggest a theoretical case for pointing beyond their horizon to the context of study. The heart of the theory is my—at this stage, tactically vague—construct of "the student" of the Bavli's composition and their "mind." This construct is multifunctional: it shows how editors could make a composition more coherent without having to fabricate, discard, or even radically reorganize any of their sources. Further, it reveals more nuanced ways of evaluating the scholastic hierarchy buried in their edits, by contrast to clearly non- or antischolastic parallels in PRK. Finally, it suggests how they linked this passage to other Bavli sources, some of which are now lost or broken beyond repair ("dead ends" that retain a heuristic value by pointing up possible routes of inner-talmudic travel). In short, this theory helps us to read in three different directions: within, between, and beyond sources.

Only a steady accumulation of cases can sustain the theory, but, given the state and direction of the field, it bears further exploration. We might say that such a theory hovers over even the most trenchantly positivistic reading: any time we invoke a source that differs from the one before us (which is always itself a composite of versions) we are reading beyond "the" text and stepping into the role of an earlier generation of students who construed the text differently. Still, it is one step to compare the sources of a single text tradition, literary unit, or set of parallels, and another step to read beyond those continuities; to look for links between texts that did *not* result in their actual combination or obvious association within any form of the work as we now have it. No one would dispute that such links continued to be formed after the Bavli and other works were edited, just as they must have once existed among the Amoraim before their traditions were edited. The question is whether they were completely obscured by the work of the editors at each stage. I argue that they were not; on the contrary, in some cases, the editors' activity provokes, directs, and preserves the *process* of correlating and reintegrating texts that has always been central to talmudic study. This process did not always result in a new text. It could highlight connections among old texts or amplify echoes to make them mutually legible in new ways (as *parashah* is to *haftarah* in midrash). Such connections were formed differently by each student, but we can recover their broad outlines by tracking traces that editors left on their sources and asking how these traces reconfigure the texts.

To situate the theory, let me reiterate that it is far from *sui generis*. Rather, it is designed to extend recent advances in Bavli poetics while mitigating their critiques of source criticism (which, if faithfully applied, could lead to a parting of ways between the two methods). It affirms recent calls for a more holistic way of reading the Bavli, beyond the legal or nonlegal passage (*sugya*), whether this entails reading across wider literary contexts,[126] across forms of discourse ("genres"),[127] across a tractate,[128] across the Bavli canon,[129] or across the Babylonian and Palestinian canons.[130] By arguing for the student, rather than the unit, as the main vehicle for mediating Bavli intertexts and making sense of their relations, I share the resistance to Fränkel's thesis regarding the hermeneutic "closure" of rabbinic stories.[131] I temper the halakha/aggada dichotomy by showing that

126. Steinmetz, "*Agada* Unbound"; Jeffrey L. Rubenstein, "Context and Genre: Elements of a Literary Approach to the Rabbinic Narrative," in *How Should Rabbinic Literature Be Read in the Modern World?*, ed. Matthew Kraus, Judaism in Context 4 (Piscataway, NJ: Gorgias, 2006), 137–65.

127. See n. 21 above.

128. Wasserman, *Jews, Gentiles, and Other Animals*; Charlotte Elisheva Fonrobert, *Menstrual Purity: Rabbinic and Christian Reconstructions of Biblical Gender*, Contraversions (Stanford, CA: Stanford University Press, 2000), 15–39.

129. Septimus, "Trigger Words and Simultexts"; Septimus, "Poetic Superstructure." Rather than adopt this model (Zellentin, "Typology and the Transfiguration," 263 n. 67: "Given the likely process of ongoing editorial revisions of the Bavli, we should read (almost) all its stories in light of (almost) all its stories"), I am revising it in two ways. First, I apply Septimus's theory, not to the "implied reader" of the Bavli as a whole, but to that of this particular loosely integrated literary unit (parts 1 and 2), as implied by particular editor(s). These editors are also a construct, but one with a thicker profile in the scholarship that can be tested against local signs of their activity. My goal is to understand not how "the" Bavli's editors created a theoretical reader but how *these* editors created *their* implied reader, using techniques akin to those that Septimus has deftly named and analyzed in his work. Second, as for these techniques, my refinement of Septimus's apparatus is that Bavli "simultexts" can emerge not only by using "triggers" between rare words but also by pairing what I call "keywords" with "catchphrases" and ideas that echo an overarching problem/theme of one simultext, turning it into a hermeneutic key that makes an earlier (adjacent) simultext newly legible. I am more tentative about extending my approach to Bavli passages that are not (or no longer) part of the same source, though I concede Septimus's point that sources were not necessarily studied in the order or configuration that were imposed by the editors of our versions. (To illustrate the distinction between our approaches, see *potential* links between b. Sanh. 100a and b. B. Bat. 75a, or *potential* polemical allegory, that I map out [nn. 113-116 above], only to label a "dead end"; Septimus's global approach is more open to such connections.)

130. See Levinson, *Twice Told Tale*, 278–93; and, for primarily legal sources, Alyssa Gray, *A Talmud in Exile: The Influence of Yerushalmi Avodah Zarah on the Formation of Bavli Avodah Zarah*, BJS 342 (Providence, RI: Brown Judaic Studies, 2005); Christine Elizabeth Hayes, *Between the Babylonian and Palestinian Talmuds: Accounting for Halakhic Difference in Selected Sugyot from Tractate Avodah Zarah* (Oxford: Oxford University Press, 1997).

131. J. Fränkel defines this concept as a double closure: the narrative is isolated from historical context, and it is an integrated, self-referential literary whole, all of its parts complementing one another (*Darkhe ha-aggadah*, 260–61; Fränkel, *The Aggadic Narrative: Harmony of Form and Content* [Hebrew] [Tel-Aviv: Ha-qibbuts ha-meuḥad, 2001], 32–39). For critique, see Rubenstein, "Context and Genre," 138–44; and literature at Binyamin Katzoff, "A Story in Three Contexts: The Redaction of a Toseftan Pericope," *AJSR* 38 (2014): 109–27, here 110–11 n. 4.

Bavli editors reworked sources with the same tool kit: stressing words, or drawing out themes, to make sources speak to one another. On the other hand, I reject binaries between poetics and source-critical interpretation. I have argued that, by focusing on how sources were used in the "live" oral context, we can access the interface between creator and audience where poetics happens—as opposed to the closed space of "the Bavli" alone (no matter how global its borders). Specifically, by comparing the reception of two exegetical complexes in Babylonian and Palestinian works during the obscure period between the Amoraim and the Bavli's more or less fixed redaction, I hope I have shown that the Bavli's editors (or, as some scholars of poetics say, "authors") could *both* retain the integrity and linear flow of their sources, according to conventions of their discourse, *and* use repeated terms, with verbal formulae, to guide the student to read differently—either retrospectively (within a large unit) or laterally (across units associated only by such terms and formulae).

These linear, retrospective, and lateral ways of reading within the Bavli need not produce split meanings or a "hermeneutics of suspicion," aimed at ferreting out suppressed counter-readings. If subordinated to a theme (in our case, the authority of vision versus exegesis), multiple reading tactics could also cooperate, as verbal correlations piqued students' interests, jogged their memories, and nudged their arguments. Nor were the editors wholly original in their uses of these techniques. Rather, my reconstruction of their activity hints that keywords and catchphrases once built bridges across traditions of the Bavli that they did not use (and that therefore turned into dead ends), while others were still alive in the academies but can be restored only with great ingenuity (e.g., as relics of oral performances).[132] One can, at least, test this profile of the Bavli's editors as creative traditionalists, guiding students through structured rereadings of inherited material; their retrospective stance may prove to be a stylistic veneer over more subversive uses of sources.

In the end, perhaps their intentions are not the point. At least on the narrow line of inner-talmudic interpretation that we have retraced here, it is less the creators of the Bavli who subsume Scripture under their unique expressive forms than the reverse: in Babylonian midrash, Scripture's iridescence spreads to the texts that it contacts. Saturated by a scriptural spectrum of possibilities, any text becomes at once supercharged and blurred, shedding traditional connections and straining its frame of reference to enfold an excess of interpretations, issuing in both new senses

132. Already Zecharias Frankel called attention to passages (b. Šabb. 147a, 148a; b. Ḥul. 106b) where the Bavli's redactors presume familiarity with oral explanations that were lost or only retained in other works ("Traditionelle Erklärung der Mischna und des Talmuds," *MGWJ* 11 [1862]: 274–75). On this phenomenon, see Rosenthal, "'Al ha-qitsur vehashlamato," 791–803.

and—no less significantly—new incomprehensibilities. Such is interpretation. Now you see it; now you don't.[133]

Appendix: Translations[134]

1. *Part 1: b. B. Bat. 73a, line 17-74b line 22 (Vilna).* (Text based on MS Hamburg 165, with minor modifications from other manuscripts, as noted.)[135]

I.
Rava[136] said:
They that go down to the sea in ships[137] recounted to me:
Between one wave and the next are three hundred *parasangs*,
the height of each wave is three hundred *parasangs*.
Once, a wave lifted us up
and I saw the cradle of a star
and it was as great as the sowing of forty *grivs* of mustard;
had it lifted us any higher, we'd have been burnt by its heat.[138]
The waves raised their voices in chorus:
"So, is there anything in the world you've left alone and not destroyed?"
"Let us go, you and I, and destroy it."[139]
And replied:
"Come see the might of your master!

133. "'When your eyes light upon it, it is gone'" (Prov 23:5, after translation and exposition in Visotzky, "Misnomers, '*Petihah*' and 'Homiletic Midrash,'" 21).

134. All translations are my own. Compare Stein, *Textual Mirrors*, 125–36. Part 1: Abramson, *Baba Batra*, 89–91; Kiperwasser, "Travels of Rabbah bar bar Ḥanah," 216–23; part 2 (2.A and 2.B only): Michael Fishbane, "The Great Dragon Battle and Talmudic Redaction," in his *The Exegetical Imagination: On Jewish Thought and Theology* (Cambridge, MA: Harvard University Press, 1998), 41–55, here 43–46; part of 2.A: Reuven Kiperwasser and Dan D. Y. Shapira, "Irano-Talmudica II: Leviathan, Behemoth, and the 'Domestication' of Iranian Mythological Creatures in Eschatological Narratives in the Babylonian Talmud," in *Shoshannat Yaakov: Jewish and Iranian Studies in Honor of Yaakov Elman*, ed. Shai Secunda and Steven Fine, Brill Reference Library of Judaism 35 (Leiden: Brill, 2012), 203–36, here 217–19; 3.A: *Pesikta de-Rab Kahana: R. Kahana's Compilation of Discourses for Sabbaths and Festal Days*, trans. William G. Braude and Israel J. Kapstein (Philadelphia: Jewish Publication Society, 1975), 461–73; 3.B: *Pesikta de-Rab Kahana*, trans. Braude and Kapstein, 318–20.

135. Based on my edition and translation of part 1, an appendix to my book in progress, *Adventures of Rabbah & Friends: The Talmud's Strange Tales and Their Afterlife* (Brown Judaic Studies).

136. The spelling of Rabbah's name varies in units 1.I–III, but not necessarily the attribution. See n. 106 above.

137. Tg. Ps. 107:23. See also n. 142 below.

138. MS Hamburg: *by its damage* [or: *by a destructive demon*]. Following all other MSS.

139. Following MS Munich Cod. Hebr. 95. Minus in MS Hamburg.

I cannot pass so much as a grain of sand[140] the width of a thread,"
as it is said:
Fear ye not me? saith the Lord. *Will ye not tremble at my presence?*[141]

II.

Rava said:
They that go down to the sea in ships[142] recounted to me:
A wave that is apt to overwhelm[143] the ship appears with a white branching flame upon its crest,
but we have poles upon which is inscribed:
I am that I am,[144] the Lord of Hosts,
and we strike it,
and it subsides.

IIIa.

And Rava said:
I myself have seen:
Hormiz, son of a Lilith, who was bounding upon the dome of Maḥoza,
as[145] a horseman raced beneath him, riding a steed,
but could not overcome him.

IIIb.

Once
two mules were saddled for him
on two bridges of the Rognag,
and he bounded from one to the other and back again
and he held two goblets of wine[146] in his hands
and he poured from one to the other and back again
but did not spill a single drop.
And upon that day,
They mount up to the heaven, they go down again to the depths:[147]
the authorities got wind of him and brought him to an end.

---

140. MS Hamburg: *mustard*. Corrected on the basis of all other MSS.

141. Jer 5:22 KJV. The verse aptly concludes: "... which have placed the sand for the bound of the sea by a perpetual decree, that it cannot pass it: and though the waves thereof toss themselves, yet can they not prevail; though they roar, yet can they not pass over it?"

142. Tg. Ps. 107:23. See also n. 137 above.

143. On this construction, see Elitzur A. Bar-Asher Siegal, *Introduction to the Grammar of Jewish-Babylonian Aramaic* (Münster: Ugarit, 2013), 288.

144. Exod 3:14 KJV.

145. Common orthographic corruption in MS Hamburg, corrected on the basis of MS Munich.

146. MS Hamburg: *water*. Following all other MSS. See, however, Reuven Kiperwasser and Dan D. Y. Shapira, "Irano-Talmudica I: The Three-Legged Ass and Ridya in B. Ta'anit: Some Observations about Mythic Hydrology in the Babylonian Talmud and in Ancient Iran," *AJSR* 30 no. 1 (2008): 101–16, here 107–8.

147. Ps 107:26 KJV. The verse concludes: "... their soul is melted because of trouble," reflected in the demise of Hormiz.

IV.

Rabbah b. bar Ḥanah said:
I myself have seen:
A day-old gazelle who was as big as[148] Mount Tabor
(And how big is Mount Tabor? —Forty *parasangs*).
The length of its neck: three *parasangs*;
The cradle of its head: a *parasang* and a half;
and it let loose a turd and stopped up the Jordan.

V.

Rabbah b. bar Ḥanah said:
I myself have seen:
A certain frog who was as big as the Fort of Hagrunya
(And how big is the fort of Hagrunya? —Sixty houses).
A serpent came, swallowed it;
A giant bird[149] came, swallowed the serpent
and flew up and settled in a tree.
Come see the strength of that tree!
How great it was!
Rav Pappa son of Shmuel said:
If I hadn't been there,[150] I wouldn't have believed it.

VIa.

And Rabbah b. bar Ḥanah said:
Once I was traveling in a ship
and I saw a certain fish[151]
whose nostril a mud worm entered, and it died
and the water cast it and hurled it ashore.
Sixty towns were destroyed by it
Sixty towns ate from it
Sixty towns salted it
From one of its eyeballs, they made
three hundred jugs of oil.

VIb.

We returned the next year, and when we arrived, we saw
they were hewing from its bones
beams to rebuild those towns.

---

148. MS Hamburg: *upon*. Following all other MSS (positing a common orthographic error).

149. On the Iranian mythological background, see Kiperwasser and Shapira, "Irano-Talmudica II," 209, and Daniel E. Gershenson, "Understanding Puškanṣa (bB.B. 73:2)," *Acta Orientalia* 55 (1994): 23–36.

150. MSS Vatican and Oxford: *seen it*.

151. On the Iranian mythological background, see Kiperwasser and Shapira, "Irano-Talmudica II," 210, 216.

VII.

And Rabbah b. bar Ḥanah said:
Once I was traveling in a ship
and I saw a certain fish
with sands settled upon its back
and a thorn-plant had sprouted on it.
We thought it was dry land
and we went up, we kneaded, and we baked;
The back of the fish got hot
and it flipped over
and if the ship hadn't been[152] close to us
it would have sunk us.

VIIIa.

And Rabbah b. bar Ḥanah said:
Once I was traveling in a ship
and the ship passed between one fin of a fish and the other
three days and three nights
it went upstream as we went downstream.

VIIIb.

And perhaps you'd say:
The ship wasn't moving much!
When Rav Dimi arrived, he said:
Like heating a kettle
the ship moved six *parasangs*.
And there is one who says:
A horseman shot an arrow
but could not overcome it.
Rav Ashi said:
That one is the *gildna* fish of the sea,
who has two fins.

IXa.

And Rabbah b. bar Ḥanah said:
Once I was traveling in a ship
and I saw a certain bird
who was standing up to its ankles in the water
and its head reached the firmament.
We thought the water wasn't deep;
we meant to go down to cool ourselves off.
A heavenly voice appeared and said to us:
Here, you mean to cool yourselves off?
For a carpenter's adze fell seven years
and has not reached the bottom;

152. Correct only in MSS. Hamburg and Vatican ebr. 115.II.2.

and not because the water is deep
but because the water is forceful.

IXb.
Rav Ashi said:
That is *ziz śāday,*
as it is written:
and the wild beasts of the field [ziz śāday] *are mine* ['immādî].[153]

Xa.
And Rabbah b. bar Ḥanah said:
Once I was traveling in the desert
and I saw those geese
whose wings drooped
because of their fat
and a stream of oil
flowed out of them.
We said to them:
Have we in you a portion of the world to come?[154]
One lifted up its thigh at me, and one lifted up its wing.

Xb.
When I came before R. Elazar, he said to me:
In time to come, Israel shall be judged on their account.

XI.
Rabbah b. bar Ḥanah said:
Once I was traveling in the desert
and with us was a certain *Tayeya'*,[155] who was sniffing the earth.
He said:
"This [path] goes to such-and-such a place,
and this goes to such-and-such a place."
We gave him some dirt.
He said: "You are eight *parasangs* from water."
We gave him some [more]. He said: "You are three *parasangs* away."
We shuffled the dirt around on him,
but we could not overcome him.

153. Ps 50:11 KJV. With different vowels, *mine* reads *my pillar;* just as the birds reach from earth to heaven. I thank Reuven Kiperwasser for correcting my theophoric gloss (*ziz šāday*), as in Eli Yassif (*The Hebrew Folktale: History, Genre, Meaning,* trans. Jacqueline S. Teitelbaum, Folklore Studies in Translation [Bloomington: Indiana University Press, 1999], 188), and others. Common orthographic error in MS Hamburg, corrected on the basis of all other MSS.

154. Common orthographic error in MS Hamburg, corrected on the basis of all other MSS.

155. An Arabian tribe; nomadic Arab in general; sometimes "Arab" in general (not distinguishing sedentary/nomadic).

XIIa.

He said to us:

"Come, I will show you the dead of the desert."

I went and I saw that they were reposing, like one who is intoxicated,[156] and they slept. And one of them was sleeping on his back, knees bent.

And the *Tayeya'* went through while riding a camel, and holding a spear in his hand,

but did not touch him.

I cut off and took a thread of *tekhelet*[157] from them

and our camel couldn't move. He said:

"Perhaps one of you took something from them? Let him return it to them."

(For it is taught that one who takes something from them can't move.)

We returned it to him, and we went on.

XIIb.

When I arrived at the house of study, I was told:

"Every Abba is an ass; every bar Ḥanah is a jackass.

Now then, those threads of the joints:

Is it according to the House of Shammai or according to the House of Hillel?

If only you'd counted them! And come and told us!"

XIIIa.

He said to us:

"Come, I will show you Mount Sinai."

I went and saw that it was surrounded by scorpions as big as Libyan donkeys.

A heavenly voice appeared and said:

"Woe is me for having sworn; and now that I have sworn, who will annul it for me?"

XIIIb.

When I arrived at the house of study, they said:

"Every Abba is an ass, every bar Ḥanah is a jackass.

You should have said, 'It's annulled for you, it's annulled for you!' "

But I figured, "Perhaps it was the oath of the generation of the Flood?"

Yet our teachers [retorted]: "'One doesn't say 'woe' [about that!]"

XIV.

He said to us:

"Come, I will show you the Maw of Qoraḥ."

156. Common orthographic error in MS Hamburg, corrected on the basis of MSS Vatican and Escorial.

157. Purple-blue thread, prescribed in the Tanakh for corners of the prayer-shawl [*tsitsit*], as well as for priestly vestments.

He showed us a certain crevice, from which a wisp of smoke was appearing.
He brought out a tuft of wool,
brushed it in water, and wrapped it around his spear, and inserted it.
He drew it out and it was charred.
He said to me: "Hear, now, what you hear from here."
And I heard them saying: "Moses and his Torah are true, and they are liars!"
He told me: "Every thirty days, Gehinnom stirs them *as flesh in the caldron.*"[158]
And they said again: "Moses and his Torah are true, and they are liars!"

XV.
He said to us:
"Come, I will show you where the firmament is overturned upon the earth."
He showed us; I saw a certain slit.
I took my basket and rested it inside until I had prayed.
The orb revolved and I could not find it.
I said: "Perhaps–God forbid–there are thieves here?"
He told me: "Wait until a day from now;
the orb will revolve to its position, and you'll take it back."

XVI.
R. Yoḥanan recounts:
Once I was traveling in a ship
and a certain fish[159] lifted up its head
and its eyes resembled two moons
and water fell from its two snouts[160]
like the two fords of Sura.

XVIIa.
Rav Safra recounts:
Once I was traveling in a ship
and a certain fish lifted up its head
and it had two horns
and upon them was engraven:
I am a small creature of the sea [Ps. 104:25]
and I am three hundred parasangs,
and designated for the mouth of Leviathan.

XVIIb.
Rav Ashi said:
That one is the goat of the sea, and it is lean.

158. Mic 3:3 KJV.
159. See n. 151 above.
160. Common orthographic error in MS Hamburg, corrected on the basis of MSS Munich, Oxford Opp. 249 (Neubauer 369), Bologna Archivio di Stato Fr. ebr. 420.

XVIII.

R. Yonatan recounts:
Once we were traveling in a ship
and I saw a certain little basket
that was studded with precious stones and pearls
and encircled by a kind of fish named *karshei* [shark].
A diver went down to bring up [the basket]. It was about to kill him.
He surfaced, held a skin-bottle of vinegar over it, and it went down.
A heavenly voice appeared and said:
What did you do with the little basket that belongs to the wife of R Ḥanina ben Dosa,
in which is tekhelet[161] *that she spins*[162] *into threads for the righteous in the world to come?*

XIX.

R. Yehudah the Indian recounts:
Once I was traveling in a ship
and I saw a certain precious stone that was encircled by a sea-serpent.
A diver went down and brought it up,
and the sea-serpent was swallowing the ship.
A giant bird[163] came and killed it:
the water was transformed into blood.
Another sea-serpent came,
took [the precious stone], placed it upon [the sea-serpent], and it revived.
Again it was swallowing the ship;
the giant bird came back and killed it,
took [the precious stone], and flew off, but as it flew,
[the precious stone] landed in the ship,
on top of some salted birds, and they revived.
They took it and they flew off.

XX.

Our rabbis taught:
A story about R. Eliezer and R. Yehoshua,
who were going by ship,
and R. Eliezer was sleeping,
and R. Yehoshua was awake.
R. Yehoshua gave a start and R. Eliezer woke up.
He asked him: "What is it, Yehoshua?"
He replied: "Rabbi, I have seen a great light in the sea."
"Perhaps it was the eyes of Leviathan you saw," he said. "As it is written of him:
and his eyes are like the eyelids of the morning."[164]

---

161. See n. 157 above.

162. Likely a common orthographic error in MS Hamburg, corrected on the basis of most other MSS (Munich, Escorial, Bologna, Paris Suppl. Héb. 1337, New York JTS Rab. 2308, 2351.20).

163. See n. 149 above.

164. Job 41:18 KJV.

XXIa.
Rav Ashi said:
Huna bar Natan recounted to me:
Once I was traveling in the desert
and with us was a thigh.
We opened it and removed the veins from it.
It lay on the grass, and it closed up;
we brought logs and roasted it.
The next year, I came back:
the coals were still glowing.

XXIb.
When I[165] came before Amemar, he said to me:
The herbs were dragon's blood, and the coals were of broom.

2. *Part 2: B. B. Bat. 74b, line 22–75b line 40 (Vilna).* (Text based on Vilna, with reference to manuscripts and commentaries, as per the notes.)

2.A. *The Leviathan*

And God created the great sea-serpents ...[166]

Here, they rendered [this as]:[167] *gazelles of the sea.*[168] R. Yoḥanan said: Those are *Leviathan the straight serpent*[169] and *Leviathan the bent serpent,*[170] as it is written: *In that day the Lord with his sore [and great and strong] sword shall take care of* [*Leviathan the straight serpent and Leviathan the bent serpent*].[171]

(Mnemonic: **All things, Moment, The Jordan**).

Rav Yehudah said in the name of Rav: **All things** that the Holy One, Blessed be He, created in his universe, *male and female created He them* [Gen. 5:2, KJV]. So, too,

---

165. MS Hamburg: *one/he.* Error by harmonization with common Bavli formula (see Redfield, "'When X Arrived, He Said…': The Historical Career of a Talmudic Formula," 10, http://www.blackfire.life), corrected on basis of all other MSS.

166. Gen 1:21 KJV (modified).

167. For all instances of this formula, see Smelik, *Rabbis, Language and Translation*, 193 n. 38. It more commonly contrasts a Babylonian translation/interpretation ("here") with one attributed to a Palestinian authority; in this case, the contrast to the Palestinian authority (R. Yoḥanan) is implicit. See further Kalmin, *Migrating Tales*, 43–44 n. 34.

168. This is not in any extant targum that I could find, but it is a variant of *aurochs/aurochs gazelle*, 1.IV (see, e.g., Rashi, b. Zebaḥ. 113b, s.v. אורזילא). It may be influenced by, or in fact reference 1.IV (Stemberger, "Münchhausen und die Apokalyptik," 69).

169. Isa 27:1 KJV (modified; translation after Rashi, ad loc.)

170. Isa 27:1 KJV (modified; translation after Rashi, ad loc.)

171. Isa 27:1 KJV (modified). For *p.q.d* + *'al* ("to take care of" in a negative sense; "to visit [punishment] upon"), see, e.g., Isa 27:3; 10:12.

Leviathan the straight serpent and Leviathan the bent serpent—*male and female created He them*. And were they to copulate, they would destroy the entire universe. What did the Holy One, Blessed be He, do? He castrated the male, killed the female, and salted her for the righteous in the world to come, as it is written: *And he slayed the sea-serpent that was in the sea.*[172]

> And so, too, *Behemoth upon a thousand hills,*[173] *male and female created He them*, and were they to copulate, they would destroy the entire universe. What did the Holy One, Blessed be He, do? He castrated the male and made the female frigid,[174] and preserved her for the righteous in the world to come, as it is said: *Lo now, his strength is in his loins*–that is the male—*and his force is in the navel of his belly*—that is the female.[175]
>
> [But] there, too, [in the case of the Leviathan], He should castrate the male and make the female frigid [rather than killing her]! —Fish are wanton [so making them frigid is not an option].[176] —Then He should do it the other way around [kill the male and preserve the female]! —[Indeed,] if you like, argue: a salted female is superb. If you like [to differ], argue: *there is that* [male] *Leviathan, whom thou hast made to play with.*[177] —[Further, because] it is not proper conduct [to "*play*"] before a female. But also [in the case of Behemoth], shouldn't he salt the female [rather than *make her frigid* and *preserve her*]?—[Not necessarily, because] salted fish is superb, whereas salted meat is not.

And Rav Yehudah said in the name of Rav: At the **moment** that the Holy One, Blessed be He, decided to create the universe, He said to the Prince of the Sea: "Open your mouth and swallow all the waters in the universe." But he said to Him: "Lord of the Universe, it's quite enough for me to swallow my own waters."[178] Immediately, He kicked[179] him and killed him,[180] as it is written: *He divideth*[181] *the sea with his power, and by his understanding he smiteth through Rahav.*[182]

---

172. Isa 27:1 KJV (modified). In its biblical context, the verse is in the future aspect and refers to a *third* kind of aquatic creature.

173. Ps 50:10 KJV (modified).

174. The same root as *cool ourselves off* (1.IXa); another verbal link back to part 1.

175. Job 40:16 KJV. To read this language as castration and sterility seems counter to the plain sense (extolling the virility and fecundity of these creatures). Rashbam (ad loc.) explains that his strength is *in* his loins because it has never been ejaculated, just as her force is *in* her belly because she has never given birth.

176. Bracketed explanations after Rashbam.

177. Ps 104:26 KJV (modified). That is, "Leviathan" is clearly marked as male, so God cannot kill him.

178. Underlined text after Rashbam, ad loc. (Vilna: *that I shall remain with what is mine*).

179. MS Paris: *yelled at*; MS Oxford: *grew angry at*.

180. Compare the defiance of the sons of Qoraḥ and their punishment (1.XIV), linked to the same verb: "swallow" (ב.ל.ע).

181. The translation *divideth* accords with Rashbam, b. B. Bat. 74b, ad loc., whereas Rashi to Job (ad loc.) renders "wrinkles," as in Job 7:5: *My skin is wrinkled* (KJV; modified).

182. Job 26:12 KJV (modified).

R. Yitsḥaq said: Learn from this that the Prince of the Sea's name is Rahav. And if waters were not covering him, no creature could remain due to his stench, as it is written: *They shall not hurt nor destroy in all my holy mountain [for the earth shall be full of the knowledge of the Lord] as the waters cover the sea.*[183] Do not read *as the waters cover the sea* but rather *cover the Prince of the Sea.*

And Rav Yehudah said in the name of Rav: **The Jordan** issues from the cave of Panyás.[184] It is also taught thus:[185] The Jordan issues from the cave of Panyás and goes through the sea of Sammək̲o and the sea of Tiberias, and circulates and runs down into the Great Sea, and circulates and runs down until it reaches the mouth of the Leviathan,[186] as it is said, *he trusteth that he can draw up Jordan into his mouth.*[187]

> Rava bar Ulla challenged:[188] That [verse] is written about *Behemoth on a thousand hills*! Rather, what Rava bar Ulla said [that the verse meant] was: When "*trusteth*" Behemoth on a thousand hills? At the moment that the Jordan penetrates the mouth of Leviathan.[189]

(Mnemonic: **Seas, Gabriel, Hungry**)

When Rav Dimi arrived,[190] he said in the name of R. Yoḥanan: What [are we to make of] what is written, *For he hath founded it upon the seas, and established it upon the rivers?*[191] Those are the seven **seas** and four rivers surrounding the Land of Israel. And these are the seven seas: The sea of Tiberias[192] and the sea of Sodom[193]

---

183. Isa 11:9 KJV. On "Prince of the Sea" see Michael Fishbane, *Biblical Myth and Rabbinic Mythmaking* (Oxford: Oxford University Press, 2003), 119.

184. Spelling of rare Palestinian and Babylonian place-names, respectively, follows Gottfried Reeg, *Die Ortsnamen Israels nach der rabbinischen Literatur*, Beihefte zum Tübinger Atlas des Vorderen Orients B.51 (Wiesbaden: Reichert, 1989); and Aharon Oppenheimer, *Babylonia Judaica in the Talmudic Period*, Beihefte zum Tübinger Atlas des Vorderen Orients B.47 (Wiesbaden: Reichert, 1983). Common place-names are spelled in accord with house style.

185. This *baraita* is paralleled at b. Bek. 55a, minus the conclusion ("until it reaches the mouth of the Leviathan, etc."), which seems to be added to harmonize it with the larger context.

186. See 1.XVIIa: *and designated for the mouth of the Leviathan*, another retrospective link between the two parts.

187. Job 40:23 KJV.

188. Vs. whoever added the conclusion about the Leviathan to the *baraita*. See n. 185 above.

189. That is, although, in the context of Job 40:23, the verse is clearly about Behemoth, not about Leviathan, according to this reinterpretation of Rava bar Ulla's challenge, he *accepts* the interpretation that it is about Leviathan, but he asserts that it is *Behemoth* who "trusteth" when *Leviathan* "drinks" (why, he does not say; perhaps because Leviathan cannot devour Behemoth while it is busy drinking the waters). Rashbam.

190. In the Babylonian Talmud, this formula is traditionally understood as implying [from Palestine], and often associated with, Rav Dimi, who transmits teachings of the Palestinian sage Yoḥanan. See n. 39 above; and Redfield, "'When X Arrived,'" 5 n. 9.

191. Ps 24:2 KJV (modified).

192. The sea of Tiberias = the Sea of Galilee.

193. The sea of Sodom = the Dead Sea.

and the sea of Shilyat[194] and the sea of Ḥulta'[195] and the sea of Sammək̠o and the sea of Apamea and the Great Sea.[196] And these are the four rivers: the Jordan and the Yarmuk̠ and the Qẹramyon and the Pẹgȧ.

When Rav Dimi arrived, he said in the name of R. Yoḥanan: In time to come, **Gabriel** shall arrange a <u>hunt</u>[197] of the Leviathan, as it is written: *Canst thou draw out Leviathan with an hook? or his tongue with a cord which thou lettest down?*[198] But if the Holy One, Blessed be He, does not help him, he will not be able to overcome him, as it is written: *he that made him can make his sword to approach unto him.*[199]

When Rav Dimi arrived, he said in the name of R. Yoḥanan: At the moment that Leviathan is **hungry**, he puts forth vapor from his mouth and boils all the seas that are in the deep, as it is written: *He maketh the deep to boil like a pot.*[200] And if he did not put his head into the Garden of Eden, no creature would be able to withstand his stench, as it is written: *he maketh the sea like a pot of ointment.*[201] And when he is thirsty, he makes furrows upon furrows in the sea, as it is written: *He maketh a path to shine after him.*[202]

Rav Aḥa bar Ya'aqov said: [Due to the Leviathan], the deep only returns to its strength after seventy years, as it is said: *one would think the deep to be hoary;*[203] and *hoary* is not less than seventy.[204]

194. Reeg identifies this with the Gulf of Eilat (*Die Ortsnamen Israels*, 303).

195. Location uncertain. Reeg locates it north of the sea of Sammək̠o (*Die Ortsnamen Israels*, 302).

196. The Great Sea = the Mediterranean.

197. *Qenigiya*, from Gk. κυνήγιον; see Samuel Krauss and Immanuel Löw, *Griechische und lateinische Lehnwörter im Talmud, Midrasch und Targum*, 2 vols. (Berlin: Calvary, 1898–1899), 2:553–54. Rav Dimi's Babylonian contemporary prized the agentive form as a rare loanword (b. Ḥul. 60b): "But was Moses our teacher a hunter [*qenigi* = κυνηγός] or an archer [*balistari*]?! … Rav Ḥisda said to Rav bar Taḥlifa bar Avina: 'Go, write *qenigi* and *balistari* in your [book of] aggada and define it." On possible Iranian background, see Kiperwasser and Shapira, "Irano-Talmudica II," 223–27.

198. Job 41:1 KJV [MT 40:30]. In the Vilna print and other witnesses, the word for *canst* has a prefixed *heh*, indicating a rhetorical question. Other manuscripts (the Genizah fragment Cambridge T-S F1[1].30; the early Spanish MS Hamburg; and the late Provençal MS Escorial) lack this feature. The same variant appears among manuscripts of the Hebrew Bible itself. (The following verses all begin with the same rhetorical prefix; perhaps it was added due to a harmonizing impulse).

199. Job 40:19 KJV, reading restrictively to imply "… [*only*] he that made him" etc.

200. Job 41:31a KJV [MT 41:23].

201. Job 41:31b KJV.

202. Job 41:32a KJV.

203. Job 41:32b KJV.

204. In other words, a person is not called *hoary* until they reach seventy. See m. 'Abot 5:21: "At the age of seventy, one is hoary" (ed. Albeck, *Shisha Sidrei Mishnah*, 4:381).

2.B. The Leviathan and The Coverings

Rabbah said in the name of R. Yoḥanan: In time to come, the Holy One, Blessed be He, will arrange a banquet for the righteous from the flesh of Leviathan, as it is said: *Shall the companions make a feast of him?*[205] For *feast* is none other than a banquet, as it is said: *And he fêted them with a great feast: and they ate and they drank;*[206] and *the companions* [*ḥabbarim*] are none other than disciples of the sages, as it is said: *Thou that dwellest in the gardens, the companions* [*ḥaverim*] *hearken to thy voice: cause me to hear it.*[207] And they divide the rest and arrange it as merchandise in the markets of Jerusalem, as it is said: *shall they part him among the merchants?*[208] For *merchants* are none other than competitors,[209] as it is said: *He is a merchant, the balances of deceit are in his hand: he loveth to oppress.*[210] Or, if you like, argue it from here: *whose merchants are princes, whose traffickers are the honourable of the earth.*[211]

And Rabbah said in the name of R. Yoḥanan: In time to come, the Holy One, Blessed be He, will arrange a booth for the righteous from the skin of Leviathan, as it is said: *Canst thou fill his skin with barbed irons* [*śukkôt*]?[212] If he is deserving, a booth is arranged for him; if not, a shading is arranged for him, as it is said: *or his head with a fish spear* [ṣilṣāl dāgîm].[213] If he is deserving, a shading is arranged for him; if not, chains are arranged for him, as it is said: *and chains about thy neck.*[214] If he is deserving, chains are arranged for him; if not, an amulet is arranged for him, as it is said: *or thou wilt bind it for thy maidens.*[215] And the rest will the Holy One, Blessed be He, spread across the walls of Jerusalem, and its radiance will shine from one end of the universe to the other, as it is said: *And nations shall walk by thy light, and kings by the brightness of thy rising.*[216]

---

205. Job 41:6a KJV [MT 40:30] (modified).

206. 2 Kgs 6:23 KJV (modified).

207. Song 8:13 KJV. These words (*hearken; hear; companions*) suggest rabbinic study of Torah, the "bride" of Israel.

208. Job 41:6b KJV.

209. The same gloss appears in the Masorah Parva to Job 41:6b ("a term for a competitor," *lashon taggerayya*). It is not necessarily pejorative (closer to "middleman"); see Friedman, "Dama ben Netinah," 465.

210. Hos 12:7 KJV.

211. Isa 23:8 KJV.

212. Job 41:7a KJV. "Barbed irons" [*śukkôt*] is a homophone of "booths" [*sukkôt*]; here, the midrash changes the consonantal text of the Masoretic tradition. To disambiguate homophones, I adopt the academic transliteration system of *The SBL Handbook of Style,* 2nd ed. [Atlanta: SBL Press, 2014], 26).

213. Job 41:7b KJV (modified). Biblical "spear" is a homophone of rabbinic "shading" (*ṣilṣāl*), from *ṣēl* ("shade; shadow"). Rather than *ṣilṣāl*, Rashbam to b. B. Bat. 75a, s.v. *sukkāh,* seems to read *ṣēl*, just as in Isa 4:6 (see 3.A below), that is, "a kind of canopy [*sikkūaḥ*] without a [vertical] partition."

214. Prov 1:9 KJV.

215. Job 41:5 KJV (translation modified in line with Rashbam's interpretation: the verse is referring not to the binding of the Leviathan but to "a small thing that he ties to wear around his throat, like an amulet"). More likely, his child's.

216. Isa 60:3 KJV (modified).

2.C. The Heavenly Jerusalem

And I will make thy windows of kadkod:[217] R. Shmuel bar Naḥmani said: Two angels are debating in the firmament, Gabriel and Michael. And some say it was[218] two Amoraim in the West. (And who are they? Judah and Ḥizkiyah, the sons of R. Ḥiyya). One said [*kadkod* is] onyx.[219] One said [*kadkod* is] jasper.[220] The Holy One, Blessed be He, said to them: Let it be both as this and as that [*kedein u-khedein*].

And thy gates of carbuncles.[221] Just as in this [tradition]:[222]

//R. Yoḥanan was expounding: "In time to come, the Holy One, Blessed be He, will bring precious stones and pearls that are thirty by thirty [cubits], and carve out [a space from] them ten [cubits wide] by twenty [high],[223] and set them up in the gates of Jerusalem." A certain disciple jeered at him: "Nowadays, we don't find them as big as a turtle-dove's egg; are we to find all that?!" Some days later, his ship went off to sea. He saw the ministering angels who were chiseling precious stones and pearls thirty by thirty [cubits] and carving out [a space from them] ten [cubits wide] by twenty high. He said to them: "Who are these for?" They replied that in time to come, the Holy One, Blessed be He, would set them up in the gates of Jerusalem. He came before R. Yoḥanan and said to him: "Expound, Rabbi, it is fit for you to expound; yea, just as you have said, thus have I seen." He replied: "Good-for-nothing! If you *hadn't* seen, you *wouldn't* have believed! You jeer at the words of the sages." He cast his eyes at him and he was transformed into a pile of bones.

It is objected:[224] *And I will make you go upright:*[225] R. Meir says: "[The word *upright* means that the height of the gates of the Heavenly Jerusalem will

---

217. Isa 54:12 KJV (modified).

218. On this introductory formula for variant attributions/traditions, see literature: Redfield, "Redacting Culture," 74 n. 92.

219. *Shoham*, an unknown gem in the priestly breastplate (see Exod 25:7; 28:9, 20; 35:9, 27; 39:6; 39:13). I translate *onyx* after LXX ὄνυξ (cf. Exod 28:9: *σμαράγδος, emerald*).

220. *Yashfeh*, an unknown gem in the priestly breastplate (see Exod 28:20; 39:12). I translate *jasper* after LXX ἴασπις (Ezek. 28:13).

221. Isa 54:12 KJV (modified).

222. The section enclosed within // // is paralleled at b. Sanh. 100a; under 2.C.i below, I translate the literary context of the parallel that is relevant to my suggestions in the essay (see n. 116 above).

223. Translation after Rashbam (ad loc.) and the clarifying wording of the repetition below ("twenty *high*").

224. That is, someone disputes R. Yoḥanan's previous claim about the height of the temple in the Heavenly Jerusalem on the basis of R. Meir's interpretation of a different verse.

225. Lev 26:13 KJV (modified from the past to the future aspect, in line with R. Meir's interpretation).

be] two hundred cubits, equalling twice the height of Adam."[226] R. Yehudah says: "[The gates of the Heavenly Jerusalem will be] a hundred cubits, matching [the height of] the Temple and its walls, as it is said: *That our sons may be as plants grown up in their youth; that our daughters may be as corner stones, polished after the similitude of a palace.*"[227] But R. Yoḥanan is only speaking about the slits of the area for a draft.[228]//

> [2.C.i = b. Sanh. 100a (Vilna): R. Yirmiyah sat before R. Zeira and he was saying: "In time to come, the Holy One, Blessed be He, will bring forth a river from the Holy of Holies, and upon it shall be all kinds of delicacies, as it is said: *And by the river upon the bank thereof, on this side and on that side, shall grow all trees for meat, whose leaf shall not fade, neither shall the fruit thereof be consumed: it shall bring forth new fruit according to his months, because their waters they issued out of the sanctuary: and the fruit thereof shall be for meat, and the leaf thereof for medicine.*[229] A certain Elder said to him: "Just so! And R. Yoḥanan said the same." R. Yirmiyah said to R. Zeira: "Does such a manner smack of irreverence?" He replied: "That's help[ful]! It's helping you[r position]!" Rather, if you've heard [about an irreverent manner], then [surely] you've heard about when R. Yoḥanan was expounding: [... //parallel to the above two paragraphs follows with minor variations]. //

And Rabbah said in the name of R. Yoḥanan: In time to come, the Holy One, Blessed be He, will arrange seven canopies [*ḥuppot*] for each of the righteous, as it is said: *And the Lord will create upon every dwelling place of mount Zion, and upon her assemblies, a cloud and smoke by day, and the shining of a flaming fire by night: for upon all the glory shall be a canopy.*[230] This teaches that for every one them, the Holy One Blessed be He will arrange a canopy, according to his honor. [But] why is there *smoke* in a canopy?[231] R. Ḥanina said that if anyone squints[232] at disciples of the sages in this world, his eyes will be filled with smoke in the world to come. [And] why is there *fire* in a canopy? R. Ḥanina said: this teaches that [if] anyone envies the canopy of his companion, Woe for such shame! Woe for such disgrace!

---

226. As Rashbam notes (ad loc.), R. Meir derives this doubled height from the doubled letter *mem* in "upright" (*qomemiyyut*). For Adam's height after the fall as 100 cubits, see sources in Louis Ginzberg, *The Legends of the Jews*, 2nd ed. (Philadelphia: Jewish Publication Society, 2003), 98 n. 137.

227. Ps 144:12 KJV. Rashbam: the height of the gates (or: God's *sons* and *daughters*) in the Heavenly Jerusalem will equal the height of God's previous *palace* [i.e., temple].

228. This unique term has a longer reading/gloss in MS Paris 1337: *Slits that a draft goes through*, that is, the ventilation ducts of the temple. The rare words "slit" and "draft" (or a homonym of the latter: "skin-bottle") already appeared in 1.XV and 1.XVIII, respectively—yet another example of verbal synergy between the two parts of the composition.

229. Ezek 47:12 KJV (modified).

230. Isa 4:5 KJV (modified).

231. That is, if it is a reward, why does it contain this noxious element?

232. That is, is stingy and does not share his assets with them. Rashbam, ad loc.

Along the same lines, you [may] say: *And thou shalt put some of thine honour upon him.*[233] But not all of your honor? Elders who were in that generation said: "The face of Moses is like the face of the sun, the face of Joshua is like the face of the moon."[234] Woe for such shame! Woe for such disgrace![235]

R. Ḥama[236] the son of R. Ḥanina said: The Holy One, Blessed be He, arranged ten canopies [*ḥuppot*] for Adam in the Garden of Eden, as it is said: *Thou hast been in Eden the garden of God; every precious stone [was thy covering: carnelian ...].*[237] Mar Zutra said: [He arranged] eleven [canopies], as it is said: *Every precious stone.*[238] R. Yoḥanan said: "And the least of them all was gold"—because it was not accounted for until the end [of the list in that verse].

---

233. Num 27:20 KJV.

234. That is, the generations had already begun to decline with Joshua. Note the inversion of the redemptive eschatological prophecy in Isa 30:26 (KJV: *the light of the moon shall be as the light of the sun, and the light of the sun shall be sevenfold*).

235. That is, the decline of the generations is shameful. Note another inversion of Isaiah (24:23 KJV: *Then the moon shall be confounded, and the sun ashamed*). Obviously, the description of Moses's shining face is already biblical (Exod 34:29; see also Deut 34:7), whereas the description of Joshua's face as "like the moon" appears to be postbiblical and is attested elsewhere in rabbinic sources (see esp. Midr. Ps. 21:179, ed. Buber). See further Elliot R. Wolfson, "The Face of Jacob in the Moon: Mystical Transformations of an Aggadic Myth," in *The Seductiveness of Jewish Myth: Challenge or Response?*, ed. S. Daniel Breslauer (Albany: SUNY, 1997), 235–70.

236. The tradition of this sage (Ḥama) may be joined to the prior tradition by association with "sun" (*ḥamah*). For somewhat similar examples (in b. Ḥul. 89a and Exod. Rab. 21, respectively), see Shamma Friedman, "*Nomen est Omen:* Dicta of Talmudic Sages Which Echo the Author's Name" [Hebrew], in *These Are the Names: Studies in Jewish Onomastics*, vol. 2, ed. Aaron Demsky, Joseph Tabory, and Y. A. Raif (Ramat-Gan: Bar-Ilan University Press, 1999), 51–77, here 74; J. D. Wynkoop, "A Peculiar Kind of Paronomasia in Talmud and Midrash," *JQR* 2 (1911): 1–23, here 14. Generally, this phenomenon of association between a sage's name and the content of a tradition has been documented *within* one tradition (e.g., the tradent's name corresponds to a rare word). But the same principles (sound-play; associations of the name with the content) could also link traditions and use common words (whether that link was forged in the original oral composition, per Friedman, or at a later stage of transmission, as earlier studies had held).

237. Ezek 28:13 KJV. The verse itself refers to Hiram, ironically contrasting him with Adam (see Rashbam; see also the beginning of this prophecy, "Son of Man" [*ben-'Adam*]). But the [bracketed continuation of the verse], not quoted in Vilna, is the key to this midrash. "Carnelian" (*'odem*) is close to "Adam," while the root of "covering" [*mĕsūkātekā*] was already used for "booth" in the midrash on Job 41:7a (see n. 212 above). Wordplay thus yields: "*every precious stone [was thy booth for Adam].*"

238. Reading "every" as an addition to the contents of the list; a standard midrashic technique (e.g. m. Ber. 1:5; ed. Albeck, *Shisha Sidrei Mishnah*, 1:15).

What [is meant by] *the workmanship of thy tabrets and of thy pipes [was prepared] in thee*?[239] Rav Yehudah said in the name of Rav: "The Holy One, Blessed be He, said to Hiram King of Tyre, '*In thee* did I look, and [upon that very day] did I create orifices upon orifices[240] within humanity.'"[241] And there is one who says, this what [the verse] is saying: "*In thee* did I look, and I imposed death upon Adam."

What [is meant by] *and upon her assemblies*?[242] Rabbah said in the name of R. Yoḥanan: "Not like Jerusalem of this world is Jerusalem of the world to come. Jerusalem of this world: anyone who wants to go up, can go up. Jerusalem of the world to come: only those who are invited[243] to it can go up."

And Rabbah said in the name of R. Yoḥanan: "In time to come, the righteous will be called[244] by the name of the Holy One, Blessed be He, as it is said: *Even every one that is called by my name: for I have created him for my glory, I have formed him; yea, I have made him.*[245] And R. Shmuel bar Naḥmani said in the name of R. Yoḥanan: "Three were called by the name of the Holy One, Blessed be He, and they are: The righteous, and the Messiah, and Jerusalem." The righteous—as we [just] said. The Messiah—as it is written, *and this is his name whereby he shall be called, The Lord Our Righteousness.*[246] And Jerusalem—as it is written, *It was round about eighteen thousand measures: and the name of the city from that day shall be, The Lord is there.*[247] Do not read *there* [*šāmmāh*] but rather *its name* [*šemāh*].[248] R. Elazar said: "In time to come, one will say 'Holy' before the righteous in the same way that one says it before the Holy One, Blessed be He, as it is said: *he that is left in Zion, and he that remaineth in Jerusalem, shall be called holy.*"[249]

And Rabbah said in the name of R. Yoḥanan: In time to come, the Holy One, Blessed be He, will raise up Jerusalem three *parasangs*, as it is said:

---

239. Ezek 28:13 KJV.

240. Combining the language of a rabbinic blessing uttered upon excretion (b. Ber. 24b = b. Ber. 60a = b. Ber. 75a) with the unique instance of this biblical noun in this verse (KJV: *pipes*, i.e. excretory "organs").

241. That is, foreseeing Hiram's rebellion and self-idolatry, God saw the need to install excretory organs to humble human beings (after Rashbam, ad loc.).

242. Isa 4:5 KJV.

243. That is, "called"; playing on the root of *assemblies* (ק.ר.א).

244. Continuing the wordplay on ק.ר.א, which links the two exegeses.

245. Isa 43:7 KJV.

246. Jer 23:6 KJV.

247. Ezek 48:35 KJV.

248. That is, "the name of the city from that day shall be, *The Lord is its name*." The proof retains the consonantal text.

249. Isa 4:3 KJV.

and He shall lift it and it shall settle in its place."[250] What is [meant by] *in its place*? [That *it shall rise* as high] as its base [is wide]. And how [do we know] that this [= three *parasangs*] is its base? Rabbah said: A certain Elder told me: I myself have seen the previous Jerusalem, and it is three *parasangs* [wide]. But perhaps you'll say: It hurts to go up? [It doesn't. That is what] the statement teaches: *Who are these that fly as a cloud, and as the doves to their windows?*[251] Rav Pappa said: "Learn from it that a cloud lifts[252] three *parasangs* atop [the earth]."[253]

R. Ḥaninah bar Pappa said: "The Holy One, Blessed be He, wanted to give Jerusalem a proper measure, as it is said: *Then said I, Whither goest thou? And he said unto me, To measure Jerusalem, to see what is the breadth thereof, and what is the length thereof.*[254] The ministering angels said before the Holy One, Blessed be He: "Master of the Universe, in your world, you made many towns[255] of the Nations of the world, and you gave them neither a measure of their length or a measure of their width. To Jerusalem—within which are Your Name, Your Holiness, and Your righteous—are you giving a measure? Immediately [God replied:] *And said unto him, Run, speak to this young man, saying, Jerusalem shall be inhabited as towns without walls for the multitude of men and cattle within.*[256] Resh Laqish said: "In time to come, the Holy One, Blessed be He, will expand Jerusalem by:[257] a thousand [times] טפ"ף gardens [= 169], a thousand [times] קפ"ל towers [= 210] a thousand [times] ליצו"י citadels,[258] [= 146] a thousand and two [times] שיל"ה four-

250. Zech 14:10 (my translation; see n. 94 above).

251. Isa 60:8 KJV.

252. From the root ד.ל.י, "to lift," yet another verbal link to part 1 (1.I; 1.XI; 1.XVI; 1.XVIIa).

253. That is, if we know from the tradition of the Elder that its base is three *parasangs*, and we know from the tradition of R. Yoḥanan that its height was the same as its base, and we know from Isa 60:8 that it is lifted up by a cloud, then we also know that a cloud rises three *parasangs* in the air.

254. Zech 2:2 KJV.

255. *Kerakhim*, which by definition actually do have walls/fortifications, contrary to the verse below. The term can also mean "city; settlement," and it seems to be used in that more general sense.

256. Zech 2:4 KJV (modified). That is, the ministering angels are challenging God's imposition of a three-*parasang*-square size upon Jerusalem. They argue that the nations' towns do not have a fixed size; God concedes and sends them to the prophet (in Zech. 2:4).

257. Rashbam (ad loc.) explains the following acronyms as a particular conventional way to express numbers in words. This understanding is already reflected in MS Hamburg 165 (1184 CE), which marks all except one (ליצוי) as numbers.

258. *Biraniyyot*; Alexander Kohut plausibly glosses "*Burg, Castell*" (*Aruch Completum* [Vienna 1880], 2:195), based on lexical equivalents in targumim, but he neglects this source (or biblical sources, e.g., 1 Chr 29:1). Translation after Stephen A. Kaufman, *The Akkadian Influences on Aramaic*, Assyriological Studies 19 (Chicago: University of Chicago Press, 1974), 44.

cornered mansions [= 345].[259] And every single one of them will be like Sepphoris at its most irenic. <u>It is taught:</u>[260] R. Yosi said: "I saw Sepphoris at its most irenic, and in it, there were a hundred and eighty thousand markets of vendors of mincemeat puddings. *And the side chambers were three, one over another, and thirty in order.*[261] What [is meant by] *three, one over another, and thirty in order*? R. Levi said in the name of Rav Pappi: Because of [what] R. Yehoshua of Siknin said: [In time to come] if it is [as big as] three Jerusalems, every single [house] will have in it thirty stories above [one another]; if it is [as big as] thirty Jerusalems, every single [house] will have three stories above [one another].

3. Parallels in Pesiqta de Rab Kahana (Text and variants in Bernard Mandelbaum edition, 2nd ed., 2 vols. Philadelphia: Jewish Publication Society, 1987).

3.A. Appendix II [ed. Mandelbaum, p. 455 line 8–line 9 … p. 456 line 22–p. 457 line 8] // Bavli 2.B]

Another matter: *and there shall be a booth* [sukkāh] *for shadow in the day time from the heat.*[262] R. Levi said: Anyone who fulfills the commandment of the [*sukkāh*] in this world, the Holy One, Blessed be He, will seat him in the *sukkāh* of the Leviathan in the time to come, as it is said: *canst thou fill his skin with barbed irons* [*śukkôt*]*?*[263]

[… long excursus, concluding with the verse just cited.]

Or his head with a fish spear [ṣilṣāl dāgîm]?[264] R. Naḥman and R. Huna the Priest and R. Yehudah the Levite the son of R. Shalom [comment]:

One of them pounds on his cymbal [*bĕṣelṣālo*] and says, "Anyone who has performed the commandment of pilgrimage [to Jerusalem] shall come and serve [him/herself] and eat from his head, and its taste is like the taste of the head of a fish from the Sea of Tiberias." And his companion says, "They pound on their cymbals and say, 'Anyone who has performed the commandment of pilgrimage [to Jerusalem] shall come and eat from his head, and its taste is like the taste of the head of a fish from the Great Sea.'" Immediately, they come and form a com-

259. טוטפראות, a corruption of טיטרפלין = τετράπυλα (see Krauss and Löw, *Lehnwörter*, 2:262).

260. Conventionally, this formula introduces a *baraita*, but in this case the *baraita* is unattested elsewhere: see Michael Higger, *Otsar ha-baraitot*, 10 vols. (New York: Hotsa'at de-be rabanan, 1938–1948), 8:92; Raphael Nathan Nata Rabbinovicz, *Diqduqe Soferim*, 16 vols. (Munich: Huber, 1868–1897), *Baba Batra*, 240 n. ס.

261. Ezek 41:6 KJV.

262. Isa 4:6 KJV, modified.

263. Job 41:7a KJV, modified. See n. 49 above.

264. Job 41:7b KJV.

pany and make a feast of him,[265] as it is said, *Shall the companions make a feast of him?*[266] [Namely,] one who has made himself a *companion* of the commandments.

Another matter: *Shall the companions make a feast of him?* Companies upon companies:[267] There are adepts in Scripture, there are adepts in Mishnah, there are adepts in Talmud, there are adepts in Aggada, there are adepts in commandments, there are adepts in good deeds. Every single company comes and serves itself a portion. And perhaps you would say that there is dissension among them? One would reply: *shall they part him among the merchants?*[268] —those are the businessmen,[269] the ones who, when they are partners in a precious stone and they sell it and they come to divide the assets, have no dissension. Rather, each of them comes and takes out his portion according to the assets that he put in. And similarly, in time to come, there will be no dissension among [the adepts]. Rather, each of the righteous will come and take out his reward according to his deeds. Hence, *shall they part him among the merchants?* [which means] not [merely] *merchants* but businessmen, as it is written: *whose merchants are princes, whose traffickers are the honorable of the earth.*[270]

3.B. 18:5 [ed. Mandelbaum, p. 296 line 4 … p. 297 line 8–p. 298 line 11] // Bavli 2.C [{Beginning of 2.C} – "pile of bones."]

And I will make [thy windows of] kadkod:[271] R. Abba bar Kahana said: as this and as that [*kedein u-khedein*]. R. Levi said: *kadkedayyanon.*[272] R. Yehoshua ben Levi said: Stones of *kadkodayyah.*[273]

[…][274]

And thy gates of carbuncles ['eqdaḥ].[275] R. Yirmiyah [said] in the name of R. Shmuel bar Yitsḥaq: "In time to come, the Holy One, Blessed be He, will

---

265. Possibly by analogy to the "company" formed to sacrifice the Paschal offering.

266. Job 41:6a KJV (modified).

267. The term "companion" also refers to a member of Palestinian rabbinic study circles, which appears to be the basis of this midrash. See Appendix 2.B above.

268. Job 41:6b KJV.

269. *Pragmatotin* = πραγματευτάδες. See Aaron Michael Butts, "Language Change in the Wake of Empire: Syriac in its Greco-Roman Context" (PhD diss., University of Chicago, 2013), 156.

270. Isa 23:8 KJV.

271. Isa 54:12 KJV (modified).

272. From καρχηδών ("carbuncle"); see Löw in Krauss and Löw, *Lehnwörter* 2:299; Sokoloff, *Jewish Palestinian Aramaic*, 251.

273. From χαλκιδική, χαλκηδών ("chalcedony"). See Jacob Levy and Heinrich Fleischer, *Neuhebräisches und Chaldäisches Wörterbuch über die Talmudim und Midraschim*, 4 vols. (Leipzig: Brockhaus, 1876–1889), 2:449.

274. The remainder of 3.B is paralleled in Pesiq. Rab. 32:8–10, in Rivka Ulmer, ed., *Pesiqta Rabbati: A Synoptic Edition of Pesiqta Rabbati Based upon All Extant Manuscripts and the Editio Princeps*, 3 vols., SFSHJ 155, 200 (vols. 1–2), Studies in Judaism (vol. 3) (Atlanta: Scholars Press, 1997–2002), 2:764–66; Midr. Ps. 87:2 (ed. Solomon Buber, Vilna, 1891), 377. The former is closer to PRK, the latter virtually identical to the Bavli.

275. Isa 54:12.

make[276] the Eastern Gate of the Temple and its two wickets from a single stone of pearl."

R. Yoḥanan was expounding inside the Great Synagogue of Sepphoris: "In time to come, the Holy One, Blessed be He, will make the Eastern Gate of the Temple and its two wickets from a single stone of pearl." And a certain pelagic[277] heretic was there. He said: "We do not even find [pearls] as big as a single egg of a turtle-dove. And someone's been talking[278] such [nonsense]?"[279]

When he set sail upon the Great Sea, his ship sank in the sea. He went to the depths, and he saw the ministering angels chiseling, etching, and hatching it, and he said to them: "What is this?" They replied: "This is the Eastern Gate of the Temple and its two wickets [being made from] a single stone of pearl." Immediately a miracle was performed for him and he departed unharmed.

A year later, he arrived and found R. Yoḥanan, who was expounding on the same matter: "In time to come the Holy One, Blessed be He, will make the Eastern Gate of the Temple and its two wickets from a single stone of pearl."

He said to him: "Elder!, Elder!, proclaim all you can proclaim, praise all there is to praise. For had my eyes not seen, I would not have believed–"

"And had your eyes not seen, you would not have believed the words that I said about Torah!" he replied.

He raised his eyes and looked at him, and immediately he was transformed into a pile of bones.

---

276. Glossing *'eqdaḥ* not as a noun, *carbuncles*, but as a verb: *I shall bore/sprout.*

277. See n. 63 above.

278. Often translated literally (Braude and Kapstein add "in a teacher's chair no less"! [*Pesikta de-Rab Kahana*, 427]), here י.ת.ב may not mean "to sit" but may rather function as a marker of progressive aspect, as in Jewish Babylonian Aramaic ("*was expounding/has been talking*"). See E. A. Bar-Asher Siegal, *Introduction to the Grammar*, 249.

279. The soundplay "somebody" (*hadein*)/"such" (*hakhdein*) echoes "bore/sprout" (*'eqdaḥ*) and *kadkod/kedein* that are prominent in this and adjacent passages.

The All-Night Seder in Bene Beraq

A Literary and Cultural History

JAY ROVNER

The Seder in Bene Beraq at which five second-century rabbinic sages reclined has inspired generations of Jews who recount that event with admiration at their own seders, year after year. Those sages enthusiastically narrated and examined the exodus and the birth of the nation all night long. This is how the standard Passover Haggadah tells story.

A story about R. Eliezer, R. Yehoshua, R. Eleazar b. Azariah, R. Akiva, and R. Tarfon, who were reclining [at a seder] in Bene Beraq, and were discussing the exodus from Egypt all that night, until their students came and said to them, "Our Masters, the time has come for reciting the morning Shema!"	מַעֲשֶׂה בְּרַבִּי אֱלִיעֶזֶר וְרַבִּי יְהוֹשֻׁעַ וְרַבִּי אֶלְעָזָר בֶּן עֲזַרְיָה וְרַבִּי עֲקִיבָא וְרַבִּי טַרְפוֹן, שֶׁהָיוּ מְסֻבִּין בִּבְנֵי בְרַק, וְהָיוּ מְסַפְּרִים בִּיצִיאַת מִצְרַיִם כָּל אוֹתוֹ הַלַּיְלָה, עַד שֶׁבָּאוּ תַלְמִידֵיהֶם וְאָמְרוּ לָהֶם: רַבּוֹתֵינוּ, הִגִּיעַ זְמַן קְרִיאַת שְׁמַע שֶׁל שַׁחֲרִית.

The dramatic effect of this narrative is heightened by its placement in the Haggadah text. For it comes to illustrate the propositions that every Jew is obligated to recount the exodus, and that in doing so they are worthy of praise (paragraph 2 below). Furthermore, it anticipates an exegesis of one of those fabulous five, Eleazar b. Azariah, who claims that the Torah itself mandates telling of the exodus at night (paragraph 4 below).

1. We were slaves to Pharaoh in Egypt, and the Lord, our God, took us out from there with a strong hand and with an outstretched arm.	1. עֲבָדִים הָיִינוּ לְפַרְעֹה בְּמִצְרָיִם, וַיּוֹצִיאֵנוּ יְיָ אֱלֹהֵינוּ מִשָּׁם בְּיָד חֲזָקָה וּבִזְרוֹעַ נְטוּיָה.

And if the Holy One, blessed be He, had not taken our fathers out of Egypt, then we, our children and our children's children would have remained enslaved to Pharaoh in Egypt.	וְאִלּוּ לֹא הוֹצִיא הַקָּדוֹשׁ בָּרוּךְ הוּא אֶת אֲבוֹתֵינוּ מִמִּצְרַיִם, הֲרֵי אָנוּ וּבָנֵינוּ וּבְנֵי בָנֵינוּ מְשֻׁעְבָּדִים הָיִינוּ לְפַרְעֹה בְּמִצְרָיִם.
2. Even if all of us were wise, all of us people of understanding, all of us learned in Torah, it would still be a *mitsvah* (meritorious activity) for us to discuss the exodus. Indeed, one who discusses the exodus at length,[1] that one is praiseworthy.	2. וַאֲפִילוּ כֻּלָּנוּ חֲכָמִים, כֻּלָּנוּ נְבוֹנִים, כֻּלָּנוּ זְקֵנִים, כֻּלָּנוּ יוֹדְעִים אֶת הַתּוֹרָה, מִצְוָה עָלֵינוּ לְסַפֵּר בִּיצִיאַת מִצְרַיִם. וְכָל הַמַּרְבֶּה[2] לְסַפֵּר בִּיצִיאַת מִצְרַיִם - הֲרֵי זֶה מְשֻׁבָּח.
3. A story about R. Eliezer, R. Yehoshua, R. Eleazar b. Azariah, R. Akiva, and R. Tarfon, who were reclining [at a seder] in Bene Beraq, and were discussing the exodus from Egypt all that night, until their students came and said to them, "Our Masters, the time has come for reciting the morning Shema!"	3. מַעֲשֶׂה בְּרַבִּי אֱלִיעֶזֶר וְרַבִּי יְהוֹשֻׁעַ וְרַבִּי אֶלְעָזָר בֶּן עֲזַרְיָה וְרַבִּי עֲקִיבָא וְרַבִּי טַרְפוֹן, שֶׁהָיוּ מְסֻבִּין בִּבְנֵי בְרַק, וְהָיוּ מְסַפְּרִים בִּיצִיאַת מִצְרַיִם כָּל אוֹתוֹ הַלַּיְלָה, עַד שֶׁבָּאוּ תַלְמִידֵיהֶם וְאָמְרוּ לָהֶם: רַבּוֹתֵינוּ, הִגִּיעַ זְמַן קְרִיאַת שְׁמַע שֶׁל שַׁחֲרִית.
4. R. Eleazar b. Azariah said: Lo, I am verily a seventy-year-old, yet I had not understood why the exodus from Egypt must be mentioned at night, until Ben Zoma explained it: "For it is stated: 'So that you remember the day you left Egypt all the days of your life'" [Deut <u>16:3</u>]; now "the days of your life" refers to the days, [and the additional word] "all" [indicates the inclusion of] the nights. The sages, however, explain: "'The days of your life' refers to this world; [and the additional word] 'all' [indicates the inclusion of the messianic era."	4. אָמַר רַבִּי אֶלְעָזָר בֶּן עֲזַרְיָה: הֲרֵי אֲנִי כְּבֶן שִׁבְעִים שָׁנָה, וְלֹא זָכִיתִי שֶׁתֵּאָמֵר יְצִיאַת מִצְרַיִם בַּלֵּילוֹת עַד שֶׁדְּרָשָׁהּ בֶּן זוֹמָא, שֶׁנֶּאֱמַר, לְמַעַן תִּזְכֹּר אֶת יוֹם צֵאתְךָ מֵאֶרֶץ מִצְרַיִם כֹּל יְמֵי חַיֶּיךָ, יְמֵי חַיֶּיךָ - הַיָּמִים, כָּל יְמֵי חַיֶּיךָ - הַלֵּילוֹת. וַחֲכָמִים אוֹמְרִים: יְמֵי חַיֶּיךָ - הָעוֹלָם הַזֶּה, כֹּל יְמֵי חַיֶּיךָ - לְהָבִיא לִימוֹת הַמָּשִׁיחַ.

1. See the following note on the addition of "at length."

2. *Marbeh* is a late addition. Just the simple act of story and discussion itself was sufficient to achieve praise. For instance, it is wanting in the early versions (see table 4, cols. 3 and 4; the formulation evolved from *ma'arikh* [cols. 5 and 6] to *marbeh* [col. 7]). This will be discussed in an analysis of linguistic aspects of this section (in preparation).

The Bene Beraq narrative is of interest from a number of perspectives. As a textual phenomenon, what is the nature of the tale? This will elicit generic and structural observations. Contextually, what is its redactional history? This will lead to literary-historical and chronological reflections. The nature of its redactional history invites a closer look at this story itself: can one trace its evolution and development? Looking at the details, seeing what is typical in this narrative and what is not, sheds light on how it came to be.

In the course of the examination, methodological issues will be mooted, and some approaches and claims will be challenged. Unique textual evidence will be utilized to clarify how this narrative originated and evolved. We will see how its theme of *sippur bi-yetsiat Mitsrayim* (recounting/discussing the exodus) contributed to the development of a new approach to the seder night's activity. Where, after the younger children had been introduced to the significance of the occasion, tradition had developed two conflicting programs, one based on halakhic discussion, another on aggadic-midrashic amplification of Scripture,[3] the Bene Beraq anecdote dramatizes a seder for adults and older children that features a less technical evening, that is, a program focused on narrative and discussion of the events.

The literary reflections of this popular, nontechnical approach for adult participants developed in a post-talmudic Babylonian milieu, probably after the seventh century. We will see that it arose in the context of the *'avadim hayinu* complex, the first four units of which were presented above (table 4 contains the entire complex). This is a significant indication of the time and place of the creation of this story. For one thing, that complex is post-talmudic and Geonic. For another, it is known only in Babylonian exemplars; it does not appear in any Erets Israel version of the Haggadah. *'Avadim hayinu* and other sections of the Haggadah from this period exemplify a desire to create texts that make this ritual accessible. Similarly, a popular literary form, Palestinian Targum, which augmented and rendered the biblical text into Aramaic for synagogue goers unfamiliar with Hebrew, developed a little earlier, in the fifth through seventh centuries in Erets Israel, after the completion of the Jerusalem Talmud. (In contrast,

3. The first is the Toseftan seder type introduced below in the next section; the second is the Scripture-oriented, semiliturgical *miqra bikkurim* midrash of the Babylonian style Haggadah. The text may be found in, e.g., Ernst Daniel Goldschmidt, *The Passover Haggadah, Its Sources and History* (Jerusalem: Bialik Institute, 1969), 120–23; on the nature of this midrash, see Jay Rovner, "Two Early Witnesses to the Formation of the Miqra Bikurim Midrash and Their Implications for the Evolution of the Haggadah Text," *HUCA* 75 (2004): 75–120.

Sagit Mor published a comparative study of both the Lod and the Bene Beraq seder stories from a conceptual point of view: "The Laws of Sacrifice or Telling the Story of the Exodus?," *Zion* 68 (2002–2003): 297–311. I discuss some of her findings and distinguish between our methodological approaches below in the appendix to this note.

classical *paytanim* had begun developing their complex and demanding poetic art form during the same period.)[4]

The Nature of This Tale

This narrative is nicely wrought. The exposition puts five sages together in a location on seder night. Their action consists of an all-night discussion. This is balanced by another group, their disciples, whose action also consists of speech, viz., the declaration that it is time to commence with the daily obligation to recite the Shema. Contrasting themes are presented through a number of complementary pairs: sages versus disciples; night versus day; unbounded all-night vigil versus time-bound liturgical obligation; the timeless versus the quotidian. Implied, as well, though unstated, is the change of location, that is, the house where sages reclined versus the synagogue or house of study, where they will join a quorum for communal prayer (submerged in this version but present in its predecessors). While the preceding paragraph (2 above) as well as the superior status of sages over disciples lead one to favor the first element in each of those opposing pairs, the reality of this-worldly obligation expressed in the liturgico-halakhic structure reminds one that the second set of elements is to be acknowledged and respected. Although Eleazar b. Azariah continues the discussion by speaking last in the extended text, the disciples get the last word in bringing the story proper to a close.

This narrative is a good example of a sage story in the form of an anecdote, which is a short narrative about an incident in the life of a rabbi (here: rabbis) of religious or moral relevance.[5] In our case, this is a tale about a group of sages engaged in *sippur yetsiat Mitsrayim*; the latter is being promoted as a praiseworthy activity. In this *maʿaseh*, the action is brought up

4. See Avigdor Shinan, "The Late Midrashic, Paytanic, and Targumic Literature," in *The Cambridge History of Judaism*, vol. 4, *The Late Roman-Rabbinic Period*, ed. Martin Jaffee and Charlotte Fonrobert (Cambridge: Cambridge University Press, 2006), 691–95.

5. Different writers tailor their definitions to the material they are dealing with. Thus, Moshe Simon-Shoshan says that an anecdote is a brief story that focuses on a single incident, generally involving only a few individuals (*Stories of the Law: Narrative Discourse and the Construction of Authority in the Mishnah* [New York: Oxford University Press, 2012], 84–85, here 85), whereas Catherine Hezser suggests that such an anecdote relates a "sequence of events in the life of a rabbi … of moral or religious relevance consisting of a number of scenes geographically or chronologically separated; the narratives can be elaborated with details, dialogue, and even rhetorical elements" (*Form, Function, and Historical Significance of the Rabbinic Story in Yerushalmi Neziqin*, TSAJ 37 [Tübingen: Mohr Siebeck, 1993], 309, 310). Actually, most of the anecdotes she presents consist of two scenes, sometimes augmented by a "pronouncement." The Bene Beraq story consists of two scenes, the one running into the other. In a sense, the ensuing citation of m. Ber. 1:5 could be seen as supplying the pronouncement in the words of Ben Zoma.

short by a surprise ending, slightly humorous but at the same time serious, which introduces a new consideration and perspective. Sages have been sequestered in a timeless nighttime activity, as it were, a wide-ranging discussion of the exodus. As a new day is dawning, the disciples (the dawning generation) call their masters from that magical world[6] to a quotidian one, a situation of temporality and this-worldly obligation, notably to a liturgical experience of the (thematically relevant) exodus.

Those messages are further enhanced by the following remarks of Eleazar b. Azariah (paragraph 4). Citing [Shimon] Ben Zoma, he shows through midrash, a rabbinic expository technique, that the Torah itself mandates that the exodus should be mentioned at night. This grounding as an obligation[7] provides rhetorical support for the activity and main topic of the preceding story.[8]

---

6. Individuals in many cultures, especially religions, experience incidents of revelation, illumination, and insight at night, often at midnight. Jewish pseudepigraphic writings report nighttime heavenly journeys in which divine secrets are revealed. As reported in a rabbinic source, a north wind would blow on a harp mounted over the bed of King David every night at midnight causing its strings to sound, and immediately he would arise and engage in Torah study (b. Ber. 3b). Engagement in *talmud torah* at night is a multifaceted theme. B. Yoma 38b praises Hillel's devotion to learning by citing an example of a nocturnal session. B. Ḥag 12b, b. ʿAbod. Zar. 3b, Midr. Prov. 31:15 (Burton L. Visotzky, *Midrash Mishle: A Critical Edition Based on Vatican MS. Ebr. 44 with Variant Readings ... an Introduction, References and a Short Commentary* [New York: Jewish Theological Seminary, 1990], 192–93) and Maimonides (*Mishneh Torah, Hilkhot Talmud Torah* 3:13) commend this nightly practice and state that its rewards extend through all areas of one's life.

The Bene Beraq *maʿaseh* portrays not an individual engaged in study or vouchsafed a revelation but a group engaged in discussion. Its immediate literary antecedent is the night-long engagement of sages at the Lod seder, on which it is based, in *hilkhot ha-Pesaḥ*. The theme of a group engaged in discussion echoes the notion of discussion and debate in rabbinic settings whose literary counterpart is the talmudic *sugya*. Although many have viewed this tale of nocturnal discussion and debate in terms of the wider cultural phenomenon of a Hellenistic nighttime symposium, David Henshke claims that discussion figures differently in the seder because of the way it structures the evening with discussion before the meal rather than, as in a symposium, after it (*"Mah Nishtannah": The Passover Night in the Sages' Discourse* [Hebrew] [Jerusalem: Magnes, 2016], 50–51 n. 42). He suggests, as well, that Geonic Babylonia is too far removed in time and place for the author of our *maʿaseh* to have been susceptible to its influence. For that reason, I would argue that Hellenistic influence cannot account for the fact that the Bene Beraq nocturnal discussion extends long after the meal.

7. In addition to Eleazar b. Azariah's "pronouncement," the nature of the obligation to rehearse and discuss the exodus was enunciated through the verb *ḥayav* in the liturgical units connecting *ʿavadim hayinu* to the Bene Beraq narrative (unit 2 on page 178 above; table 1 or 4, below, units 4–6). That approach will be examined in a study of narrative terminology of these passages (in preparation).

8. The insistence of Ben Zoma's collocutors (in the b. Ber. pericope recited by Eleazar b. Azariah at the Bene Beraq seder) that the Shema will continue to be recited in messianic times may seem irrelevant to the matter at hand, viz., that Passover night be devoted to discussion of the exodus. There are, however, two ways to understand its inclusion, an oral-stylistic one and a conceptual one. It is consistent with literatures arising in oral-literary

The artistry of this little narrative can be further appreciated when one notices that the episode at Bene Beraq was not the first all-night seder vigil in the rabbinic record. The Tosefta (t. Pesaḥ. 10:12) tells of a group of our sages' contemporaries.

A story about Rabban Gamaliel and elders, who were reclining [at a seder] at the home of Baitos b. Zonin in Lod, and were engaged in *hilkhot ha-Pesaḥ* the whole night, until cockcrow; [servants] removed the tables, and they aroused themselves and betook themselves to the *bet ha-midrash*.	מעשה ברבן גמליאל וזקנים, שהיו מסובין בבית ביתוס בן זונין בלוד, והיו עסוקין בהלכות הפסח כל הלילה, עד קרות הגבר; הגביהו מלפניהן, ונועדו (צ״ל: ניערו)[9] והלכו להן לבית המדרש.

Only one of this company, Gamaliel, is named; the location, Lod, however, is further particularized by the identification of the host in whose home those sages had reclined.

While not as tightly organized as the Bene Beraq narrative, which conveys a complex set of messages in carefully arranged contrasting pairs, the Toseftan tale is also artfully composed. A cascading chiastic structure lets the distinction between "all night long" and the moment of "cockcrow," hence the division and contrast of the nocturnal action and the diurnal obligation, break right at the center (3/3′):

0. Exposition: A story about Rabban Gamaliel and elders,	0. מעשה ברבן גמליאל וזקנים
2 and they were engaged in *hilkhot ha-Pesaḥ* (the rules of Passover)	2. והיו עסוקין בהלכות הפסח
3 the whole night,	3. כל הלילה
3′ Until cockcrow;	3′. עד קרות הגבר

contexts to cite the continuation of a passage brought to illuminate one discrete point. The other explanation is that the collocutors' point is consistent with the fulfillment of the obligation *le-sapper bi-yetsiat Mitsrayim* (to discuss the exodus). This injunction is taken in many ways in the contributions to the Haggadah of the Geonic era. Cf. the discussion of this point below, in the appendix to this note.

9. "They arose" (Paul D. Mandel, *The Origins of Midrash: From Teaching to Text*, JSJSup 180 [Leiden: Brill, 2017], 193). I follow the text as corrected by Saul Lieberman, *Tosefta ki-feshuṭah: A Comprehensive Commentary on the Tosefta* (New York: Jewish Theological Seminary, 1962), *Pisḥa* 10:12 (198, variants and comments) based the reading in the Erfurt manuscript (ונוערו) with comparison to other usages. See also Lieberman, *Tosefta ki-feshuṭah* [Hebrew], 10 vols. (Jerusalem: Bet ha-midrash le-rabanim shebe-Amerikah, 1992–2001), 4:656, lines 34–35. See the following note on Lieberman's understanding of this text.

2′ [Servants] removed the tables,	2′. הגביהו מלפניהן
1′ and the sages aroused themselves and betook themselves to the *bet midrash*	1′. וניערו והלכו להן לבית המדרש

Sages and their admirable scholastic engagement—this time *hilkhot ha-Pesaḥ* (the rules of the Passover offering and related matters)—are contrasted with the class of servants,[10] whose presence is not even mentioned save by implication, in the execution of the humble task of clearing away the remains of the rabbis' meal, which, of course, would have been their Passover seder meal, as opposed to the Passover topics discussed by the sages. The servants' undertaking, which is not a rabbinic activity, indirectly supports and enables it (2/2′). The contrast is heightened by the fact that the rules of Passover, which are collected and examined in tractate Pesaḥim, are concerned with the Passover evening meal, viz., the laws of separation from leavening and matzah, the laws of the Paschal offering, and that evening's ritual.[11] The narrator also focuses our attention on the sages by opening and closing this narrative with sages and their concerns, from reclining at the seder to attendance at the *bet midrash* (1/1′).[12]

The presence of two rabbinic seder narratives, both similar and different, invites comparison. Some questions arise right away. Which is the appropriate activity, inquiry into *hilkhot ha-Pesaḥ* or discussion of the

---

10. Ibid. Even after he corrected his understanding of נועדו/נוערו, Lieberman seems to think that Gamaliel and his party themselves picked up the (individual) tables on which lay the remains of their meal. However, m. Pesaḥ. 7:13 and t. Ber. 5:28, for example, speak of the involvement of a *shamash* (attendant, waiter) at a meal, the latter in cleaning up. Mandel also infers that "servants" were the ones who "lifted (the eating trays) from before them" (*Origins of Midrash*, 193).

11. The tractate Pesaḥim, in which they were probably engaged, covers the areas mentioned; the definite article in the term, *hilkhot ha-Pesaḥ* indicates "the Passover offering."

12. Contextually, this morning excursion would probably be to participate in the *shaḥarit* liturgy with a quorum. Mandel explains that the *bet ha-midrash* in Tannaitic literature signifies a location where sages, with disciples in attendance, made themselves available to serve the public by, for example, answering queries, providing instruction, and resolving disputes (*Origins of Midrash*, 182–90). He points out that this tended to happen on Shabbat and holidays, that is, times when people would have the leisure to come (190–96), and he cites t. Pesaḥ. 10:12 as an illustrative passage (193 and n. 64). Other examples Mandel provides indicate that liturgy was performed in *bet ha-midrash* (192), and it is probable that Gamaliel and the elders repaired there to participate in a prayer quorum, after which they would provide an audience for the public. Mandel also quotes t. Sukkah 4:5, which (anachronistically?) relates a progress from the morning sacrifice to the synagogue, then the *bet midrash*, followed by "the prayer service of the additional sacrifices," etc. (195). Perhaps Gamaliel's Lod did not have as many specialized sites as Second Temple Jerusalem. On the other hand, one might suggest that concerns about liturgy are beside the point; the creator of the Lod story simply did not have liturgy in mind as he moved the sages from their nocturnal discussion of *hilkhot ha-Pesaḥ* to the *bet midrash*, that is, the morning setting for *talmud torah* (cf. Mor, "Laws of Sacrifice,"310).

exodus? Why name Gamaliel, but not his followers, while Eliezer's whole retinue is enumerated? What is the significance of Gamaliel and Eliezer?

There are others. How did the storyteller know who was with Eliezer? If Eliezer is the chief figure, why did the other sages not come to him in Lod where he dwelt (b. Sanh. 32b)? The one sage who resided in Bene Beraq was Akiva; why not report that the sages reclined at his house as they did for Baitos b. Zonin in Lod? The Gamaliel episode is recorded in the Tosefta, a collection of early (Tannaitic) sources, while the narrative featured in the Haggadah is not known in any rabbinic composition: where did it come from, or how did it get into the Haggadah?

Many of these questions can best be resolved by a detailed analysis of the genesis and evolution of the Bene Beraq narrative. But the first, and most important, question—the primacy of halakhot versus the exodus—can best be settled by a macrocosmic examination. It is the latter, an investigation of the story in its context in the Haggadah, that can illuminate the process of the struggle for primacy, and who won, to which we now turn.

The Narrative in Context: The Redactional History of a Section in the Passover Haggadah

The tenth chapter of Mishnah Pesaḥim (ca. 200 CE) represents a major step in the formation of the Passover Seder. The most creative period subsequent to that occurs during the time of the Geonim, from the seventh to the eleventh century. During that period, there were two major liturgical families, one in Erets Israel, and another that developed in Babylonia. Each had several versions. Those versions persisted long after the Geonim had already stated their preferences. Even after one basic form would come to predominate in each family, Genizah manuscript fragments from eleventh- to thirteenth-century Haggadot show that alternative forms were still in use then.[13] I will introduce evidence below to show that extreme variations persisted in some Babylonian-derived rituals as late as the seventeenth century.

The text and context under examination occurs only in the Babylonian branch. The Babylonian Talmud reports that Rav and Shmuel,[14] two early

13. Erets Israel and Byzantine versions are listed in Safrai and Safrai, *Haggadah of the Sages*, 293 (without distinguishing versions that have absorbed Babylonian formulations), who published a conflated version alongside the standard Erets Israel text (286–92); see also Jay Rovner, "An Early Passover Haggadah according to the Palestinian Rite," *JQR* 90 (2000): 339–43. A variant (Byzantine?) recension was published by Nicholas de Lange, *Greek Jewish Texts from the Cairo Genizah*, TSAJ 51 (Tübingen: Mohr Siebeck, 1996), 29–69 (facsimiles, 322–53) and Rovner, "Two Early Witnesses," 421–53.

14. Henshke concludes that neither attribution is reliable ("*Mah Nishtannah*"); on Rav, see 439–40, 445–49, esp. n. 132; on Shmuel, see 445 n. 134, 447–49.

Babylonian Amoraim, would introduce *maggid*, the major section of the Haggadah, differently (b. Pesaḥ. 116a):[15]

[Rav] said: "In the beginning, our ancestors were idol worshipers." And [Shmuel][16] said, "We were slaves."	[רב] אמר: מתחלה עובדי עבודת גלולים היו אבותינו. ו[שמואל] אמר: עבדים היינו.

Both of those introductions came to be included in the Babylonian Haggadah, although each one was enhanced in the Geonic era by many subsidiary recitations. The Babylonian Talmud provides only the opening rubric. The Jerusalem Talmud (y. Pesaḥ. 10:5, 37d) offers a more fulsome version of what Rav may have meant, casting some doubt on whether *mi-teḥillah* was actually supposed to be part of what was originally to be said.[17]

Rav said: As formerly, one should begin [Josh 24:2–3]: "Your forefathers dwelt on the other side of the river, etc.; and I took your father Abraham from the other side of the river, etc."	רב אמר: מתחילה, צריך להתחיל (יהושע כד, ב): בעבר הנהר ישבו אבותיכם וגו' ואקח את אביכם את אברהם מעבר הנהר וגו'.

Babylonian Haggadot combine both approaches. We have no evidence for what the teaching attributed to Shmuel included, but that is important for us because *'Avadim hayinu* leads into the Bene Beraq narrative. It was certainly not the expansive version in current rites, as presented above, or even that in Saadia Gaon's *Siddur* (see below); a fragmentary text in *Ginze Schechter*[18] undoubtedly presents something closer to what might have been meant:

15. The Talmud asks how to begin *bi-genut* (with disgrace), as prescribed by m. Pesaḥ. 10:4, and each snippet commences in that vein and concludes with *shevah* (praiseworthy matter, as advised in the text).

16. See n. 14 above, on the problematic nature of these attributions.

17. See Lieberman, *Tosefta ki-feshuṭah, Zeraim* 1, Introduction, 21 n. 40; Henshke, "*Mah Nishtannah*," 439–44. Lieberman explains that *mi-teḥillah/ba-teḥillah/ka-teḥillah* = one should say or do as was originally said/done, and the scriptural source, that is, what was originally said, follows. The intervening *ṣarikh lehathil* ("one should begin" is an explanatory gloss). This explanation is borne out in the Erets Israel version of the Haggadah. For example, the Erets Israel exemplar published by Goldschmidt (*Passover Haggadah*, 78) cites, by way of *genut*, Josh 24:2ff., following a snippet from m. Pesaḥ. 10:4): לפי דעתו שלבן אביו מלמדו, מתחיל בגנות ומסיים בשבח, ואומר: בעבר הנהר ישבו אבותיכם מעלם ...

18. Louis Ginzberg, *Genizah Studies in Memory of Doctor Solomon Schechter* = גנזי שעכטער [Hebrew], 3 vols. (1928; repr., New York: Hermon, 1969), 2:252–60 (the selection under discussion may be found on 259–60). The shelfmark is Cambridge, CUL: T-S Misc.36.179 (Alternate number: T-S Loan Collection 179).

We were slaves to Pharaoh in Egypt, and the Lord took us out of Egypt with a strong hand and with an outstretched arm.	עבדים היינו לפרעה במצ[רים], ויוצ[יאנו] ה' ממצ[רים] ביד חזקה ובזרוע נטויה.

That Amoraic-period introduction is followed in *maggid* formularies from early Geonic, if not late-talmudic, versions by a pedagogic text also found in the Mekhilta of Rabbi Ishmael,[19] viz., the *baraita* of the four sons. (We can infer that it is an early element of *maggid* because both branches of the Babylonian Haggadah share it.) That text privileges *hilkhot ha-Pesaḥ* over discussion of the exodus, assigning the former to the wise son (who is mentioned first), and relegating the latter to the simple son and the one who does not know how to ask. For this hierarchical presentation, the Tosefta's all-night seder activity could be ideal.[20] On the other hand, that *baraita*'s exposition does recognize that there are four types of children, each of whom is to be taken into account in presenting a seder program for the family. The Bene Beraq episode could be an idealized recreation of what such a seder night might be like. It reminds the seder participants of the purpose of the *baraita* of the four sons, transformed albeit into venerated scholars.[21] It also disregards the Tosefta's privileging of *hilkhot ha-Pesaḥ*, concerning itself instead with the theme of the exodus.

Still, the discussion portrayed in the Bene Beraq story is a sensible precursor to that exposition. It is time to see how it came to be included in the Haggadah text. The following table illustrates the difference between a Haggadah that contains it and one that does not.

19. Mekhilta of Rabbi Ishmael, *Bo* 18 (p. 73), ed. H. S. Horovitz, I. A. Rabin (repr., Jerusalem: Wahrmann, 1970). Another version may be found in y. Pesaḥ. 10:4, 37d.

20. Judith Hauptman compares and contrasts the Tosefta's version of the seder with that of the Mishnah in "How Old Is the Haggadah?," *Judaism* 51 (2002): 5–18; and *Rereading the Mishnah: A New Approach to Ancient Jewish Texts*, TSAJ 109 (Tübingen: Mohr Siebeck, 2005), 50–63. She finds traces in the Tosefta of a form of the seder that she considers to be earlier than that of the Mishnah. The two traditions could, however, represent two contemporaneous approaches, geared to two different audiences (see n. 97 below). The differences between the two programs become obscured when the Bene Beraq discussion takes all night and the obligation to nightlong engagement in *hilkhot ha-Pesaḥ* is extended to one's son (who is the object of the mishnaic seder program), and even one's wife (*beto*, in place of *'atsmo* = himself, according to the Erfurt manuscript reading of t. Pesaḥ. 10:11; cf. Lieberman, *Tosefta ki-feshuṭah, 4: Moed*, 655, on lines 32–33).

21. The aspirational family activity is extrapolated from the comparison to the sages (transferred from the Lod seder), per unit 5 in table 1 (or table 4), below. Both seder anecdotes feature sages, though each text in its own way is addressed to the members of one's household (cf. the preceding note).

Table 1. Two Approaches to *'Avadim hayinu* in Versions of the Babylonian Haggadah

	Siddur Saadia[22]	*Ginze Schechter* Haggadah[23]	Natronai Gaon Haggadah[24]
1	עבדים היינו לפרעה במצרים ויוציאנו ה׳ אלהינו משם ביד חזקה ובזרוע נטויה	עבדים היינו לפרעה במצ[רים], ויוצ[יאנו] ה׳ ממצ[רים] ביד חזקה ובזרוע נטויה	עֲבָדִים הָיִינוּ לְפַרְעֹה בְּמִצְרָיִם, וַיּוֹצִיאֵנוּ יְיָ אֱלֹהֵינוּ מִשָּׁם בְּיָד חֲזָקָה וּבִזְרוֹעַ נְטוּיָה.
2	ואלו לא גאל המקב״ה [=המקום ברוך הוא] את אבותינו ממצרים כבר אנו ובנינו ובני בנינו משועבדים היינו לפרעה במצרים[25]		וְאִלּוּ לֹא הוֹצִיא הַקָּדוֹשׁ בָּרוּךְ הוּא אֶת אֲבוֹתֵינוּ מִמִּצְרָיִם, עֲדַיִין אָנוּ וּבָנֵינוּ וּבְנֵי בָנֵינוּ מְשֻׁעְבָּדִים הָיִינוּ לְפַרְעֹה בְּמִצְרָיִם.
3	ולא את אבותינו בלבד גאל המקב״ה אלא אף אותנו גאל שנ׳ ואותנו הוציא משם.[26]		
4		לפיכך מצוה עלינו לספר ביציאת מצ׳	
5		ואפילו כולנו חכ׳ כולנו נבונים וכולנו יודעים את התורה, מצווה עלינו לספר ביציאת מצ׳ ואפי׳ כול׳ זקנים כול׳ ישישים כול׳ יודעים את התורה, מצוה עלינו לספר ביציאת מצ׳,	וַאֲפִלּוּ כּוּלָּנוּ חֲכָמִים, כּוּלָּנוּ נְבוֹנִים, כֻּלָּנוּ זְקֵנִים, כּוּלָּנוּ יוֹדְעִים אֶת הַתּוֹרָה, מִצְוָה עָלֵינוּ לְסַפֵּר בִּיצִיאַת מִצְרַיִם,
6		וכל המספר ביצי׳ מצ׳ הרי זה משובח	שֶׁכָּל הַמַּאֲרִיךְ לְסַפֵּר בִּיצִיאַת מִצְרַיִם - הֲרֵי זֶה מְשֻׁבָּח.

22. סדור רב סעדיה גאון = כתאב ג׳אמע אלצלואת ואלתסאביח, ed. Israel Davidson, Simha Assaf, and Issachar Joel (Jerusalem: Mekitze Nirdamim, 1941), 137.

23. Cited in n. 18 above.

24. Manfred Lehman, "סדר והגדה של פסח לרב נטרונאי גאון על-פי כתב-יד קדמון שברשות המחבר," in ספר יובל לכבוד מורנו הגאון רבי יוסף דוב הלוי סולובייצ׳יק, ed. Shaul Yisraeli et al. (Jerusalem: Mossad ha-Rav Kook, 1984), 986–87.

25. "And had the Omnipresent, blessed be He, not redeemed our ancestors from Egypt, then we and our descendants would still be enslaved to Pharaoh in Egypt."

26. "And not only our ancestors did the Omniscient, blessed be He, redeem, but even us as well did He redeem, as it is said (Deut 6:23), 'And us He brought out of there.'"

7		ומעשה בר׳ אליעזר ור׳ יהושע ור׳ אלעזר בן עזריה ור׳ עקיבה, שהיו מסובין בבני-ברק; והיו מסיחים ביצי׳ מצ׳ כל אותו הלילה, עד שבאו תלמידיהם ואמרו להם: רבותינו, הגיע זמן קריאת שמע של שחרית	מַעֲשֶׂה בְּרַבִּי אֱלִיעֶזֶר וְרַבִּי יְהוֹשֻׁעַ וְרַבִּי אֶלְעָזָר בֶּן עֲזַרְיָה וְרַבִּי עֲקִיבָא וְרַבִּי טַרְפוֹן, שֶׁהָיוּ מְסֻבִּין בִּבְנֵי בְרַק; וְהָיוּ מְסַפְּרִין בִּיצִיאַת מִצְרַיִם בְּלֵיל פֶּסַח, עַד שֶׁבָּאוּ תַלְמִידֵיהֶם וְאָמְרוּ לָהֶם: רַבּוֹתֵינוּ, הִגִּיעַ לִקְרִיאַת שְׁמַע שֶׁל שַׁחֲרִית.
8		אמ׳ ר׳ אלעזר בן עזריה: הרי אני כבן שבעים שנה, ולא זכיתי שתיאמר יצי׳ מצ׳ בלילות, עד שדרשה בן זומא, שנ׳,[27] למען תזכור את יום צאתך מארץ מצ׳ כל ימי חייך, ימי חייך- הימים, כל ימי חייך- הלילו; וחכמים אומרים: ימי חייך - העולם הזה, כל ימי חייך - להביא את ימות המשיח.	אָמַר רַבִּי אֶלְעָזָר בֶּן עֲזַרְיָה: הֲרֵי [אֲנִי] כְּבֶן שִׁבְעִים שָׁנָה, וְלֹא שָׁמַעְתִּי שֶׁתֵּאָמֵר יְצִיאַת מִצְרַיִם בַּלֵּילוֹת, עַד שֶׁדְּרָשָׁהּ בֶּן זוֹמָא, שֶׁנֶּאֱמַר, לְמַעַן תִּזְכֹּר אֶת יוֹם צֵאתְךָ מֵאֶרֶץ מִצְרַיִם כֹּל יְמֵי חַיֶּיךָ, יְמֵי חַיֶּיךָ - הַיָּמִים, כָּל יְמֵי חַיֶּיךָ – הַלֵּילוֹת; וַחֲכָמִים אוֹמְרִים: יְמֵי חַיֶּיךָ - הָעוֹלָם הַזֶּה, כֹּל יְמֵי חַיֶּיךָ - לְהָבִיא לִימוֹת הַמָּשִׁיחַ.
9			*Barukh ha-Maqom*[28]
10	*Baraita* of the four sons	*Baraita* of the four sons	*Baraita* of the four sons

The *Ginze Schechter* and Saadia *Siddur* versions exemplify two Geonic-period approaches to introducing the *maggid* section of the Babylonian seder by augmenting the text attributed to Shmuel. (On the eclectic Natronai Gaon version, see below.) *'Avadim hayinu* (augmented by the pedagogical *baraita*) developed in two directions. In Saadia's *Siddur*, units 2 and 3 were added (with unit 10 following at the end). That version is designed to foster in those participating at a seder, at any point in time, an awareness of the significance of the exodus event in its implications in their own lives (2–3). Seeing the theme of freedom from bondage set out in terms of one's own situation, arouses an eagerness to find out more about the exodus. From that vantage, the seder liturgist then moves to remind everyone that there are at least four different developmental and personality types to

27. Deut 16:3.

28. The *barukh ha-maqom* peroration was added in later textualizations, such as the version here ascribed to Natronai.

keep in mind as the examination continues, and that it should be done over the Paschal meal (10, with concluding *davar ʾaḥer*).

In the *Ginze Schechter* family, *ʿAvadim hayinu* is followed by the Bene Beraq complex (7 and 8), its transitioning introduction (4–6 or, in other exemplars, just 5–6) and the ensuing *baraita* (10). In this version, the approach is to respond to the exodus event by retelling and discussing it (4, 6). Even learned elders should participate (5). In fact, the most learned and revered rabbis have done so; one session even went on for the whole night (7–8). On the one hand, this version skips over the implications of the exodus for the seder participants' own situation; on the other, it has the advantage of anticipating the need for awareness that there are at least four different developmental and personality types to keep in mind in the ensuing recounting and discussion (10). Moreover, people would come to realize through the process of narration and discussion the existential significance of the exodus event.

Later Haggadot combined the two forms, as in the rightmost column above, which borrowed unit 2 from *Siddur* Saadia, with 5–8 from *Ginze Schechter*. A Haggadah included in a seventeenth-century *Siddur* according to the Persian rite[29] provides an indication of how the transformation could have occurred for those beginning with a Saadian version. In the body of the text, units 1–3 are followed by 10, as in Saadia's *Siddur*. Items 5 and 6 appear in the upper margin, in small lettering, and 7–8 appear in the lower margin, also in small letters. One can imagine a later copyist simply copying 4 (or 5)–8 directly into their base texts. That process is reflected in the state of the Haggadah version preserved in a liturgical fragment from a different rite that was added by the copyist at the end of the *Siddur* of Shelomoh bar Natan (twelfth century) of Sijilmassa (the Sijilmassa-B version).[30] Interestingly, only units 4 and 6 are found there, suggesting that the Bene Beraq–oriented expansion of *ʿAvadim hayinu* was originally made

29. *The Persian Jewish Prayer Book: A Facsimile Edition of MS Adler ENA 23 in the Jewish Theological Seminary Library* [Hebrew], ed. Shlomoh Tal (Jerusalem: Ben Zvi Institute, 1980), 61b, 63a. The Adler (former) shelf mark of the manuscript is ENA 23; the current shelf mark is New York, The Library of The Jewish Theological Seminary, MS 4522.

30. סידור רבינו שלמה ברבי נתן זצ״ל, אב ביד דין מן העיר סיג׳ילמסה, המכונה אלגבאלי, ed. and trans. Shemuel Hagai (Jerusalem, 5755 [1994 or 1995]), 249–50. The manuscript was copied in Barca (now Marj), Libya, in 1202 (see the online catalogue of the Institute of Microfilmed Hebrew Manuscripts, Jerusalem). It is described in the introduction, 4–5; it was evidently copied in a Near Eastern hand. There is some question about whether Shelomoh b. Natan's Sijilmassa was the one in the Maghreb or the Middle East (see the discussion and bibliography in the introduction, pp. 5–6). Stefan C. Reif considers the *Siddur* to be an exemplar of an early Moroccan rite (*Judaism and Hebrew Prayer: New Perspectives on Jewish Liturgical History* [Cambridge: Cambridge University Press, 1995], 152). Uri Ehrlich writes that it was arranged in the Middle East (*The Weekday* Amidah *in Cairo Genizah Prayerbooks: Roots and Transmission* [Hebrew] [Jerusalem: Yad Ben Zvi, 2013], 9; see n. 39 there).

up of either units 4 and 6 or 5 and 6 (see table 4 at the end). Those elements could also be combined, as in the *Ginze Schechter* version.

Most of the Haggadot containing the Bene Beraq–oriented versions removed unit 3, perhaps because its contents were already present further in the Haggadah, in the paragraph beginning *be-khol dor va-dor*.[31]

This situation leaves us with a chronological conundrum regarding the text on which our inquiry is centered. The Bene Beraq sage story lies between two sets of material from widely varying periods. Depending on how closely unit 1 reflects the actual wording of the text attributed to Shmuel in the Talmud, but abbreviated there, it may be from the talmudic (Amoraic) period. Unit 8, imported from m. Ber. 1:5 is, like the following *baraita* (unit 10, from the Mekhilta of Rabbi Ishmael, as mentioned above), earlier; that is, they are found in Tannaitic-era compositions. Moreover, units 4 (or 5)–6 may well be a late addition to the "Samuel" text. For example, it has been observed that the expression *le-sapper bi-yetsiat Mitsrayim* is not to be found anywhere in talmudic writings.[32] Therefore, unless that phrase is a *hapax legomenon* in that literature, units 4/5–6 would likely be of Geonic provenance. Now, they are like our sage story in that they strongly promote speaking about the exodus, as opposed to, for example, reviewing *hilkhot ha-Pesaḥ* (championed in the Tosefta's story of the nightlong Gamaliel session). Our story's position could also be Tannaitic, however, for it seems to reflect an approach to the seder advanced by the Mishnah,[33] in contrast to the Tosefta.[34] To be sure, units 4/5–6 seem to have been formulated as a transition from the *'Avadim hayinu* declaration to the Bene Beraq narrative. So, they themselves could have been composed anytime between the Amoraic period, when that opening rubric may have been

31. It may be found in the standard text of, e.g., Goldschmidt, *Passover Haggadah,* 125. Although also found in standard editions of m. Pesaḥ. 10:5, it is not included in the Erets Israel version of the Mishnah, e.g., the Kaufmann Mishnah manuscript, nor is it contained in the original, Erets Israel version of the Haggadah, e.g., that found in Goldschmidt, 81. It seems, therefore, that the Mishnah later absorbed this passage from the Haggadah liturgy (see Safrai and Safrai, *Haggadah of the Sages,* 36; Goldschmidt suggests that it originated in a *baraita,* that is, a Tannaitic text not [originally] included in the Mishnah [*Passover Haggadah,* 53]). Goldschmidt notes that it is sometimes augmented by our unit 3's Deut 6:23 or Exod 13:5, and that the former verse has been repurposed elsewhere in some Haggadah versions as well. Moreover, unit 3 is cited in its entirety is many Haggadah versions.

32. Henshke suggests that this is an indication that the Bene Beraq text is a fabrication (*"Mah Nishtannah,"* 32–33, 392).

33. Israel Yuval argues that this narrative represents a Yavnean seder (הפוסחים על שני הספים: ההגדה של פסח והפסחא הנוצרית, *Tarbiṣ* 95 [1995]: 5–28). See the critique in Hauptman, *Rereading the Mishnah,* 51–52 n. 7.

34. It is interesting, and significant, that m. Pesaḥ. 10:4–5, framed by the three questions and Gamaliel's answers, speaks of teaching, expounding, and reciting or explaining (מלמד, דורש, אמר), appropriate to a didactic setting, whereas t. Pesaḥ. 10:11 prescribes a collegial engagement (לעסוק) with *hilkhot ha-Pesaḥ*.

composed, and the time of the Geonim, when the Bene Beraq story was incorporated into the seder liturgy and, possibly, when it was composed.

That narrative tells of Tannaitic sages engaging in an activity encouraged in a Tannaitic passage, so it does seem that it could be a genuine Tannaitic text, just like units 8 and 10, not to mention the similar story of Gamaliel's seder in Lod. It is different from these texts, however, in that all the Amoraic or Tannaitic units of this group are definite borrowings; that is, they can be traced back to actual sources in talmudic or Tannaitic documents. The Bene Beraq story has no antecedent; it cannot be traced to any late antique rabbinic source. Even though it seems like a Tannaitic text, and it is paired with one (unit 8), perhaps its genesis may be connected in some way with units 4–6. That is, it may have been created along with them as a transition element to item 8, or slightly antecedent to them, and subsequently intended by the author of 4 or 5–6 as their target.

Further cause for uncertainty is another phrase from this story, *kol ʾoto ha-lailah* (that whole night). It can be added to *le-sapper bi-yetsiat Mitsrayim* as unattested in Tannaitic literature. It does, nonetheless, occur in Amoraic literature.[35] The question then becomes, can the possible *hapax* and the Amoraic *kol ʾoto ha-lailah* be indicative of a text formulated sometime during the Amoraic period but never incorporated into a late antique composition, only to be found and conserved in the Babylonian branch of the Passover Haggadah? While unlikely, it is nonetheless a definite possibility, for rabbinic texts, even Tannaitic ones thought to have been lost, or whose existence was not even known, have been discovered and published throughout the past century. Therefore, it may not be necessary to reject this possible provenance for the Bene Beraq story.

I will show below that those linguistic concerns are not conclusive; rather, they are ultimately irrelevant; that is, they are beside the point in the quest to date this narrative because they did not appear in its original versions. Nonetheless, strong evidence can be adduced to demonstrate that the Bene Beraq episode must be an apocryphal, Geonic-era creation. Several stylistic problems and discrepancies demonstrate that the narrative as it stands clashes with expectations that one would have from reading other rabbinic sage stories. Full conclusions will be drawn through a textual study of the evolution of this passage. That study will also shed light on how those stylistic discordances came about.

Microcosmic Examination: The Nature and Evolution of the Bene Beraq Seder Narrative

Table 1 above (and the more comprehensive table 4 below) shows that the formula attributed to Shmuel (row 1) developed in two directions in

35. Henshke, "*Mah Nishtannah*," 393–94 and n. 151.

the Babylonian branch of the Haggadah. Saadia's *Siddur* added units 2–3 before proceeding with the *baraita* of the four sons/children; the *Ginze Schechter* version added rows 4–8.[36] Natronai Gaon's version, which is virtually identical with current rites, followed *Ginze Schechter* but adopted unit 2 from Saadia, as well.

Examination of these texts suggests that even the simplest version—that of *Siddur* Saadia—seems to have evolved in two ways that ultimately merged. In view of the existence of the contrasting *Ginze Schechter* form, it seems likely that the Saadia text coalesced from two (post-talmudic) augmentations, as follows.

עבדים היינו לפרעה במצרים, ויוציאנו ה׳ אלהינו משם ביד חזקה ובזרוע נטויה.	עבדים היינו לפרעה במצרים, ויוציאנו ה׳ אלהינו משם ביד חזקה ובזרוע נטויה.
ולא את אבותינו בלבד גאל המקב״ה, אלא אף אותנו גאל, שנ׳ (דברים ו, כג): ואותנו הוציא משם.[37]	ואלו לא גאל המקב״ה את אבותינו ממצרים, כבר אנו ובנינו ובני בנינו משועבדים היינו לפרעה במצרים.[38]

The two cells in the second row make the same point in two different ways. The right-hand cell claims that we and our descendants would still be slaves had our ancestors not been redeemed, while the left-hand one asserts that we were also redeemed along with our ancestors. Upon their amalgamation, the latter assertion was put in the final position in order to close with a prooftext, a rhetorically fitting way to bring the passage to a conclusion.

Close reading reveals that the *Ginze Schechter*–type version seems not to have been fully formed in this period. Units 4 and 6 do have the possibly late locution *sapper bi-yetsiat Mitsrayim*, but it is not secure. Natronai's version employs the infinitive *le-ha'arikh* in unit 6, and even *Ginze Shechter* varies in unit 7 with *mesiḥin* instead of *mesapperim/n*. The Natronai Gaon version does not contain unit 4, which is present in *Ginze Schechter*.

In his comprehensive and exhaustive study of the rabbinic Haggadah, Henshke cited many problems with the Bene Beraq narrative.[39] In addition to the linguistic anomalies mentioned above, he noted irregularities in the way that the Bene Beraq story is told. For instance, sages appear out of

36. It conflated two formulations in row 5; current versions have accepted *zeqenim* from the second one.

37. "And the Omnipresent, blessed be He, did not redeem our ancestors alone, but also us did He redeem, as is said [Deut 6:23]: 'And us He took out from there.'"

38. "And had the Omnipresent, blessed be He, not redeemed our ancestors from Egypt, we and our descendants would certainly have been enslaved to Pharaoh in Egypt."

39. Henshke ("*Mah Nishtannah*") deals with this narrative on 391–95. See also Mor, "Laws of Sacrifice"; and see my comments below, appendix to note 3.

order of superiority;[40] Akiva is presented before Tarfon.[41] Eleazar b. Azariah is placed in the middle position, out of chronological order, between Eliezer and Yehoshua, and Akiva and Tarfon. However, Henshke attributes that achronological arrangement to an aggadic tradition that Eleazar b. Azariah was promoted when Gamaliel was deposed.[42] On the other hand, since Bene Beraq is Akiva's hometown, the reclining presumably occurred at his residence. Therefore, Henshke posits that the narrative should be set out differently: "A tale of [*maʿaseh be* ...] Eliezer, etc., who reclined *chez* Akiva in Bene Beraq [*she-hayu mesubbin 'etsel R. Akiva* ...]."[43] Furthermore, he stipulates, narratives introduced by the phrase *maʿaseh be* ... never feature more than two or three sages.[44]

But there are other peculiarities, even more troublesome. For instance, Tarfon is not just out of order; he is totally wanting in the *Ginze Schechter* recension. Is this just a scribal omission, or is there another way to explain that? Eleazar b. Azariah may be important, but Eliezer, who is named first, is really the senior person in this assemblage, as well as one of Akiva's masters, so it does seem that his presence is appropriately emphasized precisely by the order in which he is presented.[45]

---

40. Precise biographical details are hard to pin down. Adin Steinsaltz groups Eliezer (b. Hyrcanus), Tarfon, and Yehoshua (b. Ḥananyah) in the generation of Gamaliel (II) of Yavneh, that is, the third generation of Tannaim (80–110 CE); and Eleazar b. Azaryah with Akiva in the one following (110–135 CE) (*The Talmud: the Steinsaltz Edition, a Reference Guide* [New York: Random House, 1989], 33). I follow his lead but note that an older arrangement compiled by Hanokh Albeck, *Introduction to the Mishnah* [Hebrew] (Jerusalem: Bialik Institute; Tel Aviv: Dvir, 5719 [1958 or 1959]), locates Eleazar ben Azariah in Gamaliel's generation (p. 224) and Tarfon in that of Akiva (p. 225). There is some disagreement in our sources with regard to the precedence of Akiva versus Eleazar ben Azariah, possibly because some texts may have been influenced by a story in both Talmuds in which the latter is chosen, on account of his priestly status, lineage that can be traced back to Ezra, wealth, and learning to be a temporary *naśi*, despite Akiva's greater knowledge and seniority (y. Ber. 4:1, 7c–d // b. Ber. 27b–28a). The representation of precedence in various sources is summarized below in table 2. Safrai and Safrai, in an alternative assessment of their sources, explain that Akiva, who follows Eleazar b. Azariah in the Bene Beraq list, is really the youngest member of the group, but he increased in prominence over time, although he did not serve as leader (*Haggadah of the Sages*, 208). Mor also assumes that Akiva was the youngest ("Laws of Sacrifice,"304 ; and see n. 34 on Eleazar's age).

41. Henshke, *"Mah Nishtannah,"* 392–93.

42. Ibid., 394–95. The aggadic tradition is cited and summarized in n. 43 above.

43. Ibid., 393.

44. Ibid., 392.

45. Mor explains that Eleazar ben Azariah's senior status is indicated by his being named in the center position in the sequence of sages; this is in accordance with the seating arrangement at a symposiastic dinner, where the most eminent person's couch is set at the apex ("Laws of Sacrifice," 304–5). Henshke's proof (*"Mah Nishtannah,"* 394–95) that Eleazar ben Azariah's placement in the center of the list of sages at Bene Beraq—following a pattern of precedence indicated by the seating at a symposium—is an indication of his prominence is questionable in two respects. It is based on a late source, Kallah Rab. 7:4 (After his survey

The solution to each sage problem is best approached from a different perspective. The inclusion or absence of Tarfon is a text-redactional problem and goes hand in hand with the previously noted linguistic variations. They can be addressed best through tracing the evolution of this narrative. The issues involving the numbers and the position of Eliezer are stylistic and formal. They can be understood through clarifying the nature of *maʿaseh be …* and *mesubbin* narratives, that is, when sages are named, and who takes precedence.

The generic and stylistic issues raised by Henshke will be clarified immediately below and I will add some others to the one I raised above. In the section after that, those problems and the linguistic issues will be addressed as the evolution of this narrative is demonstrated and conclusions drawn.

The Bene Beraq Seder Narrative as a Generic Maʿaseh

In order to assess whether this narrative could have been created in the talmudic era,[46] the number of sages present and the way the location of the gathering is recorded may be dispositive evidence. The Bene Beraq narrative names five sages. This indicates to Henshke that its author did not understand how a talmudic *maʿaseh* works, for *maʿasim* never include more than three sages. This surplus of sages is improper, for the self-identification *maʿaseh* is present in our story's opening rubric.

However, while most *maʿasim* feature only two or three sages, some do indeed include more. Thus, an exchange at Puteoli,[47] styled as a *maʿaseh*, included the four sages, viz., Judah b. Bathyra, Matteya b. Heresh,

---

of previous scholarship as well as the evidence of Kallah Rabbati itself, David Brodsky concludes that chs. 3–9 are post-talmudic or, at least, post-Amoraic (*A Bride without a Blessing: A Study in the Redaction and Content of Massekhet Kallah and Its Gemara*, TSAJ 118 [Tübingen: Mohr Siebeck, 2006], 238). The senior personage, Gamaliel, was put in the center in the Kallah Rabbati narrative because of a unique set of circumstances: the group was approaching a residence, and that way Gamaliel would be the first and primary person to be seen by the person receiving them. Nonetheless, *maʿaseh* narratives that list sages according to age and status always name Gamaliel first, not in the middle. In our story, therefore, the leader is not ben Azariah but Eliezer (b. Hyrcanus, *ha-gadol*), the sage named first, who also happens to be the oldest and revered for his knowledge. Safrai and Safrai conclude that the sequence in our *maʿaseh* follows the proper order according to status (*Haggadah of the Sages*, 117 n. 3, 208).

46. For a summary of those who regard the story as a record of an actual event, and those who do not, see Henshke, *"Mah Nishtannah,"* 391–92, and nn. 139, 143.

47. The source (Sifre on Deuteronomy, *Re'eh*, 80, p. 146) reads פלטום, which Finkelstein suggests is Platana (*Sifre on Deuteronomy*, Corpus Tannaiticum [New York: Jewish Theological Seminary of America, 1969], note on 1:5); Marcus Jastrow suggests that it is a corruption of פוטיולין, (*A Dictionary of the Targumim, the Talmud Babli and Yerushalmi, and the Midrashic Literature: with an Index of Scriptural Quotations* [New York: Choreb, 1926], 1179; the entry for which may be found on 1140).

Hananiah son of the brother of Yehoshua, and Jonathan.[48] Another *maʿaseh* finds Eleazar b. Mattiah, Ḥananiah b. Hakhinai, Simon b. Azzai, and Simon ha-Timni in discussion.[49] One more group of four, Gamaliel, Yehoshua, Eleazar b. Azariah, and Akiva is featured in no fewer than four *maʿasim*.[50] The last group, which includes three of the sages in the Bene Beraq session, will be a focus of the next section, on evolution.

Yet another passage, one in which not four but five sages appear, should be mentioned, especially because those are the same five sages as in the Bene Beraq narrative.[51] Although the latter text is not styled a *maʿaseh*—that is, it is not introduced by the term *maʿaseh be* …—it is still a talmudic-era anecdote or story and thus relevant to our concerns. Cited as a *baraita* in b. Sanh. 101a, this story comes from a Tannaitic source text that appears in both the Mekhilta of Rabbi Ishmael and the Sifre on Deu-

48. Finkelstein, *Sifre on Deuteronomy, Re'eh*, 80, p. 146. Without challenging its Tannaitic status, Finkelstein suggests that the section containing this story was not originally part of the Sifre but was added in the margins and subsequently incorporated into the text (note on line 3).

49. T. Ber. 4:18 (Lieberman says that this was interpolated by the editor of Tosefta Berakhot from a different source; see his brief commentary there, and his long commentary, *Tosefta ki-feshuṭah, Zeraim*, I:69, line 75).

50. M. Maʿaś. Š. 5:9; Sifra *Emor, parashah* 12, *perek* 16:2 (ed. Weiss, p. 102c–d) = t. Sukkah 2:11 = b. Sukkah 41b; Exod. Rab., *Mishpatim, parashah* 30:9 (reprint of ed. Vilna: Romm; undated reprint by Pe'er of reprint ed. Jerusalem, 5700 [1939 or 1940]), 106a–b; Derekh Ereẓ (Rabbah), also called *Pirqe Ben Azzai*, 3:2 (it is 5:4 in Marcus van Loopik, *The Ways of the Sages and the Way of the World: The Minor Tractates of the Babylonian Talmud*, TSAJ 26 [Tübingen: Mohr Siebeck, 1991], 100–102). Note that, while they are credited with speaking in the Exodus Rabbah narrative, they are portrayed as doing so as a group (*dareshu, ameru*); probably one spoke words with which the others concurred.

51. When the question of five (sages) has arisen, scholars have cited texts featuring five, but those citations do not reference narrative texts, that is, stories such as those being analyzed here. Thus, Safrai and Safrai observe that groups of "five sages/elders" (חמ[י]שה חכמים/זק[י]נים) are "quite common" (שכיח למדי) in Tannaitic traditions (מסורות), and in n. 4 cite three of them (*Haggadah of the Sages*, 117). Henshke correctly deletes "sages" but claims that this designation is (just) "common" in Tannaitic "texts" (מקורות) and also cites three (392 and n. 141). The following stipulations should be noted. First, the number of such occurrences is not at all large: only one in the Mishnah ('Erub. 3:4), four in the Tosefta (Šeb. 4:21, 'Erub. 2:16, Miqw. 7:10, and Ṭeh. 9:14), and one in Sifre Zuṭa on Numbers 19, 21 (p. 315). (There are also three cases in the Bavli, plus two duplications; and two in the Yerushalmi, one of them mentioned three times.) Moreover, the sages do not speak as individuals, and they are named in only one occurrence, viz., b. Sanh. 8b. In addition, there is one group of "five disciples" (תלמידים) in the Mishnah ('Abot 2:8) and one in the Bavli (b. Sanh. 43a). In the one in Mishnah 'Abot, their names and qualities are listed. Basically, when a group of five is designated, they are anonymous or, at the most, just listed by name (and quality). Thus, although it is significant that groups of five occur in this literature, such groups are not portrayed in stories; rather, rulings and traditions are ascribed to them as a collective. Finally—and this is significant for our narrative text—these (almost exclusively anonymous) groups are all composed of Tannaim (except for the list, with names, of Jesus's disciples in b. Sanh. 43a).

teronomy.[52] The Tannaitic document versions begin, כבר היה רבי אליעזר חולה ונכנסו[53] רבי טרפון ורבי יהושע ורבי אלעזר בן עזריה ורבי עקיבה לבקרו ("Rabbi Eliezer had been ailing for a while[54] when Rabbis Tarfon, Yehoshua, Eleazar b. Azariah, and Akiva entered to pay him a visit"). The storyteller simply chose to introduce his narrative with an expression that put Eliezer's ongoing condition upfront, as opposed to, for example, *maʿaseh be-rabbi … ve-rabbi …,* etc., *she-nikhnesu le-vaqer 'et Rabbi Eliezer she-hayah ḥoleh …* ("an incident about Rabbi … and Rabbi … , etc., who had come to visit Rabbi Eliezer who had taken sick"). [55] The sequence in this Tannaitic text does not necessarily reflect the eclipse of Akiva by Eleazar b. Azariah, who precedes Akiva in the list of sages (see below). Here, Akiva comes last because he speaks last in the ensuing encounter. The reason he speaks last is because his comment is the only one to which Eliezer reacts, and that with a request for more details. Thus, he alone elicits a response from the ailing master, and his ensuing reply is the longest communication in this text. Even if this episode is considered as acknowledging the hierarchical precedence of Eleazar b. Azariah, it does so in a way that celebrates the superiority of Akiva's hermeneutical insight and his favored status in the eyes of Eliezer. Indeed, that narrative-driven consideration could be sufficient in itself to account for moving Akiva to the final position.[56]

The evidence of four sages in Tannaitic *maʿasim,* as well as five in other tales, does invalidate the argument that three is the largest number of sages to appear in a *maʿaseh.* From the perspective of the number of sages, the Bene Beraq story could definitely be a Tannaitic-era tale. This possibility is enhanced by the fact that two different (and early) versions of this anecdote originally featured only four sages, as mentioned above (and

52. *Yitro, Ba-hodesh* 10 (pp. 240–41) and *Va-ethanan* 32 (pp. 57–59) respectively. Both editors stipulate that it must have been copied into the midrashic setting from another source. It is also present in two Genizah manuscript fragments of the Sifre (Menahem I. Kahana, *The Genizah Fragment of the Halakhic Midrashim* [Hebrew] [Jerusalem: Magnes, 2005, nos. 35–37 [pp. 255–56] and no. 37 [p. 257]). Although not styled a *maʿaseh,* there is an episode where *arbaʿah zeqenim* (fours elders) get together to refute Eliezer's teachings posthumously, and they are joined by a fifth (y. Giṭ. 9:1, 50a), all of whom engage in the debate.

53. The Mekhilta adds here *arbaʿah zeqenim* (four elders) and then enumerates them.

54. Jastrow, *Dictionary,* 609, s.v, II כבר, "a long time since, … already"; cf. entry כבר in Michael Sokoloff, *A Dictionary of Jewish Babylonian Aramaic of the Talmudic and Geonic Periods* (Ramat-Gan: Bar-Ilan University Press, 2002), 550–51.

55. Alternatively, one could begin *maʿaseh be-rabbi Eliezer she-hayah holeh, ve-nikhnesu Rabbi … le-vaqero.* See table 3, on alternative narrations of a dinner party hosted by Gamaliel (p. 209 below), one of which begins *kevar,* another with *maʿaseh be …,* and another simply, *keshe-ʿasah …*

56. Similarly, Henshke explains that some texts present Akiva before Tarfon, despite the latter's preeminent status (see n. 41 above), for reasons specific to the circumstances there (Henshke, "*Mah Nishtannah,*" 392–94 and n. 145]). Sources that sequence them properly are cited in n. 100 below.

see the discussion below, pages 204–5). Furthermore, an episode of five named sages,[57] in which four visit Eliezer, is Tannaitic, and our *maʿaseh* features the same sages, the only difference being that Akiva is apparently the one being visited.

What about the order in which the sages are named? As I stipulated in the preceding section, Eliezer is the most prominent person, so he is named first. Tarfon's position will be addressed in the following section, on the evolution of the Bene Beraq *maʿaseh*. What do we know about the other three—Yehoshua, Eleazar b. Azariah, and Akiva? These three appear in other *maʿasim*, along with Gamaliel II, of Yavne. The latter is the senior figure, so he is always named first (which supports the claim above that Eliezer is featured in the initial position because of his seniority). Gamaliel's eminence is further indicated in some of the narratives, namely, the ones that begin *maʿaseh be-rabban Gamaliel u-zeqenim/veha-zeqenim* … ("a story about Rabban Gamaliel and some elders/the elders …"). Some go on to enumerate them. Rabbi Yehoshua, who is also from Gamaliel's age group is the next to be named in the narratives of four, to be followed by the other two, who are members of the succeeding generation. The order there differs, and the Bene Beraq text follows the majority.

Table 2. Precedence of Akiva over Eleazar b. Azariah in Narratives

(Citations preceded by an asterisk are from narratives *not* introduced by *maʿaseh be* …)

Akiva named first	Eleazar b. Azariah named first
*T. Ber. 1:2[58]	
M. Maʿaś. Š. 5:9 (Gamaliel + *zeqenim*)[59] = y. Maʿaś. Š. 5:4, 55c	
T. Šabb. 3:3	
	*Mekhilta of Rabbi Ishmael, *Ba-Hodesh* 10 (240–41) = Sifre Deuteronomy, *Va-ethanan* 32 (57–58) = b. Sanh. 101a

57. For Safrai and Safrai, *Haggadah of the Sages*, 117, the (apparently) frequent citation of groups of "five sages" or "five elders" in Tannaitic traditions (they provide references n. 5), supports the historicity of the present account. Henshke is not persuaded of the historicity of our narrative on the basis of such phenomena ("*Mah Nishtannah,*" 391-92). Cf. n. 51 above.

58. אמ׳ ר׳ יהוד׳ פעם אחת הייתי מהלך אחר ר׳ עקיבא ואחר ר׳ אלעזר בן עזריה והגיע זמן קרית שמע.

59. In this story, Gamaliel gifts Yehoshua and Akiva, and then Yehoshua gifts Eleazar ben Azariah.

	*Mekhilta of Rabbi Ishmael, *Ki Tisa, Shabbeta* 1: *Ki*
	Sifra *Emor, parashah* 12, *pereq* 16:2 (Gamaliel + *zeqenim*; ed. Weiss, p. 102 c–d) = t. Sukkah 2:11 (sages are not named) = b. Sukkah 41b
	*Sifre Devarim, *Ekev 43, 16: Ve-akhalta* (p. 94)[60]
	*Sifre Devarim, *Ki tetse 269: Keritut she-yehe* (p. 289) // y. Keritot 9:1, 50a[61]
	Y. Sukkah 2:4, 52d[62]
	Der. Er. Rab. (*Pirqe Ben Azzai*) 3:2[63]
	Exod. Rab., *Mishpatim* 30:9 (p. 106a-b)

In two *ma*ʿ*asim* that feature just Akiva and Eleazar b. Azariah, Akiva is mentioned first in t. Šabb. 3:3 but last in y. Sukkah 2:4, 52d. Each is typical of the group of texts with which that source clusters in the above table. It could be that the editorial history of the preponderant texts reflects the conception behind the (Amoraic!) narrative of the deposition of Gamaliel, in which Eleazar b. Azariah was accorded precedence over Akiva,[64]

60. וכבר היו רבן גמליאל ורבי יהושע ורבי אלעזר בן עזריה ורבי עקיבה נכנסים לרומי.

61. לאחר מיתתו של רבי אליעזר נכנסו ארבעה זקנים להשיב על דבריו רבי טרפון ורבי יוסי הגלילי ורבי אלעזר בן עזריה ורבי עקיבה. Note that the list in the Yerushalmi Keritot version varies. Note also that Yehoshua, who is not listed there, speaks first, and, following Amoraic interventions, Yose ha-Gelili and Akiva speak last.

62. Gamaliel precedes Akiva in the parallel in b. Sukkah 23a, which is another indicator that the prominent person is conventionally named first in these stories.

63. Note that it begins *ma*ʿ*aseh be-arba*ʿ*ah zeqenim* and, as it progresses, Gamaliel takes up a position between Yehoshua and Eleazar on the right, and Akiva on the left. It should be noted that Der. Er. Rab. (*Pirqe Ben Azzai*) 3:2 is a late (Geonic) composition (see n. 94 below), hence most likely to have been influenced by the deposition story.

64. Alluded to by Henshke, *"Mah Nishtannah,"* 394–95 (and see n. 45 above). The story of the deposition of Gamaliel, in which Eleazar ben Azariah was preferred over Akiva (and Yehoshua), may be found in y. Ta'an. 4:1, 67d = b. Ber. 27b–28a. On this narrative and its traditions, see Robert Goldenberg, "The Deposition of Rabban Gamliel: An Examination of the Sources," *JJS* 23 (1972): 167–90; Haim Shapira, "The Deposition of R. Gamliel, between History and Legend" [Hebrew], *Zion* 64 (1994): 345–70; Devora Steinmetz, "Must the Patriarch Know 'Uqtzin? The Naśi as Scholar in Babylonian Agadda," *AJSR* 23 (1998): 163–90; Jeffery L. Rubenstein, *Stories of the Babylonian Talmud* (Baltimore: Johns Hopkins University Press, 2010), 77–80; Moshe Simon-Shoshan, "Creators of Worlds: The Deposition of R. Gamliel and the Invention of Yavneh," *AJSR* 41 (2017): 287–313; Simon-Shoshan, "Transmission and Evolution of the Story of R. Gamliel's Deposition," in *Jews and Christians in the First and Second Centuries: The Interbellum 70–132 CE*, ed. Joshua J. Schwartz and Peter J. Tomson, CRINT 15 (Leiden: Brill, 2018), 196–222.

The only entry in which Akiva's positioning at the end can be questioned is that of

whereas the Mishnah and the Tosefta, which were not affected, preserve the memory of Akiva's original precedence.[65]

A related issue, one pertinent to the Bene Beraq story, is whether it would be appropriate for Eliezer, the master, to visit his disciple, especially on the latter's turf. That is difficult to ascertain because narratives do not often spell out matters of precedence, but there is a case where a Rabbi Eliezer went to visit *'etsel* (on the turf of) Yose b. Peredah *talmido* (his disciple).[66] The disciple is little known but, since this visit is also recorded in a Tannaitic text (t. 'Erub. 1:2), the visiting master is undoubtedly the same eminent sage, Eliezer, who in our narrative visited Akiva at Bene Beraq.

Another consideration Henshke raised is that the proper way to indicate attendance at a party that took place at Akiva's residence, or even with him as host, would be along the lines of *hayu mesubbin 'etsel R. Akiva bi-Bene Beraq*. The following is a paradigmatic example of that that point: אורחין שהיו מסובין אצל בעל הבית וקדש עליהן היום ועקרו עם חשיכה לבית המדרש ("Guests who had been reclining *etsel* the householder when Shabbat began, and then betook themselves at nightfall to the *bet midrash*") (t. Ber. 5:3).[67] That criticism seems reasonable. The apparent obliviousness of the creator of the Bene Beraq narrative to such a fine point of style could indicate that he stands outside of the world of *baraita* creation and, therefore, could be a sign of post-talmudic composition. However, it is not even followed in all Tannaitic texts. For instance, while one of the examples in table 3 uses an

---

Mekhilta *Ba-hodesh* (and parallels), in the second column of table 2 above, where each sage speaks when his name is mentioned. It could be that Akiva speaks last there because of the significant reason that, not only does he speak longest but also in a concluding dialogue with Eliezer, on whose account they had convened (see above, pp. 195–96). One could, on the other hand, suggest that Akiva's favored speech and, by implication, predominant scholarly attainment, are coincidental indications of his political subservience to Eleazar, who is named before him. See, e.g., Simon-Shoshan, *Stories of the Law*, 219.

65. The phrase *shabbat shel [Eleazar ben Azariah]* (t. Soṭah 8:9) was adapted in b. Ber. 28a to refer to that sage's appointed day to deliver the sermon, in an arrangement worked out following the deposition and reinstatement of Gamaliel. This Toseftan passage seems, then, to imply the precedence of Eleazar ben Azariah. However, the parallel in Mekhilta R. Ishmael, *Bo, Pisḥa* 16 (pp. 58–59: *mi shavat sham?*) does not allow for the Bavli's construction. Lieberman suggests that the Tosefta refers in a general way to which master spoke on that Shabbat, which could be for a number of reasons (he refers to *Sifra, Metsora,* [Introduction], 13 [p. 70c], and to the commentary of the Raavad there [*Tosefta ki-feshuṭah, VIII: Nashim*, 679–80]). He also notes that J. N. Epstein explained that "whose Shabbat was it?" can ask which disciple's turn it was to attend upon his master (*Prolegomena ad Litteras Tannaiticas* [Hebrew] [Jerusalem: Magnes, 1957], 427).

66. B. 'Erub. 11b; ben Peredah's status is not revealed in the original Tannaitic account, t. 'Erub. 1:2.

67. This text is cited by Mandel (*Origins of Midrash*, 192) as an example of the Tannaitic *bet midrash* in which "instruction" and "sessions" took place "in the evening or during the day" (190). The host may have stayed behind to provide continuity to the meal for ritual and liturgical purposes (see Lieberman, *Tosefta ki-feshuṭah, Zeraʿim* 1:74 on lines 8–9).

'etsel formula, the other two, one of which is in the Sifre Deuteronomy, do not specify where the event occurred. I would furthermore stipulate that this incongruity may be explained, in part, by the evolutionary development of our text, as it is traced in the next section.

Nonetheless, I would claim that there is a far more telling problem with this narrative, one that marks it as incommensurate with the ways in which sage stories, *maʿasim* and others as well, were told during the talmudic period. That is, the economy of expression in aggadic tales extends even to the specification, by name, of the persons involved. This policy of narrative economy accords with the rule of Chekhov's gun;[68] that is, unless an individual character will say or do something further on in the tale, or fulfills some other function, that character's name is not to be proclaimed at the beginning.

The seder of Gamaliel and the elders in Lod (t. Pesaḥ. 10:12)[69] is a case in point. The text reads

A story about Rabban Gamaliel and elders,	מעשה ברבן גמליאל וזקנים,
Who were reclining [at a seder] at the home of Baitos b. Zonin in Lod,	שהיו מסובין בבית ביתוס בן זונין בלוד,
and were engaged in *hilkhot ha-Pesaḥ* the whole night,	והיו עסוקין בהלכות הפסח כל הלילה,
until cockcrow;	עד קרות הגבר;
[servants] removed the tables,	הגביהו מלפניהן,
And they betook themselves to the *bet midrash.*	וניערו והלכו להן לבית המדרש.

Gamaliel is named since he is the leader, but the elders remain anonymous, because no specific statement or action is attributed to any one of them; the servants whose humble task is to clear away the mess are not even denominated as a group, but merely folded by implication into the verb *higbihu*; ironically, Baitos,[70] the only person named besides Gamaliel, merited such public recognition because he hosted the event.[71]

Only two people function in the following *maʿaseh.*

68. "One must never place a loaded rifle on the stage if it isn't going to go off. It's wrong to make promises you don't mean to keep" (Leah Goldberg, *Russian Literature in the Nineteenth Century: Essays* [Jerusalem: Magnes Press, 1976], 163).

69. Discussed above, p. 182.

70. On Baitos, see Joshua Schwartz, "על זונן ובנו בייתוס," *Sinai* 103 (1988–1989): 108–22.

71. Nurit Be'eri explains that a simulated background story (סיפור דמוי־מציאות) would be constructed from borrowed and invented details and motifs, including persons and locations, into which a teaching or tradition could be incorporated; the invented narrative background with its vibrant details and emotional associations, makes the teaching easier to remember (*Exploring Ta'aniyot: Yerushalmi Tractate Ta'aniyot – Forming and Redacting the Traditions* [Hebrew] [Ramat-Gan: Bar-Ilan University Press, 5769 (2008/2009)], 88–91).

A story about R. Eleazar b. Azariah and R. Akiva, who were traveling on a ship; R. Akiva made himself a *sukkah* at the head of the ship, And a wind came and blew it away. R. Eleazar b. Azariah said to him, "Akiva, where is your *sukkah*?"	מעשה בר[בי] אלעזר בן עזריה ורבי עקיבה שהיו באין בספינה, ועשה לו רבי עקיבה סוכה בראש הספינה, ובאת הרוח והפריחתה. אמר לו רבי אלעזר בן עזריה: עקיבה איה סוכתך.[72]

This incident takes place onboard a ship. Other people may have been on that voyage, but they are not mentioned because they are not connected to the action. The sages' destination, if any, is irrelevant; they just need to be on a ship, so that the typical winds, more powerful than those experienced on land, can blow the *sukkah* away.[73] Both sages are named because each one has a role to play: one builds a *sukkah* sturdy enough to stand up to normal winds, as halakhically required in his view, but unable to withstand the strong winds on the Mediterranean; and the other emphasizes the irony of his situation.[74]

The following narrative begins with Gamaliel and the elders, also on a ship sailing to an undetermined destination, the purpose being to furnish a halakhically challenging setting. The narrator begins with "the elders," as in the Lod seder story, but he goes on to state their names.

A story about Rabban Gamaliel and the elders, who were sailing on a ship; No *lulav* was there except in the possession of Rabban Gamaliel alone. And Rabban Gamaliel gave it as a gift to R. Yehoshua, and R. Yehoshua to R. Eleazar b. Azariah, and R. Eleazar b. Azariah to R. Akiva. So, each of them fulfillled their obligation.	מעשה ברבן גמליאל והזקינים, שהיו באים בספינה, ולא נמצא לולב כי אם ביד רבן גמליאל בלבד. ונתנו רבן גמליאל מתנה לרבי יהושע, ורבי יהושע לרבי אלעזר בן עזריה, ורבי אלעזר בן עזריה לרבי עקיבא, וכולם יצאו ידי חובתם.[75]

72. Y. Sukkah 2:4, 52d. Retold with Gamaliel and Akiva in b. Sukkah 23a.

73. A *sukkah* is a temporary, impermanent dwelling. It should be sufficiently sturdy to serve as a temporary housing but, at the same time, not so substantial as to be a permanent structure. According to m. Sukkah 2:3, one may construct a *sukkah* at the top or head of a moving vessel such as a ship or a wagon.

74. The implication is that, under the circumstances, it never was a *sukkah*. Eleazar holds that a *sukkah* built onboard a ship must be able to withstand gusts typical of that setting, whereas Akiva holds that one need be able to withstand only winds typical of land. Akiva may have a considered position on this matter, but he no longer has a *sukkah*.

75. Sifra *Emor*, *parashah* 12, *pereq* 16 (p. 102c). The identities were not revealed in the following version, which chose to enrich the narrative in other ways (t. Sukkah 2:11).

Employing a practiced narrative skill, this storyteller does not reveal their names until the character's role in the action is set forth.

An apparent exception, the gun that seemingly does not get fired, may be found in t. Ber. 4:18.

A story about four sages who were sitting in the gate house of R. Yehoshua, Eleazar b. Mathia, Hananya b. [Ha]khinai, Shimeon ben Azzai and Shimeon ha-Timni. They were occupied with what R. Akiva had taught them, "Why did Judah merit kingship? Because he confessed with respect to Tamar." They added on their own [Job 15:18–19], "That which wise men have transmitted from their fathers, and have not withheld, to whom alone was given the Land, etc."	מעשה בארבעה זקנים שהיו יושבין בבית שער של ר׳ יהושע, אלעזר בן מתיא וחנניא בן כינאי ושמעון בן עזאי ושמעון התימני, והיו עסוקין במה ששנה להם ר׳ עקיבא: מפני מה זכה יהודה למלכות? מפני שהודה בתמר. הוסיפו הן מעצמן (איוב טו, יח-יט): אשר חכמים יגידו ולא כחדו מאבתם; להם לבדם נתנה הארץ וגו׳

That text, however, is a parenthetical insertion into the Tosefta there, and it is incomplete. In another version, each sage does speak.[76]

Before concluding this section, let us reexamine the evidence of two phrases undocumented in Tannaitic texts. They are *kol ʾoto ha-lailah* (which is Amoraic), and *sapper bi-yetsiat Mitsrayim* (which is unknown before this Haggadah *maʿaseh* and its surrounding texts). Henshke suggests that their lack of earlier documentation does render them suspect. Perhaps so, but it would not be sufficient to disprove a Tannaitic provenance. The phrase *sapper be-*, for example, while rare in Tannaitic literature, does occur in two settings in the Tosefta, the one *le-sapper be-maʿaseh ha-'ari* ("to talk about the episode of the lion"; t. Ber. 1:11) and t. Yoma 2:7: *le-sapper bi-genut* … ("to recount or discuss the disgrace of ..."). The first is actually pertinent because it involves recounting a salvation event; the second involves *genut* (disgrace, shame) a rhetorical perspective to be taken up during the seder

---

מעשה ברבן גמליאל וזקנים שהיו באין בספינה ולא היה עמהן לולב. לקח רבן גמליאל לולב בדינר זהב. כיון שיצא בו ידי חובתו נתנו לחבירו, וחבירו לחבירו, עד שיצאו כולן, ואחר כך החזירוהו לו.

76. See Lieberman's brief note (ad loc.); in his *Tosefta ki-feshuṭah, Zeraim* 1:69, he cites a version from a late midrash (Adolph Jellinek, *Bet ha-midrash* [repr., Jerusalem: Wahrmann, 1967], 5:95) in which all do speak.

A late example features three eminences (*gedole ha-medinah*) who were reclining with Yoḥanan b. Zakkai ('Abot R. Nat. B 13, p. 16, s.v, *davar 'aḥer*); they neither speak nor act. That text exceeds the chronological scope of this inquiry, but the publicizing of their names is not in conflict with the thesis advanced here because it does have a rhetorical purpose, for they are expounded upon in the ensuing account.

exposition. In view of those usages, each one itself a *unicum,* it would be reasonable to suggest that, if *le-sapper bi-yetsiat Mitsrayim* appeared in the Bene Beraq *ma'aseh,* there is no reason that it could not indeed be a third Tannaitic instance. One could surmise that it came to be integrated into the Haggadah by the introductory units 4–6 (or 5–6), which had borrowed that phrase from the *ma'aseh* (except that I observed above, and will further demonstrate below, that the linguistic concern is irrelevant, for this expression is not original to our narrative).

The expression *kol 'oto ha-lailah* presents a more complicated problem. On the one hand, it has no precedent in Tannaitic documents (although *kol ha-lailah* is definitely common there).[77] On the other hand, Levi, a disciple of Judah the Prince uses it,[78] as does his son, Yehoshua.[79] But those two sages are on the cusp, members of a liminal group, straddling between the Tannaitic period and that of the Amoraim. Were it not for the chronological indeterminacy, observations on linguistic usages like that might lend support to an argument but would not themselves constitute proof. A further indication, though, does negate a hypothesis that *kol 'oto ha-lailah* could not be Tannaitic. That is, a corresponding phrase concerning *yom* ("day," the opposite of night), viz., *kol 'oto ha-yom,* occurs several times in Tannaitic documents.[80] That makes it easy to imagine a Tannaitic author stipulating *kol 'oto ha-lailah* in a statement or narrative.

In light of the above considerations, one must concede that the Bene Beraq *ma'aseh* may relate an event that occurred in Tannaitic times, and it probably would not fail some linguistic tests for a possible Tannaitic provenance. However, it definitely violates certain Tannaitic literary narrative conventions. Henshke objects to the way in which the narrator chose to identify the location of the event. He thinks that there may be a problem with how Eliezer, the senior person, is presented, and Tarfon is completely out of order, at the end rather than closer to Eliezer at the beginning (as in the above-mentioned story of four sages who went to visit an ailing Eliezer [pp. 196–97 above]). True, and even more telling, is that Tarfon is totally wanting in some iterations of this incident. The other objections must, however, yield in the face of the evidence adduced above. Nonetheless, the story violates a basic rule of aggadic anecdotes in stating

77. According to the Bar Ilan Responsa Project database, there are nine occurrences in the Mishnah; twenty-three in the Tosefta; and twenth-nine in the halakhic midrashim.

78. Gen. Rab. 40:17 (*Midrash Bereshit Rabba,* ed. J. Theodor and Ch. Albeck [repr., Jerusalem: Wahrmann, 1965]), = 52:18.

79. Gen. Rab. 26:2. Citing Bar Pedayah (a contemporary of Levi, his father). = Gen. Rab. 50:5.

80. According to the Bar Ilan Responsa Project database, there are nine occurrences in the Tosefta; one in the Mekhilta of Rabbi Shimeon bar Yochai (*Mekhilta d'Rabbi Shim`on b. Yochai,* ed. J. N. Epstein and E. Z. Melamed [repr., Jerusalem: Yeshivat Shaare Rahamim and Bet Hillel, 1955], ad Exod 17:12 [p. 122]).

the names of sages even though not all of them speak or perform a specific action or function.

The demonstrable unfamiliarity of the author of this composition with some basic rules of *ma'aseh* composition leads to the conclusion that this *ma'aseh* is post-talmudic. It was, therefore, created during the Geonic period, when it shows up in the Haggadah and when so many elements of *maggid* were being composed and developed. It was undoubtedly generated in order to fill a perceived gap in *maggid*.

Interestingly, its flaws indicate that the creator of this *ma'aseh* was conversant with rabbinic literature. The following sections show how that familiarity can help us understand how it originated and developed.

The Evolution of the Bene Beraq Seder Narrative, Stage 1: An Adaptation of t. Pesaḥ. 10:12

Of the problems with the Bene Beraq *ma'aseh* raised in Henshke and added by me, the serious, unresolved ones are as follows. The exposition is formulated so that Rabbi Akiva is a participant rather than a host, even though he is the only one who dwells in Bene Beraq. Sages, rather than being treated as a collective, are named individually, even though most do not act or speak on their own. Finally, Tarfon, a senior figure, is either introduced last rather than at the beginning with Eliezer, or else he is completely wanting, as in the *Ginze Schechter* version. Are those aberrations mere scribal oversights?

Let us take a closer look at that version.

A story about R. Eliezer, R. Yehoshua, R. Eleazar b. Azariah and R. Akiva, Who were reclining [at a seder] in Bene Beraq,	ומעשה בר' אליעזר ור' יהושע ור' אלעזר בן עזריה ור' עקיבה, שהיו מסובין בבני-ברק,
and were speaking about the exodus all of that night,	והיו מסיחים ביצי' מצ' כל אותו הלילה,
until their disciples came and said to them,	עד שבאו תלמידיהם ואמרו להם:
"Our masters, the time for the morning Shema has come."	רבותינו, הגיע זמן קריאת שמע של שחרית.

This text has only four sages, a statistic less unusual than the current five. It also employs a different verbal phrase for recounting the exodus, viz. *mesiḥim + be* ... instead of *mesapperim + be* .... It could be that the above iteration represents an early form of this narrative, with fewer sages and a verb of recounting that would, in later textualizations, come to be eclipsed by another contextual expression, *mesapperim/n*. (Neither expression is common.)

Pursuant to that possibility, let us consider a companion to the *Ginze Schechter* version, a recension of this anecdote found in a Haggadah text appended by the copyist at the end of a manuscript of the *Siddur* of Shelomoh bar Natan of Sijilmassa. That Sijilmassa-B text (table 4, col. 3) is instructive.

0. A story about Rabban Gamaliel, R. Yehoshua, R. Eleazar b. Azariah and R. Akiva,	0. מעשה ברבן גמליאל ור' אלעזר בן עזריה ור' יהושע ור' עקיבא,
1. Who were reclining [at a seder] in Bene Beraq,	1. שהיו מסובין בבני-ברק,
2. and were speaking at length about the exodus,	2. והיו משיחין והולכין ביציאת מצרים,
3. until the rising of the dawn.	3. עד שעלה עמוד השחר.
4=3′. Upon the rising of the dawn,	4 =3'. כיון שעלה עמוד השחר,
5=1′. their disciples came to them;	5 =1'. נכנסו תלמידיהם אצליהם,
6=2′. they said to them, "The time for the morning Shema has just come."	6 =2'. אמרו להם: כבר הגיע זמן קריאת שמע.

It is arranged in a modified chiastic pattern, perhaps under the influence of the Tosefta Pesaḥim source it was adapting. Line 0 is the exposition. That and the action, lines 1–6, revolve around the central lines 3 and 4, which end the first scene and begin the second one, respectively. Lines 1 and 5 set out the action of the sages and of their students, respectively, while units 2 and 6 report the different topics that they addressed.

This text is even more distinctive than the previous one in several noteworthy respects. Linguistically, *mesiḥin* is used, rather than *mesapperim/n*, as before. Moreover, *kol 'oto ha-lailah* is nowhere to be found. Without mentioning its nightlong duration, the extensive nature of the recounting is conveyed by an augmented verbal construction (*mesiḥin* ***ve-holekhin***) for a process that continued until dawn (*'ad she-'alah 'amud ha-shaḥar*). The masters are not addressed as *rabbotenu*, and the specification *shel shaḥarit* does not augment *zeman qeri'at shema*[81] (the dawning of the day makes that clear). Hence, it is indeed ironic that, in critiquing the literary and linguistic competence of the Bene Beraq narrative in the Haggadah, scholars were either unaware that the original form of the tale was actually different, and lacked the linguistically problematic phrases, or they ignored the evidence. The differences, then, illuminate some of the problems and obviate others.

It seems clear that this supplementary version in the Shelomoh bar

81. The phrase *zeman qeri'at shema* appears in Tannaitic documents, e.g., t. Ber. 1:2, 1:4, and 3:19, but the specification "(*shel*) *Shaḥarit/'Arvit*" does not appear earlier than Geonic and medieval sources. While the Sijilmassa-B version could theoretically be of Tannaitic provenance, this factor would suggest that all subsequent versions are post-talmudic.

Natan *Siddur* manuscript is a preliminary form of the anecdote. Indeed, evidently taking the Lod Seder as a structural paradigm, it is longer than the others, told in six lines instead of four. The dawning of the day is stated twice, although greater dramatic effect could have been achieved if instead the all-night length of this episode had been noted. *Mesiḥin ve-holekhin*, on the other hand is a nice way to convey the long and continuous progress of the discussion in which of these sages were engaged.

There are as many problems as sages. Rabbi Tarfon is wanting, which means that only four are in attendance. (Let it be noted that this statistic comports well with our observations above that four—as well as five—fits within the numerical norm of named persons in a *maʿaseh* or other sage narrative.) The naming of Eleazar b. Azariah before Yehoshua is anomalous. Akiva is on the list of attendees when he ought to be the host. But more unusual than any of those items by far is that Gamaliel is in the first position instead of Eliezer, who is nowhere to found. Gamaliel does not appear in any of other versions of the seder at Bene Beraq.[82]

Where some have seen the Toseftan and Haggadah versions of the all-night Passover as mirror-image reflections of each other,[83] Henshke and others have gone further in suggesting that the Haggadah version is actually an adaptation of the former, which served as its model.[84] The Sijilmassa-B text, preserved in an early thirteenth-century Near Eastern or North African manuscript, appears to be a missing evolutionary link, textual evidence of that process of adaptation. The Bene Beraq narrative is not a lost Tannaitic tale at all; it began, and it developed, within the context of one family of the Babylonian branch of the Haggadah as the latter was taking form in the Geonic period.

At this point, the beginning of the Babylonian Haggadah would have been in the following state. As a way of addressing the Four Questions, the *maggid* section opened with a brief *'Avadim hayinu* declaration (table 1 or 4, unit 1) and reminded those present that the manner in which the Questions are answered should take four different styles of personal identity and learning into account (table 1 or 4, unit 10). That *baraita* favored inculcating the rules of the Passover offering to the wise son, whom it mentioned first, although it did provide for three other types. In developing this section, one group of liturgical composers interposed units 2 and 3 between *'Avadim hayinu* and the pedagogical *baraita*. Another liturgical composer interposed units 7 and 8, viz., the Bene Beraq *maʿaseh* and m. Ber. 1:5, in which Eleazar b. Azariah cites Ben Zoma to instruct people to mention the exodus at night and unnamed sages debate with him.

---

82. For this reason, Safrai and Safrai concluded that Gamaliel is simply a scribal error (*Haggadah of the Sages*, 117).

83. Henshke, "*Mah Nishtannah*," 392.

84. Ibid., 392–95.

It is not certain how the match was made. Perhaps the pedagogic text was intended to counter the emphasis on *hilkhot ha-Pesaḥ*, or simply to anticipate it by showing people in discussion; and, by way of introduction, the (Toseftan) *maᶜaseh* of Gamaliel's all-night examination of *hilkhot ha-Pesaḥ* was reworked to tell of a gathering that spent the night discussing the exodus à la Mishnah Berakhot. Alternatively, the sequence may have been reversed. In this scenario, a liturgical composer may have adapted the Toseftan *maᶜaseh* to anticipate the pedagogic text with a tale of sages engaged in discussion, and added m. Ber. 1:5 to illustrate the discussion. The pedagogic *baraita* would follow as a guide to seder participants in the application of the preceding examples (of sages) to their own seder discussion.

The adapter evidently decided to further differentiate the two Gamalielan seders by changing the location from Lod to Bene Beraq. Perhaps the latter place was chosen simply because it was the place where the sage named last, Akiva, dwelt. It was, accordingly, convenient to conclude the exposition of this *maᶜaseh* with Akiva in Bene Beraq.

With respect to that coincidence, one can suggest that it was unnecessary to specify that this was the home of Akiva. In the three versions of a festive meal hosted by Gamaliel that will be examined in the next section, one account specifies that sages were *mesubbin 'etslo* (at his house, or with him where he hosted his festivity). The other two do not.[85] The location is expressed as the occasion: *hayu mesubbin be-vet mishteh beno shel Rabban Gamaliel*. The narrators could have formulated it, for example, as *hayu mesubbin 'etsel Rabban Gamaliel be-mishteh beno*. But they did not. Similarly, the failure to stipulate *'etsel Rabbi Akiva* may not be an oversight but a consequence of the retention of the formulation of the Toseftan story in switching from Lod to Bene Beraq, but with Akiva already stipulated as a member of the group in the final position, immediately adjacent to the place-name.

The Evolution of the Bene Beraq Seder Narrative, Stage 1 Continued: Sequence of Sages

T. Pesaḥ. 10:12, the evolutionary germ of this narrative, does not identify Gamaliel's collocutors, who are simply styled *zeqenim*, because it did not report anything they independently said or did that night. The Babylonian adapter, however, did want to present something that Eleazar b. Azariah spoke about at the Bene Beraq seder as he imagined it, viz., m. Ber. 1:5, so he stipulated that sage's presence.

85. See table 3 below.

It was mentioned above that the latter, along with Yehoshua and Akiva, were reported to have accompanied Gamaliel in several *maᶜasim.*[86] Although they were never reported to have been *mesubbin* as a group in each other's company, it would certainly seem appropriate to include Eleazar b. Azariah in a seder led by Gamaliel, along with the two aforementioned colleagues.[87] On the other hand, it would not have entered the storyteller's mind to place Tarfon at that seder because the latter is never part of a group accompanying Gamaliel. Rather, in their encounters, Gamaliel seems to be portrayed as challenging Tarfon's assertions.[88]

Eleazar b. Azariah's position is noteworthy. Not only does he precede Akiva, as discussed above,[89] but he is named immediately following Gamaliel. Thus, he is given precedence with respect to Yehoshua, who was his elder, and therefore always preceded him in a sequence of named sages. This violation of a long-standing norm was probably done to promote the younger scholar, for he declaimed a message (unit 10), whereas Yehoshua did not say or do anything. Therefore, his presence would be signaled right after that of the session leader, with Yehoshua and Akiva trailing after.[90]

86. See above, p. 196 and n. 50, and p. 201 and n. 75; and table 2 (pp. 197–98 and nn. 60 and 63). They were also together in *maᶜasim* without Eleazar ben Azariah; see b. Qidd. 26b and b. B. Meṣ. 11a. All four sages travel together in Der. Er. Rab. (= *Pirqe Ben Azzai),* 3:2 (ed. van Loopik, 1991, 5:4), but only the senior figures Gamaliel and Yehoshua speak. The fact that this is a late text like our Bene Beraq narrative may explain this shared anomaly.

87. The *maᶜasim* discussed herein have halakhic implications, but they also are imaginative literary creations. Menachem Elon discusses them under a signification of *maᶜaseh,* "case" (*Jewish Law: History, Sources, Principles* [Hebrew] [Jerusalem: Magnes, 1973], 768–89; on sages as actors in cases, see 771–72, 779–82). Nurit Be'eri discusses legal *maᶜasim* in y. Ta'an. (*Exploring Ta'aniyot,* 95–105); however, she distinguishes more literary narratives as *sippurim* stories (see 95–96, nn. 92–93; 176 and n. 32). Jonah Fraenkel also distinguishes halakhic anecdotes from aggadic stories (*sippur hilkhati, sippur aggada*) (*The Aggadic Narrative: Harmony of Form and Content* [Hebrew] [Tel Aviv: Hakibbutz Hameuchad, 2001], 220–35). Moshe Simon-Shoshan demonstrates the literary qualities of "stories" (*maᶜasim*), which he divides into three types: exempla, case stories, and etiological stories (*Stories of the Law,* 45–49). He considers stories like ours (narratives of cases involving like-minded individuals) under the rubric, exempla (138–49), while his detailed analysis of case stories is devoted to stories of events that occasioned rulings that are later subverted by greater authorities (167–93).

88. He rebukes Tarfon in Sifre on Numbers, ed. H. S. Horovitz (Leipzig: Gustav Hock, 1917) *Qoraḥ* 116, s.v., *ve-'atah u-vanekha* (p. 133) = b. Pesaḥ. 72b and disputes him in Midrash Mishle, ed. Burton L. Visotzky (New York: Jewish Theological Seminary, 1970), 69–70.

89. Pp. 193–99.

90. Being accorded such a favorable position would have had nothing to do with the talmudic stories of the deposition of Gamaliel, wherein Eleazar was chosen over Akiva and even Yehoshua to replace the *nasi.* Otherwise, Eleazar would have been introduced before Yehoshua in the other narratives where they appeared with Gamaliel. For Mor ("Laws of Sacrifice") and Henshke ("*Mah Nishtannah*") this foregrounding of Eleazar by centering him is unremarkable (see n. 45 above).

What is important to conclude at this point is that the revisionist adapter seems to have chosen to update the Toseftan nighttime seder to reflect an emphasis on the exodus account. In specifying who was present, he elected to follow a different paradigm, albeit incorrectly, but he kept to a traditional choice of sages.

Indeed, this rabbinic-liturgical composer violated another norm when he named Yehoshua, the silent sage. This positional disparity was remedied by later redactors who put Yehoshua where he belongs, in the second position, followed by Eleazar b. Azariah. (The later redactor was even further from the talmudic rules of the game in naming a silent sage, as will be explained below.) One can claim that Akiva, who was also silent, was named last because—as presumptive host and, hence, active contributor—he would be appropriately juxtaposed with Bene Beraq. The story could be set out in different ways.

Table 3. Three Possible Ways to Open an Aggadic Narrative

	Mekhilta of Rabbi Ishmael, Yitro, 'Amaleq 1[91]	*Sifre on Deuteronomy, 'Eqev 38*[92]	*b. Qidd. 32b*
a	כשעשה רבן גמליאל סעודה לחכמים, היו כל חכמי ישראל מסובים אצלו.	וכבר היו רבי אליעזר ורבי יהושע ורבי צדוק מסובים בבית משתה בנו של רבן גמליאל.	מעשה ברבי אליעזר ורבי יהושע ורבי צדוק שהיו מסובין בבית המשתה בנו של רבן גמליאל.
b1	עמד רבן גמליאל ושמשן.	מזג רבן גמליאל את הכוס לרבי אליעזר.	והיה רבן גמליאל עומד ומשקה עליהם.
b2	אמרו החכמים: אין אנו כדי שישמשנו.	ולא רצה לטלו, נטלו רבי יהושע.	נתן הכוס לר׳ אליעזר ולא נטלו, נתנו לר׳ יהושע וקיבלו.
c1	אמר להן ר׳ יהושע: הניחו לו שישמש, שמצינו שגדול מרבן גמליאל שמש את הבריות.	אמר לו רבי אליעזר: מה זה יהושע, בדין שאנו מסובים וגמליאל ברבי עומד ומשמשנו?	אמר לו רבי אליעזר: מה זה, יהושע, אנו יושבין ורבן גמליאל ברבי עומד ומשקה עלינו?
[c2]	אמרו לו, אי זה זה?		

91. Pp. 195–96. There is a parallel in Mekhilta of Shimeon bar Yochai, *ad* Exod 18:12 (p. 88).

92. Pp. 74–75.

[c3]	אמר להם: אברהם אבינו גדול העולם, ששימש מלאכי השרת, והיה סבור בהן שהם בני אדם ערביים עובדי עבודה זרה, רבן גמליאל שישמש חכמים לומדי תורה, על אחת כמה וכמה.		
c2 / [d1]	אמר להן ר׳ צדוק: הניחו לו שישמש, מצינו גדול מרבן גמליאל ומאברהם ששימש את הבריות.	אמר לו רבי יהושע: הנח לו וישמש, אברהם גדול העולם שמש מלאכי שרת וכסבור שהם ערביים עובדי עבודה זרה שנאמר (בראשית יח ב) וישא עיניו וירא והנה שלשה אנשים, והלא דברים קל וחומר, ומה אברהם גדול העולם שמש מלאכי שרת וכסבור שהם ערביים עובדי עבודה זרה, גמליאל ברבי לא ישמשנו?	אמר ליה: מצינו גדול ממנו ששמש, (אברהם גדול ממנו ושמש) אברהם גדול הדור היה, וכתוב בו: והוא עומד עליהם! ושמא תאמרו, כמלאכי השרת נדמו לו? לא נדמו לו אלא לערביים, ואנו לא יהא רבן גמליאל ברבי עומד ומשקה עלינו?
d1/ [d2]	אמרו לו, אי זה זה?	אמר להם רבי צדוק: הנחתם כבוד מקום, ואתם עסוקים בכבוד בשר ודם?	אמר להם רבי צדוק: עד מתי אתם מניחים כבודו של מקום, ואתם עוסקים בכבוד הבריות?
d2 / [d3]	אמר להם: שכינה, שבכל שעה מספיק מזון לכל באי העולם כדי צרכן ומשביע לכל חי רצון, ולא לבני אדם הכשרים והצדיקים בלבד, אלא אף הרשעים עובדי עבודה זרה רבן גמליאל על אחת כמה וכמה שישמש חכמים ובני תורה.	אם מי שאמר והיה העולם משיב רוחות ומעלה עננים ומוריד גשמים ומגדל צמחים ועורך שולחן לכל אחד ואחד, גמליאל ברבי לא ישמשנו.	הקדוש ברוך הוא משיב רוחות ומעלה נשיאים ומוריד מטר ומצמיח אדמה, ועורך שולחן לפני כל אחד ואחד, ואנו לא יהא רבן גמליאל ברבי עומד ומשקה עלינו?

The versions of this anecdote consist of an exposition (a), an action and response (b1 and 2), and two speech acts with replies (c1 and 2, d1 and 2; the Mekhilta is set out differently from the other two, without Eliezer, and with extra steps). What interests us is the way the actors and speakers are introduced. Since this wedding feast was being hosted by a prominent family (the house of the *nasi* Gamaliel) many guests would have been present. The Mekhilta (which just characterizes its occasion as a "feast for the sages") reports, right in the exposition, that "all the sages of Israel were *mesubbin*" with Gamaliel (*'etslo*), but the Sifre and the Bavli report that only Eliezer, Yehoshua, and Tsadok were there, with the implication that Gamaliel, the father, would be present as host. One would expect the Sifre and Bavli composers, and their audiences, to have been aware that others would also have been present. They chose to restrict themselves to the persons who would act or speak in the ensuing action.

This convention is followed in late antique rabbinic anecdotes. Like Chekhov's gun, a character identified by name must act or speak. There is one wrinkle in the exposition that does not name the sages (as with the Mekhilta above), viz., their number may be restricted to the ones who take part in the action. For example, an exposition in Sifra *Emor*, *parshah* 12, *pereq* 16 (p. 102c), has Gamaliel and the elders (*zeqenim*) on a ship on the first day of Sukkot, with Gamaliel alone in possession of a *lulav*. The action has Gamaliel gifting the *lulav* to Yehoshua, who then gifts it to Eleazar b. Azariah, who does the same to Akiva. The sequence ends with Akiva, and the auditor infers that no one else was there, or else it would have been reported that Akiva in turn gave the *lulav* to that person.[93]

Now, our Haggadah adapter chose to use the style of the b. Qidd. 32b example. He began *maʿaseh be* ... and named all the sages in the exposition. However, even though the Chekhovian gun was loaded with four bullets, only one was fired, for Eleazar b. Azariah was the only one who spoke. Still, one can count Akiva too who, followed by the name of his town, Bene Beraq, was presumably the host; Gamaliel, the erstwhile leader, by implication would have said or done something. That leaves Yehoshua alone without a task. That fact is an indication of critical remoteness from the methods and modes of literary creativity characteristic of the talmudic period. The same anomaly occurs in an anecdote in Derekh Ereẓ Rabbah, but that is also a post-talmudic tractate.[94] The conventions of one era were eclipsed in another. That is a further sign that our story is post-talmudic.

It is indeed curious that Eliezer is missing in this early version of the adaptation, as well as Tarfon. How they came to be in this *maʿaseh*, and

---

93. This is clear in the version in b. Sukkah 41b, for Akiva returns the *lulav* to Gamaliel, completing the circuit, thereby confirming that only the named sages were in that party.

94. The dating of this tractate, which is actually composed of separate parts, has yet to be determined. Although some passages may date to Tannaitic times or derive from Tannaitic material, van Loopik reports that it is considered to be Geonic (*Ways of the Sages*, 8–10). Similarly, Myron B. Lerner notes that researchers generally follow Leopold Zunz in dating the minor ("external") tractates "to the early Gaonic Era, i.e., the eighth and ninth centuries," but suggests that more research on individual compositions, among which is Derekh Ereẓ Rabbah, is required to provide a more secure dating (Lerner, "The External Tractates," in *The Literature of the Sages*, part 1:*Oral Tora, Halakha, Mishna, Tosefta, Talmud, External Tractates*, ed. Shmuel Safrai [Assen: Van Gorcum, 1987], 367–404, here 368).

how Gamaliel dropped out, will be accounted for as a sequential evolutionary development, in the next section.

The Evolution of the Bene Beraq Seder Narrative, Stage 2: Eliezer and Tarfon

A later adapter decided that a seder that emphasizes the exodus narrative over *hilkhot ha-Pesaḥ* should have a different leader than Gamaliel (despite the fact that an adaptation of his directive in m. Pesaḥ. 10:5, which, in directly addressing the child's opening questions, is a centerpiece of the Mishnah's seder, and is prominent in all later versions).[95] Eliezer, an eminent sage, brother-in-law, and sometime antagonist of Gamaliel, was selected.[96] This choice is reflected in the *Ginze Schechter* version (table 4, col. 4), which is otherwise so similar to Sijilmassa-B (table 4, col. 3). Gamaliel's entourage, however, was preserved; just the leader changed.

In late antique rabbinic literature, Eliezer was not viewed as a leader like Gamaliel; he does not travel with an entourage of *zeqenim*. It seems that his eminence rather than his opinions got Eliezer the appointment. He agrees with Gamaliel that the evening should focus on *hilkhot ha-Pesaḥ*, although he thinks that the discussion need be engaged only until midnight, rather than Gamaliel's nightlong effort.[97] Nor is it part of a pattern

95. Henshke observes that some scholars (cited in *"Mah Nishtannah,"* n. 125) view Gamaliel's instruction in m. Pesaḥ. 10:5 as convergent with his spending the night in discussion of *hilkhot ha-Pesaḥ* in t. Pesaḥ. 10:11, but he concludes correctly that Gamaliel's explication of the evening menu is narration of the exodus rather than discussion of rules (386). Hauptman views the two sources as representing two historical moments in the evolution of the Passover seder (see n. 20 above). Henshke, on the other hand, views each as a different aspect of the Passover evening program, the Mishnaic portion purposed for children, the Toseftan one for adults (*Rereading the Mishnah,* 54–55 n. 56).

96. Perhaps, a homicidal aggadic motif is transfigured in this replacement process, for the Talmud suggests that it was the prayer of Eliezer, embittered because Gamaliel had placed him under a ban, that resulted in the latter's death (b. B. Meṣ. 59b).

97. Eliezer's view may be found in the Mekhilta of Rabbi Ishmael, *Pisḥa* 18, s.v., *Vehayah ki* (p. 74), which is consistent with his understanding that the Paschal lamb could not be consumed past midnight (Mekhilta of Rabbi Ishmael, *Pisḥa* 6, p. 19). Gamaliel, who holds that a sacrifice that must be eaten in one day may be consumed until dawn (although it is preferable to finish it by midnight; m. Ber. 1:1), spends the whole night in discussion of *hilkhot ha-Pesaḥ* (t. Pesaḥ. 10:10–11). If he was aware of Eliezer's position on the appropriate nighttime activity and of the paradigmatic midnight limit, it is not clear that the Haggadah redactor who substituted him for Gamaliel considered those matters relevant to his narrative. Tannaim can contradict themselves or be represented as espousing contradictory positions: the first-level adaptor (the Sigilmassa-B recension), who borrowed Gamaliel for the Bene Beraq *maʿaseh,* also created a contradictory scenario (thematizing discussion of the exodus instead of rules). Even before that, within the universe of Tannaitic texts, Gamaliel in t. Pesaḥ. 10:12 says to discuss *hilkhot ha-Pesaḥ* all night long; but m. Pesaḥ. 10:5's Gamaliel says

involving the sages that make up Gamaliel's entourage and who also famously got together to visit Eliezer when he was ailing. That source must be discounted because Tarfon, who was not a member of a faction that accompanies Gamaliel[98] but was a member of the party visiting Eliezer, was not included even in the *Ginze Schechter* version.[99]

As a witness to more far-reaching textual autonomy from its Toseftan model, the *Ginze Schechter* version reflects the exchange of Eliezer for Gamaliel. This version limits itself to the latter's three traveling companions (known from elsewhere), which means that Tarfon is still wanting from the entourage. He was added only in the subsequent Bene Beraq versions that were to become universally accepted. The lateness of his insertion is reflected in Tarfon's position. This colleague of Yehoshua,[100] senior to both Akiva and Eleazar b. Azariah, was simply tacked on at the end. That, of course, eclipsed the juxtaposition of Akiva with Bene Beraq. The logic of that collocation was evidently not on the mind of the final-stage redactor, who interposed Tarfon, just as his distance from classical talmudic considerations is apparent in his obliviousness to the prominence of Tarfon in view of the latter's seniority.

The reason for his addition to the group is not clear. To the possibility that the redactor, looking at m. Pesaḥ. 10 as a prototypical seder—hence a model for his Bene Beraq event—added Tarfon because he contributed there (paragraph 6), one can object that other speakers, viz., Eleazar bar Tsadoq (paragraph 3) and Yose (8) were not included. It would, rather, make more sense to look at m. Ber. 1, which is the source of Ben Azzai's dispute with the sages cited by Eleazar b. Azariah (paragraph 5, our unit 8), and where Tarfon appears in paragraph 3. Others included in our *maʿaseh* also contribute to that chapter, viz., Eliezer (1, 2) and Yehoshua (2), that is, everyone but Akiva, who was needed for his residence, and who was already part of the group. Could a post–*Ginze Schechter* redac-

---

to explicate the foods for historical/symbolic illustration (see above, n. 95). Moreover, must Bene Beraq's supererogatory activity be constrained by the time frame of when the Passover offering must be consumed (according to Eliezer and others)? Discussion of the exodus does not map onto the phenomenon of the Paschal sacrifice and meal in the same way that the rehearsal of the *hilkhot ha-Pesaḥ* functions as their analogical surrogate.

98. Cf. p. 209 above, and n. 92.

99. See p. 204 above. That is the only occasion when Eleazar ben Azariah is part of a group along with Akiva that is involved with Eliezer. Akiva was with Eliezer and Yehoshua, y. Hor. 3:4, 48a = Lev. Rab. 5:4; and with Tarfon added as well, 'Abot R. Nat. A 6 = ibid., *Hosafah 2 to Nosah A*, 8, s.v., *Mah hayah* (p. 162).

100. Henshke observes that Tarfon's opinion is presented before that of Akiva when they disagree, aside from situations that have their own logic (*"Mah Nishtannah,"* 392–93 and n. 145). Tarfon is correctly presented as senior to Akiva in t. Zebaḥ. 1:8; Sifra, *Dibburah de-Nedavah* 4:5; Sifre Numbers, *Be-haalotekha* 75; y. Meg. 1:10, 72b = y. Hor. 3:2, 47d; Kallah Rab. 1:21.

tor have imagined the sages in m. Ber. 1 as participants in a discussion that surfaced in Eleazar b. Azariah's message, and so added Tarfon to the Bene Beraq narrative? The fact that the houses of Shammai and Hillel, who are not represented in our *maᶜaseh,* appear in paragraph 3 is irrelevant, for they are too early, and merely supply background to Tarfon's contribution. What is unfortunate for this possibility, however, is that Gamaliel also appears there (1). Indeed, he takes part in a discussion with his children that is thematically suggestive, for they have been partying all night, like the Bene Beraq group, and have a question about the recitation of the Shema, albeit the evening one rather than the morning one. Perhaps Gamaliel contributed that theme, along with Ben Zoma's exegesis, to make m. Ber. 1 a source of inspiration for the third-stage redactor, who decided to add Tarfon to Eliezer's Bene Beraq group. The least problematic hypothesis for his inclusion in this third-stage revision, is that its redactor was aware that Tarfon had joined a group that had paid a visit to Eliezer on his sickbed.[101] He could accordingly, therefore, imagine that the same individuals who had participated in that incident might also have gotten together at Bene Beraq for a seder. One might challenge that possibility, as well, for Tarfon could just as easily have been inserted into his proper place unless, of course, an addition should just be interpolated at the end of the list. Certainty eludes us here.

Macrocosmic Issues Redux: The Evolution of the Bene Beraq Seder Narrative, Stage 2 Continued: Linguistic and Liturgical Matters

We have seen that, whatever its merits, concern over certain phrases of the Bene Beraq narrative that seemed anomalous, for example, *kol 'oto ha-lailah, sapper bi-yetsiat Mitsrayim,* was irrelevant. The first one does not appear until the *Ginze Schechter* revision; the second, only in subsequent ones.

The phrase *sapper bi-yetsiat Mitsrayim* also came late to the Bene Beraq story. It was adapted from units 4, 5, and 6. They were created early on to integrate the Bene Beraq narrative with Eleazar b. Azariah's exposition into the *'Avadim hayinu* sequence. When, in relation to the key units 7 and 8, the transitional units were developed will be discussed in tandem with an examination of the shift from the use of the verb *mesiḥin* to *mesapperim* in the analysis of language (in a forthcoming study).

101. See p. 196 above.

Conclusion: Overall Development and Cohesion

The Bene Beraq and Mishnah Berakhot texts are intertwined thematically and linguistically with units 4/5–6, whose authors contributed the construction, *sapper bi-yetsiat Mitsrayim.*[102] One cannot understand those three textual sets in the Haggadah without apprehending their evolution and function. It would be incorrect to simply atomize them and treat them as separate units that were imported from three different places. Doing so would affect how we comprehend their meaning and purpose. While m. Ber. 1:5 is clearly a textual borrowing, organic and evolutionary factors play a formative role in the evolution of the other units and affect our understanding of Mishnah Berakhot, as well as their intertwined relations in the Haggadah. This is especially important regarding text 7, the Bene Beraq story. Inasmuch as it is a post-talmudic composition, it is unlikely for it to have been drawn from a hypothetical, unknown rabbinic source; it seems more reasonable to suppose that it was crafted to supersede the Toseftan seder story that served as its model, with the intended function of introducing m. Ber. 1:5 (unit 8) in a way that valorized *sippur* (originally: *mesiḥin*) *bi-yetsiat Mitsrayim*. It can best be understood with reference both to its originating motivation and to its literary function. Most rabbinic *mesubbin* anecdotes do not relate to Passover, and m. Ber. 1:5 refers to all the *lelot* (nights) of the year, but there can be no doubt about the occasion for the Bene Beraq reclining incident because it is clear from its Toseftan foil—not to mention the Haggadah context in which it was formed—that a Passover seder was intended. Such a late date of composition, as well as the intended audience, moreover, put the Bene Beraq story beyond the chronological and geographical limits within which people would have reclined at meals, viz., Tannaitic Palestine. It was composed for the purpose of integrating m. Ber. 1:5 into the Haggadah liturgy, a recontextualization that would logically read it as applying to the "nights" of the seder.[103]

102. It is tempting to suppose that a connection with m. Pesaḥ. 10:4, *doresh me-'Arami 'oved 'avi*, is implied. However, even Mandel, who explains that *d-r-sh* denotes exposition, expounding, public instruction (without reference to specific exegetical techniques, "midrash"), and cites that passage as an example, stipulates that the Mishnah requires "active recitation" of Scripture, a "content-oriented reading," rather than narrative or discussion (*sapper*) (*Origins of Midrash*, 235–36).

103. Not everyone accepts the notion of this redactional move, insisting instead that it be understood as from the perspective of m. Ber. 1. See below, appendix to n. 8, and my examination of the language in this section (in preparation). It should be noted that, although instances of Babylonian sages reclining at a meal are reported in the Bavli, they are exceptions to the norm, occurring only during attendance at meals in the court of the Exilarch (Geoffrey Herman, "Table Etiquette and Persian Culture in the Babylonian Talmud [Hebrew]," *Zion* 77 [2006–2007]: 160–64).

While a date for this creation cannot be determined, an evolutionary position can be plotted. There was a point during the Amoraic period when an *'avadim hayinu* pronouncement (unit 1) and the *mi-teḥillah 'ovde 'avodah zarah* proposition were recommended, as preambles for the *miqra bikkurim* exposition (b. Pesaḥ. 116a).[104] *'Avadim hayinu* was later coupled with the *baraita* of the four children (unit 10). It subsequently came to be augmented in two directions, exemplified by Saadia's *Siddur* and by the *Ginze Schechter* Haggadah. Both of those share the aforementioned pedagogical *baraita*. That means that, at a point before either units 2–3 (Saadia, Sijilmassa-A) or 4–8 (Sijilmassa-B, *Ginze Schechter*) had developed, a Babylonian liturgical redactor had chosen to interject a passage similar to that found in the Mekhilta (10) that introduced two themes, one being that four types of personalities, learning styles, or developmental stages should be taken into account in explicating the meaning and intent of the evening ritual; and the other that, furthermore, the instruction is to be done on the seder night, "a time when *matzah* and *maror* are laid out before you."[105]

The Saadia tradition reflects further emphasis on the significance of the exodus for contemporaries assembled at a seder (units 2 and 3). In an alternative augmentation, a liturgical composer chose to reflect on *'avadim hayinu* by preceding the *baraita* of the four children with the linked pair, units 7 and 8; they combined to emphasize the importance of celebrating the exodus by articulating it (8) with a story of a conversation that went on all night (7). This narrative looks back on the theme of *'avadim hayinu* (the exodus) and forward to the Mekhilta-like *baraita* (inculcation and instruction on it).

One may question whether this composer specifically connected units 7–8 to unit 1 by means of the transition elements, units 4 and 6 (Sijilmassa-B, the earliest extant version,[106] is our point of reference here), or whether a later liturgist added them. It does seem clear that unit 4 was elaborated into unit 5 at a later point (to resonate rhetorically with the sages in Bene Beraq), which replaced 4 in most versions.[107] Be that as it may, units 4 (or 5) and 6 make explicit a theme that was acted out in unit 7, viz., talking about the exodus, while extending it to include in this practice every type of person, not just sages and elders. Unit 6 defines it as an aspi-

---

104. Although the printed edition attributes it to Shmuel, an early Babylonian Amora, other names appear in manuscript witnesses and related works, making it difficult to determine when this statement originated. See n. 14 above.

105. As instructed at the end of the pedagogic *baraita*.

106. Although it includes units 2–3 as well. Since those units are wanting, however, in the *Ginze Schechter* version, it seems that Sijilmassa-B contains an amalgamation of both traditions. The fact that all other witnesses to the Bene Beraq version include unit 2 from that of Saadia indicates the latter's continuing influence on the Bene Beraq tradition as it developed.

107. The *Ginze Schechter* text has an accumulative nature: it retained both units 4 and 5; moreover, its unit 5 consists of an amalgamation of two different elaborations.

rational practice (*kol ha-mesapper … hare zeh meshubbaḥ*). In characterizing it as praiseworthy, the liturgist acknowledges that this is either an innovation or a supererogation, or both, albeit not a requirement.

It is unlikely that units 4/5–6 developed in tandem with the inclusion of 7–8, because of the incongruous terminological differences; that is, units 4/5–6 employ the verb *sapper*, while early versions of the unit 7 use *mesiḥin*.

Appendix to Note 3: On Sagit Mor's Examination of the Two Seder Narratives, "The Laws of Sacrifice or Telling the Story of the Exodus?," Zion 68 (2002–2003): 297–311

Sagit Mor has contributed a thoughtful comparison of the narratives of Gamaliel's seder at Lod and Akiva's at Bene Beraq. Noting that one story is structurally and linguistically dependent on the other, Mor sees the Toseftan story as Tannaitic, the Bene Beraq account, unattested in talmudic literature, as very late. The latter is a conceptual polemic in opposition to the Lod story.

Mor considers the Lod story as drawing upon Palestinain Passover customs to create a description that represents a Tannaitic conceptual approach to dealing with the national crisis of destruction and defeat on a national holiday celebrating redemption. At the same time, Mor does seem to consider the Toseftan account to be historical, as when she demonstrates how it is reasonable that Gamaliel and the elders could have convened in Lod for a seder. She, furthermore, considers the anecdote to be historically accurate in its portrayal of the removal of the leftovers, which she infers would be the remains of a Passover meal consisting of a roasted kid (*gedi mequlas*). Gamaliel had famously preferred such a menu in commemoration of the scriptural Paschal offering consumed when the temple was in existence. (This practice was rejected even by some Erets Israel contemporaries, and subsequently repudiated universally by the Bavli.) By ignoring their tragic present as it recreates a glorious past, Gamaliel's observance is geared to his contemporaries, many of whom remembered the temple and had experienced the consequences of their military defeats at the hands of the Romans. His program works in two modalities, one intellectual, the other experiential, both consistent with its literary context in t. Pesaḥ. 10. Intellectually, the group engages in examination of *hilkhot ha-Pesaḥ*, the rules of the Paschal offering. On an experiential level, they reconstruct the meal with a roasted kid, similar to that consumed on this night at pre-destruction Paschal repasts and, glossing over their present-day situation, an intimation of hope for a future restoration.

On a further historical note, Mor concludes that the generic elders accompanying Gamaliel are second-tier sages, for the first-tier ones, who are named in the Bene Beraq story, were with Akiva at that seder. This is actually an anachronistic inference, since she concludes later on that the latter incident is fictional. Moreover, why would we infer that the two seders occurred on the very same night?

Mor does not consider the Bene Beraq seder to be historical because the selection of sages and depiction of their relative prominence follow the Babylonian version of the story of the deposition of (Rabban) Gamaliel (b. Ber. 27b–28a), an account that reflects Babylonian talmudic realia. The Bene Beraq seder narrative would likely be post-Amoraic because it accepts the Babylonian tamudic refusal to countenance the notion that any sacrifice could be imitated in their time. Again, how can Mor be sure that *gedi mekulas* was not on the Bene Beraq menu?

Indeed, that *maʿaseh* could even be later since it accords with Babylonian Geonic themes seen throughout the Haggadah. Just as she interpreted the Lod seder in its literary setting t. Pesaḥ. 10, Mor contextualizes the Bene Beraq seder as part of a literary complex, viz., the Babylonian Haggadah. That work takes a very different approach to Passover, on both a conceptual and an experiential level. Conceptually, history is viewed as cyclical: episodes of slavery, defeat, and exile are followed by redemption, freedom, and deliverance. Experientially, the seder discussion is opened up to everyone, not just scholars, because the evening is to be devoted to haggada/aggada, that is, to the story of the exodus from Egypt and its cyclical repetitions.

Mor observes that the distinction between the two seders is encapsulated in the contrasting conclusions of those respective anecdotes. Gamaliel and the sages of Lod repair the next morning to the *bet midrash* to study *halakhot*, focusing on the past in a setting that is a substitute for the temple. Akiva and his companions are joined by their disciples, emblems of the future and of hope, for prayer, which is a liturgical substitute for sacrifices.

This is an erudite and sophisticated article. I agree with many of its main conclusions, for example, that Gamaliel's study of *hilkhot ha-Pesaḥ* is an attempt to reconstruct conceptually a past that is no longer available in reality, and that the Bene Beraq story is post-talmudic. I agree that examination of a text in terms of its immediate literary context may be efficacious, even necessary. I would be hesitant with respect to integrating either of the two narratives into a larger set of talmudic traditions without literary warrant. My approach tends to be philological, structural, and redaction critical. Without being as doctrinaire as Jonah Fraenkel with regard to treating an aggadic narrative as a hermetically closed entity, I find no indication in the Toseftan story that the narrator imagined Gamaliel and the elders at Lod to have consumed a roasted kid in imitation of the Second Temple Paschal offering. Tables were cleared, remains removed, for any meal. This general information can be illuminated by other material on Tannaitic-era meals. That is the extent of what we can say would have been on the mind of the author of the Lod seder story. For that reason, I would not draw the lesson on the experiential level that Mor did.

Similarly, most current research agrees that the Bene Beraq narrative developed from that of Lod. There are telling differences, both stylistic and conceptual. The phenomenon of an author reworking an older work to renew and recreate that text so that it reflects new approaches, themes, and ideas is widespread in literature, certainly in rabbinic literature. Does that indicate a polemic with the source or just an opening to the recreator's own present? Is this process always an oedipal struggle, or can it also be a creative repurposing of found materials? To outsiders balancing the two texts (here abstracted, outside of their original context), it may seem like they are witnesses to a polemical debate occurring across the generations while, in their minds, the repurposer may have been indifferent to the original intentions. Mor herself acknowledges that the shift in emphasis from a seder centered on halakha to one emphasizing aggada was already present in the Mishnah. My understanding is that, if the creator of the Bene Beraq *maʿaseh* was innovating conceptually, it was not with new ideas but, rather, it was contextual. He was arguing with the pedagogic *baraita* against favoring *hilkhot ha-Pesaḥ* as the ideal seder evening program.

Aggadic composers did not work in a vacuum, but inferring details and traditions of talmudic mythology or hagiography as if they were synchronically and ubiquitously manifest throughout that body of literature even where they are unmotivated or unnecessary can lead to false conclusions. Mor follows other scholars in applying two factors to puzzling out the identity and precedence of the sages in Bene Beraq, viz., the seating arrangement at a Hellenistic symposium and the story of the deposition of Gamaliel. The order of seating in a symposium would probably be a very anachronistic guide in a tale that Mor herself claims was created in post-talmudic Babylonia. I, too, went outside the story to understand the order of the list, especially to understand how sages were removed and added to the *maʿaseh* (and moved around in it), as in the next paragraph.

The deposition narrative is used to account for particulars in both seder anecdotes. The arrangement of Akiva's companions, with Eleazar b. Azariah in the middle position favored for symposia (see n. 45 above), requires one to assume that Akiva's seder occurred at the same time as Gamaliel's. That would explain why the eminent sages, Gamaliel's erstwhile companions, were away: they were accompanying Eleazar b. Azariah at the time he was in the ascendant, leaving only second-tier *zeqenim* to keep Gamaliel company. This effort at an integrated, intertextually consistent talmudic hagiography is brilliant, but it ignores two things. One is that the order in which sages at Bene Beraq are listed, except for Eliezer at the head, is the same order in which the same sages are listed in stories of journeys with Gamaliel. He is named first because he is the primary personage; other sages are listed in order of precedence. I have shown that Gamaliel was indeed named first in the original version of the Bene Beraq story (Sijilmassa-B), but Eliezer later eclipsed him.

Talmudic-era aggadists knew the requirement of narrative economy that, just as the presence of Chekhov's gun requires it to fire, so the presence of a named sage requires him to speak or fulfill some other function. This happens in all Gamaliel stories. Sages were not specified by name in the Lod anecdote because none of the *zeqenim* did or said something that uniquely identified one over the other. The sages were, on the other hand, named at Bene Beraq, even though they did not all fulfill some unique function, because the author of the post-talmudic tale did not know or else did not observe the rule of Chekhov's gun.

It is correct to differentiate (an approach emphasizing) halakha from haggada/aggada; law from narrative; the turn in the present to the past from the vantage of a vision in the present of hope for the future. But it is difficult to pin down exactly when this shift occurred, or whether the two visions were experienced simultaneously. For instance, the Mishnah, like the Tosefta a Tannaitic work, mandates the turn from halakha to aggada in that sense, and the centering on family members and their needs, in the "seder" experience. (Mor noted that the Tosefta also mandates the inclusion of family members, albeit in *hilkhot ha-Pesaḥ*.) Moreover, some of the Haggadah passages that express a hope-filled, cyclical view of historical development and experience may be found in Erets Israel versions of the Haggadah, as well as Babylonian ones. Recognition of those passages might require a revision of both the temporal and geographical parameters of the Bene Beraq seder or elements of it.

Appendix to Note 8: The Function of m. Ber. 1:5 as a Continuation of the Bene Beraq Story

Critical readers are quick to point out that m. Ber. 1:5 refers to an ongoing nightly occurrence rather than a Passover seder. Philip Birnbaum (*The Passover Haggadah* [New York: Hebrew Publishing Company, 1953], 23) and Shmuel and Zeev Safrai (*Haggadah of the Sages: The Passover Haggadah* [Hebrew] [Jerusalem: Carta, 1998], 118–19) point to linguistic and thematic connections that may have occasioned this borrowing, but they do not suggest that it produced a new understanding of the Mishnah pericope. Still, the Haggadah liturgist may here be engaging in a sleight-of-hand performance, albeit an artful and deliberate one. Mishnah Berakhot 1:5 sets out a debate concerning the exegesis of Deut 16:3, with Eleazar b. Azariah citing Ben Zoma to demonstrate that liturgical mention of the exodus must be expressed at night[108] and anonymous "sages" following with an opposing exegesis of that passage that takes the words in a different direction, viz., the question of whether the exodus will continue to be recalled or recited in the messianic era.

The Haggadah liturgist seems to be continuing the account of Eleazar b. Azariah in Bene Beraq with the opening of that mishnah, that is, to make it seem as if the exegesis there were reported at that seder. Indeed, some Haggadah texts add into their m. Ber. 1:5 citations, "Eleazar b. Azariah said *lahem* ["to them"], i.e., to the other sages with him in Bene Beraq…." That could be taken to mean that the Shema exegesis of Ben Zoma and his collocutors was originally reported at this time (Meir Friedmann, *Meir Ayin* [reprint of ed. Vienna, 5655 [1894 or 1895]: Jerusalem: Shai, 5731 [1970 or 1971]), 86. Joseph Tabory, on the other hand, suggests that it "is incorporated here merely because it discusses the importance of remembering the Exodus" (*JPS Commentary on the Haggadah* [Philadelphia: Jewish Publication Society, 2008], 85) and would, furthermore, be typical of synoptic literature (ibid., 38-39). But many commentators correlate more intensively its Haggadah context with Eleazar b. Azariah's emphasis that Ben Zoma's exegesis teaches about a nighttime practice (Ben Zoma did speak about both night and day). For example, Joshua Kulp (*The Schechter Haggadah* [Jerusalem: Schechter Institute, 2009], 205) writes that "the editor has taken this derashah out of its original context (Shema and its blessings) and applied it to a new context (the seder)."

Despite the apparent self-contradictory nature of this construction of the exegesis, Kulp's point of view can be defended in view of the rabbinic literary background of this text. In considering the echoes and refractions of this reuse, two other factors may be relevant. One is that a Passover eve/night hovers in the background, for the original intent of Scripture's למען תזכר את יום צאתך מארץ מצרים כל ימי חייך (the crux of Ben Zoma's and his collocutors' disagreement) is that "the

108. The paragraph of the Shema that mentions it was not recited in Tannaitic (or Amoraic) times (see, e.g., the commentary of Hanokh Albeck, *Shishah Sidre Mishnah* [Jerusalem: Bialik; Tel Aviv: Dvir, 1957], 1:15 and 17, on m. Ber. 1:5 and 2:2, respectively; Lieberman, *Tosefta ki-feshuṭah, Zeraim,* 1:12).

day of your departure from Egypt" is to be remembered/commemorated through the consumption of the Paschal offering along with *matzah* (Rashi) each year (Ibn Ezra)—that is, not literally "all the days of your life" but idiomatically, every Passover eve "for as long as you live" (NJPS). The second is that recontextualization in order to produce innovative connections, and new significations, is a stylistic technique ubiquitous in rabbinic literature and in *piyyuṭ*. It is practiced in midrash with biblical phrases, and in talmudic *sugyot* with both biblical and rabbinic teachings; indeed, this technique is employed to modify or infuse new meaning into existing halakhic passages. See, for example, Shamma Friedman, "A Critical Study of *Yevamot* X with a methodological introduction" [Hebrew], in *Texts and Studies: Analecta Judaica 1*, ed. H. Z. Dimitrovsky (New York: Jewish Theological Seminary, 1978), 277–441; Moshe Halbertal, *Revolutions in the Making: Values as Interpretative Consideration in Midrashei Halakhah* [Hebrew] (Jerusalem: Magnes, 1997). It is here put into practice in the post-talmudic Haggadah through the reuse of the early (mishnaic) exegetical passage.

It may seem somewhat disconcerting to see m. Ber. 1:5, including sages' seemingly irrelevant counterexegesis, cited in full, but it is a habit of orally oriented traditions and literatures to quote a passage *in extenso* even though only one section is contextually required (see Safrai and Safrai, *Haggadah of the Sages*, 210). This practice is followed in rabbinic literature. Moreover, the Haggadah contains a lengthy example of this practice: although Psalm (113–)114 would have sufficed to rhapsodize on the exodus, the remainder of the Hallel (Pss 115–118) is (re)cited in full, even though it commemorates later historical events and concerns. In the case of the seder liturgy, one can find enriching thematic connections in both cases. For instance, the full Hallel carries the theme of redemption and salvation beyond Egypt into the ensuing Jewish historical experience; and the insistence of sages in m. Ber. 1:5 that the exodus will be recalled even in the distant future, after yet more spectacular events have culminated in the messianic era, exemplifies the exhortation to discuss the exodus. That point opens an alternative possibility of understanding the intent of the Haggadah's reuse of m. Ber. 1:5, which will be presented in an analysis of the language of this section (forthcoming).

Table 4. Evolution of the Bene Beraq Text in the Context of *Avadim Hayinu* and the Babylonian Haggadah Traditions[109]

	Babylonian branch B		***Babylonian branch A*** *with earliest versions of the Bene Beraq story*	
	1. *Siddur Saadiah* (10th century?)[110]	**2. Sijilmassa-A** (ca. 1200)[111]	**3. Sijilmassa-B** (ca. 1200)[112]	**4. *Ginze Schechter*** (11th century?)[113]
1	עבדים היינו לפרעה במצרים יוציאנו ה׳ אלהינו משם ביד חזקה ובזרוע נטויה	עבדים היינו לפרעה במצרים ויוציאנו ה׳ אלהינו משם ביד חזקה ובזרוע נטויה	עבדים היינו לפרעה במצרים ויוציאנו ה׳ אלהינו ממצרים ביד חזקה ובזרוע נטויה	עבדים היינו לפרעה במצ[רים] ויוצ[יאנו] ה׳ ממצ[רים] ביד חזקה ובזרוע נטויה
2	ואלו לא גאל המקב״ה את אבותינו ממצרים כבר אנו ובנינו ובני בניניו משועבדים היינו לפרעה במצרים	ואילו לא גאל הב״ה את אבותינו ממצרים כבר אנו ובנינו ובני בניניו משועבדים [היינו] לפרעה במצרים	ואלו לא גאל המקום ב״ה את אבותינו ממצרים כבר אנו ובנינו ובני בניניו משועבדים היינו לפרעה במצרים	
3	ולא את אבותינו בלבד גאל המקבה אלא אף אותנו גאל שנ׳ ואותנו הוציא משם.	ולא את אבותינו בלבד גאל, אלא אף אותנו גאל שנאמר: ואותנו הוציא משם.	ולא את אבותינו בלבד גאל אלא אף אותנו גאל שנ׳ ואותנו הוציא משם.	
4			לפיכך אנו חייבין לספר ביציאת מצרים	לפיכך מצוה עלינו לספר ביציאת מצ׳
5				ואפילו כולנו חכ׳ כולנו נבונים וכולנו יודעים את התורה, מצווה עלינו לספר ביציאת מצ׳ ואפי׳ כול׳ זקנים כול׳ ישישים כול׳ יודעים את התורה, מצוה עלינו לספר ביציאת מצ׳

109. Question marks following dates in parentheses following names and titles indicate (varying degrees of) uncertainty that the text presented faithfully reproduces the formulation of the (attributed) author.

110. סדור רב סעדיה גאון = כתאב ג׳אמע אלצלואת ואלתסאביח, edited by Israel Davidson, Simha Assaf, and Issachar Joel (Jerusalem: Mekitze Nirdamim, 1941), 137. To the extent that the liturgical texts are faithful representations of Saadiah's original, this is a picture of the state of a tenth-century Near Eastern Haggadah.

111. סידור רבינו שלמה ברבי נתן זצ״ל, אב ביד דין מן העיר סיג׳ילמסה, המכונה אלגבאלי edited by Shemuel Hagai (Jerusalem: Hagai?, 5755 [1994 or 1995]), 84–85. The compiler of the rite lived in twelfth-century Morocco or the Near East. It is evidence that Saadiah's version was still in use at the turn of the thirteenth century.

112. Copied following the text of סידור רבינו שלמה ברבי נתן זצ״ל, אב ביד דין מן העיר סיג׳ילמסה, המכונה אלגבאלי and published from that manuscript by Shemuel Hagai in this edition of that *Siddur* (cited in the following note), 249–50 (MS Page 230r = image 465). I corrected some of the printed readings in accordance with the manuscript. This version shows that the earliest version of the Bene Beraq seder story was being recited at the turn of the thirteenth century.

Babylonian branch A *and late versions of the Bene Beraq story*		
5. Natronai (post 9th century?)[114]	**6. Maimonides** (12th century?)[115]	**7. Modern**
עבדים היינו לפרעה במצרים ויוציאנו יי אלהינו משם ביד חזקה ובזרוע נטויה.	עבדים היינו לפרעה במצרים ויוציאנו יי אלהינו משם ביד חזקה ובזרוע נטויה.	עֲבָדִים הָיִינוּ לְפַרְעֹה בְּמִצְרָיִם, וַיּוֹצִיאֵנוּ יְיָ אֱלֹהֵינוּ מִשָּׁם בְּיָד חֲזָקָה וּבִזְרוֹעַ נְטוּיָה.
ואלו לא הוציא הקדוש ברוך הוא את אבותינו ממצרים עדיין אנו ובנינו ובני בנינו משעבדים היינו לפרעה במצרים.	ואלו לא הוציא הקדוש ברוך הוא את אבותינו ממצרים עדין אנו ובנינו ובני בנינו משעבדים היינו לפרעה במצרים.	וְאִלּוּ לֹא הוֹצִיא הַקָּדוֹשׁ בָּרוּךְ הוּא אֶת אֲבוֹתֵינוּ מִמִּצְרַיִם, הֲרֵי אָנוּ וּבָנֵינוּ וּבְנֵי בָנֵינוּ מְשֻׁעְבָּדִים הָיִינוּ לְפַרְעֹה בְּמִצְרָיִם.
ואפלו כולנו חכמים, כולנו נבונים, כולנו זקנים, כולנו יודעים את התורה, מצוה עלינו לספר ביציאת מצרים.	ואפלו כולנו חכמים, כולנו נבונים, כולנו יודעים את התורה, מצוה עלינו לספר ביציאת מצרים.	וַאֲפִילוּ כֻּלָּנוּ חֲכָמִים, כֻּלָּנוּ נְבוֹנִים, כֻּלָּנוּ זְקֵנִים, כֻּלָּנוּ יוֹדְעִים אֶת הַתּוֹרָה, מִצְוָה עָלֵינוּ לְסַפֵּר בִּיצִיאַת מִצְרָיִם.

113. Ginzberg, *Genizah Studies*, 2:252–60 (the selection under discussion may be found on 259–60). The shelfmark is Cambridge, CUL: T-S Misc.36.179 (Alternate number: T-S Loan Collection 179).

114. סדר והגדה של פסח לרב נטרונאי גאון על-פי כתב-יד קדמון שברשות המחבר, Manfred Lehmann in ספר יובל לכבוד מורנו הגאון רבי יוסף דוב הלוי סולובייצ׳יק, edited by Shaul Yisraeli et al. (Jerusalem: Mossad ha-Rav Kuk; New York: Yeshiva University, 1984), 986–87. Natronai ben Hilai flourished in the mid-ninth century. This version, which definitely exhibits some early features, does not represent an actual ninth-century recension. For instance, מאריך לספר is a conflated formulation (cf. Maimonides's text, column 6); Tarfon has joined the Bene Beraq seder; and the *barukh ha-maqom* peroration (unit 9) is included.

115. Maimonides (Moses ben Maimon) (1135–1204) copied a Hagadah formulary at the end of *Hilkhot ḥamets u-matsah* in his code, the *Mishneh Torah* (Egypt, between 1170 and 1180). Since Maimonides's text has been modified by copyists throughout the centuries, one cannot be certain that any manuscript contains his version. I have copied the one in Safrai and Safrai, *Haggadah of the Sages*, 262–84, who printed the Yemenite text published by Y. Kafih in his edition of the *Mishneh Torah*.

6			שכל המספר ביציאת מצרים הרי זה משובח	וכל המספר ביצי׳ מצ׳ הרי זה משובח
7			מעשה ברבן גמליאל ור׳ אלעזר בן עזריה ור׳ יהושע ור׳ עקיבא שהיו מסובין בבני-ברק, והיו משיחין והולכין ביציאת מצרים, עד שעלה עמוד השחר. כיון שעלה עמוד השחר נכנסו תלמידיהם אצליהם אמרו להם: כבר הגיע זמן קריאת שמע	ומעשה בר׳ אליעזר ור׳ יהושע ור׳ אלעזר בן עזריה ור׳ עקיבה שהיו מסובין בבני- ברק, והיו מסיחים ביצי׳ מצ׳ כל אותה הלילה, עד שבאו תלמידיהם ואמרו להם: רבותינו, הגיע זמן קריאת שמע של [שחרי]ת.
8			אמר להם ר׳ אלעזר בן עזריה: הריני כבן שבעים שנה, ולא זכיתי שתאמר יציאת׳ מצרים בלילות, עד שדרשה בן זומא, שנ׳, למען תזכור את יום צאתך מארץ מצ׳ כל ימי חייך, ימי חייך- הימים, כל ימי חייך- הלילות. וחכמים אומרים: ימי חייך - בעולם הזה, כל ימי חייך - להביא את ימות המשיח.	אמ׳ להם ר׳ אלעזר [בן עזריה: הרי אני כבן שבע]ים שנה, ולא זכיתי שתיאמר [יציאת מצרים בלילות], עד שדרשה בן זומא, שנ׳, למען [תזכור את יום צאתך מארץ מצרים] ימי חייך, ימי חייך הימים, וכל ימי חייך הלילות; וחכ[מים] אומ[רים]: ימי חייך העולם הזה, וכל ימי חייך להביא את ימות המשיח.
9				
10	Baraita of 4 sons	Baraita of 4 sons	Baraita of 4 sons	Baraita of 4 sons

וְכָל הַמַּרְבֶּה לְספר בִּיצִיאַת מִצְרַיִם הֲרֵי זֶה מְשֻׁבָּח	וכל המאריך ביציאת מצרים - הרי זה משבח.	שכל המאריך לספר ביציאת מצרים - הרי זה משבח.
מַעֲשֶׂה בְּרַבִּי אֱלִיעֶזֶר וְרַבִּי יְהוֹשֻׁעַ וְרַבִּי אֶלְעָזָר בֶּן עֲזַרְיָה וְרַבִּי עֲקִיבָא וְרַבִּי טַרְפוֹן שֶׁהָיוּ מְסֻבִּין בִּבְנֵי בְרַק, וְהָיוּ מְספרים בִּיצִיאַת מִצְרַיִם כָּל אוֹתוֹ הַלַּיְלָה עַד שֶׁבָּאוּ תַלְמִידֵיהֶם וְאָמְרוּ לָהֶם: רַבּוֹתֵינוּ, הִגִּיעַ זְמַן קְרִיאַת שְׁמַע שֶׁל שַׁחֲרִית.	מעשה ברבי אליעזר ורבי יהושע ורבי אלעזר בן עזריה ור׳ ור׳ עקיבא ורבי טרפון שהיו מסבין בבני-ברק, והיו מספרין ביציאת מצרים, כל אותו הלילה, עד שבאו תלמידיהם ואמרו להם: רבו־תינו, הגיע זמן קריאת שמע של שחרית.	מעשה ברבי ליעזר ורבי יהושע ורבי אלעזר בן עזריה ורבי עקיבא ורבי טרפון שהיו מסבין בבני-ברק, והיו מספרין ביציאת מצרים בליל פסח, עד שבאו תלמידיהם ואמרו להם: רבותינו, הגיע זמן קריאת שמע של שחרית.
אָמַר רַבִּי אֶלְעָזָר בֶּן עֲזַרְיָה: הֲרֵי אֲנִי כְּבֶן שִׁבְעִים שָׁנָה, וְלֹא זָכִיתִי שֶׁתֵּאָמֵר יְצִיאַת מִצְרַיִם בַּלֵּילוֹת עַד שֶׁדְּרָשָׁהּ בֶּן זוֹמָא: שֶׁנֶּאֱמַר, לְמַעַן תִּזְכֹּר אֶת יוֹם צֵאתְךָ מֵאֶרֶץ מִצְרַיִם כֹּל יְמֵי חַיֶּיךָ, יְמֵי חַיֶּיךָ - הַיָּמִים, כָּל יְמֵי חַיֶּיךָ - הַלֵּילוֹת. וַחֲכָמִים אוֹמְרִים: יְמֵי חַיֶּיךָ - הָעוֹלָם הַזֶּה, כֹּל יְמֵי חַיֶּיךָ - לְהָבִיא לִימוֹת הַמָּשִׁיחַ	אמר להם רבי אלעזר בן עזריה: הרי אני כבן שבעים שנה, ולא זכיתי שתאמר יציאת מצרים בלילות, עד שדרשה בן זומא, שנאמר, למען תזכר את יום צאתך מארץ מצרים כל ימי חייך, ימי חייך - הימים, כל ימי חייך - הלילות. וחכמים אומרים: ימי חייך - העולם הזה, כל ימי חייך - להביא לימות המשיח.	אמר רבי אלעזר בן עזריה: הרי [אני] כבן שבעים שנה, ולא שמעתי שתאמר יציאת מצרים בלילות, עד שדרשה בן זומא, שנאמר, למען תזכר את יום צאתך מארץ מצרים כל ימי חייך, ימי חייך - הימים, כל ימי חייך - הלילות. וחכמים אומרים: ימי חייך - העולם הזה, כל ימי חייך - להביא לימות המשיח.
ברוך המקום	ברוך המקום	ברוך המקום
Baraita of 4 sons	Baraita of 4 sons	Baraita of 4 sons

The Story-Cycles of the Bavli

Part 1

JEFFREY L. RUBENSTEIN

In 1990 Eli Yassif published a ground-breaking article, "The Cycle of Tales in Rabbinic Literature," in *Jerusalem Studies in Hebrew Literature.*[1] Yassif argued that the phenomenon of the story-cycle, namely, a cluster of stories told in sequence, occurs frequently in rabbinic literature but has largely been ignored, as scholarship has concentrated mostly on the individual tales. Yet a substantial number of stories appear within story-cycles, at least three hundred stories in the thirty-seven story-cycles that Yassif identified of between three and forty stories each, making the story-cycle a significant organizing structure for rabbinic stories. Yassif posed the following questions: "What were the origins of the story-cycles? Should we view them as collections of tales recorded as they were told orally by folk storytellers, or as the literary creation of those who put them in writing? In what manner were the groupings organized and edited, and by what artistic and ideological motivations were they inspired?"[2] Besides these questions, the central topic that Yassif pursued in his analysis of the individual story-cycle was "to identify its organizing principle. How can we describe the literary or ideational rationale which led the compiler to collect in one place a given set of tales and none other, in that particular order"?[3] An appendix to the article listed those thirty-seven story-cycles, the number of stories in each cycle, and the main organizing principle or theme. Yassif noted that the list was not meant to be exhaustive of all the

1. Eli Yassif, "The Cycle of Tales in Rabbinic Literature" [Hebrew], *Jerusalem Studies in Hebrew Literature* 12 (1990): 103–45.

2. English translation from Eli Yassif, *The Hebrew Folktale: History, Genre, Meaning,* trans. Jacqueline S. Teitelbaum, Folklore Studies in Translation (Bloomington: Indiana University Press, 1999), 210.

3. Ibid., 213

"collections of stories" (*qobtsei ha-sippurim*), but only the most important ones that are discussed in the article.

Yassif published his monumental *Sippur Ha-am Ha-ivri* [The Hebrew Folktale] in 1994, with 174 pages dedicated to "The Period of the Sages," of which the last thirty-seven pages focused on "The Story-cycle."[4] This section is extremely similar to the 1990 article, with a great many minor changes in style, a few corrections, and some added footnotes, but otherwise essentially a verbatim republication. The appendix containing the list of stories, however, was slightly updated and now numbered forty: 9 story-cycles in the Yerushalmi, 21 in the Bavli containing 218 stories, and another 10 in the midrashim and 'Abot de Rabbi Nathan.[5] An excellent English translation of the entire book by Jacqueline Teitelbaum was published as *The Hebrew Folktale* in 1999, which faithfully reproduced the section on "The Story-cycle" with almost no changes whatsoever.[6] Yassif republished the original article in 2004 as a chapter in his book *The Hebrew Collection of Tales in the Middle Ages*, again almost verbatim, but with a revised list of story-cycles that grew to forty-four: 9 in the Yerushalmi, 24 in the Bavli containing 228 stories, and 11 in the other rabbinic compilations. Here is his final list of the story-cycles of the Bavli:[7]

1. Ber. 18a. 3 stories [stories of the dead]
2. Šabb. 30b-31a. 4 stories [Hillel the Elder]
3. Šabb. 127b. 3 stories [one who gives his fellow the benefit of the doubt]
4. Šabb. 156b. 3 stories [righteousness saves from death]
5. Ta'an. 20b. 10 stories [shaky houses]
6. Ta'an. 21b. 6 stories [righteous commoners]
7. Ta'an. 23a-25b. 38 stories [causing rain]
8. Mo'ed Qaṭ. 28a. 7 stories [the moment of death]
9. Ketub. 62b. 7 stories [rabbinic disciples who separate from their wives]
10. Ketub. 65a. 3 stories [wives who demand an allotment of wine]
11. Ketub. 67b. 4 stories [charity "sufficient for his needs"]
12. Ned. 22b-23a. 3 stories [annulment of vows]
13. Ned. 91a-b. 4 stories [suspicion of adultery]

---

4. Eli Yassif, *Sippur Ha-am Ha-ivri: Toldotav, Sugav, uMashma'uto* (Jerusalem: Bialik Institute, 1994).

5. Ibid., 268–69. Yassif found an additional story-cycle for both the Bavli and Yerushalmi, and two more for 'Abot de Rabbi Nathan, though he removed one for Leviticus Rabbah.

6. Yassif, *Hebrew Folktale*, 209–44. However, the English translation omitted the appendix with the list of story-cycles, for reasons that are not clear to me.

7. Eli Yassif, *The Hebrew Collection of Tales in the Middle Ages* [Hebrew] (Tel-Aviv: Hakibbutz Hameuchad, 2004), 73–74. Yassif added ##10, 12, and 13 to the list of Bavli story-cycles printed in *Sippur Ha-am*.

14. Giṭ. 55b-58a. 25 stories [destruction of the temple]
15. Qidd. 39b-40a. 3 stories [sages who withstood temptation from gentile women]
16. Qidd. 81a-b. 5 stories [sages who were almost tempted]
17. B. Meṣ. 83b-84b. 22 stories [R. Eleazar b. Rabbi Shimeon]
18. B. Bat. 58a. 8 stories [R. Banaa]
19. B. Bat. 73a-74b. 22 stories [seafarers]
20. Sanh. 67b. 3 stories [stories of magic]
21. Sanh. 91a. 4 stories [Geviha b. Pesisa]
22. Sanh. 109a-b. 10 stories [the wickedness of the Sodomites]
23. 'Abod. Zar. 17b-18b. 13 stories [sins accounted as *avodah zarah*]
24. Bek. 8b-9a. 18 stories. [R. Yehoshua b. Ḥanania and the Athenian elders]

Yassif categorized the story-cycles into the following five classifications: (1) "the framework grouping"; (2) "the generic principle"; (3) "the biographical cycle"; (4) "the Bible verse as a unifying principle"; (5) "the principle of associative accumulation."[8] This last category was the most extensively discussed and contained the most story-cycles. I confess that I do not completely follow Yassif's definition of "the generic principle," and I think it more useful to employ a different category "the thematic principle" to include story-cycles that focus on a common subject, topic, or theme.[9]

Yassif emphasized that the story-cycle, as opposed to the individual aggadic tale, marked a significant change in literary production and even in culture. The impact of a series of stories on the audience was different from that of an individual story, and the impetus to organize disparate stories into a collection also reflected a new mentality. Hence the phenomenon of the story-cycle was indicative of two transitions in the history of rabbinic narrative. First, the organization of stories in a cycle entailed a transition from the original contexts of individual stories into their present contexts in larger groupings. Second, and more important: the story-cycle, Yassif suggested, "constitutes a transitional stage" between "two modes

8. Yassif, *Hebrew Folktale*, 214–27.

9. Ibid., 215. Yassif writes, "The generic conception of the groupings' compilers is ethnic, not analytic. It is a mixture of narrative themes and ideas with basic, simplistic structural distinctions. The unifying principle of several story cycles can be defined by a general, vague sense of the tales' belonging to one literary category." The examples he discusses here include the tales of magic (b. Sanh. 67b), tales of destruction (Lam. Rab. 1:45–51) and "two large aggadic cycles of humoristic tales: Those of Sodom (b. Sanh. 109a–b) and the tales of Rabbah b. Bar Hana (b. B. Bat. 73a–74b)." In my opinion the former two are better characterized as thematic (magic, destruction), and only the latter two "generic," unified by the genre of humor, not the subject matter. On the story-cycle in b. B. Bat. 73a–74b, see the article of James Redfield in this volume.

of literary expression … the transition from folktale to literary work,"[10] such as the collections of stories that emerged in the Middle Ages including *Ḥibbur Yafeh Mehayeshua* [An Elegant Composition Concerning Relief after Adversity] and *Sefer Hama'asim* [The Book of Exempla].[11]

Yassif's scholarship is innovative, breathtakingly vast, penetrating in its analysis, and masterful in its presentation of a great mass of data in a succinct and economic manner. In one and the same work he described and analyzed the story-cycles in all of classical rabbinic literature along with folktales found in all of Hebrew literature from the Bible through the modern period. Given this wide scope, Yassif's analysis of the story-cycle in rabbinic literature was extremely impressive and incredibly comprehensive. However, because of the breadth of his purview we cannot expect Yassif to have completely and exhaustively analyzed each and every story-cycle, nor comprehensively treated the story-cycles of one text such as the Bavli. As noted above, Yassif explicitly acknowledged that his list of story-cycles is incomplete. Moreover, Yassif was interested primarily in folklore, as the title of the book proclaims, and his main approach was that of a folklorist. The focus on folklore led him to select his material based on specific criteria and also to approach his material in certain ways and notions to the exclusion of other methods, although he is more attentive to the role of the compiler than are the authors of some folklore studies. And in the thirty years since the publication of Yassif's initial article in 1990, the study of rabbinic stories has progressed a great deal, as has the development of critical methods of analysis. There also have been detailed studies of some story-cycles over the course of these years, although no complete study of the phenomenon as a whole.

Here I begin a comprehensive study of the story-cycle in the Bavli, building on Yassif's pioneering publications. I will of necessity point out problems and deficiencies in Yassif's work to illustrate the path forward, but this criticism should not be understood as impugning Yassif's scholarship, which had different goals and purposes.

The first part of the essay discusses general questions, problems, and methodological issues and illustrates them through an analysis of the story-cycle in b. Ber. 18a–b, the first in the Bavli. The second part contains case studies of four other story-cycles: (2) Ketub. 67b, (3) Šabb. 30b–31a, (4) Šabb. 156b, (5) 'Abod. Zar. 10a–10b. The first three of these were discussed by Yassif; the last is new. In subsequent publications I hope to add

10. Yassif, *Hebrew Folktale*, 243; *Sippur Ha-am*, 266.

11. Moses Gaster, *Sefer Hama'asim: The Exempla of the Rabbis* (repr., New York: Ktav, 1968); *Ḥibbur Yafeh Mehayeshua*, ed. H. Z. Hirschberg (Jerusalem, 1970). On the transition to narrative as a genre with cultural capital of its own, see too Joshua Levinson, *The Twice Told Tale: A Poetics of the Exegetical Narrative in Rabbinic Midrash* [Hebrew] (Jerusalem: Magnes, 2005), 316–17.

analyses of the other story-cycles on Yassif's list as well as identify additional story-cycles. I will offer some preliminary conclusions at the end of this paper, but final conclusions will have to wait until all the story-cycles have been analyzed anew.

Case Study 1: b. Ber. 18a–b

Clearly the first step in identifying the story-cycle, or the "story-collection" (*qobetz sippurim*;Yassif uses these terms interchangeably), is a definition of the phenomenon. Yet this is no easy task. Yassif defines the story-cycle as follows: "The literary phenomenon I wish to discuss here is an unbroken sequence of tales. On occasion, a biblical verse or rabbinic saying comes between two tales ... but these fall within accepted norms in almost all story groupings, including those outside rabbinic literature." He proceeds to clarify: "in all the story cycles discussed hereafter, the tales follow one another uninterrupted (or nearly so), the compiler clearly not intending to break their continuity or intervene with a moral or with didactic sermonizing" (הסיפורים באים בזה אחר זה ברצף בלתי פוסק [או עם הפסק מזערי]).[12] Yassif distinguishes the story-cycle from the solitary tale, on the one hand, and the "aggadic *pisqa*," on the other hand, exemplified by Bavli *Pereq Heleq* (b. Sanh. ch. 11), which is "peppered liberally with tales, sages' remarks, commentary and homily, expanded biblical tales, sermons and so on" and in which the stories are not adduced for their own sake but to serve "the ethical idea or ideas developed in the course of the discussion." The compiler of this mass of aggadic material—I would prefer to call it an aggadic *sugya* or series of aggadic *sugyot*—"does not engage in telling tales for the sake of the narrative world constructed within them—rather, he uses the tales to flesh out and develop his ideas." [13]

Two criteria thus distinguish the story-cycle from the aggadic *pisqa* or aggadic *sugya*: First, the story-cycle is an uninterrupted (or almost uninterrupted) series of stories, without the incorporation of other genres of aggadic or halakhic traditions. Second, the story-cycle immerses the audience in the narrative world of the stories rather than the morals or lessons or ideas that the compiler wishes to express: "Before the reader's eyes"—note the textual model of a reader; we should probably correct this to "the audience's ears" given the consensus that the Bavli, and probably rabbinic textual production and study more broadly, were oral until the end of the Geonic period—"passes a sequence of diverse narrative worlds, each with distinct figures and/or narrative reality, but linked firmly by a clear structural and compilerial conception ... the reader is immersed for a relatively

12. Yassif, *Hebrew Folktale*, 210–11.

13. Ibid., 210.

long period in an imaginary world, attention focused on the tales' narrative qualities as opposed to their ideological significance."[14]

Both of these criteria are problematic, and in fact some of Yassif's examples do not even measure up. First, even if we acknowledge that textual interpretation always involves a degree of subjectivity, the issue of how much of an interruption a story-cycle can accommodate is tricky. When is a series of stories "almost uninterrupted" and when is it "interrupted"? What constitutes a "minor interruption" (*hefseq miz'ari*) and when does it become "major"? Yassif's formulation that the biblical verses or rabbinic sayings that come between tales in the cycles fall "within accepted norms in almost all story groupings, including those outside rabbinic literature" is equally unclear. What are these "accepted norms"? By "story groupings ... outside rabbinic literature" Yassif presumably means series of stories in other periods of Jewish history, or in the literature of other cultures, which tolerate minor interjections between the stories. But these "accepted norms" are not defined, and we are again left wondering how cohesive and continuous the series of stories must be. The second criterion, that of the audience being immersed in the narrative worlds of the stories *as opposed to their ideological significance*, is also problematic. This opposition strikes me as a false dichotomy: often the narrative world of the story contains or includes their ideological significance, even if we would not wish to reduce the meaning of stories to one particular significance. In addition, such editorial comments can direct the audience's attention to important aspects of the narrative world and thereby contribute to their "focus." They need not always distract or remove the audience from the narrative world, as Yassif seems to assume. On the other hand, even the minor interventions of the compiler, the kind that Yassif tolerates, can distract the audience from the narrative world when not directed towards its thematics but oriented to other ends.

Let us examine a concrete example that illustrates the difficulties with these criteria and also sets forth other challenges that confront the scholar when approaching this topic. The first story-cycle of the Bavli on the list above is b. Ber. 18a-b, three stories that Yassif characterizes as "stories of the dead" (סיפורי מתים). The text follows the Vilna printing for convenience, though this in itself is one of the issues that require attention, as will be discussed below, and I have included the significant manuscript variants for my purposes. The editorial comments are printed with shading to distinguish them from the stories proper. The passages preceding and following the story are labeled [0,00, etc.], as these cannot be considered interruptions of the story-cycle, though they provide contextualization.

14. Ibid., 211.

[0] תנו רבנן: המוליך עצמות ממקום למקום - הרי זה לא יתנם בדסקיא ויתנם על גבי חמור וירכב עליהם, מפני שנוהג בהם מנהג בזיון. ואם היה מתירא מפני נכרים ומפני לסטים - מותר, וכדרך שאמרו בעצמות כך אמרו בספר תורה. אהייא? אילימא ארישא - פשיטא, מי גרע ספר תורה מעצמות! אלא אסיפא. אמר רחבה אמר רב יהודה: כל הרואה המת ואינו מלוהו - עובר משום לעג לרש חרף עשהו. ואם הלוהו מה שכרו? אמר רב אסי, עליו הכתוב אומר: מלוה ה׳ חונן דל, ומכבדו חנן אביון.

[1] רבי חייא ורבי יונתן הוו שקלי ואזלי בבית הקברות, הוה קשדיא תכלתא דרבי יונתן. אמר ליה רבי חייא: דלייה, כדי שלא יאמרו למחר באין אצלנו ועכשיו מחרפין אותנו. אמר ליה: **ומי ידעי כולי האי**? והא כתיב: *[כי החיים יודעים שימותו] והמתים אינם יודעים מאומה [קהלת ט:ה]*!

[1א] אמר ליה: אם קרית - לא שנית, אם שנית - לא שלשת, אם שלשת - לא פירשו לך: *כי החיים יודעים שימותו* - אלו צדיקים שבמיתתן נקראו חיים, שנאמר: *ובניהו בן יהוידע בן איש חי רב פעלים מקבצאל הוא הכה את שני אראל מואב והוא ירד והכה את הארי בתוך הבור ביום השלג* <**יח ע״ב**> *בן איש חי*, אטו כולי עלמא בני מתי נינהו? אלא, בן איש חי - שאפילו במיתתו קרוי חי;

[1ב] *רב פעלים מקבצאל* - שריבה וקבץ פועלים לתורה; *והוא הכה את שני אראל מואב* - שלא הניח כמותו לא במקדש ראשון ולא במקדש שני; *והוא ירד והכה את הארי בתוך הבור ביום השלג* - איכא דאמרי: דתבר גזיזי דברדא ונחת וטבל, איכא דאמרי: דתנא סיפרא דבי רב ביומא דסיתוא.

[1ג] *והמתים אינם יודעים מאומה* - אלו רשעים שבחייהן קרויין מתים, שנאמר: *ואתה חלל רשע נשיא ישראל*.

[1ד] ואי בעית אימא, מהכא: *על פי שנים עדים או (על פי) שלשה עדים יומת המת*. חי הוא! אלא: המת מעיקרא

[2] בני רבי חייא נפוק לקרייתא אייקר להו תלמודייהו, הוו קא מצערי לאדכוריה. אמר לו חד לחבריה: **ידע אבון בהאי צערא? אמר לו אידך: מנא ידע?** והא כתיב: יכבדו בניו ולא ידע! אמר ליה אידך: **ולא ידע?** והא כתיב: אך בשרו עליו יכאב ונפשו עליו תאבל, ואמר רבי יצחק: קשה רמה למת כמחט בבשר החי.

[2א] אמרי: בצערא דידהו - ידעי, בצערא דאחרינא - לא ידעי.

[**אמרי:** ד. **א״ל:** פריז, מ, פ. **חסר:** א1, א2, ב]

[2ב] ולא?

[**ולא?** ד, ב, א2. **חסר:** פריז, א1. **ובצערא דאחריני לא ידעי?** מ,פ.[15]

[3] והתניא: מעשה בחסיד אחד שנתן דינר לעני בערב ראש השנה בשני בצורת והקניטתו אשתו והלך ולן בבית הקברות. ושמע שתי רוחות שמספרות זו לזו, אמרה חדא לחברתה: חברתי, בואי ונשוט בעולם ונשמע מאחורי הפרגוד מה פורענות בא לעולם אמרה לה חברתה: איני יכולה שאני קבורה במחצלת של קנים, אלא לכי את ומה שאת שומעת אמרי לי. הלכה היא ושטה ובאה. ואמרה לה חברתה: חברתי, מה שמעת מאחורי הפרגוד? אמרה לה: שמעתי, שכל הזורע ברביעה ראשונה ברד מלקה אותו. הלך הוא וזרע ברביעה שניה. של כל העולם כולו - לקה, שלו - לא לקה. לשנה האחרת הלך ולן בבית הקברות, ושמע אותן שתי רוחות שמספרות זו עם זו. אמרה חדא לחברתה: בואי ונשוט בעולם ונשמע מאחורי הפרגוד מה פורענות בא לעולם. אמרה לה: חברתי, לא כך אמרתי לך: איני יכולה שאני קבורה במחצלת של קנים? אלא לכי את ומה שאת שומעת בואי ואמרי לי. הלכה ושטה ובאה. ואמרה לה חברתה: חברתי, מה שמעת מאחורי

15. MS references: ד = Vilna printing, מ = Munich 95; פריז = Paris 671, א1 = Oxford 366 (Opp. Add. Fol. 23); א2 = Oxford-Bodleiana heb. C. 65 11; פ = Florence II-I-7; ב = Basel-Universtaetsbibliothek R III 1.1.-2.

הפרגוד? אמרה לה: שמעתי, שכל הזורע ברביעה שניה שדפון מלקה אותו. הלך וזרע ברביעה ראשונה. של כל העולם כולו - נשדף, ושלו לא נשדף. אמרה לו אשתו: מפני מה אשתקד של כל העולם כולו לקה ושלך לא לקה, ועכשיו של כל העולם כולו נשדף ושלך לא נשדף? סח לה כל הדברים הללו. אמרו: לא היו ימים מועטים עד שנפלה קטטה בין אשתו של אותו חסיד ובין אמה של אותה ריבה. אמרה לה: לכי ואראך בתך שהיא קבורה במחצלת של קנים. לשנה האחרת הלך ולן בבית הקברות ושמע אותן רוחות שמספרות זו עם זו. אמרה לה: חברתי, בואי ונשוט בעולם ונשמע מאחורי הפרגוד מה פורענות בא לעולם. אמרה לה: חברתי, הניחיני, דברים שביני לבינך כבר נשמעו בין החיים.

[3א] אלמא ידעי!
- דילמא איניש אחרינא שכיב ואזיל ואמר להו
תא שמע: ד

[4] זעירי הוה מפקיד זוזי גבי אושפיזיכתיה, עד דאתי ואזיל לבי רב, שכיבה. אזל בתרה לחצר מות. אמר לה: זוזי היכא? - אמרה ליה: זיל שקלינהו מתותי בצנורא דדשא בדוך פלן, ואימא לה לאימא תשדר לי מסרקאי וגובתאי דכוחלא בהדי פלניתא דאתיא למחר.

[4א] אלמא ידעי!
- דלמא דומה קדים ומכריז להו.
תא שמע ד

[5] אבוה דשמואל הוו קא מפקדי גביה זוזי דיתמי, כי נח נפשיה לא הוה שמואל גביה. הוו קא קרו ליה בר אכיל זוזי דיתמי. אזל אבתריה לחצר מות. אמר להו: בעינא אבא. אמרו ליה: אבא טובא איכא הכא. אמר להו: בעינא אבא בר אבא. אמרו ליה: אבא בר אבא נמי טובא איכא הכא. אמר להו: בעינא אבא בר אבא אבוה דשמואל, היכא? - אמרו ליה: סליק למתיבתא דרקיעא. אדהכי חזייה ללוי דיתיב אבראי. אמר ליה: אמאי יתבת אבראי, מאי טעמא לא סלקת? אמר ליה, דאמרי לי: כל כי הנך שני דלא סליקת למתיבתא דרבי אפס ואחלישתיה לדעתיה - לא מעיילינן לך למתיבתא דרקיעא. אדהכי והכי אתא אבוה, חזייה דהוה קא בכי ואחיך. אמר ליה: מאי טעמא קא בכית? אמר ליה: דלעגל קא אתית. מאי טעמא אחיכת? - דחשיבת בהאי עלמא טובא, אמר ליה: אי חשיבנא - נעיילוה ללוי, ועיילוהו ללוי. אמר ליה: זוזי דיתמי היכא? אמר ליה: זיל שקלינהו באמתא דרחיא, עילאי ותתאי - דידן, ומיצעי - דיתמי. אמר ליה: מאי טעמא עבדת הכי? - אמר ליה: אי גנובי גנבי - מגנבו מדידן, אי אכלה ארעא - אכלה מדידן.

[5א] אלמא דידעי! - דילמא שאני שמואל, כיון דחשיב - קדמי ומכרזי פנו מקום

[00] ואף רבי יונתן הדר ביה, דאמר רבי שמואל בר נחמני אמר רבי יונתן: מנין למתים שמספרים זה עם זה? שנאמר: ויאמר ה׳ אליו זאת הארץ אשר נשבעתי לאברהם ליצחק וליעקב לאמר, מאי לאמר - אמר הקדוש ברוך הוא למשה: לך אמור להם לאברהם ליצחק וליעקב שבועה שנשבעתי לכם כבר קיימתיה לבניכם <יט ע"א>

[000] ואי סלקא דעתך דלא ידעי - כי אמר להו מאי הוי? - אלא מאי, דידעי? - למה ליה למימר להו? - לאחזוקי ליה טיבותא למשה

This passage in fact contains five stories, labelled [1] through [5]. I assume that Yassif intends the last three, as these have the highest degree of narrativity, and several anonymous comments separate the second story from the third [א2]-[ב2]. The precise identification of the stories that form the cycle is itself a wider problem with Yassif's list, as only in a few cases does he catalog the stories themselves, stating, for example, "after the first story that features Rava ... the second and third are about such and such." In some cases the stories can be identified very easily, especially those that have relatively few stories. In other cases the breakdown is unclear and it is uncertain how Yassif arrived at his numeration. So one major need of a comprehensive study of the story-cycle in the Bavli is the precise identification of the stories within each cycle.[16] Related to this desideratum is the question of the definition of the story, which Yassif does not address. As is well known, this is not an easy question to answer, and there are competing definitions of the minimum threshold for a story as opposed to a narrative or list or dialogue (more on this below). While on this slight digression, let me note that another major question requiring attention is that of the halakhic story.[17] As a folklorist, Yassif was interested in aggada, in its rich narrative material with colorful plots and vivid imagery, some of which is paralleled in world folklore. However, the distinction between halakha and aggada is not always self-evident, nor can these modes always be distinguished easily.[18] Many series of halakhic stories, that is, halakhic story-cycles, appear in the Bavli, but are not mentioned in Yassif's work, as they are not folklore, but rather products of the rabbinic academy. Whether these halakhic story-cycles should be considered together with story-cycles of aggada, or in a separate study, is also a significant question.

Anonymous glosses appear between stories [3] and [4] and between [4] and [5] (as well as after [5]); this is what Yassif means by a story-cycle that, although not "uninterrupted," is "nearly uninterrupted." But if this is the case, why not include story [2], which is separated from story [3] by similar brief comments? Indeed, in place of the reading אמרי of the Vilna printing, several manuscripts have א"ל, indicating the response of one of R. Ḥiyya's sons to his brother *within* the story rather than the voice of the compiler or editor.[19] The next comment, ולא [ב2], is missing in several manuscripts. In this case the third story follows the second story almost directly (except for the introductory term, והתניא). In sum, there are compelling grounds to include story 2, yielding a cycle of four stories.

To push matters further, we might also include story [1], despite the fact that a few more comments separate it from the second story

16. In fact a major desideratum of scholarship of Bavli stories is a comprehensive list of all stories in the Bavli. How many stories are there in the Bavli? How many in each tractate?

17. See Moshe Simon-Shoshan, *Stories of the Law: Narrative Discourse and the Construction of Authority in the Mishnah* (New York: Oxford University Press, 2012).

18. Ibid., 2–5; Barry Scott Wimpfheimer, *Narrating the Law: A Poetics of Talmudic Legal Stories*, Divinations (Philadelphia: University of Pennsylvania Press, 2011), 31–62.

19. I think that אמרי can also be read that way, that is, as part of the dialogue within the story, although it can also be taken as the voice of the editor, or at least a level of discourse outside of the story, which would be more of an interruption, and seems to be Yassif's understanding.

[1ב, 1ג, 1ד]. I set [1ג] in standard font, unshaded, because it is undoubtedly the continuation of the words of R. Ḥiyya within the story, the conclusion of his dictum. He first responds with an explanation of the first clause of Qoh 9:5, כי החיים יודעים שימותו, underlined in [1א], and then explains the second clause of the verse, והמתים אינם יודעים מאומה in [1ג], although his words are interrupted by the Stam, which adds exegetical comments on the rest of the supporting verse, 2 Sam 23:20, in [1ב].[20] In fact, even this secondary verse seems to have been added to the original dictum of R. Ḥiyya by the Stam in [1]; that his original dictum was an explication of the first two clauses of Qoh 9:5 alone can be confirmed by the parallels in y. Ber 2:3, 4c–d (= Qoh. Rab. 9:5, with minor changes), and finds some support in Yal. Šimoni, 2 Samuel, #165:

B. Ber. 18a	y. Ber. 2:3, 4c–d (= Qoh. Rab. 9:5)[21]	Yal. Šimoni, 2 Samuel, #165
		<u>*ובניהו בן יהוידע בן איש חי*</u>, *וכי בניהו בן יהוידע בן איש חי וכולי עלמא בני מתיא נינהו*, *אלא בן איש שאפילו במיתתו קרוי חי*. *רב פעלים*.... **[1ב]** *רב פעלים מקבצאל* - שריבה וקבץ פועלים לתורה; *הוא הכה את שני אראל מואב* – שלא הניח כמותו לא במקדש ראשון ולא במקדש שני; *והוא ירד והכה את הארי בתוך הבור ביום השלג* – איכא דאמרי: דתבר גזיזי דברדא ונחת וטבל, איכא דאמרי דתנא סיפרא דבי רב ביומא דסיתוא. .
[סיפור 1] רבי חייא ורבי יונתן הוו שקלי ואזלי בבית הקברות ...	דילמא. ר׳ חייא רובא ור׳ יונתן היו מהלכין...	**[סיפור 1]** רבי חייא ורבי יונתן הוו שקלי ואזלי בבית הקברות ...
[1א] אמר ליה: אם קרית לא שנית, אם שנית לא שלשת, אם שלשת לא פירשו לך:	א״ל: לקרות את יודע, לדרוש אין את יודע	א״ל: אם קרית לא שנית ואם שנית לא שלשת ואם שלשת לא פירשו לך:

20. In theory we could read [1ב] as the continuation of R. Ḥiyya's words, and not an editorial gloss. As is often the case, the boundaries of an Amoraic dictum are difficult to discern, namely where the dictum ends and the Bavli's anonymous voice begins. In this case the presence of the double איכא דאמרי suggests the exegesis is not part of the Amoraic dictum.

21. There are minor differences between these versions.

כי החיים יודעים שימותו - אלו צדיקים שבמיתתן נקראו חיים שנאמר: ובניהו בן יהוידע בן איש חי רב פעלים מקבצאל הוא הכה את שני אראל מואב והוא ירד והכה את הארי בתוך הבור ביום השלג <**יח ע"ב**>> בן איש חי, אטו כולי עלמא בני מתי נינהו? אלא, בן איש חי - שאפילו במיתתו קרוי חי; **[1ב]** רב פעלים מקבצאל - שריבה וקבץ פועלים לתורה; והוא הכה את שני אראל מואב - שלא הניח כמותו לא במקדש ראשון ולא במקדש שני; והוא ירד והכה את הארי בתוך הבור ביום השלג – איכא דאמרי: דתבר גזיזי דברדא ונחת וטבל, איכא דאמרי דתנא סיפרא דבי רב ביומא דסיתוא.	כי החיים יודעים שימותו - אילו הצדיקים שאפילו במיתתן קרויין חיים	כי החיים יודעים שימותו- אלו הצדיקים שאפילו במיתתן קרוין חיים שנאמר: ובניהו בן יהוידע וגו',
[1ג] והמתים אינם יודעים מאומה - אלו רשעים שבחייהן קרויין מתים, שנאמר: ואתה חלל רשע נשיא ישראל	והמתים אינם יודעים מאומה - אילו הרשעים שאפילו בחייהן קרויים מתים.	[1ג] והמתים אינם יודעים מאומה - אלו הרשעים שאפילו בחייהם קרויים מתים שנאמר: ואתה חלל רשע נשיא ישראל

In the parallel story in y. Ber. 2:3, 4c–d (and Qoh. Rab. 9:5), R. Ḥiyya's response to R. Yonatan contains explications only of the two clauses of Qoh 9:5 in sequence to argue that the "living" and "dead" of the verse refer to the righteous (even if dead) and the wicked (even when living) and therefore that the "dead know." The absence of 2 Sam 23:20 in these Palestinian parallels suggests that this verse has been spliced into R. Ḥiyya's dictum by the Stam and then supplemented by additional interpretations [1ב]. Even Yalqut Shimoni, based on the Bavli, had no trouble removing most of 2 Sam 23:20 and its exegesis from R. Ḥiyya's dictum and providing it at the outset in order to underline the connection to 2 Sam 23:20, its point of departure, thereby restoring R. Ḥiyya's dictum to a form close to the more original formulation attested in y. Ber. 2:3, 4c–d and Qoh. Rab. 9:5.

After the story proper, another brief anonymous comment, an alternative prooftext (אי בעית אימא) citing Deut 17:6, appears [1ד]. Granted there is some "interruption" between stories [1] and [2] caused by the Stam adding 2 Sam 23:20 together with subsequent interpretive comments [1ב], and a slightly greater interruption created by this alternative prooftext [ד1]. Nevertheless, because [1] also concerns whether "the dead know," I would argue that it should be considered part of the story-cycle, yielding a cycle of five stories. These considerations illustrate the difficulty of defining the boundaries of the story-cycle and the need for a reassessment of Yassif's list of story-cycles that takes into account manuscript readings.

Let us now consider the nature of the anonymous editorial comments, the "minor interruptions" Yassif mentions in the second half of his definition of the story-cycle. Even if we focus exclusively on the comments between the three stories that Yassif included in his cycle, [א3] and [א4], we should note that they correlate with the particular interest of the larger *sugya* and stand in some tension with Yassif's characterization of the cycle as "stories of the dead." Within the larger *sugya* the three stories are adduced for the more specific question of whether "the dead know," that is, "whether the dead know about the living," which is exactly the focus of these two anonymous editorial comments. The comments are in fact mini-dialectical interchanges, offering a contention (אלמא ידעי), a rejection (דילמא), and the technical term adducing another proof (תא שמע). So too the framing comment in [ב2], ?ולא, that is, "Do the dead not know?"; the postscripts to the final story [א5], אלמא דידעי, "Therefore they know" (and again there are variants in the manuscripts); and the concluding anonymous interchange [000] all direct attention to this one specific issue. But this is not really the main point of the third story, the famous folktale of the "pious man in the cemetery," as Ofra Meir argued in a brilliant article about the impact of the different contexts in which the story appears on the meanings absorbed by the audience.[22] Likewise, the fourth story about Shmuel's father is a complex tale of which the deceased's knowledge of the living is but one aspect. Thus, Yassif's characterization of the topic of the story-cycle fits the stories, but not really their framing and function in the *sugya*, which is presumably how the audience would assess them. We might fairly say that the editorial interruptions (as well as the trajectory of the larger *sugya*) "constrict" the narrative world, or even remove the audience from the larger narrative world by directing their attention to this specific issue.

Now, on the one hand, this might be seen as support for Yassif's awareness of the potential gap between the "imaginary world" and "narrative qualities" of the stories "*as opposed* to their ideological significance."[23] But, on the other, without these comments there would be no story-cycle, as they signal to us the purposes for which the stories were introduced into

22. Ofra Meir, "The Literary Context of the Sages' Aggadic Stories as Analogous to Changing Storytelling Situations" [Hebrew], *Jerusalem Studies in Jewish Folklore* 13–14 (1992): 81–98.

23. Yassif, *Hebrew Folktale*, 211 (see p. 232, above).

the *sugya*. This is *not* a case of a cohesive, preexistent story-cycle that later editors appropriated and then subsequently interrupted with comments reflecting their later ideological interests or concerns. Rather, the editorial comments, the interruptions, indicate why the stories appear in proximity to one another, that is, in a series that can be characterized as a story-cycle, namely, to answer the specific question of the whether "the dead know." Compare, for example, comment [ד1] with comments [א3], [א4] that "interrupt" between stories [3] and [4] and then [4] and [5]. The former is an aside, an opportunistic gloss providing an alternative prooftext and can be removed without any negative impact on the story-cycle (i.e., the longer story-cycle of five stories that I identify above). It is fairly characterized as an "interruption" vis-à-vis the story-cycle, though of course it serves certain purposes, among then offering pentateuchal support for the claim. The latter two, on the other hand, are part of the warp and woof of the story-cycle itself, part of the intrinsic connective tissue of the *sugya*. They indicate why each story is adduced and why each is not sufficient for the purposes of the *sugya*. Without them the *sugya* presumably would have ended after story [3] or even story [2]. In Yassif's words quoted above, this is a case where the editor "does not engage in telling tales for the sake of the narrative world constructed within them—rather, he uses the tales to flesh out and develop his ideas," which, in Yassif's view, characterizes the "aggadic *pisqa*," not the story-cycle.

Thus, "interruptions" between the stories of a story-cycle are diverse and complex, and not only because of their length, whether brief ("minor") or longer. We require a taxonomy of interruptions to better understand the nature, workings, and even origins of the story-cycles. Here comments [ב1] and [ד1] can be categorized as "minor digressions." These comments simply provide alternative or additional explanations of the verses and neither add nor detract from the story-cycle. Comments [ב2]-[א2], [א3], [א4] on the other hand, should be classified as "introductory or transitional phrases." They alert the audience as to the function of the coming story and identify its importance for the compiler.

Both the analysis of interruptions and the consideration of the story-cycle in relation to the larger *sugya* lead us directly to the question of the editors of the story-cycles. Yassif regularly speaks of the עורך of the story-cycle, rendered as "compiler" or "editor" in the English translation. However, the identity of this compiler/editor is not clear, nor whether he is to be identified with the Bavli redactors/compilers/editors, the Stammaim. Or, to put the question more generally: Are these story-cycles the work of the late Bavli editors (Stammaim), or did the editors draw on existing story-cycles? If the latter, to what extent did they transmit the story-cycle unchanged, and to what extent did they rework the cycle, as they did, say, halakhic *sugyot* and stories they received from the Land of Israel? What is the relationship between the Bavli story-cycles and their sources? These questions were not really raised by Yassif, who was more interested in the folkloristic dimensions, and he may not have distinguished between two types of editors—the Bavli redactors/Stammaim and the compiler-editors of the story-cycle (Amoraim? nonrabbinic storytellers?). Yet this question potentially sheds light on the origins and development of the rabbinic story-cycle, the literary sources of the Bavli, and the Bavli editors' compositional techniques.[24]

There is little doubt that the Bavli redactors/Stammaim are responsible for the story-cycle in b. Ber. 18a–b, as intimated above. The *sugya* is made up in large part of the story-cycle, and the anonymous Aramaic phrases that gloss and introduce the stories—that is, the interruptions—are typical of the redactors. The topic of whether the dead know about the living pertains to the halakhic discussion of the proximate m. Ber. 3:1, which refers to a death, "One whose dead lies before him is exempt from reciting the Shema." In the course of the subsequent discussion (b. Ber. 18a), the *sugya* cites a tradition requiring proper respect for the dead buried in cemeteries: "One should not walk in a cemetery with tefillin on his head, and a Torah scroll in his arms and read from it, and if he does so, he violates *He who mocks the poor, blasphemes the Creator* (Prov 17:5)." It continues with two other cautions against offending the dead (one about not transporting bones in a saddle bag, the second about escorting the deceased in the funeral procession). The first story deals with walking in the cemetery and potentially offending the dead, which raises the question of how the dead would take offense, being dead, hence whether they know what transpires among the living. This question is explicitly asked of the following four stories and motivates their incorporation into the *sugya*. Thus, the story-cycle essentially constitutes an aggadic *sugya* related to a halakhic provision; the stories are adduced to address this issue and serve this purpose almost exclusively. The redactors evidently gathered the stories from other sources and brought them together into the story-cycle. That the interruptions are essentially "mini-dialectical interchanges" including the technical terminology of the Bavli (e.g. תא שמע) makes this abundantly clear.

This conclusion is supported by assessing the parallel Yerushalmi *sugya* to m. Ber. 3:1 presented above, the very *sugya* that contains the parallel story of R. Ḥiyya (the Great) and R. Yonatan [1]. This *sugya* also contains traditions about honoring and not offending the dead (though

24. See Yassif's note, *Sippur Ha-am*, 626 n. 120, on previous scholarship on collections of aggadot in rabbinic literature; and see Shamma Friedman, "La'aggadah hahisṭorit batalmud babli" [On the Historical Aggadah in the Babylonian Talmud], in *Saul Lieberman Memorial Volume*, ed. Shamma Friedman (Jerusalem: Jewish Theological Seminary of Amerca, 1993), 119–64, here 120 n. 5 on the literary sources of the Bavli. These studies have implications for the methods with which the Bavli redactors reworked their sources.

somewhat different traditions than those in the Bavli)[25] and presents this one story, but no other stories. It therefore appears that the Bavli redactors reworked and expanded the Palestinian *sugya* in part by adducing other stories pertinent to the issue of the dead's awareness of the living and in this way created this story-cycle. No Amoraic dicta appear within the entire story-cycle (although Amoraim are protagonists of the stories, and a dictum of R. Yonatan follows the story-cycle, [00]).

However, we know that other story-cycles anteceded the Bavli redactors/Stammaim and were received from earlier sources. Yassif identified story-cycles in the Yerushalmi and other Yerushalmi compilations. And Shamma Friedman's foundational article, "On the Historical Aggadah in the Babylonian Talmud," demonstrated that the Bavli redactors of the story-cycle in b. B. Meṣ. 83b–84b (#17 on the list above) received two story-cycles from Palestinian sources, one from Pesiq. Rab. Kah. *Beshalaḥ* 11, and one that appears twice in the Yerushalmi, Kil. 9:3 and Ketub. 12:3.[26] The Bavli redactors then supplemented and reworked these sources dramatically.[27] In cases such as this, the story-cycle anteceded the redactors, but they reworked it to such an extent that the Bavli version is essentially a different and novel redactorial creation. This story-cycle therefore belongs in a second category, namely, story-cycles produced by the Bavli redactors based on antecedent story-cycles.

Are there story-cycles that the redactors transmitted intact without interventions? The well-known story-cycle containing "seafarer stories" in b. B. Bat. 73a–74b, for example, a lengthy cycle of twenty-two stories (#19 on the list above), is uninterrupted by any anonymous phrases that introduce, conclude, or link the stories, and I see but a single, brief Stammaitic gloss in the entire series that clarifies one detail in one of the stories.[28] Here it is possible that the Bavli redactors incorporated this entire story-cycle in its present form from an earlier source. If so, we have a third type of story-cycle, namely, a story-cycle incorporated wholesale into the Bavli with no (or almost no) redactorial contribution. It is equally possible, however, that the redactors created this story-cycle by combining seafarer stories from disparate sources but left us no non-

25. For example, the *baraita* in the Bavli prohibits performing certain commandments in the cemetery, whereas the parallel *baraita* in the Yerushalmi prohibits relieving oneself in the cemetery.

26. Yassif, *Hebrew Collection*, 73–75, ##44, 5, 9.

27. See n. 24 above.

28. B. B. Bat. 74a: כי אתאי לקמיה דרבנן אמרו לי כל אבא חמרא כל בר בר חנה סיכסא היה לך לומר מופר לך *והוא סבר דלמא שבועתא דמבול הוא ורבנן א"כ אוי לי למה*. "When I came before the sages, they said to me: Every Abba is a donkey, and every Bar Bar Ḥana is an idiot! You should have said to them, 'Your [oath] is annulled.' *But he [Rabba b. bar Ḥana] thought. Perhaps he was referring to the oath about the flood. And the sages? If so, why did he say, 'Woe is me?'*" See the article by James Redfield in this volume.

narrative comments or telltale technical terminology as evidence—only a detailed study can resolve question. It might be that this question cannot be resolved with certainty.

Another issue that requires detailed analysis is the function of story-cycles within their halakhic contexts, as this has much to teach us about the function of aggada in the Bavli in general, and stories in particular, and also about the processes of composition of Bavli *sugyot*. Are story-cycles always connected to the proximate halakhic contexts? If so, what is their function or functions, and what do they teach about the relationship between halakha and aggada? If they are not connected, how and why are they integrated into their present contexts? As we have seen, the story-cycle of b. Ber. 18a–b substantively relates to the laws discussed earlier in the *sugya* that require respect for the dead, which in turn appear here due to an associative link to m. Ber. 3:1, which mentions prayer after the death of a relative. Thus, the story-cycle, emphasizing connections between the dead and the living, and describing the deceaseds' knowledge of that which transpires among their descendants, helps ground the laws requiring proper behavior in cemeteries and other measures of respect for the dead. We have a good example of the deep connections between an aggadic story-cycle and its halakhic context.

The following four case-studies of Bavli story-cycles build on Yassif's scholarship to address the questions delineated above and other issues. These include the identification and definition of the story-cycle, the function of the story-cycle, the contextualization of the story-cycle and relationship to the halakhic context, the role of the Bavli redactors, and the relationship to earlier sources. I will then offer some preliminary conclusions. Of course comprehensive treatment of these questions will have to wait until study of all of the Bavli's story-cycles has been completed.

Case Study 2: b. Ketub. 67b. Four Stories. [Giving to the poor "sufficient for his needs"][29]

[א] ת״ר יתום שבא לישא שוכרין לו בית ומציעין לו מטה וכל כלי תשמישו ואחר כך משיאין לו אשה שנאמר {דברים ט״ו} די מחסורו אשר יחסר לו די מחסורו זה הבית אשר יחסר זה מטה ושלחן לו זו אשה וכן הוא אומר {בראשית ב׳} אעשה לו עזר כנגדו:

29. Vilna text; significant variants are discussed below and in the notes. Apart from Yassif's comments, see the analysis of the story-cycle in the article by Dov Kahane, "Problematizing Charity," in this volume and the secondary references there. Kahana also provides a translation. For literature on individual stories and charity in general, see Alyssa Gray, "The Formerly Wealthy Poor: From Empathy to Ambivalence in Rabbinic Literature of Late Antiquity," *AJSR* 33 (2009): 101–33; Gregg Gardner, *The Origins of Organized Charity in Rabbinic Judaism* (New York: Cambridge University Press, 2016), 124, 136, 153, 184; Yael Wilfand, *Poverty, Charity and the Image of the Poor in Rabbinic Texts from the Land of Israel,*

[ב] תנו רבנן די מחסורו אתה מצווה עליו לפרנסו ואי אתה מצווה עליו לעשרו אשר יחסר לו אפילו סוס לרכוב עליו ועבד לרוץ לפניו

[1] אמרו עליו על הלל הזקן שלקח לעני בן טובים אחד סוס לרכוב עליו ועבד לרוץ לפניו פעם אחת לא מצא עבד לרוץ לפניו ורץ לפניו שלשה מילין:

[2] תנו רבנן מעשה באנשי גליל העליון שלקחו לעני בן טובים אחד מציפורי ליטרא בשר בכל יום
[א2] ליטרא בשר מאי רבותא **אמר רב הונא** ליטרא בשר משל[30] עופות ואיבעית אימא בליטרא בשר ממש **רב אשי אמר** התם כפר קטן היה בכל יומא הוה מפסדי חיותא אמטולתיה:

[3] ההוא דאתא לקמיה דרבי נחמיה אמר ליה במה אתה סועד א״ל בבשר שמן ויין ישן רצונך שתגלגל עמי בעדשים גלגל עמו בעדשים ומת אמר אוי לו לזה שהרגו נחמיה
[א3] אדרבה אוי לו לנחמיה שהרגו לזה מיבעי ליה אלא איהו הוא דלא איבעי ליה לפנוקי נפשיה כולי האי

[4] ההוא דאתא לקמיה דרבא אמר לו במה אתה סועד אמר לו בתרנגולת פטומה ויין ישן אמר ליה ולא חיישת לדוחקא דציבורא א״ל אטו מדידהו קאכילנא מדרחמנא קאכילנא דתנינא {תהלים קמ״ה} עיני כל אליך ישברו ואתה נותן להם את אכלם בעתו בעתם לא נאמר אלא בעתו מלמד שכל אחד ואחד נותן הקב״ה פרנסתו בעתו אדהכי אתאי אחתיה דרבא דלא חזיא ליה תליסרי שני ואתיא ליה תרנגולת פטומה ויין ישן אמר מאי דקמא א״ל נענתי לך קום אכול

[ג] תנו רבנן: אין לו ואינו רוצה להתפרנס, נותנין לו לשום הלואה וחוזרין ונותנין לו לשום מתנה, דברי רבי מאיר; וחכמים אומרים: נותנין לו לשום מתנה וחוזרין ונותנין לו לשום הלואה.
לשום מתנה הא לא שקיל! אמר רבא: לפתוח לו לשום מתנה.
יש לו ואינו רוצה להתפרנס, נותנין לו לשום מתנה וחוזרין ונפרעין ממנו.
חוזרין ונפרעין הימנו, תו לא שקיל! אמר רב פפא: לאחר מיתה.
ר״ש אומר: יש לו ואינו רוצה להתפרנס - אין נזקקין לו, אין לו ואינו רוצה להתפרנס - אומרים לו הבא משכון וטול, כדי שתזוח דעתו עליו.

[ד] ת״ר: העבט - זה שאין לו ואינו רוצה להתפרנס, שנותנים לו לשום הלואה וחוזרין ונותנין לו לשום מתנה, תעביטנו - זה שיש לו ואינו רוצה להתפרנס, שנותנין לו לשום מתנה וחוזרין ונפרעין הימנו לאחר מיתה, דברי ר׳ יהודה; וחכ״א: יש לו ואינו רוצה להתפרנס - אין נזקקין לו, ואלא מה אני מקיים תעביטנו? דברה תורה כלשון בני אדם

[5] מר עוקבא הוה עניא בשיבבותיה דהוה רגיל כל יומא דשדי ליה ארבעה זוזי בצינורא דדשא יום אחד אמר איזיל איחזי מאן קעביד בי ההוא טיבותא ההוא יומא נגהא ליה למר עוקבא לבי

SWBA 2/9 (Sheffield: Sheffield Phoenix, 2014); and Wilfand, *The Wheel That Overtakes Everyone: Poverty and Charity in the Eyes of the Sages in the Land of Israel* [Hebrew] (Tel Aviv: Hakibbutz Hameuchad, 2017).

30. Several manuscripts read ליטרא בשר מוח עופות, "A litra of meat of the brains of birds," which magnifies the expense. Saul Lieberman suggests that meat was readily available in Babylonia, prompting the comments of the Babylonian Amoriam to the story (*Studies in Palestinian Talmudic Literature,* ed. David Rosenthal [Jerusalem: Magnes, 1991], 336). See too Kahane, "Problematizing Charity," n. 54.

מדרשא אתיא דביתהו בהדיה כיון דחזיוה דקא מצלי ליה לדשא נפק בתרייהו רהוט מקמיה עיילי להוא אתונא דהוה גרופה נורא הוה קא מיקליין כרעיה דמר עוקבא אמרה ליה דביתהו שקול כרעיך אותיב אכרעאי חלש דעתיה אמרה ליה אנא שכיחנא בגויה דביתא ומקרבא אהנייתי

[5א] ומאי כולי האי דאמר מר זוטרא בר טוביה אמר רב ואמרי לה אמר רב הונא בר ביזנא אמר ר״ש חסידא ואמרי לה א״ר יוחנן משום רבי שמעון בן יוחי נוח לו לאדם שימסור עצמו לתוך כבשן האש ואל ילבין פני חברו ברבים מנא לן מתמר דכתיב {בראשית ל״ח} היא מוצאת

[6] מר עוקבא[31] הוה עניא בשיבבותיה דהוה רגיל לשדורי ליה ארבע מאה זוזי כל מעלי יומא דכיפורא יומא חד שדרינהו ניהליה ביד בריה אתא אמר ליה לא צריך אמר מאי חזית חזאי דקא מזלפי ליה יין ישן אמר מפנק כולי האי עייפינהו ושדרינהו ניהליה

[7] כי קא ניחא נפשיה אמר אייתו לי חושבנאי דצדקה אשכח דהוה כתיב ביה שבעת אלפי דינרי סיאנקי אמר זוודאי קלילי ואורחא רחיקתא קם בזבזיה לפלגיה ממוניה

[7א] היכי עבד הכי והאמר ר׳ אילעאי באושא התקינו המבזבז אל יבזבז יותר מחומש הני מילי מחיים שמא ירד מנכסיו אבל לאחר מיתה לית לן בה

[8] רבי אבא הוה צייר זוזי בסודריה ושדי ליה לאחוריה וממצי נפשיה לבי עניי ומצלי עיניה מרמאי

[9] רבי חנינא הוה ההוא עניא דהוה רגיל לשדורי ליה ארבעה זוזי כל מעלי שבתא יומא חד שדרינהו ניהליה ביד דביתהו אתאי אמרה ליה לא צריך מאי חזית שמעי דהוה קאמרי ליה במה אתה סועד <סח ע״א> בטלי כסף או בטלי זהב אמר היינו דאמר רבי אלעזר בואו ונחזיק טובה לרמאין שאלמלא הן היינו חוטאין בכל יום שנאמר {דברים טו} וקרא עליך אל ה׳ והיה בך חטא

The stories are contextualized with m. Ketub. 6:5, which specifies that a minimum of fifty *zuz* should be spent on the marriage of an orphan girl and adds that, if the charity fund has sufficient resources, then she should be provided "according to her honor." After a brief halakhic discussion, the *sugya* cites the two *baraitot* above ([א], [ב]). The first complements the Mishnah in specifying the minimum charity funds to be spent on an orphan boy and invokes the standard of "sufficient for his needs" (די מחסורו) based on Deut 15:8. This standard seems to correspond to the Mishnah's standard for the orphan girl, "according to her honor": it is the amount required to preserve the orphan boy's dignity. The second *baraita* applies this standard to charity for the poor in general, setting forth a tension between excessive charity ("you are not commanded to enrich him") and the appropriate amount, which, somewhat surprisingly, is indexed according to "his needs," even to the point of a horse (typically owned only by aristocrats) and a slave.[32] This *baraita* also furnishes the first two stories of the cycle, which illustrate this surprising high standard

31. MSS Firkovich 187 and Vatican 130 have "and also" (ותו), in place of the proper name.

32. The *baraita* appears in t. Pe'ah 4:10, Sif. Deut. #116 (p. 175) and y. Pe'ah 8:8, 21a in slightly different form (without Hillel himself running before the poor), as has often been

of charity, with "real-life" descriptions. The Bavli introduces the second story with תנו רבנן, as if it is a different *baraita*, but in the Tannaitic parallels it appears together with the first.[33] The cycle continues with two stories that provide further illustrations of how far the principle of "sufficient for his needs" should be taken. In the third story, a rabbi fails to provide the fine food the man eats each day, offering him lentils instead, which results in his death. The story thus illustrates the danger of neglecting this high standard (though the anonymous gloss nuances the idea [2א]). In the fourth story, a rabbi's objection that the expensive food a poor man requests will place a heavy burden on the community is disputed, and the food is supplied by providence, thus justifying the request. The first and second stories contain the common phrase: שלקח/ו לעני בן טובים אחד. The third and fourth story both contain the formulation ההוא דאתא לקמיה ד ... אמר לו/ליה[34] במה אתה סועד ... יין ישן.[35] Taken together, the four stories form a well-constructed story-cycle that illustrates the importance and extent of the halakhic principle "sufficient for his needs," or, in other words, how much expense (and personal effort, as in the case of Hillel) should be extended to preserve a poor person's honor.[36] At the same time, the latter two stories flag potential difficulties of living up to this standard, thereby giving voice to countervailing considerations. The third story's contrast between the rabbi's daily fare of lowly lentils and the poor man's (appropriate) request for fatty meat and old wine leads one to wonder about whether it is fair and just to provide for the poor so lavishly when others go with far less. (The Stam's gloss, which essentially blames the man for his own death, clarifies this potential unfairness.) Rava articulates a related concern explicitly in the fourth story, namely, the burden imposed on the community to supply such expensive food.

Yassif offers no analysis of this story-cycle. His only comment classifies it under the fifth of his categories "the principle of associative accu-

---

noted by scholars; see Kahane, "Problematizing Charity," above p. 61. It also appears in almost the same form as the Bavli in Midrash Tannaim to Deut 15:8.

33. This may be because the Bavli embellishes the account by having Hillel run before the poor man and not only supplying a slave to do so; see the previous note. It is worth noting that the second story is extremely terse and would not even qualify as a story by some definitions, as it reports one event without much conflict or change, typically considered necessary for the minimum threshold of a story. It should probably be classified as a "case story." See the taxonomy of forms in Simon-Shoshan, *Stories of the Law*, 23–49. See Yassif, *Hebrew Folktale*, 226. The comments to the story, especially those of Rav Ashi, however, add something to its degree of narrativity.

34. The manuscripts of both stories vary in אמר לו / אמר ליה as well as א"ל so the difference is not significant.

35. See Shalom Arbiv, n. 38 below.

36. Granted that the first two stories come together as a ready-made unit from the *baraita*.

mulation."[37] But since all four stories deal with charity and more narrowly with high levels of charity for the formerly wealthy in order to preserve their honor, I believe it should be classified under the category I propose above, the "thematic principle." These four stories, together with the following five stories, are also analyzed in Dov Kahane's contribution to this volume, and by Shalom Arbiv in a fine article, "Charity and Honor."[38]

Worth noting are the brief comments following [2] and [3], including two Amoraic dicta following [2]. Evidently these comments did not constitute a sufficient interruption to disrupt the story-cycle in Yassif's view. True, the comments keep us within the narrative world in that they provide additional narrative details (the meat was from fowl,[39] or cost an entire litra of coins, or they had to slaughter an entire animal [2א]) or clarifications (exactly what R. Neḥemiah meant [3א]) rather than adducing other exegetical traditions or the "morals and didactic sermonizing" of the compiler. Nevertheless, one wonders about the limits of how many comments there can be, and how extensive the comments, before the stories should no longer be considered part of a cycle. These comments are no less interruptive than those between the first three stories in the expanded series of five stories I propose above for b. Ber. 18b. I will address this question presently in reconsidering the boundaries of the cycle.

Yassif does not comment on the continuation of the passage, but there is much more to say. These four stories are followed by two additional *baraitot* ([ג], [ד]) that address other concerns related to communal charity, namely (1) those who require charity but refuse to accept it, and (2) those who do not require charity but wish to take it anyway.[40] The first addresses the same problem of preserving the dignity of the poor; here the poor refuse to accept charity at all so as to preserve their honor, but thereby risk devastating themselves and their families. The *baraita* proposes a method of supplying them funds while avoiding embarrassment, a kind of charity legal fiction. The second includes a danger related to that implicitly raised in stories [3]–[4]. This individual, like the destitute formerly wealthy of those stories, uses resources that could otherwise support many other

---

37. Yassif, *Hebrew Folktale*, 226.

38. Shalom Arbiv, "Hatsedaqah vehakavod" [Charity and Honor], *Derekh Aggadah* 11 (2011): 79–99. I am grateful to Menaḥem Katz for bringing this article to my attention. While Arbiv's focus is broader than the story-cycle, he discusses many of the relevant issues, including the structure and organization of the *sugya*, the role of the redactors, and the meaning of the composition as a whole. See too Moshe Halbertal, who discusses several of these stories in the context of the story-cycle ("Addressing the Needs of Others: What Is the Stance of Justice?," in *Radical Responsibility: Celebrating the Thought of Chief Rabbi Lord Jonathan Sacks,"* ed. Michael J. Harris, Daniel Rynhold, and Tamra Wright [Jerusalem: Maggid, 2012], 95–109).

39. Or "brains of fowl"; see n. 30 above.

40. Both of the *baraitot* have parallels in Tannaitic sources; t. Pe'ah 4:12 and Sif. Deut. 116 (p. 175).

indigents. The first *baraita* is accompanied by two brief Amoraic comments (and the anonymous questions that contextualize their statements). There follow five more stories: [5]–[9].

Story [5] illustrates one of the issues raised by the *baraitot*, that of the embarrassment the poor experience when receiving charity and how to mitigate it. The importance of this principle is emphasized both by Mar 'Uqba's heroic, and almost self-sacrificial, efforts not to be seen and by the gloss explaining his behavior [5א].[41] This concern of not embarrassing the recipient also features in story [8], which also has a rabbi give charity in a manner that avoids his being seen by the recipient, namely, throwing the money over his shoulder. (Note that both of these stories share the expression שדי ליה and מצלי; this word means "push [the door]" in the former and "tilt/turn aside" [his eyes aside] in the latter.[42]) Between stories [5] and [8], however, we find two more stories about Mar 'Uqba—the redactor evidently received these three stories ([5]–[7]) as a unit and could not (or chose not to) separate them.

Story [6] like the first four stories, illustrates the principle "sufficient for his needs," and also justifies an extremely high level of "need." [43] Mar 'Uqba sees a poor man to whom he annually gives 400 *zuz* squandering old wine for its fragrant scent, but decides—counterintuitively to the audience's initial expectation—that since the man is accustomed to such luxury, he requires double this amount! Like stories [3] and [4], this story mentions "old wine" as the mark of expensive food and drink.[44] And it too raises a potential problem with the high standard, that it seems to allow for excessive self-indulgence. Whereas stories [1]–[4] and [6] focus on preserving the dignity of a poor person with monetary and material support (even at a surprisingly high level, such as running before him), stories [5] and [8] focus on preserving the dignity of the poor through the way charity is given (even to a surprisingly high degree, such as jumping into an oven).[45] Story [7], also about Mar 'Uqba, addresses a different

---

41. On this story, see Admiel Kosman, "Balash Talmudi," *Sifrut Aggadah* 2 (2004): 132–35; Kosman, "Al hashimush beshem hagibor ke'emtsa'i sifruti basippur hatalmudi beheqsherim migdariyim," in *Ve'eleh shemot: meḥḳarim be-otsar hashemot hayehudiyim*, vol. 4, ed. A. Demsky (Ramat-Gan: Bar-Ilan University Press, 2011), 51–80.

42. See Michael Sokoloff, *A Dictionary of Jewish Babylonian Aramaic of the Talmudic and Geonic Periods*, Publications of the Comprehensive Aramaic Lexicon Project (Ramat-Gan: Bar-Ilan University Press; Baltimore: Johns Hopkins University Press, 2002), 964–65.

43. There is no evidence for Arbiv's claim that the protagonist in [6] exemplifies the *baraita*'s case of one who has no money yet does not want to take charity. This man is happy to receive charity daily but at a certain point wants to know the identity of the benefactor. See too Halbertal's analysis of the story as a lesson to the son, who may be thinking of his inheritance ("Addressing the Needs," 99).

44. Note too that the anonymous gloss to story [3] paraphrases the words מפנק כולי האי ("pamper [himself] so much") from story [6], though to make the opposite point.

45. See Arbiv, "Charity and Honor," 93.

question about charity, the maximum that one should give so as not to risk impoverishing oneself. Story [8], besides addressing the issue of embarrassment, raises the problem of "deceivers" who take charity but do not need it, as the sage "turned aside his eyes," that is, he looked in a furtive and oblique manner, to make sure the recipients were legitimate. Story [9] then features poor deceivers and concludes with the rueful expression of gratitude for such swindlers.

The awkward order of these five stories [5]–[9] probably resulted from the integration of a preexistent grouping of three Mar ʿUqba stories with the other two, as noted above. Yassif offers numerous examples of the logical or theme-based order of stories in a cycle interrupted due to the incorporation of a preexistent unit, or because of "associative accumulation."[46] Indeed, several manuscripts begin the second Mar ʿUqba story ([6]) with "And also, he …," without providing the proper name "Mar ʿUqba" again, and the third Mar ʿUqba story ([7]) also uses the pronoun without the proper name, suggesting these two stories accompanied the first, otherwise we would not know the identity of the protagonist.[47] Indeed, it is likely that this unit accounts for why the compiler followed the first four stories with the two *baraitot* ([ג], [ד]). He wished to follow stories [1]–[4] with story [6], another story of "sufficient for his needs" (and also mentioning "old wine"), but this story came in a preexistent unit of three Mar ʿUqba stories, the first of which [5] deals with the issue of not embarrassing the poor.[48] So he inserted the two *baraitot*, which address this issue, as preparatory material before continuing the story-cycle with the Mar ʿUqba unit.[49] As noted, story [8] follows the Mar ʿUqba unit because it deals with the problem of not embarrassing the poor (like [5]). It also connects to the problem of potential deceivers raised in [6] by Mar ʿUqba's son, though in that story Mar ʿUqba ignores his son's concern. Story [9] then continues with a case of deceptive poor. So [6], [8], and [9] form a cohesive sequence of three stories evincing a concern for deception: potential deception is overridden due to the importance of charity [6]; potential deception requires caution when giving charity [8]; outright deception

46. Yassif, *Hebrew Folktale*, 234.

47. See n. 31.

48. Arbiv divides the unit into two stories by considering [7] as a continuation of [6]. However, the shift to a completely different time (Mar ʿUqba's death) and lack of direct connection between the plots suggest that we should count the second as an independent story, as does Kahane, "Problematizing Charity," in this volume.

49. It should be observed, however, that in story [5], ironically, the recipient does not care about the embarrassment of receiving charity and tries his best to see his benefactor. Mar ʿUqba attempts heroically to preserve the dignity of the poor man against his wishes! Nevertheless, the story, especially with the gloss, rehearses the idea at the root of the *baraitot* of preserving dignity. See Kosman, "Al hashimush beshem hagibor," 66–79; Arbiv, "Charity and Honor," 86.

occurs but its utility is recognized [9]. Story [7], as noted, interrupts this unit because it is the third story of the Mar 'Uqba unit. Though not immediately apparent, the structuring and ordering of the passage are not only understandable, but brilliant.[50]

The openings of stories [5] and [6] are very similar and also resemble the opening of [9]: all three have: ההוא עניא (בשבבותיה)[51] דהוה רגיל ... לשדורי/לשדי ליה ארבע (מאה) זוזי.[52] Stories [8] and [9] both mention the "deceivers" (רמאין / רמאי). Stories [6] and [9] share the phrase אתא(י) אמר(ה) ליה לא צריך אמר מאי חזית; and, while [6] tells of charity given "every eve of the Day of Atonement," [9] tells of charity given "every Friday evening."[53] These shared phrases suggest that the editors may have played a role in shaping the stories (see below).

As mentioned in passing above, I wish to consider whether we might view the entire collection of nine stories as one story-cycle. Yassif evidently considered the two *baraitot* too much of an interruption of non-narrative material. In addition, there are brief editorial comments to stories [5] and [7] that might be considered interruptions, as they not only gloss the stories but also adduce other traditions that appear elsewhere in the Bavli.[54] However, because the *baraitot* relate directly to the themes of the story-cycle, and even prepare the audience for the following stories, they need not be considered an interruption as much as preparatory material. And the comments to stories [5] and [7] are not much longer than or different from those to [2] and [3], which did not violate the story-cycle for Yassif, and these comments too contribute to the themes of the *sugya*, rather than digress to other matters.[55] That [6] is also about "sufficient for his needs," like [1]–[4], is another reason to consider the nine stories part of a single story-cycle. Moreover, [9] offers an elegant conclusion to the entire unit by featuring deceivers who take advantage of the charity precept, a potential problem that also applies to the opening stories of "sufficient for

---

50. Arbiv's summary ("Charity and Honor," 91) has much to recommend it. He suggests that the stories, until the final one, "create an unbearable burden for the" audience, as they give "the unambiguous message that an individual must do everything in his power to respond to the needs and requests of the poor. But the average individual, who does not always act this way, is liable to see himself as wicked. The final story comes to soften this message: it does not reduce the obligation but provides a moral escape."

51. In [5] MS Munich 95 omits בשבבותיה; in [6] MSS Munich 95 and Firkovitch 187 omit בשבבותיה; in [7] MSS Vatican 130 and Firkovitch 187 have בשבבותיה, while the other MSS omit.

52. See Arbiv, "Charity and Honor," 87.

53. In fact, the stories are so similar it is unclear why in the first the former are considered deserving and in the latter they are considered deceivers. See Tosafot, ad loc., s.v., *batlei*, and other commentators.

54. The first appears in b. Ber. 43b; b. Soṭah 10b; b. B. Meṣ. 59a (with minor variations); the second b. Ket. 50a; b. 'Arak. 28a; and is paralleled in y. Ket. 4:8, 28d.

55. The first explains the importance of not causing embarrassment, while the second adds the possibility of posthumous charity.

his needs"; yet the story concludes with a silver lining, mitigating the seriousness of this danger.[56] That all the stories are part of the same literary unit is essentially the conclusion of both Arbiv and Kahane, though they analyze the *sugya* more broadly and do not focus on the question of the story-cycle per se. Alternatively, if the *baraitot* are considered an interruption, then stories [5]–[9] should be considered an independent story-cycle about charity and added to the list.

Ultimately this is a question of definition—how one chooses to define the story-cycle, and how much other material, or what kind of other material (e.g., brief comment vs. independent *baraitot*) can interpose. It may be useful to distinguish types of story-cycles: (a) interrupted; (b) almost uninterrupted; (c) uninterrupted (though of course there would have to be some limits on the "interrupted" category). The larger story-cycle of nine stories can be classified as an "interrupted story-cycle," as the nine stories function analogously to other story-cycles in presenting different and varying aspects of a topic in a narrative mode and in a cohesive manner.[57] On the one hand, how does one preserve the honor/dignity of the poor when giving charity? How far does the standard of "sufficient for his needs" extend ([1]–[4], [6])? What are the dangers if one fails to provide charity at this standard ([3])? How should charity be given so as not to embarrass the recipient ([5], [8])? On the other hand, does the standard of "sufficient for his needs" impose too heavy a burden on the community ([4])?[58] Does it cater to self-indulgent excess ([3], [6])?[59] How do deceivers and swindlers impact this standard or the commandment to give charity in general ([6],[8],[9])? Are there preferred methods of giving to minimize the danger of unworthy recipients and deception ([8])? In addition, how much charity should one give ([7])? What is the punishment for refusing to give ([9])?[60]

It is also important to continue developing the taxonomy of interrup-

56. Cf. Arbiv's comment on the concluding story, above n. 50.

57. On the other hand, if we consider the last five stories an independent story-cycle, I would categorize both as "almost uninterrupted," given the comments identified above.

58. See Halbertal, "Addressing the Needs," 98: "And yet the reader is left with an open question. Should we learn from this story that reckless giving is recommended, since in matters of charity there is no set limit? … Or maybe such extravagant giving ought to be practiced only when an immediate, miraculous supply is provided, but caution should be the rule in the daily and common experience of shortage?"

59. And if we include the glosses—which the audience of the redacted Talmud would have considered together with the stories—the ambivalence is more pronounced. See Halbertal, "Addressing the Needs," 96–97, who does not distinguish the glosses from the stories and therefore is more conscious of the ambivalence.

60. See too Kahane, "Problematizing Charity," above, p. 71. Kahane suggests "a movement from stories which simply report the ostensibly meritorious acts of charity as performed by a number of rabbis towards a discernible trend at complicating and problematizing that giving." And see Halbertal, "Addressing the Needs," 99: "As in many such talmudic discussions, the issue is left unsettled. The Talmud does not provide a fixed point of view

tions I began above in the analysis of b. Ber. 18a–b. The interruptions here can be classified as follows: (i) Relatively prominent interruptions: the *baraitot* that prepare the audience for additional stories ([ג], [ד]). (ii) Brief explanatory comments clarifying aspects of a story ([2א], [3א], [5א]). The first of these contains Amoraic dicta of Rav Huna and Rav Ashi, unlike [3א] and the comments in b. Ber. 18a-b which were all anonymous. Presumably the compilers received this story (a *baraita*) together with these Amoraic explanations. Comment [5א] explains Mar 'Uqba's behavior based on the tradition attributed to various rabbis about the importance of not shaming others found in b. Ber. 43b and elsewhere. (iii) Opportunistic difficulties and responses that introduce other sources as putative contradictions and resolve the conflict ([7א]). This category resembles the previous one but imports a source from elsewhere and involves a dialectical exchange. In this case, R. Ilai's dictum is found in b. Ket. 50a and several other places. This type of interruption, typical of redactorial activity in halakhic *sugyot,* also functions to clarify an element of the story.

Sources of the Story-Cycle and the Role of the Redactors

This story-cycle bears some relationship to the story-cycle found in y. Peʾah 8:9, 21b, eight stories of "deceitful poor" (עניים לא הגונים).[61] Yassif comments briefly on this cycle and identifies three of the stories, though I am still not sure exactly which eight stories he considers in the cycle, as the Yerushalmi passage in fact contains twelve stories.[62] Even assuming Yassif means the first eight stories, the characterization as a cycle about "deceitful poor" is inaccurate, as only the first two are about poor swindlers, while the others deal with other aspects of charity.[63] The following is a brief outline of the cycle. (Hebrew/Aramaic texts and translations of several of the stories appear in Kahane's article above):

---

on the matter, but rather offers a spectrum of reactions that aims to exhibit the plethora of considerations relevant to assessing such practice."

61. #2 on Yassif's list (*Hebrew Collection*, 73). Part of the story-cycle (beginning with the third story) is paralleled in y. Šeqal. 5:5, 49b, with minor differences.

62. Yassif, *Hebrew Folktale*, 238.

63. This story-cycle deserves a reassessment together with other story-cycles in the Palestinian Talmud. In fact, the first nine stories deal with charity: although the beggar in [9] is not characterized as poor but as "afflicted with boils" (מוכה שחין), he requests charity and is obviously sick and wretched, as evident from his imminent death. Moreover, both this story and [2] involve the trope of the giver(s) promising to give "when I/we return" only to find the recipient dead. Stories [10] and [11] deal with the blind, another bodily affliction, though not with indigents per se, though in [11] the blind man is given charity. Story [12] returns to a different type of charity, to support Torah scholars—perhaps we are to assume they are poor—followed by a quotation from m. Peʾah 8:9, a fitting conclusion to the cycle. Many of these stories are discussed in the course of Gardner, *Origins of Organized Charity;* Yael Wilfand, *Poverty, Charity and the Image of the Poor*.

1. Shmuel and his father (deceitful poor). Conclusion about gratitude for deceivers.
2. R. Yoḥanan and Resh Laqish (deceitful poor).
3. Abba b. Ba's son Samuel saw a poor man eating meat and drinking wine. The sage instructed his son to give him more due to this need. (This story is about "sufficient for his needs," though this phrase does not appear.)

4a–b. R. Ḥama, father of R. Oshaya, and R. Zekharia, son-in-law of R. Levi, took funds from other sages as charity but were really distributing them to the poor.

5. R. Ḥinena b. Papa's method of distributing charity at night. He met a spirit/ghost.[64]
6. R. Yonah's method of distributing charity to the formerly wealthy to spare them embarrassment.
7. R. Ḥiyyah b. Adda tells of elderly people who only take charity between Rosh Hashanah and Yom Kippur.
8. Neḥemiah of Sikhnin gave money to a poor man, who requested a chicken, to buy a piece of meat. The man died.
9. Naḥum of Gamzu delayed giving charity to a man afflicted with boils, who then died, and Naḥum called sufferings upon himself as punishment.
10. R. Hoshaya the Elder and his son's blind teacher. (This story is about honor for the blind, not charity.)
11. R. Eliezer b. Ya'aqov showed honor to a blind man, and the people therefore gave him abundant charity.
12. R. Ḥama b. Ḥananiah and R. Hoshaya the Elder and discussion about donating money for synagogues or to support Torah study (a more complete version of the story is in the parallel at y. Šeqal. 5:5, 49b. The story itself is not about charity to the poor, but charity for these other purposes, so related to "standard" charity.)

The Bavli story-cycle exhibits parallels to some of this material.[65] BT [9] is a version of PT [1].[66] BT [6] is a version of PT [3].[67] BT [3] is very sim-

64. See Yassif, *Hebrew Folktale*, 238.

65. See the collection of Talmud parallels compiled by Bar Ilan University, https://www.biu.ac.il/js/tl/yerushalmi/files/Pe'ah.pdf, and *Yafe 'Eynaim* to b. Ket. 67b. And see David Assaf, "Let's Thank the Crooks: On the Shaping of Charity Stories in the World of the Sages" [Hebrew], in *Iturim: Studies in Honor of Moshe Krone* (Jerusalem: Torah Education Department of the World Zionist Organization, 1986), 248–62. And see Dov Kahane's article in this volume.

66. Although different Amoraim are the protagonists, both overhear the poor deliberating whether to use silver or gold vessels, and both conclude with gratitude for poor deceivers. See *Mar'eh hapenim*, ad loc.

67. Both feature a poor man enjoying fine wine, and the sage replying to the witness

ilar to PT [8], a man/sage named Neḥemiah who did not give a poor man the fine chicken he requested, resulting in the other's death.[68] Although they are not different versions of the same source, both BT [8] and PT [5] are about the sages' methods of giving charity.[69] In addition, parallels to BT [1–2] appear in the previous *sugya* in the PT, y. Pe᾿ah 8:8, 21a, though not in a story-cycle. All this material appears in connection with m. Pe᾿ah 8:7-9, which deals with communal charity institutions; the Bavli, lacking Tractate Pe'ah, placed it in connection with m. Ket. 6:5, charity for orphan marriages, as noted above. Thus of the nine stories in the Bavli, versions of five appear in the Yerushalmi (including the first two that originate in Tannaitic sources), though in two different passages. That BT [3], from the first group of four stories (= Yassif's cycle) and BT [9], from the second group of five, come from the same Yerushalmi story-cycle might be an additional reason to see the Bavli passage as one story-cycle of nine stories (though clearly this consideration is not decisive in itself).

The compiler of the Bavli story-cycle thus seems to have had access to some of the same sources as the editor of the Yerushalmi cycle, if not the cycle itself, together with other Babylonian sources (e.g., the three stories of Mar 'Uqba).[70] We should identify that compiler with the Stammaim; here, as is typical, they collected the disparate sources and juxtaposed them in the present order, thereby radically reworking their Yerushalmi materials. The introduction of the two *baraitot* to prepare for incorporating additional sources indicates a redactional hand at work. Whether we consider the two Bavli story-cycles independently or as part of one larger cycle, the traditions function as an aggadic *sugya* similar to other Bavli *sugyot* that the Stammaim created.[71]

Some of the interruptions are also signs of redactional processes. The anonymous comment [3א] clarifies a source in the question-and-answer style characteristic of the Stammaim. More significantly, the anonymous comments [5א] and [7א] import sources from elsewhere, and that of [7א] creates a contradiction, which is then immediately resolved, as is typical of the Stammaim. It is possible, however, that these comments were added by still later Stammaim after the initial story-cycle was constructed,

---

counterintuitively that this poor man requires even finer sustenance. The Bavli version has been integrated into the Mar 'Uqba unit.

68. As noted already by *Yafe 'Eynayim*, ad loc. See too Gray, "Formerly Wealthy Poor," 124; Wilfand, *Wheel That Overtakes Everyone*, 261–62; Arbiv, "Charity and Honor," 84; Kahane, above, p. 67.

69. PT [4a–b] can also be understood as stories about a method of giving charity, namely, through a third party.

70. See Gray, "Formerly Wealthy Poor," 123–27.

71. The Yerushalmi story-cycle has no interruptions—the stories follow directly one after another. Whether this is the case of Yerushalmi story-cycles in general is a question for further study.

in theory by an Amoraic compiler. Hence, they do not constitute clear evidence of the identity of the compiler of the story cycle. (The comments of Rav Huna and Rav Ashi [2א] pertain to that source alone, and the compiler integrated them into the cycle along with that story—the same applies to the Amoraic comments of Rava and Rav Pappa to the *baraitot* [ג],[ד]. So these comments do not necessarily point to redactional processes.) The phrases shared by groups of stories delineated above add to the evidence of Stammaitic compilation, as they probably reflect efforts by the compiler to create links between the sources in the process of integrating them and constructing the *sugya*.[72] Moreover, some of these phrases appear to have been changed from their parallels. Thus, the version of [2] in y. Pe'ah 8:8, 21a and t. Pe'ah 4:10 is about an "elder" (*zaqen*), not a "poor aristocrat" (*'ani ben tovim*) as in [1], and the verb is מעלין, not לקחו, and there are other changes too.[73] The version of [3] in the Bavli has language in common with [4], though the Yerushalmi parallel [PT 8] reads differently. Story [9] in the Bavli, as we have noted, shares language with [5] and [6], which does not appear in the Yerushalmi parallel [PT 1]. This standardized language is not a smoking gun, as some standardization is found in all rabbinic texts. But in the context of a *sugya* such as this it often indicates the reworking of sources by the Stammaim.

Conclusion

We can either identify a long story-cycle of nine stories, or two story-cycles of four and five stories; my preference is for the former. The stories should be classified under the category of the "thematic principle," engaging questions relating to the *mitzvah* of charity in general for the longer cycle of nine (and more specifically the standard "sufficient for his needs" for the first cycle of four, as Yassif noted). The cycle was compiled by the Stammaim, though they may have drawn on an earlier story-cycle in the Yerushalmi, or on the same sources. The story-cycle has some interruptions, but these serve the purposes and themes of the cycle, rather than digressing into other matters; the cycle therefore can be categorized as an "interrupted story-cycle." The story-cycle is associated with the proximate Mishnah and halakhic discussion, which mentions charity for the marriage of orphans so as to preserve their honor. While the story-cycle

---

72. See Arbiv, "Charity and Honor," 84–85, who sees the phrases in common as a structuring device that divides the composition into several pairs of stories.

73. See Lieberman, *Tosefta ki-feshuṭah,* 1:58 and 1:185–86. In Sifre Deut. 116 (p. 175) the protagonist is a "guest" (*ore'aḥ*), and Hillel "gives" (*natan*) rather than "takes." On the versions of these two stories, see Gray, "Formerly Wealthy Poor," 114–15, 123; Arbiv, "Charity and Honor," 80–84. As noted above, the major Bavli innovation is that Hillel himself runs before the poor.

also centers mostly on preserving honor and dignity while bestowing charity, it is not about orphans but about charity in general, and therefore it constitutes a self-contained unit.

Case Study 3: b. Šabb. 30b-31a. Four Stories. [Hillel the Elder][74]

[א] תנו רבנן לעולם יהא אדם ענוותן כהלל ואל יהא קפדן כשמאי

[1] מעשה בשני בני אדם שהמרו זה את זה אמרו כל מי שילך ויקניט את הלל יטול ארבע מאות זוז אמר אחד מהם אני אקניטנו

[1.1] אותו היום ערב שבת היה והלל חפף את ראשו הלך ועבר על פתח ביתו אמר מי כאן הלל מי כאן הלל נתעטף ויצא לקראתו אמר לו בני מה אתה מבקש אמר לו שאלה יש לי לשאול אמר לו שאל בני שאל מפני מה ראשיהן של בבליים סגלגלות אמר לו בני שאלה גדולה שאלת מפני שאין להם חיות פקחות

[2.1] הלך והמתין שעה אחת חזר ואמר מי כאן הלל מי כאן הלל נתעטף ויצא לקראתו אמר לו בני מה אתה מבקש אמר לו שאלה יש לי לשאול אמר לו שאל בני שאל מפני מה עיניהן של תרמודיין תרוטות אמר לו בני שאלה גדולה שאלת מפני שדרין בין החולות

[3.1] הלך והמתין שעה אחת חזר ואמר מי כאן הלל מי כאן הלל נתעטף ויצא לקראתו אמר לו בני מה אתה מבקש אמר לו שאלה יש לי לשאול אמר לו שאל בני שאל מפני מה רגליהם של אפרקיים רחבות אמר לו בני שאלה גדולה שאלת מפני שדרין בין בצעי המים אמר לו שאלות הרבה יש לי לשאול ומתירא אני שמא תכעוס נתעטף וישב לפניו אמר לו כל שאלות שיש לך לשאול שאל אמר לו אתה הוא הלל שקורין אותך נשיא ישראל אמר לו הן אמר לו אם אתה הוא לא ירבו כמותך בישראל אמר לו בני מפני מה אמר לו מפני שאבדתי על ידך ארבע מאות זוז אמר לו הוי זהיר ברוחך כדי הוא הלל שתאבד על ידו ארבע מאות זוז וארבע מאות זוז והלל לא יקפיד:

[2] תנו רבנן מעשה בנכרי אחד שבא לפני שמאי אמר לו כמה תורות יש לכם אמר לו שתים תורה שבכתב ותורה שבעל פה אמר לו שבכתב אני מאמינך ושבעל פה איני מאמינך גיירני על מנת שתלמדני תורה שבכתב גער בו והוציאו בנזיפה בא לפני הלל גייריה יומא קמא אמר ליה א״ב ג״ד למחר אפיך ליה אמר ליה והא אתמול לא אמרת לי הכי אמר לו לאו עלי דידי קא סמכת דעל פה נמי סמוך עלי

[3] שוב מעשה בנכרי אחד שבא לפני שמאי אמר לו גיירני על מנת שתלמדני כל התורה כולה כשאני עומד על רגל אחת דחפו באמת הבנין שבידו בא לפני הלל גייריה אמר לו דעלך סני לחברך לא תעביד זו היא כל התורה כולה ואידך פירושה הוא זיל גמור:

[4] שוב מעשה בנכרי אחד שהיה עובר אחורי בית המדרש ושמע קול סופר שהיה אומר {שמות כח} ואלה הבגדים אשר יעשו חושן ואפוד אמר הללו למי אמרו לו לכהן גדול אמר אותו נכרי בעצמו אלך ואתגייר בשביל שישימוני כהן גדול בא לפני שמאי אמר ליה גיירני על מנת שתשימני כהן גדול דחפו באמת הבנין שבידו בא לפני הלל גייריה אמר לו כלום מעמידין מלך אלא מי שיודע טכסיסי מלכות לך למוד טכסיסי מלכות הלך וקרא כיון שהגיע {במדבר א} והזר הקרב יומת אמר ליה מקרא זה על מי נאמר אמר לו אפילו על דוד מלך ישראל נשא אותו גר קל

74. #2 on the list above.

וחומר בעצמו ומה ישראל שנקראו בנים למקום ומתוך אהבה שאהבם קרא להם {שמות ד} בני
בכורי ישראל כתיב עליהם והזר הקרב יומת גר הקל שבא במקלו ובתרמילו על אחת כמה וכמה
בא לפני שמאי אמר לו כלום ראוי אני להיות כהן גדול והלא כתיב בתורה והזר הקרב יומת בא
לפני הלל אמר לו ענוותן הלל ינוחו לך ברכות על ראשך שהקרבתני תחת כנפי השכינה

[א'] לימים נזדווגו שלשתן למקום אחד אמרו קפדנותו של שמאי בקשה לטורדנו מן העולם
ענוותנותו של הלל קרבנו תחת כנפי השכינה

Yassif describes this story-cycle as four stories about Hillel the Elder and categorizes it in his third category, "the biographical cycle." That there are four stories in this unit is straightforward, though the number of stories in the larger passage is more complex and will be addressed below. Both of his other points are open to question. Amram Tropper understands the common element as how to handle annoying questions, though since they all feature Hillel, we might specify "Hillel's responses to annoying questions," assuming that is not too narrow.[75] As to the "biographical cycle," Yassif writes that "only the first story is clearly biographical, focusing on an event that actually took place during the protagonist's life." The other three stories, Yassif suggests, are "scholarly" tales (Yassif's scare quotes) of a "literary-learned nature"; because of the repeated literary pattern, Yassif speculates that the "author" or "compiler" composed these three tales on the basis of the first one, which he knew from "folk tradition."[76] It is not completely clear to me whether Yassif means to distinguish between a real biographical event and three fictional stories, or between a real folk tradition (albeit fictional) and three stories that emerged from the rabbinic academy. Both are false dichotomies, at least insofar as the present form of the stories, though Yassif's observations on the common literary pattern are insightful. I think these stories may be more profitably categorized along thematic lines as stories about the optimal character for a sage, and about humility (*'anavah*) in particular, as stated almost explicitly in the opening and closing lines. However, Tropper's description better suits the larger context, as we will see.

Yassif also makes the astute observation that the form of the story-cycle, a single biographical anecdote followed by a set of three stories with repeated phrases and structure, also is found in the four stories of Geviha b. Pesisa (b. Sanh. 91a, #21). This is part of his evidence for delineating the role of the compiler in creating the story-cycles.

At first glance it seems possible, at least theoretically, that the Bavli redactors/Stammaim found the story-cycle intact, in this very form, and

75. Amram Tropper, "On Condition That You Teach Me the Entire Torah while I Stand on One Foot: The Inception of a Story" [Hebrew], in *Between Babylonia and the Land of Israel: Studies in Honor of Isaiah M. Gafni*, ed. Geoffrey Herman et al. (Jerusalem: Zalman Shazar Center, 2016), 267–86.

76. Yassif, *Hebrew Folktale*, 218–19.

incorporated it unchanged in the Bavli. (As noted, Yassif does not clearly distinguish between the compiler/editor of a story-cycle and the compilers/redactors of the Bavli. And he says nothing of the relationship of the stories to parallel sources, further complicating the ambiguity.) Tropper, however, has compellingly argued that the Bavli story-cycle is a reworking of three stories found in 'Abot de Rabbi Nathan, and that the famous third story is a "collage" composed by a Bavli compiler through a process of literary reworking.[77] The following are the important observations and conclusions that emerge from his comprehensive study (which also provides manuscript variants and references to previous research):[78]

- The opening and closing lines, [א'] and [א], which enclose the unit in a self-contained envelope structure, contrast the patience of Hillel with the impatience of Shammai, but Shammai does not appear in the first story, indicating that this contextualization is the result of a later reworking (270–71).[79] The closing line is similar to the final line of the fourth story, which suggests it was formulated on the basis of that story (272).
- Stories 2–4 have a similar literary structure (as also observed by Yassif). Story 2 opens with תנו רבנן, as does the opening line of the first story, which indicates that the four stories divide into two units (1 and 2–4), which perhaps points to different provenances. Despite this terminology, the stories appear in no Tannaitic compilations and cannot be considered authentic *baraitot* (271).
- Stories 1, 2, and 4 appear in 'Abot R. Nat. B 29 and 'Abot R. Nat. A 15, in the order 1, 4, 2, with some minor variations but with such striking similarities to the Bavli indicating that they are versions of the same source.[80] Tropper provides a number of persuasive arguments to show that the Bavli has borrowed from 'Abot R. Nat. B 29 (which is earlier than 'Abot R. Nat. A 15), among them the absence of story 3 in 'Abot R. Nat. (277–79). (This helps explain the תנו רבנן, as the Bavli editor may have considered 'Abot R. Nat. to be a Tannaitic source.)
- The Bavli style is more uniform, with repeated phrases, and also contains clarifications and expansions, heightened drama, and omission of noncritical details, which all suggest that it is the later version (278–79).[81]
- Story 3 appears in a different version, and told of R. Akiva, in 'Abot R. Nat. B 26. The Bavli compilers transferred the story to Hillel for

---

77. Tropper, "On Condition That You Teach," 268.

78. Ibid.; for variants see 268–69 nn. 6–9. Other studies are discussed throughout the article.

79. See too Jeffrey L. Rubenstein, *Talmudic Stories: Narrative Art, Composition, and Culture* (Baltimore: Johns Hopkins University Press, 1999), 350 n. 37.

80. Ed. Schechter, 60–62. A different version of story 2 appears in Qoh. Rab. 7:8. See Tropper, "On Condition That You Teach," 279 n. 40, and the references there.

81. See the references in ibid., 276 nn. 28–30.

various reasons, including the fact that 'Abot R. Nat. B 26 includes sayings attributed to Hillel (280-84).

- The reworked version of story 3 combines elements from that story of R. Akiva of 'Abot R. Nat. B with phrases from story 4 in the Bavli (underlined in the text above).
- The reordering of the stories in the Bavli creates an increasing progression of the problematic nature of the questions and their degree of implausibility. The questions in the first story are legitimate, and only the time of the questioning is inappropriate.[82] The question in the second story is problematic and threatens the holiness of the Torah. The question in the third story is empirically impossible, and the question in the fourth absolutely impossible and absurd.

To these observations it should be added that the three stories (2–4), when considered in and of themselves, engage serious theological questions, perhaps displaced onto gentiles, to render them less threatening than if articulated by a rabbi or disciple.[83] Story 2 deals with the authority and trustworthiness of the oral Torah: what guarantees its divine origin and integrity? Story 3 inquires whether there is an essence of Torah, a most important element. Story 4 grapples with the privileges of lineage, especially priestly, and whether some Jews are more beloved by God than others.[84]

Tropper refers to a "Bavli composer" (מחבר בבלי) or simply "the Bavli" or the "Bavli editor" (עורך) as the creator of the unit (268, 276, 280). He does not take a position on whether this editor/compiler should be identified with the late Bavli editors or simply the Bavli editor of this unit, in theory an Amora. In my opinion, however, his excellent study leaves little doubt that the unit was composed by the redactors/Stammaim. The compositional processes, including the reworking of earlier sources, combination of disparate sources, stylistic uniformity, recycling and repetition of phrases, sophisticated literary artistry (yet with some incongruities that remain from the reworking process, such as absence of Shammai in the first story despite the opening)—all point to the Bavli redactors.

82. I am not sure whether the storytellers consider these questions legitimate. I would think they consider them silly, hence doubly provocative on account of both their lack of substance and the timing.

83. See Christine E. Hayes, "Displaced Self-Perceptions: The Deployment of Minim and Romans in B. Sanhedrin 90b–91a," in *Religious and Ethnic Communities in Later Roman Palestine*, ed. Hayim Lapin (Bethesda: University Press of Maryland, 1998), 249–89.

84. The convert realizes that even King David cannot serve as priest, and that he himself has entered under the wings of the divine presence. See Jeffrey L. Rubenstein, *Rabbinic Stories*, Classics of Western Spirituality (New York: Paulist, 2002), 182.

Context

The story-cycle has no connection to its Mishnaic context, m. Šabb. 2:5, which deals with extinguishing a lamp on the Sabbath for the benefit of the sick and for other good reasons, nor a connection to its halakhic context, the brief discussion of that Mishnah found in b. Šabb. 30a. It is included through the associative process of talmudic discourse. In the course of the halakhic discussion, a question related to the Mishnah is asked of R. Tanḥum, who begins his answer with a long aggadic discourse, the opening of which is an accusation that King Solomon (the putative author of Qohelet) contradicted himself with Qoh 4:2 and Qoh 9:4 (and also contradicted Ps 115:17, authored by his father, David).[85] R. Tanḥum then introduces various other traditions about Kings David and Solomon (in which Solomon also quotes Qoh 9:4 directly). Part of this aggadic section is very tangentially related to the halakhic material in that it deals with King David's death on the Sabbath and whether the corpse can be moved—hence a matter of Sabbath law and whether certain circumstances (David's corpse rotting in the sun) overrides certain Sabbath prohibitions. This passage ends with R. Tanḥum finally resolving the halakhic question posed to him. Because R. Tanḥum raised the issue of contradictions within Qohelet, the Talmud then segues to a report that the sages considered suppressing the book of Qohelet because of its internal contradictions. Several apparently contradictory verses are proposed and the contradictions resolved. The Talmud then notes that the sages also considered suppressing Proverbs because of its internal contradictions and adduces, as an example, the contradiction between Prov 26:4 ("Answer not a fool according to his folly, lest you also be like him") and Prov 26:5 ("Answer a fool according to his folly, lest he be wise in his own eyes.") This problem is resolved by distinguishing foolish statements about general matters (which should not be answered) from foolish statements about Torah (which should be answered). The distinction is exemplified first by two stories of R. Yehudah HaNasi and R. Ḥiyya and then by three stories of Rabban Gamaliel. The former two rabbis do not deign to answer foolish and insulting assertions but rather offer their interlocutors to drink, which they do and burst open (and presumably die). Rabban Gamaliel, on the other hand, responds to students who scoff at his incredible interpretations (e.g., "in the future a woman will give birth every day") by pointing out empirical precedents (e.g., a hen, which lays eggs every day.) There follows the story-cycle about Hillel.

Here is the text of these preceding stories (b. Šabb. 30b):

85. Scholars generally consider this discourse as an example of a talmudic *she'ilta* in the form typically encountered in Geonic sources.

[0א]<לא קשיא הא בדברי תורה הא במילי דעלמא> כי הא ד[86]

[1] ההוא דאתא לקמיה דרבי. אמר ליה: אשתך אשתי ובניך בני. אמר ליה: רצונך שתשתה כוס של יין? שתה ופקע.

[2] ההוא דאתא לקמיה דרבי חייא. אמר ליה: אמך אשתי ואתה בני. אמר ליה: רצונך שתשתה כוס של יין? שתה ופקע.

[2א] אמר רבי חייא: אהניא ליה צלותיה לרבי דלא לשווייה[87] ממזירא. דרבי כי הוה מצלי, אמר: יהי רצון מלפניך ה' אלהינו שתצילני היום מעזי פנים ומעזות פנים.

[2ב] בדברי תורה מאי היא?[88] כי הא ד

[3] יתיב רבן גמליאל וקא דריש: עתידה אשה שתלד בכל יום, שנאמר הרה ויולדת יחדיו. ליגלג עליו אותו תלמיד, אמר: אין כל חדש תחת השמש! אמר לו: בא ואראך דוגמתן בעולם הזה, נפק אחוי ליה תרנגולת.

[4] ותו יתיב רבן גמליאל וקא דריש: עתידים אילנות שמוציאין פירות בכל יום, שנאמר ונשא ענף ועשה פרי, מה ענף בכל יום - אף פרי בכל יום. ליגלג עליו אותו תלמיד, אמר: והכתיב אין כל חדש תחת השמש! אמר לו: בא ואראך דוגמתם בעולם הזה, נפק אחוי ליה צלף.[89]

[5] ותו יתיב רבן גמליאל וקא דריש: עתידה ארץ ישראל שתוציא גלוסקאות וכלי מילת, שנאמר יהי פסת בר בארץ. ליגלג עליו אותו תלמיד, ואמר: אין כל חדש תחת השמש! אמר ליה: בא ואראך דוגמתן בעולם הזה, נפק אחוי ליה כמיהין ופטריות, ואכלי מילת - נברא בר קורא.

The characterization of the story-cycle of Hillel as "a sage answers annoying/foolish questions" is thematically related to the topic of foolish statements posed to a sage of these five stories. It is possible that the editors meant to contrast Hillel's policy of politely entertaining all such questions/requests with the perspective of the previous stories, which rejects this policy by limiting it to "matters of Torah." Alternatively, the three questions of the converts, which have to do with matters of Torah, perhaps are meant to correlate with Rabban Gamaliel's policy of courteously responding to the student scoffers who doubt him, and thus to be consistent with the policy. In his edition of the Talmud, Adin Steinsaltz perceptively noted, "And while on the topic of the tolerance of the sages to

86. MSS Munich 95 and Vatican 127 omit הא ד; fragment T-S F2(2).11 omits כי הא ד.

87. Vilna reads בני ממזירי rendering the prayer about Rabbi's sons. However, the Venice and Italian printings, and MSS Vatican 127 and Friedberg read לישוייה ממזירא (with minor variations). MS M reads איהו ממזרין, which again seems to be about Rabbi himself, or about Rabbi and his family. See Raphael N. Rabbinowicz, *Diqduqei Soferim*, 16 vols. (Munich: Huber, 1868–1897), ad loc., n. 10, who explains that R. Ḥiyya means that the slander against Rabbi calls into question the lineage of Rabbi's children, not Rabbi himself, unlike the slander against R. Ḥiyya, whose own lineage is called into question. The advantage of this explanation is that the implied contrast connects the dictum to both stories, not only that of Rabbi.

88. MS Munich 95 omits היא.

89. Other minor variants are not relevant for my purposes here.

listen to trifling comments and remain silent, they brought other stories of this type, and concluded that 'One should always be patient like Hillel....'"[90] Certainly the presence of the preceding stories of Rabban Gamaliel expands the audience's purview on this issue.

Having come this far, we might consider all nine stories as a single story-cycle consisting of three subunits: the two stories of foolish-insulting charges and death, the three stories of Rabban Gamaliel, and the four stories of Hillel. The first two stories share a common pattern and differ only in minor respects, as do the three stories of Rabban Gamaliel (see the underlined portions), and as do the stories of Hillel, at least the concluding set of three, all of which point to the heavy redactional hand. The brief anonymous Aramaic comments ([א0], [ב2]) that introduce the two units are akin to those of our first example of b. Ber. 18a–b.[91] At first glance the comment at [א2] could be considered more of an "interruption," as it appears to be an Amoraic dictum reflecting on the story. Upon closer scrutiny, however, this comment enhances the first story, and possibly both stories,[92] by providing a prologue, informing us that, prior to the events of the story proper, Rabbi had prayed that his sons not be "insolent," understood by R. Ḥiyya as equivalent to being *mamzerim* (who are associated with insolence).[93] In other words, Rabbi's successful dispensing of the man, thus exposing the man's claim as baseless, was the fulfillment of this earlier prayer. Although R. Ḥiyya also offers a kind of non-narrative comment by explaining that this event was the fruition of that prayer, we remain firmly within the narrative world. Hence I do not think this comment need be considered an interruption at all.

Yassif probably ignored these stories because they are not "folkish"; the first two are brief, of low narrativity and concern rabbinic policies; the three of Rabban Gamaliel are set in the academy, also of low narrativity, and center on rabbinic exegesis. Nevertheless, all five qualify as stories by just about any definition, so they should not be overlooked.[94] Minimally,

---

90. *Talmud Bavli, Masekhet Shabbat,* ed. and trans. Adin Steinsaltz (Jerusalem: Israel Institute for Talmudic Publications, 1989), 1:125.

91. Both comments involve the technical term כי הא ד to illustrate the two halves of the Bavli distinction that resolves the contradiction of the previous discussion, which I have set in the angled brackets. We might even consider the word ותו, that introduces stories 4 and 5, as a kind of introductory word, though it is not the typical technical terminology of the Bavli as in the introductory comments [א0] and [ב2].

92. See n. 87.

93. See Rashi ad loc.

94. Yassif may have been influenced by the Vilna printing placing a ":" before the first story of Hillel, which often signifies a *pisqa* or the beginning of a new *sugya.* The colon appears in the first complete printing too (Venice, 1520), but not in MSS Munich 95, Friedberg, or the Geniza fragment T-S F2(2).8, though all three leave an empty space (*vacat*) before continuing with the Hillel stories. MS Vatican 127, however, has neither a colon nor a space. The printers apparently (mistakenly) believed that the Hillel traditions have no connection

we have a story-cycle of seven stories, as there is no interruption between the stories of Rabban Gamaliel and those of Hillel. However, since the stories of Rabban Gamaliel essentially form a unit with the two previous stories, as exemplifications of the twin directives of Prov 26:4–5, and because the interruptions are minimal, we should recognize a story-cycle of nine. Moreover, the cycle displays a high degree of thematic unity in delineating situations of sages confronted by annoying utterances, varying the types of protagonists (troublemakers, students, potential converts), locations (the academy, the sage's own house), the nature of the utterances (insulting slander, scoffing disbelief, provocative questions, unreasonable demands), and the sages' responses (punishment for the insult, evidence against the disbelief, patient answer, didactic lesson).

In sum, I would categorize this story-cycle as "almost uninterrupted." The only real interruption, [ב2], is a brief introductory phrase, which parallels the introductory phrase of the whole cycle, [א0]. It informs the audience why the following stories of Rabban Gamaliel are introduced and focuses attention on the salient aspect of the story, viz., answering foolish questions that relate to matters of Torah. In terms of our developing taxonomy of interruptions, it can be categorized as an "introductory or transition phrase," similar to those of b. Ber. 18a. Both [א0] and [ב2] are clearly the work of the redactors and, together with Tropper's observations of the Bavli's reworking of the Hillel unit, suggests that the Stammaim compiled this story-cycle.

It is noteworthy that the lack of a substantive connection to the halakhic context renders the cycle more of a self-contained unit, a freestanding collection of stories, hence a transition to the medieval narrative compilations.

Case Study 4: b. Šabb. 156b. Three Stories. [Righteousness saves from death]

[1][א] ומדשמואל נמי אין מזל לישראל

[ב] דשמואל ואבלט כי הוו יתבי ואזלי הנך אינשי לאגמא א׳ל אבלט לשמואל האי גברא אזיל ולא אתי וטריק ליה חיויא ומאית

[ג]א׳ל שמואל אי ברישראל הוא אזיל ואתי

[ד] אדיתבי קא עסקי ביה אזי[ל] ואתא קם אבלט שדייה לטוניה אשכח ביה חיויא דפסיק ושאדי בתרתי גובי

with the previous material and were presumably included simply due to the fact that m. Šabb. 2:5 deals with the Sabbath, and the provocateur approaches Hillel on the Sabbath eve in the first story, or because some of the previous mishnahs also deal with preparations for lighting the Sabbath lamps, which will take place on the Sabbath eve, or possibly because the previous aggadic traditions mention the Sabbath, as detailed above.

[ה] א״ל שמואל מה עבדת א״ל כל יומא הוינא מרמינן ריפתא בהדי הדדי ואכלינן והאידנא הוה איכא חד גבן דלא הוה ליה ריפתא בהדיה והוה מכסיף אמינא לחבראי אנא קאימנא ומרמינא ליה ריפתא כי מטאי לגביה שוי נפשאי כמאן דשקלי מיניה כי היכי דלא ליכסיף

[ו] א״ל מצוה קא עבדת ואתצלת נפק שמואל לבי מדרשא ודרש וצדקה תציל ממות ולא ממיתה משונ׳ אלא אפי׳ ממית׳ עצמה

[2][א] ומדר׳ עקיבא נמי אין מזל לישראל

[ב] דר׳ עקיבא הויא ליה ברתא אמרו ליה כלדאי ההוא יומא דעיילא לבי גנאנה טריק לה חויא ומתה

[ג] הוה דאיג עלה דמילתא טובא

[ד] ההוא יומא דעיילה שקלה למכבנתא דעציתה בביזעא איתרמי לה עיילה בעיינא דחויא לצפרא כי קא שקלה ליה הוה קא סריך ואתי חיויא בתרה

[ה] אמ׳ לה אבוה מה עבדת אמרה ליה בפניא אתא ענייא קרא אבב׳ והוו טרידי כולי עלמא בסעודתא וליכא דשמעיה קמית אנא שקלית ואמרי׳ הדין דסתאנא דיהביתו לי הבו ניהליה

[ו] א״ל מצוה קא עבדת ואתצלת נפק ר׳ עקיבא לבי מדרשא ודרש וצדקה תציל ממות ולא ממיתה משונה אלא ממיתה עצמה

[3][א] ומדרב נחמן בר יצחק נמי אין מזל לישראל

[ב] דאימיה דרב נחמן בר יצחק אמרו לה כלדאי בריך גנבא יהא

[ג] לא שבקתיה גלויי רישיה אמרה ליה כסי רישך כי היכי [ד]ליהוי עלך אימתא דשמיא ובעי רחמי לא הוה ידע אמאי קאמרה ליה

[ד] יומא חד הוה קא גריס ויתיב תותי דיקלא נפל גלימא מעילוי רישיה דלי עייניה חזייה לדיקלא אלמיה יצר הרע סליק פסקיה לקיבורא בשיניה

Yassif summarizes this cycle as "Righteousness saves from death" (צדקה תציל ממות)[95] and places it in his fourth category of story-cycle types: "The Biblical Verse as a Unifying Principle."[96] Both of these points require revision.[97] Indeed, Yassif himself noted,

> The first two tales in the cycle of BT *Shabbat* suit the verse "righteousness delivers from death." … The third tale, however, tells of the woman whose son, according to the astrologers' predictions, would be a thief.… This tale has nothing to do with the verse, and hence the compiler chose not to conclude this tale with it. Why then was the third tale included here, if it did not fit the topic of the cycle? The answer lies in the principle of "associative accumulation," one of the main unifying means in rabbinic story cycles.[98]

95. Cycle #4 on the list above.

96. Yassif, *Hebrew Folktale*, 223–25.

97. Interestingly, in the English translation, the translator first translated the verse, "Charity delivers from death" (ibid., 223), but subsequently—and more accurately—"righteousness delivers from death" (224). Apparently she realized from Yassif's summary that the good deed of the first story was not charity and therefore altered the translation.

98. Ibid., 224–25.

But this analysis is hard to accept, as the cycle comprises but three stories total, the minimum for a cycle, hence there should be a common unifying principle to all three. By "associative accumulation" Yassif means that the stories share some common element (e.g., another story about the same sage), even if it has nothing to do with the subject of the story-cycle, and was incorporated on that basis. Yet Yassif does not identify the common element. But clearly that comment element is astrology, which in fact points to the real issue of the story-cycle.

All three stories are about astrology, as the compiler of the *sugya* explicitly informs us by introducing each of the three stories with the phrase: "And from [the case of] Shmuel/R. Akiva/Rav Naḥman b. Yitsḥaq too [we learn that] 'Israel has no *mazal* (אין מזל לישראל).'" Moreover, these three stories conclude a *sugya* of seven traditions about astrology that grapples with whether or not astrology exclusively determines the fate of Jews, expressed in the Bavli with the shorthand אין מזל לישראל / ויש מזל לישראל, as I have shown elsewhere.[99] The story-cycle should not be categorized under "The Biblical Verse as Unifying Principle" but under the "thematic principle," namely, astrology.

The three stories conclude this tightly structured seven-tradition *sugya* about astrology, which is important, as it demonstrates not only their shared topic but also (together with other considerations) the role of the redactors/Stammaim in constructing the cycle.[100] The larger passage consists of three major units. The first unit argues for the power of astrological influences, offering two different schemas. The second unit offers two exegetical traditions which argue that "Israel has no *mazal*," while the third unit, our story-cycle of three stories, makes this same claim. Although it does not use the expression itself, the first unit obviously assumes "Israel has a *mazal*." The second unit reveals that this point is the subject of an Amoraic debate by introducing the opinions that contravene those of the first unit. The stories in the third unit are unanimous that "Israel has no *mazal*."[101]

The three stories exhibit a common structure, although the third story is abbreviated:

A. An introductory line states the theme of the story.
B. Astrologer(s) predict(s) that an unfortunate event will befall a Jew.
C. A Jew reacts to the prediction.
D. The event fails to occur as predicted.[102]

---

99. Jeffrey L. Rubenstein, "Talmudic Astrology: Bavli Šabbat 156a–b," *HUCA* 78 (2007): 109–48.

100. See ibid., 112–18, for translation and structure of the entire unit.

101. This paragraph is based on my article referenced in n. 99 above.

102. In the third story Rav Naḥman b. Yitsḥaq does become a thief as predicted. Appar-

E. The sage questions the protagonist, who responds with the description of the meritorious deed; the sage explains why s/he was saved.
F. The sage then expounds (*darash*) that lesson in midrashic form, that is, based on Scripture.

This pattern suggests that the redactors reworked the stories, as it is unlikely they collected three disparate stories that happened to feature a common structure. The introductory lines, sections A, not part of the story, are typical of the Bavli redactors. A different version of the first story appears in y. Šabb. 6:9, 8d, which may have been reworked by the redactors for their present purposes.[103] In addition, Shamma Friedman has shown that the text of the story seems to have continued to develop in Babylonia, and an earlier form, somewhat closer to that of the Yerushalmi, is preserved in one Geniza fragment.[104] That the final exposition (F) exhibits some textual variants and does not read well also suggests the redactors adapted it from another source.[105]

That the stories share a number of repetitions and features, together with variations of the same elements, suggests a deliberate process of composition and reworking.[106] I have noted the following variations:

> Sections A adduce the cases of three rabbis, the first an unrelated party to the subject of the prediction (Shmuel); the second a close relative (Akiva); the third the party himself (Rav Nahman b. Yitsḥaq). We shift from a father and daughter in the second story to a mother and son in the third. Sections B vary the nature of the unfortunate event from an imminent death that very day, to a distant death on a defined day sometime in the

---

ently, the compiler holds that he was free of planetary influence as long as he covered his head, which demonstrates that astrology is not determinative of fate.

103. See Jeffrey L. Rubenstein, *The Culture of the Babylonian Talmud* (Baltimore: Johns Hopkins University Press, 2003), 68–70

104. Shamma Friedman, "Anaf-nosah hadash bemasekhet Shabbat batalmud habavli," *Oqimta* 1 (2013): 147–76. Cf. Rubenstein, "Talmudic Astrology," 147–48.

105. See Rubenstein, "Talmudic Astrology," 138, n. 92; Friedman, "Anaf-nosah hadash," 161–62. What does it mean to be saved from "death itself"?

106. Friedman argues that the story of R. Akiva's daughter was adapted from the story of Shmuel and Avlat ("Anaf-nosah hadash," 162–63). On the variation of elements, see Rubenstein, "Talmudic Astrology," 136: "The first two stories share the phrase 'a snake will bite him/her and s/he will die' about the predicted disaster (B). The second and third stories share the phrase 'astrologers said to him/her' about the forecasters of the disaster, in that same section (B). The first and third stories both use 'cut' in the description of the event in sections D: the snake is cut (*paseeq*) into two halves, and Rav Nahman b. Yitsḥaq cut off (*pasqeih*) the date cluster. So we have linguistic ties between each pair of stories. Moreover, the man tells his companions that he will throw (*marmina*) the bread into the basket in the first story, and regarding R. Akiva's daughter 'it happened (*itrami*) for her' that the wedding-crown pierced the snake's eye, from the same root (sections D). In the first story the man recounts that he pretended to take (*shaqli*) bread from the man; in the second story the daughter recounts that she took (*shaqlit*) the portion of food given to her (sections E)."

> future, to crime and descent into a criminal life (thus the omission of sections E and F in story 3, as the verse deals with death).... Sections C vary the reactions from rejection (Shmuel), to inaction, perhaps fatalistic acceptance (Akiva), to an effort to avoid the fate (the mother). In sections D the prediction fails to occur through the inadvertent actions of the heroes of the first two stories, but through the constant vigilance of the character (and his mother) in the third story (always keeping his head covered). Yet it is through an inadvertent event (the head covering happens to fall off) that the prediction comes true. This variation, to a certain extent, is a product of the diverse predictions of sections B. Head coverings appear in both the second and third stories, though they function in almost opposite ways: the removal of a head covering (the wedding crown) obviates the predicted outcome in the second story, whereas the removal of the head covering causes the predicted outcome in the third (sections D). Also in sections D the meritorious deed shifts from 'commandments between man and his fellow' in the first two stories to 'commandments between man and God' in the third. While the deeds in the first two stories vary from preventing humiliation to almsgiving, both involve poor men and food. Whereas in the first story the hero *pretends* to *take* food from the poor man, in the second the heroine *actually gives* food to the supplicant.[107]

These similarities and variations are what make the stories here function as a superb example of a story-cycle, multiplying cases, situations, characters, and other narrative elements to achieve a thorough engagement with the topic, the way astrology influences life and its limitations. The story-cycle was created by the Bavli redactors, reworking one story that originated in the Yerushalmi, and likely generating the other two stories on its basis.[108]

Another interesting structural feature that may be indicative of the Bavli redactors is the two complete stories followed by an abbreviated third story. A similar structure characterizes the three stories in the Geviha b. Pesisa unit (b. Sanh. 91a, #21) and a subunit of three stories in the long story-cycle of "stories of destruction" (b. Giṭ. 5b–58a, #14), as noted above.[109]

This story-cycle too can be categorized as "almost uninterrupted." The only interruptions are the brief redactional comments that introduce each story, which function to focus attention on astrology (sections A). As in the first and third case studies, such editorial comments almost explicitly state the topic of the story-cycle and thus provide valuable direction to the audience. In terms of our taxonomy of interruptions, they are "intro-

---

107. Rubenstein, "Talmudic Astrology," 136-37.

108. See n. 99.

109. On the three stories of destruction, see Pinḥas Mandel, "The Tales of the Destruction of the Temple: Between the Land of Israel and Babylonia" [Hebrew], in *Israel-Diaspora Relations in the Second Temple and Talmudic Periods*, ed. Isaiah Gafni (Jerusalem: Zalman Shazar Center, 2004), 141–58.

ductory or transitional phrases" that alert the audience why the story is introduced and focus attention on the salient aspect.

Context

The entire unit on astrology bears no relation to its halakhic context. It appears in chapter 24 of Tractate Shabbat, which deals with feeding animals. The *sugya* quotes a pertinent tradition about kneading bran with the introductory phrase, "It was written in the notebook of Zeira." There follows a short discussion and then a tradition about an unrelated matter of Sabbath law with a similar introductory phrase, "It was written in the notebook of Levi ..." Immediately thereafter comes the opening phrase of our unit, "It was written in the notebook of R. Yehoshua b. Levi ..." followed by his astrological schema. Thus the astrology unit is contextualized in this chapter of this tractate purely for formal reasons, the parallel introductory formulae.[110]

This is significant because it indicates a step in the freeing of narratives from the documentary contexts of classical rabbinic literature to their new contexts in the Middle Ages, including collections of stories, as in *Hibbur Yafe meha-Yeshua*, as noted in the introduction. Here the story-cycle is part of a self-contained and independent unit, a kind of topical essay on astrology, and not a part of the talmudic or halakhic context, except insofar as it is perforce included in the text.

Case Study 5: b. 'Abod. Zar. 10a–11a. Three Stories. [Righteous gentiles]

A story-cycle not discussed by Yassif appears in b. 'Abod. Zar. 10a–11a, three (or more) stories of righteous gentiles: Antoninus, Qetia b. Shalom, and Onqelos b. Qalonymos. These gentiles either converted (Qetia, Onqelos) or joined the Jewish people in body and spirit (Antoninus; see below). Alyssa Gray published a superb analysis of this entire passage, and the following is indebted to her study.[111]

---

110. It should be noted, however, that the passage mentions the astrological fate of those born on each day of the *shabta* (week) and also those born on the Sabbath itself. Yet this does not seem to be the reason for its inclusion in Tractate Shabbat. And even if the mention of Shabbat is relevant to its contextualization, why in this chapter and not elsewhere?

111. Alyssa Gray, "The Power Conferred by Distance from Power: Redaction and Meaning in b. AZ 10a-11a," in *Creation and Composition: The Contribution of the Bavli Redactors (Stammaim) to the Aggada*, ed. Jeffrey L. Rubenstein (Tübingen: Mohr Siebeck, 2005), 23–69. See too Ofra Meir, *Rabbi Judah the Patriarch: Palestinian and Babylonian Portrait of a Leader* [Hebrew] (Tel-Aviv: Hakibbutz Hameuchad, 1999): 277–91; Meir, "Ha-terumah hahistorit shel aggadot hazal: le'or aggadot Rabbi ve'antoninos," *Mahanayim* 7 (1994): 8–25; Daniel Boyarin, "Homotopia:

[1]

[1.1] א״ל אנטונינוס לרבי: בעינא דימלוך אסוירוס ברי תחותי ותתעביד טבריא קלניא, ואי אימא להו חדא - עבדי, תרי - לא עבדי. אייתי גברא ארכביה אחבריה ויהב ליה יונה לעילאי [בידיה], וא״ל לתתאה: אימר לעילא דלמפרח מן ידיה יונה. אמר, שמע מינה הכי קאמר לי:[112] את בעי מינייהו דאסוירוס ברי ימלוך תחותי, ואימא ליה לאסוירוס דתעביד טבריא קלניא.

[2.1] א״ל: מצערין לי חשובי [רומאי]. מעייל ליה לגינא, כל יומא עקר ליה פוגלא ממשרא קמיה. אמר, ש״מ הכי קאמר לי: את קטול חד חד מינייהו, ולא תתגרה בהו בכולהו.
[2.1א] ולימא ליה מימר [בהדיא]! אמר: שמעי (בי) חשובי רומי ומצערו ליה. ולימא ליה בלחש! משום דכתיב: כי עוף השמים יוליך את הקול.

[3.1] הוה ליה ההוא ברתא דשמה גירא, קעבדה איסורא, שדר ליה גרגירא, שדר ליה כוסברתא; שדר ליה כרתי, שלח ליה חסא.

[4.1] כל יומא הוה שדר ליה דהבא פריכא במטראתא וחיטי אפומייהו, אמר להו: אמטיו חיטי לרבי. אמר [ליה רבי]: לא צריכנא, אית לי טובא. אמר: ליהוו למאן דבתרך דיהבי לבתראי דאתו בתרך, ודאתי מינייהו ניפוק עלייהו.

[5.1] ה״ל ההיא נקרתא דהוה עיילא מביתיה לבית רבי,כל יומא הוה מייתי תרי עבדי, חד קטליה אבבא דבי רבי וחד קטליה אבבא דביתיה, א״ל: בעידנא דאתינא לא נשכח גבר קמך.

[6.1] יומא חד אשכחיה לר׳ חנינא בר חמא דהוה יתיב, אמר: לא אמינא לך בעידנא דאתינא לא נשכח גבר קמך? א״ל: לית דין בר איניש. א״ל: (אימא) [לימא] ליה לההוא עבדא דגני אבבא דקאים וליתי. אזל ר׳ חנינא בר חמא אשכחיה דהוה קטיל, אמר: היכי אעביד? אי איזיל ואימא ליה דקטיל, אין משיבין על הקלקלה! אשבקיה ואיזיל, קא מזלזלינן במלכותא! בעא רחמי עליה ואחייה ושדריה. אמר: ידענא, וודאי דאית בכו מחיה מתים, מיהו בעידנא דאתינא לא נשכח איניש קמך.

[7.1] כל יומא הוה משמש לרבי, מאכיל ליה, משקי ליה, כי הוה בעי רבי למיסק לפוריא הוה גחין קמי פוריא, א״ל: סק עילואי לפורייך, אמר: לאו אורח ארעא לזלזולי במלכותא כולי האי, אמר: מי ישימני מצע תחתיך לעולם הבא. א״ל: אתינא לעלמא דאתי? א״ל: אין. א״ל, והכתיב: לא יהיה שריד לבית עשו! בעושה מעשה עשו.

[7.1א] תניא נמי הכי: לא יהיה שריד לבית עשו - יכול לכל? ת״ל: לבית עשו, בעושה מעשה עשו.[113]

א״ל, והכתיב: שמה אדום מלכיה וכל נשיאיה! א״ל: מלכיה - ולא כל מלכיה, כל נשיאיה ולא כל שריה.[114]

The Feminized Jewish Man and the Lives of Women in Late Antiquity," *differences: A Journal of Feminist Cultural Studies* 7 (1995): 41–71; Mira Beth Wasserman, "The Humanity of the Talmud: Reading for Ethics in Bavli 'Avodah Zara" (PhD diss., University of California at Berkeley, 2014), 73–75 (on the Qetiah story); Wasserman, *Jews, Gentiles, and Other Animals: The Talmud after the Humanities*, Divinations (Philadelphia: University of Pennsylvania Press, 2017), 57–60; Shlomo Zuckier, "Cutting a Peace: The Story of Ketiah Bar Shalom," 25 January 2018; https://www.thelehrhaus.com/scholarship/cutting-a-peace-the-story-of-ketiah-bar-shalom/.

112. This line is missing in MS Munich.

113. MS Paris omits this section.

114. MSS Munich and JTS omit the "he said to him" between what I have labeled as [7.1א] and [7.1ב] in both the question and response (although they are found in the Pessaro

[7.1ב] תניא נמי הכי: מלכיה - ולא כל מלכיה, כל נשיאיה - ולא כל שריה; מלכיה ולא כל מלכיה - פרט לאנטונינוס בן אסוירוס, כל נשיאיה ולא כל שריה - פרט לקטיעה בר שלום.[115]

[7.1ג] קטיעה בר שלום מאי (הוי) [היא]?

[2] דההוא קיסרא דהוה סני ליהודאי, אמר להו לחשיבי דמלכותא: מי שעלה לו נימא ברגלו, יקטענה ויחיה או יניחנה ויצטער? אמרו לו: יקטענה ויחיה. אמר להו קטיעה בר שלום: חדא, דלא יכלת להו לכולהו, דכתיב: כי כארבע רוחות השמים פרשתי אתכם, מאי קאמר? אלימא דבדרתהון בד׳ רוחות, האי כארבע רוחות, לארבע רוחות מבעי ליה! אלא כשם שא״א לעולם בלא רוחות, כך א״א לעולם בלא ישראל; ועוד, קרו לך מלכותא קטיעה. א״ל: מימר שפיר קאמרת, מיהו כל דזכי (מלכא): [למלכא] שדו ליה לקמוניא חלילא. כד הוה נקטין ליה ואזלין, אמרה ליה ההיא מטרוניתא: ווי ליה לאילפא דאזלא בלא מכסא! נפל על רישא דעורלתיה קטעה, אמר: יהבית מכסי חלפית ועברית. כי קא שדו ליה, אמר: כל נכסאי לר״ע וחביריו. יצא ר״ע ודרש: והיה לאהרן ולבניו - מחצה לאהרן ומחצה לבניו. יצתה בת קול ואמרה: קטיעה בר שלום מזומן לחיי העוה״ב. בכה רבי ואמר: יש קונה עולמו בשעה אחת, ויש קונה עולמו בכמה שנים.

[2א] אנטונינוס שמשיה לרבי; אדרכן[116] שמשיה לרב. כי שכיב אנטונינוס, א״ר: נתפרדה חבילה; כי שכיב אדרכן, אמר רב נתפרדה חבילה.

[3] אונקלוס בר קלונימוס[117] איגייר. שדר קיסר גונדא דרומאי אבתריה, משכינהו בקראי, איגיור. הדר שדר גונדא דרומאי [אחרינא] אבתריה, אמר להו: לא תימרו ליה ולא מידי. כי הוו שקלו ואזלו, אמר להו, אימא לכו מילתא בעלמא: ניפיורא נקט נורא קמי פיפיורא, פיפיורא לדוכסא, דוכסא להגמונא, הגמונא לקומא, קומא מי נקט נורא מקמי אינשי? אמרי ליה: לא. אמר להו: הקדוש ברוך הוא נקט נורא קמי ישראל, דכתיב: וה׳ הולך לפניהם יומם וגו׳, איגיור [כולהו]. הדר שדר גונדא אחרינא אבתריה, אמר להו: לא תשתעו מידי בהדיה. כי נקטי ליה ואזלי, חזא מזוזתא [דמנחא אפתחא], אותיב ידיה עלה ואמר להו: מאי האי? אמרו ליה: אימא לן את. אמר להו: מנהגו של עולם, מלך בשר ודם יושב מבפנים ועבדיו משמרים אותו מבחוץ, ואילו הקדוש ברוך הוא, עבדיו מבפנים והוא משמרן מבחוץ, שנאמר: ה׳ ישמר צאתך ובואך מעתה ועד עולם, איגיור. תו לא שדר בתריה.

[3א] ויאמר ה׳ לה שני גוים בבטנך - אמר רב יהודה אמר רב: אל תקרי גוים אלא גיים, זה אנטונינוס ורבי, שלא פסקו מעל שולחנם לא חזרת ולא קישות ולא צנון לא בימות החמה ולא בימות הגשמים, דאמר מר: צנון מחתך אוכל, חזרת מהפך מאכל, קישות מרחיב מעיים.

---

printing. MS Paris has "he said to him" before the question, not the response.) If so, then the line can be read as part of the anonymous discourse and would make for a longer "interruption." However, often "he said to him" is understood, and appears in some manuscripts and not others, so the omission is not probative. Note that Rabbi's response also lacks the "he said to him" in the previous line. MSS Munich and JTS read שמה אדום מלכיה ושריה מלכיה - ולא כל מלכיה שריה - ולא כל שריה, which was emended in the printings to conform to Obad 1:18. The Pessaro printing has: שמה אדום מלכיה ושריה וכל נשיאיה. On these variants, see Shaye J. D. Cohen, "The Conversion of Antoninus," in *The Talmud Yerushalmi and Graeco-Roman Culture*, vol. 1, ed. Peter Schäfer (Tübingen: Mohr-Siebeck, 1998), 141-171, here 165–66.

115. MSS JTS and Paris add דלאו שריה הוא דהא איגייר. Clearly this is a nonhalakhic type of conversion and caused the commentaries difficulties, for which reason the line may have been removed in the printings.

116. MS JTS reads ארטבן; MS Paris reads ארדבן.

117. MSS Munich, JTS, Paris read "Qaloniqos."

The story-cycle consists of three main units: stories of Rabbi Yehudah HaNasi and Antoninus [1], the story of Qetia b. Shalom [2], and the story of Onqelos b. Qalonymos [3]. These units can be considered three stories, with the saga of Rabbi and Antoninus including many episodes. Alternatively the first unit can be subdivided in several ways, such as into the seven brief stories indicated above, which would make for a numerically larger story-cycle. Or it can be divided into three subunits: [1.1]–[2.1] face-to-face political consultation; [3.1]–[4.1] interactions at a distance (both episodes contain the phrase שדר ליה); [5.1]–[7.1]; Antoninus's secret visits through the tunnel. Another possible division, following Gray, is: [1.1]-[3.1] political advice; [4.1]–[6.1] what Antoninus did "every day"; [7.1] the conversation about the world to come.[118] (On unit [א2], see below).

Admittedly, the story-cycle is interrupted by brief, non-narrative sections, and Yassif may have rejected it for this reason. But these interruptions are minor, comparable to some interruptions found in Yassif's story-cycles, and serve the purposes of the story-cycle. [א2.1] is a brief anonymous interchange addressing an obvious difficulty and perhaps even contributing to the story by implying that the Roman notables, or others who might inform the Roman notables, were present or sufficiently close to observe. (In our taxonomy, it is a "brief explanatory comment.") [א7.1] is a brief gloss, a pseudo-*baraita* that supports Rabbi's congenial response. (This pseudo-*baraita* is missing in MS Paris, which would eliminate this problem of an interruption completely. I would categorize this interruption as a "minor digression," that is, a digression from the narrative, though in content it supports the story's contention.) [ב7.1], another pseudo-*baraita,* provides support for Rabbi's next response, and at the same time brilliantly provides a segue to the next story by detailing the identities of the exceptions with the names of Antoninus and Qetia b. Shalom. [ג7.1] then introduces the story of the just-mentioned Qetia. This second pseudo-*baraita* is clearly a construction of the redactors; its artificiality can be seen in that it first repeats Rabbi's response verbatim and then repeats it again with the addition of the two names to link the stories. We might even recognize such comments as part of the art of the story-cycle, a variant mode of introducing another story with a brief introduction rather than proceeding directly. (These two comments together can be categorized as an "anonymous segue" that links the previous story to the next.)

The comment following the second story [א2] differs, however, in that it actually constitutes a double narrative, even a double story by some

---

118. Note the threefold repetition: "Every day" [4.1], "one day" [5.1], and again "every day" in [6.1] and [7.1]. However, the conversation about the world to come in and of itself may not qualify as a story. It could be considered part of the previous story, as I have outlined above. Meir divides the unit into six stories, considering my [7.1] -[5.1] as two parts of a single story (*Rabbi Judah the Patriarch,* 283–84).

definitions: both references to the emperors include two actions, service and death, and the deaths in turn cause expressions of lament, which in fact signify change: "the bundle is undone." There are thus two actions and a verbal response, causality, and change, which generally qualify as a story. Even if this section is considered a narrative, not a story, it is clearly related to the thematics of the story-cycle, and keeps the audience firmly within the narrative world. So it need not be considered an interruption. The story of Onqelos follows this comment without segue or introduction, and is linked to the previous story through the motifs of the evil Caesar and conversion.

There are numerous verbal connections among the Antoninus episodes and also among the three stories. In both [1.1]-[2.1] Antoninus responds to Rabbi's symbolic act, שמע מינה הכי קאמר לי ("Hear from this: thus he is telling me ..."). Antoninus "sends to him" (שדר ליה) in both [3.1] and [4.1], R. Hanina b. Hama "sends" the servant back to Antoninus in [6.1], and the Caesar "sends" the troops in [3]. Sections [2.1], [3.1], [5.1], and [7.1] have the phrase "every day" (כל יומא). The "notables of Rome/the Kingdom" appear in [4.1] and [2]. The story of Qetia relates "While they were taking him and going" (כד הוה נקטין ליה ואזלין), while the story of Onqelos relates "when they took him and went" (כי נקטי ליה ואזלי); and earlier that story states, "while they were taking him and going" (כי הוו שקלו ואזלו).[119] The "servicing" of Rabbi of [7.1] is revisited in [א2] with Adrakhan's servicing Rav added to provide a Babylonian parallel. Rabbi's comment on the Qetia story, his weeping and rueful observation, connects this story to [1], where Rabbi features as the main character. Section [7.1] centers on whether Antoninus will enter the world to come, and the *bat qol* states that Qetia is invited into the world to come. Stories [2] and [3] start with mentions of the "Caesar." Gray has noted that the *qalonya* (colony) that Antoninus asks Rabbi about [1.1] sounds like the name Qalonymos in [3].

There are also a number of motifs in common: the concern over "demeaning the Kingdom" (מזלזלינן במלכותא) in [7.1] is similar to the charge that Qetia "defeated the king" (דזכי למלכא) in [2]. The secrecy thematized in episodes [4.1]-[7.1] is designed to avoid anyone seeing Antoninus behave as an inferior to Rabbi, which is precisely the problem caused by Qetia's public defeat of the emperor [2]. Antoninus's financial support of Rabbi features in [4.1] and Qetia donates his estate to support R. Akiva and his colleagues [2].

This story-cycle centers on the righteous gentile, his respect for the Jews/Judaism, the dangers of disclosing this respect, yet the great reward for doing so. The narrative elements are varied in the stories to manifest different possibilities, permutations, and eventualities, as in other highly

---

119. See Gray, "Redaction and Meaning," 57.

developed story-cycles. The protagonists vary from the Roman emperor, to the Persian/Parthian emperor, to a Roman notable (Qetia), to an important Roman. (Onqelos must be an important Roman, as the Roman Caesar knows him and attempts to arrest him. And an Onqelos b. Qalonymos in b. Git. 56b is Titus's nephew, so if we are to identify the two, and assume the audience knew some version of that story, he is a relative of the emperor.[120]) The protagonists' respect for Judaism takes different forms: conversion (Onqelos), quasi-conversion/circumcision (Qetia),[121] and subservience to the Jewish leader as a proxy for the Jewish God (Antoninus, Adrakhan). The order seems deliberately to progress from Antoninus's service and affiliation, to Qetia's belated circumcision/conversion-cum-martyrdom, to Onkelos's full-fledged conversion. The main three (ignoring Adrakhan for now) face danger from different sources: Antoninus is afraid of the notables of Rome, who cause him difficulties and trouble him in the first two episodes and are presumably the source of the danger requiring the great secrecy; Qetia is obviously threatened by the emperor, and perhaps by the notables he addresses and contradicts; Onqelos is threatened by the emperor and the Roman troops. All three serve and support Jews/Judaism: Antoninus services Rabbi and sends him gold; Qetia persuades the Romans not to "cut off" the Jews; Onqelos joins the Jewish people and converts Roman soldiers. The stories emphasize the rewards for these courageous actions: both the world to come (which Antoninus and Qetia enter), and the this-worldly divine protection (which Onqelos explicates so convincingly to his audience and benefits from in that the emperor abandons efforts to arrest him).

Ultimately the stories argue for the truth and superiority of Judaism, which these leading gentiles recognized. Rabbi, representing Judaism, knows more than the great gentile emperor, who solicits his advice and turns to him to solve political and even familial problems. The emperor tries to support Rabbi monetarily and acknowledges the great powers of the Jews (resurrecting the dead is no big deal). He even comes to serve Rabbi every day, providing him food and drink, letting Rabbi step on him and wishing to be Rabbi's mattress in the world to come! Boyarin points out that these are the services a woman performs for her husband, so the story essentially construes the Roman emperor as desiring to be Rabbi's wife, with all the inferiority entailed in ancient patriarchal society.[122] Providing food and drink are also two elements of the honor due to parents, and the Bavli includes a story of R. Tarfon bending down so that his mother could step on him when she ascended to her bed using strik-

120. See Gray, "Redaction and Meaning," 62–63, and the references there.
121. Some MSS state explicitly that he converted; see n. 115.
122. Boyarin, "Homotopia," 47-49.

ingly similar language.[123] Antoninus is thus also construed as a son giving appropriate honor to his (spiritual) father. Section [א2] makes the same point of Ardakhan (Artaban in some MSS), presumably the Parthian/Persian emperor, servicing Rav, the leading Babylonian rabbi of his time. We are dealing with a full-fledged fantasy of political and religious reversal.

Qetia b. Shalom likewise recognizes the immortality and indestructability of the Jews and succeeds in a type of conversion and entrance to the next world. Onqelos goes through the standard conversion and easily convinces gentiles of the superiority of the Jewish God.

Parallels

There are parallels to parts of the Antoninus story in other sources, and their deployment in the Bavli indicates a process of extensive and deliberate reworking, as Ofra Meir and Alyssa Gray have documented.[124] To note just a few examples:

1. The parallel to [2.1] in Gen. Rab. 67:6, has Antoninus send word by messenger to Rabbi that his treasury is empty. Rabbi takes the messenger to the garden, uproots the radishes, and explicitly refuses to give him a written answer.[125] When the messenger returns to Rome, Antoninus, not receiving a written response, asks what Rabbi did, learns of the uprooting, and decodes the meaning. The Bavli reworked the source so that it could be a continuation of [1.1], where Rabbi and Antoninus are together (in Genesis Rabbah it is an independent story). In the Bavli's face-to-face encounter there is no need to conceal the solution, no reason for Rabbi not to answer directly, prompting the Stammaitic question and requiring the forced explanation (i.e., the interruption [א2.1].) Scholars have noted that the Bavli's reworking of its sources sometimes produces difficulties and incongruities.[126] It is possible that the efforts of Bavli redactors to produce story-cycles out of originally disparate stories are a particular manifestation of this phenomenon.

2. A parallel to the story of R. Ḥanina b. Ḥama resurrecting the slave appears in Lev. Rab. 10:2, told of R. Shimon b. Ḥilfuta, again as an independent story.[127] Here Antoninus naturally encounters Rabbi teaching his

---

123. B. Qidd. 31b: רבי טרפון הוה ליה ההיא אמא דכל אימת דהות בעיא למיסק לפוריא גחין וסליק לה.

124. See Meir, "Ha-terumah ha-historit," 8–25; Gray, "Redaction and Meaning," 35, 68–69.

125. *Bereschit Rabba*, ed. Julius Theodor and Ḥanokh Albeck (Berlin: Poppeloyer, 1903–29; repr., Jerusalem, 1965), 761–62; see the note on 762 about parallels to the story in classical literature.

126. As noted above in the analysis of the Hillel story-cycle; and see Rubenstein, *Talmudic Stories*, 260–61.

127. *Midrash Wayyikra Rabbah*, ed. M. Margalioth (1953–60; repr; New York: Jewish Theological Seminary, 1993), 203–4

students and Rabbi tells Antoninus that the least among them can resurrect the dead. Some time later Antoninus requests that Rabbi send someone to revive his servant who died, taking Rabbi up on this assertion. The Bavli has awkwardly integrated this story into the series of "tunnel" events, with the bizarre and contrived double murder of servants "each day," Antoninus coming upon R. Ḥanina b. Ḥama when he should not have been there, and Rabbi explaining that Ḥanina b. Ḥama is "not a man." In this version Antoninus, not Rabbi, states that the least of Rabbi's students can raise the dead as an indication of his great respect for the Jews.[128]

3. The discussion of whether Antoninus will enter the world to come is probably based on y. Meg. 1:12, 72b (= y. Sanh. 10:6, 29c), where the larger question is whether Antoninus converted. A story there recounts that Antoninus once asked Rabbi if he could eat of Leviathan in the world to come, and Rabbi answered affirmatively.[129]

4. The odd expression "the bundle is undone" is probably borrowed from b. B. Meṣ. 59b, where it refers to the situation when no *kohen* (priest) is present for the Torah reading.

These and other sources were reworked and integrated into a longer series of Antoninus–Rabbi stories. As in other cases, the Bavli has fashioned an extended and more sustained passage by combining and reworking disparate sources.

5. The Qetia story has no parallel. However, the midrashic proof that the world cannot endure without Israel, just as it cannot endure without winds, is borrowed directly from a teaching attributed to R. Yehoshua b. Levi in b. Ta'an. 3b. The postscript where Rabbi weeps and comments on inheriting the next world in one hour appears verbatim in two other Bavli stories that appear later in the tractate, b. 'Abod. Zar. 17a and 17b. Michal Bar-Asher Siegal has argued that the passage is original in b. 'Abod. Zar. 17a and was transferred both to our story and the story in b. 'Abod. Zar. 17b.[130] (The heavenly voice proclaiming entrance to the world to come is also a common motif found elsewhere in the Bavli.[131])

Halakhic Context

The story-cycle is contextualized with m. 'Abod. Zar. 1:3, which mentions gentile festivals including the birthday and deathday and "the *yom genusiya*" of gentile kings/emperors. Gray has argued that the redactors

128. Gray, "Redaction and Meaning," 42; Meir, *Rabbi Judah the Patriarch*, 284–85.

129. See Cohen, "Conversion of Antoninus"; Gray, "Redaction and Meaning," 54–56.

130. Michal Bar-Asher Siegal, *Early Christian Monastic Literature and the Babylonian Talmud* (Cambridge: Cambridge University Press, 2013), 193–98.

131. See ibid., 196–97.

"subtly" and "deftly" created a segue to the story through the back-and-forth of the halakhic discussion, which clarifies the meaning of *yom genusiya*.[132] First, an anonymous response to a putative redundancy answers: "there is no difficulty ... this one is his [the emperor's] coronation ... this one is his son's coronation." In this way the Bavli introduces the issue of the emperor's son. After raising some difficulties in this solution, the Bavli tweaks it as follows: "And if this is difficult for you ... they coronate [a son] through a request [of the father] like the case of Asverus b. Antoninus who ruled." The Bavli then proceeds to [1.1] as proof, and the rest of the story-cycle follows. Clearly this is an artificial sequence intended to prepare the ground for the story-cycle, although the introduction of Asverus b. Antoninus is hardly subtle.[133]

The story-cycle is thus superficially or associatively connected to the Mishnah and halakhic discussion, but not substantively related. The stories, rather, are related to larger questions occasioned by the tractate as a whole. Although called 'Avodah Zarah, "Idolatry" or "Foreign Worship," the tractate focuses equally, if not more, on gentiles and interactions between Jews and gentiles. The dominant view of gentiles is negative: they are violent, sexually immoral, hostile, and dangerous; and hence a great deal of halakhic effort is directed to creating boundaries and distance between Jews and gentiles.[134] The term *'evah,* "hatred," functions in several contexts as a quasi-halakhic term used to explain or justify certain laws of social distancing (b. 'Abod. Zar. 6b, 26a; b. B. Meṣ. 32a). The long story at the beginning of the tractate portrays gentiles negatively and denies them entry into the world to come.[135] Against this background, these stories manifest a different, more hopeful possibility—an alternative view that gentiles can be righteous, support Judaism, and even enter the world to come. This alternative view surfaces periodically in the tractate and throughout the Bavli and perhaps is entailed in the very possibility and institution of conversion, obviously a mechanism for boundary crossing.[136] As Mira Wasserman has noted, the Qetia story (and I would say the story-cycle as a whole) "subverts the boundary between Jews and non-Jews."[137]

---

132. Gray goes into more detail ("Redaction and Meaning," 30–32). See too Meir, *Rabbi Judah the Patriarch*, 278–79.

133. See Rubenstein, *Talmudic Stories*, 235–38, for a similar example, also from 'Avodah Zarah.

134. See m. 'Abod. Zar. 2:1; Rubenstein, *Talmudic Stories*, 237–38.

135. See Rubenstein, *Talmudic Stories*, 212–35.

136. Ibid., 238–40; Wasserman, *Jews, Gentiles, and Other Animals*, 40–43; Jenny R. Labendz, "Rabbinic Eschatology: Complexity, Ambiguity, and Radical Self-Reflection," *JQR* 107 (2017): 269–96.

137. Wasserman, "Humanity of the Talmud," 7.

Composition

There is solid evidence that the story-cycle was composed by the Stammaim. The profound reworking of sources both from elsewhere in the Bavli and from Yerushalmi compilations points to the redactors, as does the construction of the larger, more developed story of Antoninus with multiple episodes that derive from briefer sources. The transition from the Antoninus story to that of Qetia is clearly a redactional construction. The verbal links and repeated phrases among the units also suggest composition by the redactors, as does the borrowing from other Bavli sources. So too does the non-narrative midrashic tradition that follows the story-cycle [א3], which returns to Rabbi and Antoninus, thereby creating a neat "envelope" structure.[138]

Summary

This is a story-cycle of at least three, and up to eleven stories, depending on how the units are divided. I prefer the maximum enumeration: seven stories of Rabbi and Antoninus, the story of Qetia, the story of Onqelos, together with the two skeletal stories in unit [א2] of the deaths of the emperors; without those borderline two stories the count is nine. Given the minor interruptions, the story-cycle can be categorized as "interrupted." The cycle was constructed by the Bavli redactors/Stammaim and has only a superficial connection to its halakhic context.

Preliminary Conclusions

I will refer to the story-cycles by the following numbers for convenience.

1. Ber. 18a–b (do the dead know about the living?)
2. Ketub. 67b (charity)
3. Šabb. 30b–31a (how to answer annoying questions)
4. Šabb. 156b (astrology)
5. 'Abod. Zar. 10a–10b (righteous gentiles)

(I). The characterizations, or general topics, of some of the story-cycles identified by Yassif require reevaluation, and some should be revised. The topic of 1 is whether the dead know about the living. The topic of 3 is better understood as "how to answer annoying questions" or "Hillel's

138. This comment also features vegetables, as mentioned in the first two units. Of course the comment can be considered a later addition to the story-cycle, hence evidence of later redaction, rather than composition of the story-cycle proper.

wise responses to annoying questions" and not as a biographical cycle about Hillel. The topic of 4 is astrology, not "righteousness saves from death." The topic of 2 perhaps should be considered "charity" rather than "sufficient for his needs," though this depends on the boundaries of that story-cycle and whether that cycle is expanded.

(II). The boundaries of the story-cycles identified by Yassif require reassessment—in particular, whether additional stories should be included in the story-cycles, as we saw in cases 1, 2, and 3. This issue is related to the following.

(III). The nature and extent of the "interruptions" between stories that violate the sequence such that it cannot be considered a story-cycle require more attention. Yassif, as noted, allows for "minor interruptions." But this is subjective, not defined, and varies a great deal among his own examples. It is also a product of Yassif's focus on folklore and the idealization of an oral context of a storyteller telling stories to an audience. If we focus, rather, on the context of rabbinic tradition, the *sugya,* and its sources, our perspective on interruptions may differ. Ultimately there is no right or wrong answer: the larger the interruption tolerated, the more story-cycles will qualify, but the less concentrated will be the density of narrative and impact of the narrative world on the audience. My preference is to allow for somewhat longer interruptions provided that the purposes of the interruptions serve the interests of the story-cycles, such as brief glosses that clarify problems, anonymous comments that create segues to the following story, and even *baraitot* that prepare the audience for the stories to follow. These types of digressions are a characteristic of Bavli *sugyot,* and the story-cycle is, at root, a specific type of *sugya.* But I grant that these, too, are subjective and messy criteria. Perhaps more coherent criteria will emerge from analysis of all the story-cycles; certainly this question has to be revisited.

Meanwhile, a preliminary taxonomy of different types of interruptions that emerges from the story-cycles analyzed thus far is as follows.

(a) *Minor digressions such as additional explanation of verses, often introduced by the term* איכא דאמרי. These do not contribute to the story-cycle but are stimulated by the elements of the stories. Examples include the explanation of the subsequent clauses of the verse quoted by R. Ḥiyya and the alternative prooftext for his claim in 1 (comments [ב1], [ד1]).

(b) *Brief explanatory comments clarifying aspects of a story.* These are a product of the Bavli's propensity to interrogate all statements and sources and are typical of both halakhic and aggadic *sugyot.* Such comments generally remain within the "narrative world" of the story and the story-cycle. But clearly an extended discussion of an element of a story will disrupt the audience's focus and remove it from the narrative world. A good example of this category in 5 is the questions why Rabbi does not tell the emperor directly or whisper his advice but rather makes a symbolic gesture that the emperor must decode (comment [א2.1]).

(c) *Opportunistic difficulties and responses that introduce other sources as apparent contradictions and resolve the conflict.* For example, comment [א7] in 2 objects that Mar 'Uqba should not have pledged half his resources to charity on the basis of R. Ilai's dictum, found elsewhere in the Bavli, that one should give away no more than one-fifth. These interruptions function to clarify aspects of an individual story, similar to type (b), but adduce other sources. They too are characteristic of the Bavli's love of dialectic argumentation and tendency to juxtapose conflicting sources and work out the contradictions.

(d) *Anonymous segues that bridge from one story to the next with a link or series of links.* A good example is comments [ג7.1]-[ב7.1] in 5, the pseudo-*baraita* that mentions Qetia b. Shalom, who then features in the subsequent story. These segues can be removed without causing much problem in appreciating the relevance of the next story or the coherence of the story-cycle. They too are standard redactional techniques commonly found in the Bavli.

(e) *Relatively prominent interruptions including baraitot and other sources that prepare the audience for the incorporation of additional stories.* These are similar to type (d) but include other sources that are necessary to understanding the subsequent stories. For example, the two *baraitot* interrupting the larger story-cycle of nine stories about charity in 2, together with brief Amoraic comments on the *baraitot*.

(f) *Introductory or transitional phrases that alert the audience why the story is adduced and focus attention on the salient aspect of the story.* Although these bridging phrases can be brief, they are crucial, since they disclose why the compilers created the story-cycle and what they intend the audience to absorb. Indeed, from this point of view, they are an equally important part of the cycle as the stories themselves. Examples include the transitions between the stories in 1, debating whether the stories prove that "the dead know," and the introductions to the stories about astrology in 4. The presence of this type of interruption, to my mind, is strong evidence of the redactors' role in creating these story-cycles.

(IV). Story-cycles are not all of one cloth, but can be categorized according to the extent and type of interruptions. Provisionally I suggest we categorize story-cycles as (a) interrupted, e.g, 1, 2, 5; (b) almost uninterrupted (3, 4); and (c) uninterrupted (none in our sample). This question is related to the following point.

(V). The role of the redactors/Stammaim in compiling the story-cycle. The Stammaim seem to be responsible for all of these story-cycles. In some cases, this conclusion seems beyond doubt, such as 1 and 4, where the stories are adduced and linked through the anonymous comments, and without the anonymous comments there would be no cycle. In other cases the evidence of the Stammaitic composition comes from the reworking of parallel sources and verbal connections among the stories, such as 2, 3, and 5. (These criteria are not mutually exclusive.) This may not be all that surprising in that a story-cycle is a type of aggadic *sugya,* and to say that the Stammaim are responsible for the *sugya* borders on a tautology. Nevertheless, it is possible that the Bavli redactors received story-cycles from earlier compilations and included them in the Bavli as received, without reworking, as discussed above; analysis of the other story-cycles may identify such cases. (This is occasionally the case for halakhic *sugyot* too.) The reworking and compilation of story-cycles therefore can illuminate the methods of reworking, composition, and even narrative art of the redactors. Some of the examples, such as the reworking of the Antoninus stories in 5, provide striking evidence of these methods.

(VI). Story-cycles vary in their relationship to their Mishnaic and halakhic contexts. (a) Some have no relation to the proximate Mishnah or halakhic discussion that follows it, such as 3 and 4. These are integrated into the talmudic context through associative links (e.g., the same formula "it was written in the notebook of x" in 4; the elaborate series of aggadic associations to reach the Hillel stories in 3). (b) Others, such as 2 and 5, have some superficial association with the mishnaic or halakhic contexts but really engage other issues (in 2, the general questions of charity relate to the Mishnah's law that charity be provided for orphan marriages; in 4, the story of the righteous gentile king Antoninus is associated with the Mishnah's mention of holidays of kings and the artificial halakhic discussion based on it). (c) Still others, such as 1, are directly related to the halakhic context (the laws requiring respect for the dead.) Other examples of this category include the very well-studied *sugya* of b. Ketub. 62b, stories of sages leaving home to study Torah, which directly relates to the mishnaic ruling about how long sages may leave their wives to study, and essentially functions as its *sugya* (#9 on the list above).[139] The stories in b. Ta'an. 23a–25b about rain and drought also fall into this category (#7 on the list). On the one hand, this taxonomy is probably applicable to Bavli aggada as a whole and is hardly unexpected.[140] On the other, a classification of all story-cycles may reveal interesting conclusions about this phenomenon. Those self-contained story-cycles with no substantive connection to their halakhic contexts resemble a type of topical essay and also represent a move toward the medieval narrative collections such as *Hibbur Yafeh meha-Yeshua,* where stories have a cultural capital of their own and need not be subordinated to rabbinic compilations organized according to halakha (e.g., the Talmuds) or biblical verses (e.g., midrashim). It

139. See Rubenstein, *Culture of the Babylonian Talmud,* 102–18, and the references there.

140. See now Yonatan Feintuch, *Face to Face: The Interweaving of Aggada and Halakha in the Babylonian Talmud* [Hebrew] (Jerusalem: Maggid, 2018).

also appears that some of these story-cycles were compiled in order to address larger theological issues, such as 5, about righteous gentiles; 4, about astrology and fate; and the stories of destruction in b. Giṭ. 55b–58a (#14 on the list above) about destruction and theodicy. These can also be considered a type of transition to philosophical and theological writings of the post-talmudic period.

(VII). A definition of a story is required, as the Bavli contains many dialogues and brief narratives that may or may not qualify as stories. Given that the Bavli is overwhelmingly dialogical, I think a more expansive definition that accepts speech acts is most useful. I have in mind a definition along the same lines as Moshe Simon-Shoshan in his work on the Mishnah, who defines a story as "any representation of a sequence of at least two interrelated events that occurred once and only once in the past."[141] However, he also acknowledges that some dialogues can be considered stories, despite the absence of "events," provided they involve significant change:

> Reported dialog in and of itself represents a borderline case in the classification of narratives and stories. Speech acts are the most ephemeral of actions. By themselves, they make no physical mark on the world around them.... Other dialogs contain a stronger dynamic element and can be classified as narratives.... Dialogs in which one of the speakers either makes a significant discovery or changes his or her opinion in the course of the conversation are sufficiently dynamic and specific to be considered stories.[142]

(VIII) Additional story-cycles must be identified (such as 5), beyond those on Yassif's list. As noted, the question of halakhic story-cycles needs to be addressed.

These preliminary conclusions and other unresolved issues will continue to be addressed in supplements to this study.

---

141. Simon-Shoshan, *Stories of the Law*, 20.
142. Ibid., 22–23.

The Deposition of Rabban Gamaliel

Talmud and the Political Unconscious

ZVI SEPTIMUS

> The history of all hitherto existing society is the history of class struggles: freeman and slave, patrician and plebian, lord and serf, guild-master and journeyman—in a word, oppressor and oppressed—stood in constant opposition to one another, carried on and uninterrupted, now hidden, and now open fight, a fight that each time ended, either in a revolutionary reconstitution of society at large or in the common ruin of the contending classes.
>
> —Karl Marx and Friedrich Engels, "The Communist Manifesto"[1]

The Babylonian Talmud (hereafter Bavli or BT) in b. Ber. 27b–28a tells a story about a revolution within the rabbinic academy shortly after the destruction of the Second Temple (70 CE). This story, which scholars refer to as The Deposition of Rabban Gamaliel,[2] "is one of the better-known incidents in Rabbinic history."[3] It takes place during the Yavneh period of rabbinic Judaism and is one of the historiographical texts that make up the Yavneh story-cycle, the stories of which, taken together, point to a reorganization of rabbinic society and a restructuring of its leadership dynamic

---

I thank Jonathan Boyarin, David Henkin, and Jeffrey L. Rubenstein for their insightful comments on an earlier draft of this paper. I also thank those who participated in the "Rabbinic Narratives" conference at New York University in June 2018. I benefited greatly from all of those who joined in the lively debate.

1. Karl Marx, *On Revolution*, ed. and trans. Saul K. Padover, Karl Marx Library 1 (New York: McGraw-Hill, 1971), 81 (quoted in Fredric Jameson, *The Political Unconscious: Narrative as a Socially Symbolic Act* [1981; repr., London: Routledge, 2002], 4.)

2. This appellation dates from as early as Philip Blackman's 1951–56 translation of the Mishnah (*Mishnayoth*, 2nd ed., vol. 1 [Gateshead: Judaica Press, 1990], 510).

3. David Stern, *Midrash and Theory: Ancient Jewish Exegesis and Contemporary Literary Studies*, Rethinking Theory (Evanston, IL: Northwestern University Press, 1998), 34.

after the destruction of the Second Temple in the late first century CE. The story tells of a power struggle within the rabbinic academy between the ruling Rabban Gamaliel and his subordinate colleagues. In the context of a student-led revolt, Rabban Gamaliel is seen as abusing his authority and is voted out of his position as leader. Later, upon realizing the error of his actions and apologizing for his abuse, he is given most of his power back, albeit over an academy whose enrollment policy is formed along more populist lines. Since it is difficult to set the individual stories within the Yavneh story-cycle into a precise chronology, it is unclear whether the revolution depicted in this story is a reaction to earlier Yavneh reforms or simply represents the defining moment of a reform era.[4] Shaye Cohen, in a groundbreaking 1984 essay, opts to read the Yavneh narratives synchronically and sees the sum of this body of texts as representative of a new paradigm in Jewish history defined by mutual tolerance.[5] Yet, even if the deposition story is read independent of the Yavneh story-cycle, it still can certainly be viewed as buttressing Cohen's thesis that "the major contribution of Yavneh to Jewish history [was] the creation of a society which tolerates disputes without producing sects. For the first time Jews 'agreed to disagree.'"[6]

The deposition story, with its depiction of a revolution and the overthrow of a ruling elite followed by a reorganization of the rabbinic power structure is ripe for a Marxist reading. As seen in the epigraph to this essay, Karl Marx saw the story of history as one of class struggle, about domination and subjugation. In order to make sense of a life organized along the lines of oppressor and oppressed, societies invent stories to explain the reason for an existing power structure. These stories, called ideologies, conceal the true source of the power dynamics within society.[7] For Marx, what really determines the nature of class struggle in any moment of history and the particular ideologies that develop is the evolution of economic conditions—an approach known as "historical materialism."[8]

4. It seems that Daniel Boyarin would argue that it is both. See Daniel Boyarin, *Border Lines: The Partition of Judaeo-Christianity*, Divinations (Philadelphia: University of Pennsylvania Press, 2004), 186–89.

5. Shaye J. D. Cohen, "The Significance of Yavneh: Pharisees, Rabbis, and the End of Jewish Sectarianism," *HUCA* 55 (1984): 27–53, here 49–50. Other scholars following Cohen, such as David Stern, place this story diachronically within the story cycle. Stern dates the story to "around the years 100–110 C.E." and notes that another story in the cycle, b. Ḥag. 3a–b, follows up on the events of the story (*Midrash and Theory*, 35).

6. Cohen, "Significance of Yavneh," 29.

7. For a history of this term in general, and its use in Marxist theory, see Raymond Williams, *Marxism and Literature* (Oxford: Oxford University Press, 1977), 55–71. For the relationship between ideology and false consciousness in the development of Marxist thought, see Ron Eyerman, "False Consciousness and Ideology in Marxist Theory," *Acta Sociologica* 24 (1981): 43–56.

8. Marx outlines pre-capitalist modes of production in three stages, based on different

That is, for Marx, it is the economic structure of a society that drives its thought processes and not the other way around. The material conditions of a society create the power structure, which is in turn stabilized through an ideology invented by members of the ruling class.[9] These ideologies work to conceal the true economic cause of exploitation—the organization of both the material means of production within a society and the mechanisms for the distribution and exchange of products.[10] At the risk of an oversimplification of Marx's position, in a feudal society, where the economic system relies on land ownership and its relationship to labor, the ideology that develops in the service of maintaining the power structure of the ruling class is religious (or Catholic) in nature; a capitalist society develops legal and social democratic (or interventionist state) ideologies.[11] It is the effectiveness of the ideology in concealing the economic system's role in the subjugation of the nonhegemonic class that prevents revolution. Revolution, therefore, occurs when the ideology produced by the hegemonic class is no longer effective in concealing the true nature of what works to subjugate the other classes. After such a revolution, the

---

forms of ownership: tribal ownership, ancient communal and state ownership, and feudal or estate property; see Karl Marx and Friedrich Engels, *The German Ideology: With Selections from Parts Two and Three, Together with Marx's "Introduction to a Critique of Political Economy"*, ed. Christopher John Arthur (London: Lawrence & Wishart, 1970), 43–46. For a more complicated picture, see Marx's notes from 1857–1858 compiled together with supplemental writings in Karl Marx, *Pre-Capitalist Economic Formations*, ed. Eric Hobsbawm, trans. Jack Cohen (New York: International Publishers, 1965). Jameson lists the modes of production according to the "'stages' of human society" according to the development of Marxist theory in seven stages as "include[ing] the following: primitive communism or tribal society (the horde), the gens or hierarchical kinship societies (neolithic society), the Asiatic mode of production (so-called Oriental despotism), the polis or an oligarchical slaveholding society (the ancient mode of production), feudalism, capitalism, and communism (with a good deal of debate as to whether the 'transitional' stage between these last—sometimes called 'socialism'—is a genuine mode of production in its own right or not)" (*Political Unconscious*, 74–75). For extensive analysis of the characteristics of precapitalist modes of production, see Barry Hindess, *Pre-Capitalist Modes of Production* (London: Routledge and K. Paul, 1975). The terminology "historical materialism" derives from Friedrich Engels, *Socialism: Utopian and Scientific*, trans. Edward Aveling (1882; repr., New York: Cosimo, 2008), 10–16.

9. Marx and Engels, *German Ideology*, 65.

10. Marxism uses the terms *base* and *superstructure* to express these ideas. The material means of production within a society and how products are distributed and exchanged is called the *base*. The *superstructure* is the ideology developed by the hegemonic class of that society to hide the effects of the *base* on the position of the subjugated. The *superstructure*'s concealment of the *base* works to prevent revolution at the hand of the subjugated. For the historical development of this terminology and its development in the transition from Marx to Marxism, see Williams, *Marxism and Literature*, 75–82.

11. See Bryan S. Turner, Nicholas Abercrombie, and Stephen Hill, *The Dominant Ideology Thesis (RLE Social Theory)* (London: Routledge, 2014), 7–29 and 59–94, for the positions of various Marxist theorists, a detailed analysis of the sources in Marx and Engels for their positions, as well an in-depth critique of such a reading of these sources.

material means of production within a society becomes organized along a different scheme and products are distributed and exchanged according to this new scheme. Does such a view, with its emphasis on economic conditions, help us understand the shift in the structure of power relations within the rabbinic society of which the story tells?

It would be very convenient to map the revolution told in this story onto Karl Marx's epochal scheme of history, as the result of an evolution from one dominant economic system to another. The story, which starts out as a discussion about prayer and evolves into one about the politics of the rabbinic academy would then likewise be explained in terms of a transition from a feudal culture to a capitalist one, where, according to Marx's scheme, a religious ideology with its centralized top-down authority is replaced by a more democratic one.[12] If a transition from a religious ideology to a legal and democratic one in rabbinic society of the late first century CE coincided with a shift from a feudal to a capitalist society, then the student-led revolution would fit neatly into Marx's scheme. It does not make sense, however, to look in this direction for several reasons. First, even if such a transition was found, it would have to first be used to explain a more basic and important revolt, the First Jewish Revolt against the Romans (66–70 CE), which led to the destruction of the Second Temple. Only then could an understanding of the shift in economic systems be secondarily related to the student revolt within the academy a mere decade or two later. Second, in Marx's scheme of successive economies viewed in epochal terms, Roman Judea would most likely belong to the category of a slave society, not a feudal or capitalist one.[13] Third, though the prominence in rabbinic texts of the Second Temple–era schools of Shammai and Hillel point to the existence of some established form of predestruction rabbinic society, it certainly does not appear that this subset of Second Temple Judaism would have in any way been considered hegemonic at the time. Yet rather than telling of a revolt that led to the rise of the rabbinic class over competing forms of Second Temple–era hegemony, the deposition story instead tells of a revolution in the context of a ruling postdestruction rabbinic class and a reorganization of its internal power structures, ones that are quite distinct from those of Second Temple Judaism. Fourth, the story

12. See n. 51, below.

13. Rabban Gamaliel himself was a noted slaveowner. See m. Ber. 2:7. For the characteristic features of a slave society, see Hindess, *Pre-Capitalist Modes of Production*, 109–77. It should be noted, though, that Marx understood "societies characterized by the dominance of the slave mode of production [as] ones in which 'ancient religions' were dominant"; see Turner, Abercrombie, and Hill, *Dominant Ideology Thesis*, 61. However, attempting to map Marx's conceptions of Roman, Catholic, and Protestant religious ideologies onto late antique Jewish ones has little value for the current analysis.

itself was produced by storytellers who lived many centuries after the events depicted in the story, with both Sasanian and later Islamic-era Babylonian rabbis in all likelihood contributing to the form of the text we now read. Consequently, even if the story was the product of some accurate historical memory of some economic transition, it is not likely that a memory that had percolated in a foreign economic system would directly cohere with the actual economic conditions in Roman Judea in the late first century. At the same time, there is ample evidence that in the late talmudic period, Jewish society had undergone (or was undergoing) a process of urbanization.[14]

Fredric Jameson provides an avenue for applying Marx's basic system of economic materialism to a historical situation that does not neatly fit into his epochal scheme. At face value it would seem counterintuitive to apply his methodological approach to the Talmud. Jameson's work seeks to establish how the novel is the ultimate expression and definitive artistic output of capitalist society and its fragmented and alienated psyche. While the Talmud itself is narrated in a fragmented manner, it represents, as will later be argued, the anti-novel; and while Jameson, in search of a narrative's absent cause, goes to great lengths to justify the weaving into his analysis of the personal biography of a novel's author and the precise historical moment in which that author lived,[15] we know very little about the

---

14. Maristella Botticini and Zvi Eckstein, *The Chosen Few: How Education Shaped Jewish History, 70–1492*, Princeton Economic History of the Western World 42 (Princeton, NJ: Princeton University Press, 2012), 124–52 (see p. 124 n. 2 of this chapter for earlier proponents of this view); Michele Campopiano, "Seventh–Tenth Centuries," *Studia Islamica* 107 (2012): 1–37; Campopiano, "Land Tenure, Land Tax and Social Conflictuality in Iraq from the Late Sasanian to the Early Islamic Period (Fifth to Ninth Centuries CE)," in *Authority and Control in the Countryside: From Antiquity to Islam in the Mediterranean and Near East (Sixth–Tenth Century)*, ed. Alain Delattre, Marie Legendre, and Petra Sijpesteijn, Leiden Studies in Islam and Society 9 (Leiden: Brill, 2018), 464–99; I. M. Lapidus, "The Evolution of Muslim Urban Society," *Comparative Studies in Society and History* 15 (1973): 21–50; Abdelwahab Meddeb and Benjamin Stora, *A History of Jewish–Muslim Relations: From the Origins to the Present Day* (Princeton, NJ: Princeton University Press, 2013), 79–81; Michael G. Morony, "Landholding in Seventh-Century Iraq: Late Sasanian and Early Islamic Patterns," in *Islamic Middle East, 700–1900: Studies in Economic and Social History*, ed. A. L. Udovitch, Princeton Studies on the Near East (Princeton, NJ: Darwin, 1981), 135–75; Morony, "Landholding and Social Change: Lower al-ʿIraq in the Early Islamic Period," in *Land Tenure and Social Transformation in the Middle East*, ed. Tarif Khalidi (Beirut: Syracuse University Press, 1985), 209–22; Michael G. Morony and Khodad Rezakhani, "Markets for Land, Labour and Capital in Late Antique Iraq, AD 200–700," *JESHO* 57 (2014): 231–61. Phillip Ackerman-Lieberman argues against the view of the importance of urbanization on Jewish culture of this period ("Revisiting Jewish Occupational Choice and Urbanization in Iraq under the Early Abbasids," *Jewish History* 29 [2015]: 113–35).

15. See, e.g., his chapter "Realism and Desire: Balzac and the Problem of the Subject," in Jameson, *Political Unconscious*, 137–71. For A. J. Greimas on the "relationship between presence and absence," see Jameson, 33.

biographies of the authors of a particular talmudic story or precisely when or where they lived. Therefore, a direct application of Jameson's analytical model would leave us at a loss in trying to discover the hidden and missing characters, so important to Jameson's method, in both historical figures and the author. The little we do know about the Talmud's authors and the historicity of the characters contained in its pages only makes matters worse. Jameson, and indeed most Marxist literary theory, is focused on what in Marx's historical scheme represents the third and fourth epochal stages of history: the feudalist and capitalist societies of medieval and modern Europe. By all accounts, the stories in the Talmud were produced prior to and outside of those markedly European historical stages.

Jameson's approach to literature leans heavily on psychoanalytic theory, but he argues that the theory itself fails to recognize the historical contingency of its own semiotic system. The sexual symbolic system put forth by Freud only makes sense in the context of the type of nuclear family structure in which the mode of interpretation itself was developed. Freud's theory would therefore not make sense in a society that existed prior to notions of privacy and individuality.[16] Yet Jameson argues that, once we identify the historical contingency that informs Freud's master code, the particularities of its sexual orientation, we can uncover his most profound insight. That is, that the very nature and necessity for interpretation lie in the relationship between the conscious and the unconscious that it represses. While, for Freud, the object of interpretation is the individual subject, for Jameson it is the collective unconscious of a culture; and narratives are the key to understanding this collectivity because they can exist only in the context of a society in which they are told and received. Jameson is interested in narratives because he sees them as a mode through which a society's collective consciousness represses its intolerable organization along the lines of domination and subjugation. Through a method of looking for the absent cause behind a narrative, Jameson seeks to discover a society's hidden political unconscious, to uncover the latent meaning behind what is openly manifest in a culture's literary production.[17]

Jameson is not unaware that Marx too suffered from an inability to overcome his own historically contingent interpretive horizon.[18] He there-

16. Jameson, *Political Unconscious*, 46–51.

17. Ibid., 45. The core project of Jameson's book *The Political Unconscious* is to demonstrate the problematics of reading according to a master code by showing how all master codes (except, of course, his own) are blind to their historical contingency. Therefore, rather than using Jameson as a master code through which to read this text, I will instead draw upon his insights and methods as they might be productively put to use in the context of the analysis of the Talmud as a cultural artifact quite distinct than that of the nineteenth- and early twentieth-century European novels he analyzes.

18. For the concept of interpretive horizons, see Hans Georg Gadamer, *Truth and Method* (New York: Seabury, 1975), 299–306.

fore provides a reading of Marx's theory that, like his reading of Freud's, seeks to free it of its own master code and uncover the deep insight that lies beneath. For Jameson, Marx should not be read as giving an account of history, but rather an account of capitalism, the dominant economic condition of the historical moment in which he wrote. Therefore, Marx's true insight is not to be found in his story about the successive economic stages of history but rather in his approach to viewing all social phenomena within a given historical framework of the economic. Though Marx analyzes capitalism, the other modes of production in his diachronic historical scheme remain synchronically present, and antagonistic toward one another, within the capitalist historical period he studies, whether they exist in a concrete form, as memory, or as potential. It is through this idea, what Jameson calls metasynchronicity, that Marxist theory can most productively be put to use in analyzing b. Ber. 27b–28a—where Marxist theory provides the basis for a more complex understanding of what previous scholarship has somewhat uniformly read in this story as a binary class struggle between aristocratic and populist leaning factions. The purpose of the somewhat lengthy analysis in this essay is not to provide a strict Jamesonian reading of the Talmud but rather to think through a talmudic narrative with him, to push the boundaries of interpretation and demonstrate how Jameson can be used to find in that narrative cultural insight that more traditional academic talmudic approaches might ignore.

The Story

The Bavli, in Ber. 27b–28a, narrates an episode that recounts the deposition of Rabban Gamaliel as *Nasi* (patriarch/president).[19] The academic scholarship on this story is rich. At least a dozen articles or chapter-length studies have been devoted to this story. The story, too, plays a prominent role in additional studies more generally focused on a description of rabbinic Judaism during the Yavneh period (late first century CE) or other periods in rabbinic Judaism that might have produced the stories of the Yavneh cycle.[20] The scholarship on b. Ber. 27b–28a, together with

19. The fact that the word *Nasi* does not actually appear in the story, though the office is inferred, buttresses Robert Goldenberg's understanding of Rabban Gamaliel's position in this story as "the presidency over the Rabbinic gathering." (See n. 65 below.) See Goldenberg, "The Deposition of Rabban Gamliel II: An Examination of the Sources," *JJS* 23 (1972): 167–90, here 171.

20. Shaye Cohen's 1984 article "The Significance of Yavneh," 28–29, was groundbreaking in establishing this academic discursive sphere. Cohen argues against the previously regnant view that Yavneh represented a moment of sectarian crisis where the rabbis "ejected all those who were not members of their own party." Instead, Cohen posits that the Yavneh era reforms were inclusionary rather than exclusionary.

its Palestinian Talmud (hereafter Yerushalmi or PT) parallel (y. Ber. 4:1), therefore represents a subdiscourse within the larger academic discourse on the Yavneh era of rabbinic Judaism, with later scholars directly engaging the work of earlier ones.[21] Previous scholarship has approached this story with two basic strategies. The first focuses on detailing how the text evolved from its Yerushalmi iteration into the final form that appears in the Bavli. The second uses the divergences between the parallel accounts to make historical arguments about the people who produced each story. Most scholars working with this story have used a combination of the two approaches with differing emphases. Additionally, there is great disparity in the dating that scholars posit for these texts and therefore much discrepancy in the historical periods for which these scholars want to use this story to make claims. What all of these scholars in their readings share is a very narrow view of the characters contained in the drama. I therefore will summarize the story according to the information deemed pertinent by previous scholars in order to later contrast how a distant reading approach would view the story differently.

The basic outline of the story begins with an unnamed student who plots to bring about a public confrontation between Rabban Gamaliel

---

21. I therefore list the most comprehensive of these studies, as well as a few more that are either central to the discourse created by these treatments or were written in dialogue with them, in chronological order: Louis Ginzberg, *Perushim Ve-Hidushim Bi-Yerushalmi*, 4 vols., Texts and Studies of the Jewish Theological Seminary of America 10–12, 21 (New York: Jewish Theological Seminary of America, 1941), 3:174–220; Goldenberg, "Deposition of Rabban Gamliel II"; Devora Steinmetz, "Must the Patriarch Know 'Uqtzin'? The 'Nasi' as Scholar in Babylonian Aggada," *AJSR* 23 (1998): 163–89; Menachem Ben Shalom, "The Story of the Deposition of Raban Gamliel and the Historical Reality" [Hebrew], *Zion* 66 (2001): 345–70; Haim Shapira, "Between Literature and History: A Response to M. Ben Shalom" [Hebrew], *Zion* 66 (2001): 371–78; Jeffrey L. Rubenstein, "The Thematization of Dialectics in Bavli Aggada," *JJS* 54 (2003): 71–84; Daniel Boyarin, "The Yavneh-Cycle of the Stammaim and the Invention of the Rabbis," in *Creation and Composition: The Contribution of the Bavli Redactors (Stammaim) to the Aggada*, ed. Jeffrey L. Rubenstein, TSAJ 114 (Tübingen: Mohr Siebeck, 2005), 237–89; Devorah Steinmetz, "Agada Unbound: Inter-Agadic Characterization of Sages in the Bavli and Implications for Reading Agada," in Rubenstein, *Creation and Composition*, 293–337; Jeffrey L. Rubenstein, *Stories of the Babylonian Talmud* (Baltimore: Johns Hopkins University Press, 2010), 77–90; Richard Hidary, *Dispute for the Sake of Heaven: Legal Pluralism in the Talmud*, BJS 353 (Providence, RI: Brown Judaic Studies, 2010), 241–95; Boaz Shpigel, "Did Rabban Gamliel See a Real Dream? Studies in Babylonian Talmud in Tractate Brachot, 28, a" [Hebrew], *Sinai* 148 (2014): 29–72; Geoffrey Herman, "Insurrection in the Academy: The Babylonian Talmud and the Paikuli Inscription" [Hebrew], *Zion* 79 (2014): 377–407; Moshe Simon-Shoshan, "Transmission and Evolution of the Story of R. Gamliel's Deposition," in *Jews and Christians in the First and Second Centuries: The Interbellum 70–132 CE*, ed. Joshua Schwartz and P. J. Tomson, CRINT 15 (Leiden: Brill, 2017), 196–222; Moshe Simon-Shoshan, "Creators of Worlds: The Deposition of R. Gamliel and the Invention of Yavneh," *AJSR* 41 (2017): 287–313; Shraga Bar-On, "The Art of the Chain Novel in b. Yoma 35b: Reconsidering the Social Values of the Babylonian Yeshivot," *HUCA* 88 (2017): 55–88.

and his rabbinic subordinate R. Yehoshua about a matter of law in which the two rabbis differed. Rabban Gamaliel attempts to exert his unilateral authority over matters of law and humiliates R. Yehoshua in the process. Those who are present take offense at Rabban Gamaliel's treatment of R. Yehoshua, and Rabban Gamaliel is deposed from his leadership role. In deciding between possible successors, R. Elazar b. Azariah (a wealthy, priestly descendant of the biblical Ezra) is chosen over R. Yehoshua (a party to the dispute) and R. Akiva (the progeny of poor genealogy) for pragmatic reasons. "On that day,"[22] the guard at the door of the study-house is removed and Rabban Gamaliel's restrictive admissions policy is overturned, granting many new students entry. Rabban Gamaliel eventually decides to apologize to R. Yehoshua and, upon reaching his house, he discovers that R. Yehoshua sustains himself through a lowly profession. After Rabban Gamaliel's apology is accepted, R. Yehoshua sends word to the study-house in an attempt to have Rabban Gamaliel reinstated, but R. Akiva locks the doors. When R. Yehoshua himself goes to the study-house and successfully intervenes, R. Akiva decides to go together with R. Yehoshua to inform R. Elazar of a compromise position they had reached. Moving forward, Rabban Gamaliel and R. Elazar will share the leadership position, with Rabban Gamaliel in charge for three weeks a month and R. Elazar for one. (The full text of the story is provided in the appendix.)

The Academic Discourse

While earlier treatments of the narrative, such as Wilhelm Bacher's entry on Gamaliel II in the *Jewish Encyclopedia*, took the historicity of the events recounted for granted, Robert Goldenberg, writing in 1972, positioned himself against Bacher and Louis Ginzberg in arguing that the story was not a historical record of events in the first century of the common era.[23] Goldenberg's stated aim in analyzing the parallel Bavli and Yerushalmi versions of the account of Rabban Gamaliel's deposition was to "evaluate the two reports as historical sources."[24] In the end, he concedes that, though the story is full of anachronism, and is certainly not a contem-

22. I have put these words in quotation because they are cited in my review of Daniel Boyarin's reading of this story.

23. Wilhelm Bacher, "Gamliel II," in *The Jewish Encyclopedia: A Descriptive Record of the History, Religion, Literature and Customs of the Jewish People from the Earliest Times to the Present Day*, ed. Isidore Singer and Cyrus Adler (New York: Funk & Wagnalls, 1925); Ginzberg, *Perushim Ve-Hidushim Bi-Yerushalmi*; Goldenberg, "Deposition of Rabban Gamliel II," 189 nn. 98–99, though Goldenberg (176 n. 58) does cite J. N. Epstein as an earlier example of a scholar who questioned aspects of the historicity of the story (J. N. Epstein, *Mevo'ot Le-Sifrut Ha-Tana'im: Mishnah, Tosefta u-Midrashe-Halakha* [Jerusalem: Magnes, 1957], 424–25).

24. Goldenberg, "Deposition of Rabban Gamliel II," 167.

poraneous account, the story might still contain a memory of an actual historical disturbance, where the factions of R. Yoḥanan b. Zakkai, the priests, and the Hillelites vied for power.[25] According to Goldenberg's speculation, "[t]he patriarchal regime was just beginning to consolidate its power. The rabbinic conclave in general must have resented this. At least two rival groups … are likely to have had aspirations of their own."[26] Given the large stakes involved, Goldenberg posits that the actual events of the late first century must have been far more complex than those narrated in this story and "[t]he men who created the Talmud forgot as much of their own past as they remembered."[27]

By 1999, Haim Shapira was arguing "that the story's historical value lies far less in what it has to say about the Yavneh period than as a fabricated legend that bespeaks the historical and sociological context of its composition: the Yerushalmi version—that of third century Palestine; the Babylonian version—that of fourth century Babylonia."[28] Despite their differences in this regard, Shapira's reading of the story is the product of a trend set in motion by Goldenberg that continues to this day. That is, since Goldenberg's 1972 article, scholars who have dealt at length with the b. Ber. 27b–28a story have universally sought out both the meaning of the story and its function within society by comparing it to its earlier Yerushalmi iteration (y. Ber. 4:1).[29] By comparing both versions of the story, Goldenberg argued that, while both the BT and PT versions of the story are composites, the BT version is based directly on the PT version. Additionally, within the PT version itself there are earlier and later strata, and Goldenberg postulates that the first part of the narrative, with its extremely negative depiction of Rabban Gamaliel, was told independently from the rest of the story. Yerushalmi authors sympathetic to

25. Ibid., 190.

26. Ibid.

27. Ibid.

28. Haim Shapira, "The Deposition of Rabban Gamaliel — Between History and Legend" [Hebrew], *Zion* 64 (1999): 5–38, here, iv of the English summary. See also Menachem Ben Shalom's rejoinder and Shapira's response to that rejoinder in *Zion* 66 (2001): Ben Shalom, "The Story of the Deposition of Raban Gamliel and the Historical Reality"; Shapira, "Between Literature and History: A Response to M. Ben Shalom."

29. In most of these studies, the parallels are presented side by side in synoptic fashion or in their entireties consecutively. The theoretical underpinning of such an approach is found in the process folklorists call ecotypification, when oral narratives are modified "as they are transferred and retold from one cultural context to another"; see Boyarin, *Border Lines*, 154. In the words of Rubenstein, the tellers of these stories "refracted them through the prism of their experience. Many changes occurred unintentionally or subconsciously as transmitters replaced outmoded ideas with those more familiar to them. However, recent studies have shown that numerous changes resulted from a process of deliberate, intentional reworking" (*The Culture of the Babylonian Talmud* [Baltimore: Johns Hopkins University Press, 2003], 6).

Rabban Gamaliel chose the most favorable depiction of the initial episode available and "gave it a conclusion putting the whole incident in the best possible light."[30] Since Goldenberg's aim was a literary comparison and structural analysis for the purposes of understanding the historical veracity of the two accounts, his conclusions do not push much beyond noting the differences between the emphases found in each version. While the PT version is political, containing no moral component, the BT changes the overall tone of the story in presenting a personal dispute between two rabbis that focuses more on "what might be called the Rabbinic life-style," in particular, the display of dialectics.[31]

Devorah Steinmetz, writing in 1998, used both versions of the story to argue that meaning, for each story, is to be found in the differences between the two.[32] She focused on both stories' depictions of the requirements associated with the authority position of the *Nasi.* While the Yerushalmi sees heredity as the sole determining factor for this position, the Bavli takes a more pragmatic approach, combining wisdom and practical considerations in its depiction of the requirements for a more academic position. Steinmetz notes that Rabban Gamaliel's own level of scholarship is never questioned, only his position on the value of debate.[33] She states that "clearly the authors of the BT were further from the historical reality of the patriarchate and the society within which it functioned than the authors of the PT."[34] She therefore posits that the BT idealizes the position of the *Nasi* as both a political and academic one because their own Babylonian Jewish political leader, the Exilarch (*resh geluta*), mostly operated in a purely political capacity outside of the academic circle.[35]

Writing just five years later in 2003, Jeffrey L. Rubenstein, in a wide-ranging examination of dialectic as value in Bavli stories, built on Goldenberg's observation that the Bavli version of the story displays a shift from what was originally a story that was political in nature to one that highlighted dialectical skill as a value.[36] David Weiss Halivni and Shamma Friedman had independently proposed that most of the dialectical argumentation found in the Babylonian Talmud is contained in the anonymous, rather than Amoraic, layer of the text.[37] While Friedman

30. Goldenberg, "Deposition of Rabban Gamliel II," 189. So even in the earliest of the scholarship reviewed here a view of the material evidence representing one of many possibilities is posited.

31. Ibid., 176.

32. Steinmetz, "Must the Patriarch Know 'Uqtzin?," 170.

33. Ibid., 189.

34. Ibid., 187.

35. Ibid. For the position of the Exilarch more generally, see Geoffrey Herman, *A Prince without a Kingdom: The Exilarch in the Sasanian Era*, TSAJ 150 (Tübingen: Mohr Siebeck, 2012).

36. Rubenstein, "Thematization of Dialectics."

37. See ibid., 71 n. 1 for Halivni and Friedman bibliography.

tends to take a purely literary approach in his analyses of the anonymous layer of the BT—"The Stam"—Halivni reads that layer in historical terms, dubbing the composers of that stratum of text the "Stammaim."[38] While the Amoraim were active from the beginning of the third century CE until the mid-fifth century, Halivni has pushed the dating of the activity of these Stammaim later and later in time over the course of the publication of his multivolume running commentary on the Talmud, *Meqorot u-Mesorot* (1968–2012). His earliest work dated the Stammaim to the mid-sixth century, but his most recent work has posited their activity as taking place in several stages through the mid-eighth century.[39] The purpose of Rubenstein's article was to test Halivni's theory that the shift in styles between Amoraic literary output, which consisted mostly of apodictic statements devoid of accompanying argumentation, to Stammaitic output, which "contains most of ... the logical analysis often considered the essence of the Bavli," points to "a shift in values that transpired in Stammaitic times."[40] What drove Rubenstein's inquiry was the fact that Halivni's voluminous commentary deals almost exclusively with legal sections of the Talmud and all but passes over the Talmud's narrative passages. Rubenstein asks if Halivni's theory applies to the aggadic portions of the Talmud as well and answers in the affirmative.[41] By arguing that the value of dialectic is not only a Bavli phenomenon but a late-Bavli one, Rubenstein takes issue with Shapira's fourth-century dating of the Babylonian version of the story and moves it a few centuries later into the era of the Stammaim.[42] The result is that we now have a story that can tell us about a historical period concerning which we have no external records and little or no explicitly contemporaneous internal data. What used to be a lacuna in the Jewish historical record has now been filled with much data that can

38. For an analysis of the philosophic underpinnings of each approach, see Sergey Dolgopolski, *The Open Past: Subjectivity and Remembering in the Talmud* (New York: Fordham University Press, 2012).

39. For a summary of Halivni's work and a description of how his views changed over a forty-year period, see Jeffrey L. Rubenstein's introduction to his translation of David Weiss Halivni's, *Meḳorot u-masorot: be'urim ba-Talmud: Masekhet Bava Batra* (Jerusalem: Magnes, 2007), in David Weiss Halivni, *The Formation of the Babylonian Talmud*, trans. Jeffrey L. Rubenstein (New York: Oxford University Press, 2013), xvii–xxx.

40. Rubenstein, "Thematization of Dialectics," 71 n. 2, summarizing the position of Halivni, first laid out in David Weiss Halivni, *Midrash, Mishnah and Gemara: The Jewish Predilection for Justified Law* (Cambridge, MA: Harvard University Press, 1986), 86–92.

41. On the distinction between halakha and aggada as it relates to the Talmud, see Barry Wimpfheimer, *Narrating the Law: A Poetics of Talmudic Legal Stories*, Divinations (Philadelphia: University of Pennsylvania Press, 2011), 31–62.

42. Later, Rubenstein argued that b. Ber. 27b–28a "contains numerous late elements ... and seems to have been composed or at least reworked well into the Stammaitic period" (*Stories of the Babylonian Talmud*, 82). There, Rubenstein provides a taxonomy for establishing late elements in Bavli narratives (86–90).

be culled from texts that recount earlier periods. Where Shapira argued that the stories do not tell us anything about the period in which they were set (late 1st century CE) yet can be used to tell us about the period in which they were composed, Rubenstein has moved that period of composition forward in time from Shapira's fourth-century CE to as late as Halivni's mid-eighth century.

Daniel Boyarin, in contrast, proposed dating the Babylonian Talmud's Yavneh story-cycle, of which this story is a part, to "somewhere in the fifth and sixth centuries," when the resolutions established in the Nicaean Council of 325 CE were finally taking effect.[43] For Boyarin, the Yavneh cycle of stories represents fabricated myths, a rabbinic mythopoesis. Rather than forming from centuries of oral traditions, they are instead the product of a "single redactional (stammaitic) layer and carry a similar ideologically freighted (or even driven) tendency."[44] According to Charlotte Fonrobert, whom Boyarin quotes, the mythology put forth in these stories posits "the institution that is not yet but has always already been."[45] The stories themselves, therefore, represent the product of a particular moment in the history of rabbinic Judaism rather than its founding essence or prehistory. Rabbinic pluralism is actually a later development than initially thought and its institutionalization can be dated to the stammaitic era.[46] For Boyarin, it is not dialectic that is thematized in the Yavneh cycle but rather an understanding of the essence of Torah as the "multiplicity of interpretations as well as the multiplicity of halakhic views,"[47] a stammaitic value that could be posited only once the possibility for any real opposition had been vanquished.[48] B. Ber. 27b–28a is the exceptional case of the entire Yavneh cycle of stories, where the "Talmud itself is preserving/constructing a memory of when things were not quite as they are now … in order to deal with or dispense with that alternative memory."[49]

43. Boyarin, *Border Lines*, 155. Boyarin points to the work of Richard Paul Vaggione for the dating of the Christian context (Vaggione, *Eunomius of Cyzicus and the Nicene Revolution* [Oxford: Clarendon, 2001], 151–57, as cited in Boyarin, *Border Lines*, 308 n. 17).

44. Boyarin, *Border Lines*, 154.

45. Boyarin (ibid.) cites Charlotte Elisheva Fonrobert, "When the Rabbi Weeps: On Reading Gender in Talmudic Aggadah," *Nashim: A Journal of Jewish Women's Studies & Gender Issues* 4 (2001): 56–83, here 58.

46. Boyarin, *Border Lines*, 155.

47. Ibid., 183. See also Hidary, *Dispute for the Sake of Heaven*, 269. In his treatment of the Berakhot story, Hidary is interested in understanding "what the two versions of this story might reveal about the attitude of the Yerushalmi and the Bavli toward multiplicity of practice." Hidary concludes that the Bavli narrative focuses "on the value of debate, inclusiveness of multiple opinions, and the right of an individual rabbi to dissent" (272). He uses legal pluralism as the lens through which to read this story as indicating the value of debate and the right of the individual to dissent.

48. Boyarin, *Border Lines*, 188.

49. Ibid.

B. Ber. 27b–28a therefore is the location within the Talmud where "[a] currently dominant institution (… the rabbinic House of Study) established its authority via a myth of foundation that represents the bad old days that it displaced and replaced."[50] The "'That day' [of the Berakhot story] is the day on which a shift took place to a 'democratic' and 'pluralistic' form of rabbinism from Rabban Gamaliel's version of Judaism in which there was a central authority" who has the power to decide who is in and who is out.[51]

In 2017, Moshe Simon-Shoshan published two articles that provided a fresh take on both the history of the transmission of b. Ber. 27b–28a and its relation to history. In "Transmission and Evolution of the Story of R. Gamliel's Deposition," Simon-Shoshan takes issue with the notion that the Bavli story is based on the Yerushalmi version.[52] Introducing a distinction between textual and performative modes of transmission,[53] Simon-Shoshan posits that the performative tradition included a basic plot structure, some key phrases, and rules for the inclusion of thematic content, which in the case of both the Bavli and Yerushalmi was a focus on political aspects of the study-house together with critical perspectives.[54] For Simon-Shoshan,

> a textual approach assumes a mode of transmission in which traditions are transmitted in a fairly fixed fashion, with great concern for maintaining the precise wording of the tradition as it was received … [and] texts develop through a process … in which they undergo a series of conscious revisions at various points in their history.... A performative approach, on the other hand, assumes that parallel passages each represent an original instantiation of a common set of received guidelines rather than a reworking of a previously formulated text.[55]

Simon-Shoshan sees the very first part of the narrative, the confrontation in the study-house between Rabban Gamaliel and R. Yehoshua over a matter of law and the latter's humiliation, as exhibiting features of a textual transmission mode, and the rest of the story as displaying charac-

---

50. Ibid.

51. Ibid., 187.

52. Simon-Shoshan, "Transmission and Evolution of the Story," 207–11.

53. Ibid.,196–206.

54. Ibid., 218.

55. Ibid., 197–98. Simon-Shoshan points to, on the one hand, Jeffrey L. Rubenstein, Shamma Friedman, and Amram Tropper as presuming a textual model in their analyses of the evolution of the text of talmudic stories, and, on the other hand, folklorists such as Ofra Meir and Jonah Fraenkel as assuming an oral-performative model to the texts they analyze. He also states that "a similar argument was made by Martin S. Jaffee, *Torah in the Mouth: Writing and Oral Tradition in Palestinian Judaism, 200 BCE–400 CE* (Oxford: Oxford University Press 2001). However, Jaffee conflates the textual/performative dichotomy with the oral/written one" (200).

teristics of a performative mode. "If the Bavli story tellers had before them the entire story in a fairly fixed form, they would have had no reason to preserve the opening scenes with such care while radically altering the formulation of the rest of the story."[56] The fact that a small part of the story was transmitted in a textual transmission mode and the rest in a performative mode leads Simon-Shoshan to conclude that "the most reasonable explanation of the evidence is that the two versions of the Deposition story emerged independently from a common performative tradition."[57]

In "Creators of Worlds: The Deposition of R. Gamliel and the Invention of Yavneh," Simon-Shoshan further argues that the Yavneh cycle of stories cannot be viewed "as direct reflections of historical circumstance—as relatively transparent commentaries on the dominant social and political systems in the worlds of their authors in later amoraic or postamoraic Palestine and Babylonia.... [I]t may be nearly as problematic to use these texts as sources for later rabbinic history as it is to use them as evidence for the earlier period they purport to portray."[58] He introduces the idea of "narrative worlds as autonomous literary phenomena" to explain his point.[59] "Theorists of narrative worlds ... frequently emphasize the gap between fully constructed narrative worlds and the 'real world' of the creators and consumers of a given story."[60] Authors create narrative worlds by cannibalizing elements of possible worlds, such as: the authors' primary world (their subjective interpretation of the real world in which they live); contiguous worlds (worlds that the author believes to really exist though they sit at some temporal or geographic distance from their direct experience); ideological worlds ("conceptualizations of how the world should, or should not, work"); and "the narrative world of a preexisting story or stories."[61]

> To create narrative worlds, authors and readers draw on aspects of a set of possible worlds of the types here described. Narrative worlds are inevitably interconnected with the historical, cultural, intellectual, and emotional worlds of their creators. But once created, narrative worlds cannot be so easily reverse engineered into their constituent parts. Each narrative world is a new creation, which synthesizes components of other worlds together with new material into an original unity. Narra-

56. Simon-Shoshan, "Transmission and Evolution of the Story," 206.

57. Ibid.

58. Simon-Shoshan, "Creators of Worlds," 297–98.

59. Ibid., 299.

60. Ibid. Simon-Shoshan points to Richard J. Gerrig as one of these theorists; see Gerrig, *Experiencing Narrative Worlds: On the Psychological Activities of Reading* (New Haven: Yale University Press, 1993).

61. Simon-Shoshan, "Creators of Worlds," 299–300.

tive worlds tend to blur the distinctions between the possible worlds on which they draw.[62]

For Simon-Shoshan, the Yerushalmi's narrative world is aristocratic, based on heredity; the Bavli's narrative world is volatile, with people rising and falling based on their abilities.[63] But neither story even mentions the word *Nasi* and therefore the stories' relationship with any historical *Nasi* is tenuous at best.[64]

While Steinmetz and Shapira read the parallel Berakhot stories as contemporaneous reflections of real political conflict, though each highlighted different time periods in which to locate the story, and Boyarin and Rubenstein, despite their divergent datings, read the Bavli stories as a reflection of the type of intellectual activity valued in stammaitic academies, Simon-Shoshan instead looks for the function the stories might have served within the societies in which they were told. Boyarin, too, had read the Bavli story as serving a function within the society that created it, but Simon-Shoshan critiques Boyarin's conclusions by arguing against his assumption that the elements of the story can be so neatly disentangled.[65] For Simon-Shoshan, rather than putting forth "a clear-cut agenda," the story engages issues[66] as it combines two opposing ideological worlds into its narrative world.[67] Performers of such stories use narrative worlds to play with assumptions and opinions in order to view them in a different light.[68] At the same time, the telling and retelling of these stories instilled in the performers "an organic sense of connection between their own circles and their endeavors and those of the first generation of rabbis"; and this activity worked to "legitimate the regnant social and political structures and ideologies in late antique rabbinic societies by creating the impression that these arrangements go back to the times of the earliest rabbis."[69]

Simon-Shoshan has introduced two ideas that are useful for my analysis of b. Ber. 27b–28a. The first relates to performance and the second, by extension, to genre. While the emphasis of Simon-Shoshan's foray into the theoretical realm of narrative worlds focuses on the materials that a performer might draw upon in forming a narrative, the byproduct of his analysis is the introduction of a new understanding of how to think about the form of these texts in terms of genre. While previous scholars have argued about how to properly excavate the historical information con-

62. Ibid., 300.
63. Ibid., 295.
64. Ibid., 298.
65. Ibid., 307.
66. Ibid. Shraga Bar-On takes a similar approach. See n. 116, below.
67. Ibid., 305.
68. Ibid., 308.
69. Ibid.

tained in the text, Simon-Shoshan, in both recasting the setting in which the stories were crafted and reimagining the materials from which they were crafted, has drawn our attention to the possibility that rabbinic narratives are neither historical accounts, folklore, nor mythology, but rather something entirely different.[70]

Talmudic Narrative as Walter Benjamin's Ideal Story

For Walter Benjamin, the novel is the death of the story.[71] The novel, through its one-time diachronic unfolding of events, is consumable. The novel is a material genre of literature made possible by the printing press. It is written in solitude and read in solitude and, when finished, disposed of. As such, upon completion, it answers all of its questions. A story, in contrast, is never done; it goes on forever.

> There is nothing that commends a story to memory more effectively than that chaste compactness which precludes psychological analysis. And the more natural the process by which the storyteller forgoes psychological shading, the greater becomes the story's claim to a place in the memory of the listener, the more completely it is integrated into his own experience, the greater will be his inclination to repeat it to someone else someday, sooner or later.[72]

"[I]t is half the art of storytelling to keep a story free from explanation as one reproduces it."[73] What is a story? Benjamin gives an example, as told by Herodotus:

---

70. For an exploration of genre as it relates to the Babylonian Talmud, see Daniel Boyarin, *Socrates and the Fat Rabbis* (Chicago: University Of Chicago Press, 2009). Boyarin is interested in discovering the genre to which the Talmud as a whole is most similar and he settles on the *spoudogeloion* of Menippean satire, the Greek seriocomic "literary mood" found in writers such as Lucian of Samosata (c. 125–180 CE) (28–29).

71. Walter Benjamin, "The Storyteller," in *Illuminations*, ed. Hannah Arendt, trans. Harry Zohn (New York: Schocken, 1969), 87. This essay, first published in 1936, has been reprinted many times. Benjamin does not distinguish between narrative and story. What he is after is what makes a story good. He locates good stories within a tradition of storytelling, when a story's telling encourages its retelling. For the classic definition of a story, see E. M. Forster, *Aspects of the Novel* (New York: Harcourt, Brace & Co., 1927), 83–104. Forster, there distinguishes between "story" and "plot." For a distinction between "narrative" and "story," as well as relevant bibliography on the subject, see Moshe Simon-Shoshan, *Stories of the Law: Narrative Discourse and the Construction of Authority in the Mishnah* (New York: Oxford University Press, 2012), 15–22. Ultimately, different theorists use terms like "narrative," "story," "event," and "plot" differently.

72. Benjamin, "The Storyteller," 91.

73. Ibid., 89.

> When the Egyptian king Psammenitus had been beaten and captured by the Persian king Cambyses, Cambyses was bent on humbling his prisoner. He gave orders to place Psammenitus on the road along which the Persian triumphal procession was to pass. And he further arranged that the prisoner should see his daughter pass by as a maid going to the well with her pitcher. While all the Egyptians were lamenting and bewailing this spectacle, Psammenitus stood alone, mute and motionless, his eyes fixed on the ground; and when presently he saw his son, who was being taken along in the procession to be executed, he likewise remained unmoved. But when afterwards he recognized one of his servants, an old, impoverished man, in the ranks of the prisoners, he beat his fists against his head and gave all the signs of the deepest mourning.[74]

What is the meaning of this story? Why did the king react in the way he did? Each listener of the story must decide for themselves, is encouraged to decide for themselves. The story is noteworthy precisely because the storyteller refrains from offering up more than an image. The hearer of this story is motivated to process the story through the act of its retelling. Benjamin contrasts the "story" with the morning news, the primary mode in which information was disseminated in his era. (The essay was written in 1936.) The news contains no noteworthy stories because it presents events "already … shot through with explanation."[75] The events therefore do not remain with us because they require no meditation; they have no reason to be retold. They have already been consumed at the moment they are read.

Biblical narratives are stories in the Benjaminian sense.[76] Talmudic narratives, too, follow this tradition of storytelling. They do not tell us what they mean while they are dictating events. So, where do we look for meaning in a story? How do we find it? Structuralists argue that meaning is most easily found in difference; and for many rabbinic stories we are given two or more different versions to compare.[77] These versions appear in the Bavli and its material precursors and successors—the Yerushalmi and various other rabbinic texts. It is the very materiality of the rabbinic books we now read that creates the illusion that they are finished products

74. Ibid., 89–90.

75. Ibid., 89.

76. For an example of critics who highlight this aspect of biblical narratives, as not "already shot through with explanation," see Robert Alter, *The Art of Biblical Narrative* (New York: Basic Books, 1981), 114–30, on "reticence" in biblical narrative; and Meir Sternberg, *The Poetics of Biblical Narrative: Ideological Literature and the Drama of Reading*, Indiana Literary Biblical Series (Bloomington: Indiana University Press, 1985), 186–229, on gaps and ambiguity in biblical narrative and their impact on the reading process.

77. This idea was proposed for linguistics in Ferdinand de Saussure, *Cours de linguistique générale* (Paris: Payot, 1916); and for mental structures in Claude Lévi-Strauss, *Anthropologie structurale* (Paris: Plon, 1958).

in their own right, making it difficult to ignore the discrepancies between two tellings of a story as the starting point on a quest for the meaning. Since Friedman's methodological breakthrough, and Rubenstein's extensive application and development of that method for rabbinic narratives, this approach has become ubiquitous among academic Talmudists.[78] But the texts' materiality, and mass production, creates an illusion that allows for, or even encourages, the viewing of two concrete forms of a story as representative of two distinct moments in the time of a storytelling, and that these two moments, when compared, supply the key to the meaning of the story.[79] More likely, the talmudic storyteller worked within an oral performative tradition similar to that "atmosphere of craftsmanship"[80] described by Paul Valéry and quoted by Benjamin. For Valéry, the craftsman imitates the "patient process of Nature" as "the precious product of a long chain of causes similar to one another" and produces "lacquer work or paintings in which a series of thin, transparent layers are placed

---

78. Examples of this approach for the deposition story, though each scholar moves in different directions, can be found in Steinmetz, "Must the Patriarch Know 'Uqtzin?"; Rubenstein, *Stories of the Babylonian Talmud*, 77–90. Friedman's programmatic statement can first be found in Shamma Friedman, "A Critical Study of Yevamot X with a Methodological Introduction," in *ʿAṭarah le-Ḥayim: Meḥḳarim ba-sifrut ha-Talmudit yeha-rabanit li-khevod Profesor Ḥayim Zalman Dimiṭrovsḳi*, ed. Daniel Boyarin et al. (Jerusalem: Magnes, 1977), 275–441. He later applied his methodology to rabbinic narratives, and a good example of that application can be found in Shamma Friedman, "The Further Adventures of Rav Kahana: Between Babylonia and Palestine," in *The Talmud Yerushalmi and Graeco-Roman Culture*, ed. Peter Schafer and Catherine Hezser, 3 vols., TSAJ 71, 79, 93 (Tübingen: Mohr Siebeck, 2001), 3:247-71; and Friedman, "A Good Story Deserves Retelling: The Unfolding of the Akiva Legend," *JSIJ* 3 (2004): 55–93. For Rubenstein, see his trilogy on rabbinic narratives: *Talmudic Stories: Narrative Art, Composition, and Culture* (Baltimore: Johns Hopkins University Press, 1999); *The Culture of the Babylonian Talmud*; and *Stories of the Babylonian Talmud*. David Weiss Halivni should also be noted in the same conversation as Friedman's methodological breakthrough, and his innovative work can be found starting in 1968 in his multivolume Dayid Halivni, *Meḳorot U-Masorot: Be'urim Be-Talmud* (Tel Aviv: Devir, 1968). The drive behind Halivni's method is different from Friedman's, as Halivni is more interested in explaining the reasons for forced interpretations in the Bavli. In his commentary, Halivni almost completely ignores the aggadic sections of the Talmud. See Rubenstein's comment in his introduction to, and annotation of, his translation of Halivni's most extensive programmatic statement, in Halivni, *The Formation of the Babylonian Talmud*, xviii–xix, 270.

79. Jameson presents the problem presented by the printed text as follows: "For one thing, the illusion or appearance of isolation or autonomy which a printed text projects must now be systematically undermined. Indeed, since by definition the cultural monuments and masterworks that have survived tend necessarily to perpetuate only a single voice in this class dialogue, the voice of a hegemonic class, they cannot be properly assigned their relational place in a dialogical system without the restoration or artificial reconstruction of the voice to which they were initially opposed, a voice for the most part stifled and reduced to silence, marginalized, its own utterances scattered to the winds, or reappropriated in their turn by the hegemonic culture" (*Political Unconscious*, 71).

80. Benjamin, "Storyteller," 92.

one on top of the other."[81] For Benjamin, likewise, "the perfect narrative is revealed through the layers of a variety of retellings."[82]

If, as Benjamin suggests, "stories" are dynamic, formed by "that slow piling one on top of the other of thin, transparent layers,"[83] then talmudic stories represent only examples of versions of the stories that have been told in a long history of their storytelling. Is there a way for us to analyze the meaning of such stories in a way that highlights the variability rather than stability of a particular text? An approach that seeks to downplay a single instantiation of a story would resist the temptation to compare it to other known versions, because such a comparison reifies the notion of two separate and distinct concrete artifices that are meant to stand in stark contrast. On an interpretive level, even if we do not begin with an assumption that the author of the later version of a story was reading the same version of the earlier story that we now have before us, the very act of lining up the two extant versions side by side skews the reader's analysis in the direction of difference. What happens if, instead of reading two texts as representing a transition between two distinct, already entrenched and defined, historical moments, we read a single text as composed over centuries in a transitionary environment? At the same time, even if we were to assume that the plot of a given story was somewhat stable throughout the history of its storytelling, narratological analysis of a structural variety should also be downplayed. That too would direct attention to how particular portions or lines of the text relate to the entirety of the narrative in a single stabilized recording of a dynamic text. However, since we do not now have access to the missing performances, whether because they were never recorded in writing or simply because they were lost to time, resorting to imagined versions of a story runs the risk of skewing our analysis in a different direction, toward blindly erasing, or shifting the focus away from, what might have been important and central to the storytelling tradition.[84] How is one to solve this bind? Is there another avenue for analyzing the essence of a text while trying to read it not as text but as story, to look beyond what it says to find what it means?

A distant reading approach, one that resists reading the story and instead reads a map of its characters and their relationships, is useful in finding a way to read, with fresh eyes, a story that has been extensively analyzed so many times that it has become hard to view it outside of the

81. Ibid.

82. Ibid., 93. See also Robert Kawashima's use of this Benjamin passage in *Biblical Narrative and the Death of the Rhapsode*, ISBL (Bloomington: Indiana University Press, 2004), 167–68.

83. Benjamin, "Storyteller," 93.

84. See Jameson, *Political Unconscious*, 71, for his approach to this problem as it relates to his overall project.

established academic discourse.[85] In my quest to rethink this story, I first began by creating such a map and trying to tell anew the story of the map.[86] While it would be significant to merely highlight what data this approach yields—and in this instance it is a realization that the plot of a particular story contains many more characters, representing many more social positions, than previous readings have noticed—I will further read the story through a Marxist lens. The relevance of using such a lens for the deposition story will become clear once a key subtext is elucidated and thereby the context for the text's production and development is laid bare. Following Benjamin's conception of a story, it is necessary to find a methodology through which to view a text not only in terms of what is present in an individual performance, what is not, and what is only partially present, but also in the totality of those relationships in the culture that produced both the story being read and its undocumented, or absent, iterations. Such a method does not seek to discover what is missing from the text through diachronic analysis, by appealing to information contained in its Palestinian precursor version, but rather through synchronic analysis within the Babylonian milieu. Frederic Jameson provides the entry point for such analysis.

Jameson's method of interpretation involves passing progressively through three interpretive stages, which he calls "distinct semantic horizons."[87] In the following extended analysis, I will follow Jameson through these three horizons in an attempt to delve more deeply into what this text can reveal about the society in which it was produced and that society's relationship to its past and imagined future. These horizons are "also distinct moments of the process of interpretation, and may in that sense be understood as … successive 'phases' in our reinterpretation—our rereading and rewriting—of the literary text."[88] As one moves through the three stages, the object of interpretation—what might be called "the text"—becomes reconstructed. In the first stage, the object of interpretation is the individual narrative, which, in this case, is a historical narrative about a

85. This approach was proposed by Franco Moretti as a solution to a similar question as it relates to literature as a whole (*Distant Reading* [London: Verso, 2013], 211). Moretti argues counterintuitively that we cannot understand literature by reading books. For no matter how many books we read there would be others we necessarily did not read. To solve this problem, he turned to the quantitative analysis of literature and to, most importantly for the present study, network theory, the study of relationships. When he tried to apply quantitative analytical methodologies to plot, he admittedly failed and found himself slipping back into qualitative analysis of a different kind. However, his application of network theory to plot yielded a method for using distant reading to analyze narratives, character maps.

86. The map can be found on page 321, below.

87. Jameson, *Political Unconscious*, 61.

88. Here, Jameson (*Political Unconscious*, 61) invokes Northrop Frye (*Anatomy of Criticism* [Princeton, NJ: Princeton University Press, 1957], 71–130) and views his own approach as a dialectical equivalent of Frye's method.

revolution and its resolution. In the second stage, the individual text is no longer the object of interpretation. Rather, it is "the essentially antagonistic collective discourses of social classes," within which the narrative is but one utterance.[89] In the third stage, this individual expression is viewed in its relationship to the entirety of human history, where, in accordance with Benjamin's understanding of how stories are produced, "sedimented content" can be viewed "as carrying ideological messages of their own, distinct from the ostensible or manifest content of the works."[90] By moving progressively through these three interpretive horizons, a story that at first appears to tell of a particular historical revolution instead becomes one that reveals the ever-present potential for cultural revolution that existed within the rabbinic society that produced, altered, and retold the story.

Rabbi Shimeon's Biography as the Absent Present

In reading within the first of his three semantic horizons, Fredric Jameson views a literary work as a single expression within a diachronic view of political history, "in which history is reduced to a series of punctual events and crises in time ... the rise and fall of political regimes."[91] As such, the individual text as object of study is seen, much as in Claude Levi-Strauss's reading of myths, "as symbolic resolutions of real political and social contradictions."[92] The production of a narrative is not informed by an ideology but is rather "an ideological act in its own right, with the function of inventing imaginary or formal 'solutions' to unresolvable social contradictions."[93] Such a view sees the text as political allegory, as "a sometimes repressed ur-narrative or master fantasy about the interaction of collective subjects," using "class representatives or 'types.'"[94] In the case of the deposition story, this would amount to viewing the revolution within the academy as an invention used to resolve a social issue through the restructuring of the political system. It is this approach that, as we have seen, is taken by some of the academic scholarship on this story. Jameson, however, moves one step beyond and seeks out the source of the contradiction that the narrative seeks to solve not in the narrative itself but in its absent subtext—to read a narrative not for the text's visible structure but for its

89. Jameson, *Political Unconscious*, 61.

90. Ibid., 84. Jameson himself is speaking of form and genre, as vestiges of past systems, within a literary work. Our analysis will focus on content.

91. Ibid., 62.

92. Ibid., 65; Claude Lévi-Strauss, "The Structural Study of Myth," *Journal of American Folklore* 68 (1955): 428–44.

93. Jameson, *Political Unconscious*, 64.

94. Ibid., 65.

absent cause.[95] In this way, he looks to the text's "signifying absence" in order to discover the semantic precondition of the text's meaning.[96] While Jameson uses Greimassian semiotics to locate the absent subtext in history, such an approach is far more difficult for the Talmud, owing to our uncertainty both about when it was produced and the particular environment in which it was produced.[97] I therefore look to the Talmud itself in search of the subtext of the deposition narrative. The most glaring clue for where to find this subtext is in the first line of the story. B. Ber. 27b–28a begins with a *baraita*, the first line of which, מעשה בתלמיד אחד שבא לפני רבי יהושע אמר ליה, can be translated either as:

> 1. "A story, with one student who came before R. Yehoshua, saying to him …"

Or:

> 2. "A story about a certain student who came before R. Yehoshua. He said to him …"

What is this story about? The answer to this question, at least in an overt sense, depends on how we interpret this first line.[98] Is it simply a story, a story about a student, or a story about a decidedly unnamed student who came before R. Yehoshua? It is not until the final line of the narrative that this question is answered:

> ואותו תלמיד ר׳ שמעון בן יוחאי הוה
>
> And that student was R. Shimeon b. Yoḥai.

This final line that names the unnamed student is quite jarring because, prior to its appearance, the story is focalized around a conflict in the academy between two rabbis, R. Yehoshua and Rabban Gamaliel, and the political ramifications of the conflict as they relate to leadership of the academy.[99] Without this final line of the narrative, the above questions raised by the opening line would probably recede into the background. However, the fact that the story is bookended in this manner calls attention to itself. It alters the focus of the story and brings the trope of a student-led revolution to the fore. But at the same time the revelation serves the function of making this a story in the Benjaminian sense. Though this final sentence appears to tie up a loose end, it nonetheless, much like with

95. Ibid., 66–67.
96. Ibid., 124.
97. This point will be elaborated below.
98. I thank Ely Behar for first bringing this point to my attention.
99. MS Oxford of b. Ber. 27b is an outlier among the manuscripts and printed editions of this text. There, the name of the student is revealed as parenthetical comment in the beginning of the narrative.

the Herodotus text cited by Benjamin, prevents the audience from consuming the narrative and moving on. The fact that the student is identified as R. Shimeon, that this identification seems significant for the story, and that the significance of R. Shimeon's identification is left unexplained within the confines of the story, leaves a gap in the text that forces the story's audience to look beyond its boundaries for interpretation and illumination. It is R. Shimeon's action that puts the events of the story in motion; but what about R. Shimeon is the cause of the story itself?

Benjamin describes the novel, with its one-time diachronic unfolding of events, as consumable. The Talmud as a whole resists such a description. When viewed in its entirety, the Talmud's events unfold neither diachronically nor chronologically. Each new page read cannot be understood without information contained on a page not yet read in the diachronic unfolding of events. But even after the entirety of the book is read and known, the chronology of events contained therein remains hidden[100]—this despite the many short narratives that independently develop along a definite chronology, as does the narrative presently under investigation. While the Talmud is certainly interested in rabbinic biography, in telling biographical tales, its fragmented representation of the biographies of its heroes does not allow the reader the possibility of consuming those biographies. Of the characters in our story, some are given the space within the Talmud for an elaborate biographical narrative (by talmudic standards), and it is in those biographical texts that we can look to discover the significance of the gaps in our story. The story's unconscious drive, the underlying tension that the plot of the narrative serves to obscure, can be found by filling in these gaps. It is the very fact that these biographical tales stand outside of a decipherable chronology of other talmudic events in which those rabbis appear—that they stand in an atemporal relationship to the events in other stories—that lends them their significance in the context of a narrative focalized around other primary characters.[101] As the plot of one story develops, and the reader attempts to consume that narrative, the

100. In the terminology of Russian formalism, the fabula of the Talmud cannot be reconstructed from its syuzhet. These terms roughly translate to "story" and "plot," respectively. They were first used by Viktor Shklovsky in a 1921 essay, which can be found in English translation in Viktor Shklovsky, "Sterne's Tristam Shandy: Stylistic Commentary," in *Russian Formalist Criticism: Four Essays*, trans. Lee T. Lemon and Marion J. Reis (Lincoln: University of Nebraska Press, 1965), 25–60.

101. Devorah Steinmetz takes a different approach but similar enough to warrant a comparison. In her essay "Agada Unbound: Inter-Agadic Characterization of Sages in the Bavli and Implications for Reading Agada," Steinmetz argues that the Bavli as a whole characterizes certain sages in particular ways and shows how reading talmudic passages in which a number of rabbinic characters appear is enriched by an understanding of how those sages are characterized throughout the Bavli.

texts that recount events external to that story remain unchanged.[102] In the b. Ber. 27b–28a narrative, R. Akiva and R. Shimeon are minor characters in terms of their screen time, but their biographical tales, ubiquitous in the cultures that produced, listened to, and retold this story, provide a deeper and more complex structure for the tensions and antagonisms that truly drive the storytelling. For R. Akiva, two parallel biographical narratives are most prominent, and we will return to their contents later. For R. Shimeon, it is the tale told in b. Šabb. 33b–34a that supplies the clue to the deposition story's latent discourse. R. Shimeon's external biographical tale reveals what his character stands in for in our story, the hidden cause of the social and political tensions that underlie the storytelling: urbanization.[103]

Rabbi Shimeon's Biography and Urbanization

The overt themes of the b. Šabb. 33b–34a story are obvious: foreign domination, materialism, and the delicate balance required to be a successful spiritual being in a political world. [104] The story begins with R. Shimeon debating R. Yehudah as to the value of Roman infrastructure. R. Yehudah praises the actions of the Romans in their establishment of markets, bridges, and bathhouses. R. Shimeon, in response, argues that all that the Romans have established they have done for selfish reasons: markets as a place in which to establish prostitutes, bathhouses to refresh themselves, and bridges in order to collect taxes. When R. Shimeon's statement is

102. For biographical tales of rabbis as a stratum of the Talmud text that stands as a dialogical countervoice to the Stam of the halakhic *sugya*, see Boyarin, *Socrates and the Fat Rabbis*, 174–91.

103. Marina Rustow writes, "An apocryphal piece of academic lore recounts the story of a graduate seminar at Columbia in which the late Yosef Yerushalmi asked his students to name the single most important event in Jewish history. 'The destruction of the second Temple?' one hazards. 'No!' Yerushalmi thunders; 'you're thinking like yeshiva *buchers*.' 'The founding of the state of Israel?' 'No!' he bellows; 'you're thinking like Zionists. Think like historians!' The answer he seeks: the imposition of the land tax after the Islamic conquests. An answer more pedestrian, even *boring*, his students think, cannot be imagined; they are perplexed, but no one dares object. He explains: the land tax brought Jews to cities, changing Jewish history forever" (Marina Rustow, "Baghdad in the West: Migration and the Making of Medieval Jewish Traditions," *AJS Perspectives* [Fall 2010], http://perspectives.ajsnet.org/the-iran-iraq-issue-fall-2010/baghdad-in-the-west-migration-and-the-making-of-medieval-jewish-traditions/). James Loeffler, in an oral communication, revealed to me that this story is not in fact apocryphal. He had the very same interaction with Prof. Yerushalmi during his qualifying exams.

104. For detailed analysis of this story, see Lee Levine, "R. Simeon b Yohai and the Purification of Tiberias: History and Tradition," *HUCA* 49 (1978): 143–85; Ofra Meir, *Sugiyot ba-poʾeṭiḳah shel sipure Ḥazal*, Poʾeṭiḳah u-viḳoret (Tel-Aviv: Sifriyat poʿalim, 1993), 11–35; and Rubenstein, *Talmudic Stories*, 105–38.

brought to the attention of the Roman government he is forced to flee for his life and hide in a cave for thirteen years. There, he studies Torah all day, free from the distraction of seeing to his own material needs. Through events that transpire upon his leaving the cave (twice), R. Shimeon comes to soften his position. He now realizes that materiality and spirituality are not mutually exclusive pursuits. If one directs one's material energies toward attaining spiritual heights, then the two pursuits can indeed coexist in the political realm. R. Shimeon attempts to practice this approach by appropriating the very things the denial of which sent him to the cave in the first place: he makes use of a bathhouse to heal his wounds; builds a virtual bridge over a graveyard to allow others easier access to markets;[105] and he even makes use of prostitutes, albeit rhetorically. But R. Shimeon's epiphany is short lived. He never finds true balance and the story ends with him killing two men. In this story, too, the narrator is reticent and neither excoriates nor exonerates R. Shimeon for causing the death of two morally ambiguous characters whose culpabilities remain in question.

In order to discover what R. Shimeon's biographical tale contributes to our understanding of the b. Ber. 27b–28a story with which we began, it is helpful to focus first on a narrative interlude between the time that he uses the bathhouse to heal his wounds and when he builds his virtual bridge. This interlude is presented in what appears to be an inner monologue.

> אמר הואיל ואיתרחיש ניסא איזיל אתקין מילתא דכתיב ויבא יעקב שלם ואמר רב שלם בגופו שלם בממונו שלם בתורתו ויחן את פני העיר אמר רב מטבע תיקן להם ושמואל אמר שווקים תיקן להם ור׳ יוחנן אמר מרחצאות תיקן להם

> [R. Shimeon] said [to himself]: Since a miracle happened, I will go and repair [*'atqin*] something, as it is written, "And Jacob came complete [to the city of Shechem…]" (Gen 33:18)
> And Rav said [in explication of this verse]: Complete in his body; complete in his money; complete in his Torah.
> "… and he encamped before the city." (continuation of Gen 33:18)
> And Rav said [in explication of this verse]: He established [*tiqen*] coinage for them.
> And Shmuel said [in explication of this verse]: He established [*tiqen*] markets for them.
> And R. Yoḥanan said [in explication of this verse]: He established [*tiqen*] bathhouses for them.

105. Markets are not specified in the text. Rather this is how Rashi explains R. Shimeon's motivation, explicitly relying on Palestinian versions of the story. In the versions of the story in the Yerushalmi, Pesiqta de Rab Kahana, and Lamentations Rabbah, R. Shimeon establishes markets as his first act of reform upon leaving the cave. In the version in Genesis Rabbah, markets also play a role in R. Shimeon's purification of Tiberias.

R. Shimeon's use of a verse explicated by three rabbis who postdated him by a century betrays that this story, when viewed in its entirety, is a later retelling of an earlier story.[106] The positioning of this achronological interlude within the story highlights the Talmud's synchronic notion of history, with multiple historical moments being brought into dialogue in the present of the text. This feature of talmudic storytelling, I will later argue, proves essential for understanding the nature of the cultural work talmudic stories and their retelling performs. The interlude, itself playing with time, serves to pass judgment on what comes before and after it in the text's internal narrative time. Rav's first statement uses the patriarch Jacob as an exemplar of what it means to be a whole man, to be complete. This entails a balance of materiality, physicality, and spirituality, what, perhaps, R. Shimeon had come to learn at this point in the story. The tripartite exegesis of the second part of the verse, by Rav, Shmuel, and R. Yoḥanan, takes a biblical context that appears to be the exemplification of the anti-urban bias of the book of Genesis, the Shechem narrative, and turns it on his head.[107] According to the interpretation of these three rabbis, it was the patriarch Jacob who is the father of the modern city. Jacob established the material conditions necessary for urban life—the commoditization of goods through the use of markets and coins, as well as the hygienic reforms that allow for dense populations to thrive.

---

106. In fact, there are a number of different Palestinian rabbinic compilations, ranging from the late fourth through the eighth centuries that contain an account of the story of R. Shimeon and the cave. While the dating of rabbinic texts is a hotly contested issue, I will list these sources in chronological order and provide the range of dates given for each text as found in Hermann Leberecht Strack, *Introduction to the Talmud and Midrash*, trans. Markus Bockmuehl (Philadelphia: Fortress, 1996), 164–326: y. Šeb. 9:1 (between ca. 360 and ca. 430, Palestine); Gen. Rab. 79:6 (first half of fifth century, Palestine); Pesiq. Rab Kah. 11:16 (ed. Mandelbaum; late fifth–early eighth century); Esth. Rab. 3:7 (sixth–eleventh century, Palestine); Qoh. Rab. 10:8 (sixth–eighth century, Palestine); Midr. Ps. 18:13 (contains earlier material but continues to be edited through the thirteenth century, Palestine). Yal. Shim. *Beshalaḥ* (twelfth–thirteenth century) and Midrash Hagadol 18:22 (thirteenth–fourteenth century, Egypt or Yemen) also contain this story, but it is derivative of the version found in the Babylonian Talmud. As Lee Levine has noted, "the Palestinian material is strikingly homogeneous" ("R. Simeon b Yohai and the Purification of Tiberias," 144). Though the Palestinian versions of the story do not explain that R. Shimeon was in the cave because he was fleeing the Roman government, they all either have R. Shimeon reflecting on the patriarch Jacob establishing duty-free markets with efficient pricing or have R. Shimeon himself establish a market. The Genesis Rabbah version opens with this information and ties it into the idea that one should be grateful to a place from which one derives benefit.

107. See Phillip Michael Sherman, *Babel's Tower Translated: Genesis 11 and Ancient Jewish Interpretation*, BibInt 117 (Leiden: Brill, 2013), 67–69. Sherman, with a focus on Genesis, takes issue with Robert R. Wilson's rebuttal to the academic consensus on this topic ("The City in the Old Testament," in *Civitas: Religious Interpretations of the City*, ed. Peter S. Hawkins [Eugene, OR: Wipf & Stock, 2016], 3–14). Wilson sees the attitude toward the city in the Old Testament as a whole as ambivalent.

While it is unclear whether Rabbi Shimeon's initial claim that the Romans did everything for self-interest implies that Rabbi Yehudah thought them to be benevolent and philanthropic, there is another possibility for understanding Rabbi Yehudah's praise, one that relates to the development of the rabbinic power structure over time in the context of a shift in the economic structure of the society of the storytellers. Though in the time of Rabbi Shimeon, the power source of Palestinian Jewish society might have been slowly shifting from one based on an agrarian economy to an urban one, the memory of such a shift, if such a memory existed, was already in the distant past by the time of the late Babylonian storytellers.[108] What is more likely reflected in this tale is the grafting of a contemporary Babylonian experience onto stories told and retold over time in the course of the transmission process. Since we really have no idea when the particular version of this Shabbat story (or, for that matter, the deposition story) that we now read was produced, other than prior to when line commentaries began to be written on the Talmud in the early eleventh century, we cannot place it in a precise historical moment. At the same time, in following Benjamin's understanding of what a story represents, this text should not be read in terms of its association with a particular historical moment that is marked in contrast to another concrete historical moment—as a text situated in a moment of rupture—but rather as part of a process. The text therefore reflects one moment within many moments of transition, and it is the centuries-long process of urbanization rather than a year in which urbanization took place that is reflected in the text. In light of this, two factors should be considered. First, there is ample evidence that Babylonian Jewry had already been undergoing a process of urbanization by the late eighth century, where an earlier sharecropper economy had given way to a merchant class economy, at least among the ruling class.[109] Second, contemporaneous versions of this story were being told in Palestinian circles with different emphases. Most importantly for our purposes, those versions do not contain the opening section of the story, the discussion between the three rabbis about the value of Roman urban infrastructure.[110] The BT story, therefore, appears to retroject the transitioning socioeconomic organization of the society in which the storytellers lived onto a

108. For discussion of rabbinic urbanization in the Palestinian context, see Seth Schwartz, *Imperialism and Jewish Society: 200 B.C.E. to 640 C.E.*, Jews, Christians, and Muslims from the Ancient to the Modern World 32 (Princeton, NJ: Princeton University Press, 2009), 162–76; Hayim Lapin, "Rabbis and Cities: Some Aspects of the Rabbininc Movement in Its Graeco-Roman Environment," in Schäfer and Heszer, *Talmud Yerushalmi and Graeco-Roman Culture*, 2:51–80; Hayim Lapin, "Rabbis and Cities: The Literary Evidence," *JJS* 50 (1999): 187–207; and Catherine Hezser, *The Social Structure of the Rabbinic Movement in Roman Palestine*, TSAJ 66 (Tübingen: Mohr Siebeck, 1997), 157–84.

109. See n. 14 above.

110. See n. 106 above.

rabbinic society that was much different from their own, and altogether different from that of the patriarch Jacob, their imagined founder of the urban economy. Therefore, when the character of R. Yehudah extols the value of the contribution the Romans had made to the quality of life of the Palestinian rabbis, he stands in for a position extant in the sociopolitical culture of the hegemonic Babylonian storytellers. These storytellers, having experienced a transition toward urbanization, reveal to us the environment in which they imagined the rabbis of R. Shimeon's era too to have thrived.[111] Of course, the Shabbat story is not about R. Yehudah but is rather focalized on the evolving position of R. Shimeon's character. The story therefore more directly reflects the anxiety associated with the disruption of an entrenched economic system, even if the new structure itself is what allows for the class of which the storytellers were a part to consolidate power.

What this b. Šabb. 33b–34 biographical tale of R. Shimeon and its interpolated homiletics on the establishment of coinage, markets, and bathhouses therefore provides is the subtext of the deposition story. R. Shimeon's momentary presence at the end of the b. Ber. 27b–28a story is what marks his absence at the start of that story; and his absence highlights urbanization as the subtext that clues us into the true source of the tensions that underlie the revolution he leads. Though the revolution takes place in a narrative rather than in history, the semantic precondition for understanding the revolution, which the narrative's plot and form conceal, is found in the socioeconomic impact of a market economy on the way the rabbis conceptualize their own power structures and the role Torah study plays in that equation. It is urbanization that supports rabbinic hegemony through the centralization of its power structures, yet at the same time urbanization also leads to a different kind of relationship between the labor force and the modes of production and exchange within a society. But it is not the ramifications of the transition to an urban environment of the time of R. Shimeon, whether historically representative or not, that are the object of our study but rather the ramifications of the time of the later Babylonian storytellers. In order to unpack the effect of this transition in terms of both the traditional market economy and the place of Torah study within the rabbinic economy, I turn to theorists who develop and expand on Karl Marx's initial concepts.

111. The Babylonian storytellers were no doubt unaware of the picture of the early second-century rabbinic movement constructed by modern scholarship, that the rabbis had defeated the many competing claims to religious authority that existed prior to the destruction of the Second Temple less than a century before the time in which this story is set. They most probably understood, based on the proliferation of named rabbis in the Mishnah during this period, as well as other factors, that it was with the destruction of the Second Temple that the rabbinic movement began to prosper.

Reading beyond Historical Materialism: An Economics of Torah

In order for Marx to be a productive lens through which to view the revolution in this story, it is necessary to abandon his understanding of history in epochal terms—where a series of successive economic structures with determinate features replace one another whole scale—yet at the same time retain his emphasis on history and modes of production and exchange as central guiding features for our analysis. To do so, we must first revise our understanding of "economic conditions" as it relates to the power structure under which this text was produced. Then, we can address ways of retaining Marx's focus on history while avoiding the epochal scheme that seems at odds with the historical time line of both the narrative and those who produced it.

Louis Althusser, in his expansion of Marxism, borrowed Freud's term "overdetermination" and challenged orthodox Marxism's notion that everything can be traced back to a single cause, economic factors.[112] If we attempt to look beyond traditional material economic factors in trying to understand the organization of rabbinic society as it relates to a power scheme, the most obvious direction would be to simply map Marx's historical materialism onto the distinctly "rabbinic" economy, where Torah as the life-blood of both spiritual and material existence is considered the dominant mode of production. Those who control the means of production and exchange of this society's essential necessity, Torah, therefore control the power relations of domination and subjugation within that society. B. Ber. 27b–28a is certainly, on its surface, a story about control over the means of production as it relates to Torah, and the scholarship outlined above tilts in this direction without explicitly invoking Marxism. But let us bracket for a moment the notion of Torah study as a spiritual necessity and focus first instead on the material and political implications of Torah study output. A Jew living within rabbinic society cannot eat, let alone perform any other necessary function required for living, without rabbinic authorization of what is permitted and what is forbidden. Even the type of sandal strap one is permitted to wear is strictly enforced in the rabbinic legal system (b. Sanh. 74b). Here too Althusser is useful in his differentiation between "repressive" and "ideological" structures.[113]

Repressive structures, such as the police and law courts, control soci-

---

112. Louis Althusser, *For Marx* (1969; repr., New York: Verso, 2005), 87–128, esp. 105 n. 23 and 112.

113. Louis Althusser, "Ideology and Ideological State Apparatus (Notes Toward an Investigation)," in *Lenin and Philosophy, and Other Essays* (1971; repr., New York: Monthly Review Press, 2001), 85–126. Althusser (95 n. 7) builds on the distinction between "civil society" and "political society" or "the State" posited by Antonio Gramsci (*Selections from the*

ety through the use of external force. Ideological structures work through internal force, by inculcating a value system within the minds of the subjugated. This value system works to maintain the status quo in terms of the power relations between the dominators and those they subjugate.[114] In the case of practice, the repressive structures of rabbinic society would translate to whatever judiciary institutions enforce the practice of rabbinic law, such as those responsible for the administration of lashes to violators of Jewish law. At moments when repressive structures fail to control, ideological structures remain operative. The inculcation of a belief in the minds of the subjugated that the rabbis were the true interpreters of divine law is an effective device even in instances where courts are for whatever reason unable to enforce the law. Built into the rabbinic judicial system is the notion that it is God who fills in the administrative gap in situations where the rabbinic court is powerless. So, for example, if one committed a crime punishable by burning and escaped conviction in the rabbinic courts through a technicality, such as a lack of two witnesses to the infraction, God would ensure that such a person would fall into a fire or be bitten by a snake. The criminal would thus suffer the prescribed punishment of burning extrajudicially (b. Ketub. 30b; b. Sotah 8b; b. Sanh. 37b). Though not stated explicitly in the Talmud, one would assume the same principle to apply in cases where corporal punishment is warranted. Therefore, even when repressive structures are absent, the prospective violator of rabbinic law always lives in fear because there is no way to escape punishment. For, even if one were to escape justice in the court of law, it is impossible to escape divine retribution.[115] What becomes lost in this psycho-theological control scheme, what the ideology conceals, is that it is the rabbis themselves who have defined precisely what constitutes a violation of divine law. Ideological structures, therefore, work more effectively as a strategy of control because they are less visible than repressive ones, which, because of their visibility, can be confronted head on and thwarted.

Let us now return to the deposition story and shift our focus to Torah study rather than practice as life's necessity. In this view, the study of Torah is not seen merely as a means to an end, a practical necessity

---

Prison Notebooks of Antonio Gramsci, ed. and trans. Quintin Hoare and Geoffrey Nowell Smith (New York: International Publishers, 1971), 12–13; Williams, *Marxism and Literature*, 109–20.

114. According to Gramsci's theory of ideological hegemony, the ruling class not only controls the legal system but also establishes a system of values learned by those they oppress (*Selections from the Prison Notebooks*, 206–76).

115. In fact, one would not even want to escape divine punishment, because punishment itself was understood to be absolution of sin and without such absolution one would not be able to enter the world to come. See Beth A. Berkowtiz, *Execution and Invention: Death Penalty Discourse in Early Rabbinic and Christian Cultures* (New York: Oxford University Press, 2006), 53–61 and 83–86.

required for the organization of material, political, or even spiritual life; instead, Torah study itself is viewed as life's prime necessity. In the deposition story, it was the visibility of repressive structures, both in terms of physical presence and metaphorical language, that led to the "student revolution." While the guard at the door stood as a physical barrier who controlled access to the academy, those on the inside who sought to dissent were still left to contend with the metaphorical shield bearers, a linguistically employed militaristic force. At the start of the story, Rabban Gamaliel controlled both repressive structures.[116] As the story has it, it is

---

116. It is noteworthy that a study-hall guard appears in only one other Bavli story, b. Yoma 33b. In that story, Hillel, the ancestor of Rabban Gamaliel who established the hereditary line of the position Rabban Gamaliel holds in the b. Ber. 27b–28a story, is blocked from entrance into the academy prior to his appointment as *Nasi* by a guard because he cannot afford to pay the entrance fee. Several generations later, it is Hillel's progeny who is now on the inside, wielding the very power that excluded his ancestor. [I thank Jeffrey L. Rubenstein for pointing this out to me.] In his analysis of b. Yoma 33b, Shraga Bar-On argues for an understanding of Babylonian stories about Tannaim as reflecting a debate between an aristocratic orientation and a popular one at the time of the storytellers ("Art of the Chain Novel," 57 n. 3). For Bar-On, the Yoma story is a chain novel that is authored in three stages. The conception of a legal corpus as a chain novel was introduced by Ronald Dworkin: "Each [writer] has the job of writing his chapter so as to make the novel being constructed the best it can be" (*Law's Empire* [Cambridge, MA: Belknap Press of Harvard University Press, 1986], 229, cited in Bar-On, "Art of the Chain Novel," 57 n. 3). As Bar-On explains, "The chain novel is a work of literature and of criticism. The writer, who depends upon the words of his predecessors, serves both as a critic and as an author. He adopts or opposes the words of his predecessors, and on the basis of their words he creates the next chapter of the book. Moreover, he structures the next stage of engagement with that which he wishes to promote or instill. His integrity is not expressed by repeating the words of his predecessors. Rather, it is manifest in the responsibility that he bears toward the past and toward the future: toward the literary and human tradition upon which he bases himself and which he carries on, and toward the community for whom he provides the next identity-forming story in the chain" (58). For Dworkin, jurists working in a legal tradition interpret the past legal corpus with a commitment to the integrity of a coherent whole and an eye toward future interpretations, which they leave to the next set of jurists. Bar-On's interest in the chain novel is that, by viewing the Talmud analogically, he makes an argument for scholars to shift their focus "from identification of the units that constitute stories and discussion of their relative earliness or lateness, to a discussion of the moral, educational, and identity-related meanings that are reflected in the multi-generational rabbinic production of stories of the sages" (60). It is therefore curious that Bar-On chooses to emphasize, in his own treatment of b. Yoma 33b, the relative earliness and lateness of strata in that text. In doing so, however, he has identified a number of points that are pertinent to the present discussion. First, he points to the work of Ze'ev and Chana Safrai, who argue that the rabbinic notion that Torah study is a value above all others (m. Pe'ah 1:1) arose out of a need for the previously non-elite rabbis to establish a monopoly on power by introducing an ideological shift. See Ze'ev Safrai and Chana Safrai, "תלמוד תורה וערכיה: הורתו ולידתו של המשאב החיוני למעמדם של חכמים," in *Meḥuyavut Yehudit mitḥadeshet: ʿal ʿolamo ve-haguto shel David Harṭman*, ed. Abraham Sagi and Tsevi Zohar (Jerusalem: Ha-Ḳibuts ha-meʾuḥad, 2001), 880, as cited in Bar-On, "Art of the Chain Novel," 63. Second, Bar-On shows how a story that was originally about devotion to this ideal was later turned into a story about a conflict with the guard (76). Third, he shows how the adja-

through a particular historical moment, the student revolution, that the domain of Torah is opened to all (males) of Jewish society, even the formerly excluded Moabites. While the story of the student-led revolution is designed to appear as though the revolution was successful, as more people have been granted access to the academy, in reality the greatest impact of the revolution is that the power of the dominant class has now been extended beyond the academy's walls to a larger subjugated population of newly indoctrinated insiders. It is the very focalization of the story as an argument over inclusion that conceals the reality that the story is an insider debate between five named rabbis. It is these rabbis who struggle for control over those most greatly affected by the outcome of the debate, a subordinated population that remains nameless and powerless. This population has been brought into the academy and under the direct control of the ideological state apparatus by means of no action of their own. While in the story, as told, the academy represents the ideological state apparatus, and the story recounts a shift in the power dynamics associated with that apparatus, it is the telling of the story that inculcates in the minds of its audience the ideology that Torah study is itself a necessity to be sought by all (males).

This is a very effective use of the tools of ideological structure. Before the events of the story there was a clear demarcation between insiders and outsiders, those who were allowed to participate in the power structures of the realm of Torah and those who were not. Yet, even as the events unfold and the power structure shifts, it is only a group of five named rabbis, a priori insiders, who hold any real claim to power. By inviting a new and larger population into the realm of "Torah" while at the same excluding them from power, the story conceals its intention and therefore its effect. The narrative hides its ideological structure by focalizing the removal and reinstatement of Rabban Gamaliel and conceding his loss of one quarter of his power. Since Rabban Gamaliel eventually gets reinstated to most of his position of authority, in the final sum of events the prime effect of the revolution is the dispatching with Rabban Gamaliel's personal shield bearers and the removal of the guard from the door. Yet, while these highly visible repressive structures are removed, a lock remains on the door. For, even after the masses are allowed access, the door lock ensures that entry into the actual power structure remains guarded; entry into the group of named rabbis is still closed off to all who threaten their hegemony.[117] Only now, the exclusionary tactic is less visible. Both a locked and unlocked door look the same to the observer, whether inside or out. It is not until

cent story of R. Elazar b. Ḥarsom was similarly altered from an earlier version that was originally about devotion to Torah study to a later version that critiques R. Elazar's treatment of his own slaves (77).

117. This develops the idea put forth by Boyarin, *Border Lines*, 187, cited above.

approaching the door and attempting to enter that the door is discovered to be locked. In the story, the lock on the door, as another form of absent presence, a physical one, signals that the visible repressive structure is erased in the service of an invisible ideological structure that dominates.

Here, we have moved into Jameson's second horizon, where he views the text not in terms of a reflection of the diachronic shift between two distinct power structures but rather as an individual expression of a synchronic struggle between two competing classes of the social order, a dominant and subjugated class of society. In this horizon, the antagonistic dialogical relationship between the struggling classes "is one in which two opposing discourses fight it out within the general unity of a shared code."[118] The shared code, the characteristics of which derive from the particular mode of production dominant in any given society, presents the illusion that the text represents a single unified culture.[119]

As mentioned earlier, the body of scholarship on this story reads it as a reflection of an actual revolution, a diachronic change in the structure of the academy that took place in either the first, fourth, fifth, or eighth century, depending on whose view we follow. From the vantage point of Jameson's second horizon, however, the story rather reflects a synchronic state of affairs. The revolution depicted in the story relies on the fact that majority rule itself already exists as the shared code between the hegemonic and revolutionary classes. This is a direct outcome of a rabbinic economy where Torah is the means of production. For Torah output cannot proliferate outside of a system that allows multiple voices to express their differing opinions. Democratic principles were already entrenched in the society in which the revolution depicted took place. This can be seen in the fact that Rabban Gamaliel is simply voted out of office in a way that implies that it was with democratic election that he was seated in that office to begin with.[120] In the case of our story, the oppositional voices, through a process of cultural universalization, have already been reabsorbed into the hegemonic class, now a group of five named rabbis who operate according to the rules of the shared code of an open academy and democratic rule. But the idea of democratic rule is what is itself used to justify why those in power remain so and those who are oppressed likewise accept their predicament. Yet, as we have moved from the first horizon to the second, from the narrative of a historical revolution to a single narrative expression within a class discourse fought out through a unified

118. Jameson, *Political Unconscious*, 70.

119. Ibid., 72.

120. Ibid.: "[Hegemonic forms] can be grasped as a process of the reappropriation and neutralization, the cooptation and class transformation, the cultural universalization, of forms which originally expressed the situation of 'popular,' sub-ordinate, or dominated groups."

code, the subjugated class has shifted from those rabbis who opposed Rabban Gamaliel to the masses who remain nameless. The story is therefore not about the shift from one power structure to another but rather a reflection of an ever-present conflict between the oppressor and the truly oppressed, those members of society whose subjugation the focalization of the story on the five named rabbis has obscured. The telling and retelling of this story about a revolution of inclusion only further conceals how the story itself has worked to dominate and subjugate the larger populace now included.

A Return to Historical Materialism

What is lacking in the above analysis from a Marxian perspective is that, in reading Torah as life's necessity, in both material and spiritual terms, it ignores history and traditional economics. In order to move on to Jameson's third horizon it is necessary to reengage with both of these elements. Jameson's third horizon focuses on the relationship between multiple modes of production within a single culture. As mentioned above, Marx's epochal scheme of historical materialism does not map neatly onto the era in which the story takes place. And even if it did, the producers of the story were quite far removed, both geographically and chronologically, from the setting depicted in the story. At the same time, though we cannot pinpoint precisely when the storytellers were active, there is ample evidence that they lived in a culture undergoing a process of urbanization, where a society that at the very least exhibited features of a feudal society was undergoing (or had undergone) a transition to one that exhibited features of a capitalist one. So how can Marx be used productively in this context? Raymond Williams's critique of epochal analysis provides a fruitful framework for the application of Marx's historical economic paradigms in just such an environment. Epochal analysis, as proposed by Marx, relies on notions of determinate dominant features such as "feudal culture" and "socialist culture." It therefore tends to overlook stages and variations within a general system, especially when the object of analysis is a multicentury cultural process.[121] Williams explains that, when speaking of a capitalist economic system, "'bourgeois culture' is a significant generalizing description and hypothesis, expressed within epochal analysis by fundamental comparisons with 'feudal culture' or 'socialist culture.' However, as a description of cultural process, over four or five centuries and in scores of different societies, it requires immediate historical and internally comparative differentiation."[122] In epochal analysis, the dom-

121. Williams, *Marxism and Literature*, 121.

122. Ibid.

inant, or hegemonic, are viewed "as a static type against which all real cultural process is measured."[123] The very idea of a determinate "feudal culture," "capitalist culture," "socialist culture," and so on, turns what is a dynamic cultural process into a static cultural system. While analyses of static cultural systems do recognize stages and variations, they deemphasize internal dynamic relations.[124]

Any analysis of rabbinic cultural production must consider that the production itself takes place in a society where its foundational text, the Hebrew Bible, presents a radically different structure of the hegemonic institutions of Jewish society from those of the society in which rabbinic texts were produced. The rabbinic cultural project of developing an oral law consists of two textual components, the productive (or generative) (re)reading of biblical texts and the supplemental filling in of gaps where the biblical text is silent. While oral texts are malleable, subject to a re-remembering of the past, the biblical record remains fixed. Since the creative reading of biblical texts is central to the supplementary oral tradition, a dual oral-written legal system has much flexibility in adapting to changing political, social, and economic climates. At the same time, despite the effort of creative reading practices, the biblical text itself cannot be altered or erased from memory. No matter how developed a creative reading practice becomes the text itself always remains in a position of antagonistic relation to its subsequent interpretation. In the Hebrew Bible, after the transition from the rule of judges to that of kings, it is the hereditary kings and priests, and the charismatic prophets, who vie for control and dominance.[125] For the rabbis, after the destruction of the Second Temple, it is the (somewhat) hereditary *Nasi* (and later the Exilarch) and the dialectical rabbi who operate in a system where caste is seen as decreasingly determinate of social and political standing. In this hegemonic rabbinic culture, kingship has already been abolished and the prophet erased, yet the priest (and other hereditary castes) still weigh as valid stakeholders in claims

123. Ibid.

124. Jameson would probably call Williams's approach a meta-synchronic approach to the analysis of social development; see *Political Unconscious*, 84. "What is synchronic is the 'concept' of the mode of production; the moment of the historical coexistence of several modes of production is not synchronic in this sense, but open to history in a dialectical way. The temptation to classify texts according to the appropriate mode of production is thereby removed, since the texts emerge in a space in which we may expect them to be crisscrossed and intersected by a variety of impulses from contradictory modes of production all at once" (81).

125. In the Hebrew Bible itself, this system emerges with Samuel's appointment of the first king, Saul. Prior to this moment, Israel was ruled by judges. Samuel was himself a (nonhereditary) priest, prophet, and judge, and with his appointment of Saul, these power sources became for the most part dispersed among separate competing groups.

for dominance.[126] The historical *Nasi*, rather than his narrative reflection, represents a complicated case within this new system since the hereditary nature of the position is itself an invention of the period of Rabban Gamaliel (or later) and a retrojection onto the past.[127]

This complex sociological matrix is epitomized in the final Mishnah of tractate Horayot (3:8):

> The priest is prior to the Levite; the Levite to the Israelite; the Israelite to the *mamzer* [bastard caste]; and the *mamzer* to the *Natin* [descendants of Gibeonite converts]; and the *Natin* to the convert; and the convert to the freed slave. When [is this the case]? When they are all equal (in terms of their sagacity). However, if a *mamzer* was a *talmid ḥakham* [sage] and a high priest an *'am ha'arets* [unschooled], then the bastard sage is prior to the unschooled high priest. (b. Hor. 13b–14a)

It is illuminating that, of the two stories in the Bavli that relate an attempted *coup* of the *Nasi* in office, the second one, in terms of the chronological order of the events depicted, appears in a discussion attached to this Mishnah.[128] In the Horayot story it is R. Shimeon the son of Gamaliel who is the subject of the *coup*, where the appellation "son of Gamaliel" reminds the audience that the issues played out in the first story were not resolved and that heredity remains a central component of the power dynamics in play in both the societies that produced and retold the story.

Williams argues that it is necessary not only to examine the "dominant" or hegemonic within a society but also their relationship to the "residual" and "emergent" elements operating as internal dynamic relations within a process of cultural formation.[129] In such a view, the dominant is itself a dynamic category, and the instability of the role of the *Nasi* within the rabbinic class, as negotiated in the deposition story, is testament to this point. Williams defines the residual as the remnants of the value system of a past social formation that still exists within a society, where these values are ones that cannot be expressed in terms of the dominant culture. The emergent is when a new value system arises out of the dominant culture, but where these values are not considered wholly novel and in opposition to that culture. The emergent class always incorporates elements of the

126. See Reuven Kimelman, "The Conflict between the Priestly Oligarchy and the Sage in the Talmudic Period" [Hebrew], *Zion* 48 (1983): 135–47.

127. David M. Goodblatt, *The Monarchic Principle: Studies in Jewish Self-Government in Antiquity*, TSAJ 38 (Tübingen: Mohr Siebeck, 1994), 131–230.

128. Though this story presents as Tannaitic, David Goodblatt brings much evidence in arguing that it is a late Babylonian invention ("The Story of the Plot against R. Simeon B. Gamliel II" [Hebrew], *Zion* 49 [1984]: 349–74).

129. Williams, *Marxism and Literature*, 121–22.

dominant and the dominant therefore "already conditions the limits of emergence."[130] Therefore, the residual within a culture is always easier to locate than the emergent.[131] In the case of our narrative, the dominant represents those who rule by majority and the residual those who have a hereditary claim on power. The values upon which these competing parties stake their claims to power are unrelated and, in fact, oppositional to each another. In order to locate the emergent class, the work of recent scholarship, outlined above, is quite valuable. The notion of an emergent dialectic class makes sense within Williams's scheme because it operates within the established rules of the hegemonic order, which, in turn, conditions its limitations. Therefore, using Williams's categories, the deposition story depicts an emergent class vying to restructure the hegemonic order of a dominant society whose primary occupation is the study and interpretation of texts that stand as a constant reminder of residual power structures. What Williams has contributed here is the possibility for a conception of a cultural formation that struggles along synchronic lines. Such a conception leads directly into Jameson's third semantic horizon, which allows for the reintroduction of historical materialism into the interpretive framework of our story.

The starting point of Jameson's third horizon is the relationship between the shared code, which in our case is democratic rule, and the entirety of history—"from prehistoric life to whatever far future history has in store for us."[132] This is not a historiographic frame, where causes are ordered in narrative form in relation to their effects, but rather an exploration of history that is designed to highlight how the signifying textual artefacts originating out of several distinct periods, each dominated by its own economic determinants, can be found in a single text.[133] Following Marx, Jameson is interested in the specific dominant ideology that typifies the mode of production of the society in which the text was produced.[134] Yet he, much like Williams (and Althusser),[135] critiques the idea that a given historical moment contains "monolithic models of cultural unity" and instead sees competing modes of production coexisting within any historical moment.[136] Therefore, in order to further analyze the deposition story in the full complexity of the power relations and vestiges of past

130. Ibid., 124.
131. Ibid., 123–25.
132. Jameson, *Political Unconscious*, 60.
133. Ibid., 84. Jameson's interest and, therefore, formulation are quite different from that of the current study. Jameson wants to find in the genre of the novel, which he says is a product of capitalist modes of production, remnants of other genres that derive from other modes of productions.
134. Ibid., 74–75.
135. Ibid., 75.
136. Ibid., 76.

economic systems they contain, it is necessary to consider not only the economic transformations the society that produced the text were undergoing (or had undergone) but also the various modes and phases of domination and subjugation in the prehistory of the text's culture.

History itself develops in an unbalanced manner, with different antagonistic power relations finding their source in different historical economic formations. So while the domination of capital modes of production finds its source in the industrial revolution, the domination of men over women has its root in tribal society.[137] Contemporary society is structured along the antagonistic relations between both of these dominations and deals with them metasynchronically.[138] Metasynchronicity is the idea "that a given social formation consist[s] in the coexistence of various synchronic systems or modes of production, each with its own dynamic or time scheme."[139] As Jameson sums up his discussion of Nicos Poulantzas's idea of "social formation,"

> every social formation or historically existing society has in fact consisted in the overlay and structural coexistence of *several* modes of production all at once, including vestiges and survivals of older modes of production, now relegated to structurally dependent positions within the new, as well as anticipatory tendencies which are potentially inconsistent with the existing system but have not yet generated an autonomous space of their own.[140]

Therefore, for Jameson, since power structures derived from different economic formations coexist in the same historical moment, "texts emerge in a space in which we may expect them to be crisscrossed and intersected by a variety of impulses from contradictory modes of cultural production all at once."[141] In Jameson's final horizon, the object of interpretation is cultural revolution, but not one that manifests itself in the reordering of society.[142] Here, the text is read as part of a "permanent process in human

137. Ibid., 85.

138. Ibid., 75–78.

139. Ibid., 82. Jameson arrives at his metasynchronic approach through a critique of the synchronic "total-system" approaches applied to the social and historical analyses of Max Weber, Michel Foucault, and Jean Baudrillard (75–78).

140. Ibid., 80. Poulantzas distinguishes between mode of production, which is an abstraction, and social formation, which is a lived historical situation. For Poulantzas, no actual historical situation is ever lived exclusively under any particular mode of production.

141. Ibid., 81.

142. Ibid., 83. When such a political reorganization does take place it is just a diachronic manifestation of a constant struggle that was synchronically there all along. Here, "diachronic" refers to differences between modes of production and their respective consequent ideologies from one time period to the next; "synchronic" refers to such differences within a single society.

societies,"[143] in which the power structures derived from different economic formations coexist and become "visibly antagonistic, their contradictions moving to the very center of political, social, and historical life."[144] As Jameson writes near the conclusion of his chapter "On Interpretation," "The task of cultural and social analysis thus construed within this final horizon will then clearly be the rewriting of its materials in such a way that this perpetual cultural revolution can be apprehended and read as the deeper and more permanent constitutive structure in which the empirical textual objects know intelligibility."

A Metasynchronic Reading of the Narrative

Let us now read b. Ber. 27b–28a through a lens that takes a broader view of class struggle, the transformation of economic systems, internal and external political realities, and ideology. To examine the deep structure of the story along lines of domination and subjugation and reveal repressed anxieties that the narrative seeks to work out, it is necessary to examine the nature of, and relationships between, the historical power dynamics at play in the text. Once we step away from the linear structure of the narrative as diachronic plot and instead plot all of the characters presented in the story on a character map, the relationships between the characters (both in the story and) as symbolic values across the synchronic structure of the society in which the story was told will move into deeper focus. Though the story is focalized around the dispute between Rabban Gamaliel and R. Yehoshua, there are more than twenty characters or symbols in the narrative, representing many more social positions and relationships.[145] Such a scheme can be presented visually as in Figure 1 (p. 321).

Let us begin from outside, in the supernatural realm, and work our way in. Though the catalyst of the story is a discussion of laws of prayer, the story is a decidedly political rather than religious one. While in a Marxist scheme religion is generally viewed as an ideology that works to explain circumstances of oppression, the story does not use God in this manner. God intervenes as a rational actor at moments in the narrative through miracles and dreams, but there is another supernatural force that operates in a more primal manner, one that echoes a time before the introduction of the Jewish God into the religious imagination. It is the possibility of *'anish lei* ("he [might] harm him") that is given as the rationale for why R. Akiva must not lay claim to political power, why his position as a

143. Ibid., 83.
144. Ibid., 81.
145. If the reader is not already familiar with the story in its entirety, it would be helpful to read the text provided in the appendix at this point.

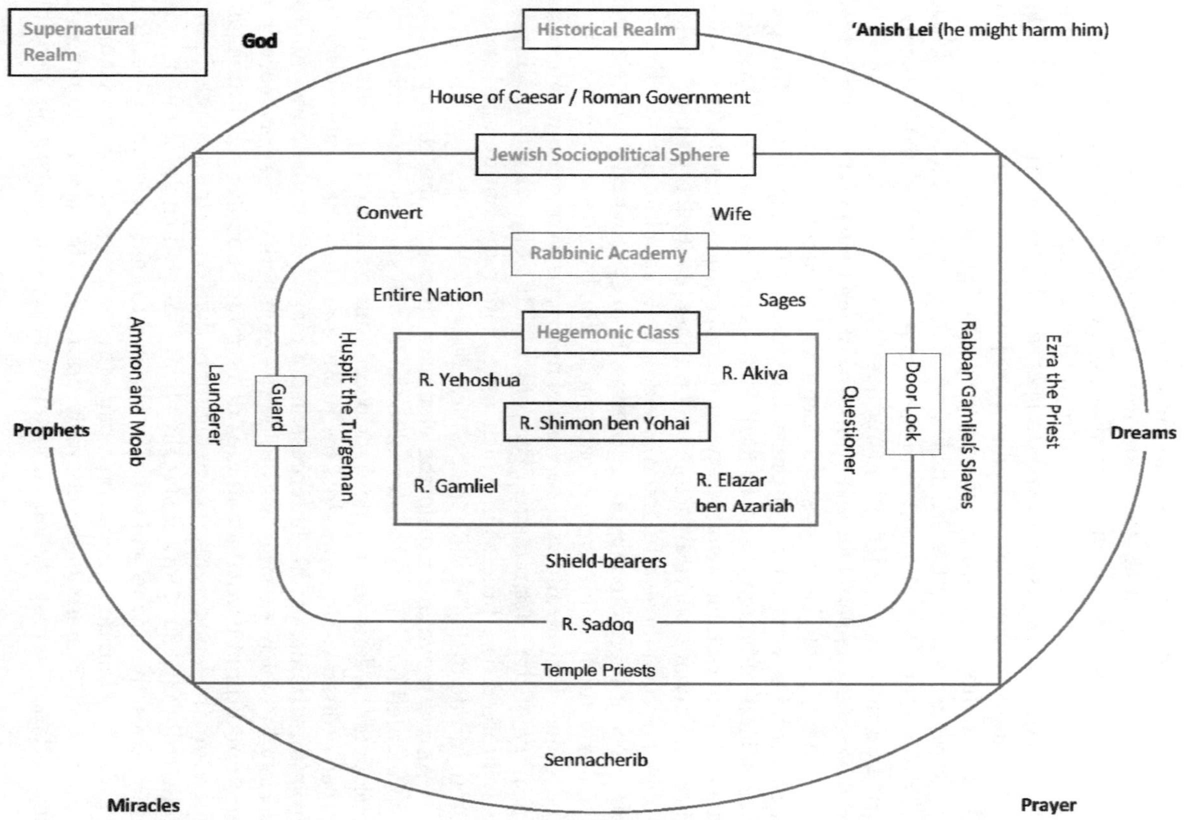
Supernatural Realm
God
Historical Realm
'Anish Lei (he might harm him)
House of Caesar / Roman Government
Jewish Sociopolitical Sphere
Convert
Wife
Rabbinic Academy
Entire Nation
Sages
Hegemonic Class
R. Yehoshua
R. Akiva
R. Shimon ben Yohai
R. Gamliel
R. Elazar ben Azariah
Prophets
Ammon and Moab
Launderer
Guard
Ḥuṣpit the Turgeman
Questioner
Door Lock
Rabban Gamliel's Slaves
Ezra the Priest
Dreams
Shield-bearers
R. Ṣadoq
Temple Priests
Sennacherib
Miracles
Prayer
Figure 1

subjugated class vis-à-vis the dominant one must remain in place. While it is unclear precisely in what way, and through what mechanism, Rabban Gamaliel might harm R. Akiva, the implication is that it is through supernatural forces rather than material or political means.[146] The idea that R. Akiva can be physically impacted by irrational supernatural forces, ones that belie just cause, is not theological per se but can be seen as functioning in the same manner as Marx's religion, to justify why a particular political structure allows for some members to dominate others.

Next, we move in toward the historical oppressors Ammon and Moab, whose potential for physical dominance can be erased with rabbinic rhetoric through ethnic redefinition. Yet this distant historical memory is set in relief of the violent external oppressor of the time in which the story is set, the house of Caesar as synecdoche for the Roman Empire. This juxtaposition between past and present, in historical time, serves two purposes. First, although the story itself focuses on how the rabbis negotiate the ordering of their own society, in the background lies the reality that there are always political factors beyond their control, ones that work to subjugate even those who internally dominate rabbinic society. The rabbinic leader therefore must be chosen with an eye toward Rome. Second, the memory of Ammon and Moab placed side by side with the reality of the Roman Empire allows for a view of history as a continuum, where the memory of the past remains ever present. This outlook toward history is reinforced by a process in which a meditation on foundational texts is brought into dialogue with the political present.

As we move inward on the character map into the class positions represented by characters internal to the Jewish sociopolitical sphere, we encounter the launderer, whose socioeconomic position is a product of the urban economy. He represents the proletariat class that is all but absent from this drama, yet likely represented a majority population within the society in which the story was told. The members of this socioeconomic stratum did not participate in the "democratic" populist revolution, and therefore the launderer serves to highlight that, while the struggle itself is only within the academy, it is really about those whom the academy truly dominates, those who will never be allowed to gain access to the realm of power. The launderer is put on a par with the slaves of Rabban Gamaliel and as such represents the eternally oppressed, those who do not even understand the root of their subjugation because it has become invisible

146. Perhaps a curse is implied. See b. B. Bat. 22a. There, several rabbis accept responsibility for Rav Adda bar Abba's death, using terminology similar to *'anish lei*. Rav Yosef claims responsibility because he cursed him. Other rabbis claim responsibility citing instances where Rav Adda insulted them, the implication being that God took pity on their honor at the expense of Rav Adda. Finally, Rav Naḥman bar Yitsḥaq claims to be responsible for Rav Adda's death simply by speaking of his death.

to them.[147] Like the launderer, the wife and the convert occupy a liminal space at the walls of the academy.[148] These characters can exert pressure on the ruling class while standing outside the regnant power structure. The story is effective in allowing these voices to penetrate the walls of the academy from the outside. If these marginal figures were fully excluded, it would be impossible to subjugate them. By hearing this story, the launderer, the convert, and the wife can imagine themselves as players in the academic realm even when facing a locked door.

Finally, we shift focus to the internal workings of the academy itself. Inside these walls, we find a few of the central named rabbis of the Mishnah. In the rabbinic imagination, these four Yavneh-era rabbis dominate the historical period in which the story takes place. Yet a fifth Yavneh-era rabbi is conspicuously absent from this narrative, and the significance of this lacuna will later be addressed. Of the four Yavneh-era rabbis who are named, the socioeconomic position of three is given in the text, while that of R. Akiva remains as subtext. It is within the academy walls and among the named rabbis that we find our power struggle, the agon of the story, in the embodiment of R. Yehoshua and Rabban Gamaliel. R. Yehoshua, the subjugated, is a poor craftsman.[149] Rabban Gamaliel, his oppressor, represents the political leadership of the new rabbinic regime after the destruction of the Second Temple, though his position of *Nasi* is imagined to have existed in the old regime of the priests.[150] He exerts his power over the academy through a control of the physical apparatus of power symbolized by the guard and the symbolic assignment of his source of political power to the shield bearers. The two candidates presented as potential replacements for Rabban Gamaliel are R. Elazar b. Azariah and R. Akiva. R. Akiva's socioeconomic status is pointed to in the text and is found in his external biographical tale. In the deposition story, R. Akiva is turned down for the position of *Nasi* due to his lack of hereditary status. In the next line of the text, R. Elazar b. Azariah is put forth as a candidate because he not only is rich and a sage but also has hereditary status, implying that R. Akiva possessed two of the three qualities that R. Elazar possessed but not the third. R. Akiva represents a kind of nouveau riche and is upwardly

---

147. In the story about R. Judah the Patriarch's death (b. Ketub. 103b), the launderer is also depicted as one who is utterly reliant on the patriarch. In that story, the launderer commits suicide upon hearing of the patriarch's death, and it is only through this act that he receives life in the world to come. I thank Jeffrey L. Rubenstein for pointing out to me the pertinence of this enigmatic text.

148. R. Tsadoq's role in this story will be addressed later.

149. On the difference between the wage laborer, represented in this story by the launderer, and the craftsman in a Marxist scheme, see S. H. Rigby, *Marxism and History: A Critical Introduction* (Manchester: Manchester University Press, 1998), 19.

150. T. Pesaḥ. 4:13–14; y. Pesaḥ. 6:1; b. Pesaḥ. 66a. For the pre-Yavneh patriarchate as retrojected fiction, see Goodblatt, *Monarchic Principle*, 176–231.

mobile in a number of ways. He began his career in the agrarian economy, as a shepherd for a large landowner (b. Ketub. 62b–63a). He subsequently became wealthy by marrying rich (twice), finding hidden treasures (over and over), and being bequeathed money (b. Ned. 50). R. Akiva is also upwardly mobile within the rabbinic economy of Torah, beginning his life as an outsider and eventually reaching great heights within the academy (b. Ketub. 62b–63a). His being denied the position of *Nasi* sets the limits on the possibility for transgressing the boundaries of hereditary class and station of origin in this society. In contrast, R. Elazar represents the old priestly regime and (ostensibly) old money. More importantly, though, R. Elazar's heritage is traced back to the biblical Ezra, the priest who was responsible for organizing proto-rabbinic society into hereditary castes. While R. Akiva's biography acts as subtext, R. Elazar b. Azariah's position is openly marked in the text. Though m. Hor 3:8, discussed earlier, argues against a conception of heredity being a determinate of social standing, this story indicates that the social reality is quite different from that mishnah's idealized conception of mobility.

Besides the named rabbis, within the academy there are four other class symbols: the generic questioner;[151] the generic sages; the generic "entire nation"; and Ḥutspit, Rabban Gamaliel's mouthpiece. The generic questioner and Ḥutspit act as administrators within the academy. They serve the purposes of setting Rabban Gamaliel at a distance from his colleagues and constituents, respectively.[152] The anonymity of the sages and the entire nation should be viewed together with another piece of information found in R. Akiva's external biography, his twenty-four thousand students, all but a handful of those who remain nameless throughout the Talmud. The story thus conceals the scale of the included excluded population (b. Yebam. 62b; b. Ketub. 63a). The anonymity of the sages and the entire nation indicates that, while the rabbinic legal system promoted a social democracy, the political reality is that very few are given a voice within that system. It is this unnamed body that represents the ever-present forces of revolution. It is their "protopolitical impulses" that must be 'managed' and defused."[153] It is the murmurs of this anonymous population that symbolize antagonistic energy bubbling to the surface. Their murmurs are converted into power when they speak with one collective voice: "Stop!"

Finally, we move to the center of the map and R. Shimeon. As detailed

---

151. This questioner could very well be the anonymous student (Rubenstein, *Stories of the Babylonian Talmud*, 81) or a functionary of academic procedure within the academy.

152. Ḥutspit's tragic end, with his tongue being dragged through the street by a pig, serves as another reminder of the fragile state of inner-rabbinic politics while under foreign rule (b. Qidd. 39b)

153. Jameson, *Political Unconscious*, 277.

above, he signals the history of transformation from an agrarian society to an urban market economy and the possibility for revolution inherent in that shift. The later Babylonian composers of this story processed the impact of urbanization upon their current economic, and therefore social, environment by (re)developing an older narrative that dramatized an event set immediately after the destruction of the Second Temple. Therefore, what is important is not the actual economic structure of late Second Temple Judaism and how the destruction of the Second Temple might have altered that structure, but how the rabbis of the late talmudic period might have imagined that transition as it related to their own transitional economic environment. While the pre-rabbinic era would not be considered feudal in the sense in which Marx intended, as existed in medieval Europe, the economic structure of late Second Temple Judaism certainly shared a number of characteristics that would align it with feudal society;[154] and it would make sense that the storytellers viewed it that way.[155] Late Second Temple Judaism was a monarchy, ruled by the priestly Hasmonean dynasty.[156] When that dynasty gave way to the lay Herodian dynasty, the theocracy of the priests who controlled the temple yet remained. This society was organized by hereditary castes, originally established by the priests in the time of Ezra, centuries earlier.[157] Its economy was primarily an agrarian-based one. This economy was not reliant on slave labor, as was the larger Roman economy of which late Second Temple Judaism was a subset, though slavery certainly existed.[158] What is more essential for understanding how the rabbis of the late Babylonian talmudic era would conceive of this society's economic structure is the role of the priests in the economy. In Marx's understanding of feudalism, a ruling aristocracy exploited the peasant class by offering them land use in exchange for labor, produce, or rent.[159] Though the Second Temple–era priests did not actually own land, they essentially played an identical role to that of a ruling class in a feudal society. For, if a Second Temple Jew owned land, his position vis-à-vis the priest was akin to the relationship

---

154. For the characteristics of feudal society, see Hindess, *Pre-Capitalist Modes of Production*, 221–59.

155. See n. 159, below.

156. On the priestly monarchy of the Second Temple period, see Goodblatt, *Monarchic Principle*, 6–29. On the theory of a doctrine of diarchic constitution, consisting of a king-like figure and a priestly ruler, in Second Temple Judaism, see ibid., 57–76.

157. See m. Qidd. 4:1 for a full list.

158. For this general topic, see E. E. Urbach, "Halakhot Regarding Slavery as a Source for the Social History of the Second Temple and the Talmudic Period" [Hebrew], *Zion* 25 (1960): 141–89. See also n. 13, above.

159. See, e.g., Karl Marx, *Capital: A Critique of Political Economy*, introduction by Ernest Mandel, trans. Ben Fowkes, 3 vols. (repr., New York: Penguin Classics, 1992; German original, 1867), 344–48 [1:10:1].

between a medieval feudal farmer and the owner of the land he farmed. In the late Second Temple period, the priest was the virtual lord of an actual landowner's land and the landowner was a virtual serf to the priest. The Second Temple Jewish landowner, in practicality, paid the priest a percentage of his agricultural and livestock output in return for land use. At least this would be the economic, rather than theological, understanding of this relationship by the later rabbis of the Talmud looking back at the texts that describe the laws of that era.[160]

Once the Second Temple was destroyed the system of priestly gifts, given as a percentage of a farmer's agricultural output, became decentralized.[161] Additionally, livestock production became completely free of priestly tariffs.[162] In Babylonia, the entire system was completely inoperative;[163] and, while the Babylonian curriculum did include the study and development of mishnaic laws related to the temple, laws relating to agriculture had already been removed from the course of study. At the same time, laws relating to market economy, private property, and wage labor were a central focus of Babylonian academic discourse. It therefore would make sense that the late Babylonian storytellers would retrojectively map the urbanization of their own times and the shift in the economic structure of their own society onto a similar shift that they imagined to have taken place in the Land of Israel after the destruction of the Second Temple.

With this in mind, let us turn to two other absent causes referenced in the deposition story. This story is not the first instance in which Rabban Gamaliel used his political position to dominate R. Yehoshua. Two

---

160. For the Babylonian Exilarch as occupying a role similar to that of the feudal lord, see Morony, "Landholding in Seventh-Century Iraq," 147–48. It should be cautioned that Morony relies on Julius Newman, *The Agricultural Life of the Jews in Babylonia between the Years 200 C.E. and 500 C.E.* (London: Oxford University Press, 1932), and dated scholarship of this sort is in need of reconsideration. Isaiah Gafni too relies on Newman in his discussion of tenant farmers; see Gafni, "The Political, Social, and Economic History of Babylonian Jewry, 224–638 CE," in *The Cambridge History of Judaism*, vol. 4, *The Late Roman-Rabbinic Period*, ed. Steven T. Katz (Cambridge: Cambridge University Press, 1984), 810.

161. Aharon Oppenheimer, *The 'Am Ha-Aretz: A Study in the Social History of the Jewish People in the Helenistic-Roman Period.*, trans. I. H. Levine, ALGHJ 8 (Leiden: Brill, 1977), 36–38. It is difficult to assess with precision the manner in which the priestly-gift system became altered in actual practice after the destruction of the Second Temple. For an extensive bibliography of scholars who address this question, see Philip S. Alexander, "What Happened to the Jewish Priesthood after 70?," in *A Wandering Galilean: Essays in Honour of Seán Freyne*, ed. Zuleika Rodgers, Margaret Daly-Denton, and Anne Fitzpatrick McKinley, JSJSup 132 (Leiden: Brill, 2009), 5–33, here 6 nn. 3–5. For our purposes, it is important to state only that the Babylonian storytellers must have understood the priestly-gift system to have undergone dramatic changes with the destruction of the Second Temple.

162. The very fact that the starting point for the revolt centers on a discussion of prayer, a replacement for temple sacrifice, highlights this transformation.

163. However, see Jacob Neusner, *A History of the Jews in Babylonia*, vol. 4, *The Age of Shapur II* (Leiden: Brill, 1969), 143–49.

other stories are mentioned. Taken together, these two referents work to highlight a hidden social antagonism that is being worked through in this story: the impact of a restructuring of the rabbinic economy from an agrarian one to an urban one and the development of a new power structure organized around social democracy. I will address the second story (b. Bek. 36a) first as it is practically identical to our b. Ber. 27b–28a story aside from the legal content of the query.[164] In that story, too, someone poses a question first to R. Yehoshua and then, independently, to Rabban Gamaliel. In that case the question is posed by R. Tsadoq rather than an anonymous student, but the story plays out in a nearly identical manner. Rabban Gamaliel tells R. Tsadoq to wait until the shield bearers enter, R. Yehoshua reverses his original private opinion, is forced to acknowledge that reversal, and is made to stand; the populace murmurs and eventually demands that Ḥutzpit stop speaking. It is the fact that R. Tsadoq is the character who poses the question and the very topic of his question, the law of the firstling,[165] that is central to how the Berakhot story reveals to us the true nature of what it is trying to work through. R. Tsadoq is a Second Temple figure, a priest, and his question deals with priestly gifts, the laws of which have been dramatically altered in a post-temple society.[166] To have R. Tsadoq submit to the authority of Rabban Gamaliel—a rabbi many years his junior—and his regime signals a number of the hidden features of the restructuring of rabbinic society at play in our story.[167]

164. See Rubenstein, *Stories of the Babylonian Talmud*, 77–90.

165. On this law, see Shmuel Shilo, "Evasion of the Law in the Talmud," in *Authority, Process, and Method: Studies in Jewish Law*, ed. Hanina Ben-Menahem and Neil S. Hecht, Jewish Law in Context 2 (Amsterdam: Harwood Academic, 1998), 188–89.

166. While there is certainly more than one R. Tsadoq mentioned in rabbinic texts, it makes sense that the storytellers understood this R. Tsadoq to be the one mentioned in b. Git. 56b. There, R. Tsadoq is associated with R. Yoḥanan b. Zakkai and the story of the destruction of the Second Temple. In that story, R. Yoḥanan makes three requests of Vespasian, the general (and later emperor) who laid siege to Jerusalem: to allow Yavneh and its sages to survive; to allow Rabban Gamaliel's dynasty to survive; and to provide R. Tsadoq with a doctor. As juxtaposed, these three highlight the complexity of the dynamics of the power structure on display in the Berakhot story. The destruction of the temple symbolizes the end of a priestly order supported by what amounted to a virtual feudal economy with its priestly agricultural gifts and a supply of cattle. It is R. Yoḥanan b. Zakkai who negotiates the terms of that transfer, and it is R. Yoḥanan who assumes the leadership of Yavneh. (There is debate among the Rishonim whether or not R. Yoḥanan was himself a priest. See Rashi to b. Šabb. 34a and Tosafot to b. Menaḥ. 21b.) Yavneh itself symbolizes the new order of rabbinic democratic rule, but it is, in this story, retrojected onto the past, as if such leadership already maintained control outside of Jerusalem at the time of the destruction of the temple. Finally, the political organization of rabbinic society with *Nasi* as leader, is also retrojected onto the past, with Rabban Gamaliel's dynasty going back several generations to the time of his great ancestor Hillel.

167. Such a reading helps illuminate R. Yehoshua's cryptic statement to R. Akiva: "R. Yehoshua said to him: 'Let the sprinkler son of a sprinkler sprinkle; but shall he who

What is most important though, for our analysis, is that R. Tsadoq stands as a reference to the agrarian economy and priestly rule of the past.

Let us now return to the first story about Rabban Gamaliel's domination of R. Yehoshua that is referenced. This story supplies an important clue to a central paradox of the new regime: the role of rule of the majority in the rabbinic political structure and its relation to truth as a source of authority. In the referenced story (m. Roš Haš. 2:8–9), Rabban Gamaliel accepted witnesses who testified to viewing a new moon even though their testimony defied the logical possibility of being accurate. Dosa b. Harkinas disagreed with Rabban Gamaliel, denying the testimony of such witnesses, and R. Yehoshua sided with Dosa. Rabban Gamaliel forced R. Yehoshua to submit to his ruling in quite a violent manner. He demands that R. Yehoshua appear before him carrying his staff and money belt on a day that would be Yom Kippur according to R. Yehoshua's own calculation of the new moon. Both R. Akiva and Dosa convince R. Yehoshua to submit to Rabban Gamaliel's authority for the sake of political stability. It appears that Rabban Gamaliel is operating within a system of the court, where it is his court that has supplied a majority ruling of its own. This might have represented some historical reality during the time in which the story is set, but it does not reflect the rabbinic system as it has developed by the time of the story's telling. The story is itself at odds with the rabbinic ideological system as expressed in the Mishnah, where it is the majority of rabbinic opinions who control the law, not the *Nasi*'s court (see m. ʿEd. 1:5–6). In the world of the Mishnah it is, in actuality, only a very limited number of players who get to vote; and it is the very named rabbis in these stories who are among those granted that right, whose voices are given equal standing. In this case, it would be Dosa and R. Yehoshua who would get to outvote Rabban Gamaliel. The silencing of these voices, a majority inside the system, calls into question whether the very notion of a democratic system is a ruse that hides an alternate power structure. In this case, therefore, democratic rule is the ideology that the rabbis have developed to conceal the true power structure and suppress a populist revolt. Once again, this story tells of a populist revolt while disguising an ideology that actually suppresses such a possibility.

While the story of the new moon is at face value a story about the rule of truth versus the rule of what is politically practical, the reference to this theme in the text points to the historical era of the First Temple and the dominance of the prophets. In the convert scene, Rabban Gamaliel and R. Yehoshua use biblical texts, dueling back and forth. The outcome is to erase Ammon and Moab from history, but in the course of the debate the

---

is neither a sprinkler nor the son of a sprinkler say to the sprinkler son of a sprinkler: Your water is cave water, and your ashes are from roasting'?"

role of God and the prophets in determining truth is called into question.[168] It is worthwhile to take a closer look at the nature of the arguments in this section of text, which has mostly been glossed over by both traditional and academic scholars. When the Ammonite convert inquires whether he can enter the congregation of Israel, Rabban Gamaliel denies him entry but R. Yehoshua accepts his conversion. Rabban Gamaliel defends his position by quoting the Pentateuch, "Neither shall an Ammonite nor Moabite enter the congregation of God" (Deut 23:4). R. Yehoshua responds by citing a verse from the book of Isaiah that speaks of the Assyrian king Sennacherib displacing local populations during his conquests. However, R. Yehoshua does not cite an actual prophecy. Rather, he uses the words of the Assyrian king Sennacherib to make his point. "I have removed the boundaries of nations and have robbed their treasures and, as a mighty one, I have brought down their inhabitants" (Isa 10:13). But the citation of this verse alone does not suffice. R. Yehoshua then appeals to a rabbinic legal principle to support his argument. When faced with an object of questionable provenance, such as a piece of meat found in the street, the rabbis assume the object to have the status of the majority group. The kosher status of the piece of meat follows the majority of the number of kosher and non-kosher butchers in a town. So too, this Ammonite is not to be considered a native Ammonite but rather his status follows the majority of the (post-Sennacherib) residents of that land, dislocated foreigners. He is therefore deemed to be a non-native Ammonite. R. Yehoshua has thus used the words of a gentile king coupled with a rabbinic legal principle to undo the command of the Pentateuch regarding the acceptance of converts from the land of Ammon.

Rabban Gamaliel, next, revives the debate by appealing to prophecy. He quotes from the prophet Jeremiah, "But afterwards, I will bring back the captivity of the children of Ammon, says God" (Jer 49:6). Though Sennacherib had displaced the nation of Ammon, God proclaims that He will return them to their place of origin. R. Yehoshua himself responds by citing a prophecy. In the book of Amos, the prophet states, "And I will bring back the captivity of My people Israel" (Amos 9:14). R. Yehoshua argues

168. R. Yehoshua here plays a role similar to the one he plays in b. B. Meṣ. 59b, where he rejects God's intervention in matters of truth by citing God against Himself. In that story, after God reveals his position through the medium of a heavenly echo (*bat qol*) and says that the law is in accordance with R. Eliezer, R. Yehoshua stands up and rejects God's authority to make such a proclamation. R. Yehoshua does so by citing a verse from Deuteronomy, "it is not in heaven" (30:12). These words in their actual biblical context, however, mean something quite the opposite of the use to which R. Yehoshua has now put them. There, the words are used to argue that the revealed law is self-evident and accessible to all. God's revelation should therefore need no intermediary. Yet, in proclaiming these words, R. Yehoshua has rejected God's authority to convey the intent of the divine words to humans unmediated by the rabbis.

that this prophecy states that God will return the people of Israel from captivity, yet they have still not returned. With this retort, R. Yehoshua wins the argument. On its face, however, R. Yehoshua's argument is quite remarkable. The prophet Amos, a native of the southern kingdom of Judea, directed his writings to the northern kingdom of Israel. He was active in mid-eighth century BCE, prior to both the Assyrian conquest of the northern kingdom of Israel and the Babylonian conquest of the southern kingdom of Judea during the time of Jeremiah. Though Amos 9:11 speaks of the restoration of King David's house, it is safe to assume that the "Israel" referred to in verse 14 is the northern kingdom.[169] Therefore R. Yehoshua's argument is that, since the ten lost tribes have still not returned, how can one assume that the prophecy in Jeremiah has already been fulfilled? R. Yehoshua has, in effect, pointed to an unfulfilled prophecy to question the veracity and reliability of prophecy in general.

While the story speaks of one revolution and its containment, it at the same time hides another far more dangerous revolution that must be contained, the overthrow of the rabbinic system altogether. Essential to the shared code of the battling parties within this rabbinic culture is a rejection of the regime of the prophet.[170] Even the dream, posed as a form of prophecy, is simply stamped out as unreliable. The symbolic Yavneh-era prophetic figure in the rabbinic academy, R. Eliezer b. Hurqanus (see b. B. Meṣ. 59b), is nowhere to be seen in this drama.[171] Whereas for R. Shimeon and R. Akiva, whose appearance in the text points to a hidden subtext, R. Eliezer is completely erased. Jameson would call this type of absence a "negative intertextuality."[172] The negative intertext highlights that the class struggle itself, represented by all of the opposing voices in the story, exists only within a hegemonic discourse united by a single shared code. R. Eliezer operates outside of this code. The shared code of rabbinic culture is built upon a system that constantly points to God while simultaneously rejecting Him.[173] This culture cites the words of God but controls those words through the use of rabbinic rhetoric. Therefore, in imagining revolution, this text sees only one possibility, the return to the political past of the period of the Second Temple but not the First Temple. It is the rule of the priest and not the prophet that threatens return; and it is

---

169. Source-critical scholars have much debated the precise dating of this section, as it appears to be a later addition to the text.

170. The story of the Oven of Akhnai (b. B. Meṣ. 59b) is the *locus classicus* in the Talmud for the working through of this problem.

171. Though the b. B. Meṣ. 59b story is one that deals with the problems of a prophetic-type figure operating within the rabbinic system, it does not entertain the possibility of a cultural revolution that would lead to the revival of that system.

172. Jameson, *Political Unconscious*, 124.

173. This idea is epitomized in R. Yehoshua's statement, "it is not in heaven," found in b. B. Meṣ. 59b. See n. 168, above.

priestly rule that therefore must be contained and managed. So, is this a text that consciously seeks to reify the shared code among the competing parties, or is it a text that unconsciously displays a more deeply rooted fear, the return to the referent of the negative intertext, the prophet? While Jameson writes that a story must be read not for its visible structure but for its absent cause,[174] I leave this question open. If my retelling of this story were to answer this question, then it would be no story at all.

Appendix: Translation of the Deposition Story

[The Mishnah states:] The evening prayer has no fixed time. What [does] "has no fixed time" [mean]? If I say [it means] that if one wants one can pray [any time during] the entire night, then let [the Mishnah] state "[the time for] the evening prayer [is] the whole night"! Rather, what [does] "has no fixed time" [mean]? [The Mishnah's ruling] follows the one who says that the evening prayer is optional. As Rav Yehudah said that Shmuel said: Regarding the evening prayer, Rabban Gamaliel says it is obligatory; R. Yehoshua says it is optional.

Abaye said: The law follows the one who says it is obligatory; Rava said the law follows the one who says it is optional.[175]

Our Rabbis taught [in a *baraita*]:[176] A story about a certain student who came before R. Yehoshua.
[The student] said to [R. Yehoshua]: "[Is] the evening prayer optional or obligatory?"
[R. Yehoshua] said to [the student]: "Optional."
[The student then] came before Rabban Gamaliel.
[The student] said to [Rabban Gamaliel]: "[Is] the evening prayer optional or obligatory?"
[Rabban Gamaliel] said to [the student]: "Obligatory."
[The student] said to [Rabban Gamaliel]: "But, did not R. Yehoshua tell me that it is optional?"
[Rabban Gamaliel] said to [the student]: "Wait until the shield bearers[177] enter the *(beit midrash)* study hall."

174. Jameson, *Political Unconscious*, 20.

175. Abaye and Rava are fourth-century Babylonian Amoraim. They often dispute in the Talmud. In almost all occurrences, the law follows Rava.

176. Extracanonical rabbinic source, similar to a Mishnah.

177. That is, debaters. The Talmud here uses language associated with warriors in depicting the intellectual activity of the rabbis in the study hall.

When the shield bearers entered [the study hall], the questioner[178] stood and asked: "Is the evening prayer optional or obligatory?"
Rabban Gamaliel said to [the questioner]: "Obligatory."
Rabban Gamaliel [then] said to the Sages: "Is there anyone who disagrees on this matter?"
R. Yehoshua said to [Rabban Gamaliel]: "No."
[Rabban Gamaliel] said to [R. Yehoshua]: "But did they not, in your name, say to me that [the law] is [that the evening prayer is] optional?"
[Rabban Gamaliel then] said to [him]: "Yehoshua, stand on your feet and they shall testify against you!"
R. Yehoshua stood upon his feet and said: "If only I were alive and [the witness] dead, the living could contradict the dead. [However,] now that I am alive and [the witness] is alive, how can the living contradict the living?"[179]
Rabban Gamaliel was sitting and expounding and R. Yehoshua [remained] standing upon his feet until the populace murmured and said to Ḥutspit the Turgeman,[180] "Stand [still]!"
[Ḥutspit] stood [still].

[The populace[181] then] said: "How long will [Rabban Gamaliel] go on vexing him [R. Yehoshua]! On New Year's day last year he vexed him.[182] In [the matter of] the firstborn, in the story involving R. Tsadoq, he vexed him;[183] now too he vexes him! Come, let us depose him [as *Nasi*]!"[184] [They continued,] "Whom shall we appoint [in his stead]? Shall we appoint R. Yehoshua? [We cannot because] he is involved in the matter. Shall we appoint R. Akiva? [We cannot because] perhaps [Rabban Gamaliel] will harm him [*'anish lei*][185] because [R. Akiva] has no ancestral merit. Rather, we shall appoint R. Elazar b. Azariah because he is wise and he is rich and

---

178. Literally: "the asker stood and asked," implying there was an official inquisitor in the study hall whose job it was to pose questions for official review and discussion. Alternatively, this could refer to the aforementioned student.

179. This is just a complicated way of saying: "Though I might want to lie to you about this, I cannot, because there are people here who heard me say it." In other words, "Okay, you got me."

180. A Turgeman is either an interpreter, a translator, or a human loudspeaker. It was the practice for an old rabbi to speak softly to those around him and for a Turgeman to broadcast his words to the crowd. It is unclear if the Turgeman also translated (e.g., from Hebrew to Aramaic) and/or further explained the rabbi's words.

181. Or, perhaps, the other Sages present.

182. R. Yehoshua and Rabban Gamaliel had debated the date of the New Year. Rabban Gamaliel forced R. Yehoshua to submit to R. Gamaliel's position in a public manner, by making R. Yehoshua travel to Rabban Gamaliel with his money belt on the day that was Yom Kippur according to R. Yehoshua's, but not Rabban Gamaliel's, reckoning.

183. In a story that is in many ways identical to this one.

184. That is, remove Rabban Gamaliel from the office of the presidency.

185. See n. 146, above.

he is a tenth [generation descendant] from Ezra.[186] He is wise, so that if anyone puts a question to him he will be able to answer it. He is rich, so that if he has to bribe the Roman government (house of Caesar),[187] he will also be able to go and bribe. And he is a tenth [generation descendant] from Ezra, so that he has ancestral merit and [Rabban Gamaliel] will not be able to punish him."[188]

They[189] came and said to [R. Elazar b. Azariah,] "Do you, sir, consent to become head of the Academy?"
[R. Elazar b. Azariah] said to [the populace]:[190] "I will go and consult with the members of my household."

[R. Elazar b. Azariah] went and consulted his wife.
She said to him: "Perhaps they will [also] depose you [at some later point]."
He said to her [quoting a proverb]: "[Let a man use][191] a cup of honor for one day and let it be smashed the next."[192]
She said to him: "You have no white hair."[193]

That day, [R. Elazar b. Azariah] was eighteen years old. A miracle happened for him and eighteen rows of his [beard] hair turned white.

That is why R. Elazar b. Azariah said [in an earlier Mishnah], "Behold I am <u>like</u> seventy years old," and [did] not [say] "[I am] seventy years old."[194]

[A Tanna][195] taught: On that day, they removed the [study hall's] entrance guard and the students were given permission to enter. For Rabban Gamaliel used to proclaim [during his tenure as president], saying: "Any student whose inner self (i.e., character, substance, or appearance) does not align with his outer self may not enter the study hall." On that day many benches were added [to the study hall].

---

186. Ezra was is a biblical character who was involved in the restructuring of Israelite society after the mass return of exiles from Babylon. Ezra was a priest and was allied with the Persian government. He therefore is a figure that marks the transition from Israel being led by kings from the tribe of Judah to Israel being led by priests who were regents of an external sovereign.

187. Literally, house of Caesar.

188. Rashi, cited in *Ein Ya'akov* adds "and cause him to die" in parentheses.

189. Either the populace or, perhaps, the other sages present.

190. Either the populace or, perhaps, the other sages present.

191. These words appear in brackets in the Vilna edition of the Talmud.

192. That is, it is better to experience honor if only for a day.

193. That is, you are too young. They will never respect your decisions.

194. In a Mishnah (Ber. 1:5) quoted in the Passover Haggadah.

195. Rabbi living in the time of the Mishnaic period (50 BCE–200 CE).

R. Yoḥanan[196] said: Abba Yoseph b. Dostai[197] and the [rest of the] Rabbis dispute this matter: one [of these two disputing authorities] says four hundred benches were added; and the other says seven hundred benches [were added].

Rabban Gamaliel was dispirited. He said, "Perhaps, God forbid, I withheld Torah from Israel!" White casks full of ashes[198] were shown to him in a dream.

But the [message of the dream] is not [a reflection of the truth of the matter.] The [dream] was only shown to him to calm his spirit.

[A Tanna][199] taught: Eduyyot[200] was taught[201] on that day. Additionally, wherever the expression "on that day" is used [in rabbinic literature] it designates that very day. And [on that day] there was no law left pending [decision] in the study hall which was not fully explicated. And even Rabban Gamaliel did not absent himself from the study hall [on that day] for even a single moment, as is taught [in a Mishnah]:[202] On that day Yehudah, an Ammonite[203] convert, came before the [Rabbis] in the study hall.
[Yehudah the Ammonite convert] said to [the Rabbis]: "What [is the law] for me as far as entering the congregation [of Israel]?"[204]
Rabban Gamaliel said to [Yehudah the Ammonite convert]: "You are forbidden to enter the congregation [of Israel]."
R. Yehoshua said to [Yehudah the Ammonite convert]: "You are permitted to enter the congregation [of Israel]."
Rabban Gamaliel said to [R. Yehoshua]: "But is it not already stated [in the Pentateuch],[205] 'Neither shall an Ammonite nor Moabite enter the congregation of God'?"
R. Yehoshua said to [Rabban Gamaliel]: "Do Ammon and Moab [still] reside in their [original] territories?[206] Sennacherib king of Assyria already [long ago] arose and mixed up all the nations,[207] as it is stated [in the books

196. Third-century Palestinian Amora.
197. A second-century Tanna who, though not mentioned in the Mishnah, is named in the Tosefta.
198. Implying his policy of exclusion was warranted.
199. Rabbi living in the time of the Mishnaic period (50 BCE–200 CE).
200. A Mishnah tractate.
201. Or formulated; or redacted.
202. M. Yad. 4:4.
203. Ammon was a nation that, according to the biblical account, was not allowed to convert to Judaism.
204. That is, convert to Judaism.
205. Deut 23:4.
206. That is, the people living in those lands nowadays are not related to the original inhabitants of those lands in biblical times.
207. That is, he forcibly relocated all indigenous populations.

of the Prophets],[208] 'I have removed the boundaries of nations and have robbed their treasures and, as a mighty one, I have brought down their inhabitants.' And [there is a talmudic principle] that whatever parts [from a group is assumed] to have parted from the majority [of the group.]"[209]
Rabban Gamaliel said to [R. Yehoshua]: "But is it not already stated [in the books of the Prophets],[210] 'But afterwards, I will bring back the captivity of the children of Ammon, says God'? And [the captives, the original inhabitants of Ammon,] have [therefore] already returned!"[211]
R. Yehoshua said to [Rabban Gamaliel]: "But is it not already stated [in the books of the Prophets],[212] 'And I will bring back the captivity of My people Israel'? And [the captives of Israel] have not yet returned!"

Immediately, [the Rabbis] permitted [Yehudah the Ammonite] to enter the congregation [of Israel].

Rabban Gamaliel said [to himself]: "Since this is how it is, I will go and appease R. Yehoshua."

When [Rabban Gamaliel] reached [R. Yehoshua's] house he saw that the walls of his house had blackened.
[Rabban Gamaliel] said to [R. Yehoshua]: "From the walls of your house it is apparent that you are a charcoal-burner."
[R. Yehoshua] replied: "Woe to the generation of which you are the leader, because you do not know of the pain of [its] scholars, how they support themselves and how they are sustained!"
[Rabban Gamaliel] said to [R. Yehoshua]: "I apologize; forgive me."
[R. Yehoshua] paid no attention to him.
[Rabban Gamaliel tried again,] "Do it out of respect for my father."
[R. Yehoshua] was appeased.
They[213] said: "Who will go and tell the Rabbis?"
A certain clothing launderer said to them: "I will go."

R. Yehoshua sent [a message] to the study hall: "[Let] the one who wears the robe wear it; shall the one who does not wear the robe say to him who wears the robe, 'Take off your robe and I will wear it?"[214]

---

208. Isa 10:13.

209. In this case, this man has separated himself from the current residents of Ammon; and these residents are not the original inhabitants. They therefore are allowed to convert. So too, this man may convert.

210. Jer 49:6.

211. This man from Ammon is therefore a descendant of the original Ammonites and consequently may not convert to Judaism.

212. Amos 9:14.

213. Perhaps "they" refers to the two rabbis, perhaps to those present.

214. The robe here represents the garment of the presidency.

R. Akiva said to the rabbis, "Lock the doors so that the slaves of Rabban Gamaliel should not come and bother the Rabbis."

R. Yehoshua said [to himself]: "It is best that I get up and go to them."
[R. Yehoshua] came and knocked at the door [and] said to them: "The sprinkler son of a sprinkler shall sprinkle; shall one who is neither a sprinkler nor the son of a sprinkler say to a sprinkler son of a sprinkler, 'Your water is cave water and your ashes are oven ashes'?"[215]
R. Akiva to him: "R. Yehoshua, have you been appeased? We only did [what we did] for the sake of your honor. Tomorrow, you and I will rise early [and go] to [R. Elazar b. Azariah's] door.

[The Rabbis] said: "How shall we go about this? Shall we depose [R. Elazar b. Azariah]? [We cannot because] we have a tradition [that] 'we may elevate the sanctity [of an object] but we may not degrade [the sanctity of an object.][216] Shall we let one master lecture on one Sabbath and the other [the next] Sabbath? [We cannot because] this will lead to jealousy. Rather, let Rabban Gamaliel lecture three weeks [per month] and R. Elazar b. Azariah one week [per month]."

And it is in reference to this [resolution of the matter] that a Master[217] said: Whose week was it? It was the week of R. Elazar b. Azariah.

And "that student"[218] was R. Shimeon b. Yoḥai.

---

215. Here, once again, R. Yehoshua uses a metaphor implying hereditary leaders should lead. Ironically, he uses priestly imagery in an effort to convince the rabbis to depose R. Elazar b. Azariah (who is a priest) and replace him with Rabban Gamaliel (who is not a priest, but rather a member of the tribe of Judah). Cave water and oven ashes are both disqualified for temple purification procedures. Running water and ashes of the red heifer must be used for purification.

216. In this case the "object" being R. Elazar and the "sanctity" being R. Elazar's leadership status.

217. Referring to a quotation from elsewhere in the Talmud.

218. Referring to the student who, at the start of the story, caused the controversy by pitting R. Yehoshua and Rabban Gamaliel against each other in asking about the status of the evening prayer.

Jews, Gentiles, and Gehinnom in Rabbinic Literature

DOV WEISS

In 1985, the renowned Pauline scholar E. P. Sanders (b. 1937) excoriated the German Lutheran theologian Joachim Jeremias (1900–1979) for unfairly portraying the rabbis as gentile haters who denied salvation to non-Jews.[1] Contra Jeremias, Sanders argued that the rabbis were not monolithic as they debated whether non-Jews were fated for the fiery torments of hell. According to Sanders, Jeremias ignored those inclusivist rabbinic voices that regarded righteous gentiles as destined for heaven. Contra Jeremias, Sanders regarded Paul's mission to the gentiles, and his belief that all people could achieve salvation through Christ as not opposing the xenophobic rabbinic view, as Jeremias had argued, but rather as paralleling the inclusive voices found in rabbinic literature. Following Sanders, Paula Fredriksen argued that the rabbis had "dissenting views"

Unless otherwise noted, rabbinic texts mentioned in this article rely on the best manuscripts as selected by the Historical Dictionary Project of the Academy of the Hebrew Language, which can be found at https://maagarim.hebrew-academy.org.il/Pages/PMain.aspx. I accessed these texts in May 2018. While taking full responsibility for the translations that appear herein, I have relied on the following works, freely making changes to them as deemed necessary: *Midrash Rabbah*, ed. H. Freedman and Maurice Simon, 13 vols. (London: Soncino, 1939); William G. Braude, *Pesikta Rabbati: Discourses for Feasts, Fasts, and Special Sabbaths*, vol. 18, YJS (New Haven: Yale University Press, 1968); Reuven Hammer, *Sifre: A Tannaitic Commentary on the Book of Deuteronomy*, YJS (New Haven: Yale University Press, 1986); Jacob Z. Lauterbach, *Mekhilta de-Rabbi Ishmael : A Critical Edition, Based on the Manuscripts and Early Editions*, 3 vols. (Philadelphia: Jewish Publication Society, 1976).

1. Joachim Jeremias, *Jesus' Promise to the Nations* (1958; repr., Philadelphia: Fortress, 1982); E. P. Sanders, *Jesus and Judaism* (Philadelphia: Fortress, 1985), 213–21. The term *salvation* typically means the state of being saved from (1) hell, (2) alienation from God, or (3) annihilation. In this essay, I use the term *salvation* in its first sense: being saved from hell. See Jeffrey A. Trumbower, *Rescue for the Dead: The Posthumous Salvation of Non-Christians in Early Christianity*, OSHT (New York: Oxford University Press, 2001), 3.

on the question of gentile salvation. She then maintained that, ultimately, the inclusivist view prevailed as "for the most part [the rabbis] concurred: Gentiles could be righteous, and as such they would have a place in the world to come."[2] Scholars of ancient Judaism, too, have largely agreed with Sanders. Christine Hayes, for example, argued that "there was no rabbinic consensus on the question of the ultimate destiny of humankind [i.e. gentiles]."[3] In this respect she follows a long list of scholars of Judaism beginning with George Foot Moore (1851–1931) and Claude Montefiore (1858–1938), who, a century ago, presented the question of gentile salvation as simply a matter of debate between two rabbinical schools.[4] The above scholars (excluding Jeremias) could then posit that the rabbis of late antiquity preserved the diverse opinions on the fate of gentiles as found in the Hebrew Bible and Second Temple Jewish literature.[5] Concurring with this perspective, Jeffrey L. Rubenstein remarked that "in many ways the tensions concerning the eschatological fate of the gentiles in rabbinic sources mirrors tensions within the biblical corpus."[6]

This essay argues that the above scholars accurately captured only half of the picture. While the rabbis, indeed, debated the question of gentile salvation in the Tannaitic period (first and second centuries), the exclusivist position—which regarded the gentiles as destined for Gehinnom—reached near-unanimous consensus in the later rabbinic periods (third to tenth centuries).[7] This fact—that the rabbinic belief in gentile damnation

---

2. Paula Fredriksen, "Judaism, the Circumcision of Gentiles, and Apocalyptic Hope: Another Look at Galatians 1 and 2," *JTS NS* 42 (1991): 532–64, here 535. A similar stance is taken by Alan F. Segal, *Life after Death: A History of the Afterlife in the Religions of the West* (New York: Doubleday, 2004), 198. David Novak also implied that the inclusivist rabbinic view prevailed soon after the Tannaitic period, stating that "the affirmation ... of gentile righteousness by R. Yehoshua laid the theological foundation for the [widespread and accepted] Noahide laws *a generation later*" (*The Image of the Non-Jew in Judaism: The Idea of Noahide Law*, 2nd ed. [Oxford: Littman Library of Jewish Civilization, 2011], 148; my italics).

3. Christine Hayes, "The 'Other' in Rabbinic Literature," in *The Cambridge Companion to the Talmud and Rabbinic literature*, ed. Charlotte Elisheva Fonrobert and Martin S. Jaffee (Cambridge: Cambridge University Press, 2007), 257.

4. C. G. Montefiore and H. Loewe, *A Rabbinic Anthology* (New York: Schocken, 1974), 582; George Foot Moore, *Judaism in the First Centuries of the Christian Era: The Age of the Tannaim*, 3 vols. (1927–1930; repr., Cambridge: Harvard University Press, 1954), 2:386. For similar presentations, see Segal, *Life after Death*, 635; Efraim E. Urbach, *The Sages: Their Concepts and Beliefs*, trans. Israel Abrahams (Cambridge, MA: Harvard University Press, 1987), 543.

5. See, e.g., Sanders, *Jesus and Judaism*, 214.

6. Jeffrey L. Rubenstein, *Talmudic Stories: Narrative Art, Composition, and Culture* (Baltimore: Johns Hopkins University Press, 1999), 386.

7. Rabbinic texts often state that the gentiles are destined for Gehinnom but do not indicate for how long. When I note in this essay that the rabbis "damn" the gentiles I mean only that the rabbis believed that gentiles would go to hell. I am not weighing in on the question of duration. In fact, it is in the realm of possibility that the Tannaim reserved an eternity in hell only for Jewish apostates, but not gentiles, as evidenced in the Tosefta (see t. Sanh. 13:2).

intensified over time—has gone unnoticed in prior scholarship (both Jewish and Christian). We have around twenty-five rabbinic texts attributed to named sages, found in both the midrash and Talmud, that posit this exclusivist soteriology. These anti-gentile teachings rely on diverse biblical prooftexts and conceptual justifications, as well as employing highly derogatory metaphors to describe gentiles. The sheer number, size, diversity, and complexity of these midrashic texts solidify their centrality for rabbinic thinking and culture. Until now, none of this material has been collected, let alone analyzed. By presenting a close reading of these anti-gentile texts, this essay challenges Robert Goldenberg's claim that "the dispute over gentiles [and the afterlife] ... attracted remarkably little attention from later generations of rabbinic masters."[8] It also questions Sanders's claim that "rabbinic literature is addressed to members of the covenant [and thus] ... the gentiles [in rabbinic literature] are dealt with only sporadically ... and different Rabbis had different opinions about their destiny."[9] As this essay posits that rabbinic xenophobia—at least in its soteriological context[10]—intensified over time, it challenges Goldenberg's assertion that we can detect little change between Tannaitic and Amoraic documents toward gentiles.[11]

Christian theology offers a nice parallel and might even have served to reinforce the transformations we encounter in rabbinic theology. As on the Jewish side, in early Christianity we see a shift from a stance of soteriological inclusivism or universalism to exclusivism. In the second and third centuries *some* Christian theologians, such as Clement of Alexandria (150–215) and Origen (184–253), as well as select Gnostics (the authors of the Secret Book of John and the Tripartite Tractate) adopted, in different ways

8. Robert Goldenberg, *The Nations That Know Thee Not: Ancient Jewish Attitudes towards Other Religions*, Reappraisals in Jewish Social and Intellectual History (New York: New York University Press, 1998), 84.

9. E. P. Sanders, *Paul and Palestinian Judaism: A Comparison of Patterns of Religion* (London: SCM, 1977), 207.

10. I recognize that rabbinic literature contains many positive statements concerning gentiles. My contention, here, is that these sentiments do not appear in soteriological contexts, where the stakes could not be higher. For a collection of some of these "pro-gentile" sources, see Montefiore and Loewe, *Rabbinic Anthology*, 556–65; Efraim Elimelech Urbach, *Collected Writings in Jewish Studies*, ed. Robert Brody and Moshe David Herr (Jerusalem: Magnes, 1999), 269–98.

11. Goldenberg, *Nations That Know*, 97. In this regard, this essay dovetails nicely with Marc Hirshman's claim that the Amoraim adopted the particularistic worldview of R. Akiva, while rejecting the universal approach of R. Ishmael; see Marc G. Hirshman, "Rabbinic Universalism in the Second and Third Centuries," *HTR* 93 (2000): 101–15. It also aligns with Moshe Lavee, "'Sarah Nursed Children': Different Models of Jewish–Gentile Relations in the Metamorphosis of Midrashic Traditions" [Hebrew], in *"On the Well's Mouth": Studies in Jewish and Halakhic Thought* [Hebrew], ed. Howard T. Kreisel, Daniel J. Lasker, and Gerald J. Blidstein (Be'er Sheva: Ben Gurion University Press, 2008), 269–91.

and degrees, the possibility, or eventuality, of non-Christian salvation.[12] By contrast, the subsequent view that dominated from the fourth century and on, best epitomized in the writings of John Chrysostom (349–407) and Augustine of Hippo (354–430), proclaimed that only through faith in Jesus Christ could a person achieve salvation.[13] In other words, there is no salvation outside the church (*extra ecclesiam nulla salus*); only righteous Christians could be saved.

I will further argue that a rabbinic anti-gentile soteriology worked in tandem with a new rabbinic doctrine that advocated a radical vision of Jewish supremacy: all Jews—even the sinners—would escape the fiery torments of hell. As Ishay Rosen-Zvi and Adi Ophir have recently shown, theological attitudes toward Jews and gentiles are two sides of the same coin.[14] Identity is established via highlighting differences. In this case, several rabbis from the third to the eighth century damned the gentiles and offered salvation to the Jews. By doing so, Amoraic and post-Amoraic rabbis discursively engage in a double act of theological discrimination: (1) unlike sinning gentiles, sinning Jews go to heaven; and (2) unlike righteous Jews, righteous gentiles go to hell. With this emerging soteriology, the rabbis went further than the regnant Augustinian view, which damned all non-Christians to suffer eternally in hell (for Adam's sin). That is because Augustine did not, inversely, proclaim immunity for all Christians. For Augustine, bad Christians who did not make proper use of their faith were destined to end up in hell. (Recall that Dante has many Christians in his inferno.) Indeed, this new Jewish soteriology would have no analogs in the Christian world until the sixteenth century when Martin Luther averred that, by definition, every Christian would be saved.

Put together, both emerging phenomena—an intensified anti-gentile soteriology and a Jewish supremacist soteriology—represent a marked shift in rabbinic discourse. While in early rabbinic times the primary binary of righteous versus wicked determined salvation for every human being (focus on action and belief), in later rabbinic texts a new binary emerges—not wicked versus righteous, but Jew versus gentile (focus on ethnicity). With this in mind, George Foot Moore's claim that "the predominant religious and moral interest of the rabbis in the Last Judgement was … not in the fate of the heathen, but in the individual retribution which there awaits [the] Israelites" rings hollow.[15] This is because not only do we have much rabbinic material on gentile salvation but also because

12. Michael James McClymond, *The Devil's Redemption: A New History and Interpretation of Christian Universalism*, 2 vols. (Grand Rapids: Baker Academic, 2018), 1:144–54, 239–67.

13. See ibid., 1:235–433; Trumbower, *Rescue for the Dead*.

14. Adi Ophir and Ishay Rosen-Zvi, *Goy: Israel's Others and the Birth of the Gentile*, Oxford Studies in the Abrahamic Religions (New York: Oxford University Press, 2018).

15. Moore, *Judaism in the First Centuries*, 2:386–87.

rabbinic attitudes toward Jews should not be seen in isolation from rabbinic attitudes toward gentiles.

The new binary of Jew versus gentile emerged over a long span of time. During this period, and even after, it did not completely supplant the older soteriology that Jewish sinners would be punished in Gehinnom, at least for a period of time. As the rabbis seldom strive for consistency, these two mutually exclusive battles—one to promote Jewish righteousness and the other to promote Jewish supremacy—were waged simultaneously. While the rabbis do not explicitly flag the obvious internal contradiction, many of their narratives highlight an attempt to balance these competing aims. As I will show below, the rabbis craft narratives in part to express not only their soteriological beliefs and hopes but also their self-contradictory projects and impulses. These stories could also express the rabbis' ethical unease with a soteriology (their very own!) that unfairly discriminates against gentiles. In short, unlike theological propositions or doctrines, stories have the capacity to carry competing voices that represent the rabbis' own ambivalences.

I. Early Rabbinic Inclusivism

In m. Sanh. 10:1, only specific gentiles are denied a place in the world to come, implying that gentiles in general have a place in the world to come. Unlike the Mishnah, which does not address our issue explicitly, t. Sanh. 13:2 (ca. early third century) presents the following debate between two well-known students of R. Yoḥanan b. Zakkai (first century CE).

> R. Eliezer says: All the gentiles have no portion in the world to come, as it says, *the wicked shall return to Sheol, [all the nations] that forget God* (Ps 9:18). *The wicked shall return to Sheol*—this refers to wicked Israelites; [and *all the nations that forget God*—this refers to the nations of the world].
> R. Yehoshua replied: if Scripture had said *the wicked shall return to Sheol, all the nations* (ibid.) and kept silent, I would have agreed with you. But now that Scripture says, *that forget God* (ibid.)—this implies that the righteous among the nations [who do not forget God] will receive a portion in the world to come.[16]

In Ps 9:18, the petitioner expresses his hope that "God will send [literally, return] wicked people to Sheol and those nations that reject [literally, forget] God." In the Hebrew Bible, Sheol does not signify hell; rather, it is a dark, murky place where all the dead, both the righteous and the wicked,

16. T. Sanh. 13:2 according to MS Erfurt accessed through https://www.biu.ac.il/JS/tannaim/.

reside.[17] The dead live in a shadowy, half-conscious state and cannot praise God (see Ps 6:6). In Ps 9:18, the psalmist is articulating a wish that the wicked and idolatrous nations be destroyed.

The rabbis, however, consistently interpret Sheol as referring to Gehinnom (hell), a place where some of the dead will be punished through fire (and, in some sources, snow). Sheol in Psalms thus, for the rabbis, no longer connotes simply death, but the experience of torture after death. Moreover, *goyim* ("nations") denotes not only the non-Israelite nations, as used in the Hebrew Bible, but also individual non-Jews. With these interpretive transformations, R. Eliezer reads Ps 9:18 not as a plea leveled at God to kill the wicked and idolatrous nations, as a simple reading suggests, but as pronouncing a theological fact: wicked Jews along with the gentiles—even the righteous ones—are destined for hell. He reads the verse as if it says, "God sends the wicked (Jews) to Gehinnom, and also all the gentiles [כל גוים]." R. Yehoshua disagrees and argues that one must not elide the concluding phrase of the verse: only gentiles who "forget" God are destined for hell. Righteous gentiles, in R. Yehoshua's view, will be spared such agony.

In the following section of the Tosefta (Sanh. 13:3), an anonymous teaching includes a rather innocuous phrase that seems to concur with the inclusive approach of R. Yehoshua.[18] Only sinning gentiles will be punished in hell, not righteous ones.

> Israelites who sinned with their bodies and gentiles who sinned with their bodies go down to Gehinnom and are judged there for twelve months. And after twelve months their souls perish, their bodies are burned, Gehinnom absorbs them, and they are turned into dirt. And the wind blows them and scatters them under the feet of the righteous, as it is written, *And you shall trample down the wicked; for they shall be ashes under the soles of your feet on the day that I shall do this, says the Lord of hosts* (Mal 3:21).

17. On Sheol in the Hebrew Bible, see Alan E. Bernstein, *The Formation of Hell: Death and Retribution in the Ancient and Early Christian Worlds* (Ithaca, NY: Cornell University Press, 1993), 133–67; Segal, *Life after Death*, 134–40; Jon Douglas Levenson, *Creation and the Persistence of Evil: The Jewish Drama of Divine Omnipotence*, Mythos (Princeton, NJ: Princeton University Press, 1994), 35–66.

18. Here, I follow Chaim Milikowsky's reading that this section should be read as a later anonymous interpolation ("Gehinnom and the Sinners of Israel according to 'Seder Olam'" [Hebrew], *Tarbiṣ* 55 [1985–1986]: 311–43, here 328 n. 69). Arthur Marmorstein, by contrast, read this Tosefta passage as a continuation of Beit Hillel's view (*Studies in Jewish Theology: The Arthur Marmorstein Memorial Volume*, ed. J. Rabbinowitz and M. S. Lew [London: Oxford University Press, 1950], 181). Lawrence H. Schiffman assumes that it is the view of Beit Shammai (*Who Was a Jew? Rabbinic and Halakhic Perspectives on the Jewish Christian Schism* [Hoboken, NJ: Ktav, 1985], 46).

Note the Tosefta's egalitarianism: it asserts that gentiles (and Jews) who sin "with their bodies" will be tormented in Gehinnom for twelve months before being burned to ashes. By implication, the Tosefta maintains that non-sinning gentiles, or gentiles who sin but not "with their bodies" (whatever that means) will not be punished in Gehinnom. This general orientation accords with the inclusivist position of R. Yehoshua noted above.[19]

II. Rabbinic Exclusivism: Early and Late

Sages and Exegetical Strategies

R. Yehoshua's inclusivist position offering salvation to gentiles virtually disappears from rabbinic culture after the Tannaitic period. Strikingly, no trace of this position can be detected in any of the writings of Amoraic literature, which includes the Jerusalem Talmud, Genesis Rabbah, Leviticus Rabbah, Lamentations Rabbah, Songs of Songs Rabbah and Pesiqta de Rab Kahana. By contrast, R. Eliezer's exclusivist position emerges as the dominant one and appears often in Amoraic and post-Amoraic literature. Besides R. Eleazar, subsequent rabbinic texts attribute the anti-gentile position to the following Palestinian sages: R. Eleazar ha-Moda'i (second century), R. Yoḥanan (third century), R. Levi (third century), R. Yehoshua b. Levi (third century), R. Tanḥum b. Ilai (third century), and R. Yehudah b. Simon (fourth century). Other anti-gentile soteriological teachings—especially in post-Amoraic literature—go unattributed.

From Specific Nations to All Gentiles

The rabbinic penchant and proclivity to regard the gentiles as destined for hell can be exposed by measuring the gap between a rabbinic Gehinnom teaching and its biblical prooftext. Consider, for example, an anonymous teaching in Sifre Deut. 311 (ca. third century CE) that imposes its anti-gentile soteriology onto Ezek 32:17–32. In these biblical passages, God declares—through the prophet Ezekiel—that Pharaoh and his people will shamefully descend to Sheol (= rabbinic Gehinnom) where they will lie in an inferior section reserved for the uncircumcised and those murdered by the sword. The Egyptians will not be alone, as they will join the Assyrians, the Sidonians, the Edomites, and others. According to a contextual reading of this chapter, Sheol contained a specific and undignified section for the uncircumcised where select non-Israelite nations (and even some

19. Notably, the phrase "nations of the world" does not appear in a parallel teaching preserved in S. 'Olam Rab. 3 (ca. 300 CE). This omission might be purposeful, reflecting Seder 'Olam Rabbah's attempt to break down the Tosefta's egalitarianism.

circumcised ones such as the Egyptians and Edomites) shamefully abided.[20] Sifre Deuteronomy and other rabbinic texts, however, read Ezek 32 as positing that Gehinnom is the abode for all gentiles, as they are deemed "the uncircumcised ones." This rabbinic move—to lump many nations into the one category of *goyim* or "nations of the world"—is typical of their literature.

From Universal to Anti-Universal

At other times, the rabbis take a biblical passage welcoming non-Israelites and transform it into a passage that damns non-Israelites. In these cases, as the gulf between biblical text and rabbinic teaching is immense, the teaching more acutely exposes the rabbis' anti-gentile agenda. Take, for example, the second prooftext adduced by the above text (Sifre Deut. 311):

> *When the Most High gave to the nations their inheritance* [... *He set the borders of the people according to the number of the children of Israel*] (Deut 32:8): When God gave the peoples their inheritances, He made Gehinnom their portion [חלקם לגיהנם] ... Should you ask, who will possess their wealth and honor? The answer is Israel: *He set the borders of peoples [according to the number of the children of Israel]* (ibid.)

In Deut 32:7–14, Moses before his death recalls the wondrous things God did for the Israelites. In verse 8, Moses declares that, when "the Most High (God) gave to the nations their inheritance ... He set the borders according to the number of the children of Israel." Scholars, however, have shown that the MT reflects a textual emendation. The original version, as evidenced in the Septuagint and one of the Qumran scrolls, had "according to the number of divine beings."[21] In the original formulation, Moses describes how God divided the nations of the world and accorded to each an angelic or heavenly protector. The statement highlighted that the Israelites would live under the direct aegis of the Supreme God, and the non-Israelite nations would be governed by junior deities. The statement carried a universal message: non-Israelites had local gods to which they owed allegiance.

The original version, however, posed theological problems to ancient Jews, who revised the biblical verse and replaced it with "according to the number of the children of Israel." The revised sentence, however, perplexed traditional commentators. In what sense did God "give an inheritance" to the nations of world according to the "number" of Israelites?

---

20. See Moshe Greenberg, *Ezekiel 21–37: A New Translation with Introduction and Commentary*, AB 22A (New York: Doubleday, 1997), 659–70.

21. See Jeffrey H. Tigay, *Deuteronomy* דברים*: The Traditional Hebrew Text with the New JPS Translation*, JPS Torah Commentary (Philadelphia: Jewish Publication Society, 1996), 514–15.

What does that mean? Sifre Deut. 311 offers several solutions. According to one counterintuitive reading, the passage does not refer to a gentile inheritance in this world but rather to the gentiles' "inheritance" of Gehinnom in the next world. In messianic times, God would designate Gehinnom as a place for gentiles, and then grant the Jewish people permission to take the gentiles' property, wealth, and prestige. According to Sifre Deuteuronomy, the verse communicates this very point when stating, "He sets the borders [i.e., belongings] of peoples toward ... the children of Israel." Thus, while the original (pre-Masoretic) verse highlighted the celestial protection of the non-Israelites, and the MT highlighted God's gracious gift to the gentiles (as it accorded them an immense geographical landscape), the Sifre's reinterpretation of the Masoretic verse underscores the celestial damnation of non-Israelites.

A second example of this type of interpretive inversion—from universal biblical passage to anti-universal rabbinic teaching—can be found in Song Rab. 2:1:3. Here, R. Eleazar ha-Moda'i (second-century Palestine) has God announce that only the gentile nations would remain in Gehinnom, together with their gods. Remarkably, the midrashic prooftext is Mic 4:5, where the First Temple prophet optimistically states that, at some future point, all the nations of the world will march toward the Lord's temple in Jerusalem with their gods: "For let all the peoples walk each one in the name of its god." Recontextualizing the location and purpose of the march, however, the midrash no longer has the nations walking triumphantly with their gods to the Temple Mount but has the nations marching with their gods to hell. Put differently, the midrash transforms one of the most famous biblical expressions of universal salvation into a strident declaration of universal damnation.

A similar rabbinic hermeneutical inversion (from universal to anti-universal) occurs with regard to another famous biblical section: Isa 56. Here, Deutero-Isaiah has God declare that foreigners attracted to the beliefs of the Judeans could offer prayers and sacrifices at the Temple Mount because God's "house" is a "house of prayer for all the nations" (Isa 56:7). An anonymous Tanḥuma-Yelammedenu (TY) tradition, preserved in Exod. Rab. 19:4, however, defangs the universal force of Isa 56:

> *Neither let the alien, that has joined himself to the Lord, speak [saying: The Lord will surely separate me from his people]* (Isa 56:6). This refers to Jewish converts who are circumcised; but these that I (God) have disqualified are uncircumcised. For God detests [מואס] the uncircumcised and brings them down [ומורידן] to Gehinnom, as it says: *Son of man, wail for the multitude of Egypt and cast them down* (Ezek 32:18). Isaiah also says: *Therefore the netherworld has enlarged her desire, and opened her mouth without measure* [בלי חוק] (Isa 5:14), that is, for the heathen who has no circumcision, as it says: *And He established it unto Jacob for a statute [to Israel for an everlasting*

> *covenant]* (Ps 105: 10). For no [Israelite] who is circumcised goes down to Gehinnom.

Exodus Rabbah argues that the "foreigners" [בני הנכר] who should be embraced in Isa 56:6 refer only to newly converted circumcised Jews. Gentiles, by contrast, would be sent to hell because their men are uncircumcised.

From Israelites to Gentiles

The above Exodus Rabbah text further substantiates its anti-gentile sentiments by rereading another section of Isaiah. In its own context, Isa 5:11–17 has God complaining about Israelite party-goers who, while ignoring the real "victims of hunger" (5:13), exhibit a hunger that is unquenchable. For these Israelite sinners, God cleverly declares that "Sheol has opened wide its gullet and parted its jaws without measure [בלי חוק]." In other words, these people will meet their death. The TY midrash, however, reads בלי חוק not as "without measure" but for those who are not circumcised, that is, non-Israelites. And because the rabbis, as they typically do, read "Sheol" as Gehinnom, the verse is now understood to mean that the uncircumcised, that is, the gentiles, will be sent down to Gehinnom [i.e., שאול]. Here we see a different rabbinic interpretive move to produce its anti-gentile teaching: the rabbis impose an anti-gentile soteriology onto biblical texts that have nothing to do with gentiles. The biblical passage only deals with Israelites. In other words, beyond inverting universal texts into anti-universal ones, here the rabbis also transform a common biblical binary of righteous Israelites versus sinning Israelites into a new binary: Israelites versus non-Israelites.

A second example of this hermeneutical shift—from wicked versus righteous Israelites to gentiles versus Jews—can be found in the TY midrash of Exod. Rab. 25:7, where an anonymous sage declares that the gentile nations of the world will sit depressed in Gehinnom as they watch the Israelites at peace eating joyfully in the Garden of Eden. Exodus Rabbah's prooftext, however, is Isa 65:13 where, according to a straightforward reading, God details the differing fates of the righteous Judeans in contrast to the wicked Judeans: "My servants shall eat, and you shall be hungry.... My servants shall rejoice, and you shall be shamed." This late midrash, however, realigns the categories: the binary is no longer an internal division between Israelites (good and bad) but an ethnic division between Israelites and non-Israelites.[22] And, as is typical in rabbinic theology, the shaming and rejoicing take place not in this world but in the next one.

---

22. For another example, see Tanḥ. (Buber), *Shoftim* 10 and its reinterpretation of Zech 13:8.

The chart below summarizes some of the exegetical moves the rabbis make to produce their anti-gentile soteriology:

Biblical Texts	*Rabbinic Reading*
Punishment in "This World" (Sheol)	Punishment in the "Next World" (Gehinnom)
Sheol for Specific Gentile Nations	Sheol for All Gentiles
Universal Force	Anti-Universal Force
Binary: Righteous vs. Wicked Israelites	Binary: Jew vs. Gentile

Conceptual Basis

Theological

The rabbis offer four different rationales to explain their anti-gentile view. The first is a theological one. Leviticus Rabbah (ca. fifth century) posits that the gentiles will be damned because they rejected God and His Torah at Sinai. The midrash relies on Hab 3:3–15, where the prophet describes a mythological theophany that has no clear historical referent. When God revealed Himself from "Teman" and "Mount Paran" (3:3), He brought with Him "plague" and "pestilence" (3:5) so that when "He glanced," He "made the nations tremble" [ראה ויתר גוים] (3:6).

Whereas in Hab 3:6, God's wondrous appearance causes the nations to tremble [ויתר] in awe, the early (Tannaitic) text of Mekhilta de-Rabbi Ishmael reinterprets the Habakkuk passage to mean something wholly different:

> R. Eliezer the son of R. Yossi the Galilean used to say ... what had those wretched nations done that He [God] would not give them the Torah? ... They [the nations] were unwilling to accept them [the *mitsvot*], as it says: *God comes from Teman.... He stands and the earth shakes, He glances* [ראה] *and released* [ויתר] *the nations* [גוים] (Hab 3:6) (Mek. R. Ish. to Exod 19:2, *Bahodesh* 1 [ed. Lauterbach, p. 295]).

In the Mekhilta's rereading, Habakkuk's theophany takes place at Mount Sinai when the nations of the world refused God's offer to accept even the most basic Torah laws. Only Israel accepted the *mitsvot*, doing so unconditionally. As a result, God "freed up" or "released" [ויתר] the nations from any contractual obligation to fulfill Torah law. In other words, the gentiles' rejection of Torah has positive ramifications, as it exempts them from incurring any liability for their noncompliance. To produce this new reading, Mekhilta reads ויתר according to its second possible meaning: not "to tremble," as the biblical context would suggest, but "to free up."[23]

The author of Leviticus Rabbah cites the earlier Mekhilta tradition of R. Eliezer the son of R. Yossi but inserts a crucial dimension that reflects a new religious attitude:

> *And He released nations* [ויתר גוים] (Hab 3:6) …
> R. Yoḥanan said: He caused them [the nations] to leap [הקפיצן] into Gehinnom, as it says: *He glanced, and caused the nations to leap* [ויתר גוים] (Hab 3:6).[24]

Attributing its teaching to R. Yoḥanan (Palestine, third century), Leviticus Rabbah inverts the force of the Mekhilta by having God throw the gentile nations to Gehinnom for rejecting the Torah and *mitsvot*.[25] This expresses a more aggressive anti-gentile sensibility. In the earlier view of the Mekhilta, God merely dissociates Himself from entering a covenant with the nations (because of their refusal to accept Torah) and frees them from *mitsvot*. God does not punish them. In sharp contrast, R. Yoḥanan has God causing the gentile nations to leap to their torture in hell. In this reading, R. Yoḥanan revives the straightforward sense of ויתר as meaning "to leap." Here, though, the gentiles experience more than just a trembled leap, as we have in Hab 3:6 itself, but a dramatic leap into the fiery underworld. Note again how in Leviticus Rabbah the rabbis invert a universal biblical passage into an anti-universal one. A verse stressing divine revelation to the nations now becomes a verse about God damning the nations.

Following Leviticus Rabbah, the Bavli ('Abod. Zar. 2a–3a) imagines God denying the gentiles a share in the world to come because they rejected the Torah. The Bavli's teaching, attributed to R. Hanina b. Papa, nuances R. Yoḥanan's claim. For in the Bavli, it is not the gentiles' failure to accept the *mitsvot* of the Torah that causes their damnation but rather their neglect of Torah study.[26] Strikingly, the Bavli imagines God bringing a Torah and, placing it on His lap, declaring "whoever busied himself

23. For full discussion of the Mekhilta text and Tannaitic parallels, see Steven D. Fraade, *From Tradition to Commentary: Torah and Its Interpretation in the Midrash Sifre to Deuteronomy* (Albany: State University of New York Press, 1991), 25–68.

24. Lev. Rab. 13:2 according to MS Munich 117. I retrieved this manuscript through Bar Ilan University's synoptic Leviticus Rabbah project that can be accessed here: https://www.biu.ac.il/JS/midrash/VR/outfiles/OUT13-02.htm. Besides MS Munich 117, R. Yoḥanan's teaching also appears in various MS Oxford manuscripts. It does not appear, interestingly, in our printed editions, nor in MS London 169, MS Vatican 32, and MS Paris 149.

25. Conversely, Arthur Marmorstein notes that early Christian "synods and pulpits" told their "incumbents and representatives to threaten with the fire of hell … all those who adhered to the law of Moses" (*Studies in Jewish Theology*, 209).

26. On the centrality of Torah study for the Bavli, see Jeffrey L. Rubenstein, *The Culture of the Babylonian Talmud* (Baltimore: Johns Hopkins University Press, 2003), 31–35.

with it [the Torah] could come and take his reward [in the next world]." In response, the Romans, Persians, and then the rest of the nations, argue that their various building projects—marketplaces, bathhouses, bridges, and so on—afforded the Jews ample time to study Torah. God, too, denies this rejoinder because the gentiles did not engage in their construction for that altruistic purpose. Later in the talmudic narrative, God points to yet a third reason why the gentiles are denied salvation: not because they refused to accept Torah (as per Leviticus Rabbah's R. Yoḥanan), nor their lack of Torah study (as per the Bavli's Ḥanina b. Papa), but because they failed to fulfill the seven Noahide laws.[27]

Political

In the eschatological narrative above, Bavli 'Avodah Zarah raises, but quickly dismisses, a completely different reason why gentiles might not be capable of achieving salvation: they oppress Israel. This second (potential) reason explains, for the Bavli, why the other nations thought they had a chance of achieving salvation even after the Romans and Persians had been rebuffed. Perhaps, they thought, God rejected these two nations because only "they subjugated the Jewish people [הנך אישתעבדו בהו בישראל]"; but the other nations of the world did not. But, alas, God denies their entry too because the driving explanation for the gentiles' damnation is not political, as the other nations had hoped, but theological.

Whereas Bavli 'Avodah Zarah denies a political explanation, other rabbinic texts adopt one. Here, God damns the gentiles not because they rejected Torah and *mitsvot* but because they oppressed the Jewish people. Consider this teaching from Gen. Rab. 20:1, attributed to R. Levi (third century):

> *A slanderer shall not be established in the earth; let the evil violent man drive him [the slanderer] to his overthrow* (Ps 140:12).
> R. Levi said: At a future time [in the messianic era] the Holy One, Blessed be He, will take the nations of the world and hurl them down into Gehinnom, saying to them: Why did you oppress [קונסין] My children? And

27. Already at the end of the first century CE, 4 Ezra 7:36–37 has God declare that the nations of the world are fated for hell because they did not serve God nor fulfill the *mitsvot*. See also the (early medieval) Midrash Otiyot de-Rabbi Akiva, which damns the gentiles because they "did not accept the Torah and failed to fulfill the *mitsvot*." This text can be found in Shlomo Wertheimer, ed., *Batei Midrashot* (Jerusalem: Ktav Wasepher, 1968), 2:418. Also see Tanḥ. (Buber), *Nitzavim* 3 which gives a novel theological explanation: the gentiles are fated for destruction [כלייה] because, unlike the Jews, they are critical of God when experiencing suffering. I have noted elsewhere that Tanḥuma-Yelammedenu (TY) literature is uniquely interested in the question of theological protest. Strikingly, instead of embracing theological protest, as other TY texts do, this TY teaching describes it as a gentile practice worthy of destruction. See Dov Weiss, *Pious Irreverence: Confronting God in Rabbinic Judaism*, Divinations (Philadelphia: University of Pennsylvania Press, 2017), 79–84.

> they [the nations of the world] will answer Him: Some of them spoke evil gossip [לשון הרע]. Then the Lord will take both [the Jewish slanderers and gentile oppressors] and hurl them into Gehinnom.

At the moment of redemption, God will damn the gentiles because they oppressed Israel. No distinction is made between righteous and wicked gentiles. In an ensuing encounter, the nations of the world tell God that they subjugated the Jews because of Jewry's penchant for slanderous speech. In reaction, God throws both of them—the Jewish slanderers and the gentile oppressors—to hell. According to R. Levi, this narrative explains the verse from Ps 140:12 that has the "evil violent man" [איש חמס] (now understood to refer to gentiles) overthrowing the "slanderer" (now understood to be the Jews). It is important to note that Ps 140:12 makes no mention of gentiles. The verse merely describes various types of sinners, such as slanderers and robbers. The biblical reader does not know if these people are Israelites or not. It is only the rabbis who impose a Jew–Gentile binary onto Ps 140. The rabbis assume this "overthrowing" relates to hell because of the prior verse, which expresses a desire that "coals of fires drop down upon [the violent man]" and that they be "cast into pits, never to rise again."

Two early medieval midrashim echo the political explanation. The first, Midr. Ps. 49, relies on Ps 49:15 to make this claim: "Like sheep they head for Sheol [כצאן לשאול שתו] with Death as their shepherd. The upright shall rule over them at daybreak and their form shall waste away in Sheol." In its context, the verse states that arrogant wealthy Israelites (mentioned in v. 7 and 14) are headed, like sheep, to their death (Sheol). Midrash Psalms, however, assumes that the subject of the passage is not sinning Israelites but the "nations of the world," who will be placed in Gehinnom (= Sheol). Important for our purposes, the midrashist reinterprets the metaphor of the "slaughter of sheep." It no longer describes the punishment of the (Israelite) sinners, as a simple reading implies, but rather it now describes the very nature of the gentiles' sin: "[they] slaughter the Israelites as if they [the Israelites] are sheep [שטבחו ישראל כצאן]." In this reading, "sheep" does not modify the Israelites who will be thrown into Sheol, but the way the Israelites were treated by the gentiles, who are destined for hell. In short, according to Midrash Psalms, the gentiles are worthy of Gehinnom because they "slaughter Jews like sheep."

Like the above two midrashim (Leviticus Rabbah and Midrash Psalms), S. Eli. Rab. 1:5 justifies its anti-gentile soteriology by highlighting the historical oppression of the Jews: "The nations of the world are liable [נתחייבו] to be destroyed from the world and thrown down into Gehinnom because they sent forth their hand [ששילחו יד] against Israel, Jerusalem, and the Temple.... The Holy Spirit called out to them [the nations of the world]: you fools! Until that moment, you were not liable to be thrown down into Gehinnom." Seder Eliyahu Rabbah hooks this teaching onto Jer

50, where God predicts that Babylonia's "mother will be utterly shamed" [בושה אמכם] (v. 12) because they [the Babylonians] "plundered My [God's] possession [i.e., Israel]." While God, in Jeremiah, initially rebukes the Babylonians alone, the end of the verse expands this derision to all the nations: "Behold the end of the nations—wilderness, desert, and steppe."[28]

Sacrificial

Like the former two explanations (the theological and the political), Exod. Rab. 11:2 links gentile damnation to a historical transgression. But, in this early medieval midrash, we are dealing with the transgressions of the Jews, not the gentiles:

> Also in the time to come, God will cast [משליכן] the nations of the world into Gehinnom instead of Israel [תחת ישראל], as it says: *For I am the Lord your God, the Holy One of Israel, your Savior; I have given Egypt as your ransom* [כפרך], *Ethiopia and Seba for you* (Isa 43:3).

In Isa 43, the anonymous prophet has God telling Israel not to fear because He will redeem them. Highlighting His love and protection, God tells the Israelites that they will not be harmed by fire or flames as they walk through it (v. 2) because, as their Savior, God "will give Egypt, Ethiopia, and Seba" as their "ransom" (v. 3). According to Joseph Blenkinsopp, in these verses God proudly boasts that, in order to free the Judeans from Persian control, He would have the Egyptians and other African peoples take the Judeans' place.[29] Instead of the Judeans subject to Persian control, the Egyptians and other Africans would be enslaved to Persia. In short, God ransomed or exchanged Judean bondage for Egyptian bondage. Historically, the Persians indeed would conquer major parts of Egypt and Africa shortly after Cyrus's reign.

Strikingly, however, Exodus Rabbah reads Isa 43:3 as if God declares that the gentile nations will go to Gehinnom to expiate the sins of the Jews. To accomplish this reading, Exodus Rabbah makes two interpretive moves. First, this exchange—or ransom—no longer refers to a past bondage to Persia, but rather a future bondage to the flames of Gehinnom. The exegetical hook for Exodus Rabbah is that the prior verse (43:2) mentions the Judean immunity to fire, which, naturally, is now understood to refer to the fires of hell. And, second, while Isa 43:3 mentions only three nations that would be used to free the Judeans, the author of Exodus Rabbah extends the ransom to all of the nations. According to Exod. Rab. 1:2,

---

28. Also see 'Ag. Ber. 20, where Israel tells the prophet Malachi that the gentiles should not be simply destroyed but should be tortured in Gehinnom because "they made [Israel's] lives miserable."

29. Joseph Blenkinsopp, *Isaiah 40-55*, AB (New Haven: Yale University Press, 2008), 222.

gentile nations go to hell not because of anything they or their ancestors did, but rather, disturbingly, because gentile anguish in Gehinnom would atone for, or expiate, the sins of the Jews. Note that the Hebrew word כפר can mean ransom, atone, or some blurred combination of the two. That is how sacrifices typically work in the ancient world. Instead of the sinner being punished, he or she sends an animal as a "ransom" for his sins. That is how atonement is achieved. While Exod. Rab. 11:2 is the first rabbinic source to make this claim explicitly, it builds on two earlier (Tannaitic) sources—Mekhilta de-Rabbi Ishmael and Sifre Deuteronomy—that point in that direction, although its meaning is less than fully clear.[30]

Ontological

The prior three explanations for gentile damnation—theological, political, and sacrificial—are connected to transgression and are historically contingent. Either the gentiles are destined to hell because they rejected God and Torah (theological), because they subjugated Israel (political), or because their sufferings in Gehinnom atone for the sins of the Jews (sacrificial). In late rabbinic literature, by contrast, a new explanation emerges, one that I would call ontological. Here, the gentiles are damned not because of some historical sin (gentile or Jewish), but rather because the link between gentiles and Gehinnom is built into the very structure of the universe. Consider Pesiq. Rab. 20 (96a), where God explains to the Prince of Darkness the names He granted to the planets, and why He created them in the manner that He did:

> "Jupiter" [צדק]–for the Holy One, Blessed be He, will deal strictly [with the nations of the earth]. And you may mistakenly think that the nations of the world will be saved [ניצולים] from judgment. But the fact is that the Holy One, Blessed be He, in creating Mars [the Red Star—מאדים], meant it to symbolize the red-hot [fire] of Gehinnom into which they will fall.

According to Pesiqta Rabbati God tells the Prince of Darkness that He created Jupiter and named it [in Hebrew] "Justice" [צדק] because He will, without mercy, apply strict justice against the nations of the world. After Jupiter, God created Mars and named it [in Hebrew] the "Red Star" [מאדים] because that symbolizes that the nations of the world are destined to descend into a fiery red hell.

Whereas Pesiqta Rabbati sees gentile damnation in the cosmos, the Bavli sees it in the very structure of the Hebrew language. B. Šabb. 104a crafts a dialogue between God and Gehinnom wherein Gehinnom demands that God send her both Jews and gentiles.[31] Defending Jewish sinners, God refuses by declaring that Gehinnom has no "share in them"

30. See Mek. R. Ish. *Nezikin* 10 and Sifre Deut. 333.

31. The Bavli describes Gehinnom as a "she."

because the Jews are not adulterers and, moreover, are free of sin. Relenting, the Minister of Gehinnom demands again that God damn the Jews. After God refuses for a second time, Gehinnom itself bemoans the fact that it is tired, presumably due to its hunger. In response, God compassionately replies that He would send Gehinnom "whole companies of gentiles [כתות כתות של אומות העולם]." Remarkably, the Bavli regards this discrimination against gentiles to be embedded within the very structure of the Hebrew letters via various forms of the *at-bash* decoding method. No scriptural passage is necessary. The eternal Hebrew language itself reveals—via a complicated decryption method—this anti-gentile soteriological fact, albeit through a mythic narrative.[32]

Metaphors for Doomed Gentiles

We have traced how the rabbis exegetically justified and conceptually explained their anti-gentile soteriology. Now we turn to examine the various metaphors applied by the rabbis to the damned gentiles. These derogatory descriptions convey that the rabbis did not have a stoic-like and value-neutral attitude toward the gentiles fated for hell: it was steeped in antipathy. In Lev. Rab. 13:2, R. Tanḥum b. Ḥanilai compares the fact that gentiles will be denied the world to come to a terminally sick person who has no hope for recovery [לחולה שאין בו כדי לחיים].[33] Midr. Prov. 17 goes even further by having R. Yehoshua tell R. Eliezer that, unlike Jews, gentiles cannot escape hell's torments because the Torah's method of salvation only speaks of living people (= Jews) but not dead people (= gentiles). Unlike Leviticus Rabbah and Midrash Proverbs, a Tanḥuma-Yelammedenu teaching found in Pesiq. Rab. 10 (36b) and attributed to R. Levi, deems the nations of the world as living and healthy but incapable of salvation because they do not "belong to God." Citing Isa 32:12 as its prooftext, the Pesiqta has God telling Moses that the gentiles "are not Mine [אינם שלי] but belong to Destruction [טימיון] and Gehinnom." Levi's prooftext is Isa 33:12: "Nations will be turned into heaps of burnt-out ash, like thorns cut down and set on fire." While a contextual reading of this Isaiah passage would include sinning Israelites (see 33:14), the midrash deems only the gentiles as "set on fire."[34]

Other midrashim compare gentiles to various animals when announcing gentile damnation. In Gen 22:2, God tells Abraham to sacrifice Isaac

32. For a similar decoding and dialogue, see Midrash Otiyot de-Rabbi Akiva (ed. Wertheimer, 416).

33. Tanḥ. (Buber), *Shemini* 10 has a stronger formulation that the gentiles "are [destined] for Gehinnom" (not merely denied the world to come as in Leviticus Rabbah).

34. Also see Midrash Otiyot de-Rabbi Akiva (ed. Wertheimer, 418), where God damns the gentiles because, citing Isa 40:17, "they are like nothing in front of Him [כאין נגדו]."

on one of the mountains in "the land of Moriah." The Bible does not tell us the etymology of the word "Moriah." Second Chronicles 3:1 identifies Mount Moriah as the site of Solomon's temple in Jerusalem, although contemporary Bible scholars reject such an association. A variety of translations for "Moriah" are offered in Amoraic texts,[35] such as the following teaching from Gen. Rab. 55:7 (ca. fifth century), attributed to the Amora R. Yehoshua b. Levi (third century, Palestine):

> *Go to the land of Moriah* (Gen 22:2): ... R. Yehoshua b. Levi said: For from there, the Holy One, Blessed be He, decided [מורה] [the fate of] the nations of the world, and brought them down to Gehinnom. [Gen. Rab. 55:7, ed. Theodor-Albeck, 591]

R. Yehoshua b. Levi provides the following etymology for the name "Moriah." It connotes the area of Temple Mount where God sends the gentiles to hell. According to this view, Moriah comes from the word *moreh*, meaning "deciding" the gentile's fate, or possibly "shooting" the gentiles down to Gehinnom.[36] This teaching likely bases itself on the biblical tradition that the Valley of Hinnom stood in proximity to the Jerusalem temple (see Jer 19:2). Attributing Genesis Rabbah's teaching to Shmuel b. Naḥman (instead of R. Yehoshua), Tanḥ. (Buber), *Vayera* 45 adds the following prooftext from Ps 49:15: "Sheeplike they head to Sheol, with Death as their shepherd." As we noted above, in its own context, the verse illustrates the ultimate end for those Israelites who "trust in their own riches" (Ps 49:7) or who are overly confident (Ps 49:14). In Tanḥuma, however, these sheep are the gentile nations, whose shepherd is Death.[37]

Whereas Tanḥuma (Buber) likens gentiles to sheep, Midr. Ps. 104:18 compares them to lions when describing how the Messiah will one day hurl the nations of the world to Gehinnom.[38] Midrash Psalms exegetically anchors its teaching onto Ps 104:21–22, which highlights God's wondrous creation as even the wild lions behave in a timely and orderly

35. The Septuagint and Jubilees designate the term as "high land" (τὴν γῆν τὴν ὑψηλήν) suggesting that the underlying Hebrew text might have been *erets ramah* (high land) instead of *erets moriah*. And Targum Onqelos renders the phrase as "the land of worship" [לארע פלחנא]. For a full discussion, see Nahum M. Sarna, *Genesis* בראשית: *The Traditional Hebrew Text with the New JPS Translation*, JPS Torah Commentary (Philadelphia: Jewish Publication Society, 1989), 391–92.

36. The root of מורה is ירי and can mean either "deciding" or "shooting." Other manuscripts, such as MS Paris 149, MS Oxford 147, and MS Oxford 2335 have מורא (fear). If we follow the latter, then the meaning would be that God brings fear to the gentiles in that place.

37. Notably, t. Sanh. 13:3 uses Ps 49 to damn *Jewish* heretics and apostates. In Tanḥuma, it is used to damn the gentiles. As noted above, this type of exegetical shift is typical of rabbinic theology.

38. Generally, the rabbis have God damning the gentiles and their gods (as in Tanḥuma [Buber], *Shoftim* 10). Here, and in Pes. Rab. 36, p. 161, however, the Messiah serves this function. And see b. 'Erub. 101a where the Israelites fill this role.

fashion when returning to their nightly abode: "the lions roar for prey, seeking their food from God. When the sun rises, they gather and couch in their dens." However, rather than reading the verses as punctuating God's marvelous universe—as God even provides for the lions—Midrash Psalms reads them as predicting how the Messiah will one day damn the nations of the world. To produce his teaching, the midrashist reinterprets the "rising of the sun" as the coming of the Messiah; "the dens" as a reference to "Gehinnom"; and, important for our purposes, the "lions" as the nations the world. In this teaching, Midrash Psalms regards the connection between gentiles and Gehinnom as a highly natural one, just as a lion by nature returns to his den. One last animal metaphor used to describe the doomed gentiles can be found in Gen. Rab. 21. This text, as we noted above, has the "violent" gentiles slated for Gehinnom because they oppressed the Israelites. To accentuate its teaching, the midrashic author compares gentiles to the snake in the Garden of Eden who caused the downfall of Adam (who represents the Jews).

The rabbis also deploy a type of metaphor used by Jesus in the New Testament (see, e.g., Matt 13:24–30). The early medieval Midr. Ps. 2:14 compares the gentiles to the unused parts of an ear of wheat: straw, chaff, and weeds. These items, now personified, initially boast that the field was grown for them. When harvest came, however, these parts were destroyed and only the wheat itself was "brought in for safekeeping." According to the midrash, the nations of the world similarly declare that the world was created for them, but, ultimately, they too will be exiled to Gehinnom [נטרדין לגיהנם]. Israel, by contrast, "will remain" in the future world, as God, according to a rabbinic reading of Song 7:3, compares Israel to a "heap of wheat."[39] Similarly, Pirqe R. El. 28 has R. Azaryah posit that God created the Babylonians, Persians, Greeks, and Arabs only to serve as "wood" for the fires of Gehinnom.

III. The Babylonian Talmud: Whispers of Inclusion

Most Bavli texts unequivocally have gentiles destined for Gehinnom, or more moderately, denied a place in the world to come:

a. B. Šabb. 104a, as noted above, has God refusing Gehinnom's desire to "feed upon" Jews and gentiles, and God sends her, instead, only gentiles.

b. B. 'Erub. 101a records a conversation between a heretic [מינא] and

39. Three more prooftexts are adduced to ground this soteriological discrimination: Isa 33:12, Joel 4:12–14, and Deut 32:12.

R. Yehoshua. Referencing Mic 7:4, which describes a scenario of social upheaval in Judea where the "best of them [the Judeans] are like a prickly shrub" [טובם כחדק], the heretic lashes out at R. Yehoshua by calling him a "prickly shrub" [חדקאה]. The Stam then offers two explanations as to how R. Yehoshua would have reinterpreted the phrase "best of them [the Judeans] are like a prickly shrub" so as not to defame him or other Israelites. In the second one, the Stam links the term "the best of them [the Judeans] are like a prickly shrub" with the eschatological vision of Mic 4:13 where the prophet predicts how Israel would ultimately "pulverize many peoples": והדיקות עמים רבים. The Talmud here links the word כחדק in Mic 7:4 to the word והדיקות in Mic 4:13. Both words have similar core letters: (חדק and הדק). Thus, the phrase from Mic 7:4 should be read, according to the Bavli, to mean that the "best of them [the Jews] crush [שמהדקין] the gentile nations to Gehinnom." Note here, again, how the Bavli inverts an original biblical passage that chastises Israel into a text that damns the gentiles. Also, in this talmudic passage, it is not God or the Messiah but all of Jewry who are responsible for the gentiles' ultimate fate.

c. B. B. Bat. 10b has Rabban Gamaliel declare that even the charitable acts of the gentiles should be regarded as sins because the gentiles only perform such actions to bolster their image. This idea—of equating gentile kindness with arrogance and sin—is already attributed to Rabban Gamaliel (and R. Eliezer) in the earlier amoraic text of Pesiq. Rab Kah. 5. The Stam of the Bavli extends the implications of Rabban Gamaliel's teachings: Not only are these gentile acts of kindness really acts of "arrogance," but these "sins" will drive the gentiles to Gehinnom.

d. B. Meg. 15b and b. Sotah 35b maintain that gentiles will be denied entry to the world to come because they have failed to study Torah.

Bavli Avodah Zarah: Voices of Dissent

Toward the end of his examination of the narrative in b. 'Abod. Zar. 2a–3a (discussed briefly above) Jeffrey L. Rubenstein argues that the Bavli in general contains conflicting voices on the issue of gentile salvation. According to Rubenstein, as "rabbinic theology was neither systematic nor monolithic ... BT provides different perspectives on the interrelationship" between "eschatology, gentiles and Torah."[40] He further argues that R. Yehoshua's inclusive soteriology, as found in t. Sanh. 13:2, "probably [represents] the majority rabbinic opinion."[41] To support his contention that "BT culture exhibits tensions concerning the ... salvation of gentiles,"[42]

40. Rubenstein, *Talmudic Stories*, 238.
41. Ibid., 240.
42. Ibid., 241.

Rubenstein highlights those voices in Bavli Avodah Zarah that are sympathetic to non-Jews. Recall that, in this Bavli text, God embraces Jews in the world to come only because, unlike the gentiles, Jews have studied and fulfilled the Torah. Rubenstein notes several times where the Talmud's commentator (the Stam) interrupts the story's flow to "mobilize dissenting voices from within the tradition."[43] For example, Rubenstein notes how the commentator pushes back against the idea that (1) gentiles fail to keep the Noahide *mitsvot* or that (2) the gentiles should not be rewarded at all for fulfilling these *mitsvot*. Moreover, in the commentarial back-and-forth, the universal (Tannaitic) dictum of R. Meir is brought: "a gentile who studies Torah is like the High Priest."[44]

For Rubenstein, these retorts "demonstrate that the issues are more complex than they appear … [that] the many voices in the comment[s] provide ample testimony of the deep tensions in the view of gentiles within the culture of the BT."[45] Here, I agree with Rubenstein. Within the editorial layer, b. 'Abod. Zar. 2a–3a evinces a sustained moral unease with the Talmud's own story that rejects gentile salvation. Yet, I would argue, the talmudic pericope as a whole (narrative plus comments) does not affirm gentile salvation. In other words, despite a more sympathetic attitude toward gentiles in the later layers of the Bavli text, the commentarial level of discomfort does not reach the level of rejecting the narrative's soteriology. Moreover, the Bavli editors' inability to overturn the accepted rabbinic view on gentile salvation—despite its universal sensibilities—only reconfirms how entrenched the exclusivist view had become. Thus, while I agree with Rubenstein that, in Bavli Avodah Zarah, we encounter unease with the accepted rabbinic soteriology, this unease does not rise to the level of theological retraction.

Two other Bavli texts might evince whispers of inclusion. As Mira Wasserman has recently shown, the first chapter of Bavli 'Abodah Zarah contains two narratives (10b and 18a) wherein a heavenly voice (*bat qol*) declares that a specific gentile is granted a place in *'olam haba* (world to come).[46] One could argue that these texts represent a new moment of soteriological inclusion in a late rabbinic world (sixth–seventh century) dominated by gentile exclusion. B. Sanh. 105a would bolster this reading. There, the Stam argues that, because m. Sanh. 10:1 rejects the world to come for specific gentiles such as Balaam, it must have adopted the inclusivist Tosefta position of R. Yehoshua against the exclusive view of R. Eliezer:

43. Ibid., 239.

44. Ibid.

45. Ibid.

46. Mira Wasserman, *Jews, Gentiles, and Other Animals : The Talmud after the Humanities*, Divinations (Philadelphia: University of Pennsylvania Press, 2017), 50–60.

> Balaam is the one who does not come into the world to come; but other [gentiles] come [into the world to come]. Whose [opinion is expressed in] the Mishnah? R. Yehoshua (b. Sanh. 105a).

This talmudic line should not be overlooked or downplayed. While it does not produce a new pro-gentile soteriology (only acknowledging a Tannaitic one), it does not neutralize or deny the Mishnah's inclusive implication. Otherwise put, had the Bavli wanted to reject R. Yehoshua's inclusivist opinion it could have found other ways to reconcile the Mishnah with R. Eliezer's exclusivist view. By reading the Mishnah in such a fashion, this Bavli passage likely represents the beginnings of a more inclusive soteriological outlook that would reach its apex in the medieval period.

Nevertheless, I would not read the two narratives that Wasserman examines (b. 'Abod. Zar. 10b and 18a) as evidence for a pro-gentile soteriology in the Bavli. That is because they present themselves as exceptions to the rule (hence the need for a heavenly voice). They are unusual cases wherein a gentile courageously sacrifices himself for the rabbis. In other words, these are not cases of gentile righteousness per se, but gentile righteousness in support of Jews. In b. 'Abod. Zar. 18a, an executioner expresses empathy for R. Ḥanina b. Tradyon, who was about to be murdered, and ultimately martyrs himself together with this great rabbi. Moreover, the origin of this tradition is not a talmudic one but can be found centuries earlier in Sifre Deut. 307.[47] Thus, this inclusivist soteriological narrative does not belong to the later talmudic era but to the earlier Tannaitic period, where, as I have noted, the pro-gentile position dominated. The other martyrological narrative, found in b. 'Abod. Zar. 10b, has a non-Jew, Qetia b. Shalom, sentenced to death for challenging the Caesar's disparaging remarks about Jews, and, before his death, Qetia transfers all of his possessions to R. Akiva. He then deliberately falls on his penis to cut off his foreskin and declares that now he can "pass over" (presumably to the world to come) because he has paid his "tax." Whereas some scholars see Qetia's circumcision as a formal act of conversion,[48] I read it as transforming Qetia, the gentile, into, at least symbolically, "a

47. Note, however, that Sifre Deut. 307 only has the gentile (here a "philosopher") express hope that he would receive a share in the world to come. More strongly, in b. 'Abod. Zar. 18a, by contrast, a divine voice announces this as a theological fact (not just a hope).

48. MS Munich 95 does not mention that Qetia converted, but MSS JTS 15 and Paris 1337 do. See Alyssa Gray, "The Power Conferred by Distance from Power: Redaction and Meaning in b. A.Z. 10a–11a," in *Creation and Composition: The Contribution of the Bavli Redactors (Stammaim) to the Aggada*, ed. Jeffrey L. Rubenstein, TSAJ 114 (Tübingen: Mohr Siebeck, 2005), 23–69, here 58. See also Daniel Boyarin, "Homotopia: The Feminized Jewish Man and the Lives of Women in Late Antiquity," *A Journal of Feminist Cultural Studies* 7 (1995): 41–81, here 50–51.

Jew" for now his destiny is the world to come. Thus, if he is to be saved, he must become like a Jew.[49]

IV. Jewish Immunity

Fifth-century Amoraic documents such as Genesis Rabbah and Leviticus Rabbah initiate a new theological idea that even sinning Jews would be saved from experiencing the tortures of hell. This revolutionary soteriology, one based on ethnic identity, begins to emerge at roughly the same time as the Amoraic rabbis of the Galilee consolidated R. Eliezer's anti-gentile soteriology. The correspondence here, I would argue, is by no means coincidental. It reflects a new soteriological binary that gains prominence in rabbinic thought. Whereas the early rabbis emphasized the binary of righteousness versus wickedness when deciding a person's ultimate fate, later rabbis emphasized the binary of Jew versus gentile. Put simply, in rabbinic culture we can isolate a transition from an earlier virtue-based soteriology to a later ethnic-based soteriology. This later worldview, as we have seen until now, argues for the damnation of righteous gentiles, and, as we shall soon see, the salvation of sinning Jews. We now turn to the textual evidence to back my latter claim.

The Salvific Power of Circumcision

As we have seen, t. Sanh. 13:2 states that wicked Jews and Jews who "sin with their body" descend to Gehinnom—at least for a short period of time. By contrast, Amoraic texts produce a new discourse that points in a very different direction. In some Amoraic texts, male Jewish sinners automatically escape Gehinnom so long as they are circumcised, a physical feature that, in late antiquity, served as a marker of Jewish identity. Consider the following teaching found in Gen. Rab. 48:8 and attributed to R. Levi (third century, Palestine):

> *In the tent opening* (Gen 18:1):
> R. Levi said: In the future, Abraham will sit at the entrance to Gehinnom and permit no circumcised person[50] to descend therein. What then will he do to those who have sinned too much [שחטאו יותר מדיי]? He will remove the foreskin from babes who died before circumcision and set it upon them [the repeated offenders], and then bring them down into Gehin-

49. This narrative represents the exact inverse of the sinning Jew in Gen. Rab. 48:8 (noted above), who descends to Gehinnom only after losing his "Jewishness," that is, his circumcision.

50. Based on MS Vatican 30. However, see MS British Museum 27169 which has "no circumcised *Israelite*."

nom; hence it is written, *He has sent forth his hands to those that were whole; he has profaned his covenant* (Ps 55:21).

"In the heat of the day" (Gen 18:11): [this is an allusion to the time] when that day will come of which it is written, *For, behold, the day comes, it burns as a furnace* (Mal 3:19).

According to R. Levi, Abraham at the end of days will sit next to Gehinnom's opening and refuse to allow circumcised people (or "Israelites" according to MS British Museum) to enter its gates. R. Levi's prooftext derives from the subsequent phrase in Gen 18:11, which describes Abraham sitting in the "heat of the day" and which R. Levi takes symbolically to refer to the "Day" of the Lord described in Mal 3:9. At this time, according to the rabbis, God will send the wicked to Gehinnom. The "heat" of that day refers to the eschatological hell.

If circumcision saves male Jews, even the sinners among them, from experiencing the torments of hell, an obvious question emerges: What about the most wicked Jews? Here, R. Levi provides a novel solution: a foreskin transplant. Abraham will take the foreskin of uncircumcised Jewish babies and attach them to Jews who "sinned too much." That would maintain the soteriological principle that only uncircumcised men—that is, those who are not physically "Jewish"—would face afterlife torments.[51] While R. Levi leaves room for the worst Jews to suffer torments in the afterlife (so long as they do not carry the primary marker of Jewishness in males), this soteriological position inches closer to a more extreme formulation we will encounter in other Amoraic and post-Amoraic texts. Nonetheless, here we have the more moderate formulation that no circumcised male Jews go to Gehinnom.[52]

The Protests of the Gentiles

A more radical expression of this new theology (exempting sinning Jews from hell) can be found in four Amoraic texts that explicitly exclude Jews—even those engaging in the most serious of sins—from experiencing Gehinnom's torments. Strikingly, these now non-damning sins include murder, idolatry, and adultery/incest. These three sins constitute the worst sins in rabbinic Judaism, ones for which a person is obligated

51. For other rabbinic sources that mention this principle, see Exod Rab. II 19:4, Tanḥ. (Buber), *Lekh Lekha* 27, Tanḥ. (Buber), *Ḥayye Sarah* 3, Tanh. *Lekh Lekha* 20 and *Tazria* 5, S. Eli. Zut. 25.

52. Shaye J. D. Cohen argues, based on t. Ber. 6:13, for an earlier dating of this tradition (that circumcision saves) (*Why Aren't Jewish Women Circumcised? Gender and Covenant in Judaism* [Berkeley: University of California Press, 2005], 17). However, I follow other scholars who deny that this Tosefta tradition has anything to do with Gehinnom. See, e.g., David Flusser and Shmuel Safrai, "Who Sanctified the Beloved in the Womb," *Immanuel* 11 (1980): 46–55.

to die rather than transgress. While exempting these grave sinners, these four texts (two from Song of Songs Rabbah, and one each from Leviticus Rabbah and Ruth Rabbah) express moral ambivalence about the apparent discrimination this new soteriology would promote: Why should Jewish sinners be exempt when committing these crimes, but not gentile sinners? The rabbis do not express these anxieties in their own voices but, as they are wont to do, through the literary medium of narrative. In all four texts, the heavenly representatives of the gentiles criticize God for instituting a discriminatory soteriology based on ethnicity. Here I quote from Lev. Rab. 21:4, but the other three midrashim have almost the exact same protest formulation:

> For the Princes of the nations of the world come and bring charges against Israel before the Holy One, Blessed be He, saying to Him: "Sovereign of the Universe! These are idol worshippers and those are idol-worshippers; these commit sexual immorality and those commit sexual immorality; these are shedders of blood and those are shedders of blood. For what reason do those descend [into Gehinnom[53]] and these do not descend [into Gehinnom[54]]?"

In Leviticus Rabbah, God does not respond to these charges. Only the angelic representative of Israel intervenes by noting that Satan, the angelic persecutor of the Jews, only works 364 days a year. (This is derived from the numerological sum of the Hebrew word השטן [the Satan] which is also 364.) Israel regards this numerical correspondence not as coincidental but as signifying that on one day a year, on Yom Kippur, God will remove Israel's guilt without having to contend with Satan's accusations of discrimination (which mirrors the critiques of the angelic representatives). Leviticus Rabbah also cites a supporting verse from Ps 27. There, the psalmist responds to the apparent fear of enemy encroachment by declaring that "my heart is not afraid" because "in this [בזאת] I have confidence" (Ps 27:3). While contextually the phrase denotes that, despite his fears, the psalmist remains confident, the rabbis intertextually connect the word זאת to the זאת of Yom Kippur: "with this [בזאת] shall Aaron come to the Holy Place" (Lev 16:3). In other words, the rabbis now have the psalmist announce that he does not fear his enemy, Satan, because the psalmist has זאת, that is, Yom Kippur to offer atonement. In short, Yom Kippur is Satan's day off, so on that day the Jews as well as God are immune to charges of favoritism. Because of Satan's day off, sinning Israelites would be saved.

Like Leviticus Rabbah, Song Rab. 8:8:1 also invokes the power of Yom

53. Added in MS Paris 149

54. Ibid.

Kippur as a response. In this midrash, however, attributed to R. Azariah in the name of R. Yehudah b. Simon, the retort comes from God Himself: "However much Israel may be defiled by their iniquities throughout the year, the Day of Atonement comes and atones for them, as it says, 'For on this day shall atonement be made for you (Lev 16:30).'" In Ruth Rab. Proem 1, according to R. Yoḥanan, God also responds to the angels of the gentiles but does so only after berating Israel's defense angel, Michael, for his unexplained silence. God declares that He will "save" Israel due to their ancestral merit as it was Israel, not the angels, who accepted God's Torah at Sinai.

In all three midrashim, the gentiles' accusation is rejected, and God's soteriological favoritism toward the Jews is maintained. However, in an earlier section of Song Rab. 2:1:3 referenced above, we encounter a very different conclusion. Here, R. Eleazar ha-Moda'i has Israel accept the moral merits of the gentile argument, declaring that the Israelite sinners will, indeed, descend to hell:

> Israel[55] responds saying: If that is so, let all the peoples go down with their gods to Gehinnom, and so it is written, *For let all the peoples walk each one in the name of its god* (Mic 4:5).

According to Song Rab. 2:1:3, Israel concedes and proclaims that God would revise His soteriological policy: sinful Jews and non-Jews alike will face the same horrifying eschatological fate. Unmerited salvation will no longer be possible, for anyone. Moreover, Israel announces that all the nations—including the Jews—would go to Gehinnom with their gods, and that includes the God of Israel! To ground this claim, R. Reuben cites Isa 66:16, wherein, according to the plain sense, God is presented as judging Israel with fire. R. Reuben, however, exploits the fact that Isa 66:16 uses the unusual passive form for the verb "to judge," *nishpaṭ*, instead of the active form, *shopheṭ*.

> Said R. Reuben: Were it not written in Scripture, it would be impossible to say such a thing, so to speak: *For by fire will the Lord be judged* [nishpaṭ] (Isa 66:16): It does not say *God judges* [shopheṭ] *but the Lord is judged* [nishpaṭ].

R. Reuben reads the verse not as "God judges with fire," but rather "God who is being judged in fire" (together with Israel).[56] After recogniz-

55. All of the Song of Songs Rabbah manuscripts have Israel responding. Tamar Kadari has recently put online a synoptic edition of this midrash, which can be found here: https://www.schechter.ac.il/wp-content/uploads/2018/04/5.pdf. Probably because of the theological audacity of this proclamation, the printed editions emend the text to "God responds."

56. The assumption seems to be that people, including their gods, are tried by ordeal using fire.

ing the radical nature of his teaching and prefacing his remarks with the oft-stated disclaimer of "had Scripture not said so, it would be impossible to say it," R. Reuben inverts the normal hierarchical structure wherein God judges, and argues that, in this mythic encounter, God is the one being judged together with Israel.[57]

Had this midrash only stated the above texts, it would truly be scandalous. However, the framing of the midrash, in both its introduction and its conclusion, makes clear that, while, remarkably, God descends to Gehinnom with Israel, He quickly ascends and rescues them. Consider the start of the midrash where the Israelites declare, "I am plunged into the depths of Gehinnom, but when the Holy One, blessed be He, shall deliver me from its depths, I shall blossom forth in good deeds and utter song before Him." And, likewise, the midrash on Song of Songs concludes with this optimistic note: "And this is what David said through the Holy Spirit: "Yea, though I walk through the valley of the shadow of death, I will fear no evil, for You are with me" (Ps 23: 4). Because God accompanies Israel to Gehinnom, the implication is that He will surely rescue them.[58]

I would argue that these gentile protest narratives express both an emerging rabbinic belief in unmerited salvation for sinning Jews and, paradoxically, a deep moral discomfort with that very premise. The midrashim expose these anxieties not only via ventriloquism by having the gentile representatives lambast God's judicial discrimination but also in the diverse responses the midrashim have Israel, the angel Michael, and God take. Ruth Rabbah is the only text that points to some actual merit performed by Israel that would justify salvation, albeit that the merit is a vicarious one performed by Israel's ancestors. But, even here, recall that the angel Michael is silent in the face of the gentile critique, which only bolsters the merits of the accusation. (Even Israel's defense attorney is silent!) God's response in Leviticus Rabbah and Song Rab. 2:1:3 that Yom Kippur absolves Israel of sin is not rationally defended. By contrast, Israel's answer in Song Rab. 8:8:1 expresses the moral-theological ambivalence most starkly. In this midrash, Israel (and seemingly God) concedes to the moral critique. God brings the sinning Israelites (and Himself) to Gehinnom. However, the midrash implies that, as God would join the Israelites in hell, He would soon rescue them from the depths of despair. In short,

57. On these sorts of theological–human hierarchical inversions, see Moshe Halbertal, "If the Text Had Not Been Written, It Could Not Be Said," in *Scriptural Exegesis: The Shapes of Culture and the Religious Imagination; Essays in Honour of Michael Fishbane*, ed. Deborah A. Green and Laura S. Lieber (Oxford: Oxford University Press, 2009), 146–65.

58. Thanks to Tzvi Novick for alerting me to this crucial context. I had missed it when examining this passage in Dov Weiss, "Lawsuits against God in Rabbinic Literature," in *The Divine Courtroom in Comparative Perspective*, ed. Ari Mermelstein and Shalom E. Holtz, BibInt 132 (Leiden: Brill, 2014), 284–88.

Song Rab. 8:8:1 has sinning Israelites formerly going to Gehinnom, but not ultimately experiencing its terrors.

"All of Israel Have a Share in the World to Come"

A third post-Tannaitic text that highlights this new ethnic soteriology is the famous teaching that "All of Israel have a share in the world to come" (m. Sanh. 10:1). As scholars have noted, this phrase does not appear in most medieval manuscripts of the Mishnah.[59] Already in the sixteenth-century, Shlomo Luria (1510–1573) recognized this fact, stating that this dictum was a later insertion into the Mishnah. In his words, "this clause is not from this Mishnah but is simply an aggada that was brought here to begin [the chapter] on a positive note."[60] Undoubtedly, this dictum was superimposed onto a Tannaitic text that, contradicting the very first line, lists sinning Jews (and gentiles) who have no share in the world to come. Further, with this new insertion, the Mishnah as we have it now conflicts with t. Sanh. 13:3 (cited above), which claims that "sinning Jews with their bodies" will experience Gehinnom for twelve months and then be burned to ashes.

While Israel Yuval dates the insertion of "All of Israel have a share in the world to come" to the late Tannaitic period (he reads it as a polemic against Paul), I see no compelling reason to adopt this view.[61] More likely, the insertion was added sometime in the Amoraic period. As Ephraim Urbach has argued, we do not find serious rabbinic engagement or struggle with Christianity until the Amoraic period.[62] Either way, the insertion highlights a growing transformation in soteriological consciousness. In early rabbinic Judaism, righteous Jews were saved, and wicked Jews were not. At some later point a new sensibility emerged which maintained that all Jews—even the worst sinners—are saved. This emerging theology could be viewed as a unique Jewish response to the ubiquitous Christian claim that God had revoked His historic covenant with Israel because of Jewish sinfulness.[63] As scholars have shown, one classic rabbinic (Amoraic) response was to exonerate Jewish sinfulness altogether as we see in

59. See Urbach, *Sages*, 991 n. 11; Israel J. Yuval, "All Israel Have a Portion in the World to Come," in *Redefining First-Century Jewish and Christian Identities: Essays in Honor of Ed Parish Sanders*, ed. Fabian E. Udoh, Christianity and Judaism in Antiquity 16 (Notre Dame, IN: University of Notre Dame Press, 2008), 114–38.

60. See *Hokhmat Shelomo* to b. Sanh. 90a. My translation.

61. Yuval, "All Israel," 133.

62. Urbach, *Sages*, 303.

63. See Adam Gregerman, *Building on the Ruins of the Temple: Apologetics and Polemics in Early Christianity and Rabbinic Judaism*, TSAJ 165 (Tübingen: Mohr Siebeck, 2016).

Amoraic readings of the golden calf episode (Exod 32).[64] The rabbinic texts cited above, by contrast, accept the reality of Jewish sinfulness but largely defang it by removing the harsh punitive repercussions associated with it. Contra Christian claims, God does not abandon Israel, as evidenced in His refusal to send Jewish sinners to Gehinnom.

To be sure, this new rabbinic sensibility (Jewish immunity from hell) did not erase the older sensibility. We continue to encounter dozens of Amoraic texts that echo the older virtue-based soteriology that sinning Jews are destined for hell. But this new discourse is significant. While it is true that, when the rabbis polemicize against Jewish sinners, Gehinnom is a very live possibility, when they want to highlight the elevated status of the Jews vis-à-vis gentiles, their discourse shifts: now sinning Jews do not go to hell. The rabbis, of course, are not consistent, and these competing voices and sensibilities live uncomfortably side by side.

A New Doctrine

In Amoraic literature, we noted several rabbinic expressions that strongly implied that all Jews—even sinning ones—will not face the torments of Gehinnom. In post-Amoraic literature, this theological sensibility becomes formulized as a doctrine. These rabbinic texts, however, use different symbols and metaphors to justify this radical theology.

1. B. Ḥag. 27a and b. 'Erub. 19a have Resh Laqish maintain that "the fire of Gehinnom has no power over the sinners of Israel [פושעי ישראל]."[65] This formulation—of a carte blanche Jewish exemption from the tortures of hell—goes further than anything we have encountered until now. And this position, too, contrasts sharply with the anonymous earlier teaching in t. Sanh. 13:3 that "sinners of Israel" receive twelve months in Gehinnom and then become dust. Resh Laqish derives this soteriological principle by adopting an *ad majus* argument from the temple's altar. If the altar, which only has a limited amount of gold, nonetheless could protect it from being

64. Only in post-Tannaitic literature, do we have a sustained attempt to whitewash the Israelite sin of the golden calf. Scholars attribute this shift in rabbinic attitude to the growth of Christianity. See Irving Mandelbaum, "Tannaitic Exegesis of the Golden Calf Incident," in *A Tribute to Géza Vermès: Essays on Jewish and Christian Literature and History*, ed. Philip R. Davies and Richard T. White, JSOTSup 100 (Sheffield: JSOT Press, 1990), 207–22; Leivy Smolar and Moshe Aberbach, "The Golden Calf Episode in Postbiblical Literature," *HUCA* 39 (1968): 91–116.

65. Arthur Marmorstein has argued that "sinners of Israel [פושעי ישראל]" in rabbinic literature refers to Jewish-Christians. I see no compelling reason to adopt this view. See Marmorstein, *Studies in Jewish Theology*, 179–87.

burnt, then certainly Jews—who have *mitsvot*—will be able to withstand the fires of hell.[66]

2. In Pesiq. Rab. 11:45, an anonymous teaching cites 1 Kgs 4:20, which compares Judah and Israel to the sand of the sea. According to the Pesiqta, just as sand cannot be destroyed by fire, so too the Jewish people can never be adversely affected by the fire of Gehinnom. While the gentiles will perish there, Israel "will come forth unharmed."[67]

3. 'Abot R. Nat. A 16 attributes a teaching to R. Simeon b. Yoḥai whereby Jews will never encounter Gehinnom. Here, Israel is compared not to an altar (Bavli's Resh Laqish) or to sand (Pesiq. Rab. 11:45) but to men who purchase an inferior field from a king. Just as the king cannot get mad at the purchasers for failing to produce a significant profit, as the king's field was bad, so too God cannot fault Israel for engaging in sin because God gave them an evil inclination (= inferior field). It is unclear why the same logic would not serve as a reason to exempt gentiles from facing Gehinnom as well.

4. In 'Ag. Ber. 20:4 God announces that Jews will not be harmed by the fire of Gehinnom because the "fire of Gehinnom is not higher than the fire of Israel." Five prooftexts are deduced to support the Israel/fire metaphor (Isa 50:11; 1:31; 43:3; 33:12; and Obad 1:18).[68]

V. Narrative and Theology

As noted, the Amoraic and post-Amoraic soteriology—positing Jewish immunity from the pains of Gehinnom—did not fully supplant the older idea that sinning Jews would be tormented in Gehinnom. These mutually exclusive beliefs existed in tension with one another. This is not unusual. As I have noted elsewhere, rabbinic theology, generally speaking, is not based on comprehensive principles that demand consistency, as we have in early Christian literature, but rather on unsystematic intuitions and impulses that are locally driven, often inconsistent, and contextually dependent.[69] This allows the rabbis a high level of flexibility as they strive to balance competing values and agendas. And the multivocal anthological nature of rabbinic literature, which often evinces a weak editorial hand, is well suited to this type of thinking.

Returning to our topic, while the Talmud and midrashim generally

66. See also b. Ber. 10a, which anchors this principle onto Isa 54:1.

67. For a similar teaching based on different prooftexts, see Num. Rab. 2:13.

68. See Tanḥ. (Buber), *Pekudei* 5, where Jewish immunity from Gehinnom is based on the fact that Torah's fire extinguishes Gehinnom's fire.

69. See Dov Weiss, "Sins of the Parents in Rabbinic and Early Christian Literature," *JR* 97 (2017): 1–25.

do not flag their inconsistent views on the fate of sinning Jews, their narratives implicitly reflect the tension. Herein lies one of the beauties of narratives: they can highlight an author's uncertainties and ambiguities without having to resolve them. Multiple characters allow for competing values and opinions to interact with one another. Even without multiple voices, narratives can paint a complex story line or imagery that somehow satisfies, at least in part, dueling rabbinic agendas. In our case, it is the rabbinic project to use Gehinnom both as a rhetorical tool to motivate Jews to choose righteousness, and also as a polemical tool to highlight Jewish supremacy. We have already seen several narratives that address both pressures. Recall Gen. Rab. 48:8, where Abraham does not permit circumcised Jews to descend to Gehinnom. This aspect of the story accentuates Jewish supremacy (for all males who carry the marker of Jewishness), while the continuation of the narrative, wherein Abraham performs a foreskin transplant, allows for exceptions. Compulsive Jewish sinners, while still technically Jews, would be punished but only after losing their marker of Jewishness (circumcision).

The narrative from Song Rab. 2:1:3 (discussed above) also tries to strike a balance between constructing a Jewish theology that punishes Jewish sinners while, at the same time, arguing for Jewish supremacy and hell-fire immunity. It accomplishes that by envisioning Jewish idolaters, adulterers, and murderers being sent initially to Gehinnom together with their non-Jewish counterparts. At this point in the story, the most wicked Jews are severely punished. However, the midrashic narrative takes a sharp turn by imagining God descending to Gehinnom with these Jewish sinners. Via several prooftexts, the midrash strongly implies that God joins Jewry's worst only to rescue them. In the end, Jews—by virtue of their Jewishness—are saved.

Another midrash that paints a complex story to partially satisfy both rabbinic aims can be found in Midrash Konen (ch. 2), a text cited by Nahmanides (thirteenth century, Spain) in his influential *Gate of Retribution.*[70] Here, R. Yehoshua b. Levi (third century, Palestine) visits seven different compartments of hell. In six of them (the seventh is empty), R. Yehoshua sees people from ten gentile nations together with one known Israelite/Jewish sinner who oversees the compartment. The six Jewish sinners are (1) Doeg, (2) Koraḥ, (3) Jeroboam, (4) Ahab, (5) Micah, and (6) Elisha b. Avuyah. Strikingly, while these sinners live in Gehinnom, they do not

70. Midrash Konen can be found in *Otsar Midrashim: A Library of Two Hundred Minor Midrashim* [Hebrew], ed. J. D. Eisenstein, 2 vols. (New York: Eisenstein, 1915), 1:253–60. For a translation of this text, see Moses Gaster, "Hebrew Visions of Hell and Paradise," *JRAS* NS 25 (1893): 605–7. For more on R. Yehoshua b. Levi's tours of hell, see Martha Himmelfarb, *Tours of Hell: An Apocalyptic Form in Jewish and Christian Literature* (Philadelphia: University of Pennsylvania Press, 1983), 32–33.

suffer Gehinnom's torments because, as the midrash states, they have Jewish/Israelite lineage. Here, too, the author of midrash Konen tries to strike a balance between its rhetorical and polemical impulses noted above. These well-known Jewish sinners will, indeed, go to hell, but they, as hell's rulers, will not suffer there.

In these three midrashic stories, the rabbis try to balance their competing agendas without bringing explicit attention to them. As noted, this is due in part to the weak editorial hand that controls most of the midrashic compilations. Here, inconsistent rabbinic statements are rarely marked. By contrast, the editors of the Bavli showcase a stronger editorial hand and are, thus, more likely to be concerned with consistency and coherence.[71] It is, thus, no surprise that only in the Bavli do the rabbis flag the obvious contradiction between a soteriology that punishes Jewish sinners and a soteriology that exempts them from Gehinnom's tortures. B. 'Erub. 19a, as we have seen, cites the teaching of Resh Laqish (third century, Palestine) that "the fire of Gehinnom has no power over the sinners of Israel [פושעי ישראל]." The stam then questions this doctrine by noting a talmudic tradition that Jews recognize the justness of God's punishments when they are in Gehinnom (thus implying that Jews suffer there). To resolve the inconsistency, the Stam assumes that Resh Laqish would make one exception to the doctrine of immunity: a case where a Jew had intercourse with a female idolater because, in that case, we presume that the Israelite had his circumcision undone. As such, he is no longer recognized as a Jew. This hypothetical narrative—of a Jewish sinner who undoes his circumcision—satisfies again both rabbinic agendas. He is a Jew who suffers in Gehinnom for his misdeeds, but by virtue of growing back his foreskin he loses, in some sense, his "Jewishness." Strikingly, even according to the Stam, Resh Laqish's "non-Jewish Jew" (who loses his circumcision) does not lose his Jewishness completely because, unlike "real" gentiles, this quasi-Jew has the option of repenting while in Gehinnom.

As we have seen, rabbinic narrative pericopes sometimes express ethical unease with the new discriminatory soteriology. As Rubenstein has shown (in his analysis of b. 'Abod. Zar. 2a–3a) the talmudic editors could interrupt the flow of the story to express their universal sensibilities. But, more typically, the rabbis place their ambivalences into the mouths of others. For instance, in Lev. Rab. 2:9, R. Simeon b. Gamaliel relates how he was forcefully confronted by a gentile who complained that God unfairly damns gentiles. In the non-Jew's opinion, even if the gentiles have engaged in untoward behavior they should not be punished because there are no longer gentile prophets who could serve as guides or role models for non-Jews. In the absence of these leaders, the gentiles have a legitimate excuse

71. Weiss, "Sins of the Parents," 21–23.

to explain their malfeasance. In response, R. Simeon claims that, in place of the gentile prophets, non-Jews should be guided by those gentiles who convert to Judaism. Though cryptic in nature, the Leviticus Rabbah story expresses a moral concern that the rabbis or their gentile neighbors had with the emerging Jewish soteriology.

The four gentile protest narratives examined above (Leviticus Rabbah, Ruth Rabbah, and two from Song of Songs Rabbah) also use the medium of narrative to express their moral discomfort. Here, the midrashim have the celestial representatives of the gentiles do the work. While in all four texts the emerging soteriology is ultimately defended, in two of them, remarkably, the "Jewish side" initially concedes. In Ruth Rabbah the angel Michael's silence implies his agreement with the gentiles' accusers. This nonresponse propels God to berate Michael for neglecting his duties. And in Song Rab. 2:1:3 God Himself seemingly concedes as He brings both sinning Jews and non-Jews to Gehinnom. The divine concession, however, is short lived as, in the continuation of the midrash, God brings the sinning Jews out of hell. And, lastly, in b. Šabb. 104a, the egalitarian view is articulated not by the gentiles (or their representatives) but by a personified Gehinnom. On three separate occasions, God rejects Gehinnom's desire to "eat" the Jews.

The Qetia b. Shalom narrative (b. 'Abod. Zar. 10b) also expresses rabbinic unease with the dominant Jewish view that gentiles have no share in the world to come. It does so not by producing a mythical debate but rather by appealing to a divine revelation (*bat qol*) that announces an exception to the rule: this righteous gentile, who defends Jewish interests, will receive a place in the world to come. This revelatory exception, however, is quickly undermined as the narrative has Qetia deliberately fall on his penis and, symbolically at least, become a Jew. (And some manuscripts even have Qetia converting.)

VI. Explaining the Shifts

How can we explain the historical shifts in the rabbis' soteriological worldview: from inclusivism to exclusivism? Why did the rabbis in the early period (for the most part) divide people based on righteousness and virtue, and in the later period based on ethnicity? This is a question I hope to treat in fuller detail in a later publication. For now, at least, let me propose the following three suggestions. The first is the growing cultural and religious influence of Christianity on Judaism in late antiquity. In Greco-Roman culture, the standard to achieve salvation had been living a moral and righteous life, as attested in the writings of Plato (428–348 BCE), Virgil

(70–19 BCE), and Plutarch (46–120 CE).[72] With few notable exceptions, they do not regard the criteria for salvation as dependent on joining a particular community. Greeks and Romans do not advocate soteriological favoritism.[73] By contrast, with the rise of Christianity, a new soteriological model emerged: for many early Christians, escaping hell's tortures can be achieved only by joining the community of Christ. In his battle with the Pelagians, Augustine (354–430 CE) often cited Cyprian of Carthage's (210–258 CE, Tunisia) famous expression: "There is no salvation outside the Church."[74] This new religious exclusivist sensibility might have made its mark on Palestinian Jews who were highly acculturated.[75] As Seth Schwartz has noted, "starting in the third-century the Jews, especially in Palestine ... engaged in extensive cultural borrowing from their ... Christian neighbors."[76] This "cultural borrowing" related not only to the architectural, aesthetic, and literary sphere but also, as Guy Stroumsa has maintained, to the theological and doctrinal sphere.[77] We also have evidence that, beginning in the third century, particular rabbis and church leaders corresponded with each other on exegetical matters.[78] Thus, I would argue that Christian soteriological discourse possibly played a role in reinforcing the rabbinic move toward greater exclusivism. In other words, both groups now regarded salvation as determined by communal affiliation rather than (the previous model's) moral uprightness. On the Christian side, that community was made up of believers; on the Jewish side, it was determined largely by ethnicity. My claim here builds on, but also nuances, Israel Yuval's assertion that the Mishnah's insertion of "All of Israel have a share in the world to come" is a polemic against Paul's soteriology. Whereas Yuval regarded the Mishnah's guarantee of Jewish salvation as a second-century polemic, I would see it as part of a larger third- to fifth-century soteriological realignment among the rabbis that might have been, partially at least, effected by similar language within

---

72. Bernstein, *Formation of Hell*, 50–83.

73. Exceptions to this claim would be the Eleusinian and Orphic mystery cults, which, according to some accounts, granted salvation to their initiates only. See McClymond, *Devil's Redemption*, 130–34.

74. See Yuval, "All Israel," 119; Guy Stroumsa, "Religious Contacts in Byzantine Palestine," *Numen* 36 (1989): 16–41, here 23.

75. Saul Lieberman, *Greek in Jewish Palestine and Hellenism in Jewish Palestine* (New York: Jewish Theological Seminary of America, 1994).

76. Seth Schwartz, *Imperialism and Jewish Society, 200 B.C.E. to 640 C.E.*, Jews, Christians, and Muslims from the Ancient to the Modern World (Princeton, NJ: Princeton University Press, 2001), 182.

77. Stroumsa, "Religious Contacts," 19–21.

78. Marc G. Hirshman, *A Rivalry of Genius: Jewish and Christian Biblical Interpretation in Late Antiquity*, SUNT Series in Judaica (Albany: State University of New York Press, 1995), 83–94; Reuven Kimelman, "Rabbi Yohanan and Origen on the Song of Songs: A Third Century Jewish-Christian Disputation," *HTR* 73 (1980): 567–95.

patristic discourses. In other words, I would not limit the Christian "influence" to one mishnaic phrase alone, as Yuval does, nor would I date this new rabbinic soteriology to the second century.[79] Yuval also does not notice that the new ethnic-based rabbinic soteriology worked in tandem with an intensified anti-gentile soteriology.

Second, we should note a parallel shift in Christian thought itself that might have reinforced these rabbinic transformations. In the second and third centuries, some universally minded Christians believed that non-Christians would ultimately achieve salvation. For instance, the Gnostic author of the second-century *Secret Revelation to John* (found at Nag Hammadi) believed that non-Christians would escape hell by correcting themselves through successive reincarnations, so long as a person did not abandon the Gnostic faith.[80] Similar sentiments can be found in the Gnostic writings of the Basilideans, Carpocratians, and Valentinians.[81] Going even further, Origen of Alexandria (184–253 CE) believed that all human souls—and even the devil—would eventually achieve salvation after purgatory purified them.[82] While Origen's universalism would be echoed, to different degrees, by other early Christian Neoplatonists, such as Gregory of Nyssa (335–394 CE) and Evagrius Ponticus (345–399 CE),[83] these views came under harsh attack at the end of the fourth century by leading Christian theologians, most famously Jerome (347–420 CE), who later in life adopted a more exclusivist soteriology.[84] Augustine, too, condemned Origen's universalism, arguing that human nature was fundamentally sinful, and thus unable to escape the eternal fires of hell without Christ's help.[85] He, along with John Chrysostom (349–407 CE), Epiphanius (310–403 CE), and Pseudo-Dionysius (ca. fifth or sixth century), also adamantly rejected the possibility, raised by some early Christian texts, of posthumous salvation for non-Christians.[86] In 553 CE, the Fifth Ecumenical Council at Constantinople officially condemned Origen's universalism.[87]

---

79. Yuval, "All Israel."

80. Bentley Layton, *The Gnostic Scriptures: A New Translation with Annotations and Introductions* (London: SCM Press, 1987), 48–49.

81. McClymond, *Devil's Redemption*, 3, 144–54.

82. Ibid., 254–71.

83. Ibid., 278–98.

84. Elizabeth A. Clark, *The Origenist Controversy: The Cultural Construction of an Early Christian Debate* (Princeton, NJ: Princeton University Press, 1992), 99–100.

85. McClymond, *Devil's Redemption*, 333–38.

86. Trumbower, *Rescue for the Dead*, 8, 155.

87. It should be noted that my speculation—that Christianity's turn toward exclusivism might have effected a similar rabbinic shift—would only cohere if the ideas found in Genesis Rabbah and Leviticus Rabbah reflect the beliefs of their anonymous fifth-century editors/composer. In other words, the theory would work only if, following Jacob Neusner, we reject as unreliable the midrashic attributions to third-century named rabbis. For discussion and bibliography concerning Neusner's theory, see Shai Secunda, *The Iranian Talmud:*

Third, and quite paradoxically, while Palestinian Jews appropriated Christian culture in late antiquity, and shared a common religious discourse with Christians, their political and social standing deteriorated after the Christianization of the Roman Empire in the mid-fourth century. While revisionist scholars of the 1970s and 1980s, such as Jeremy Cohen and Saul Lieberman, successfully debunked the older "lachrymose" assumption of Heinrich Graetz that the new Christian emperors persecuted Palestinian Jewry through ecclesiastically inspired discriminatory laws and policies, Jews nevertheless faced growing hostility, and even hatred, from Christian theologians and preachers.[88] Though not rising to the level of fanatical persecution, discriminatory imperial laws, which had been transferred from earlier centuries, for the first time included derogatory descriptions of Jews and were now enforced more frequently.[89] We also have evidence that local Christian mobs attacked Jews and, on three occasions, burned down synagogues.[90] All of this must have humiliated Palestinian Jewry. Whereas pagan Roman rule emphasized the necessity of shared cultural norms, such as sacrificing to the gods, and evinced a more pluralistic attitude in matters of belief, Christian rulers placed religious "truth" and orthodoxy at the center of their political program.[91] They maintained that they were the "True Israel" and favored by God. All of these realities must have intensified Jewry's antipathy toward "the other."[92] And recall that several rabbinic texts make this sort of argument themselves as they attribute their anti-gentile soteriology to the reality of gentile rule, antagonism, and oppression.[93]

Aggravating the situation, this increased Christian hostility occurred while Christians adamantly maintained that only they, the Christians, could be saved. Thus, in the late rabbinic period, Jewish and Christian

---

Reading the Bavli in Its Sasanian Context, Divinations (Philadelphia: University of Pennsylvania Press, 2014), 29–31.

88. Jeremy Cohen, "Roman Imperial Policy Toward the Jews from Constantine until the End of the Palestinian Patriarchate," *Byzantine Studies* 3 (1976): 1–29; Saul Lieberman, "Palestine in the Third and Fourth Centuries," *JQR* 36 (1946): 329–70.

89. Schwartz, *Imperialism and Jewish Society*, 171–95.

90. Ibid.

91. Stroumsa, "Religious Contacts," 16–42.

92. The Christian context for the rabbinic turn toward an exclusivist soteriology might explain the weakening of this exclusivism in the (relatively) less Christian context of the Bavli. Alternatively, the Bavli's voices of soteriological inclusion might be related to Zoroastrian's more inclusive and universal conception of salvation. See Segal, *Life after Death*, 190, 198; Michael Stausberg, "Hell in Zoroastrian History," *Numen* 56 (2009): 217–53, here 231, 240.

93. My argument inverts Alan Segal's claim that the rabbis advocated a *universal soteriology* because of gentile intolerance. That view does not cohere with the evidence I have shown in the essay nor is it a logical one. Contra Segal, I maintain that the rabbis advocated an *exclusionary soteriology*, in part, because of gentile intolerance. See Segal, *Life after Death*, 198.

soteriological claims mirrored each other: both sides proclaimed that only their community could be saved. Here, we have a soteriological zero-sum game based on a new binary: my community versus the rest of the world, rather than righteousness versus wickedness. Several early medieval rabbinic texts gave voice to this awareness by having the gentiles and Jews parroting the other's exclusivist sensibility.[94] For example, 'Ag. Ber. 20 presents the following dispute:

> The nations of the world say, "Gehinnom is Israel's and the Garden of Eden is theirs." But Israel says, "Gehinnom is for the nations of the world and the Garden of Eden is ours."

The midrash ultimately proclaims that the arbiter of this debate will be Gehinnom's fire, which will destroy the nations of the world, much as fire can destroy only flax (gentiles) but not mineral (Jews).

VII. Conclusion

Previous scholars have maintained that the rabbis debated whether gentiles are destined for hell. What I have shown, however, is that this claim is misleading and does not properly convey rabbinic literature as a whole. While some early rabbinic texts, like the Mishnah and Tosefta, hold out the possibility of gentile salvation, and two Bavli texts note unique cases of specific gentiles reaching heaven, only one rabbi (R. Yehoshua) is recorded as having explicitly backed the principle that righteous gentiles have a place in the world to come. And only one prooftext (Ps 9:18) is brought by pre-medieval rabbis to ground an inclusivist soteriology. While there are a dozen or so biblical texts, most notably Isa 2, Isa 56, Mic 4, and Zech 2, that envision a universal salvation for the righteous nations of the world, none of these scriptural passages was used by the rabbis to develop an inclusive or universal soteriology.

By stark contrast, around twenty-five rabbinic passages state, in one form or other, that the nations of the world are destined for hell.[95] And the post-Tannaitic rabbis link gentile damnation to central biblical events and places: creation of the planets, Garden of Eden, dispersion of the nations (Gen 11), revelation at Sinai and the temple (Mount Moriah). Moreover, dozens of biblical prooftexts are adduced to back this soteriological exclu-

94. See, e.g., Midr. Ps. 2. Some early medieval midrashic texts might have been produced in an Islamic context. On Islam's soteriological attitude toward non-Muslims, see Mohammad Hassan Khalil, *Islam and the Fate of Others: The Salvation Question* (New York: Oxford University Press, 2012).

95. The breakdown is roughly as follows: Tannaitic texts (1), Amoraic texts (5), post-Amoraic texts (7), early medieval midrashim (12).

sivism. But, as I have shown, because nearly all of these prooftexts have nothing to do with the gentiles' inability to achieve salvation, the rabbinic agenda to reinterpret these passages as signaling an anti-gentile soteriology only highlights the rabbis' xenophobia. To buttress my claim, I have shown how the rabbis use various derogatory metaphors, in a soteriological context, to describe the gentiles. Thus, Joachim Jeremias's claim that the rabbis overwhelmingly rejected the notion of gentile salvation must not be dismissed completely, as Sanders claimed, but modified. Sanders's view is correct as it relates to the Tannaitic period, but Jeremias more accurately describes the consensus rabbinic view in the post-Tannaitic periods.

I also argued that the rabbis of the post-Tannaitic periods, generally speaking, discriminated against gentiles not only by imagining the damnation of *righteous* gentiles but also by positing the salvation of wicked Jews. Interestingly, in one late midrash preserved in Yal. Shim. Isa 429, the elements of this twofold discrimination soteriology do not occur simultaneously but rather surface one after the other. Initially, God discriminates by sending the righteous gentiles to Gehinnom but not the righteous Jews (= discrimination 1). But at some later point, because sinning Jews and righteous gentiles proclaim "Amen" at the end of God's teaching a "new Torah," God commands the angels Gabriel and Michael to free them from Gehinnom. Echoing Jesus's descent to Hades in the New Testament, the story accentuates God's mercy and predilection to forgive. But it does not fully succeed because in this salvation story one form of discrimination replaces another. After the angels free the righteous gentiles and sinning Jews, another form of discrimination remains. Sinning gentiles remain in Gehinnom while sinning Jews are saved (= discrimination 2).

I would like to close on a positive note, by noting one early medieval midrashic narrative that points in a new inclusive direction.[96] This ethos of this inclusive soteriology would become the dominant one in medieval rationalist Jewish circles. In Midrash Gedulat Moshe, God commands Gabriel to escort Moses to hell.[97] In Gehinnom, the Angel of Hell shows Moses all the awful and gruesome tortures that people—both Jews and gentiles—endure. In reaction, Moses returns to heaven and pleads with God:

96. Because the authenticity of the inclusivist midrash found in Mishnat Rabbi Eliezer (ed. Enelow, p. 121) is dubious, I did not include it in the present study. See the view of Samuel Atlas cited in Steven Schwarzschild, "Do Noachites Have to Believe in Revelation?," *JQR* 52 (1962): 297–308, here 306.

97. This midrash is also called "Apple in the Wood of the Forest" [תפוח בעצי היער] and can be found in Wertheimer, *Batei Midrashot*, 1:273–85. For a translation of this text, see Gaster, "Hebrew Visions of Hell and Paradise," 574–88. For more on this fascinating text, see Himmelfarb, *Tours of Hell*, 33–34. Also see Saul Lieberman, *Texts and Studies* (New York: Ktav, 1974), 29–51, who argues that Islamic conceptions of hell influenced this midrashic author's conception of hell.

> May it be Your will, O Lord, my God, and God of my fathers, that You may save ... Your people Israel from those places which I have seen in hell.
>
> God said to Moses: "Moses, my servant, I have created two places: paradise and hell. Whoever commits evil deeds goes down to hell, and whoever does good deeds comes into paradise, as it is said: *I the Lord search the heart, I try the reins, even to give every man according to his ways, according to the fruit of his doings* (Jer 17:10).[98]

Strikingly, in this midrash the typical roles are reversed. Now God argues not for Jewish supremacy, as other rabbinic texts did, but for soteriological equality. God represents the moral view that salvation shall be determined by righteousness rather than by communal association.

Medieval Jewish rationalists, such as Moses Maimonides (Egypt, 1038–1104), Menaḥem Meiri (Provence, 1249–1306), and Joseph Albo (Spain, 1380–1444) would ignore the dozens of late rabbinic texts that damn the gentiles and revive the older inclusive view as found in the Mishnah and Tosefta (according to R. Yehoshua).[99] They maintained that righteous gentiles after death would go to heaven, or, in their parlance, "will receive a share in the world to come." Salvation is, hypothetically, open to all people. At the dawn of the modern period, Moses Mendelssohn (Berlin, 1729–1786) celebrated this universal dimension of Judaism when readily contrasting it with the more exclusivist Christian worldview, which, in his reading, requires belief in the death and resurrection of Jesus for salvation.[100] From Mendelssohn onward, progressive-leaning rabbis and Jewish intellectuals were wont to repeat this inclusive theological principle: both righteous Jews and righteous gentiles would achieve salvation.

---

98. Wertheimer, *Batei Midrashot*, 1:283–84.

99. On Maimonides, see Eugene Korn, "Gentiles, the World to Come, and Judaism: The Odyssey of a Rabbinic Text," *Modern Judaism* 14 (1994): 265–87. On Albo and Meiri, see Novak, *Image of the Non-Jew*, 176-94.

100. Moses Mendelssohn, *Jerusalem, or, On Religious Power and Judaism* [1783], trans. Allan Arkush (Hanover, NH: Brandeis University Press 1986), 77–139.

Conflict over the Essential Nature of Law

Bava b. Buta's Activism in Tosefta Hagigah

BARRY SCOTT WIMPFHEIMER

When evaluating stories about Shammai and Hillel and their followers we often presume external data. We think of the two masters as rabbis even though they were functioning in a temple environment that precedes the rabbinic period. We have an unconscious bias toward Hillel and against Shammai in light of various rabbinic passages. To some extent, we elide the existence of the temple and, more importantly perhaps, the priests who would have been major religious and political authorities during the temple's time. We ignore the reality of a Judea riven by both religious sects and political factions. Because the houses of Shammai and Hillel are used so prominently to thematize ideas of pluralism in the rabbinic period, we overlook the fact that such houses, if they existed, would have been contemporaneous with that most extreme period of antipluralism—the sectarian period.

Residue of the actual politics and division emerges in rare cases in some rabbinic texts. Most notable in this group is the passage in the Palestinian Talmud that asserts that the students of Shammai *killed* the students of Hillel in the aftermath (foreground?) of the vote at Beit Nitzeh in Lod (y. Šabb. 1:4; 3c). Not only is this violence atypical for the pluralistic rabbis; there is also little record of actual violence among the religious sects during the sectarian period.[1] More to the point, while there is a record of violent banditry, and *political* and *military* violence in the first century, there is no historical evidence of ideologically motivated violence and killing. Josephus, who would have been drawn to the drama of sectarian violence, reports on the conflicts of political factions related to the destruction of Jerusalem but does not describe ideological differences coalescing into

1. It is important to distinguish between actual violence and the thematization of violence. See Alex Jassen, "The Dead Sea Scrolls and Violence: Sectarian Formation and Eschatological Imagination," *BibInt* 17 (2009): 12–44, for the example of Qumran.

violent clashes.[2] Since there is no historical basis for this kind of violence, we should understand the depiction of violence as representing a strong form of resistance to philosophical notions of tolerance that often dominate in rabbinic accounts of the halcyon days of Shammai and Hillel.[3]

This article focuses on a passage in t. Ḥag. 2 that includes a narrative account of a tense interaction between Shammaites and Hillelites in the temple. My reading will not follow the order of the text but will begin with a capsular version of the story preserved within the text, then radiate out to the more developed version of the same story before further expanding to take in the larger Tosefta context. Attention to syntactical and narrative interruptions within these texts will enable a source-critical analysis of this passage that not only is important for understanding the passage but also significantly contributes to an ongoing debate about the nature and chronology of rabbinic pluralism.

The Story

A less extreme and more realistic account of a factional Second Temple reality is found in the story of the clash of Shammai and Hillel in t. Ḥag. 2:11–12. In this story, violence produces social pressure and impacts ritual actions and the legal understandings that attach to such actions without escalating to deadly confrontation. The narrative details cut against the glorified picture of interhouse harmony first presented by the Mishnah and further developed in the Talmuds. The narrativization of strife, which makes the story a better fit with the sectarian strife of its historical period, might encourage a reader to trust the story as historiography. That would be a mistake. This story plays with realism as part of its claim to truth and authority, but it is a fictional narrative situated within a passage intensely devoted to the production of a form of legal theory. As I will demonstrate, the narrative conflicts with the passages around it and has been heavily edited to reflect editorial ideologies.

Mishnah Ḥag. 2:2 records a multigenerational debate between sets of early rabbis about the practice of laying on hands (*semikhah*) on a holiday sacrifice.

2. Richard A. Horsley, "Josephus and the Bandits," *JJS* 10 (1979): 37–63; Horsley, "Menahem in Jerusalem: A Brief Messianic Episode among the Sicarii—Not 'Zealot Messianism,'" *NovT* 27 (1985): 334–48.

3. M. Yebam. 1:4. But see t. Yebam. 1:12 for the view of R. Shimeon, who restricts the pluralism to situations of doubtful facts.

Yose b. Yo'ezer says not to lay on hands; Yose b. Yoḥanan says to lay on hands.	יוסה בן יועזר או' שלא לסמוך, יוסה בן יוחנן אומ' לסמוך.
Yehoshua b. Perahyah says not to lay on hands; Matti the Arbelite says to lay on hands.	יהושע בן פרחיה או' שלא לסמוך. מתיי הארבלי או' לסמוך.
Yehudah b. Tabbai says not to lay on hands; Shimeon b. Shetaḥ says to lay on hands.	יהודה בן טביי [אומ] שלא לסמוך. ושמעון בן שטח אומר לסמוך.
Shem'ayah says to lay on hands; Avtalyon says not to lay on hands.	שמעיה או' לסמוך, אבטליון [אומ] שלא לסמוך.
Hillel and Menaḥem did not disagree; Menaḥem exited, and Shammai entered. Hillel says to lay on hands; Shammai says not to lay on hands;.	הלל ומנחם לא נחלקו; יצא מנחם, ונכנס שמיי. הלל או' לסמוך שמי או' שלא לסמוך.
The firsts are patriarchs and the seconds to them are the chief judges.	הראשונים היו נשיאים, והשניים אבות בית דין.[4]

This Mishnah overlaps nearly perfectly with the chain of transmission found in m. 'Abot 1:4–12. Given what we know about the constructed nature of the Mishnah and the lateness of 'Abot, this overlap must be interrogated. Since the scholarly consensus has 'Abot as a text produced later than the rest of the Mishnah, it is likely that the chain we find in 'Abot stands in response to this multigenerational presentation. Contrasting the two permits one to see what is not as noticeable on its own—that the presentation of the multigenerational dispute (unique in rabbinic literature as such) makes an argument for *a dispute paradigm of law*—that law is well executed when it is presented as a discourse involving multiple competing authorities.[5] Witness what happens in the Mishnah when Hillel and Menachem do not disagree: Menachem is replaced by Shammai and the dispute rolls merrily along. This postmodern notion of law-as-dispute generates the response of the chain of transmission in 'Abot.[6] 'Abot employs

4. MS Kaufmann A50.

5. For a historical theory that the dispute model is connected to the third Tannaitic generation, see Yair Furstenberg, "Early Redactions of Purities: Re-Examination of Mishnah Source-Criticism," *Tarbiṣ* 80 (2012): 507–37.

6. The characterization of the dispute paradigm as postmodern is based on the suspicion of all grand narratives as the definition of postmodernism in Jean-François Lyotard, *The Postmodern Condition: A Report on Knowledge*, Theory and History of Literature 10 (Minneapolis: University of Minnesota Press, 1984).

the frame of an oracular law emerging from Sinai in response to the model of law-as-dispute put forward in m. Ḥag. 2:2.

The Mishnah that immediately follows the multigenerational dispute (2:3) depicts a deeper controversy that emerged between the houses associated with the final dueling pair Hillel and Shammai:

Beit Shammai says we bring peace offerings without laying on hands but not burnt offerings;	בית שמאי או׳ מביאין שלמים ואין סומכין עליהם אבל לא עולות;
Beit Hillel says we bring peace and burnt offerings and lay hands on both.	ובית הלל אומ׳ מביאין שלמים ועולות, וסומכין עליהן.

Both houses bring peace offerings, but only the Hillelites lay hands on the animal. The Shammaites do not allow burnt offerings at all. Tosefta Ḥagigah 2:11–12 contains a story that employs this secondary debate between the houses of Hillel and Shammai as its context. It has evaded notice that this story is actually a set of two versions of the story.[7] The initial version of the story is clearer and more elaborate. On this basis, I presume the second, terser narrative to be the earlier version and the first a clarification of the second. To wit, I begin with the second account:

A story[8] about a student from the students of Beit Hillel who laid hands on a burnt offering [in the sanctuary].[9] A student from the students of [Beit][10] Shammai said to [the Hillelite], "What is with the laying on hands?" [The Hillelite] said to [the Shammaite], "What is with the silence?" He silenced him in anger.	שוב מעשה בתלמיד אחד מתלמידי בית הלל שסמך על העולה מצאו תלמיד אחד מתלמידי שמיי אמ׳ לו מה זה סמיכה אמ׳ לו מה זה שתיקה שתקו בנזיפה[11]

The story dramatizes an encounter between a Shammaite and a Hillelite. The Hillelite performs a rite according to Hillelite understandings (as

7. Shamma Friedman, "A Good Story Deserves Retelling: The Unfolding of the Akiva Legend," *JSIJ* 3 (2004): 55–93, here 89: "Full appreciation of aggadic narrative and its artistry cannot be captured as a still, focusing upon the end product in splendid isolation, but requires investigating the overall kinetic unfolding of all its stages."

8. The absence of the word "again" in Erfurt suggests that this was a late addition to the text.

9. The implicit bracketed location is explicated in Erfurt and London.

10. The implicit house name is explicated in Erfurt and London.

11. בגערה in Erfurt.

per the Mishnah). The Shammaite questions this action and the Hillelite responds, somewhat cryptically, with "What is with the silence?" In addition to the cryptic nature of the retort, the story's final two words are also unusual. "He silenced him in/with anger" seems like a third-person narration of the story, and we would expect some plot advancement. The best explanation of the meaning of these words, though, is to say that they unpack the words that precede them. Recognizing the cryptic nature of "What is with the silence?," the editor has added a description of the scene so the reader understands that the Hillelite has silenced the Shammaite in anger. A more radical reading might support the possibility that the verb is not, as translated above, an indicative verb, but a plural imperative verb. The two words would best be rendered, "Be silent, [he said] angrily."[12]

While the final two words are ambiguous, the Hillelite's response is the crux of the story. Even though the meaning of the story is vague, its poetics are clear. The story works through rhetorical mirroring. The Shammaite's critique of the Hillelite is countered by the Hillelite's defensive use of similar language. One can suggest a deeper meaning in which the Hillelite's response, an angry one, calls out the rhetoric of the Shammaite's question because its *form* is inherently the issue. The question "What is with the laying on hands?" is a passive-aggressive judgment and criticism. The Shammaite knows the Hillelite position and is forcing the Hillelite to become more explicit through language. By mirroring the question in his own response, the Hillelite shocks the Shammaite into silence by labeling the implicit hostility of the opening question and refusing to succumb to its guilt inducement.[13]

The lesson communicated by this short version of the story has confounded interpreters from antiquity to modernity. Alongside its version of the story, the Bavli cites the fourth generation Babylonian Amora Abaye, who treats this brief story as a rhetorical precedent couched in moral terminology: "therefore, a rabbinical scholar to whom a colleague addresses something should not respond with more words than that colleague had said" (b. Beṣah 20a–b). The story, Abaye thinks, teaches rhetorical strategy. Saul Lieberman takes some of the teeth out of the retort when he transfers the conversation from the street to the intellectual legal arena: "in other words, you hinted to me that I was not an expert on the laws of laying on hands; I hint to you that you are not an expert in the laws of

12. The alternative form בגערה in Erfurt is synonymous with בנזיפה. Both mean in angry rebuke.

13. Richard Hidary, *Dispute for the Sake of Heaven: Legal Pluralism in the Talmud*, BJS 353 (Providence, RI: Brown Judaic Studies, 2010), 185. Hidary maintains that the Hillelite has won ("This time, however, the student responds with strength, thus allaying the need for any further intervention and establishing Beth Hillel as the norm"). I think the story is inconclusive on this matter.

silence."[14] Lieberman's interpretation undermines the passionate emotion of the retort by speaking of "hints" and makes it a clash of intellectual expertise.

In this micro-version of the story, the refined scholastic discourse is punctured by the emotional realities of lived life—by sudden anger. Both the initial action of laying on hands and the angry response inform the reader that the Hillelite is invested in fulfilling rites according to his own sense of the requirements (the Hillelite position) even when doing so engenders negative feedback. This characteristic of a commitment to one's own personal understanding of the halakha is a narrative feature often associated with Shammaites, but in this story it is the Hillelite, with the position that requires laying on hands, who insists on his own personal performance of halakha according to his own standards.[15]

The more elaborate version of the story develops the features present in the terser version and slightly reframes them:

A story of Hillel the Elder who laid hands on a burnt offering in the sanctuary.	מעשה בהלל הזקן שסמך על העולה בעזרה
Students of [the house of][16] Shammai gathered on top of him. [Hillel] said to [the Shammaites], "Come and see that she is a female and I need to make her into a peace offering."	וחברו עליו תלמידי שמיי אמ' להם בואו וראו שהיא נקבה וצריך אני לעשותה זבחי שלמים
He put them off with words[17] and they left.	הפליגן בדברים והלכו להן
Immediately the hands of Beit Shammai were winning and they sought to establish the halakha as their words.[18]	מיד גברה ידן של בית שמיי ובקשו לקבוע הלכה כמותן

14. Saul Lieberman, *Tosefta ki-feshuṭah: Beʾur Arokh La-Tosefta* (New York: Jewish Theological Seminary of America, 1955), 1304.

15. See, e.g., R. Tarfon's wish in t. Yebam. 1:10 and y. Šeb. 4:2 = b. Ned. 62a. Since the law typically follows Hillel and his house, those insisting on the performance of minority positions would usually be Shammaites.

16. The implicit bracketed house term is added in Erfurt, London, and the Palestinian Talmud. Its absence in the first print edition of Tosefta and in manuscripts of the Bavli demonstrate that it is not original.

17. Erfurt's "He put them off on the matter" may be the original.

18. The Venice print's "like them" is an editorial change to something more easily understood. The meaning is unchanged.

There was there Bava b. Buta, from the students of Beit Shammai, who knew that the halakha is [as the words of][19] Beit Hillel [everywhere].[20]	והיה שם בבא בן בוטא שהוא מתלמידי בית שמיי ויודע שהלכה כדברי בית הלל בכל מקום
He went and brought all the sheep of Qedar and stood them in the Temple Court and he said, "Whoever needs to bring [burnt and peace offerings][21] should come and take and lay on hands."	הלך והביא את כל צאן קידר והעמידן בעזרה ואמ׳ כל מי שצריך להביא עולות ושלמים יבוא ויטול ויסמוך
They came and took the animal[22] and brought burnt offerings and laid hands.	באו ונטלו את הבהמה והעלו עולות וסמכו עליהן
On that day the halakha was established according to the word of Beit Hillel and not a man objected on the matter.	בו ביום נקבעה הלכה כדברי בית הלל ולא ערער אדם בדבר[23]

The single scene of the simpler story has become two scenes. In the first scene the Hillelite is now Hillel himself, and the Shammaite is a gang of Shammaites. This transformation justifies the judgmental tone of the sole Shammaite in the smaller story by making the Shammaites a majority who have a degree of actual or de facto institutional control of the temple and thus represent consensus or normative behavior. The Hillelite of the original story is a passionate and strong advocate for his position who does not shy away from confrontation. In the expanded version, Hillel is a sneak who wants to fulfill his understanding of the rite but not at the cost of confrontation. Hillel is a trickster who explicitly lies about the sex of his animal to avoid confrontation.

Tricksters are a common character type in biblical narrative.[24] The trickster is one who slyly circumvents the limitations of their cultural position and one with whom the narrator sympathizes. In fact, the sympathy of the narrator is the major determinant of whether a character who bucks convention is considered a hero or a villain by the reader.[25] One of

---

19. The implicit bracketed term is explicated in Venice and Erfurt.

20. Venice adds "everywhere," which is likely a later additional edit.

21. The original version, as preserved in Erfurt, does not specify the sacrifices involved. In the description of the action below Erfurt (and Venice) also limits the free sacrifices to the burnt offerings that were the subjects of the controversy.

22. It is unclear why the singular noun is used here.

23. MS Wien – Oesterreichische Nationalbibliothek Cod hebr. 20.

24. Susan Niditch, *Underdogs and Tricksters: A Prelude to Biblical Folklore* (San Francisco: Harper & Row, 1987).

25. Consider the contrast case of Jeroboam's wife (named Ano in the Septuagint) in

the challenges of this expanded story is that the narrator's sympathies are hard to unpack. It is unclear whether Hillel has the narrator's sympathies.

There is an oddity surrounding Hillel's lie. The anatomical sex of animals is generally visible in their genitalia.[26] Hillel covers for the animal—claiming that his male is a female. Within the story, gender serves as a binary cultural identification and one through which Hillel can perform a different identity. The transgendered animal is a placeholder for the "transgendered" Hillel, who dresses in drag as a Shammaite to achieve his goals. This is particularly acute in light of the substitution ritual of "laying of hands" that is central to the story. In this ritual, the animal symbolically replaces the petitioner, losing its life in place of the supplicant in atonement for the supplicant's sins. Hillel's "and it is female" is an overt gender claim that, like a drag performance, calls into question the natural designation of bodies as inherently male or female by recognizing the role that verbal discourse plays in naming gender.[27] The substitution of the story asks the reader to similarly question the natural designation of an individual as a respective Hillelite or Shammaite.

The ambiguity of school identity is further developed in the story's expansion. Where the brief story allowed the Hillelite's passion to be communicated through an angry retort, the expanded story includes a second scene and a new character. While Hillel is a Hillelite who outwardly performs Shammaite rites, Bava b. Buta is a Shammaite who outwardly performs Hillelite rites. Shammaite status gives Bava b. Buta the credibility to pass unguarded. From his position inside the palace, Bava b. Buta plays the agent provocateur. Troubled by the intimidation of Hillel by the Shammaites, Bava b. Buta intimidates the Shammaites with an even greater force—the full populace of Jerusalem and all the sheep of the Qedar.[28]

There is a set of stories found in parallel in several works of rabbinic literature about Hillel's elevation to a leadership position in Judea. [29] In that account, the populace at large is a repository of memories of how

1 Kgs 14, who disguises herself before Ahijah but is recognized. See Barry Scott Wimpfheimer, "Suborning Perjury: A Case Study of Narrative Precedent in Talmudic Law," in *Fatal Fictions: Crime and Investigation in Law and Literature*, ed. Richard H. McAdams, Martha C. Nussbaum, and Alison L. LaCroix (Oxford: Oxford University Press, 2017), 41–64.

26. This is likely the rationale for the additional motif "it wagged its tail" in the Bavli's version of the story. The tail wagging might be a cultural performance of female gender and/or the explanation for the Shammaite blindness to the animal's genital sex.

27. Judith Butler, *Gender Trouble : Feminism and the Subversion of Identity*, Thinking Gender (New York: Routledge, 1990), 101–80.

28. The reference to the sheep of the Qedar is a midrashic wink at Isa 60:7, which says about a utopian apocalypse: "all the sheep of Qedar will be gathered on your behalf … they will be brought willingly to my altar and the house of my glory I will decorate." The verb for "brought" on the altar is related etymologically to the noun 'Olah, a burnt offering

29. T. Pesaḥ. 4:13–14; y. Pesaḥ. 6:1, 33a; b. Pesaḥ. 66a.

rituals are traditionally conducted—the people remember to bring the slaughtering knife to the temple via their animals and thus circumvent the challenge of carrying on the Sabbath. Communal behavior is implicitly thematized as a third basis of legal authority, contrasted with both the intellectual gymnastics employed by Hillel and the memorized traditions of the resident Judeans who challenge him. The knife-carrying practice is understood as both ontologically prior to and more authoritative than the two other techniques of legal authority. The moment of turning to the people is a transforming moment in which law shifts epistemologically from an intellectual discourse to a living habitus. Bava b. Buta employs the people in a similar way in this narrative. Invited to partake in an enticing yet expensive ritual, the masses of Jerusalem respond to the invitation and overwhelm the temple with their offerings. Notice an important difference between the two episodes, though. While the people's practice of tucking the knife in fur represents some form of communal knowledge or memory, Bava b. Buta's populace is responding to an invitation "to lay on hands." The people are not remembering an ontologically prior legal reality, but producing it in response to the invitation. Bava b. Buta creates a mass custom by inviting the people to specifically enact the Hillelite rite in the Shammaite controlled temple.

The great reader of rabbinic stories, Yonah Fraenkel, sees a contrast between characters.[30] Bava b. Buta, the story's hero, is contrasted with Hillel, who is portrayed as a figure who does not recognize the momentousness of his actions and cannot understand that there are times to code switch and times to represent. Fraenkel's reading is presaged by the Palestinian Talmud, which derives from the story the lesson that one cannot concede aspects of a fight, even in an early stage, because that may turn out to be one's only intervention opportunity. Like Abaye in the Bavli, the Yerushalmi attempts to draw a lesson from the story; Fraenkel's methodology is similarly oriented toward a clear moral or message.

The story is fascinating as a character study, and the comparison with the preserved earlier version provides further food for thought. But I'm drawn to a different aspect of the text—a set of interruptions to the storytelling that inform the reader about the stakes of the narrative for law. As Hillel is succeeding in distracting the Shammaites, the text reports that "immediately the hands of the Shammaites were winning and they wished to establish the law like Beit Shammai." When Bava b. Buta wins the day and the *'Olot* are brought with full Hillel rites in the temple, we read, "On that day the law was established with Beit Hillel and no man raised a word of objection." These two moments warrant deeper attention.

---

30. Yonah Fraenkel, *The Aggadic Narrative: Harmony of Form and Content* [Hebrew] (Tel Aviv: Hakibbutz Hameuchad, 2001), 20–23.

"Immediately the hands of the Shammaites were winning and they wished to establish the law like Beit Shammai." The third-person plural ("they") either refers to the Shammaites themselves or to a third party. The difference is not insignificant for the text's understanding of the law. If it refers to the Shammaites, the text means that the victory over the Hillelites empowered the Shammaites beyond the local scenario to establish the law permanently according to their position. It is unclear whether the text refers to *this specific legal scenario* or whether it implies that *all rabbinic legal rulings*, which generally side with Hillel, might have been altered in the direction of universal Shammaism. Even if the empowerment was only to the local case, such a reading understands the second half of the statement exegetically as a description of the ramifications of the first half. When the text says that "they wished to establish the law," it absorbs the impact of the Shammaite victory in the episode as recounted in the first half.

A more provocative—and in my view better—reading of this line understands the third-person plural ("they") to reference a third party. Because of the victory of the Shammaites, a third party wished to establish the law like Beit Shammai. Who is this third party? From a literary perspective, the third party is a presumed viewer/reader. The second half of the statement unpacks the ramifications of the story outlined in the first half; it is a mode of exegesis. "They" are the witnesses to the scenario as either enacted or read. From a legal perspective, the third party is an important participant in the establishing of law. They are the ones who establish law. Law is understood as a static state that is the result of prior actions and the third-person plural "they" are the mysterious agents that produce this state. By using a third-person plural, the text produces law as a subjectively generated essence.[31] So the fixed state of law admits to its subjective determination while insisting on its static position.[32]

Mikhail Bakhtin's notion of the superaddressee may help explain this feature of the text on a literary level. Communicative understandings of texts presume the presence of two subjectivities—the sender and the receiver of the message. Bakhtin deconstructs this binary by asserting the often-unacknowledged presence of a third party, the "superaddressee."[33] This superaddressee is an often-unacknowledged personification of a third party to the communication generated by the text. Bakhtin scholars have suggested by way of example cases in which speakers turn to an

---

31. On a subjective interpretation of law, see my "Footnotes to Carnal Israel: Infertility and the Legal Subject," in *Talmudic Transgressions: Engaging the Work of Daniel Boyarin*, ed. Ishay Rosen-Zvi et al., JSJSup 181 (Leiden: Brill, 2017), 161–200.

32. This is similar to Ronald Dworkin's embodying the law in the subjectivity of an ideal judge. See Ronald Dworkin, *Law's Empire* (Cambridge,MA: Harvard University Press, 1986), 164ff.

33. Gary Saul Morson and Caryl Emerson, *Mikhail Bakhtin: Creation of a Prosaics* (Stanford, CA: Stanford University Press, 1990), 135-36.

imagined third-party judge to indict ("Are you seeing this?" "Can you believe this?").[34] The present text's interruptions are moments in which the text's superaddressee has emerged from the shadows and is rendered visible.

This first interruption (Immediately ...) moves the narrative forward by creating a sense of crisis. This is what Roland Barthes labeled "proairetic code"—by suggesting that the law might follow Shammai, the line sets the stage for Bava b. Buta's urgent intervention.[35] Bava b. Buta acts decisively (*pace* Hillel) and invites the masses of Jerusalem to buttress the Hillelite position. The text concludes with the second interruption; "on that day the law was established with Beit Hillel and no man raised a word of objection." Like the earlier interruption, this line has two clauses; the first clause says that the law follows Beit Hillel, and the second describes the aftermath of that reality. The first half echoes the earlier interruption by establishing the law but does so by making law (and not a third person plural "they") the subject. Law is an essential object and grammatical subject. The verb "was established" communicates that the state of law was dynamic, and not original or permanent, but law as grammatical subject is more essential than when it was described in the first interruption utilizing the third-person plural "they."

There is greater ambiguity in the second clause of the second interruption. "No man raised a word of objection." The clause confuses a reader because they know that the Shammaites in the first part of the story *disagreed* with the performed rite. Taken literally, the clause makes a claim for arrival at a legal consensus (as if the action created ideational agreement on the issue), but in the context of the story the reader suspects that the refusal to object is a function of intimidation. The Shammaites acquiesced out of fear. While the law (this law or law in general) is established like Beit Hillel, the mechanism has more in common with a mafioso's "non-refusable offer" than with constructive consensus.

As with the earlier interruption, this second statement is exegetical, usurping the reader's position as interpreter of the narrative. The interruption tells the reader what they should have understood from the story—that the law was established with the Hillelites unequivocally. If one attends closely to the text, though, there is a gap in hero characterization between narrative and interruption. The narrative makes Bava b. Buta the hero for refusing to allow Hillel to be cowed by the Shammaites.[36] The second interrupting comment turns Bava b. Buta from an enabler of Hillelite practice into a bully who, like his Shammaite peers, intimidates

34. Ibid.

35. Roland Barthes and Honoré de Balzac, *S/Z*, 1st American ed. (New York,: Hill & Wang, 1974), 75–76.

36. This is supported in Fraenkel's reading.

opponents into silence. The story is understood by the interruption to implicate a final decision about the nature of halakha, and it sides with Beit Hillel to the exclusion of Beit Shammai. The interruption works well with the narrative's introduction of the character of Bava b. Buta. Bava b. Buta is "a Shammaite who knows that the law follows Beit Hillel." The problem with this introduction is that its implicit notion of law conflicts with that of the interrupting lines. Bava b. Buta's knowledge that "the law follows Beit Hillel" conceives of law as an essential static object (and grammatical subject) with no origin story. Paradoxically in this text, because Bava b. Buta *knows* that the law is like Beit Hillel he goes out of his way to *establish* the law like Beit Hillel. Meanwhile, the narrative records a notion of law-as-dispute with competing positions of Shammai and Hillel and the idea that even the minority in such a circumstance might continue to attempt to fulfill rites according to their own understandings.[37] To sum up, the text possesses three different notions of law: law-as-dispute (inherited from the Mishnah, this notion is implicit in the reality of competing schools and students who wish to follow their own positions), law-as-static and ontologically prior state (Bava b. Buta knows that the law is like Hillel) and law-as-static with a dynamic backstory (interrupting comments on the narrative).

Thus far I have employed Barthes and Bakhtin to suggest literary-theoretical ways of understanding the interruptions to the narrative in the Tosefta. There are other ways of accounting for this intriguing phenomenon. One could understand the interruptions as manifestations of a larger rabbinic textual habit: the intrusion of rabbinic compositional realities into a text's imagined space. There are many examples in rabbinic literature of a story set in pre-rabbinic times (the Second Temple and even earlier biblical periods) taking on features (Jacob's study in the *yeshiva* of Shem and Ever or the Beit Midrash on the Temple Mount) of rabbinic societal context. Passages of rabbinic literature that describe protocols of the Sanhedrin (more on this below) bear indications that the high court is modeled after an early rabbinic study hall rather than a Second Temple court. The interruptions that interfere with the reader's own interpretation of the narrative texts capture the reality of rabbis qua interpreters in the act of interpretation.

Another way of thinking of this intrusion into the imagined narrative space is to think of the interruptions as a deliberate breaking of the fourth wall. Theatrical dramatizations require actors on a stage to act as though an imaginary wall separates their world from that of the audience; the audience needs that wall to be transparent so they can watch what happens

37. Hidary (*Dispute for the Sake of Heaven,* 1–13) employs a set of fixed categories established by Christine Hayes to describe different legal philosophies. I avoid these categories because they require a dulling of some of the distinctions in play in the different sections of this story.

on stage. Deliberate breaks of the fourth wall are moments in which an actor in a play (or a film or television show) turns toward the audience and addresses it, violating the convention of separation. A staple of modernist drama and film, this breaking of the fourth wall is a deconstructive moment that makes all participants aware of the wall's existence, rendering its unacknowledged artificiality and importance extremely visible. The rendering of the visibility of the wall unmasks the audience behind it and makes the presence of that audience a part of the art on stage. One could apply the notion of "breaking the fourth wall" productively to rabbinic historical texts in which details from the compositional context find their way into the narrative. Doing so would change these moments from accidental moments of comedy to deliberate proto-modernist forms of composition. In the present context, the interruptions are breaks of the fourth wall that alert the reader to tensions within the idea of established law.

The gap between the interruptions and the story is not limited to the raised awareness of the scholastic contexts and the scholarly investment in a determined law. While the story is largely about law, it also potentially introduces the import of political and economic clout in the discourse of halakha. The story implies that the Shammaites control the temple's sacrifices and Hillel must navigate their resistance if he wants to perform the rites as he intends. Bava b. Buta resists this political power with the power of the people of Jerusalem. He can marshal that power through his economic resources—because he is wealthy enough to sponsor the expensive animals offered *gratis* to the people. Tosefta Ker. 4:4, the only other reference to Bava b. Buta in Tosefta, says that Bava b. Buta brought an atonement offering every day except for the day after Yom Kippur.[38] The expansion of the original Hillelite story utilizes Bava b. Buta *because* he is a character whose means have already been demonstrated to afford him the opportunity to sacrifice many animals. Reading against the grain of the interruptions, then, one can recognize that the events of the scenario testify as much to the economics of sacrifice as to its politics and its law. So while the interruptions would attempt to control the meaning of the episode and limit it to a legal space within which there is an expectation of a static law, the story itself resists this control and limitation and speaks to the intersection of law with both economics and politics in dynamic ways.[39]

By my historical reconstruction, the earliest text here is the shorter

---

38. The only reference to this character in rabbinic literature outside of these two episodes and their parallels is a story at b. Ned. 66b where the plot is dictated by a pun on the meaning of the name "Bava."

39. This Tosefta narrative thus possesses some of the discursive interdisciplinary features I identified in Bavli legal narratives in my *Narrating the Law : A Poetics of Talmudic Legal Stories*, Divinations (Philadelphia: University of Pennsylvania Press, 2011).

story that appears second in our text—the one with the verbal encounter between the Hillelite and the Shammaite. The more elaborate story of Bava b. Buta's amassing the Qedari animals and Jerusalemite people developed out of the terser version, clarifying the fact that the Shammaites had normative power (at least de facto) and that the Hillelite's final word is not simply a moral lesson or pyrrhic victory but achieves a widespread Hillelite practice. When one separates the larger story from the two framing interruptions on which I have thus far lavished attention, Bava b. Buta's actions become more ambiguous. Why did Bava b. Buta invite the masses to sacrifice? The interruptions presume Bava b. Buta to be a legal essentialist who knows that the Hillelites are correct; his behavior is about ensuring a correct legal ritual outcome. Without the interruptions, though, one might understand Bava b. Buta as intervening in response to the injustice of Hillel's treatment by the Shammaites. Perhaps, even, Bava b. Buta is a Shammaite[40] acting against Shammaite interests because of a fundamental commitment to goodness, tolerance, and religious freedom; he simply cannot stomach Hillel's being forced to go underground. By this reading, the ultimate outcome does not establish legal precedent for posterity but threatens those who wish to compel others into ritual submission. The hero in this story is committed to pluralism and religious freedom, not to an idea of singular law. The interrupting additions usurp the reader's position and force the reading in an entirely different direction.

The Larger Context of Tosefta

Thus far I have noted three different understandings of law implicit, respectively, in the Bava b. Buta story ("law-as-dispute"), in the introduction to this character ("law as static object with no prehistory") and in the interruptions ("law as static object with prior indeterminate state"). The larger context of the surrounding material in Tosefta complicates these three understandings; the texts adjacent to the Bava b. Buta story include some of the texts most central to historical characterizations of rabbinic legal practice and theory. Recall that the mishnaic context is a multigenerational dispute between pairs of rabbis over laying on hands. I argued above that the Mishnah's valorization of dispute as the ideal legal paradigm engendered a counterconstruction in the chain of transmission text

40. Only the interruption labels him a Shammaite, but this identity might be implicit in his presence in the temple at the time.

of m. 'Abot 1. Tosefta Ḥag. 2, like m. 'Abot 1, also attempts to curtail the model of law-as-dispute.

From its first comment t. Ḥag. 2 signals its intention to mitigate the idea that law's ideal state is permanent dispute. The opening line of Tosefta says, "In their days the *only* dispute was about laying-on-hands" (t. Ḥag. 2:8). The paradigmatic usage of a multigenerational dispute as a statement about the basis of rabbinic scholarship is transformed into an exception—the Mishnah notes this multigenerational dispute because it is the *only* one of its kind.

The attempt to suppress the idealization of dispute continues a few lines later in the well-known *baraita* of R. Yose. The bulk of the *baraita* of R. Yose is a protocol that describes both how an unknown matter of law comes to be known or established and how judges are appointed within the tiered system of courts.[41] In addition to this material, though, the *baraita* contains three other sections: an introductory statement ("originally there was never dispute in Israel"), an intermediate statement that interrupts the protocol ("when the students of Hillel and Shammai increased ... there emerged two torahs") and a final piece ("a priest who finds a blemish ...") that discusses the appointment of priests (a point touched on in the body of the protocol). The introductory statement and intermediate statement have been subject to various attempts at source-critical separation.[42] Richard Hidary follows the lead of David Zvi Hoffman in asserting that the introductory and intermediate pieces constitute a unified second source.[43]

Support for this argument comes from the Palestinian Talmud, which contains a *baraita* that places these two clauses in proximity:

41. The term *protocol* is from Ishay Rosen-Zvi, "Protocol Beit Hadin Beyavneh: Iyyun Mehudash Betosefta Sanhedrin Pereq Zayin," *Tarbiṣ* 78 (2009): 447–77. There is insightful analysis of the protocol in Menachem Fisch, *Rational Rabbis: Science and Talmudic Culture*, Jewish Literature and Culture (Bloomington: Indiana University Press, 1997), 66–68.

42. Hidary, *Dispute for the Sake of Heaven*, 303–7; David Zvi Hoffman, *The First Mishna and the Controversies of the Tannaim; The Highest Court in the City of the Sanctuary* (New York: Maurosho, 1977), 75–76; Rosen-Zvi, "Protocol Beit Hadin Beyavneh."

43. Rosen-Zvi disagrees with this reading and instead treats the introductory and intermediate clauses as unrelated clauses by impressively demonstrating that, despite appearances, the "originally" statement often does not generate a second time frame ("Protocol Beit Hadin Beyavneh"). The problem with Rosen-Zvi's reading is that, while the "originally" term *does not have to* generate a subsequent development, in a text in which a sequential arrangement appears, it makes sense to assume that the person who put the second clause in was aware of the way in which it interacts with the introductory clause.

תוספתא חגיגה ב:ט אמ׳ ר׳ יהודה כתחלה לא היתה מחלוקת בישראל [פרוטוקול חלק א׳] משרבו תלמידי שמיי והלל שלא שימשו כל צרכן הרבו מחלוקות בישראל ונעשו שתי תורות [פרוטוקול חלק ב׳]	תלמוד ירושלמי חגיגה ב:ג ,עז:ד[44] בראשונה לא היתה מחלוקת בישראל אלא על הסמיכה בלבד ועמדו שמי והלל ועשו אותן ארבע משרבו תלמיד בית שמי ותלמידי בית הלל ולא שימשו את רביהן כל צורכן ורבו המחלוקות ביש׳ ונחלקו לשתי כיתות אילו מטמאין ואילו מטהרין ועוד אינה עתידה לחזור למקומה עד שיבוא בן דוד

T. Ḥag. 2:9	**Y. Ḥag. 2:2, 77d**
R. Judah said, Originally, there was no contention in Israel [PROTOCOL Part A] When the students of Shammai and Hillel who had not served [their masters well] increased in number, contention proliferated and they became two Torahs [PROTOCOL Part B]	 Originally there was only contention in Israel about *semikhah* alone.[45] Shammai and Hillel went and made them four. When the students of Shammai and Hillel increased in number and did not serve their masters as necessary, contention increased in Israel and they were divided into two sects, these rendering impure and these purifying. And it will not in the future return to its place until the son of David arrives.

Both the Tosefta and Palestinian Talmud (PT) texts open with an "originally" statement. The PT version echoes a prior line in t. Ḥag. 2 (referenced earlier) in attempting to limit the multigenerational dispute as a paradigm by making it the sole example of disputation. Despite subtle differences in the two "originally" statements, comparison of the two texts allows us to understand that the text tells a story about the devolution of the law. Originally—in its ideal state—law was consensus and unity; one could even claim that law was static. Over time and as a result of negative behaviors, law changed and became riven by dispute. PT's text concludes with a utopian promise of the return to the ideal of unity in a messianic era.

The source-critical unification of two of the three protocol interruptions in Tosefta and the comparison of these interruptions with their parallel in PT allows us to understand these interruptions as a single editorial intervention that seeks to introduce a narrative of legal devolution into

44. MS Leiden Or. 4720.

45. PT has modified the original *baraita*'s language to accommodate the dispute in m. Ḥag. 2:2.

conversations around the multigenerational dispute preserved in the Mishnah. Having opened out of order with the Bava b. Buta story (which appears in t. Ḥag. after the protocol), we can now also note the overlap between the protocol's interruptions and the interruptions discussed above in the context of the story: the two protocol interruptions resemble the two interruptions of the Bava b. Buta narrative discussed earlier since they too discuss the nature of law through the question of the character of the category of dispute. While the interruptions to story and protocol do not fully share an understanding of law, they all resist the notion of law-as-dispute in favor of a notion of law as a singular entity. I will return to the interruptions below after dealing with the legal practice and theory that emerge from the protocol itself.

The protocol is somewhat contradictory. It reports that the main court on the Temple Mount in Jerusalem had seventy-one judges, but it also implies that this is a court of three judges. Setting aside such small matters, the protocol in general imagines a three-tiered court system with a local court outside of Jerusalem, a lower court in Jerusalem, and a higher court in Jerusalem. The protocol imagines an individual's bringing a legal question first to the local court then to the lower Jerusalem court and finally to the higher Jerusalem court. At each level, the possibility exists for the court to have heard the ruling from a higher authority (the higher court). If law is not heard (i.e., if there is no oral tradition from above), the petitioner takes it to the highest court and they rule on the matter with a majority decision. The framework of a vote conceives of law as a set of binary decisions that can be easily presented to majoritarian decision making. Hidary notes that the protocol is an extended midrash on Deut 17 and its notion of approaching the temple for justice.[46] This aspect lends the protocol an oracular quality—halakha is broadcast from the temple as though from God. But the protocol is not consistent in thinking of law in oracular terms. Opposing this oracular top-down quality is the protocol's message that the centralized system draws its energy from the representation of outlying cities or towns. Just as the first half of the protocol describes a process of the law's first approaching the local courts and then being brought before the higher courts, the second half describes the appointment of judges through a tiered system in which judges are first appointed locally before being elevated to the Jerusalem lower court and then to its higher court.[47] So while law emerges in singular terms from the temple in Jerusalem, it is

46. Hidary, *Dispute for the Sake of Heaven*, 307; Rosen-Zvi, "Protocol Beit Hadin Beyavneh," 476.

47. David Goodblatt suggests that the Roman Senate is the model of this form of democratic representation (*The Monarchic Principle: Studies in Jewish Self-Government in Antiquity*, TSAJ 38 [Tübingen: Mohr Siebeck, 1994], 128).

authorized/justified by the representation of all of Israel who make their way as judges up to the highest court.

As mentioned above, the protocol is introduced with an initial clause that states, "originally, there was no dispute in Israel." This line previews a protocol that provides for the resolution of legal uncertainty through judicial procedure. The protocol is an iterative narrative, describing a social institution through a story of law's progress from the outlying areas to Jerusalem and finally to the temple.[48] This narrative borrows in fundamental ways from the iterative narrative that describes the protocol for handling the "rebellious elder."[49] These iterative narratives respond to the inherent multiplicity of law as an intellectual and social project (multiple opinions, positions, or practices) by producing a ritual of transformation that restores the law to unity. While the rebellious elder embodies dispute, his prosecution and punishment guarantee consensus. The protocol that ends in a vote ensures that law's competing positions and opinions are sifted and sorted with only a single version's remaining viable.

The protocol interruptions ("originally ..." and "when the students ...") mirror the protocol's iterative narrative. Both the interruptions and the protocol describe a static reality and a dynamic process. Where the protocol goes from a state of initial multiplicity to resolution through a vote, the interruptions assert a state of initial harmony followed by a process of devolution owing to poor apprenticeship and leading to the chaotic reality of multiple legal positions. The two are not technically inconsistent, but it seems that the protocol ascribes chaos to the lack of a Sanhedrin, and the narrative interruptions attribute primordial legal unity to the great figures who used to speak for the law (and not to a procedural vote). Neither narrative of legal discourse reflects on the irony of their preservation within a law code—Tosefta, rife with disputed law that supplements another law code, the Mishnah, which has its own multiplicity and with whom Tosefta often disagrees.

Having established that the protocol and its interruptions represent diverging models of the chronology of law as unified or disputed, let us return to the story of Bava b. Buta and its two interruptions. Recall that the story of Bava b. Buta is a story of law-as-dispute. The interruptions introduce the character of Bava b. Buta as one who knows that the law is singular (and follows Hillel) and explain the outcome of the story as one in which law is established like Hillel. These interruptions overlap with

48. For the concept of iterative narrative, see Naftali Cohn, *The Memory of the Temple and the Making of the Rabbis*, Divinations (Philadelphia: University of Pennsylvania Press), 60–65.

49. Hidary, *Dispute for the Sake of Heaven*, 297–325; Rosen-Zvi, "Protocol Beit Hadin Beyavneh," 475; Aharon Shemesh, "Halakhah unevuah: Navi sheqer vezaqen mamre," in *Mehuyavut Yehudit mithadeshet: al olamo vehaguto shel David Hartman*, ed. Avi Sagi and Zvi Zohar (Jerusalem: Hakibbutz Hameuchad, 2002), 2:923–41.

the iterative narrative of the protocol and the story of legal devolution that interrupts that protocol. Like the iterative narrative, which ends in legal resolution, the second interruption of the Bava b. Buta story claims that the law is resolved and follows the Hillelites. Like the story of legal devolution, which maintains that law is originally singular, Bava b. Buta is introduced as a character who understands an ontologically prior notion that the law follows Hillel.

By now it should be clear that an editorial war is raging within Tosefta Ḥagigah. An editor bothered by the notion of law-as-dispute shared by both the Mishnah and the core version of the more elaborate of the two animal sacrifice stories has produced supplements to the Mishnah, the protocol of R. Yose and the story to produce a counterparadigm to law-as-dispute. This editor imported a preexisting unit (paralleled in PT) that similarly refuses to celebrate the law-as-dispute paradigm without realizing that this devolutionary story of legal multiplicity cuts somewhat against the protocol. The presence of the protocol and its interruptions with their competing vectors around legal unity generated the two interruptions in the Bava b. Buta story that push in opposite directions with respect to the notion of legal unity.

The Ramifications

To review, a story that began as a slice of life describing factional verbal conflict over disputed ritual practice was developed into a morality play in which individual rights to conduct rituals were defended by using the hoi polloi to bully the dominant elite faction. At some point, the more developed story received editorial interventions that usurped the power of the reader and removed some of the ambiguity around the story's actions. Rather than a defender of religious freedom, Bava b. Buta became a defender of the correct Hillelite ritual practice against the threat of deviant Shammaism. And all of this was included in a text that supplements a Mishnah with the strongest articulation of dispute as the ideal paradigm of the discourse of rabbinic law. The last bit of interpretation (the narrative interruptions) is analogous to a set of interruptions that appear in an adjacent text—the protocol of how new laws are produced in ancient Israel. The overlap in these interruptions allows us to see that these interruptions were motivated by the need to shift law from the dispute paradigm found in the Mishnah to an essential unified model that was also the basis for the chain of transmission at Mishnah 'Abot 1. Though the motivation was unified, in practice there are differences among these interruptions in the way they understand law as an essential and unified entity. Some texts (introduction of Bava b. Buta) understand the law to be static. Others perceive the law to be dynamic and process driven, with stories of different moments of time. Sometimes law was unified before corruption ("When the students of Shammai ..."); sometimes it is unified by a procedure (the iterative narrative of a law going to Jerusalem); and sometimes it will be unified in a utopian future (PT *baraita* about the son of David).

Thirty-five years ago Shaye Cohen published a landmark article that reframed historiographic understanding of the collective rabbis.[50] The bias of prior scholarship on the basis of the early Christian evidence was to equate the rabbis with their Pharisaic predecessors and consider the rabbis to have furthered a Pharisaic doctrine of law and created a Jewish orthodoxy. Focusing on the inherent multiplicity in rabbinic genres of literature, Cohen highlighted a major discontinuity: while their Pharisee forebears were engaged in a factional intellectual reality riven by strife and disagreement among the sects, the rabbis collectively produced a comparative utopia of competing positions remaining in dialogue within the same intellectual and even physical space. Cohen associated this transition with Yavneh because of a number of rabbinic stories that highlight the role of the third generation of Tannaim, legendarily situated at Yavneh, responsible for the production of rabbinic norms of dispute. At least since the publication of this article, the rabbis have been characterized and celebrated for multiplicity (the citation to competing viewpoints alongside one another), pluralism (the authorization of competing and even contradictory viewpoints) and their polysemic (capable of fundamentally meaning more than one thing) understanding of the Hebrew Bible. These features have been embraced in popular theologies and Jewish political science, while academics have spent considerable efforts to unpack and complicate this large hypothesis.

Cohen's article compares two moments in time: the sectarian period and the rabbinic period. Yavneh becomes for Cohen the pivotal moment that shifts the intellectual and social climate. One of the ways scholars have been enriching Cohen's thesis since its publication is by reflecting more deeply on the question of chronology. Since Cohen's writing of the article, the field has shifted away from the basic assumptions under which Cohen was operating and in the direction of Jacob Neusner's skepticism about the historical reliability of biographical materials in rabbinic literature. Even among Israeli scholars, who have tended to be more maximalist in their trust of sources that they examine primarily using philological tools, it is no longer accepted that one can treat talmudic stories about Yavneh as accurate historic depictions. Comparisons between parallel versions of materials that appear in multiple sources are often the best way to craft a multipoint tale of historic development.

One of the most influential works in this area has been Shlomo Naeh's

---

50. Shaye J. D. Cohen, "The Significance of Yavneh: Pharisees, Rabbis, and the End of Jewish Sectarianism," *HUCA* 55 (1984): 27–53.

linguistic work on the evolution of the term "Maḥloqet," typically translated as "dispute."[51] Naeh notes that originally the term "Maḥloqet" meant factions or parties and only later developed the more commonly employed definition of dispute. But Naeh does not stop at the linguistic point that nearly every Tannaitic use of the word "Maḥloqet" means faction or factionalism. Much of the debate around pluralism/polysemy/multiplicity consists of competing close readings of a circumscribed set of explicit passages. Naeh compares one of the classic Bavli passages about pluralism with a prior Tannaitic parallel from Tosefta and demonstrates that the Tannaitic original has no trace of notions of multiplicity and pluralism; in fact, the passage is committed to a vision of rabbinic law that makes no space for debate and doubt. Naeh's philology both confirms and complicates Cohen's work. Echoing Cohen, Naeh describes a historical evolution from factionalism to internal dispute. But, while Cohen firmly divides the rabbis from their sectarian predecessors, Naeh places the break more firmly within the rabbinic period.[52] With proper philological caution, Naeh refuses to speculate over responsibility for the ideological change. It is possible that the Talmud's editors are responsible or that they inherited the changes in their version. Nevertheless, one can definitively say that the Tannaim of Yavneh are *not* to be credited with a shift that postdates the Tannaitic period.

Daniel Boyarin threw philological caution to the wind when he wedded Naeh's work to the source-critical paradigm introduced by David Weiss Halivni and Shamma Friedman and further developed, particularly in the narrative context, by Jeffrey Rubenstein.[53] Accepting Cohen's basic two-point framework and Naeh's linguistic critique, Boyarin credits the Stammaim with rewriting the Yavneh story. So, while Cohen says the break is between Second Temple and rabbinic and Naeh (I'm reading between his lines) understands the transition to be between the Tannaim and Amoraim, Boyarin pushes the transition to the Stammaim. So the large-tent rabbinic pluralism that stands as the hallmark of rabbinic Judaism does not date from the second century, but from the fifth or the sixth century.[54]

More recently, Yair Furstenberg has employed the sharpest of philological tools to revisit this question and answer the question on which Naeh

51. Shlomo Naeh, "'Make Yourself Many Rooms': Another Look at the Utterances of the Sages about Controversy" [Hebrew], in Sagi and Zohar, *Mehuyavut Yehudit mithadeshet*, 2:851–75.

52. Though Cohen uses Yavneh as the pivot point, Yavneh is a synecdoche for the entire rabbinic period.

53. Daniel Boyarin, *Border Lines: The Partition of Judeo-Christianity*, Divinations (Philadelphia: University of Pennsylvania Press, 2004), 149–226.

54. This shift is important to Boyarin's larger claims in *Border Lines* that they are roughly simultaneous with the production of Christian orthodoxy.

refused to speculate.[55] Furstenberg identifies the generation of Yavneh, the third generation of Tannaim, as inventing what I referred to above as the dispute paradigm. Ironically, the field has returned to Cohen's Yavneh as a historical time and place if not on the basis of the same sources. While Cohen selected Yavneh because of the highly developed talmudic stories about pluralism, Furstenberg chooses it because of the evidence of Tannaitic source criticism.

The four scholars I have mentioned (Cohen, Naeh, Boyarin, and Furstenberg) all work within a linear diachronic model even as they disagree over the pivot point. Menachem Fisch is a scholar of the history of science who occasionally forays into rabbinic literature to make observations about the nature of rabbinic discourse as a field of thought.[56] Fisch's work benefits significantly from its grounding in a discipline committed to reflecting on paradigms of epistemology. At the same time, Fisch does not employ the lower-critical or higher-critical toolkits that are basic for proper academic work on rabbinic literature. In his book *Rational Rabbis,* Fisch argues for a consistent philosophical hermeneutic debate between Mishnah and Tosefta in which Mishnah is antitraditionalist (all human interpretation is conjectural, tentative and subjective; ergo, multiplicity) and Tosefta is traditionalist (ideal knowledge is transferred from generation to generation; multiplicity is a product of a hiccup in transmission). Fisch does not claim that this argument represents a thorough review of all of Mishnah and Tosefta; he acknowledges that both texts are produced within a genre of multiplicity. Fisch's claim about Mishnah (antitraditionalist) and Tosefta (traditionalist) emerges primarily from a comparison of t. Ḥag. 2 (= t. Sanh. 7:1) (the protocol) and m. Sanh. 11:2 (which discusses the procedures of the rebellious elder).[57]

Though Fisch is not careful in his comparison of Mishnah and Tosefta and is not sensitive to source-critical divisions within these corpora, his work attempts to produce a synchronic debate that undermines the narrative of linear development that has been assumed since Cohen's article. My reading above of t. Ḥag. 2 and the story of Bava b. Buta combines Fisch's synchronic approach with a historical understanding of development and resistance. My source-critical reading of t. Ḥag. 2 instantiates a Tannaitic resistance to the progress narrative that moves from the negative example of sectarian factionalism to the positive paradigm of irenic disputes for the sake of heaven.

In positing the latest understanding of the embrace of pluralism, Boyarin produced a dichotomy that separates the phenomena of multiplic-

55. Yair Furstenberg, "Early Redactions of Purities: Re-Examination of Mishnah Source-Criticism" [Hebrew], *Tarbiṣ* 80 (2013): 507–37.

56. Fisch, *Rational Rabbis.*

57. Ibid., 66–69.

ity/polysemy/pluralism from the explicit thematized celebration of such ways of thinking found primarily in late Bavli narrative. Steven Fraade counterargued for a tannaitic dating of even thematized pluralism on the basis of texts from Tannaitic midrash that can be read as speaking directly to these themes.[58] Azzan Yadin-Israel defended Boyarin's approach by pointing to the Amoraic provenance of Fraade's best examples and noting the sizable conceptual gap between these midrashic texts and the late Bavli ones.[59] Between the lines one can see that the midrashic texts could yield Fraade's readings but that such readings feel more like reading backwards from the later, more explicit thematized texts. This debate reaches something of a consensus around the divide between Tannaim and Amoraim. Tosefta Ḥag. 2 provides us with an opportunity to more precisely date the epistemological shift in the discourse.[60] Combining t. Ḥag. 2 with Naeh's passage from t. Git., one can see that at the tail end of the Tannaitic period there existed at least one voice resisting a dispute paradigm and attempting to keep the law in its ideal form as philosophically unified and without the cloud of doubt.

The Function of Shammai and Hillel

Critical rabbinics scholarship once understood Hillel and Shammai to be historical personages whose biographies could be reconstructed out of the massive archive of textual evidence about them. The field has moved past this kind of stable biography, but we still find references to Hillel and Shammai and their houses as historical realities. Today, it would be more accurate to say that Hillel and Shammai are founding figures of the rabbinic movement who date to temple times. The problem with such a statement is that the rabbinic movement itself postdates temple times. Temple times are the era of competing sects, not of rabbis. The rabbis were invented on the embers of Jerusalem. Who exactly were Hillel and Shammai?

---

58. Steven Fraade, "Rabbinic Polysemy and Pluralism Revisited: Between Praxis and Thematization," *AJSR* 31 (2007): 1–40.

59. Azzan Yadin-Israel, "Rabbinic Polysemy: A Response to Steven Fraade," *AJSR* 38 (2014): 129–41.

60. Steven Fraade ("Rabbinic Polysemy") introduces this passage and its story of the devolution of law because of poor apprenticeship as an instance of "thematization." As Yadin-Israel points out in a response ("Neither Practitioners nor Preachers: A Final Response to Steven Fraade on Tannaitic Polysemy," https://www.academia.edu/12214951/2014_Neither_Practitioners_Nor_Preachers_A_Final_Response_to_Steven_Fraade_on_Tannaitic_Polysemy, 11–12) this thematization pushes against the dispute paradigm and supports the idea that thematization that celebrates dispute is late as Boyarin argues. My reading complicates this by understanding the devolution narrative to itself be employed as part of an editorial polemic against an *implicit* celebration of the dispute paradigm.

In an appendix to his book on legal pluralism, Paul Heger suggests that the opinions attributed to Hillel, Shammai, and their houses are the results of a process of legal philosophical pigeonholing.[61] At a certain point in early Tannaitic history, the names Hillel and Shammai were associated with specific legal philosophies (Shammai was traditional, retrograde, punctilious to a fault; Hillel was creative, willing to employ legal fictions, flexible) that were also the basis for narrative traditions of these founding figures. By this account, the famous leniencies of Beit Shammai are some kind of correction to an original miscategorization. Heger provides little proof for this hypothesis, but the hypothesis is appealing because it recognizes the extent to which Hillel and Shammai might be understood as historical fictions. As Steven Wald puts it more mildly, "When dealing with rabbinic or proto-rabbinic figures of Hillel's stature, it is always important to distinguish between the earlier and more historically reliable Tannaitic sources, and the later talmudic traditions which often have a more legendary character. In the case of Hillel, however, *even the earliest extant rabbinic sources are highly legendary in nature*."[62]

The story of Bava b. Buta tempts one to treat it as history because it is a rabbinic text that acknowledges a realistic (not a murderous) factional past in the Second Temple period. Recent work by Yaakov Zussman and Vered Noam has confirmed the general reliability of properly read rabbinic texts for their descriptions of Second Temple positions and practices.[63] Even while Aharon Shemesh has demonstrated that rabbinic legal philosophical characterizations of the relative liberalism and conservatism of the Sadducees and Pharisees must often be flipped, his work still strongly connects rabbinic discussions of halakhic content with material originating in the Second Temple period.[64] Despite these points, my analysis here demonstrates how the elaborate Bava b. Buta story develops out of the smaller kernel story that appears second in our text. Moreover, this text demonstrates the way that Hillel and Shammai function as ciphers for working out what the law should be. The explicit narrative of devolution ("when the students increased ...") and the interrupting introductory

61. Paul Heger, *The Pluralistic Halakhah: Legal Innovations in the Late Second Commonwealth and Rabbinic Periods*, Studia Judaica 22 (Berlin: de Gruyter, 2003), 355–84.

62. Stephen G. Wald, "Hillel," in *Encyclopaedia Judaica*, ed. Michael Barenboim and Fred Skolnick (Detroit: Macmillan Reference USA, 2007), emphasis mine.

63. Vered Noam, "Beit Shammai and the Sectarian Halakhah" [Hebrew], *Jewish Studies* 41 (2002): 45–67; Yaakov Sussman, "The History of 'Halakha' and the Dead Sea Scrolls: Preliminary Observations on Miqsat Ma'ase Ha-Torah (4QMMT)" [Hebrew], *Tarbiș* 59 (1990): 11–76.

64. Aharon Shemesh, *Halakhah in the Making: The Development of Jewish Law from Qumran to the Rabbis*, Taubman Lectures in Jewish Studies 6 (Berkeley: University of California Press, 2009).

framing of the character of Bava b. Buta ("who knew that the law was like Hillel") demonstrate the ways in which the divide between Hillel and Shammai became representative of all divides for purposes of articulating an ideological position on the nature of law and disputation. Even if there is a residue of a historical Hillel and Shammai in rabbinic materials, it is evident that already in the Tannaitic period the names Hillel and Shammai were placeholders for conceptualizations of how competing ideas should exist in rabbinic culture.

The Legal Argument

Scholarship about law often presumes that law is a simple, static, essential, and easily comprehended entity. Just as lawyers practice law without questioning the coherence of the enterprise, scholars often presume law to be a field, discourse, or technique when it is better understood as a social practice and space that enables actors to execute a finite number of circumscribed actions. Scholarship that asks after the nature of rabbinic or Jewish law is limited by the mistaken assumption that either rabbinic or Jewish law is a stable finite entity. Philosophical reductions of rabbinic law to specific legal theoretical doctrines can be a productive enterprise, but it ultimately forces subtle and layered texts to be flattened down to reflect a single position.

While the law should not be presumed to be an essential entity, it might be valuable to show that individual rabbis or specific rabbinic texts *understood* law as essential. The research question is then not whether rabbinic law follows a specific legal doctrine, but whether specific authorities or documents adhere (knowingly or not) to a specific theoretical paradigm. And the best way to execute such research is with the realization that disparities of doctrine may manifest across corpora within the same time period (Mishnah/Tosefta) or, as illustrated above, within the gaps of the editorial layers of a specific document (Tosefta). And, while there certainly is a triumphal linear narrative in which pluralism emerges at the close of the rabbinic period as uniquely characteristic of the rabbis, the above textual discussion demonstrates the existence of at least one figure who sought to contest the dispute paradigm to produce an understanding of law as a universal and doubt-free unity.

In his book *Dispute for the Sake of Heaven*, Richard Hidary critiques earlier scholarship on pluralism both for not being precise in its characterizations and for synecdochically relying on a handful of self-conscious and explicit texts to speak for the whole of rabbinic literature.[65] Building

65. Hidary, *Dispute for the Sake of Heaven*, 13–31.

on Hidary, I want to note that debates about the nature of rabbinic law do not just pit different books (Bavli vs. Yerushalmi) or different sources within those books; individual sources, and particularly narratives, speak out of two sides of the mouth when discussing loaded issues like the unified/plural nature of law.

The rhetoric of the Bava b. Buta story claims that one of its characters knows the law (law is thus permanent, and its ontology is prior) while the plot of the same story models both the scholastic and the practical instabilities of law as a singular object. And this within a passage-long context that drives toward an ideal of law as a unified entity while contending with the challenges of historical contingency ("when the students of Hillel and Shammai multiplied …") and ignorance ("if they heard … if they did not hear …") and suppressing the evidence (the rebellious elder, m. Ḥag. 2:2's notion of a dispute culture and the historical memory of sectarianism) of law's plurality.

The Tosefta passage demonstrates the ways in which some of the categories we use to think about law bleed into one another. After the protocol asserts that judges in the high court do not judge on Sabbaths or holidays, it inserts a clause to indicate that the judges still report to their chamber—only now the chamber is a *beit midrash* and the study is theoretical.[66] This aside in the protocol allows us to glimpse the overlap of the juridical and the scholastic. That same overlap is visible in the interruption to the Bava b. Buta story that interprets the transpiring events as determinative of a scholastic sense of the proper final legal position. Similarly, the setup of the plot of the Bava b. Buta story forces an interaction between scholastic understandings of law and the lived realities that law inscribes. But it is the narrative texts—the protocol, the short historical myth of devolution ("when the students of Hillel …") and the story of Bava b. Buta—that articulate the greatest complex depiction of law. Because of the inherent temporal dynamism of narrative (and the potential for diversity among characters), narratives present their views of the law in self-deconstructing, unstable ways. In addition, the temporal and character diversity creates space for editorial interventions that bring the editor into the narrative. The interruptions to the Bava b. Buta story can be understood, in addition to the ways we have understood them so far, as generated by the narrative and its energy. The surprise of the behaviors described in the story encourages the editor to jump in and participate in the story.

The story of Bava b. Buta is an important text for current academic conversations about the relationship between sects and the rabbis, about the nature of law, and about rabbinic pluralism and its limits. It also

66. For more on the overlap between the behaviors within a single space, see Wimpfheimer, *Narrating the Law*.

constitutes an example of literary source criticism of Tosefta, a work of rabbinic literature that rarely achieves this kind of attention.[67] The point is not to describe a historical gap between the editing of Tosefta and its received materials. Rather, identifying qualitatively different features in the sources allows one to isolate the aim of the editing process. It also contributes to awareness of the historiographic unreliability of these materials and the resultant possibility that this story about a debate among the houses masks a rare rabbinic reflection on Second Temple sectarianism.

67. Other source-critical treatments of Tosefta on related topics include Naeh, "'Make Yourself Many Rooms'"; and Rosen-Zvi, "Protocol Beit Hadin Beyavneh."

Notes on Contributors

Julia Watts Belser is an Associate Professor of Jewish Studies in the Department of Theology and Religious Studies at Georgetown University, as well as a Senior Research Fellow at Georgetown's Berkley Center for Religion, Peace, and World Affairs. Her research centers on gender, sexuality, and disability in rabbinic literature, as well as contemporary Jewish feminist ethics. She has held faculty fellowships at Harvard Divinity School and the Katz Center for Advanced Jewish Studies at the University of Pennsylvania. Her most recent scholarly book is *Rabbinic Tales of Destruction: Gender, Sex, and Disability in the Ruins of Jerusalem* (Oxford University Press, 2018).

Beth A. Berkowitz is Ingeborg Rennert Professor of Jewish Studies in the Department of Religion at Barnard College. She is the author of *Execution and Invention: Death Penalty Discourse in Early Rabbinic and Christian Cultures* (Oxford University Press, 2006); *Defining Jewish Difference: From Antiquity to the Present* (Cambridge University Press, 2012); and *Animals and Animality in the Babylonian Talmud* (Cambridge University Press, 2018). She is co-editor with Elizabeth Shanks Alexander of *Religious Studies and Rabbinics: A Conversation* (Routledge, 2017). Her area of specialization is classical rabbinic literature, and her interests include animal studies, Jewish difference, Bible reception history, and rabbinic authority.

Dov Kahane is a PhD student at the Jewish Theological Seminary in the field of Rabbinic Texts and Cultures. His primary interest is the narratives of the Babylonian Talmud and what these stories can tell us about the cultures that produced them.

Jane L. Kanarek is an Associate Professor of Rabbinics at Hebrew College. Her research focuses on law and narrative in rabbinic literature, feminist theory and the Babylonian Talmud, and Talmud pedagogy. She is the author of *Biblical Narrative and the Formation of Rabbinic Law* (Cambridge University Press, 2014), and co-editor of *Learning to Read Talmud: What It Looks Like and How It Happens* (Academic Studies Press, 2016), and *Mothers* *in the Jewish Cultural Imagination* (The Littman Library of Jewish Civilization, 2017).

Tzvi Novick is the Abrams Chair of Jewish Thought and Culture Professor in the Department of Theology at the University of Notre Dame. He is the author of books on the Hebrew Bible (*An Introduction to the Scriptures of Israel: History and Theology* [Eerdmans, 2018]), normativity in early rabbinic literature (*What Is Good, and What God Demands: Normative Structures in Tannaitic Literature* [Brill, 2010]), and the relationship between midrash and early liturgical poetry (*Piyyuṭ and Midrash: Form, Genre, and History* [Vandenhoeck & Ruprecht, 2018]), and the author of numerous articles on the Hebrew Bible, Second Temple literature, rabbinic literature, and *piyyuṭ*.

James Adam Redfield is Assistant Professor of Biblical and Talmudic Literatures at Saint Louis University, a Fellow in Cornell University's Society for the Humanities and Program in Jewish Studies (2019–2021), and a Humboldt Foundation Fellow of the School for Jewish Theology at the University of Potsdam (2020–2021). James earned his PhD from Stanford in Religious Studies (2017) and did concurrent graduate work in Anthropology at UC Berkeley, earning an MA in 2010. His research brings the study of rabbinic literature together with the history of cultural theory and description. He has published articles in both fields, and others, as well as translations of Judaic scholarship and literature.

Jay Rovner is the Manuscript Bibliographer Emeritus, Library of the Jewish Theology Seminary of America, New York. His work focuses on Jewish literature produced in the Land of Israel and Mesopotamia in the late antique and Geonic eras, and on Hebrew manuscripts from the Cairo Genizah to nineteenth-century Eastern Europe. He has published literary and cultural studies of rabbinic stories and talmudic *sugyot* (debates) and traced the evolution of Jewish liturgy as evidenced in Passover Haggadah leaves and quires found in the Genizah. He is the editor and author of נא סייעני לעשר אליך = Na Saye'eni Le-aśer Elekha *(Please Help Me Tithe unto You): the* Ma'sar Kesafim *(Income Tithe) ledger of Mordecai Zeev Ehrenpreis of Lvov: with an examination of the practice, and its meaning for the donor* (New York, Jerusalem: JTS Press, 2003).

Jeffrey L. Rubenstein is the Skirball Professor of Talmud and Rabbinic Literature in the Department of Hebrew and Judaic Studies of New York University. His research focuses on the festival of Sukkot, talmudic stories, the development of Jewish law, and topics in Jewish liturgy and ethics. His books include *The History of Sukkot in the Second Temple and Rabbinic Periods* (1995); *Talmudic Stories: Narrative Art, Composition and Culture*

(1999), *Rabbinic Stories* (Classics of Western Spirituality, 2002), *The Culture of the Babylonian Talmud* (2003), and *Stories of the Babylonian Talmud* (2010).

Zvi Septimus is Lecturer in Hebrew Literature at Shanghai International Studies University and Adjunct Assistant Professor of Jewish Studies at New York University Shanghai. He previously has held research and teaching positions at Harvard University, the University of Toronto, Cornell University, and Harvard Law School. He received his PhD in Jewish Studies from the University of California, Berkeley.

Dov Weiss is an Associate Professor of Jewish Studies in the Department of Religion at the University of Illinois at Urbana-Champaign. He completed his PhD at the University of Chicago Divinity School as a Martin Meyer Fellow in 2011 and was the Alan M. Stock Fellow at Harvard University's Center for Jewish Studies in 2012. Specializing in the history of Jewish biblical interpretation and rabbinic theology, Dov's first book, *Pious Irreverence: Confronting God in Rabbinic Judaism* (University of Pennsylvania Press), won the 2017 National Jewish Book Award in the category of Scholarship. His recent articles include "Sins of the Parents in Rabbinic and Early Christian Literature" (*Journal of Religion* 97:1), "Divine Concessions in the Tanhuma Midrashim" (*Harvard Theological Review* 108:1), and "The Sin of Protesting God in Rabbinic and Patristic Literature" (*AJS Review* 39:2).

Barry Scott Wimpfheimer is Associate Professor of Religious Studies and Law at Northwestern University. Wimpfheimer has authored *Narrating the Law: A Poetics of Talmudic Legal Stories* (Philadelphia: University of Pennsylvania Press, 2011) and *The Talmud: A Biography* (Princeton, NJ: Princeton University Press, 2018). Wimpfheimer's work focuses on law as literature and the history and theory of Jewish law.

Source Index

Hebrew Bible

Genesis
1:21 163n166
6:12 22, 23
6:16 24
8:11 29
9:3–5 21n58
9:11 148n120
11 373
13:3 11, 12n34
16:29–30 34n10
18:1 359
18:12 360
18:20 6
18:21 6, 8
22:2 353, 354
33:18 306
38 82n14

Exodus
1:8–2:9 79n1, 90
1:14 86n25
2 82n14
3:14 156n144
13:5 190n31
15:2 85
15:3 90
18:4 97
20:9–10 32
20:10 33
20:11 32n4
23:10–12 33
25:7 168n219
28:9 168n219
28:20 168n219, 168n220
31:12–17 32n4
32 365
34:21 32n4
34:29 170n235
35:2–3 32n4
35:9 168n219
35:27 168n219
39:6 168n219
39:12 168n220
39:13 168n219

Leviticus
13 95
16:2 97
16:3 361
16:30 362
23:3 32n4
23:9–14 94
26:13 168n225

Numbers
12 110
12:14 96
12:15 96
19:2 103n16, 105, 106
19:3 103n16
19:4 103n16
27:20 170n233

Deuteronomy
5:14 33
5:15 32n4
6:23 187n26, 190n31, 192n37
15:8 61, 72, 73, 78, 244
15:11 47
16:3 188n27, 220
17:6 237
22:25 89n37
23:4 329, 334n205
30:12 329n168
32:12 355n39
32:7–14 344
32:8 344
32:13 86
34:7 170n235

Joshua
24:2 85n17

2 Samuel
12:11–12 86n26
23:20 236, 237

1 Kings
4:20 366
14 384n25

2 Kings
6:23 167n206

Isaiah
1:31 366
2 373
4:3 141, 171n249
4:5 127, 128n46, 130n53, 141, 169n230, 171n242
4:5–6 126, 128n44
4:6 128, 173n262
5:11–17 346
5:14 345
10:12 163n171
10:13 239, 335n208
11:9 165n183
23:8 126, 127, 129, 167n211, 174n270
24:23 170n235

Isaiah (*continued*)
27:1 163nn169–171, 164n172
27:3 163n171
30:23 170n234
32:12 353
33:12 353, 355n39, 366
33:14 353
40:17 353n34
43:2 351
43:3 351, 366
43:7 171n245
47:2–23 86n26
50:11 366
54:1 366n66
54:9 148n120
54:11 134n65
54:12 132, 134n65, 168n217, 168n221, 174n271, 174n275
56 373
56:6 345, 346
56:7 345
60:3 167n216
60:7 384n28
60:8 142n95, 147n118, 172n251
65:13 346
66:16 362

Jeremiah
5:22 148n119, 156n141
17:10 375
17:21–22 33
19:2 354
23:6 171n246
49:6 329, 335n210
50:12 350–51

Ezekiel
7:16 149n124
16 86, 86n27 89n35
16:1–14 87
16:3–13 85, 86
16:4 85
16:7 85
16:8 86, 86n23
16:10 85n20
16:13 86
16:15–63 88
16:49 4
20 86n27
23 86
23:30–34 88
23:48 87
28:13 131n57, 168n220, 170n237, 171n239
32 344
32:17–32 343
32:18 345
41:6 173n261
42:15–18 142n97
47 146n114
47:12 169n229
48:35 171n247

Hosea
12:7 129n52, 167n210

Joel
4:12–14 355

Amos
9:11 330
9:14 329, 330, 335n212

Obadiah
1:18 269n114, 366

Micah
3:3 161n158
4 373
4:5 345, 362
4:13 356
7:4 356

Nahum
3:5–6 86n26

Habakkuk
3:3 347
3:3–15 347
3:5 347
3:6 347, 348

Zechariah
2 373
2:2 172n254
2:4 172n256
13:8 346n22
14:10 141n94, 144n104, 147n117, 172n250

Malachi
3:9 360
3:19 360
3:21 342

Psalms
5:1 111n34
6:6 342
9:18 341, 342, 373
23:4 363
24:2 165n191
27:3 361
31:9 34n12
49 354n37
49:7 354
49:13 21n62
49:14 354
49:15 350, 354
50:10 164n173
50:11 159n153
55:21 360
68:14 84
78:43 86n25
104:26 164n177
105:10 346
107:26 156n147
113–114 221
115–118 221

115:17 259
129:3 85
140:12 349, 350
144:12 169n227

Proverbs
1:9 167n214
5:3 10
17:5 240
23:5 155n133
26:3 34n12
26:4 259
26:4–5 262
26:5 259
30:8 29

Job
7:5 164n181
14:4 106n23
26:12 164n182
28:4–9 12n35
29:18 27
40:16 164n175
40:19 166n199
40:23 165n187, 165n189
40:30–31 126–27, 129
40:30 166n198, 167n205
40:31 1280129, 129n51
41:5 167n215
41:6 167nn208–209, 174n266, 174n268
41:7 167nn212–213, 170n237, 173nn263–264
41:18 162n164
41:23 166n200
41:31 166n201
41:32 166nn202–3

Song of Songs
1:6 111n32
3:6 114n42
4:11 10
6:9 105

7:3 355
8:5 84, 85, 86n23
8:13 167n207

Lamentations
2:1 149n124

Qoheleth
4:2 259
8:1 131n57
9:4 259
9:5 236, 237

Ezra
7:6 102, 111n35

Nehemiah
13:15 34

1 Chronicles
29:1 172n258

2 Chronicles
3:1 354

Second Temple Sources

Dead Sea Scrolls
4Q554 III, 20–21 142n97
4Q554a 2 II, 16 142n97

2 Maccabees
1 104
1:18–36 104
12 104n17

4 Ezra
7:36–37 349n27

2 Baruch
(Syriac Baruch)
6:7–9 104n17

Christian Bible

Matthew
6:1–4 76n82
13:24–30 355

John
20:29 136n77

Revelation
21:16 142n97
21:19 132n58
21:21 133n61

Rabbinic Literature

Mishna

Berakot
1 214, 215n103
1:1 212n97
1:5 170n238, 180, 190, 207, 215, 220, 220n108, 221, 333n194
2:2 220n108
2:7 284n13
3:1 240, 242

Peʾah
1:1 312n116
8:7–9 253
8:9 251n63

Kilʾayim
8:6 39

Maʿaśer Šeni
5:9 195n50, 197

Šabbat
1:1 35
2:5 259
3:3 197
5:2 41n28
5:3 41
5:4 41n28

ʿErubin
3:4 195n51

Pesaḥim
1:1 107, 108

m. Pesaḥim (*continued*)
1:4 108, 113n38
2:1 108, 113n38
2:7 109, 112n37
2:8 112n36
3:4 112n36, 113n38
3:4–5 108
4 109
4:6 113n38
7:13 183n10
9:1–4 109
9:5 109, 109n27, 113nn39–41
10 213
10:4 185n15, 185n17, 215n102
10:4–5 190n34
10:5 113n38, 190n31, 212, 212n95, 212n97

Roš Haššanah
2:8–9 328

Yoma
5:6 147n115

Sukkah
201n73

Beṣah
1:1 99

Ḥagigah
2:2 378–80, 392, 402
2:3 380

Yebamot
1:4 378n3

Ketubbot
6:5 61, 244, 253

Soṭah
1:1 80n4, 91n44
1:1–2 80n6
1:2 89
1:5–6 87
1:6 80n4, 87, 87n29
1:7 87, 89
3:4 87

Qiddušin
4:1 325n157

Sanhedrin
4:3 110n30
6:1 62
10:1 1, 341, 364
11:2 398

'Abodah Zarah
1:3 274
2:1 275n134

'Eduyyot
1:1 99
1:2 99
1:5–6 328

'Abot
1 109, 391
1:1 99
1:4–12 379
2:8 98, 195n51
2:14 115n3
5:21 166n204

Horayot
3:8 317, 324

Menaḥot
10:4 94

Middot
3:2 147n115

Nega'im
2:4 97
2:4–5 95, 97
2:5 96, 96n5, 97

Parah
1:1 97, 99, 110
3 100, 101, 103
3:1 100
3:2–4 100, 102, 103
3:3 103
3:5 101
3:6 103
3:6–11 100

Yadayim
4:4 334n202

Tosefta

Berakot
1:2 197, 205n81
1:4 205n81
1:11 202
3:19 205n81
4:18 195n49, 202
5:3 199
5:28 183n10
6:13 360n52

Peʾah
4:10 52, 61, 62, 62n36, 63, 63n41, 244n32, 254
4:12–13 53
4:12 76n85, 246n40

Kilʾayim
5:7 39

Šebiʿit
4:12 195n51

Šabbat
3:3 198
4:1 38
4:2–3 38
4:3 34n12, 41
4:3–4 38

4:5 38, 38n22
4:11 35n13
5:8 38n22

'Erubin
1:2 199, 199n66
2:16 195n51

Pesaḥim
4:13–14 323n150, 384n29
10 218
10:10–11 212n97
10:11 186n20, 190n34, 212n95
10:12 xiv, 182, 183n12, 200, 204, 207, 212n97

Šeqalim
2:6 76n82

Yoma
2:7 202

Sukkah
2:11 195n50, 198, 201n75
4:5 183n12

Ḥagigah
2 391, 398–99
2:8 391
2:9 392
2:11–12 378

Yebamot
1:10 382n15
1:12 378n3

Soṭah
8:9 199n65
11:16 142n94

Baba Meṣi'a
6:3 66n56

Sanhedrin
7:1 398
13:2 338n7, 341, 341n16, 356, 359
13:3 342, 354n37, 364, 365

'Eduyyot
1:1 99, 99n11

Zebaḥim
1:8 213n100

'Arakin
4:27 65n51

Keritot
4:4 389

Parah
3 100, 101, 103
3:2–5 100
3:4 103

Ṭeharot
9:14 195n51

Miqwa'ot
7:10 195n51

Palestinian Talmud

Berakot
2:3, 4c–d 236–37
4:1 xxv, 288, 290
4:1, 7c–d 93n40
9:5, 14b 135n70

Peʾah
1:1, 15b 134n70
8:6, 21a 67
8:7–8:9, 21a–b 68n59
8:8, 21a 244n32, 253, 254
8:8–9, 21a–b 58–60, 63
8:9, 21b 76n82, 76n86, 251

Kilʾayim
9:3 241
9:4, 32c 125n39

Šebiʿit
4:2 382n15
9:1 307n106

Ma'aśer Šeni
3:6, 54b 143n101
5:4, 55c 197

Šabbat
1:4, 3c 377
5:4, 7b 39n24
5:4, 7c 41n29
6:2, 8b 35n13
6:9, 8d 265
8:1, 11a 134n70

'Erubin
10:1, 26a 35n13

Pesaḥim
5:3, 32a 116n5
6:1, 33a 323, 384n29
10:1, 37c 134n70
10:4, 37d 186n19
10:5, 37d 185

Šeqalim
5:5, 49b 251n61, 252

Sukkah
2:4, 52d 198, 201n72

Ta'anit
2:1, 65a 104n17, 104n18
4:1, 67d 198n64

Megillah
1:10n 72b 213n100
1:12, 72b 274
2:1, 73a 134n70

Ḥagigah
1:8, 76d 134n70
2:2, 77d 392

Ketubbot
4:8, 28d 249
12:3 241

Soṭah
2:5, 13a 66n55
5:5, 20c 134n70

Giṭṭin
9:1, 50a 196n52

Qiddušin
1:7, 61b 134n70
4:4, 65d 143n99

Sanhedrin
10:6, 29c 274

Horayot
3:2, 47d 213n100
3:4, 48a 213n99

Keritot
9:1, 50a 198

Babylonian Talmud

Berakot
3a 131n56
3b 181n6
10a 366n66
18a 228, 236–37, 240, 262
18a–b xxv, 230, 231–34, 240, 242, 250, 261, 276
18b 246
27b–28a xxv, 193n40, 198n64, 217, 281, 287, 290, 292n42, 293–94, 296, 303, 305, 306, 309, 310, 312n116, 320, 327
27b 303n99
28a 199n65
39a 138n82
43a 143n100
43b 249n54, 251
55–57a xx

Šabbat
22a 145n108
24b 171n240
30a 259
30b 259–60
30b–31a xxv, 228, 230, 255–56, 276
33b 142n96, 146n112
33b–34a 305, 309
34a 140n87, 327n166
45b 143n100
51b 35–36, 38–39, 41n28, 44n39
51b–52a 41–43
52a 39, 40, 40n25, 41n28
52b 41n28
53a 41n28
54a 40, 41, 41n28
54b 40, 41n28, 44n39
59b–60a 35n13
60a 171n240
61a 35n13
75a 171n240
82a 145n109
104a 355, 369
127b 228
141b 143n100
147a 154n132
148a 154n132
151b 21n62
156a 42n31
156b xxv, 228, 230, 262–63, 276

ʻErubin
11b 199n66
19a 365, 368
21b 138n82
51a 66n56
55b 145n110
63a 141n92
95b 35n13
101a 354n38, 355

Pesaḥim
50a 127n41, 143n100
53b 145n111
66a 323n150, 384n29
72b 208n88
115a 140n89
116a 185, 216

Yoma
20a 145n110
33b 312
38b 181n6
39b 145n110
52b 104n17, 104n18
75b 145n110

Sukkah
23a 198n62, 201n72
41b 195n50, 198, 211n93

Beṣah
20a–b 381

Taʻanit
3b 274
19a 21
20b 228
21b 228
23a–25b 228, 279
24b 124n33
30a 65n51

Megillah
6a 145n110
10b–16b 79n1
14b 11n30
15b 356

Mo'ed Qaṭan
28a 228

Ḥagigah
3a–b 282n5
12b 181n6
15b 138n81
25b 143n100
27a 365

Yebamot
62b 324
65a xviii
120b 145n109

Ketubbot
30b 311
50a 249n54, 251
57b 61
62b xiii, 228
62b–63a 324
63a 324
65a 228
67b xxv, 228, 230, 242–44, 252n65, 276
67b–68a xiv, xx, xxiii, 47, 51–58, 78
103b 323n147
111b 145n108, 145n110

Nedarim
22b–23a 228
50a xiii
50a–b 324
62a 382n15
66b 389n38
91a–b 228

Soṭah
8b 87, 311
9b–14a 79, 82n14
10b 249n54
11a–13a 79
11b xxiv, 79, 83–85
35b 356
47b 131n56
58a 145n108

Giṭṭin
55b–58a 229, 266, 280
56b 327n166
57a 145n108
79a 141n92

Qiddušin
26b 208n86
31b 273n123
32b 209–10, 211
39b 324n152
39b–40a 229
71a 143n100
81a–b 229

Baba Qamma
21a 108, 145
114a 143n100

Baba Meṣi'a
11a 208n86
30b 63n40
32a 275
59a 249n54
59b 212n96, 274, 329n168, 330, 330nn170–71, 330n173
83b–84b 229, 241
83b–86a xii, xvi
85b 145n108
110a 143n100

Baba Batra
3b 10n29
10b 76n86, 356
16b 67n58
22a 322n146
58a 229
73a 148n121, 155–63
73a–74b 229, 229n9, 241
73a–75b xxiv
74a 140n86, 241n28
74b 163–73, 164n181
74b–75b 122
75a–b 146n112
75b 145n107, 146n112

Sanhedrin
8b 195n51
17b 134n70
32b 184
37b 311
43a 195n51
67b 145n108, 229, 229n9
90a 364n60
91a 229, 256, 266
95a xii
100a 125, 146n112, 168n222, 169
101a 195, 197
105a 357–58
108a 22–23
108a–109b xxiii
108b 24–29
109a 11, 12
109a–b 13, 229, 229n9
109b 5–6, 12, 13–14

Makkot
11a 143n100

'Abodah Zarah
2a–3a 348, 356–57, 368
3b 181n6
4a 116n3
6b 275

b. 'Abodah Zarah (*cont.*)
10a–b 230, 276
10a–11a xxv, 267–69
10b 357, 358, 369
17a 274
17b 274
17b–18b 229
18a 357, 358, 358n47
26a 275

Horayot
13b–14a 317

Zebaḥim
62a 105n19
101b 96n5
101b–102a 96
113b 163n168

Menaḥot
21b 327n166
29b 98n6, 106

Ḥullin
18a 141n92
28b 143n100
84a 65n51
89a 170n236
106b 154n132
126a 21n61

Bekorot
8b–9a 229
36a 327
55a 165n185

'Arakin
28a 249n54

Niddah
27b 143n100
61b 141n92

Minor Tractates

'Abot de Rabbi Nathan
A6 213n99
A15 257
A16 366
B13 (16) 202n76
B26 257–58
B29 257

Kallah Rabbati
1:21 213n100
7:4 194n45

Derekh Ereṣ Rabbah
3:2 195n50, 198, 198n63, 208n86

Midrašim

Tannaitic Midrašim

Mekilta de-Rabbi Ishmael
Bahodesh 1 347
Bahodesh 10 197, 196n52
Bo 16 199n65
Bo 18 186n19
Ki Tisa, Shabbeta 1 198
Nezikin 10 352n30
Pisḥa 6 212n97
Pisḥa 14 127n44
Pisḥa 18 212n97
Yitro, Ba-hodesh 10 196n52
Yitro, 'Amaleq 1 209–10

Mekilta de-Rabbi Shimeon bar Yoḥai
Exod 17:12 203n80
Exod 18:12 209n91

Midrash Tannaim
Deut 15:8 245n32

Sipra
Dibburah de-Nedavah 2:5 213n100
Emor 16 (102c) 201n75, 211
Emor 16:2 (102c–d) 195n50, 198
Metsora 13 (70c) 199n65
Nega'im 4:1 (63b) 95

Sipre Numbers
75 213n100
105–6 96, 96n5
106 96n5
116 (133) 208n88

Sipre Zuta
Numbers 19:21 (315) 195n51

Sipre Deuteronomy
32 196n52, 197
38 209–10
43 198
80 194n47, 195n48
116 52, 53, 61n30, 62, 62n36, 63, 244n32, 246n40, 254n73
222 63n40
307 358, 358n47
311 343, 344–45
333 352n30
269 198

Amoraic and Later Midrašim

ʾAggadat Berešit
20 351n27, 372
20:4 366

Deuteronomy Rabbah
15 84n20

Esther Rabbah
3:7 307n106

Exodus Rabbah
11:2 351–52
19:4 345–46, 360n51
21 170n236
25:7 346
30:9 195n50, 198

Genesis Rabbah
7:1 140n89
20:1 349–50
26:2 203n79
40:17 203n78
48:8 359, 359n49, 367
49:6 5n14, 6, 8
50:5 203n79
52:18 203n78
55:7 354
64 138n80
67:6 273
79:6 307n106
98:10 111n33

Lamentations Rabbah
1:45–51 229n9

Leviticus Rabbah
2:9 368
5:4 213n99
10:2 273
13:2 348n24, 353
15:8 95, 110
21:4 361
21:7 97
25:5 135n70
28:1 94n3
34:10 68n60

Midrash Hagadol
18:22 307n106

Midrash Proverbs
17 353
31:15 181n6

Midrash Psalms
2 373n94
2:14 355
18:13 307,106
21:179 170n235
23:3 66n53
49 350
87:2 174n274
104:21–22 354

Numbers Rabbah
2:13 366n67
21:25 66n53

Pesiqta de Rab Kahana
4 98, 106n23
4:3 140n89
4:4 131n57
4:7 (73) 97, 98, 99, 105, 106, 109
5 356
8:1 (137) 94, 110
11 241
11:16 307n106
11:22 135n70, 142n96, 146n112
15 122n24
18:5 132n60, 142n96, 146n112, 174–75
20:7 142n94
Appendix
(pp. 455–57) 173–74

Pesiqta Rabbati
10 353
11:45 366
14:33–36 131n57
20 352
32:8–10 174n274
36 354n38

Pirqe Rabbi Eliezer
10 148n120
25 5n14, 8
28 355

Qoheleth Rabbah
3:1 94n3
3:6 133n63
7:8 257n80
9:5 236
10:8 307n106

Ruth Rabbah
Proem 1 361

Seder Eliyahu Rabbah
1:5 350

Seder Eliyahu Zuta
25 360n51

Seder ʿOlam Rabbah
3 343n19

Song of Songs Rabbah
2:1:3 345, 362–63, 367, 369
8:8:1 361, 363–64

Tanḥuma
Lekh Lekha 20 360n51
Tazria 5 360n51

Tanḥuma (Buber)
Ḥayye Sarah 3 360n51
Lekh Lekha 27 360n51
Nitzavim 3 349,27
Pekudei 5 366n68
Shemini 10 353n33
Shoftim 10 346n22, 354n38
Vayera 45 354

Yalkut Šimoni
Beshalaḥ 307n106
2 Samuel, #165 236–37
Isaiah, #429 373

www.ingramcontent.com/pod-product-compliance
Lightning Source LLC
Chambersburg PA
CBHW031324230426
43670CB00006B/227
* 9 7 8 1 9 5 1 4 9 8 7 9 5 *